Don Troiani's

CIVIL WAR UNIFORMS OF UNION AND CONFEDERATE SOLDIERS

Don Troiani's

Don Troiani's

CIVIL WAR UNIFORMS OF UNION AND CONFEDERATE SOLDIERS

Don Troiani
Ron Field

STACKPOLE
BOOKS

Essex, Connecticut

STACKPOLE BOOKS

An imprint of The Globe Pequot Publishing Group, Inc.
64 South Main Street
Essex, CT 06426
www.globepequot.com

British Library Cataloguing in Publication Information available

Library of Congress Cataloging-in-Publication Data
Names: Troiani, Don author | Field, Ron author
Title: Don Troiani's Civil War uniforms of Union and Confederate soldiers
 / Don Troiani, and Ron Field.
Description: Essex, Connecticut : Stackpole Books, [2026] | Includes
 bibliographical references. | Summary: "Details every aspect of the
 Civil War soldier's uniform and headgear-coats, trousers, caps and
 epaulettes, badges, buckles, buttons, and boots, along with the weapons
 and equipment each soldier carried"— Provided by publisher.
Identifiers: LCCN 2025032547 (print) | LCCN 2025032548 (ebook) | ISBN
 9780811775700 paperback | ISBN 9780811775717 epub
Subjects: LCSH: United States—Armed Forces—Uniforms—History—19th
 century—Pictorial works | Confederate States of America—Armed
 Forces—Uniforms—History—Pictorial works | United
 States—History—Civil War, 1861-1865—Pictorial works
Classification: LCC UC483 .T76 2026 (print) | LCC UC483 (ebook)
LC record available at https://lccn.loc.gov/2025032547
LC ebook record available at https://lccn.loc.gov/2025032548

Printed in India

Contents

Introduction

A T THE OUTBREAK OF THE CIVIL WAR in April 1861, clothing and equipping the vast numbers of soldiers that swelled the ranks of both Union and Confederate armies presented tremendous logistical problems. The United States Quartermaster Department was capable of supplying only the small Regular Army of approximately sixteen thousand men, and it consisted of an authorized staff of thirty-seven officers, including Quartermaster General Montgomery C. Meigs and seven military storekeepers. The United States Clothing and Equipage Depot at the Schuylkill Arsenal on Gray's Ferry Road in Philadelphia had been the chief depository of clothing and equipage since 1800.

With the onset of war, the Schuylkill Arsenal was under the direction of the elderly Colonel Charles Thomas as assistant quartermaster general. As demands on the establishment increased, he was superseded by Deputy Quartermaster General George H. Crossman, although Thomas was kept in place as an assistant.

Purchased under contract from manufacturers, cloth was received, cut according to pattern by government cutters and trimmers, and distributed to tailors and seamstresses who returned hand-finished garments to the Arsenal for inspection and approval. Although the first sewing machine specially designed for domestic use, commonly known as "the Turtle Back," was produced by Isaac Singer beginning in 1856, it was not generally used in the production of uniforms during the Civil War. Handsewn garments were considered to be more durable, although machines were used for sewing those articles, such as caps and chevrons, that would not be exposed to as much hard wear.[1]

The Schuylkill Arsenal was unable to supply the 75,000 militiamen called into three-months service on April 15, 1861. As a result, it was recommended that the militia provide its own clothing, the cost of which was not to exceed that of Regular Army clothing and was to be paid for with funds appropriated by Congress. Meanwhile, the Quartermaster Department had to clothe three-year volunteers under the proclamation of May 3, 1861, plus a Regular Army increasing in size, which reached approximately 21,700 by 1865. The facility was quickly expanded as thousands more outworkers were employed, and new clothing depots were established in New York, Cincinnati, and Saint Louis; in addition, so-called government halls or branch depots were established in Quincy, Illinois, and Steubenville, Ohio.[2]

---

1. Erna Risch, *The History of the Quartermaster Corps, 1775–1939*, Quartermaster Historian's Office, 1962, 348.
2. Risch, 350.

Realizing he could not depend solely upon production in Quartermaster Department facilities that he did not wish to expand further, Meigs decided to rely more heavily on the contract system, and he supplied cloth to the large clothing houses; this cloth could then be made up into complete garments and returned to the Department.

However, much of the cloth procured by the Quartermaster Department early in the war was of inferior quality. Too often contractors, such as Brooks Brothers of New York City, increased profits by skimping on the material, producing low-grade yarn by tearing to shreds refuse woolen rags and mixing this yarn with a lesser quantity of new wool. Known as "shoddy," uniforms made of this material rapidly deteriorated in the field and were subsequently replaced by better-quality uniforms. Also, with a shortage of dark-blue Army-standard goods, cloth of various colors was purchased by the Quartermaster Department during the first few months of the war. This resulted in numerous volunteer regiments in the Union Army wearing gray, green, or black. Several eastern and western states, such as New York and Wisconsin, clothed their early war regiments in gray out of choice, regarding it as the militia color. This led to serious confusion and incidents of "friendly fire" on battlefields, such as Big Bethel and Bull Run in 1861. The popularity of the Garibaldi, or fireman's, red shirt and of the red fez and full pantaloons of the Zouave, which were in use throughout the war, also made the soldier an easier target for the enemy.

It was not until August 1861 that the Union Army took the first steps to standardize as much as possible blue as the color of uniform for its troops. On the 21st of that month, Major General George B. McClellan, commanding the Military Division of the Potomac, issued orders forbidding the purchase of gray uniforms, which he called "the rebels' color."[3] Four days later, McClellan wrote to Secretary of War Simon Cameron, suggesting that no more Union troops be uniformed in gray.[4] As a result, on September 23, 1861, Acting Assistant Secretary of War Thomas A. Scott issued the following War Department Circular to State Governors: "The Department respectfully requests that no troops hereafter furnished by your State for the service of the Government be uniformed in gray, that being the color generally worn by the enemy. The blue uniform adopted for the Army of the United States is recommended as readily distinguishable from that of the enemy."[5]

By the second year of the war, most Union troops were adequately clothed and equipped, and the Quartermaster Department had next to concentrate on accumulating a reserve and maintaining the supply to clothing depots. By mid-1862, 6 months' supply of clothing was on hand throughout the system, and about 3,200,000 yards of cloth were in storage at the Schuylkill Arsenal.[6] However, when, on July 2, 1862, Pres-

---

3. *Boston Herald*, August 22, 1861, 4:1.

4. US War Department, *The War of the Rebellion: A Compilation of the Official Records of the Union and Confederate Armies*, 1899, series III, vol. 1, 453. Hereafter cited as ORs with series, volume, and page number.

5. *ORs*, series III, vol. 1, 532.

6. Risch, 356.

ident Abraham Lincoln called for 300,000 volunteers for three years' service, then in August called for 300,000 militia for nine months, the demand was too great for the Department. By agreement with the individual states, Meigs sent cloth and trimmings for coats and trousers either to the US quartermaster stationed within each state or, if such were not available, to the governor of the state.

To replace depleted stocks, Meigs ordered the publication of advertisements inviting proposals for cloth, headgear, and every type of equipment in Philadelphia, New York, and Cincinnati, and he directed Colonel Crossman to accumulate at the Schuykill Arsenal a surplus stock sufficient to clothe and equip 100,000 men. By 1863, with reserve stocks accumulated, the supply of clothing was well in hand, and, by the end of 1864, Meigs could report that "the supply was ample, the quality is excellent, and the complaints few."[7]

Uniform supply to the Confederate army faced its own challenges. The Confederate Quartermaster Department was established on February 26, 1861, with Colonel Abraham C. Myers as quartermaster general and Captain John M. Galt as assistant quartermaster general. Concentrating their efforts on clothing the small regular Confederate army of 10,600 men, the needs of the six-month volunteers and of the 100,000 twelve-month state volunteers, who were called out on March 6, 1861, presented an overwhelming task.[8] Meanwhile, in each of the eleven states that seceded from the Union and formed the Confederacy in 1861, floods of volunteers donned pre-war militia dress or had new uniforms made by local tailors or by their own womenfolk, based on patterns provided. The cut and color of this early war garb varied greatly. As with the Union Army, confusion reigned on the battlefield as friend mistook foe, often with fatal consequences.

A Clothing Bureau was established on Pearl Street in Richmond, Virginia, on September 6, 1861, to manufacture uniform clothing for Confederate troops. This bureau operated a system similar to that of its northern counterpart; cloth was cut and trimmed according to pattern and was distributed to tailors and seamstresses who returned hand-finished garments for inspection and approval. Other clothing bureaus were set up at places including Nashville, Tennessee; Athens, Atlanta, and Columbus, Georgia; Montgomery, Tuscaloosa, and Marion, Alabama; Jackson and Enterprise, Mississippi; and Shreveport, Louisiana. Not all of these manufactories operated throughout the war, and by 1863 the major centers were Richmond, Athens, Atlanta, and Columbus.[9]

Although uniform suits including coats rather than jackets were being issued from some of these establishments before the end of 1861, the number made was not nearly enough to supply the whole army. With the central government making too little avail-

---

7. Risch, 357.

8. Leslie D. Jensen, "A Survey of Confederate Central Government Quartermaster Issue Jackets," part 1, in *Military Collector & Historian*, vol. XLI, no. 3 , 110.

9. Jensen, 111.

able and providing it too slowly, some states produced their own distinctive pattern of uniform, generally funded by the commutation system approved by the Confederate Congress on March 6, 1861, which provided that each enlisted man should receive $21 every six months for clothing.[10]

With the approach of the winter of 1861–1862, the first appeal for winter clothing for troops was issued in the Southern press.[11] With the aid of countless volunteer and aid societies, composed mainly of wives, daughters, and sweethearts of those defending the Confederacy, many soldiers received a new homemade "uniform suit" of gray plus a blanket, which enabled recipients to survive the rigors of the first winter of war. By October 8, 1862, the Clothing Bureau system was finally considered capable of providing for Confederate troops, and the Commutation System was officially ended. It took some time for the Clothing Bureau system to be fully implemented, but it was in general use in the main armies by 1863.

Meanwhile, clothing shortages again occurred following the campaigns of 1862, and the Quartermaster Department became embarrassed and assailed with criticism. Soldiers wrote home for clothes, and a second appeal for warm winter clothing was issued. Individual states—with the exception of North Carolina and Georgia—again responded. North Carolina and Georgia shut out speculators and Quartermaster agents and declared that they would uniform their own

men first and that the Confederate government could have what was left. In Georgia, this led to "[a]n Act to appropriate money to procure and furnish clothing, shoes, caps or hats, and blankets for the soldiers" and the establishment of a state clothing bureau in Augusta under the supervision of Captain George W. Evans.[12]

By mid-1863, the Clothing Bureau system was generally capable of meeting the demands of the sprawling Confederate armies, although, with increasing disruption of supply lines, it was difficult for some troops to receive readily available uniforms. From June 1863, an increasing amount of imported uniform clothing, weapons, and equipment slipped through the Union naval blockade from Britain and Europe via Bermuda and the Bahamas, into Wilmington, North Carolina, and, to a lesser extent, into Charleston, South Carolina. By January 1865, when Fort Fisher fell, North Carolina is believed to have imported, at an approximate total, wool cloth sufficient for 250,000 suits of uniforms, and 12,000 overcoats; 50,000 blankets; and leather and shoes for 250,000 pairs.[13] Much of the cloth imported is believed to have been a dark bluish-gray shade and of the type worn by the British Army, which was quite distinct from the drab grays and browns of the Confederate-made jeans cloth of the period. This is sometimes referred to as "English blue," after "English blue denim," which ran though the blockade into Charleston as early as November 1862.[14]

---

10. *ORs*, series VI, vol. 1, 126.
11. *Daily Nashville Patriot*, August 9, 1861, 3:2; *Macon Telegraph* (Macon, GA), September 3, 1861, 2:1.
12. *Daily Constitutionalist* (Augusta, GA), December 18, 1862, 3:2.
13. *Southern Historical Society Papers*, vol. 24 (Southern Historical Society, 1896), 36.
14. *Southern Confederacy* (Atlanta, GA), November 5, 1862, 2:6.

By the end of the year, some Confederate troops were described as being better dressed than their counterparts in the Union Army. During 1864, both the armies of Northern Virginia and Tennessee were in plentiful receipt of Quartermaster-issued uniforms of a similar pattern, if not of the same color and kind of cloth. According to quartermaster reports, Confederate troops defending Petersburg remained well clothed during the last winter of the war. When it was all over and the army under General Joseph E. Johnston surrendered at Bennitt's House, near Durham Station, on April 26, 1865, North Carolina had on hand a five-month supply, which could have clothed and equipped 60,000 men for many months.[15]

---

15. *Southern Historical Society Papers,* 36.

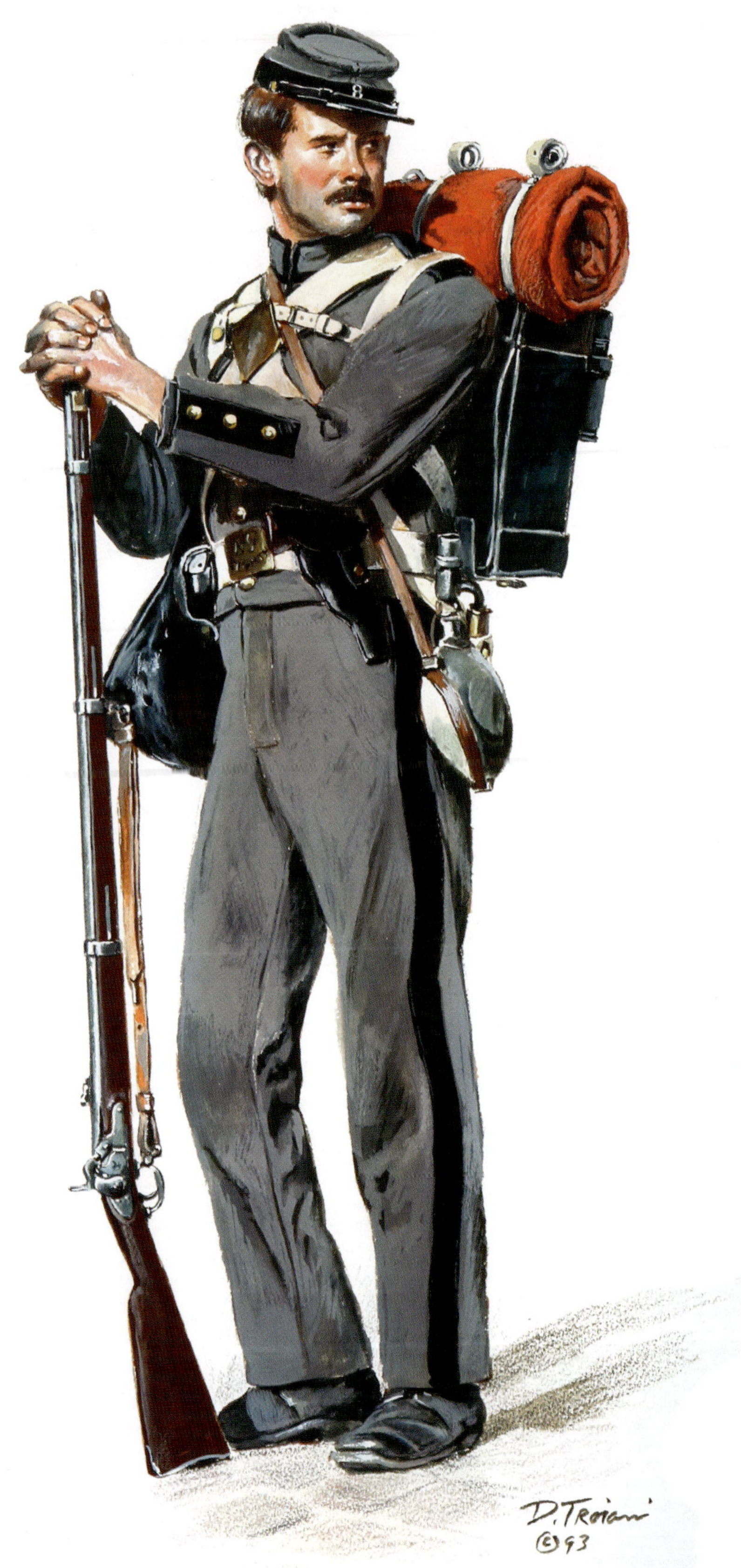

EARLY WAR MILITIA AND VOLUNTEERS

8th Company, 7th New York State Militia, 1861

WHEN PRESIDENT ABRAHAM LINCOLN CALLED FOR VOLUNTEERS to defend the Union on April 15, 1861, the *elite* 7th New York State Militia, or National Guard, commanded by Colonel Marshall Lefferts, was among the first to respond, being mustered in the service of the United States for thirty days. On April 19, the regiment left New York en route to Washington, D.C. As secessionists in Baltimore, Maryland, were hostile to the passage southward of Union troops and had attacked the 6th Massachusetts Volunteer Militia, the 7th regiment was ordered to take a more circuitous route to the Capitol.

Colonel Lefferts chartered the steamer *Boston* and sailed his men southward around Cape Charles, continuing up the Chesapeake Bay to Annapolis, Maryland. With the assistance of the 8th Massachusetts, they repaired twenty-five miles of railroad extending to Annapolis Junction, which had been destroyed by secessionists, and reached a stretch of the Baltimore and Ohio Railroad still under Union control, finally arriving at the beleaguered Capitol weary and exhausted on April 25, 1861.[1] According to one news report, "The march of the 7th was a hard one—100 men fell from sun stroke; the heavy knapsacks, weighing 80 pounds, were all thrown away."[2]

On arrival in Washington, members of the 7th New York marched up Pennsylvania Avenue to the White House and then initially took up residence in the Hall of the House of Representatives, taking their meals at the National Hotel. Subsequently establishing Camp Cameron, in honor of Secretary of War Simon Cameron, on Georgetown Heights, they were photographed profusely by Matthew Brady and his assistants.

Wearing the regimental fatigue uniform of cadet gray with black facings and trim, this private of the Eighth Company, commanded by Captain Henry C. Shumway, is distinguished by his belt plate bearing the letters "NG" above "EIGHTH." He is fully equipped for field service, with white buff leather belts supporting a cap pouch and a black leather cartridge box with a brass script monogram "NG" on its outer flap. His rigid militia knapsack is painted with the white regimental number "7" and has a red blanket roll and mess tin attached. He is armed with a Model 1855 rifle musket with a Maynard tape primer and has a privately purchased holstered revolver attached to his waist belt.

Returning to New York City at the end of its thirty days' service, the 7th New York was mustered out on June 3, 1861. A regimental history recorded, "With the streaming flags and bunting and inscriptions of welcome, the streets thronged with men heartily cheering, every building bright with women waving handkerchiefs, the booming of cannon, and the merry peal of the bells of Trinity . . . the Seventh knew that it had not lost its old place in the love and respect of the Empire City."[3]

---

1. William Swinton, *History of the Seventh Regiment, National Guard* (Charles T. Dillingham, 1886), 110.
2. *Buffalo Courier Express*, April 30, 1861, 2:2.
3. Swinton, 222.

Charleston Zouave Cadets

INSPIRED BY THE DRILL TOUR OF ELMER E. ELLSWORTH'S United States Zouave Cadets during the summer of 1860, the Charleston Zouave Cadets were organized during August of that year with Charles E. Chichester in command. Although a full-dress uniform similar to that of the "Chasseurs D'Vincennes," of the French Army, was at first considered, the Zouave Cadets eventually decided on both full-dress and undress uniforms of gray cloth made by military tailor and company member Thomas Whiley, whose premises were at 154 East Bay in Charleston.[1] The unit paraded for the first time in their "neat undress grey suit, with white cross-belts" on October 23, 1860.[2] A "full dress Zouave uniform," which was actually of chasseur pattern, was adopted during a meeting at their armory on November 23. Referred to as their "winter uniform," it was worn for the first time with black caps on December 18, 1860.[3]

The Zouave Cadets entered state service on New Year's Day, 1861, and were posted on Morris Island in Charleston Harbor when the steamer *Star of the West* attempted unsuccessfully to reinforce the beleaguered Federal garrison in Fort Sumter. After a spell of leave in Charleston they were ordered to relocate to Sullivan's Island during the bombardment of Fort Sumter on April 12th and 13th, 1861. Following Lincoln's proclamation calling on the state militia to suppress the rebellion, many of the Zouave Cadets volunteered for one year's war service as the South Carolina Zouave Volunteers. However, their ranks were soon replenished, and a virtually all-new company was formed. On September 12, 1861, the unit was ordered out to guard Federal prisoners who had been captured at First Manassas and who were quartered in the casemates at Castle Pinckney in Charleston Harbor, and they remained there until the end of 1861 even though their prisoners had been returned to Virginia for exchange.

Presenting arms with his Model 1842 musket at Castle Pinckney during September 1861, the Zouave Cadet wears the undress uniform worn by his company throughout its period of active service. His round jacket and straight-legged trousers are trimmed with red facings. His red cap, with a blue band and a Palmetto device pinned to its top, is of the pattern adopted by the company in 1860. His shoulder and waist belts are of white buff leather.

The officer's dress conforms to that prescribed by the company in 1860 and consists of a dark-blue, nine-button uniform coat with red collar and cuffs edged with gold braid. Rank is indicated by Federal-style shoulder straps with red ground. A crimson net waist sash is tied under his white sword belt. Matching trousers are trimmed with broad red seam stripes edged with gold trim. Of the same pattern as those worn by the enlisted men, his cap is embellished with gold lace.

---

1. *Charleston Daily Courier*, July 22, 1861, 1:4.
2. *Charleston Mercury*, October 24, 1860, 2:2.
3. *Charleston Mercury*, November 23, 1860, 2:7; and December 18, 1860, 2:5.

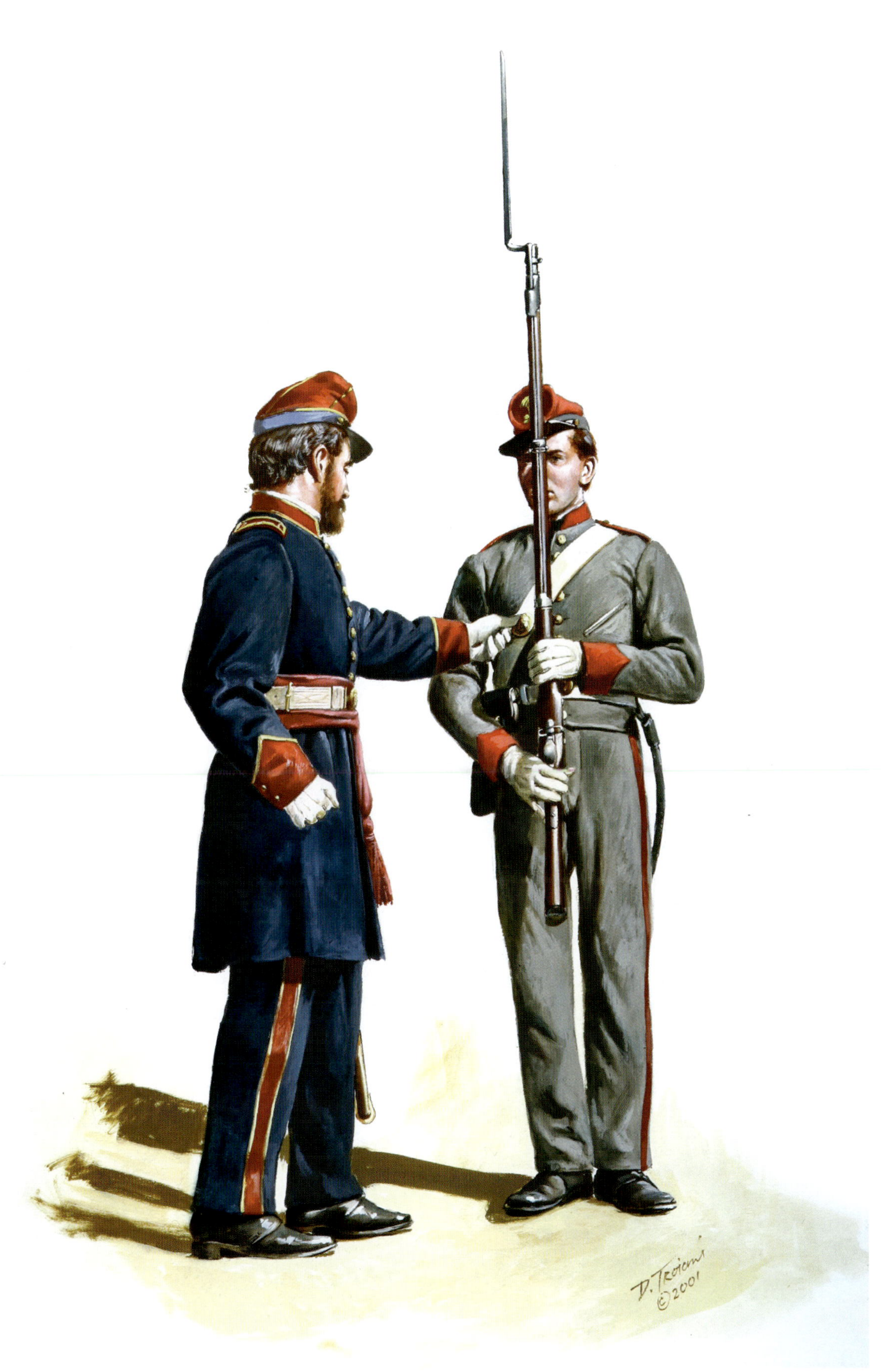

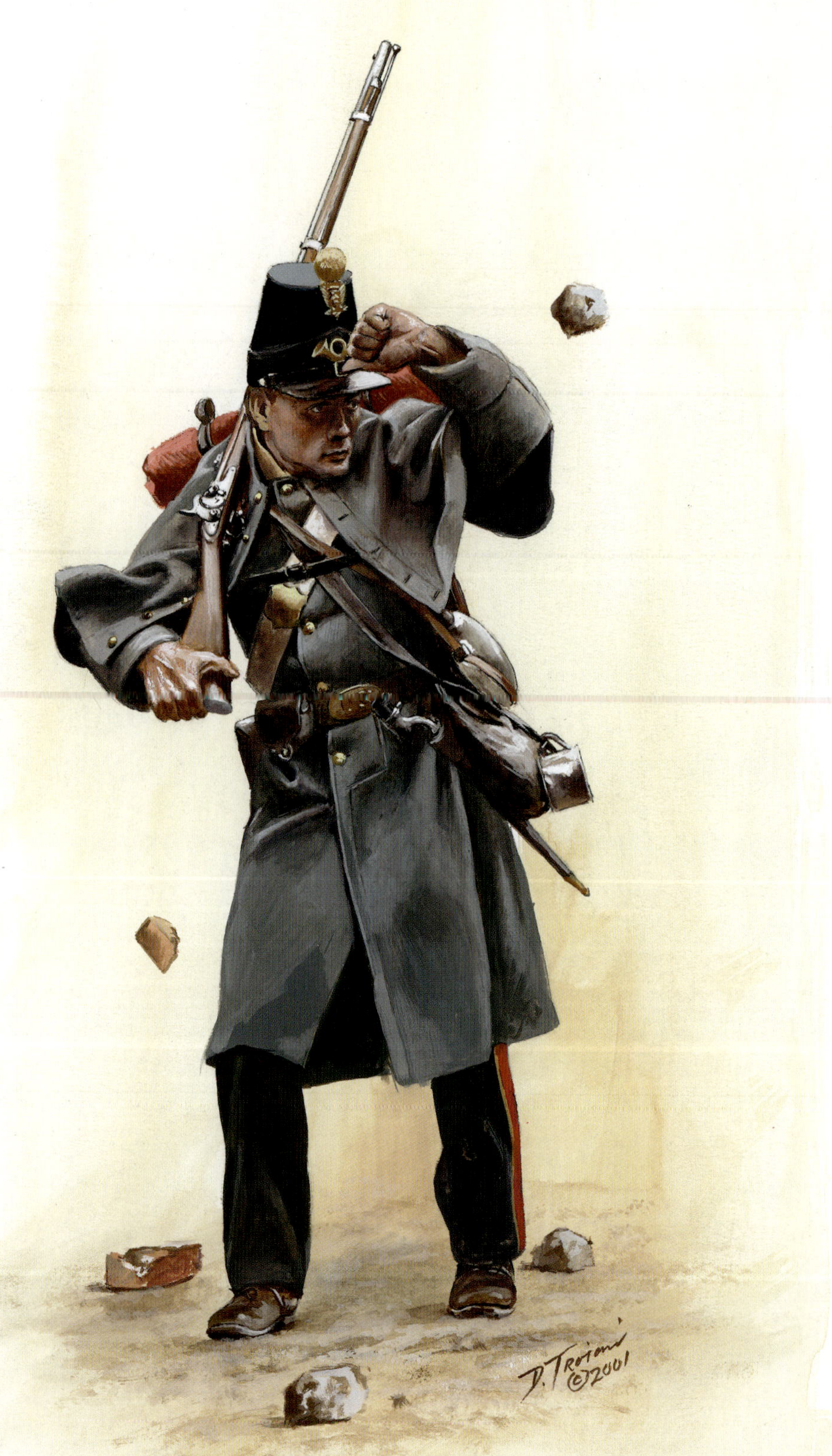

6th Massachusetts Volunteer Militia

NUMBERING 624 OFFICERS AND MEN COMMANDED BY Colonel Edward F. Jones, the 6th Massachusetts Volunteer Militia (MVM) was one of the first units to rush to the defense of the nation's capital in 1861. As it passed along Pratt Street to Camden Station in Baltimore, Maryland, on April 19, a detachment of the regiment consisting of companies C, I, L, and D, under Captain Albert S. Follansbee, was attacked by a pro-Southern mob. Four enlisted men were killed and thirty-six wounded.[1]

Being pelted with rocks and brickbats in Baltimore, this volunteer wears an example of the overcoat of medium–iron-gray beaver cloth worn by the 6th MVM. Based on a pattern obtained after consultation with the US Army Quartermaster Department, it was made by order of the Quartermaster General of the Commonwealth of Massachusetts during February 1861, in anticipation of "the inevitable conflict." At the insistence of Brigadier General Benjamin F. Butler, Governor John Andrews provided the whole regiment with these overcoats in order to achieve a greater appearance of uniformity, as each of its companies wore different uniforms.

The Pattern 1851 dress cap worn has an enlisted man's brass eagle plate attached, above which is a round yellow pompon. A Pattern 1858 infantry looped horn insignia is secured to the cap's pointed band. Worn under his overcoat is a dark-blue uniform coat of Pattern 1851 with sky-blue trim. He wears trousers, which were described by the *Evening Star*, on arrival at Washington, as "black pants, with red . . . stripes down the sides."[2]

The 6th MVM was armed with Model 1855 rifle muskets, two thousand of which had been issued to the state by the General Government in 1858.[3] Accoutrements include a waist belt of bridle leather with brass US oval Pattern 1839 plate. On this belt is a frog carrying a bayonet in scabbard and a percussion cap pouch, the latter being necessary when tape was unavailable for the Maynard primer system on his musket. Attached to a white buff leather shoulder belt with shield-shaped breast plate is a Pattern 1857 cartridge box carrying forty rounds of .58-caliber Minié balls. Also carried is a waterproof haversack with a tin cup secured through its leather strap and a Pattern 1858 canteen with a cloth cover. His militia box knapsack has a red blanket roll strapped to its top.

Enlisting for a ninety-day term of service, which lasted from April 16 to August 2, 1861, the 6th MVM returned to Baltimore after duty at the Federal capital to guard locations within the city as well as the Baltimore and Ohio Railroad station at Elkridge, Maryland.

---

1. John W. Hanson, *Historical Sketch of the Old Sixth Regiment of Massachusetts Volunteers* (Lee and Shepard, 1866), 47.
2. *Evening Star* (Washington, DC), April 20, 1861, 3:2.
3. George D. Moller, *Massachusetts Military Shoulder Arms, 1784–1877* (Andrew Mowbray Inc., 1988), 91.

Stanly Marksmen, Company H, 14th North Carolina Infantry

DEFENDING THE RIGHTS OF THEIR STATE AND THE SOUTH, the people of Albemarle, in Stanly County, North Carolina, raised a volunteer company of 104 men fifteen days before the "Old North State" seceded from the Union and joined the Confederacy on May 20, 1861. While the recruits trained and drilled outside the courthouse, the community set about clothing and equipping the Stanly Marksmen. The womenfolk turned the courthouse and other buildings into workshops where uniforms were cut out, and local tailors John Williams and Tommy Haskell worked night and day sewing them.

The outfit chosen for the Stanly Marksmen was described in the local press as being "different from the uniform of the United States, or the State of North Carolina," consisting of "a grey, thigh-length frock coat, with high collar, a chest full of red braid, and light grey trousers."[1] Providing further detail, the minute book of the organizing committee recorded that gray cloth was procured for uniforms, with a darker gray for the coats and a lighter gray for the trousers. A red grosgrain ribbon was used for the facings. Local merchant James D. Hearne was charged with acquiring hats and shoes for the company. An early war image of Private DeMarcus Palmer confirms that the Stanly Marksmen received a six-button uniform coat with a plain standing collar, plain cuffs with three small decorative buttons, and six broad red bars across the chest.[2]

Commanded by Captain Richard Anderson, the Stanly Marksmen enlisted for twelve months at Garysburg, North Carolina, as Company H, 4th North Carolina Infantry. On November 14, 1861, the state legislature passed an act raising ten regiments of State troops, which were numbered from one to ten, and the 4th Regiment was redesignated as the 14th North Carolina Volunteers.

After the arrival of his regiment at Camp Bragg, near Suffolk, Virginia, this private of the Stanly Marksmen takes a rest with his Model 1842 musket, metal drum canteen, knapsack, and equipment by his side. Placed in the Department of Norfolk, his regiment was later assigned to the Army of Northern Virginia, and ended the war at Appomattox Court House, surrendering seven officers and 107 men.

---

1. *Stanly News and Press* (Albemarle, NC), October 10, 1952, 8A:3.
2. Greg Mast, "A Few Good Tarheels," *Military Images* 16, no. 2 (September–October 1994): 27.

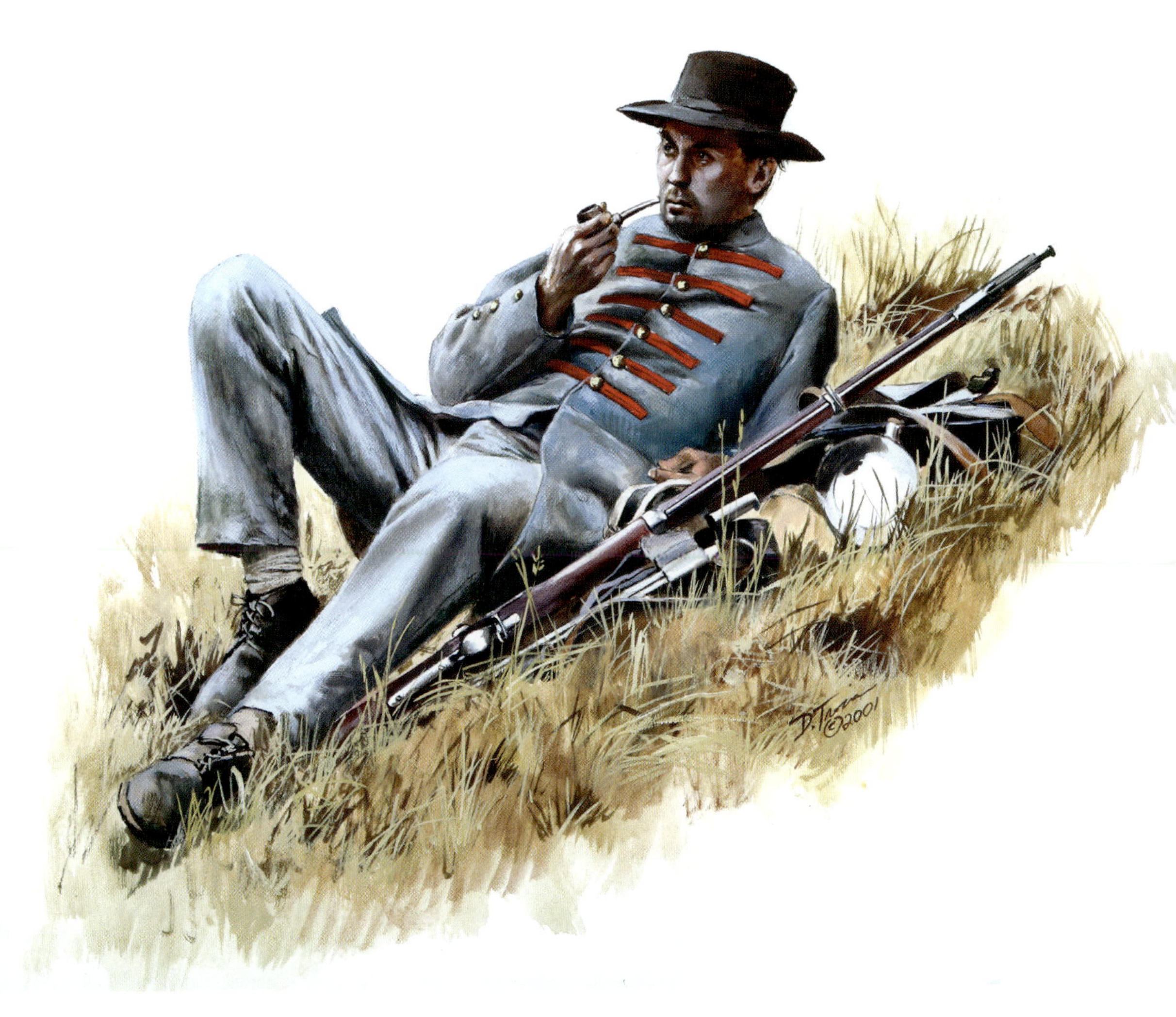

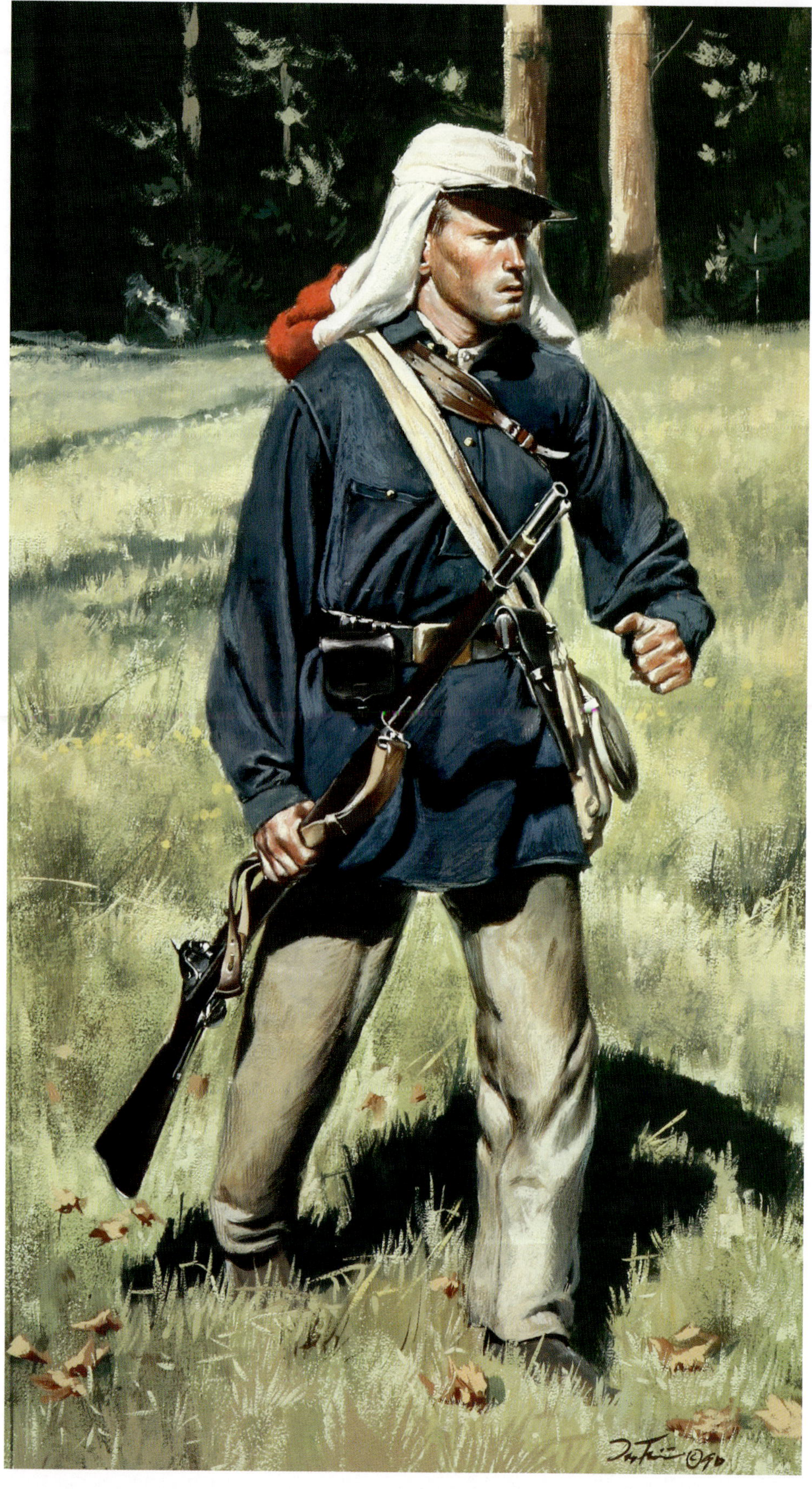

1st Rhode Island Detached Militia, 1861

THE 1ST RHODE ISLAND DETACHED MILITIA WAS organized for three months' service on April 15, 1861, and left the state for Washington five days later. Attached to the 2nd Brigade, 2nd Division, of General Irwin McDowell's Army of Northeastern Virginia, it saw action at First Bull Run on July 21, where it sustained thirteen killed, thirty-nine wounded, and thirty captured or missing, totaling eighty-two casualties. The regiment returned home on July 25 and mustered out on August 2, 1861.

The ten companies that formed the 1st Rhode Island were drawn from existing volunteer, or active, militia within the state. This included the First Light Infantry, Woonsocket Guards, Mechanic Rifles, and Newport Artillery. Prior to the Civil War, these units wore distinctive dress and fatigue uniforms. When mustered into the regiment, they received a service dress uniform that was more suitable for campaigning purposes. Suggested by their commander Colonel (later Major General) Ambrose Burnside, their blouse or overshirt was supplied in haste from cloth that was likely produced by the Boston firm of Macullar, Williams & Parker. Rushed to the clothing store of Henry A. Prescott in Providence, the local ladies were advised, "The work must be done by to-night."[1]

According to a news report published four days later, work on blouses to be worn by the first detachment of the regiment was undertaken by the ladies of the local congregations. Writing on April 19, one of those involved commented in a letter to her children in Albany, New York, "To describe the scenes of yesterday is impossible. Indeed we have no time for words, nor even for thought—only for action. We, the ladies of Providence, made a thousand blue flannel tunics for the Infantry yesterday."[2] The blouses produced had a fold-down collar and a placket front that was closed by small brass state buttons. Cuffs and a breast pocket were closed by a single button of the same type. Trousers were plain gray. On campaign in Virginia, this regiment wore white linen Havelock covers over their blue chasseur-pattern forage caps. Instead of receiving overcoats, the 1st Rhode Island was issued with scarlet blankets that were carried diagonally on the soldier's back and suspended from a leather strap. By order of Colonel Burnside, these were slit at the center so they could be worn as a poncho or cloak.

This private is armed with a US Model 1855 rifle musket with a Maynard tape primer. He has a holstered revolver attached to his waist belt, and out of view is a socket bayonet in its scabbard. Belt plates were of militia pattern of plain brass with clipped corners. Accoutrements consist of a Pattern 1858 oblate spheroid canteen and a white canvas haversack.

---

1. *Providence Daily Journal*, April 18, 1861, 2:3.
2. *Providence Daily Evening Press*, April 25, 1861, 3:6.

Flat River Guards, Company B, 6th North Carolina State Troops Infantry

ORGANIZED AT FLAT RIVER IN NORTH-EASTERN ORANGE COUNTY, North Carolina, on February 4, 1860, with Mexican War veteran Robert F. Webb in command, the Flat River Guards were accepted into state service in Hillsborough, North Carolina, on May 1, 1861.[1] On April 23, 1861, the company was ordered to go to Raleigh by Brigadier General John F. Hoke, adjutant general of North Carolina, where they were mustered in "for the war" as Company B, 6th North Carolina State Troops, commanded by Colonel Charles Fisher.[2] Sent to Virginia, the 6th North Carolina was assigned to the brigade led by Brigadier General Barnard E. Bee, and it received its baptism of fire at First Manassas where it charged Rickett's and Griffin's Federal batteries on Henry House Hill, sustaining heavy losses, including the loss of its colonel.

The uniform worn by the Flat River Guards at First Manassas was likely that originally acquired by the company during June 1860.[3] Made from "North Carolina gray cassimere," it consisted of a triple-breasted jacket with black trim on collar and cuffs and matching trousers with narrow welts of black trim on the outer seams. Headgear was a Pattern 1858 dress hat with its brim looped up on the left and a single black ostrich feather on the opposite side of the crown. The hat's insignia was composed of a gilt Pattern 1834 militia hunting horn, beneath which were the metal letters "F.R.G."[4]

The Flat River Guards were one of six companies of the 6th North Carolina that were armed with Model 1822 conversion muskets. These would have been part of the 37,000 arms seized at the Fayetteville Arsenal by the state on April 23, 1861.[5] Many of the accoutrements issued to the regiment were supplied by Colonel Fisher. A man of wealth, he had been a state senator from 1854 to 1855, and had been president of the North Carolina Railroad since 1855. Worn by the whole regiment, and likely paid for by Fisher, the unique cast belt plate shown in this painting, bearing the regimental designation "6th INF. N.C.S.T.," was manufactured by a railroad workshop in Burlington, North Carolina.

1. *Hillsborough Recorder*, February 15, 1860, 3:1, 2.
2. *Weekly Raleigh Register*, May 1, 1861, 1:6.
3. *Hillsborough Recorder*, June 27, 1860, 3:1.
4. Greg Mast, *State Troops and Volunteers: A Photographic Record of North Carolina's Civil War Soldiers*, vol. 1 (North Carolina Department of Cultural Resources, Division of Archives and History), 54.
5. Claud E. Fuller and Richard D. Steuart, *Firearms of the Confederacy* (Quarterman Publications, Inc., 1944), 19.

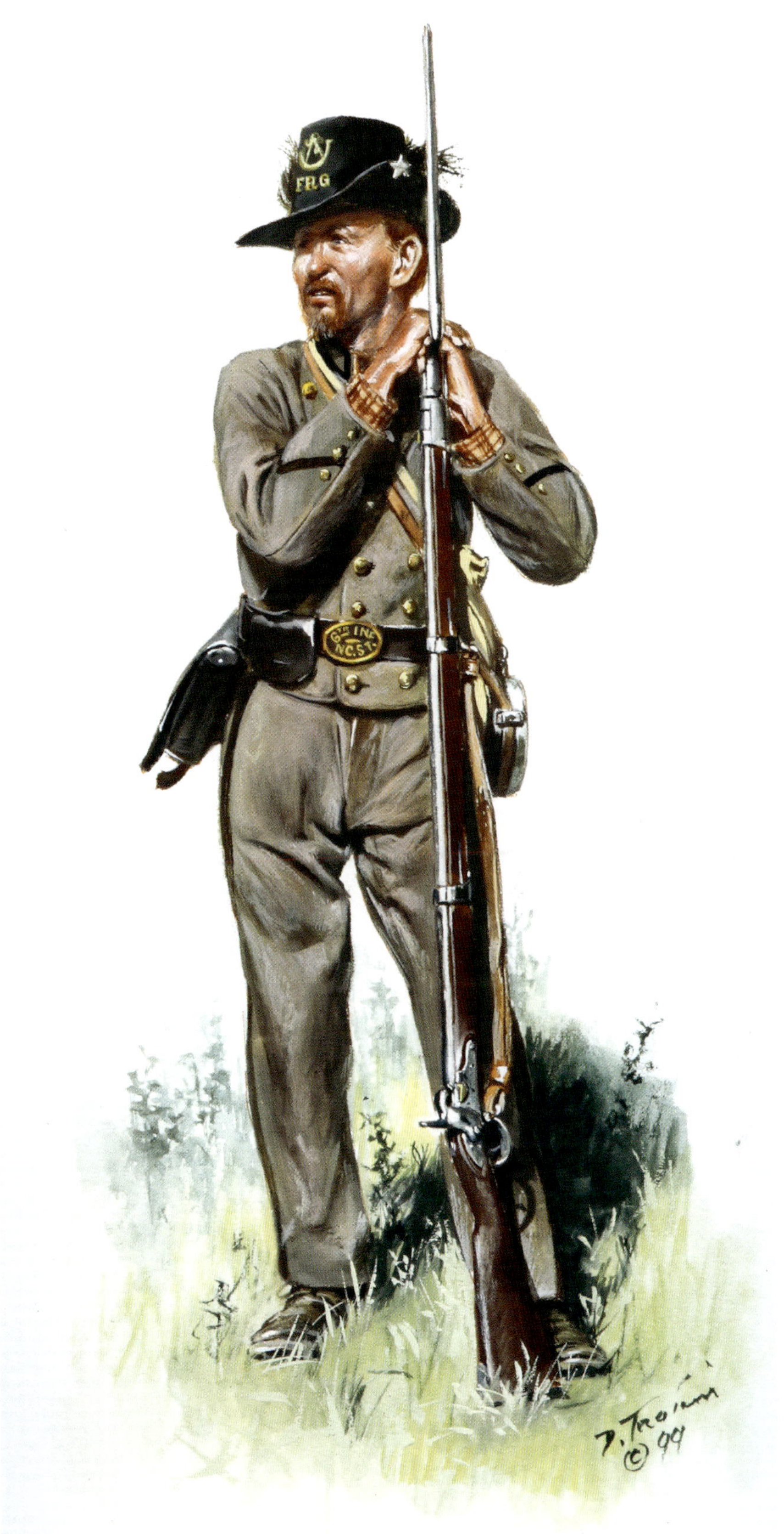

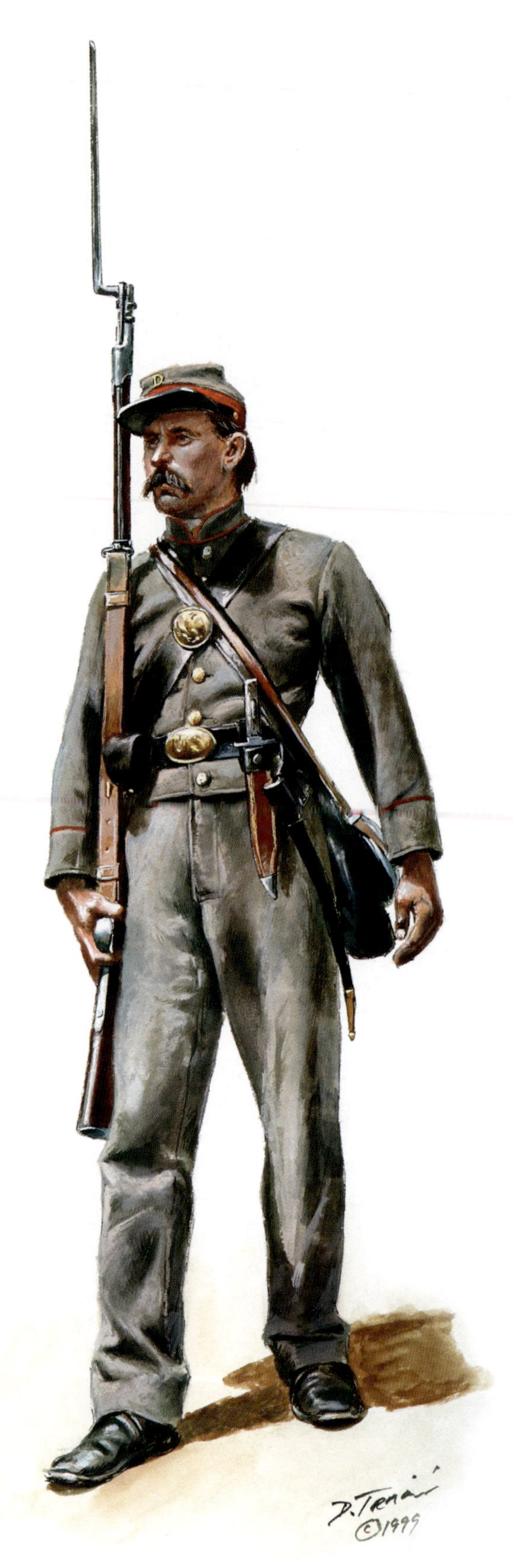

2nd New Hampshire Volunteers, 1861

THE FIRST REGIMENT FROM THE GRANITE STATE to volunteer "for the war," the 2nd New Hampshire Infantry was organized in Portsmouth, New Hampshire, under the command of Colonel Gilman Marston, between May 31 and June 8, 1861. In May, it was issued with a uniform of "grey military cloth," which was made in Boston, Massachusetts, by clothiers Whiting, Galloupe, Bliss & Co. and Whitten, Hopkins & Co.[1] This private of Company D, also known as the Dover Volunteers, wears an example of the coatee provided, which was of "swallow-tail" pattern with plain tails and a high-standing collar and cuffs trimmed with narrow red cord. The six large buttons fastening its front bear the New Hampshire coat of arms. Trousers are plain gray. The gray overcoats supplied with this uniform were of the dismounted pattern, with a cape falling to the elbow and with only five buttons in front. Of chasseur pattern, his gray cap with red band is of the type made for the regiment by hatter S. Klous & Co., of Boston, and supplied by George A. Barnes, a merchant based in Manchester, New Hampshire.[2]

Belonging to one of nine battalion or center companies of his regiment, this private is armed with a Model 1842 smoothbore musket to which he has fixed his bayonet. The remaining two flank companies carried Pattern 1853 Enfield rifle muskets and Model 1859 Sharps rifles, respectively. He also carries a nonregulation Bowie knife in a red leather sheath. Accoutrements consist of a cartridge box, percussion cap pouch, belt, bayonet scabbard, and musket sling, all of which were made by James R. Hill, who owned a large harness manufactory on Main Street, Concord, New Hampshire.[3] His black waterproofed haversack and canteen were acquired from military suppliers Haughton, Sawyer & Co., of Boston, and Horace H. Day, of 91 Liberty Street, New York.

The 2nd New Hampshire also received blue flannel four-button sack coats before leaving their home state. On arrival in Washington they wore "gray caps and pants and blue jackets," and likely fought in this dress at Bull Run on July 21, 1861.[4] By September 13, 1861, the 2nd New Hampshire had been re-uniformed in "the dress of the regular army."[5]

This regiment served through the Peninsula Campaign of 1862, Pope's Campaign in Northern Virginia, Gettysburg, and Grant's Overland Campaign, and lost 15 officers and 163 enlisted men, who were killed or mortally wounded, and 6 officers and 166 enlisted men to disease. After performing provost duty in Virginia during the summer of 1865, it was finally mustered out on December 19, 1865.

1. *New Hampshire Patriot & State Gazette* (Concord, NH), July 3, 1861, 3:1.
2. Receipt dated May 3, 1861, box marked 2nd New Hampshire, State Archives, Concord, NH.
3. *New-Hampshire Statesman* (Concord, NH), May 18, 1861, 2:6.
4. *National Republican* (Washington, DC) June 24, 1861, 3:1.
5. *Farmer's Cabinet* (Amherst, NH), September 20, 1861, 2:6.

Private, Company I, 4th Virginia Infantry, Liberty Hall Volunteers

A GROUP OF STUDENTS OF WASHING-TON COLLEGE, in Lexington, Virginia, petitioned the faculty to permit them to form a military class at least a month before the Dominion State seceded from the Union on April 17, 1861. As numbers grew sufficient to form a military company under the command of Captain James J. White, a professor of Greek at the College, the students decided to call themselves the Liberty Hall Volunteers, in honor of Liberty Hall Academy, the original name for Washington College. Drilled by cadets of the Virginia Military Institute, a neighboring institution, not all the members of the Liberty Hall Volunteers were students. Of the original company of seventy-three, seventeen were farmers or tradesmen.

On June 18, after the company repeatedly applied to be accepted for active service, Governor John Letcher ordered it to report to Winchester, where it was incorporated into the Army of the Shenandoah as Company I, 4th Virginia Infantry, First Brigade, under the command of Colonel Thomas J. Jackson. Becoming known as the "Stonewall Brigade" after its decisive action on Henry House Hill at First Manassas on July 21, 1861, this brigade preserved its identity up to the Battle of Spotsylvania Court House in May 1864, where its numbers were so depleted by capture, death, or wounds at the "Bloody Angle" that its remnants were consolidated with other brigades of the division.[1]

The youthful soldier in this painting is depicted as he would have looked on the battlefield at First Manassas. Made from cloth produced at a local woolen mill, his gray shirt has black trim down its buttoned front and along the pocket tops. Trim on shirts worn by the Liberty Hall Volunteers slightly differed from one man to the next, illustrating that they were homemade. His cadet-gray trousers have narrow black seam stripes, and headgear consists of a high-crowned, Pattern 1858 dark-blue forage cap. Linen gaiters were originally worn by the Liberty Hall Volunteers, but these would have been abandoned during the heat of the day on the battlefield.

He is armed with a .69 caliber smoothbore musket converted to percussion. The muskets carried by his company were reported to be "in good condition" on June 18, 1861. As they were considered to be "old," cartridge boxes issued were likely Pattern 1839. Captain White purchased bayonet scabbards and cap pouches for the whole company as they had not been supplied by the state.[2] A sheathed spear-pointed knife with a German silver cutlery handle is attached to his belt via a red leather frog.

---

1. James I. Robertson, *4th Virginia Infantry* (H. E. Howard, Inc., 1982), 32.

2. Janet B. Hewett, ed., *Supplement to the Official Records of the Union and Confederate Armies*, part II, record of events, serial no. 82, 826. Hereafter cited as *Supplement* plus volume and page number.

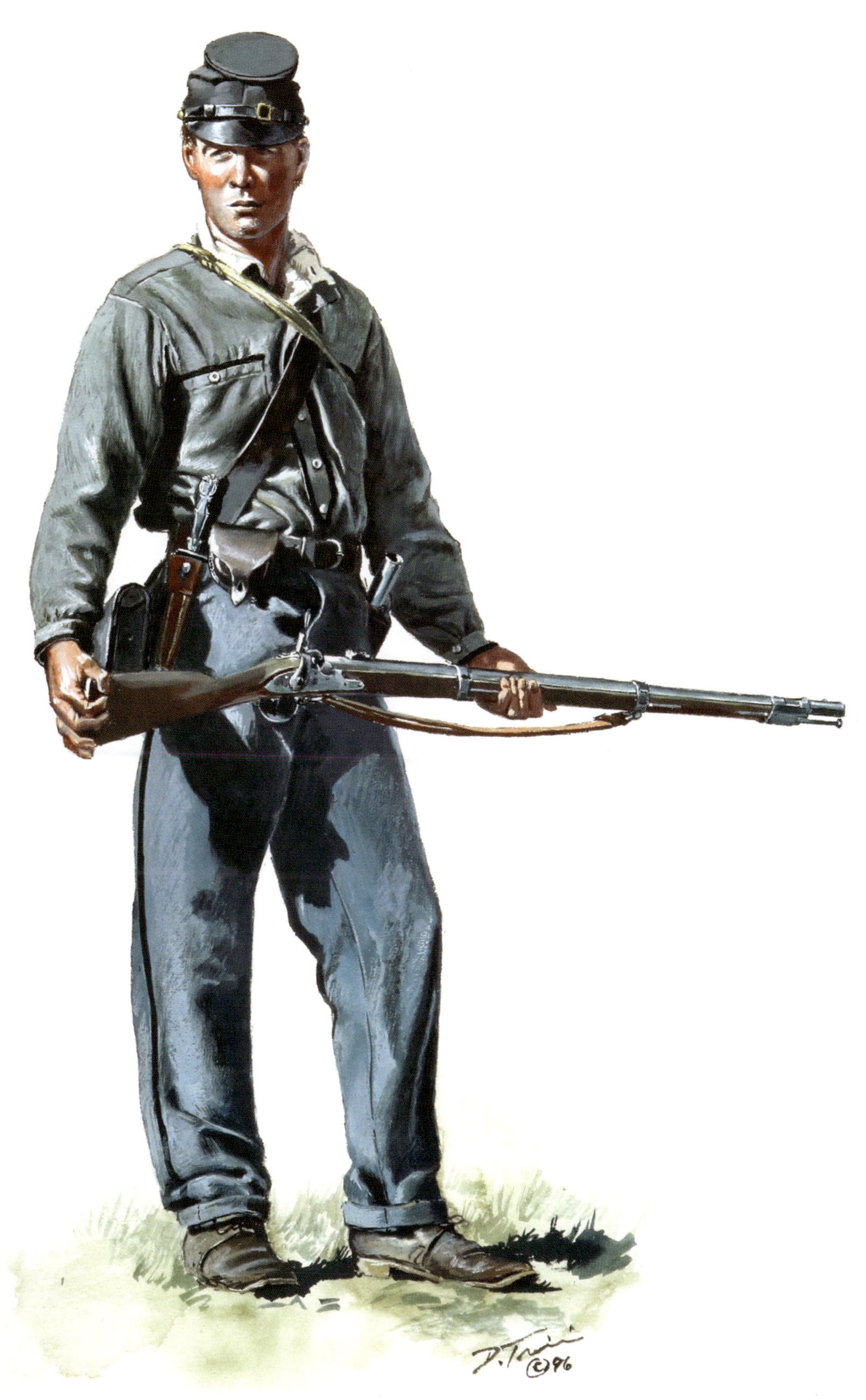

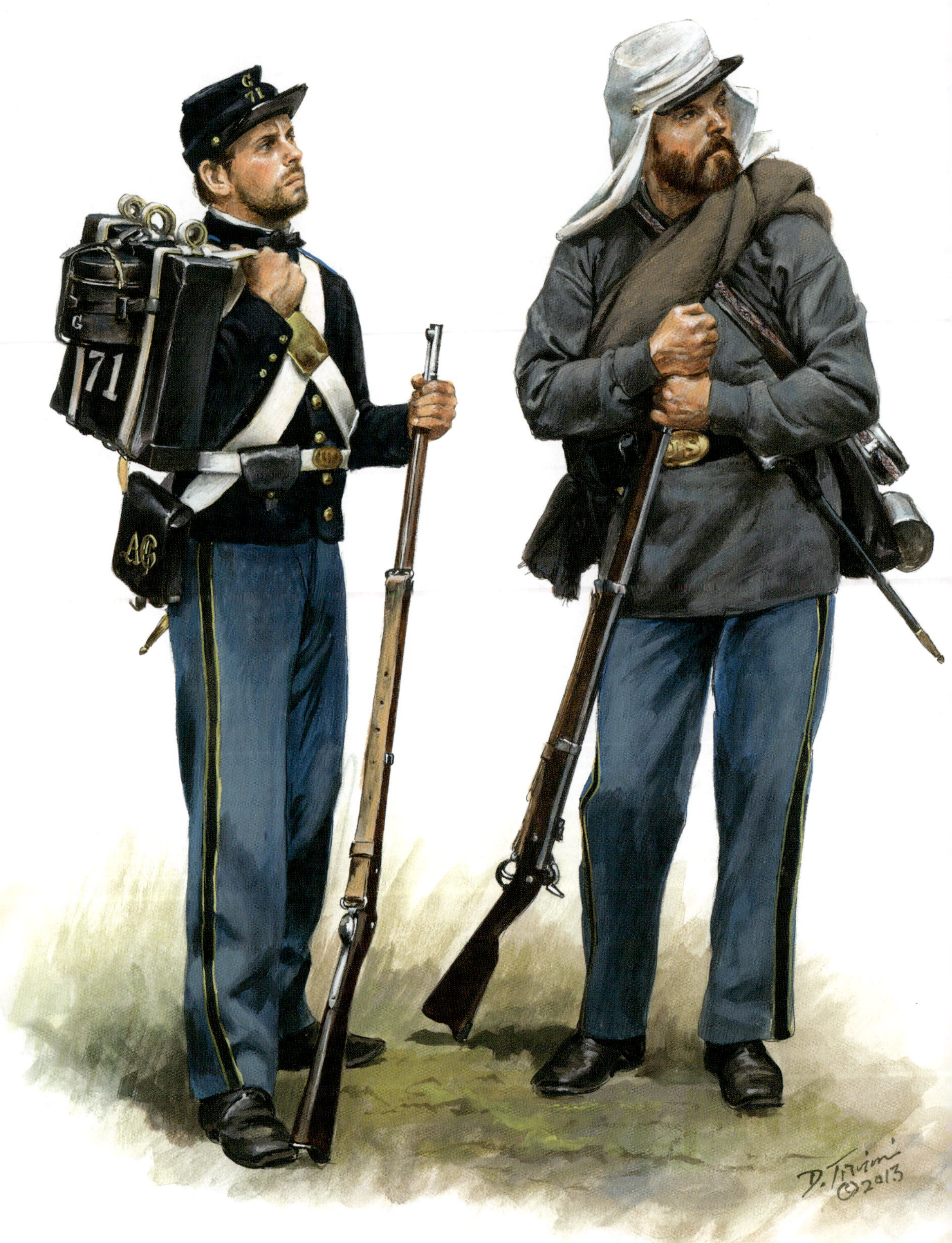

71st New York State Militia

FORMED AS A BATTALION AMONG THE AMERICAN-BORN CITIZENS of New York City in September 1852, the American Rifles were expanded into the 71st New York State Militia (NYSM) during the following month. In 1856 this regiment altered its name to the American Guard due to a change of arms from rifle to the musket.[1] The prewar full dress for the 71st NYSM consisted of a dark-blue frock coat with a sky-blue collar and cuffs trimmed with black cord and gold lace; sky-blue trousers with black seam stripes edged in gold; and a National Guard–pattern cap topped with a white wool pompon. With the outbreak of the Civil War, the bulk of unit members arrived at the capital wearing their regimental fatigue uniform, which consisted of a "dark-blue coat [jacket], [sky-] blue pants with black stripe and gilt borders, and blue fatigue cap."[2] About three hundred recruits with the regiment lacked uniforms and were "dressed as taste and fancy dictated," presenting "a most motley appearance."[3]

According to the regimental history, when the 71st NYSM members marched out of the Navy Yard at Washington on July 16, 1861, to join Burnside's brigade prior to the Battle of Bull Run, their dark-blue jackets were left in their knapsacks, and they wore bluish-gray blouses sent from New York City, with white cotton Havelock covers over their forage caps.[4]

The figure on the left is in the regimental fatigue uniform worn by the regular members of the regiment when it left for the capital on April 21, 1861. His cap bears brass letters and numerals indicating his company and regimental designation. His white buff leather shoulder belts support a Pattern 1857 cartridge box with brass "Old English" letters, "AG," on the outer flap and a bayonet in scabbard. His waist belt is fastened with a small version of the 1839 oval "US" plate, which would have previously accompanied the flask and pouch carried by the regiment when armed with rifles from 1852 through 1856. He carries a rigid militia-pattern knapsack with a mess tin attached, with white-painted regimental and company designations.

The figure at right appears as he would have when marching toward Manassas in July 1861. A brown blanket roll, a haversack containing three days' rations, and a canteen are worn over his blouse, and the ubiquitous Havelock covers his cap, while black leather belts support his cap pouch, cartridge box, and bayonet scabbard. Both men carry Model 1855 rifle muskets.

---

1. *New-York Times*, October 22, 1852, 8:3; and *New York Evening Express* (New York, NY), September 5, 1856, 3.

2. *Evening Star* (Washington, DC), April 27, 1861, 2:1.

3. *New York Herald*, April 22, 1861, 1:4.

4. *History of the 71st Regiment, N.Y.N.G.* (Veterans Association 71st Regiment, N.Y.N.G.: 1919), 160; and letter written by a member of Co. A.

8th Georgia Infantry, Company E, Miller Rifles

ORIGINALLY UNSUCCESSFUL IN OF-FERING ITS SERVICES to the state of Georgia as the Floyd Cavalry, this company reorganized as infantry and adopted the name Miller Rifles, for Senator Dr. Homer V. M. Miller, who volunteered as a surgeon with the 8th Georgia Infantry with the rank of major and who was appointed Chief Surgeon of the District of Georgia in May 1863.[1] Commanded by Captain John R. Towers, the Miller Rifles were accepted in Confederate service for the war on May 14, 1861, at Sheibley's School House, one mile northeast of Rome, Floyd County, Georgia. They were mustered in "for the war" as Company E, 8th Georgia Infantry, commanded by Colonel Francis S. Bartow, in Richmond, Virginia, on June 3, 1861.

Based on surviving images of the 8th Georgia early in the war, this private of the Miller Rifles wears a plain gray uniform coat fastened with eight Georgia state seal buttons, plus matching gray pants with black seam stripes and a forage cap. The coat was likely supplied by a tailor in Rome, Georgia, who also provided uniforms for the Rome Light Guards, Company A, 8th Georgia. He cradles a Model 1841 Mississippi rifle, indicating that the Miller Rifles was a flank company, and is also armed with a Bowie knife in a red leather sheath and a holstered revolver. Accoutrements include a waist belt with a brass frame buckle, a white canvas haversack, and a knapsack with a brown blanket roll.

As senior colonel, Bartow took command of the brigade at First Manassas on July 21, 1861, while Lieutenant Colonel William M. Gardner commanded the 8th Georgia. Including Colonel Bartow, the regiment lost 201 men, with 42 killed and 159 wounded, on the Plains of Manassas.

The regiment was involved in the campaigns of the Army of Northern Virginia from the Seven Days' Battles to the Battle of Cold Harbor, except when with Longstreet at Suffolk, in Georgia, and in Knoxville, Tennessee. The unit participated in the siege of Petersburg, south and north of the James River, and lastly in the Appomattox Campaign.[2]

The record shows that a total of 145 men enlisted in the Miller Rifles throughout the war, of whom 14 were killed in battle, 7 died of wounds, and 29 died of disease. Only 16 of the company were present during the surrender at Appomattox Court House on April 9, 1865.

---

1. Hooper Alexander, "A Sketch of the Life and Character of Dr. H. V. M. Miller," *Atlanta Medical and Surgical Journal* XIII, no. 5 (July 1896): 293.

2. Joseph H. Crute Jr., *Units of the Confederate States Army* (Derwent Books, 1987), 89.

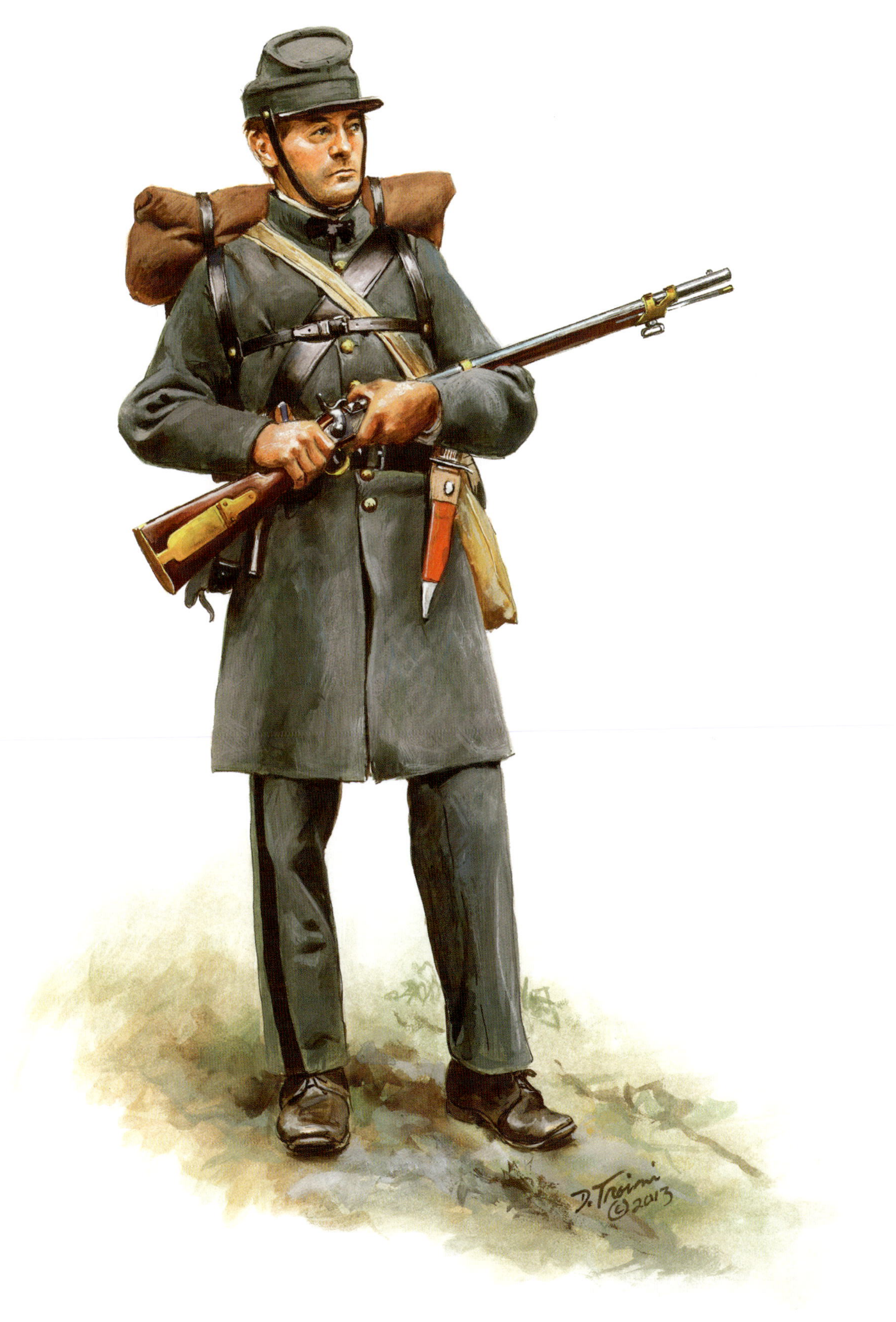

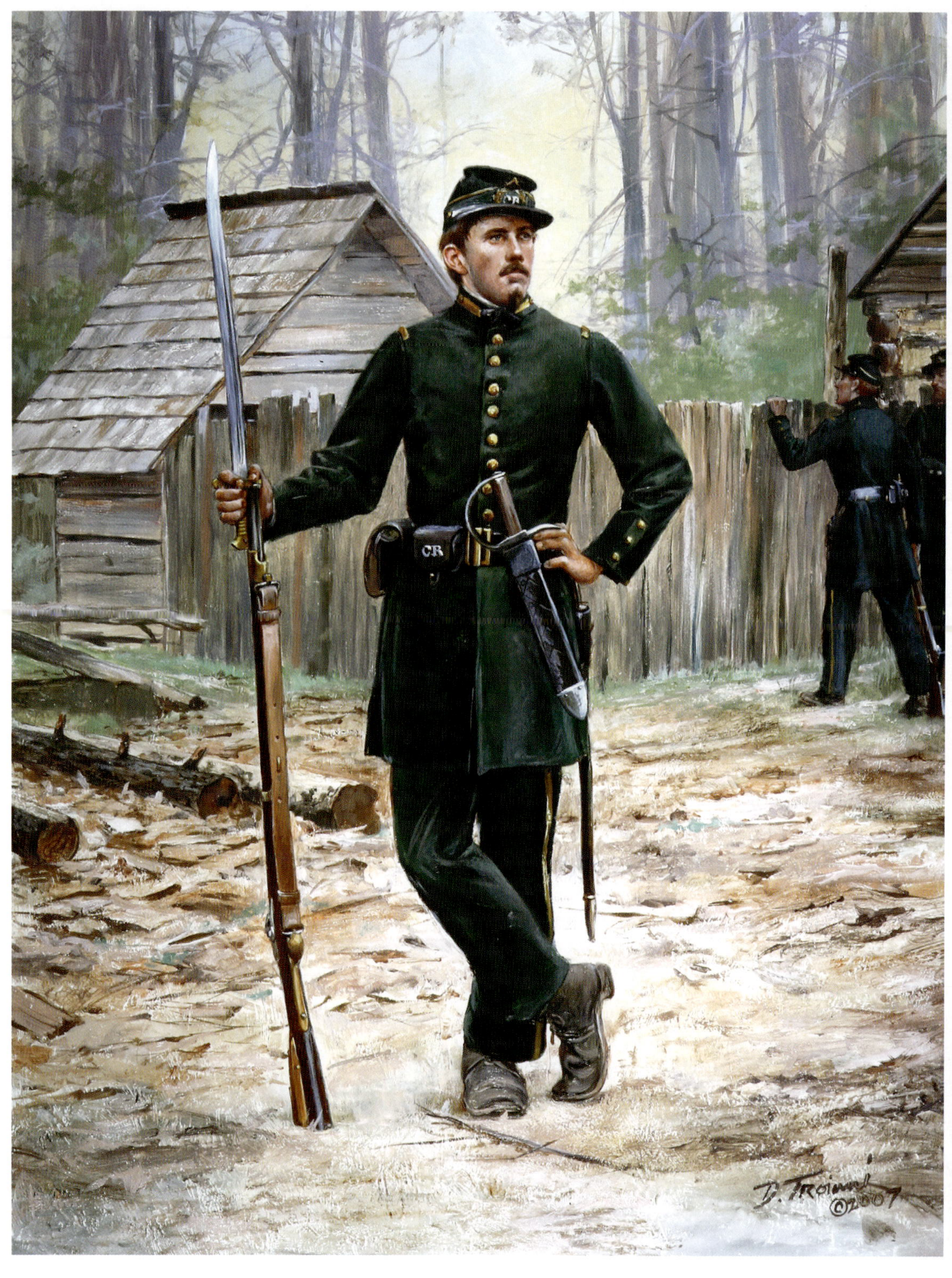

Clinch Rifles, Georgia Militia, April 1861

ORGANIZED AS AN "INDEPENDENT RIFLE COMPANY" by the Clinch Engine Fire Company No. 2, of Augusta, Georgia, on March 25, 1851, the Clinch Rifles formed part of the Augusta Independent Volunteer Battalion, Georgia Militia, and were mustered into Confederate service for twelve months on May 11, 1861, as Company A, 5th Georgia Volunteers. This unit was also known as the "Pound Cake Regiment" because of its members' smart appearance.

The "regular rifle green" uniform worn by the Clinch Rifles was adopted on February 10, 1860, and made by Merchant and Military Tailors Haigh & Andrews, of 220 Broad Street, Augusta.[1] Based on the dark-blue pattern introduced by the US Army in 1851, his uniform coat has a single row of nine brass buttons bearing the Georgia state coat of arms, with three smaller buttons of the same pattern on each plain cuff patch. His matching trousers have one-inch–wide gold strips of lace on the outer seams. Headgear consists of a high-crowned forage cap with a thin welt of gold cord around the band, which meets in a point above the company insignia, which is composed of the letters "CR" within a laurel wreath.

He is armed with a Model 1841 Mississippi rifle, with a russet leather strap, altered to accommodate the brass-handled saber bayonet. This firearm is an example of those acquired by his company from the two thousand of this model surrendered to state forces at the Federal Arsenal in Augusta on January 23, 1861. The saber bayonet was not well liked as it made the Mississippi rifle difficult to load quickly and added to the weight of the weapon.

His accoutrements consist of a Pattern 1855 US Rifleman Enlisted waist belt fastened by a brass rectangular loop and clasp plate. Of French design, this was copied from the 1847 *chasseur a pied* accoutrements with a frog for the saber bayonet and slides that were designed to be linked to the Pattern 1855 knapsack. Compatible with the Model 1841 rifle because it had only vertical belt loops, a Pattern 1839 cartridge box is out of view on the right-hand side of his belt. His percussion cap pouch was likely of the Allegheny Arsenal pattern with longer back straps to fit the riflemen's belt.

Exchanging their green for gray uniforms, members of the Clinch Rifles saw their first combat with the 5th Georgia on Santa Rosa Island off the coast of Florida on October 9, 1861. Following this, their regiment fought in and around Corinth until the end of May 1862, and lost 32 percent of its men as casualties at Murfreesboro on July 13, besides its colonel and regimental battle flag. Continuing to serve with the Army of Tennessee throughout the remainder of the war, the 5th Georgia joined the rest of the Confederate army in its retreat through North Carolina in 1865, and fought at Bentonville with 256 effectives, following which remnants of the regiment surrendered with the Army of Tennessee on April 26 of that year.

---

1. *Daily Chronicle and Sentinel* (Augusta, GA), May 17, 1861, 3:2; and December 30, 1859, 3:4.
2. Crute, *Units of the Confederate States Army*, 86.

1st Minnesota Infantry, July 1861

THE 1ST MINNESOTA VOLUNTEER MILITIA ASSEMBLED AT Fort Snelling in Saint Paul on April 27, 1861, and two days later was mustered in for three months' Federal service. As such they were the first volunteers to respond to the Union cause as Governor Alexander Ramsey of Minnesota was visiting Washington, DC, at the time and immediately offered President Lincoln one thousand men.

In order to uniform the regiment quickly, the State purchased from wholesale dealers in Indian trade goods Culver & Farrington, of Saint Paul, 800 flannel shirts of various colors; 868 black hats; and 868 pairs of dark-blue or black pants. A further 50 red flannel shirts were purchased from Farrington and Hughson of the same city.[1] According to the regimental historian, "The shirts were woolen, but of various colors, red predominating. Generally the shirts were of the kind then affected by steamboat men and men of the frontiers, and some of them were very fancifully ornamented with crescents, stars, trefoils, etc."[2] Later in July, Lieutenant Colonel Stephen Miller wrote that this was "the best temporary and practical uniform that could be obtained promptly, in our poor and sparsely settled State."[3] Regarding equipment, Culver and Farrington supplied the 1st Minnesota with 970 haversacks, 132 canteens and 500 canteen straps.[4]

Although four companies also received US regulation uniforms before they departed for the Federal capital, and the Winona Company was clothed in gray suits with black trim courtesy of their local community, most members of the 1st Minnesota wore the State-purchased clothing for fatigue and campaign duty throughout their first few months of service.[5] As a parting gift, the regiment received white cotton havelocks courtesy of the womenfolk of Saint Paul and other towns throughout the State.[6]

Witnessing their drill after arrival in the Federal capital, where the regiment was remustered for three years of service, a report in the *Evening Star* observed the 1st Minnesota as a "long line of white havelocks, red shirts, blue pants and glistening arms."[7] Part of the First Brigade, Third Division, commanded by Colonel W. B. Franklin, the 1st Minnesota fought alongside the 11th New York, or First Fire Zouaves, at Bull Run on July 21, 1861, and suffered the loss of 10 officers and 177 enlisted men who were killed in action or later died of their wounds.

The 1st Minnesota fought with distinction throughout the war in the Army of the Potomac. It suffered significant casualties at Antietam during General John Sedgewick's ill-fated assault on the West Woods. During the second day at Gettysburg it bravely charged into a brigade of approximately 1,200 Confederates belonging to Longstreet's Corps. During Pickett's charge on July 3, Private Marshall Sherman of Company C captured the colors of the 28th Virginia Infantry and later received the Medal of Honor for this accomplishment. In 1863, 1st Minnesota participated in the Bristoe and Mine Run campaigns. The regiment mustered out at Fort Snelling, Minnesota, on April 29, 1864, although many men continued to serve as the 1st Minnesota Infantry Battalion and went on to fight in the Appomattox Campaign.

---

1. *Annual Report of the Adjutant General to the Legislature of Minnesota. Session of 1862* (Wm. R. Marshall, Incidental Printer, 1862), 197, 206.

2. Retsen L. Holcombe, *History of the First Regiment Minnesota Volunteer Infantry, 1861–1864* (Easton & Masterman Printers, 1916), 12.

3. *The Weekly Pioneer and Democrat* (Saint Paul, MN), August 16, 1861, 4:5.

4. Daybook, 1858–1862, Culver and Farrington Store, MNHS, locator: Bc1.1/C968, Minnesota Historical Society, 468, 472, 480.

5. *The Weekly Pioneer and Democrat*, August 16, 1861, 4:4.

6. *Chicago Daily Tribune*, June 24, 1861, 4:2.

7. *Evening Star* (Washington, DC), June 29, 1861, 3:2.

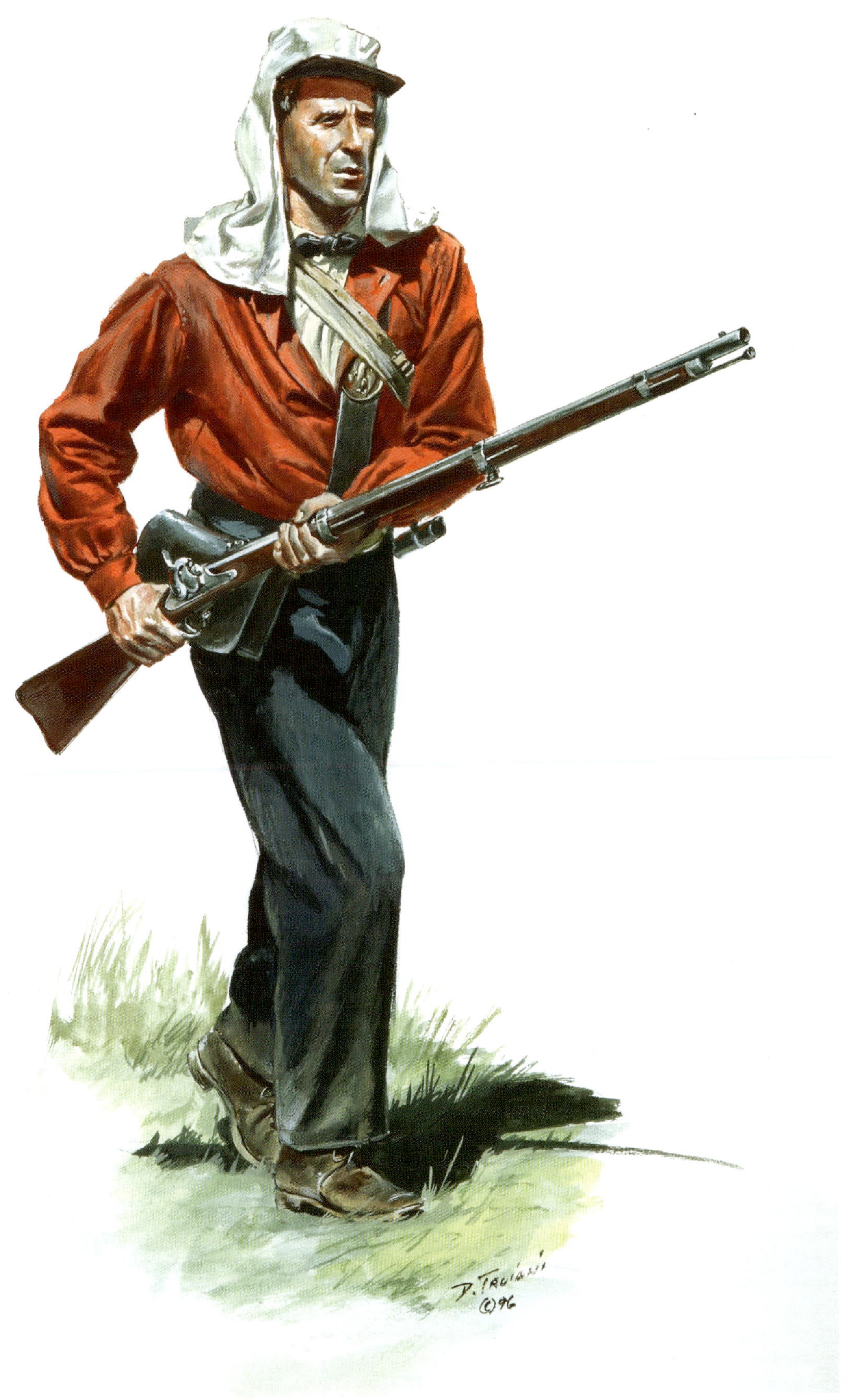

D. Troiani
© 96

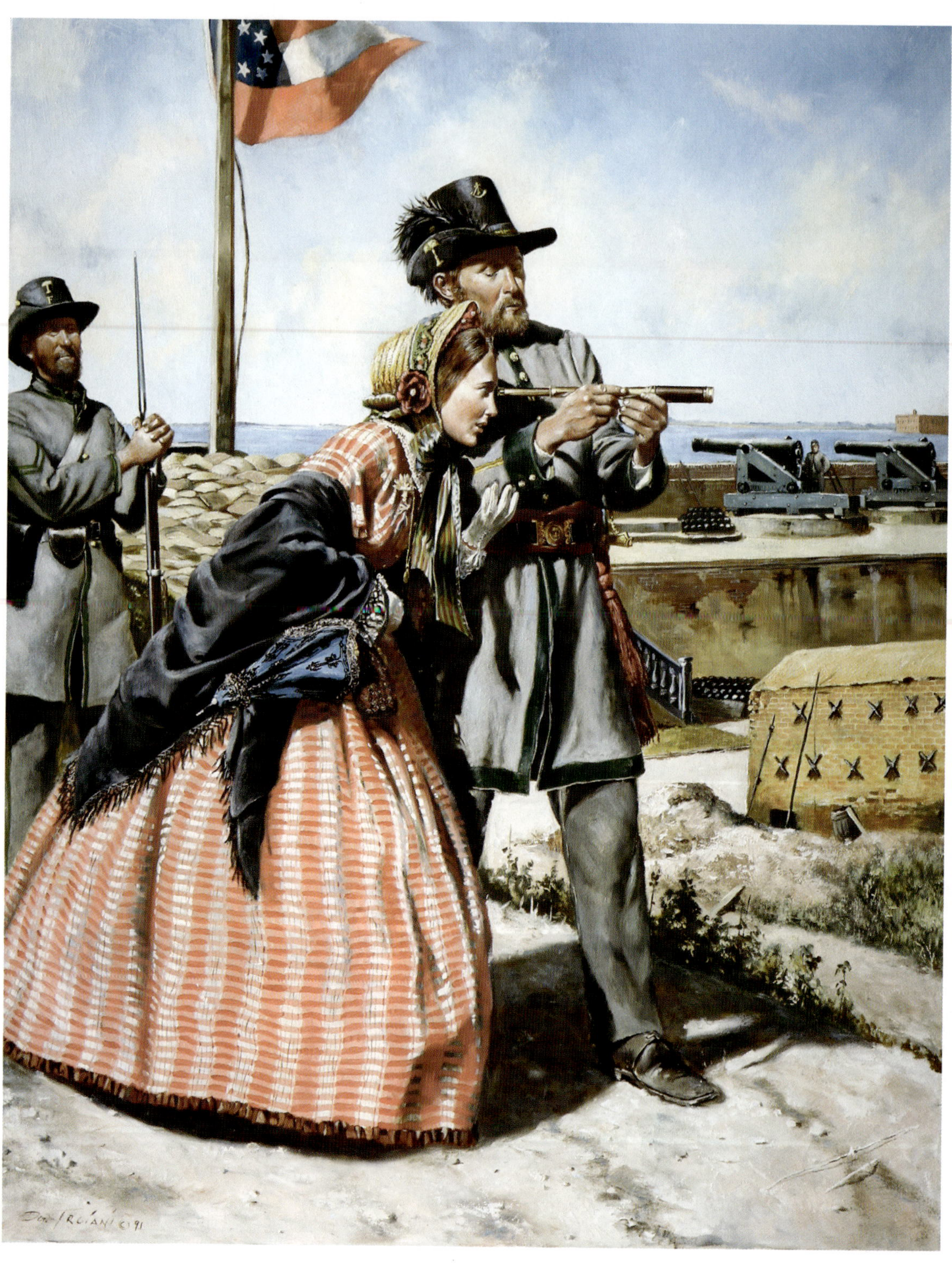

1st Regiment South Carolina Rifles, 1861

RECRUITED IN THE EXTREME WEST-ERN PART OF the state, the 1st Regiment of South Carolina Rifles, also known as Orr's Rifles, was commanded by politician and diplomat James L. Orr. Originally enlisting for twelve months, it was the first regiment from the Palmetto State to enlist "for the war," being mustered into Confederate service on July 20, 1861. The first uniforms provided for this regiment were paid for by "the good and patriotic citizens" of the respective districts of South Carolina from which the companies came. Although based on a full set of uniform regulations first published in the *Keowee Courier*, of Pickens District, on July 13, 1861, a certain amount of variation occurred in cut and trim from company to company as uniforms were made up by tailors, seamstresses, and local womenfolk in the various districts. This was compounded by a second set of slightly different regulations published in the *Abbeville Press* on August 2, 1861. Uniform coats and trousers were to be of dark-blue cloth trimmed in the branch service color of green, with velvet for officers and dark-blue jeans trimmed with green worsted lace for enlisted men.[1] Headgear was based on the dress hat prescribed for the US Army in 1858, but with the addition of a gilt Palmetto tree insignia.

As their regiment was influenced by the promulgation in June 1861 of Confederate States uniform regulations that stipulated use of cadet-gray uniforms, the captain and corporal in this plate wear a gray rather than dark-blue version of Orr's Rifles uniform.[2] Both display a Palmetto tree on the looped-up brim of their hats, while the officer has a Pattern 1834 infantry horn insignia on the crown of his hat. Based on the Abbeville set of regulations, his rank is indicated by two narrow strands of gilt lace on the outside of his coat sleeves, which were accompanied by two horizontal gilt bars on his collar. The green worsted trim on the corporal's uniform is much more modest compared with the green velvet worn by the officer. The officer's sword belt has a tongue and wreath plate with a Palmetto device, while that of the corporal is fastened with a brass frame buckle.

Toward the end of August 1861, and with the winter approaching, Colonel Orr appealed in the *Abbeville Press* for "the Ladies of Pickens, Anderson and Abbeville Districts" to make warmer uniforms for his regiment. To be provided by October 15, 1861, these were to consist of a "Frock coat, Pants and Overcoat, of brown home made woollen goods."[3] By October 1862, these began to be replaced with Confederate Quartermaster–issue jackets, trousers and overcoats.[4] Although Orr's Rifles were established as a rifle regiment, the arms first received by the unit were old smooth bore muskets. These were later replaced by Model 1842 muskets and, later still, by rifled arms.

The 1st South Carolina Rifles served the Confederacy throughout the war, seeing action in nearly every important battle fought by the Army of Northern Virginia and surrendering only 157 officers and men at Appomattox Court House on April 9, 1865.

---

1. Ron Field, "First South Carolina Regiment of Rifles (Orr's Regiment of Rifles), 1861–62," *Journal of the Confederate Historical Society* 16, no. 3 (Autumn 1988): 66–72.

2. *Uniform and Dress of the Army of the Confederate States* (Chas. H. Wynne, Printer, 1861).

3. *Abbeville Press*, August 23, 1861. 1:4, 1:5.

4. National Archives & Records Administration (NARA), Compiled Military Service Record (CMSR)—Confederate—South Carolina, 1861–1865, M267, First (Orr's) Rifles, Co. H, First Lieutenant John H. Tolar, 35.

8th and 20th New York Volunteer Infantry, 1861

GERMAN-AMERICANS PROVIDED THE LARGEST ETHNIC contingent to fight for the Union during the Civil War. Of approximately two hundred thousand volunteers provided, two regiments recruited in 1861 wore uniforms reflecting the German tradition of the rifleman and marksmanship. Commanded by Colonel Louis Blenker, members of the 8th New York Volunteers, or First German Rifles, received their uniforms on May 12, 1861. These uniforms consisted of "a loose frock coat of cadet gray, faced with green," plus matching pantaloons. Their uniforms were further reported as consisting of "a gray sack with a strap and buckle behind, green cord facings and green shoulder straps, gray pantaloons with a broad green stripe down the side, and a gray cap with green cord. The officers' uniform is the same, with a red cap."[1] Passing through Wilmington, Delaware, en route for Washington, DC, the regiment wore "gray pants and a loose gray coat, with a short belt, by which it can be loosened or tightened about the waist." It also had "an engineer corps, [and] a band of 13 pieces and a full corps of buglers."[2] Despite expectations of being a rifle regiment, this unit was issued Model 1842 muskets.

Named for the German Turnverein athletic societies that encouraged the use of firearms for marksmanship, the 20th New York Volunteers, or United Turner Rifles, were recruited in New York and New Jersey and were under the command of Colonel Max Weber. Members were supplied by New York State with "the United States regulation outfit," consisting of dark-blue coats and pants with rifle-green trim and with shoulder straps and belt loops added.[3] Initially armed with Model 1842 smoothbore muskets, by July 1861 these had been exchanged for .54-caliber Model 1841 Remington rifles that were altered to accommodate either a socket or a saber bayonet, which the regiment carried throughout its two-year term of service. On December 5, 1861, the *New York Times* reported that the regiment presented a fine appearance at Camp Hamilton, near Fortress Monroe, Virginia, with "their bright rifles and green decorated uniforms."[4]

The enlisted man of the 8th New York represents the engineer corps of the regiment. Trained to work with axes, pickaxes, and spades, they repaired roads for the passage of troops, cleared away obstructions, and dug entrenchments. He wears over his green-trimmed gray uniform an India Rubber apron, and he holds a large axe.

In full dress, the corporal of the 20th New York wears a Federal-style uniform consisting of a Hardee hat with Pattern 1858 Rifleman's brass insignia at front, with company letter above and regimental designation below, plus rifle-green hat cord; a dark-blue uniform coat with shoulder straps; and matching pants, also trimmed with rifle-green. A Germanic marksman lanyard, or aiguillette, is worn looped over his left shoulder, and his M1841 rifle has a socket bayonet attached.

1. *New York Tribune*, May 13, 1861, 8:3.
2. *Evening Star* (Washington, DC), May 29, 1861, 3:1.
3. *New York Herald*, May 7, 1861, 8:2.
4. *New-York Times*, December 5, 1861, 4:6.

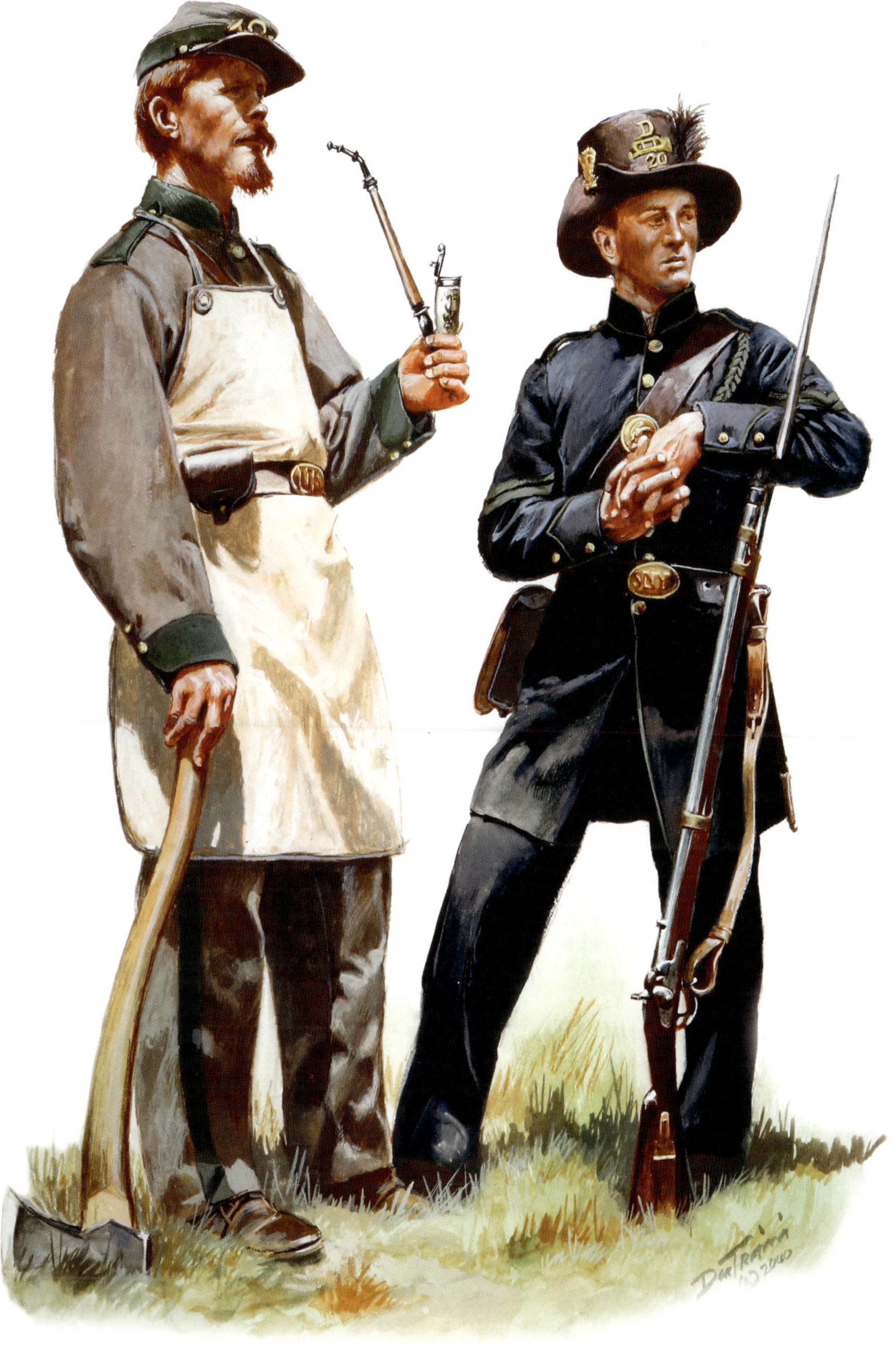

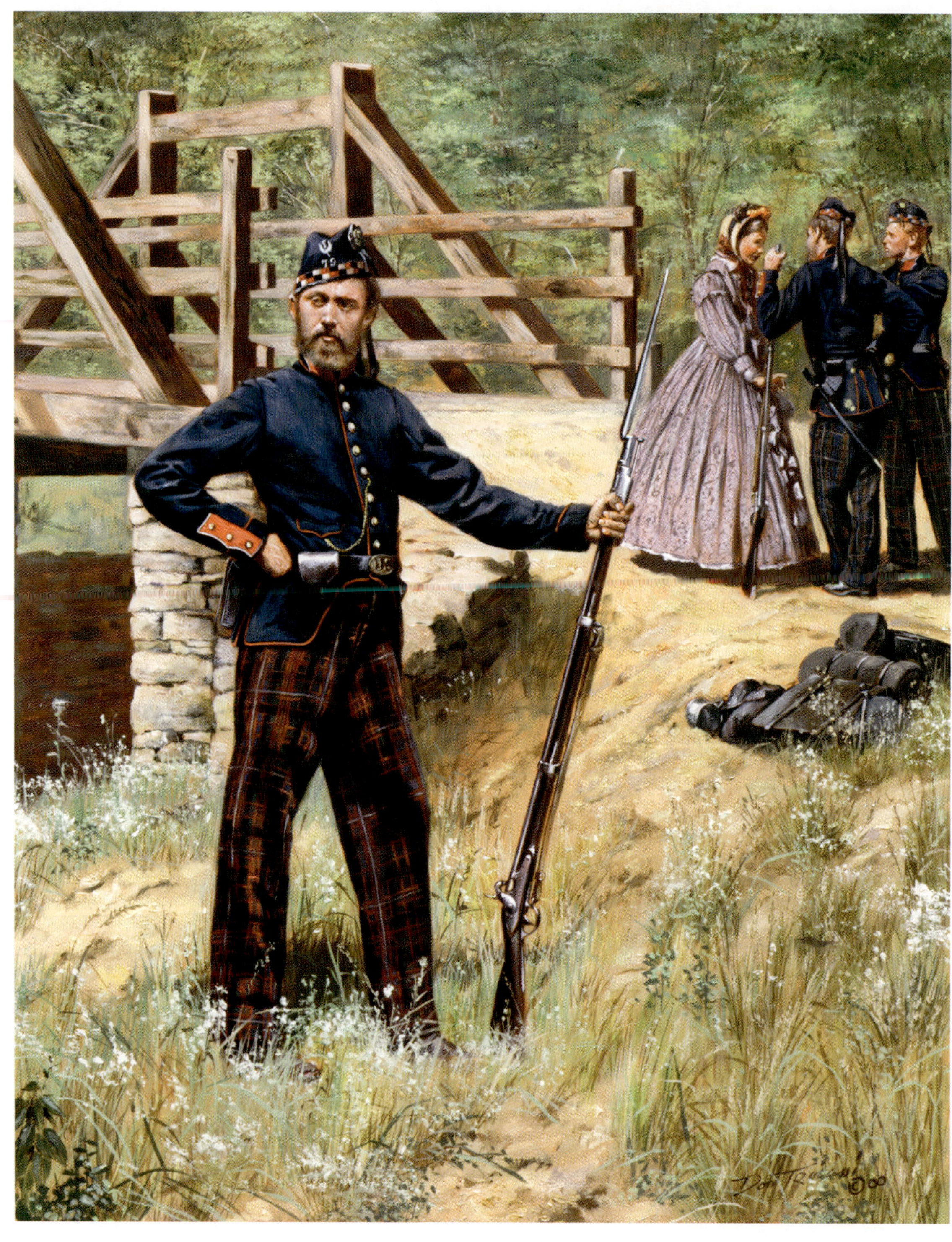

79th New York Infantry (Highlanders), 1861

ORGANIZED IN NOVEMBER 1858, AMONG THE Scottish community of New York City, the Highland Guard were designated the 79th New York State Militia (NYSM) in honor of the 79th Regiment, The Queen's Own Cameron Highlanders of the British Army.[1] Adopting the Cameron of Erracht tartan specially shipped from Scotland, the 79th New York ignored requests from New York's governor Edwin D. Morgan to wear a uniform based on 1858 regulations, which included a dress hat and frock coat, despite the concession of being permitted to wear plaid pants. Instead it paraded in full Highland dress, including kilts, on July 4, 1860, marching to the skirl of the pipes provided by the Caledonian Club of New York City.[2] The Highlanders also acquired tartan trews as fatigue dress, and 109 of them paraded as part of the Fourth Brigade, NYSM, in "plaid pants, polka jackets and small caps" on September 17 of that year.[3] This uniform was further described by the regimental historian William Todd as consisting of "handsome State jackets with red facings, blue fatigue caps and Cameron tartan pants."[4]

Increased in regimental size to 895 officers and men when mustered into Federal service for three years as a volunteer unit on May 29, 1861, the 79th New York found difficulty in providing its whole complement with kilted full dress. When the regiment departed for Washington, the press reported that "the kilted pipers were seen treading their way through the multitude . . . Then came the officers, variously clad in the tartans of their clans . . . then the men, dressed in dark jackets tipped with red, and plaid pantaloons."[5]

Uniformed as he would have appeared at the Federal capital in June 1861, this Highlander wears a Glengarry bonnet with diced band, cockade, and black silk ribbon. His nine-button doublet has red piping and red facings trimmed with white on collar and cuffs. Note the doublet worn by one of the Highlanders in the background displays the "flaming bomb" attached to its rear skirt. His tartan trews are of the Cameron of Erracht tartan. He holds a Model 1842 musket with a fixed bayonet.

According to William Todd, when McDowell's Army marched into Virginia as part of the Third Brigade of Brigadier General Daniel Tyler's First Division on July 17, 1861, members of the 79th New York wore "regulation dark blue blouses and light blue pants" and left knapsacks containing their doublets and tartan pants at camp in charge of "the Invalid Corps."[6] Nevertheless, during the next three years of war service, the Highlanders made every effort to wear their doublets and tartan trews whenever possible to carry on their Scottish heritage.

1. *New York Herald*, November 10, 1858, 4:6; and *ibid.*, December 12, 1858, 1:6.

2. Ron Field, "The Last Parade," *Military Images* 38, no. 3 (Summer 2020): 66.

3. *New York Herald*, September 19, 1860, 2:4.

4. William Todd, *The Seventy-Ninth Highlanders: New York Volunteers in the War of the Rebellion, 1861–1865* (Press of Brandow, Barton & Co., 1886), 5.

5. *New-York Times*, June 3, 1861, 8:4.

6. Todd, 18.

12th Illinois Infantry, 1st Scottish Regiment

COMMANDED BY COLONEL JOHN MCARTHUR, the 12th Illinois Infantry was one of the six three-month Illinois regiments reorganized for three years of service on August 1, 1861. It became known as the "1st Scotch Regiment" as its commander had migrated to the United States from Erskine, Scotland, in the mid-1850s and formed a volunteer militia company in Chicago, Illinois, called the Highland Guard. In 1856 this company was reported as wearing "the regular old style, with red frock coats, tartans, huge overhanging caps, bare continuations, and other paraphernalia."[1]

As a reward for reenlistment for three years, all six Illinois regiments were supplied with a dress and an undress uniform produced by Haughton, Sawyer & Co., of Boston, Massachusetts, via state agent Oliver M. Shannon. Made of "fine firm gray doeskin cassimere," the coat for the dress uniform had "a short skirt, midway to the knee" and was "trimmed with . . . blue for infantry." The fatigue uniform consisted of "a shirt, pantaloons and Zouave cap of firm hickory cloth."[2]

Likely chosen by Colonel McArthur, the distinctive headgear for the 12th Illinois consisted of a tam o' shanter with a narrow plaid band attached, which was described in the Chicago press as "the regular Scotch cap or bonnet with the thistle."[3] Organized in May 1862, the 65th Illinois, or "2nd Scotch Regiment/Cameron Highlanders," adopted a similar style of cap.

This commissary sergeant of the 12th Illinois wears an example of the gray dress uniform issued to his regiment. The cuffs of his coat have narrow light-blue panels with three nonfunctional buttons attached. His rank is indicated by 1½-inch–wide light-blue stripes on the outer seams of his trousers and sleeve chevrons of the same color with one tie, as required by Regimental Special Order No. 21 issued at Paducah on October 9, 1861, as opposed to the three prescribed for a commissary sergeant for the US Army in 1861. His blue tam o' shanter is topped with a small red pompom and has a black silk ribbon tied in a small bow at rear. A Pattern 1840 noncommissioned officers' sword is attached via a leather frog to his waist belt.

The 12th Illinois served with distinction in the Midwest, sustaining heavy losses at Fort Donelson, Shiloh, and Corinth in 1862. In the defense of Allatoona, Georgia, on October 5, 1864, it had 57 casualties among the remaining 161 men. Survivors and replacements marched to the sea with General William Tecumseh Sherman and then into the Carolinas to finish the war.

1. *Chicago Tribune*, August 16, 1856, 3:3.
2. *Illinois Daily State Register* (Springfield, IL), August 14, 1861, 2:1.
3. *Chicago Tribune*, February 13, 1862, 4:2.

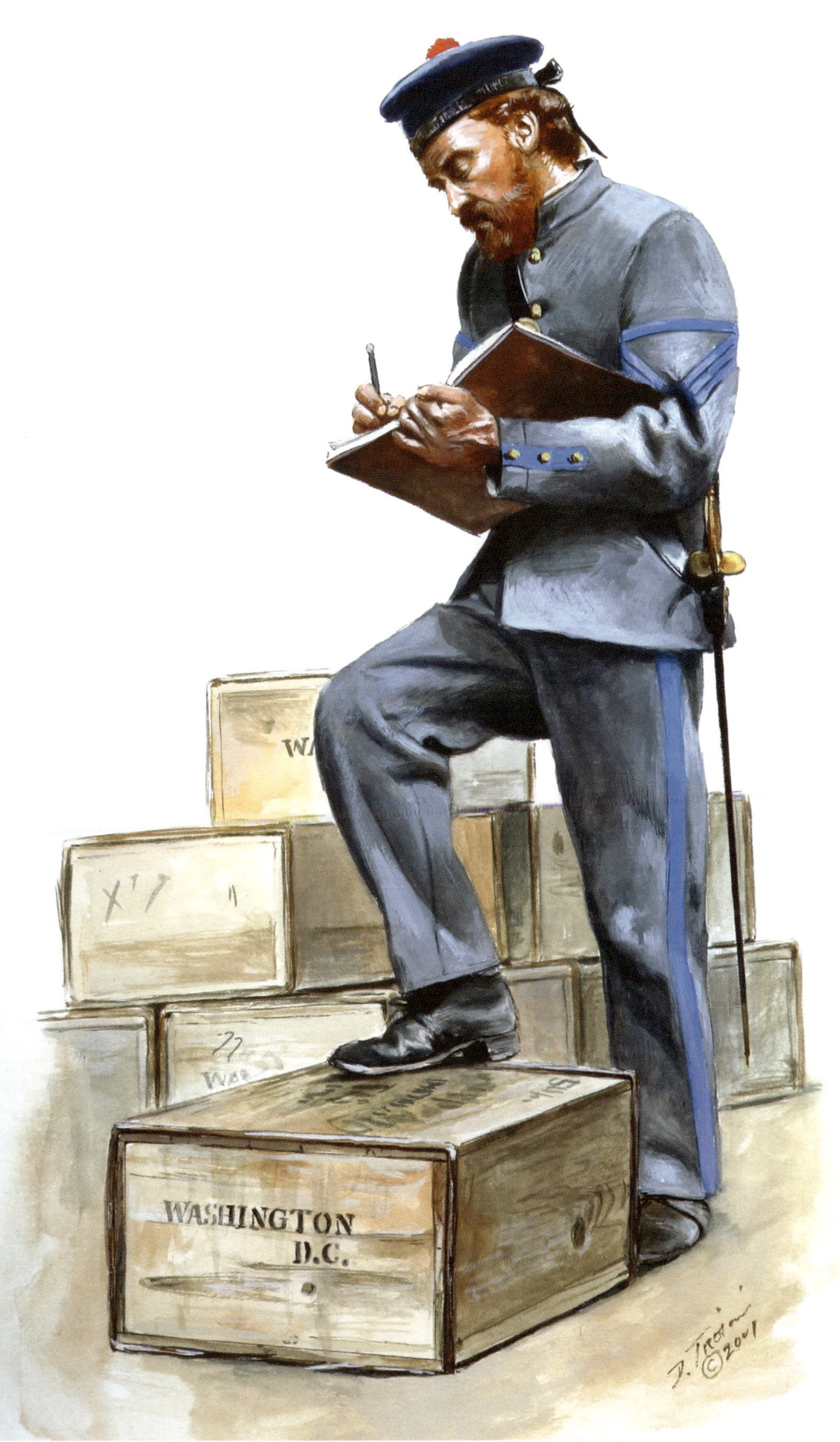

WASHINGTON
D.C.

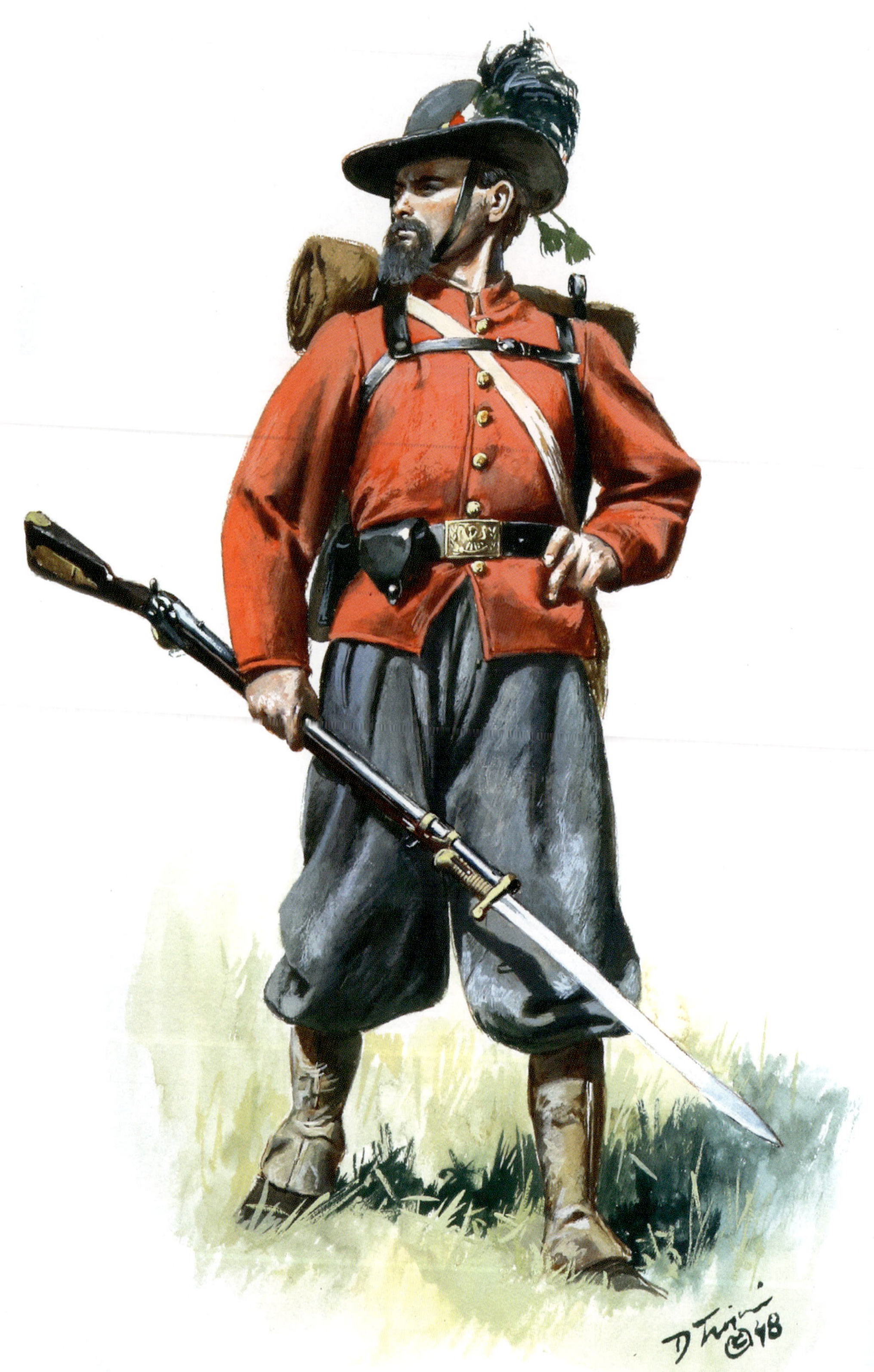

Garibaldi Legion, 1861

THE ITALIAN COMMUNITY IN NEW ORLEANS WAS thrilled by the exploits of Giuseppe Garibaldi and his "Expedition of the Thousand," which landed at Marsala, Sicily, on May 11, 1860, to conquer the Kingdom of the Two Sicilies and fight for Italian Unification. The threat to the sovereignty of their adopted southland further inspired Italians in the Crescent City to organize a Garibaldi Legion. Formed several days prior to the secession of Louisiana on January 26, 1861, the roll quickly included 270 names, with Captain Joseph Santini in command.[1]

Chosen by the end of the month, the uniform of the Legion was "to be much like that worn by Garibaldi's soldiers."[2] Ready to parade through the streets of New Orleans, this private of the Garibaldi Legion wears an example of what his unit had acquired by February 26, 1861. Reported in the city press in some detail, this consisted of a "black cocked hat, with a black plume on the cocked side, the stem of the plume (in front) being covered with little feathers of red, green, and white, (the colors of Italy) and the whole secured with a pelican button. A red jacket, tight fitting to the waist but spreading out at the hips; a black belt around the waist, with cartouche-box behind, and the jacket buttoned up to the chin with Pelican buttons. Gray trousers, of the largest Zouave style, bulging out as low as the knee; and then buff leather leggins, strapped and buckled the rest of the way down to the gaiters."[3]

His black felt hat is based on that worn by the *bersaglieri*, or riflemen, of Sardinia, formed in the 1840s by General Alessandro Ferrero La Marmora. His red chasseur-pattern jacket with six Pelican buttons is inspired by the red shirts acquired by Garibaldi's original Italian Legion in 1843. His pantaloons are gray rather than the bottle-green ones originally prescribed by the company uniform committee. His black leather waist belt is fastened with a state seal Pelican plate and carries a percussion cap pouch and a cartridge box. He is armed with a Model 1841 Mississippi rifle musket with a fixed sword bayonet. Strapped to his back is a knapsack of the type received by his unit by March 18, 1861.[4]

Maintained as a volunteer militia company for the defense of New Orleans, members of the Garibaldi Legion drilled and paraded throughout the remainder of 1861 in their "dashing red uniform and plumed hats."[5] By May, the Garibaldi Legion had been designated the Fourth Company of the Orleans Rifle Battalion and may have adopted a plainer fatigue outfit as all the companies in this unit were reported to have "adopted the same uniform."[6] Along with the rest of the volunteer militia in the city, the Garibaldi Legion surrendered to Farragut's United States Marines on April 28, 1862.

1. *New Orleans Daily Crescent*, January 23, 1861, 1:6.
2. *Daily Delta* (New Orleans, LA), January 29, 1861, 2:4.
3. *New Orleans Daily Crescent*, February 26, 1861, 1:5.
4. *Daily Delta*, March 19, 1861, 4:2.
5. *Daily Picayune* (New Orleans, LA), June 11, 1861, 2:1.
6. *New Orleans Daily Crescent*, May 10, 1861, 1:4.

39th New York Volunteers, Garibaldi Guard

THE GARIBALDI GUARD WAS THE FIRST OF FOUR REGIMENTS uniformed and armed by the Union Defense Committee, formed in Union Square, New York City, on April 20, 1861. They were commanded by Colonel Frederick George D'Utassy, who was a veteran supporter of Giuseppe Garibaldi and who joined the "Italian Legion" formed at Montevideo, Uruguay, in 1843, and subsequently saw service in Italy and the Crimea. Described as "an adventurer," D'Utassy's military career finally ended on May 29, 1863, when he was charged with dereliction of duty. Found guilty of numerous offences, including selling commissions and "plotting against officers under his command so as to cause them to resign," he was eventually sentenced to one year's hard labor at Sing Sing Prison.[1]

By May 4, 1861, the ranks of the Garibaldi Guard were full and consisted of 830 officers and men. Of its ten companies, only one was Italian, while five were German; one was Swiss; one, Spanish and Portuguese; one, Hungarian, Slav, and Prussian; and one, French and French Canadian.[2] On May 11, 1861, the regiment was mustered into state service for three years as the 39th New York Volunteer Infantry with the prospect of being put into active service immediately.

Several days later the New York newspapers reported the Garibaldi Guard wearing fatigue uniforms. The *Daily News* commented, "Dressed in their blue Zouave pantaloons and red shirts, they presented a remarkably fine appearance."[3] On May 25, a *New-York Times* correspondent observed the whole regiment uniformed in "a suit of blue-black, the pants having a narrow red stripe, and the facing of the frock coat being of red. Their hats are black, round-topped, wide, stiff brims, with a black feather and eagle. They have shoes with gaiters protecting the ankle and calf."[4]

Recruited as "a rifle regiment of sharpshooters," the Garibaldi Guard expected to receive Model 1855 US rifles with saber bayonet. Instead they were issued Model 1842 muskets with the promise of receiving better weapons once they reached Washington. They carried militia box-type knapsacks that bore the painted letters "GG."[7]

Eventually the 39th New York rid itself of corrupt leadership, and its distinctive uniform was replaced by New York State clothing. It served with honor in the Army of the Potomac, losing 8 officers and 107 enlisted men, who were killed or mortally wounded, and one officer and 158 enlisted men, who died from disease.

1. Michael Bacarella, *The 39th New York Infantry, Lincoln's Foreign Legion* (White Mane, 1997), 128.
2. Bacarella, 204–7.
3. *New York Daily News*, May 17, 1861, 1:6.
4. *New-York Times*, May 26, 1861, 8:5.
5. Bacarella, 34.
6. *New-York Times*, July 9, 1861, 1:1.
7. *New-York Times*, May 26, 1861, 8:5.

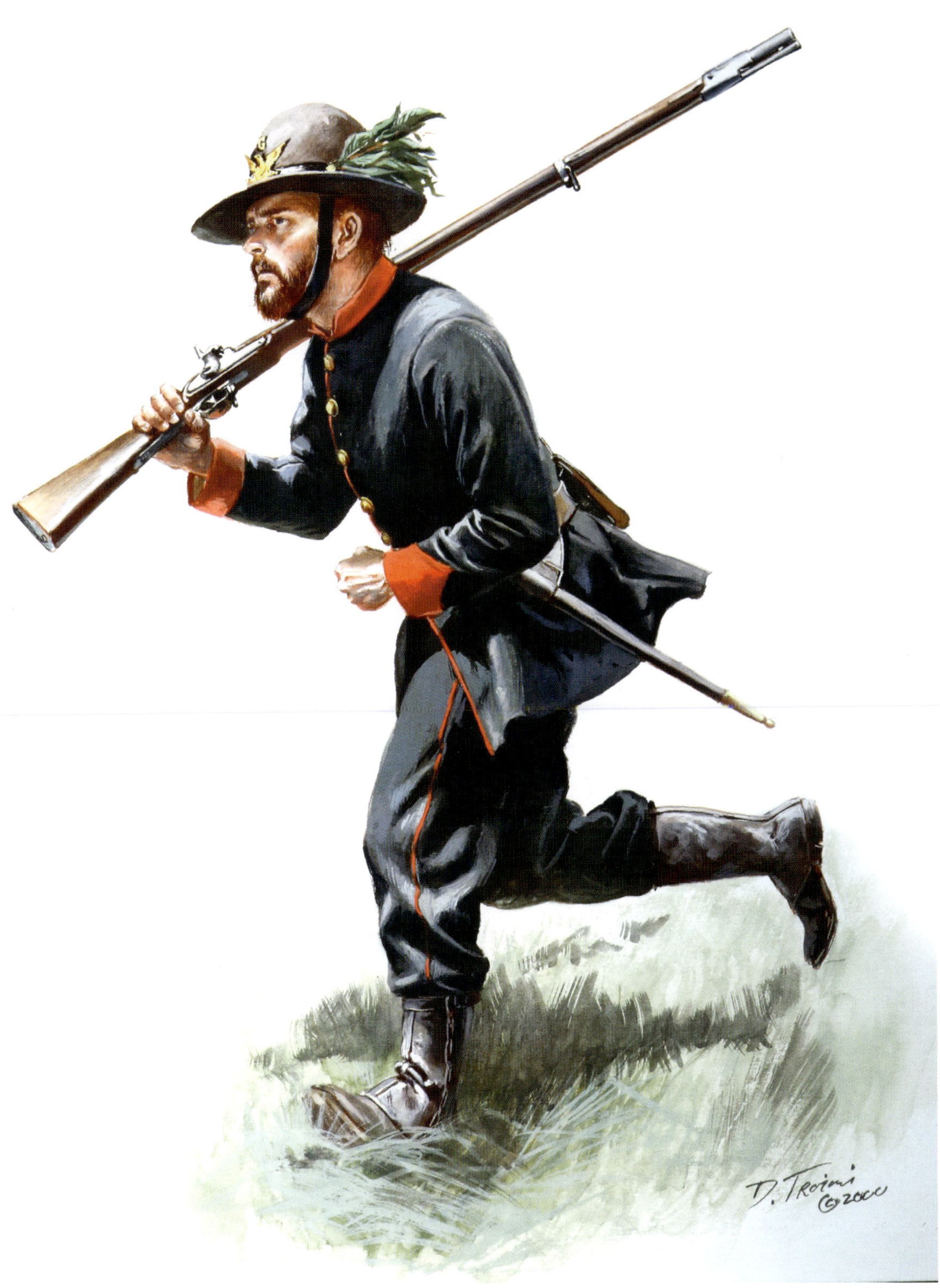

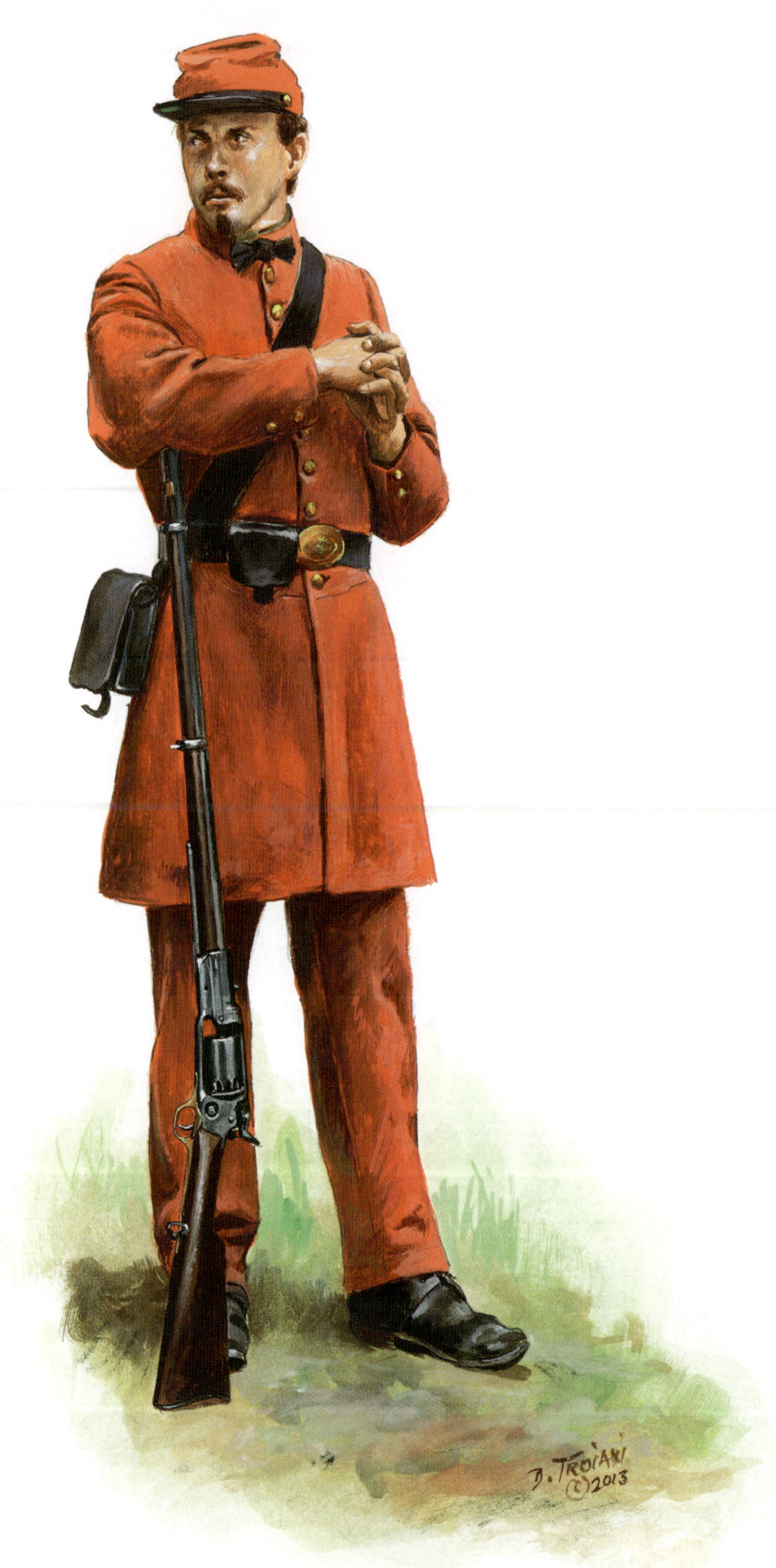

11th Mississippi Infantry (Van Dorn Reserves)

RECRUITED IN ABERDEEN, MONROE COUNTY, MISSISSIPPI, under the command of Captain William H. Moore during December 1860, the Monroe Light Infantry soon after changed its name to the Van Dorn Reserves in honor of Major (afterward Major General) Earl Van Dorn. Members of the Van Dorn Reserves were mustered into the Army of Mississippi for twelve months on February 20, 1861, as Company I, 11th Mississippi Infantry. The Company was called into the service of the Confederate States for twelve months in Lynchburg, Virginia, on May 13, 1861.[1] William Moore had been appointed colonel of the 11th Mississippi in Corinth, Mississippi, nine days earlier. As a result, Reuben O. Reynolds replaced him as captain of the Van Dorn Reserves. Reynolds would later serve as lieutenant colonel of the regiment.

According to the diary of twenty-four-year-old Private Mason Monroe Cummings, the Van Dorn Reserves were "handsomely uniformed," as "the citizens subscribed very liberally to the company—more than $7,500 having been raised" for clothing and equipment.[2] On March 4, 1861, the *Daily Evening Citizen* of Vicksburg reported that the unit wore a uniform of "red jeans," which was a type of cloth mainly used to clothe slaves during the 1850s.[3] Based on an image of Private Cummings, this included a nine-button frock coat with a standing collar and a chasseur-pattern forage cap of the same color of cloth. The Van Dorn Reserves were initially armed with "Colt's Five Shooting Rifles," while the rest of the 11th Mississippi carried old flintlock muskets converted to percussion.[4]

The first uniforms worn by the Van Dorn Reserves, and the rest of the 11th Mississippi, were in need of replacement by mid-1861 and were exchanged for plainer gray clothing produced as a result of a virtual monopolization of the state textile industry by the Mississippi military. Cloth produced in local mills was turned into uniform suits composed of frock coats and matching pants by Ladies' Soldier Sewing Societies, and the uniforms were transported to the Mississippi Depot in Richmond for distribution to the troops.[5] By 1863, the regiment began to receive Confederate Quartermaster-issue clothing.

The 11th Mississippi saw action at First Manassas, following which it was assigned to the Army of Northern Virginia. During 1862, it fought at Seven Pines, Seven Days Battles, and Second Manassas, and suffered heavy losses at Antietam. During the second day at Gettysburg, it sustained further losses at Cemetery Ridge. In 1864, it fought at the Wilderness, Spotsylvania Court House, and Cold Harbor, following which it served in the Petersburg Campaign until the Union breakthrough in early April 1865. Only sixty-four strong, most of the surviving men of the 11th Mississippi were captured, and the regiment was disbanded.[6]

---

1. *Supplement*, part 2, vol. 33, 243.
2. Diary of Mason Monroe Cummings, private collection.
3. *Daily Evening Citizen* (Vicksburg, MS), March 4, 1861, 2:1.
4. *Daily Evening Citizen*, March 4, 1861, 2:1.
5. Ron Field, *The Confederate Army 1861–65 (1), South Carolina and Mississippi* (Osprey Publishing, 2005), 39.
6. Dunbar Rowland, *Military History of Mississippi 1803–1898* (The Reprint Company, Publishers, 1908), 58.

41st New York Volunteers (De Kalb Regiment)

RAISED AMONG THE GERMAN-BORN OF NEW YORK, the 41st New York Volunteer Infantry was one of four three-year regiments the Union Defense Committee was authorized to recruit and equip. As such, it was free from state regulations and could tailor its original uniforms as the regiment desired. From its beginnings the 41st New York was also known as the De Kalb Regiment after the Prussian general Johann de Kalb who died fighting for American independence. It was also referred to as the 2nd Yaeger Regiment since the 8th New York Volunteer Infantry was known as the 1st German Rifles.[1]

The uniform chosen for all but one Zouave company of the 41st New York was based on that worn by the Prussian Yaegers, or Riflemen, of the time and consisted of dark-green coats of "very fine quality," faced with red cloth on collar and cuffs and edged with red trim. Trousers were gray with red cord on the outer seams, and forage caps the same color as the coat had a red band. In addition the regiment wore overcoats of "gray pilot cloth" made after "the Prussian Army regulation," with skirts that "looped up with hooks in order to cause the wearer no inconvenience in marching."[2] Officers wore the same uniform, with the addition of shoulder straps, and had gold lace on their caps. Equipment included two smaller-than-regulation cartridge boxes worn in Prussian jaeger-style on the front of their waist belts. The cost of outfitting the regiment was $35,648.30 for clothing and equipment.[3]

Commanding the 41st New York, Colonel Leopold von Gilsa was at first authorized to draw muskets from the Federal depot on Governor's Island, but a visit there on June 16, 1861, revealed that these weapons were "unfit to be carried by any military, even in peacetime, much less to take to the battlefield." About a week later, a shipment of Model 1842 Springfield muskets arrived, and the regiment could begin perfecting its manual of arms.[4]

The first indication that the 41st New York adopted a more regulation uniform occurred as a result of a requisition order dated July 4, 1862, for "dark blue blouses, light blue infantry pants [and] great coats."[5] By August 1862, members were wearing a mixture of Pattern 1861 New York State fatigue jackets and dark-blue trousers, four-button sack coats, and Pattern 1858 uniform coats. Many adopted the popular fashion of wearing cavalry boots, which caused foot problems resulting in orders prohibiting their use by infantry.

The 41st New York served in the XI Corps of the Army of the Potomac and was transferred to South Carolina after the Gettysburg campaign. Reenlisting in 1864, it continued as a veteran regiment and fought at Cedar Creek in the Shenandoah Valley, and in the trenches at Petersburg, following which it was on duty in the Department of Virginia until mustered out on December 9, 1865.

---

1. Ron Field and Roger Sturke, "41st New York Volunteer Infantry Regiment (De Kalb Regiment, or 2nd Yaeger Regiment), 1861–1865," *Military Collector & Historian* 39, no. 2 (Summer 1987): 76–77.
2. *New York Herald,* June 17, 1861, 8:1.
3. "Fourth Annual Report of the Bureau of Military Statistics," State of New York, 59.
4. *New York Herald,* June 22, 1861, 5:2; and June 25, 1861, 3:5.
5. NARA, Record Group 94, 41st NYVI Company Order Books.

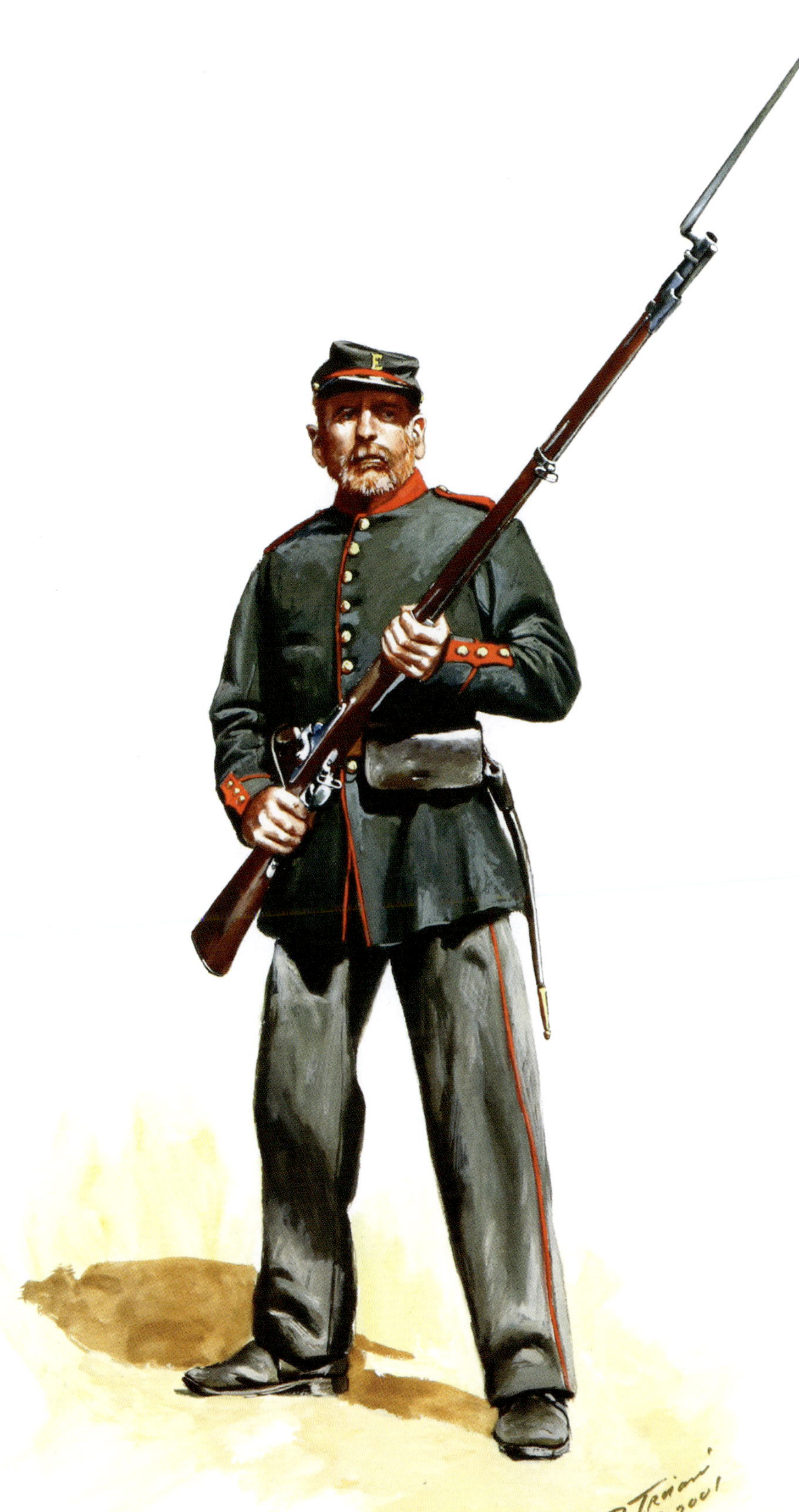

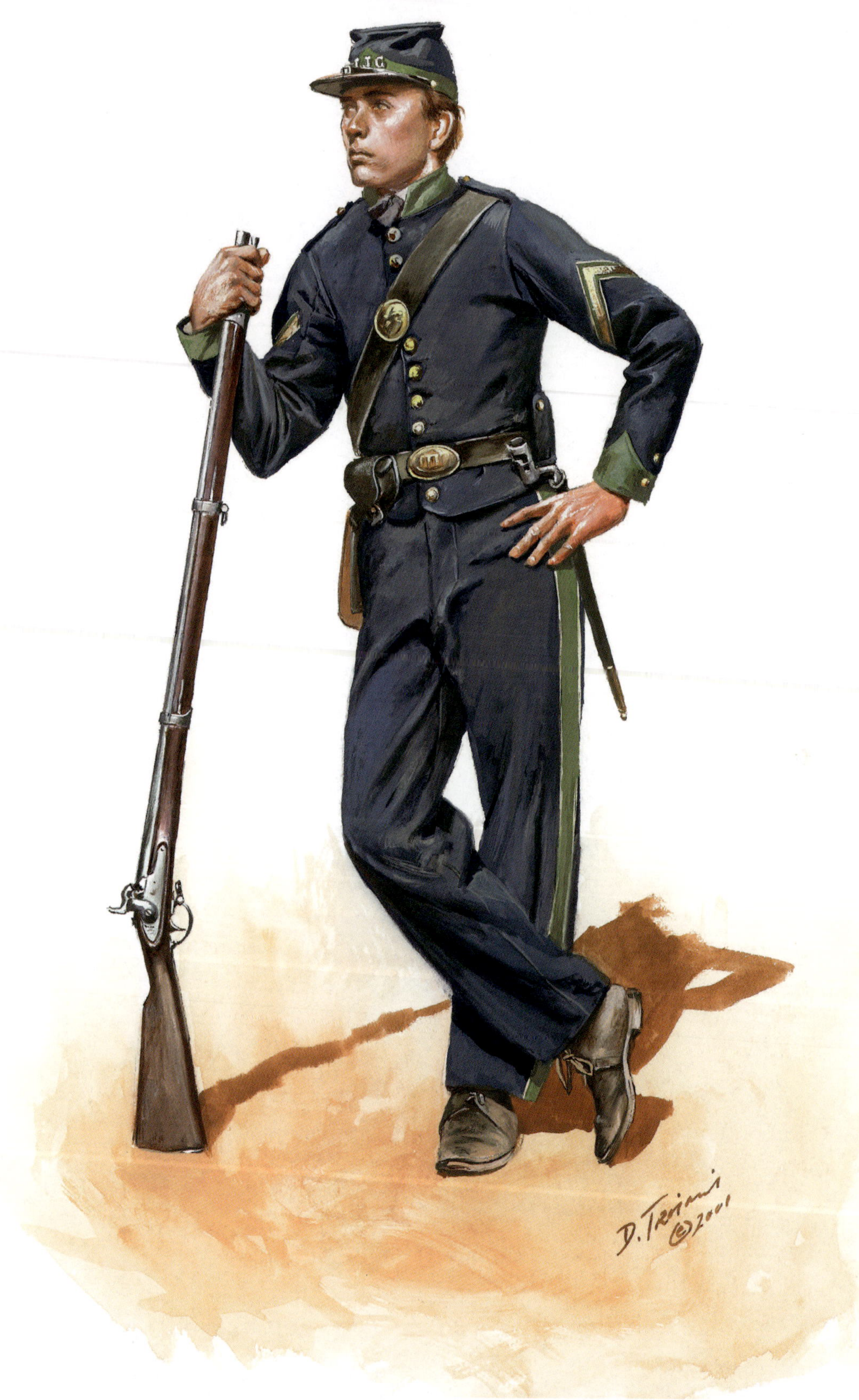

D. Troiani
© 2001

Irish Jasper Greens, Lance Corporal, 1861

NAMED FOR SERGEANT WILLIAM JASPER, WHO RECOVERED a South Carolina flag and raised it back up on a temporary staff during the Battle of Sullivan's Island on June 28, 1776, the Irish Jasper Greens was formed as a Volunteer Company in Savannah, Georgia, during 1842.[1] In 1860, as a well-established military unit commanded by Captain John Foley, it formed Companies A and B of the 1st Regiment Georgia Volunteers, which was commanded by Colonel Alexander R. Lawton. It was part of a state force that took possession of Fort Pulaski on January 12, 1861.

As with most well-established volunteer militia companies of the 1850s, the Irish Jasper Greens had both a full dress and a fatigue uniform. Adopted in July 1842, its full dress uniform originally included "a green Cloth Coat with buff trimmings."[2] In 1855 the unit changed this for a ten-button dark-blue uniform coat with green facings on collar and cuffs. Matching trousers had 1½-inch–wide green seam stripes edged with buff trim. Headgear consisted of "the regular United States Army Cap," which would have been a Pattern 1854 dress cap with worsted pompon.[3]

Depicted is a lance corporal of the Irish Jasper Greens as he would have looked as part of the force that occupied Fort Pulaski in 1861. He wears the fatigue uniform of the unit, which consisted of a dark-blue forage cap, of the type acquired by the unit in April 1860, with a green pointed band and the letters "IJG" at the front; a dark-blue jacket with a ten-button front and green facings on the collar and cuffs; "straps on the shoulders to pass the belts under"; and pants of the same pattern as on those worn with full dress. The rank of lance corporal is indicated on the upper sleeves by a single point-up chevron of green army lace on green cloth laced with buff with green backing.

He is armed with a US Model 1842 smoothbore musket with a socket bayonet, which was provided to the Irish Jasper Greens by the State of Georgia. His accoutrements include a Pattern 1839 cartridge box carried on a shoulder belt with a Pattern 1826 "eagle" plate attached. His waist belt is fastened by an oval brass plate displaying the "pillars and arches" state seal of Georgia. Produced specifically for his unit, his jacket buttons bear an eagle perched on an Irish harp with the letters "IJG" above.

The Irish Jasper Greens continued to serve with the 1st Georgia Volunteers intermittently at Fort Pulaski until April 12, 1862, when, following a heavy Federal bombardment, the regiment surrendered along with the rest of the garrison. Imprisoned on Johnson's Island, Ohio, the 1st Georgia was exchanged in October 1862. Arriving back at Savannah, it manned various city fortifications until the spring of 1863 when it was ordered to go to Charleston, South Carolina, where it formed part of the garrison defending Fort Wagner during the Federal attack on July 17. During 1864 it participated in the Atlanta Campaign and fought under Hood in Tennessee, having only fifty-two officers and men present for duty on December 21 of that year. Following its last action at Bentonville, North Carolina, it surrendered on April 26, 1865.[4]

---

1. *Georgia Journal and Messenger* (Macon, GA), January 19, 1843, 2:3.

2. Irish Jasper Greens papers, vol. 1: minutes, June 30, 1842–January 21, 1856, collection #416, box 1, Georgia Historical Society, Savannah, GA, GHS 0416, entry for July 14, 1842.

3. Minutes, March 1, 1855.

4. Crute, *Units of the Confederate States Army*, 81.

17th Mississippi Infantry, Company I, Pettus Rifles

RECRUITED DURING APRIL 1861, THE PETTUS RIFLES were named for Governor John J. Pettus and commanded by Captain Marmaduke Bell. While the company was awaiting orders at Camp Pettus, two miles north of Cockrum, in De Soto County, Mississippi, State Representative J. C. Culbertson wrote to Governor Pettus on May 8, inquiring when the Rifles would be called into service and adding that it was "Composed of Good Men."[1] Ordered to Camp Mott in Corinth, the Pettus Rifles was assigned as Company I to the 17th Mississippi Infantry, which was mustered into Confederate service for one year on June 7, 1861.

This private of the Pettus Rifles is based on an image of Private Josiah A. Lee.[2] Wounded at the Peach Orchard in the Battle of Gettysburg, he was captured and sent to Point Lookout prisoner-of-war camp. Exchanged in 1864, he survived the war and lived until 1907. He wears an example of the first uniform acquired by many Mississippi volunteer companies, which was based on "Orders" produced for the Army of Mississippi by the military board established in March 1861. These prescribed crimson as a branch service color for infantry and riflemen, with braid the same color as the facings on collar and cuffs running on each side of nine coat buttons.[3] Typical of soldiers in other Mississippi units, he wears a brimmed hat that is loosely based on the dress hat adopted by the US Army in 1858, which was occasionally referred to in Confederate ranks as a "Beegum" hat.[4] Received before his regiment left for Virginia, his full equipment includes a cartridge box, cap pouch, waist belt with frame buckle, and knapsack.

The early war uniforms of the 17th Mississippi were wearing out by October 1861, and, according to a pocket diary kept by Private Robert A. Moore of Company G, the regimental officers arranged for cloth to be purchased and taken back to the homes of the different companies "to have the goods made up." Likely plainer than their first uniform, this homemade clothing was received by October 30, 1861, after their involvement in the fight at Leesburg.[5] By May 1862, the regiment began to receive Confederate Quartermaster–issue clothing, including jackets, pants, and caps.

The 17th Mississippi served with the Third Brigade, Army of the Potomac, under Brigadier General David R. Jones at First Manassas. Following involvement at Leesburg, Virginia, the regiment fought from Seven Pines to Cold Harbor, except when detached to Chickamauga and Knoxville. It was later involved in Early's Shenandoah Valley operations and the Appomattox Campaign, where only three officers and sixty-two men surrendered.[6]

1. Governor John J. Pettus correspondence and papers, record group 27, vol. 37, letter dated May 8, 1861, written by J. C. Culbertson, De Soto County, to Pettus.

2. Bruce Reith, "Josiah Archibald Lee," *Military Images* 21 (January–February 2000): 18–19.

3. *Orders of the Military Board of the State of Mississippi* (E. Barksdale, State Printer, 1861).

4. William F. Fulton Jr., "Family Record and War Reminiscences" (1919), 63.

5. James W. Silver, ed., *A Life for the Confederacy* (McCowat-Mercer Press, Inc., 1959), 56, 74–75.

6. Crute, *Units of the Confederate States Army*, 176–77.

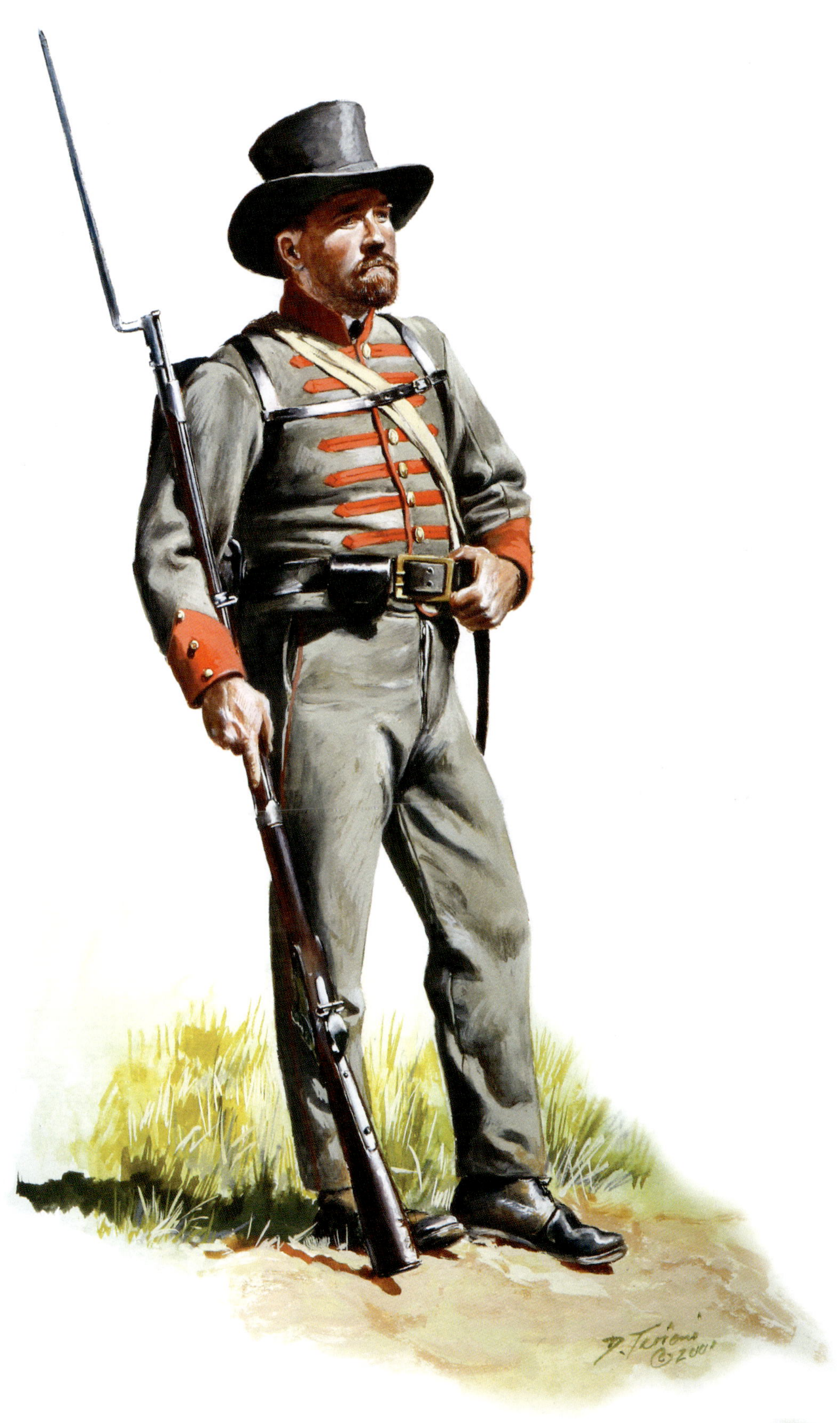

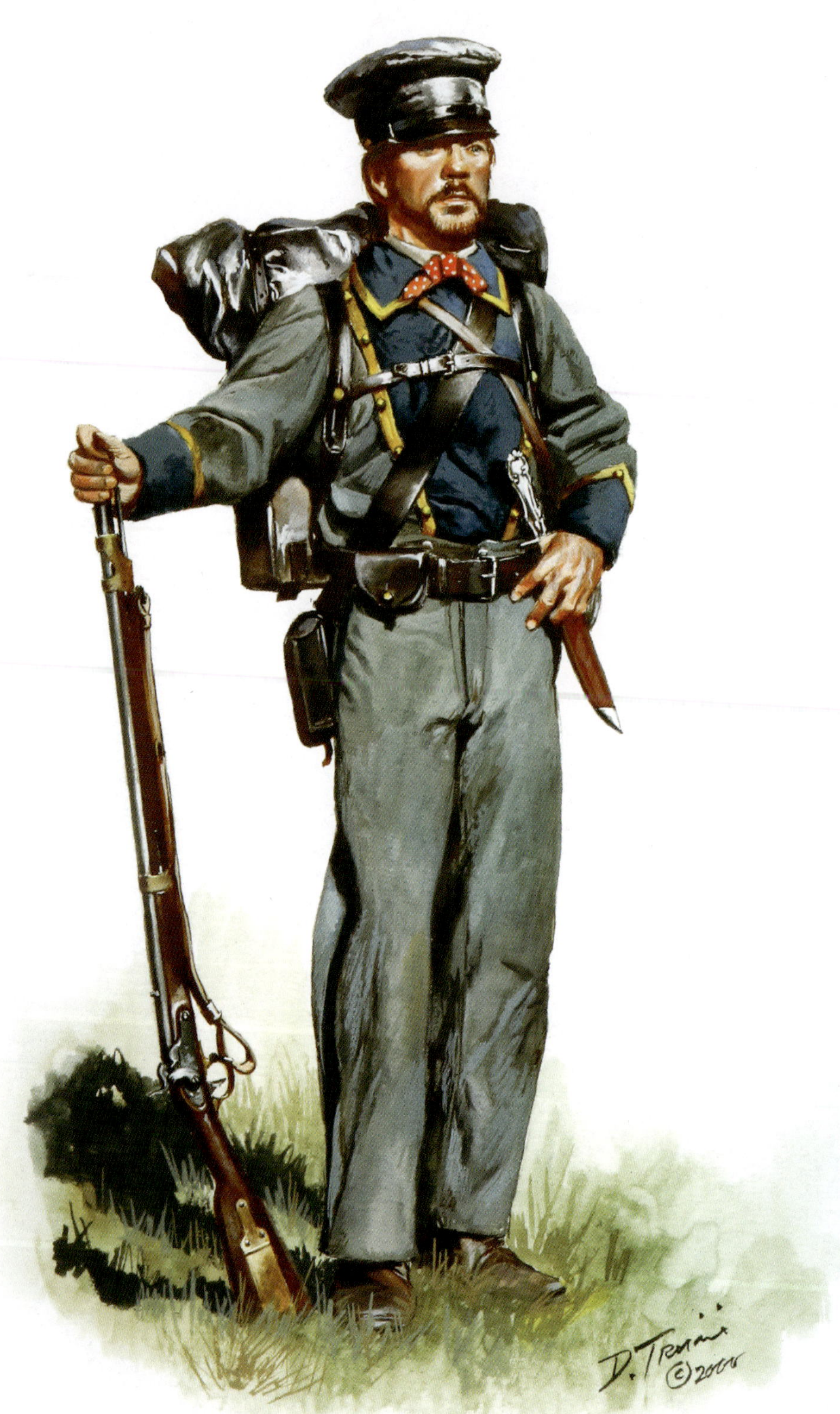

Lynchburg Rifles, Company E, 11th Virginia Infantry, July 1861

COMMANDED BY CAPTAIN JAMES E. BLANKENSHIP, a graduate of the Virginia Military Institute and Professor of Mathematics and Instructor of Tactics at the Lynchburg College, the Lynchburg Rifles were organized on April 19, 1861. Included in its ranks were ex-students, farmers, and local artisans who were "ready to go wherever their services may be needed in defence of the South."[1] Mustered into state service at Camp Davis near Lynchburg on June 3, 1861, the Lynchburg Rifles left for Richmond and joined other companies of the battalion under the command of Captain, later Colonel, Samuel Garland, Jr., at Camp Pickens, near Manassas. There they were accepted into Confederate service for twelve months on June 20, 1861, as Company E, when Garland's battalion was expanded into the 11th Virginia Infantry.

This private of the Lynchburg Rifles wears the uniform received by his company during May 1861, which was described as being of "Gray goods trimmed with blue."[2] His battle shirt is of the type likely made by tailor Charles J. Raine at 130 Main Street, Lynchburg, who advertised having "sample suits for Cavalry, Riflemen, and Infantry always on hand" before the war.[3] It has a dark-blue collar and cuffs trimmed with yellow and a dark-blue plastron front that could be unbuttoned and removed to show three broad strips of vertical yellow trim down the shirt front.

Headgear consists of a Pattern 1839 forage cap with a rainproof cover. His gray trousers have a broad dark-blue welt on the outer seams. He is armed with a Model 1841 Mississippi rifle and has a Bowie knife with a German silver handle and a cross guard in a red leather sheath tucked in his belt. Accoutrements include a waist belt, with roller buckle, on which is slid a cap pouch. A Pattern 1857 cartridge box is carried on a shoulder belt, and he shoulders a rigid militia knapsack with a rubberized blanket roll attached.

The 11th Virginia was reorganized "for the war" on April 26, 1862, and mostly fought in the Army of Northern Virginia from May 1862, through Five Forks in April 1865. Of 252 men who served in the Lynchburg Rifles, 27 died in action or of disease, and 10 were wounded. When the regiment laid down its arms at Appomattox Court House on April 9, 1865, one officer and twenty-eight men remained in its ranks.[4]

---

1. R. Harrison Daniel, "Old Lynchburg College, 1855–1869," *The Virginia Magazine of History and Biography* 88, no. 4 (October 1980): 471; and *Lynchburg Daily Virginian*, April 22, 1861, 3:1.

2. *Lynchburg Daily Virginian*, May 1, 1861, 3:1.

3. *Lynchburg Daily Virginian*, January 23, 1860, 2:4.

4. Robert T. Bell, *11th Virginia Infantry* (The Virginia Regimental Histories Series) (H. E. Howard, Inc., 1985), 56.

3rd Alabama Infantry, Company A, Mobile Cadets, 1861

FORMED IN 1845 FOR SERVICE IN THE MEXICAN WAR, the Mobile Cadets became a prominent volunteer militia company in Mobile, Alabama, during the antebellum years. Commanded by thirty-five-year-old Captain Robert M. Sands, the Cadets volunteered for twelve months of state service on April 27, 1861, as Company A, 3rd Alabama Infantry, which was the first Alabama unit to leave the state for Virginia. Mustered in to Confederate service at Lynchburg with Colonel Jones M. Withers in command on May 4, 1861, it was described as being composed of "the very best material" with some of the wealthiest citizens of Mobile in its ranks.

For full dress the Mobile Cadets wore gray shakos, coatees, and pants, all with black trim, as inspired by the US Military Academy at West Point.[1] This private wears the service uniform adopted by the Mobile Cadets by 1861. His cadet-gray chasseur-pattern cap has a black band and the brass letters "MC" at its front. His jacket has a single row of nine brass buttons. The tall standing collar, cuffs, and shoulder straps are faced with black cloth. Two small buttons are attached to the cuffs, and each shoulder strap, unusually, has three buttons arranged, with one at the neck end and two at the shoulder seam.

His cadet-gray pants have one-inch–wide black welts on the outer seams.

He is armed with a Model 1841 Mississippi rifle with a saber bayonet, some of which were likely received by the Cadets while at Lynchburg, having been shipped from the Mount Vernon Arsenal in Alabama.[2] Accoutrements consist of a waist belt with the letters "ACC" on an oval Pattern 1839 belt plate, indicating the wearer was previously a member of the Alabama Corps of Cadets, of the University of Alabama.[3] Carried on his belt is an Allegheny Arsenal–pattern cap pouch and a frog for his saber bayonet. A Pattern 1839 cartridge box is suspended from a shoulder belt of bridle leather.

The 3rd Alabama served in the Department of Norfolk, Virginia, and was then assigned to Rodes's, O'Neal's, and Battle's Brigade, Army of Northern Virginia. The regiment fought in numerous battles from Seven Pines to Cold Harbor. It then moved with General Jubal A. Early to the Shenandoah Valley and was involved in the campaign that ended at Appomattox.[4] Of 1,651 men who served in the regiment, about 260 perished in battle, 119 died of wounds or disease, and 605 were discharged or transferred.

---

1. Berlon E. Sullivan, *A History of the Mobile Cadets from the Organization of the Company in October, 1845, through April, 1925* (Press of Merchants Printing Co., 1925), 5.

2. NARA, M331, record group 109 (CMSR), confederate officers, 1861–1865, James L. White, 273.

3. Gerald G. Hovater, "ACC Boxplate of John Morgan Smith, C.S.A.," *North South Trader* (November–December 1985): 16.

4. Crute, *Units of the Confederate States Army*, 4.

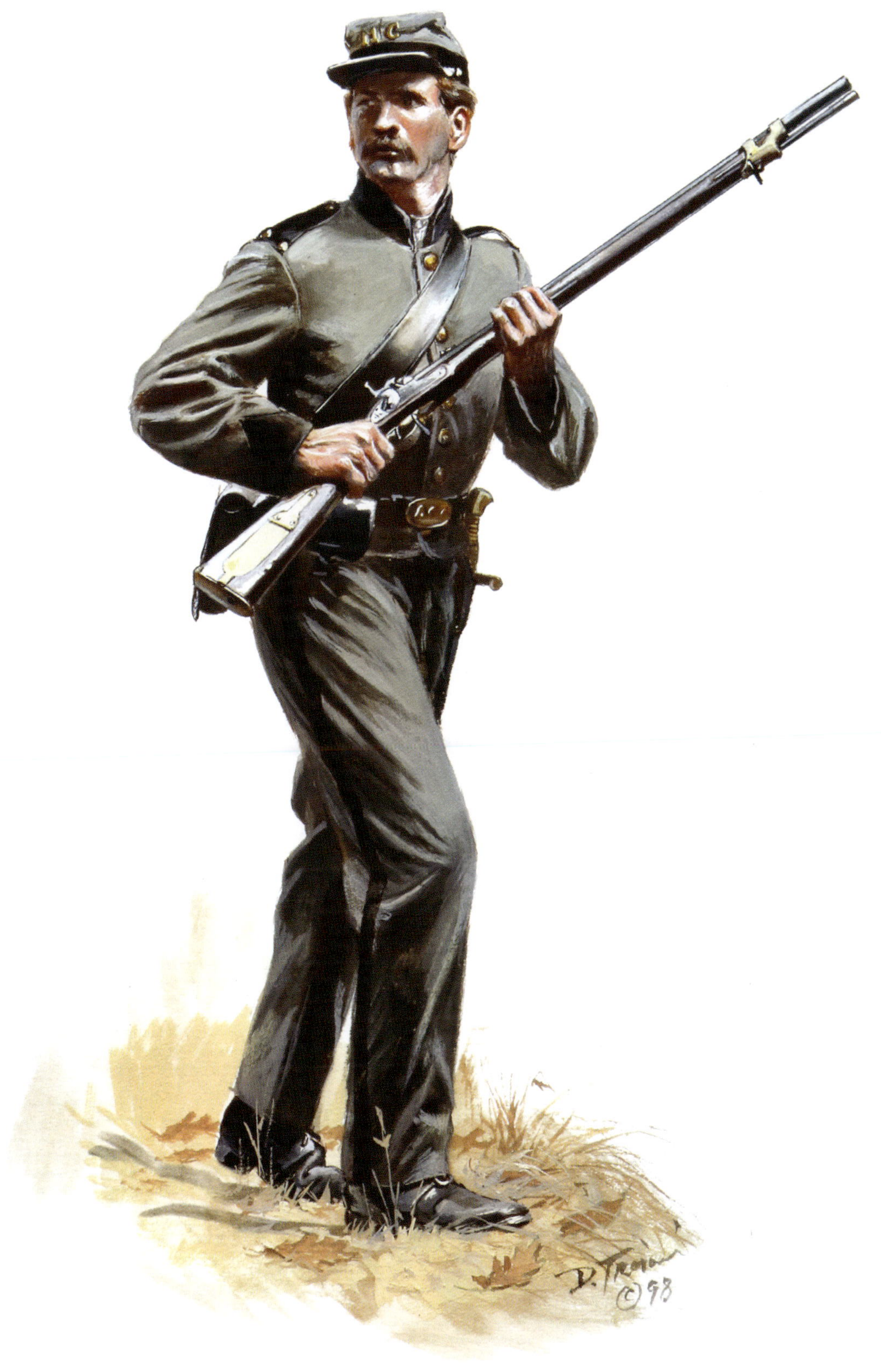

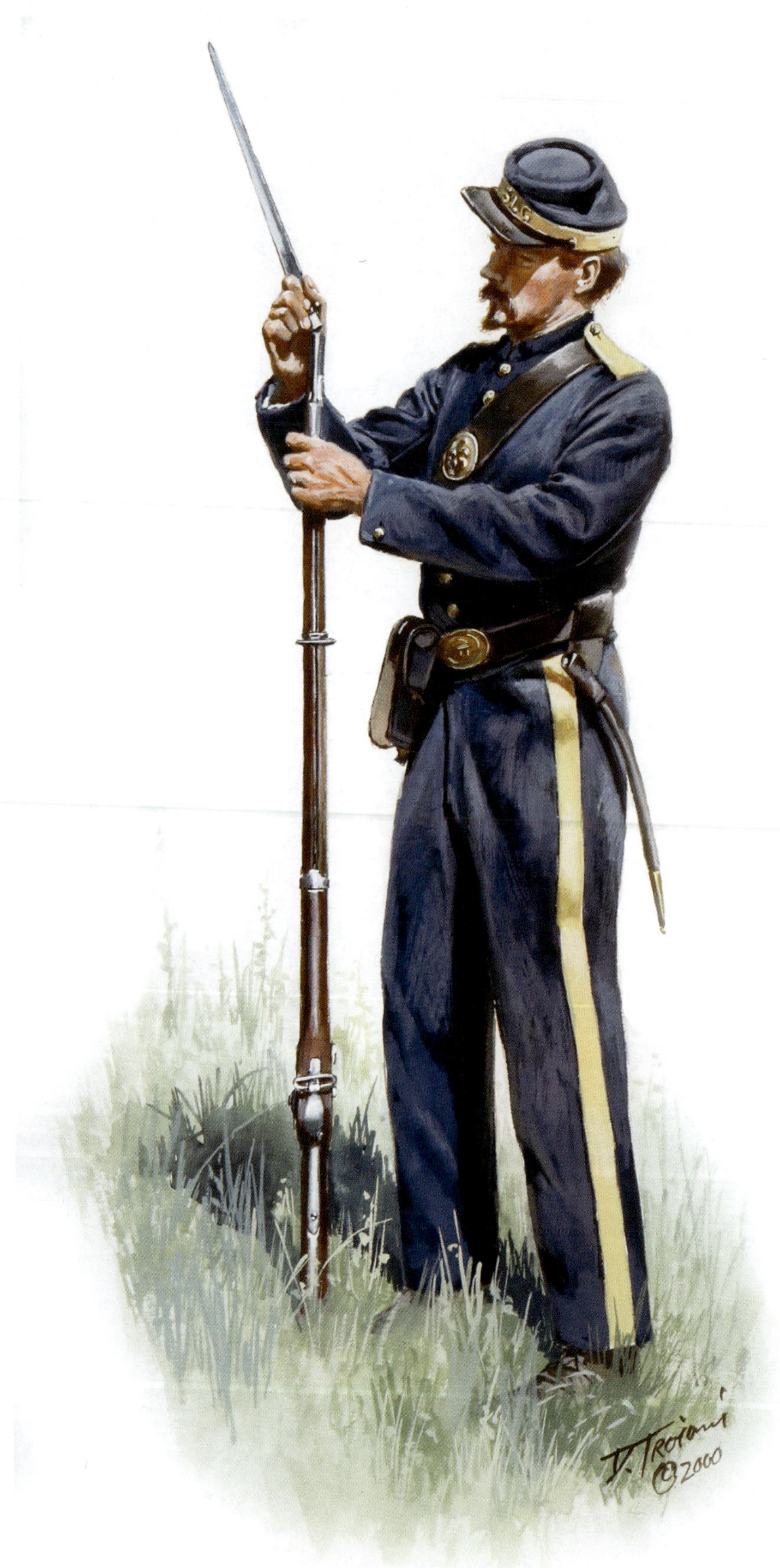

Sumter Light Guard, Company K, 4th Georgia Infantry, 1861

THE 4TH GEORGIA INFANTRY, ALSO KNOWN AS THE Sumter Light Guard, composed of volunteer companies from nine different counties, was one of the units organized in response to the Confederate call on April 16, 1861, for 32,000 volunteers. Initially mustered in for twelve months on May 9 under Colonel George Doles, the regiment was sent to Virginia and eventually went on to serve as the senior unit of the Doles-Cook Brigade of the II Corps, Army of Northern Virginia.

Commanded by Captain William L. Johnson, the Sumter Light Guard was assigned as Company K, and was one of the most highly regarded companies in the 4th Georgia. Many members of the unit came from Americus, in Sumter County, as did the thirteen-man Americus Brass Band, led by Professor Loui Zitterbart, which served with the regiment throughout the war and beside many a campfire played the "Sumter Light Guard March," composed by Friedrich Erdman.

The private in this plate wears the uniform worn by members of the Light Guard when they set out from Americus on April 27, 1861, to join the 4th Georgia at Portsmouth, Virginia. This was briefly described in the press as "dark blue jackets, for the privates, trimmed with buff."[1] His jacket has nine Georgia state-seal buttons at the front and smaller buttons of the same pattern fastening cuffs and buff-colored shoulder straps. Matching trousers are of a straight cut and have a 1½-inch–wide buff stripe running uninterrupted up to the bottom edge of the jacket. His forage cap has the brass letters "SLG" on its buff band. Supporting a cap pouch and a bayonet scabbard, his black leather waist belt has an oval state-seal plate. His Pattern 1839 cartridge box is carried on a leather sling with a round "eagle" plate.

The 4th Georgia was initially armed with smoothbore muskets, and the private shown here is fixing his bayonet on a US Model 1842 musket. Slings were not issued to the regiment at this stage. Also, on leaving for the seat of war, the regiment received no ammunition. On arrival at Portsmouth, it borrowed one round of fixed ammunition and three caps per man from the 2nd Georgia Battalion.[2] Later in the war these muskets would have been replaced with Enfield or Springfield rifle muskets.

1. *Daily Chronicle and Sentinel* (Augusta, GA), April 30, 1861, 2:4.
2. Richard Warren, Plate 15R, "The Sumter Light Guards, 1861–1862," in *Uniforms of the Confederacy* (Confederate Historical Society Press, 1990).

3rd Missouri Infantry

DURING THE EARLY MONTHS OF 1861 THE PRO-UNIONIST movement in Saint Louis, Missouri, led by Congressman Francis Preston Blair Jr., formed several unofficial militia units in semi-secrecy. Largely composed of ethnic Germans who were generally opposed to slavery, one of these units evolved into the 3rd Missouri Infantry. Enlisted for three months' service on April 22, 1861, with Colonel Franz Sigel in command, this unit was also known as the "Lyon Standard Guard" after Brigadier General Nathaniel Lyon, who would be killed at Wilson's Creek later that year.

Originally consisting of two battalions, the 3rd Missouri was composed of eleven infantry and three artillery companies.[1] According to Private August Reimers, Company B, the regiment did not have accoutrements and was in citizen's dress when ordered to capture the secessionist Camp Jackson at Lindell Grove on the western side of Saint Louis on May 10, 1861. "All we had was Harpers Ferry muskets," Reimers recalled, "with bayonets fixed to the guns for the good reason that we had no scabbards, with 40 rounds of ammunition in my pants pocket, and the caps for my gun in my vest pocket."[2]

Following the action at Camp Jackson the 3rd Missouri was mainly stationed at the Saint Louis Arsenal until it began reorganization "for the war" during mid-June 1861. Before this could be completed the regiment was ordered to take the field, and it participated in the Union defeat in Carthage, Missouri, on July 5, prior to which it had been uniformed and partially equipped, as shown in this plate. Private Reimers recalled that its uniform consisted of "a gray hat, gray shirt and gray pants, all trimmed up in red." Sergeant Otto C. Lademann, Company G, remembered, "Our equipment for field service was a very poor one. We had no blankets, no great coats, and barely any camp and garrison equipage. Our whole outfit consisted of an uncovered tin canteen and a white sheeting haversack, rotten white belts condemned since the Mexican War and contract cartridge boxes—flat shaped like cigar boxes, without tins . . . We were armed with the old 69-caliber rifle muskets."[3]

The reorganized 3rd Missouri served in the Army of Southwest Missouri until July 1862; within the District of Eastern Arkansas until December 1862; and with the Army of Tennessee until November 1864. During this time 3 officers and 89 enlisted men were killed or mortally wounded, and 3 officers and 145 enlisted men died from disease, totaling 240 deaths.

---

1. *Daily Missouri Democrat* (St. Louis, MO), May 6, 1861, 2:5.

2. Hartman McIntosh, ed., "The Memoirs of a Missouri Soldier: August Reimers," *Military Images* (May–June 1992), 18–19.

3. Otto C. Lademann, "The Battle of Carthage, Mo. in War Papers Read Before the Commandery of the State of Wisconsin," vol. 4 (Burdick & Allen, 1914).

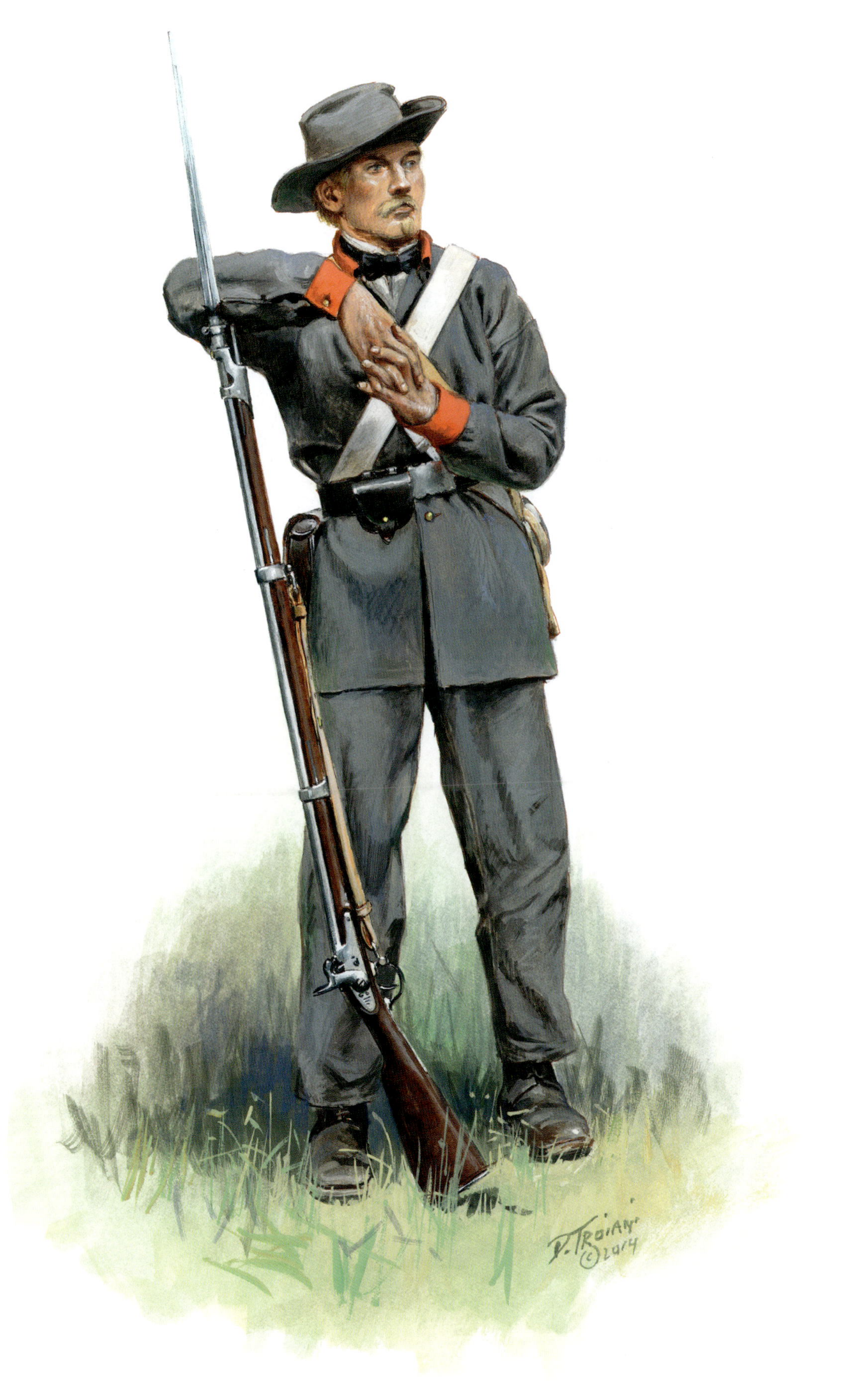

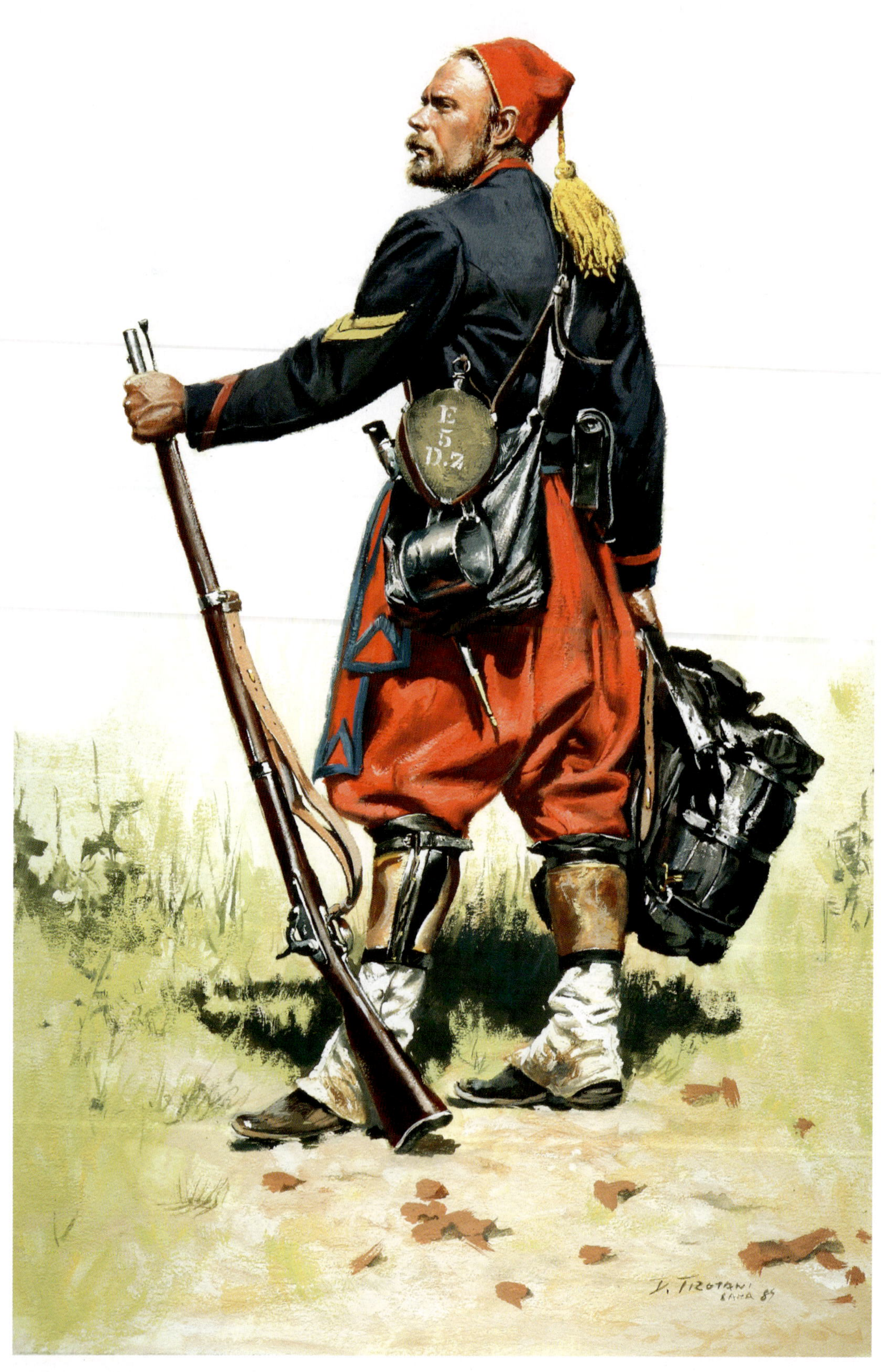

E
5
D.z

ZOUAVES AND CHASSEURS
5th New York Infantry (Duryée's Zouaves)

ORIGINALLY KNOWN AS THE ADVANCE GUARD, THE 5TH New York Infantry, or Duryée's Zouaves, was formed as a two-year regiment in New York City during April 1861, with Colonel Abram Duryée in command. Its first uniform, which had been supplied to most members of the regiment by May 7, was based on the traditional dress of the Franco-Algerian Zouaves rather than on the pattern popularized in 1859 by Elmer E. Ellsworth and his United States Zouave Cadets of Chicago, Illinois. The New York City firm of Devlin, Hudson & Co. supplied most of the jackets, vests, pantaloons, and sashes, while William Seligman & Co. provided an additional 209 sets of uniform. The fezzes were produced by the Seamless Clothing Manufacturing Company in Matteawan, New York.[1] There was much dissatisfaction with the clothing Duryée's Zouaves received. In response to complaints that the pantaloons were not large enough, Devlin, Hudson & Co. advised Colonel Duryée on May 8, 1861, that many of his men wore "the uniform pants over others, which will of course destroy the fit."

On September 10, 1861, the regiment received new uniforms of similarly poor quality. Colonel Gouverneur K. Warren, who succeeded Duryée in command, wrote to Colonel David H. Vinton, Deputy Quartermaster General for the United States in New York City, complaining that the breeches were "not nearly large and full enough" and the lining of the jacket was made of "stuff not shrunk" so that wetness pulled the garment out of shape.[2]

The Zouave depicted in this painting wears an example of the uniform mostly issued to the 5th New York from February 1862, and worn until its muster-out in May 1863. Thereafter, the blue jacket, red pantaloons, and fez were continued but with the trefoil or *tombeau* on the jacket front cut from one piece of red flannel rather than made of the braid used on the earlier uniform. Noncommissioned officers' sleeve chevrons were of gilt rather than in red. The red pantaloons no longer bore the blue cord decoration, and the fez was surmounted by a yellow tassel rather than a blue one. Since at least July 1862, leather *jambières*, or greaves, were worn over knee-length cloth leggings.

This Zouave is armed with an M1861 Springfield rifle musket. Accoutrements include a single-bag knapsack of the type produced by the Gutta Percha Co. of New York. Likely fastened by an "SNY" oval plate, his waist belt supports a Pattern 1861 .58-caliber rifle musket cartridge box. His Pattern 1858 tin canteen covered with gray cloth is personalized with the painted designation "E 5 D.Z.," and has a brown leather strap. It is accompanied by a waterproofed haversack and a tin cup.

1. NARA, record group 94, records of the Adjutant General's Office, regimental papers.
2. "Letter from Col. Warren to Col. Vinton January 8, 1862," in Todd New York files, Anne S. K. Brown Military Collection, Brown University, Providence, RI; and NARA, record group 94, regimental papers.

Salem Zouaves, 8th Massachusetts Volunteer Militia, 1861

IN 1860 ARTHUR F. DEVERAUX, A FORMER BUSINESS PARTNER of Elmer E. Ellsworth, was elected captain of the Salem Light Infantry, a Massachusetts uniformed militia company originally formed on September 22, 1805. Doubtless due to his association with Ellsworth and an adjutancy in the Illinois National Guard, Captain Deveraux had acquired an interest in the Zouave drill and uniform, especially after they hosted the US Zouave Cadets during their drill tour in 1860. Adopting the name Salem Zouaves, the unit was attached to the 8th Massachusetts Volunteer Militia as Company I and was formally mustered in on April 30, 1861. During their three-month campaign they served as marines aboard the USS *Constitution* while she was sailed from Annapolis, Maryland, to a safer haven at the Brooklyn Navy Yard. Following this they were posted at Relay House and in Baltimore until July 29, 1861.[1]

From September 9, 1862, to August 1863, the Zouaves were on duty as Company A, 50th Massachusetts Volunteer Militia, and, on May 13, 1864, they were again called out as the "13th Unattached Company M.V.M." and were garrisoned at New Bedford, Massachusetts.[2]

Their semi-Zouave uniform was delivered to them in Baltimore on June 26, 1861. Based on an original uniform and items of the Salem Zouaves in the collection of the Essex Institute, Salem, which belonged to Corporal Charles F. Williams, this consisted of a Zouave jacket, vest, and pants of a navy-blue woolen twill fabric. The braid was crimson throughout, while the collar of the vest was trimmed with red leather. The vest buttons were of the plain brass bell pattern. The cap had a scarlet top and sides with a dark-blue band and was quartered with gold braid. The brass letters "SZ" were attached to its front. Completing the uniform was a scarlet woolen sash with plum-red tassels. The gaiters were of a coarsely woven white cotton duck material with white porcelain buttons to secure the lace-up outer seams.

Prior to receipt of their Zouave dress, the unit wore a fatigue uniform reported on arrival in Washington as consisting of "dark blue jackets and pants, trimmed with scarlet braid, and red fatigue caps."[3] This was composed of a nine-button jacket of medium blue with a standing collar, shoulder straps, and nine double rows of scarlet braid across the chest. Pants of the same color had narrow scarlet piping down the outer seams. Worn out by the end of May 1861, this was replaced by a plain gray suit of similar cut. Havelock cap covers were also received "the use of which was short lived."[4] Arms consisted of Model 1855 rifle muskets and accoutrements, including a drum canteen with the black stenciled letters "S.Z." and a nonrigid black oilcloth knapsack with the painted white serif letters "S.Z."

---

1. Ron Field et al., "Salem Zouaves, Massachusetts Volunteer Militia, 1861," *Military Collector & Historian* XXXVII, no. 2 (Summer 1985): 87.

2. George M. Whipple, *History of the Salem Light Infantry from 1805–1890* (Essex Institute, 1890), 64–69.

3. *Daily National Intelligencer* (Washington, DC), May 11, 1861, 3:4.

4. "Essex Institute Historical Collections," July to December, 1899, 293–94.

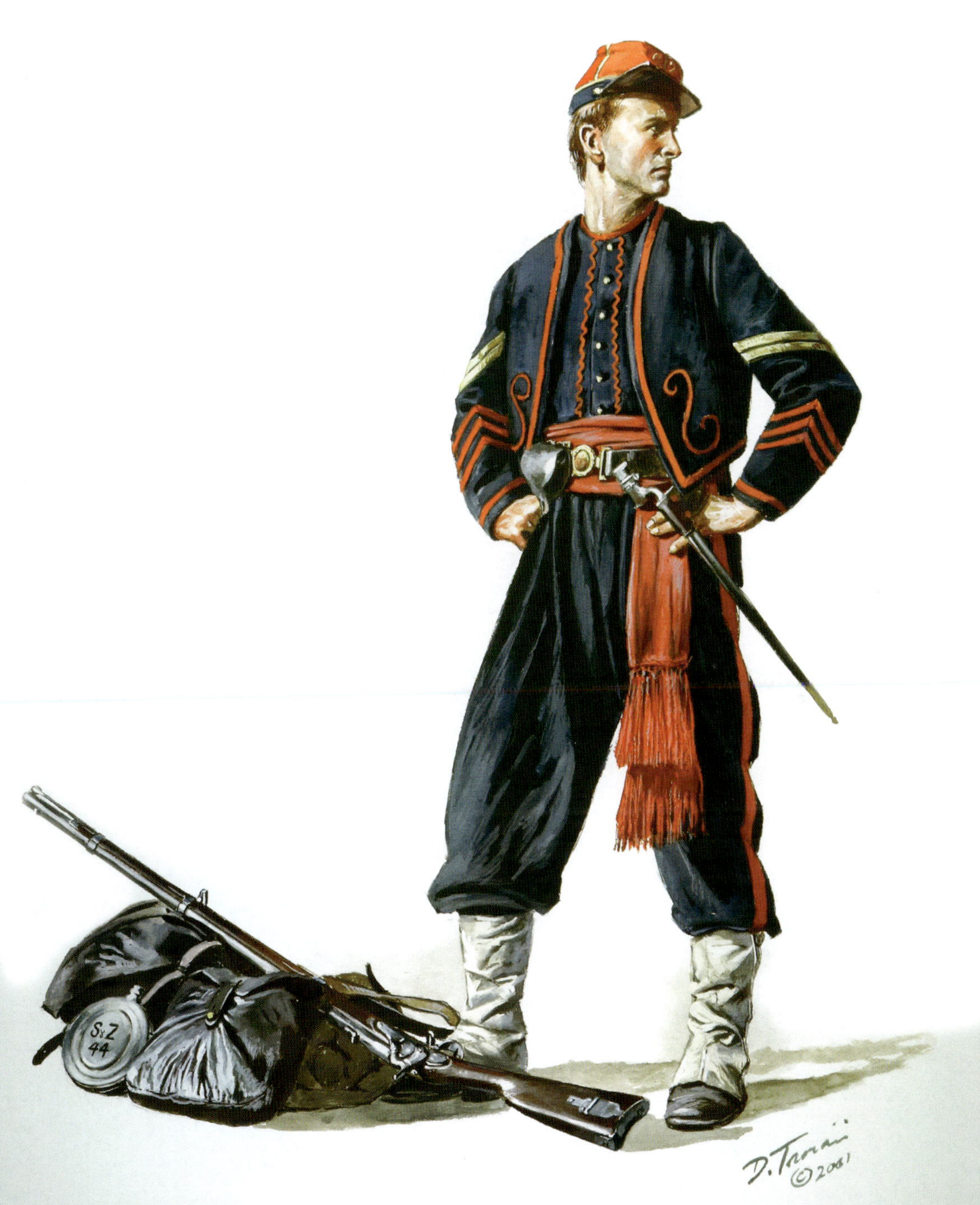
S&Z
44

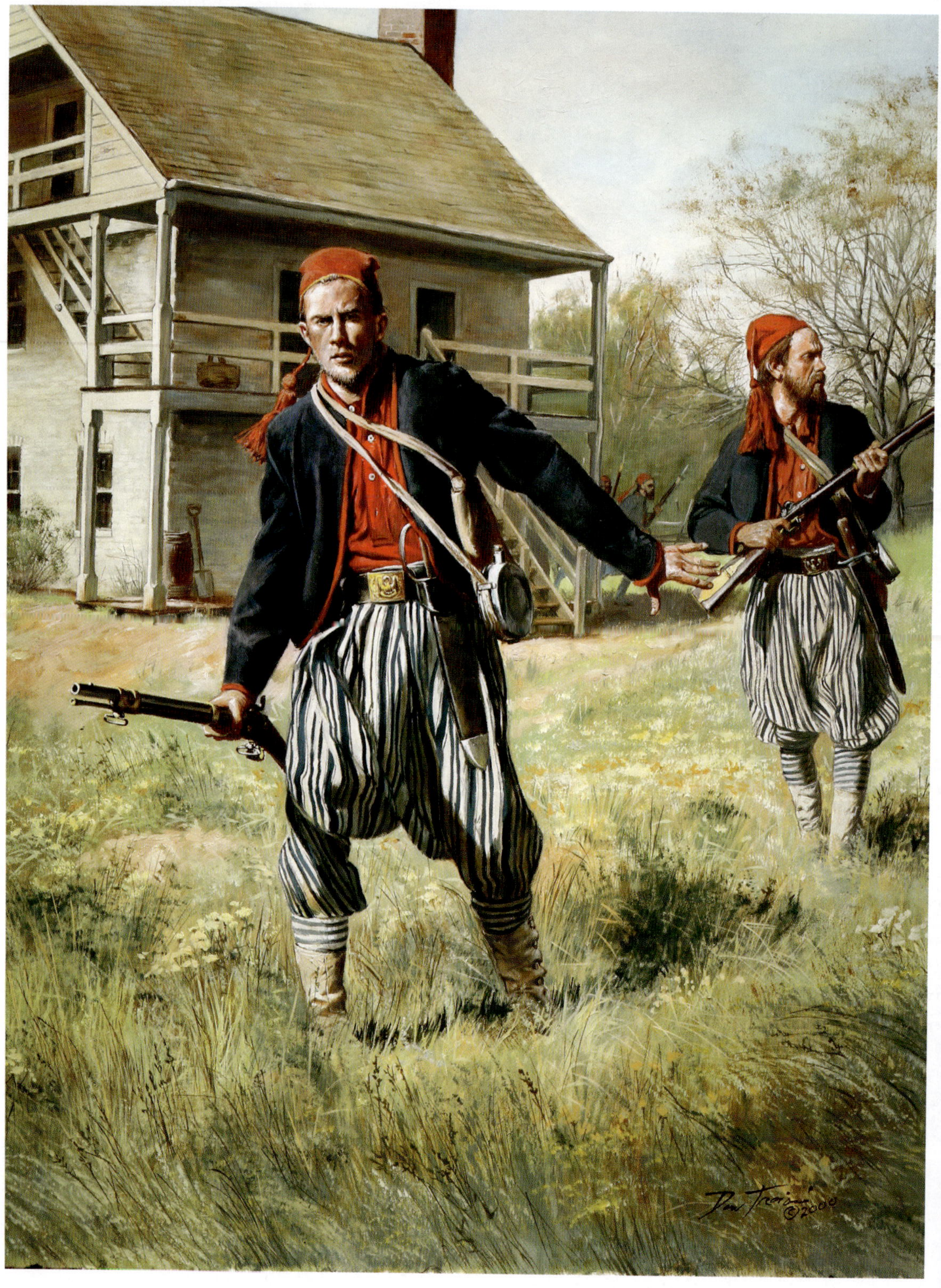

Tiger Rifles, Wheat's 1st Special Battalion, 1861

WITHIN HOURS OF THE SECESSION OF LOUISIANA FROM the Union on January 26, 1861, a volunteer company called the Tiger Rifles began to recruit and organize in New Orleans, with volunteers found mainly among the laborers, river boatmen, and longshoremen of the city. On April 21, 1861, Mexican War veteran Alexander B. White was elected to command.[1] On May 4, the Tiger Rifles were joined by other companies to form a battalion at Camp Walker within the grounds of the Metairie Ridge racecourse outside New Orleans. Officers' elections took place on May 10, with mercenary, adventurer, and Mexican War veteran Chatham Roberdeau Wheat elected as major in command. The Battalion moved to Camp Moore, near Tangipahoa, on May 14 to complete organization. There it was designated the 1st Special Battalion, Louisiana Volunteer Infantry, and it was mustered into Confederate service on June 9, 1861.

The 1st Special Battalion took part in fierce fighting at First Manassas on July 21, 1861, making several desperate charges brandishing knives as their Model 1841 Mississippi rifles had not been fitted with bayonets. Wheat was severely wounded during this action, and command of the Battalion passed to Captain Robert Harris, Company A, Walker Guards.[2] Following a relatively uneventful winter at Centreville, Virginia, the unit joined Major General Thomas J. Jackson's Army of the Valley on March 9, 1862, following which it was transferred to the Army of Northern Virginia. Wheat, who had recovered from his wound, was killed at Gaines' Mill on June 27, 1862. His much-reduced Battalion was disbanded during the following August, and its men were transferred to other Louisiana units.

Shown as they would have looked at First Manassas, these Zouaves wear the uniform provided by wealthy Kentucky horse breeder Alexander Keene Richards. Received in early June 1861 to replace their first clothing, this consisted of a red fez with a red tassel, a dark-blue jacket trimmed with red braid, and blue-and-white–striped pantaloons. Evidence for the color of the jackets is based on fragments of cloth found with exhumed remains in 1978–1979, which were tentatively identified as those of Tiger Rifles Michael O'Brien and Dennis Corcoran, who were shot by firing squad for mutiny on December 9, 1861. Forensic findings indicated their jackets were of "blue wool, twill weave . . . with red, plain weave wool binding on the edge."[3] Further research indicates the jacket color may have been more of a "dark steel gray."[4]

Their red Garibaldian-style overshirts have three small porcelain buttons on a placket front, and their striped Zouave-style pantaloons were reported to have been made from "Hamilton [mattress] ticking," which was produced by the Hamilton Manufacturing Company of Lowell, Massachusetts.[5] These are tucked into horizontally striped stockings over which white canvas leggings are worn. Armed with Model 1841 rifles, they have large, cased knives attached to waist belts that are fastened with state seal "Pelican" plates. Accoutrements include tin drum canteens and haversacks.

---

1. *Sunday Delta* (New Orleans, LA), April 21, 1861, 7:2.

2. *Supplement*, part 1, vol. 1, 194–95.

3. Mike Thomas, "Unearthing the Tigers' Graves," *Northern Virginia Heritage* II, no. 2 (June 1980): 8; and A. C. Deegan, "Archaeological Textile Evidence for Historic Costume Study: Louisiana Tiger Rifles 1861," *Clothing and Textiles Research Journal* 5, no. 4 (Summer 1987): 23–27.

4. See Ross Brooks, "'Physically Splendid Material Morally Dreadful'—The Uniforms of the New Orleans 'Tiger Rifles,'" *Military Collector & Historian* 73, no. 2: 177–80.

5. *Daily True Delta*, June 30, 1861, 4:2.

9th New York Infantry (Hawkins Zouaves)

INSPIRED BY THE VISIT OF ELMER ELLS-WORTH'S UNITED STATES Zouave Cadets to New York City on July 14–19, 1860, Rush C. Hawkins began to organize a company called the New-York Zouaves four days after the departure of Ellsworth's crack drill unit. It adopted a uniform consisting of a sparsely trimmed dark-blue jacket and straight-legged trousers, plus a red fez.[1]

With the outbreak of the Civil War nine months later, Hawkins recruited a volunteer regiment initially dubbed the First Lightening Regiment of New York Zouaves, which was officially designated the 9th New York Volunteers and mustered into US service for two years on May 4, 1861. Serving on the North Carolina coast, Hawkins's Zouaves were involved in the first main amphibious landings of the Civil War at Hatteras Inlet during August 1861. They next fought on Roanoke Island as part of Burnside's Expeditionary force in February 1862. Brigaded with the 89th New York and 6th New Hampshire under Hawkins, the regiment participated in the expedition to Elizabeth City and sustained seventy-five casualties at South Mills, including the wounding of their colonel. Following further service in Virginia and Maryland in the battles of South Mountain, Antietam, and Fredericksburg, the two-year men of the 9th New York Infantry were mustered out in New York City on May 20, 1863.

Likely based on that worn by the original New York Zouaves in 1860, and acquired by private contract from T. Menzesheimer & Sons of New York City, the first uniform worn by Hawkins's Zouaves consisted of dark-blue Pattern 1858 forage caps with white cotton havelocks; dark-blue satinette, *tombeau*-less, Zouave jackets with red trim; matching, pleated chasseur-pattern trousers; dark-blue vests trimmed with light blue; and a light-blue merino-wool waist sash.[2]

Wearing the regiment's second uniform received from the US Quartermaster Department in April 1862, this Hawkins's Zouave has a red fez cap with a dark-blue tassel, a dark-blue jacket and vest with magenta trim, plus matching trousers, a magenta waist sash, and white canvas leggings. Armed with a Springfield Model 1842 rifled musket with a leather sling and a socket bayonet, his accoutrements include a French-pattern knapsack, Model 1858 canteen, and French-style waist belt plate with an "exploding bomb" device adopted as the regimental emblem.

Surplus Hawkins's Zouave uniforms produced by the Quartermaster Department were issued to other later war units; see artwork and text on the 17th New York Veteran Infantry, 164th New York Infantry, 33rd and 35th New Jersey Infantry, and 10th US Colored Troops.

---

1. "By-Laws of the 'New-York Zouaves' (Independent Corps)" (L. H. Frank, Book & Job Printer, No. 3 Cedar Street, 1860).

2. "Early Uniforms of the Hawkins' Zouaves, 9th New York Volunteer Infantry 1861–1862," notes by Dennis C. Schurr.

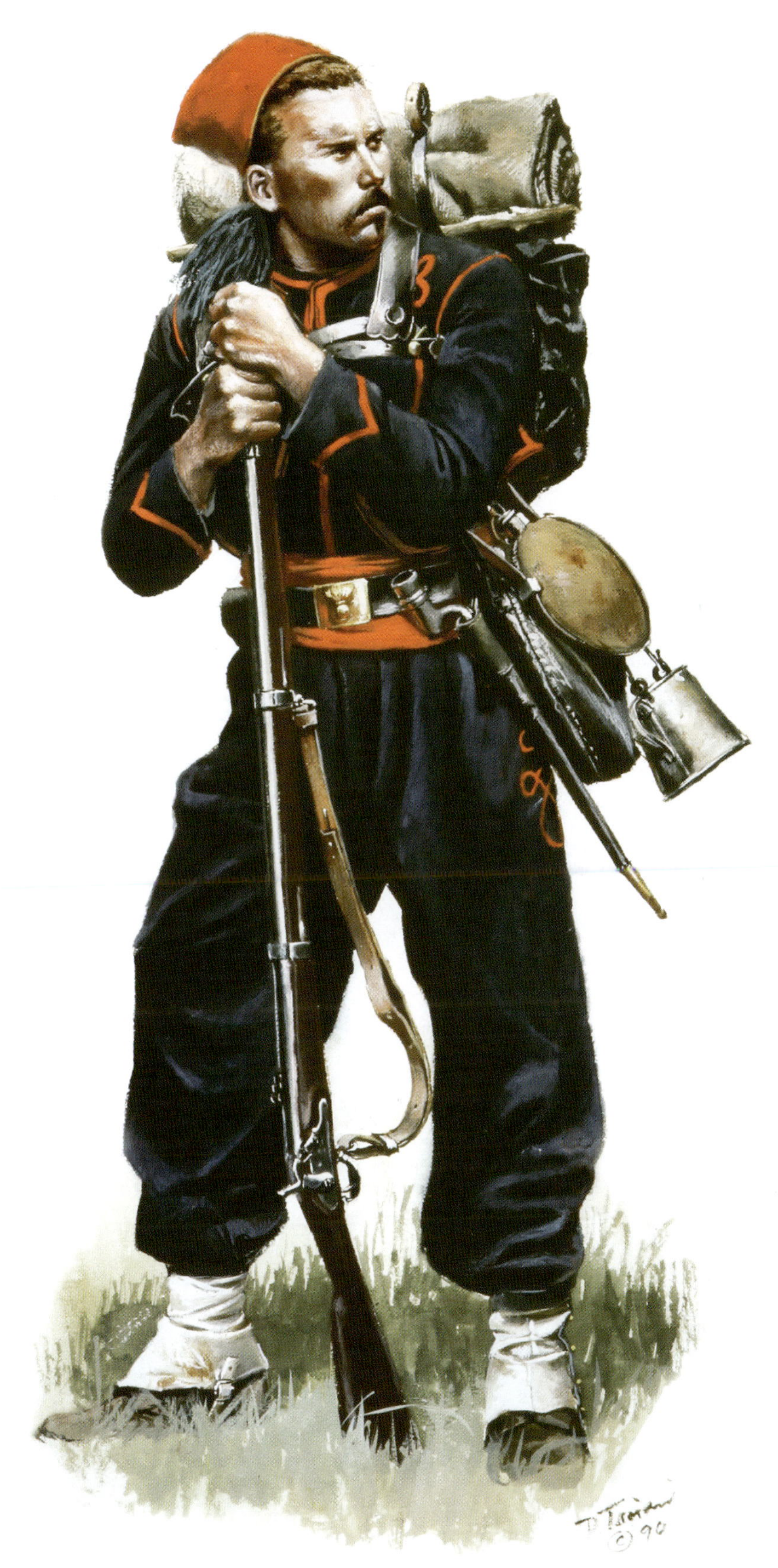

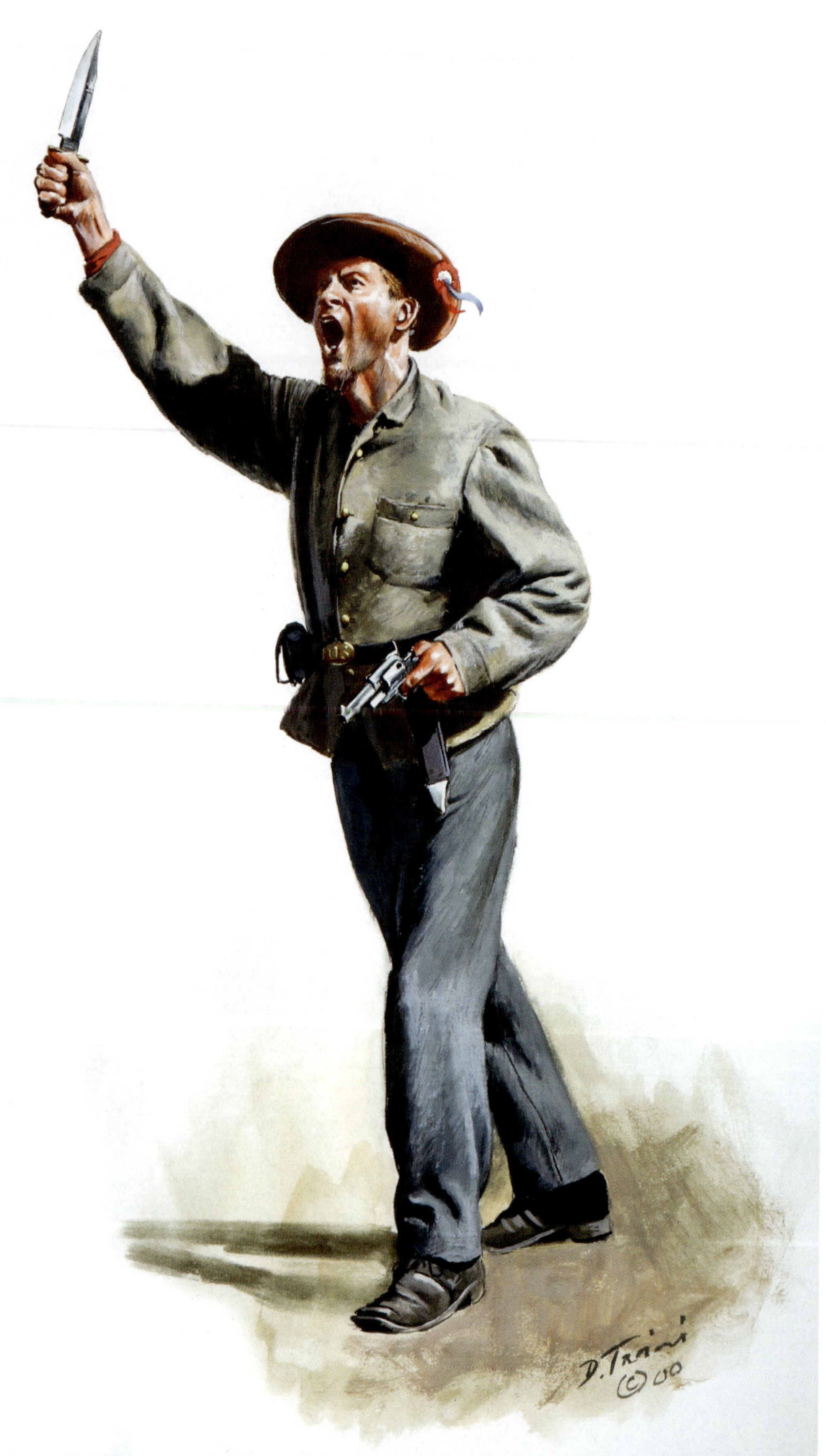

6th New York, Wilson's Zouaves, 1861

COMPOSED OF SOME OF THE ROWDI-EST ELEMENTS OF New York City, Wilson's Zouaves, or the Union Battalion of Zouaves, was organized by William Wilson, who was reputed to have been a notorious pugilist, pawnbroker, and street brawler. The unit was mustered for two years' service as the 6th New York Infantry on May 25, 1861.[1] On arrival at its first posting on Santa Rosa Island in Pensacola Bay, Florida, the regular army officers stationed at Fort Pickens were appalled at the indiscipline of the unit. Drunkenness, brawls, and arguments among its officers were followed by a disorganized defense when a Confederate force led by Brigadier General Richard Anderson crossed from the mainland to Santa Rosa Island on October 9, 1861, and mounted a surprise attack.

The indiscipline of Wilson's regiment was further demonstrated during operations against Port Hudson in Louisiana on March 26, 1863, when elements of the regiment being transported aboard the steamer *Morning Light* broke open the vessel's bar and supposedly attempted to throw Brigadier General William Dwight Jr. overboard.[2] As a result, several line officers were arrested and twenty-four men were imprisoned at Donaldsonville.[3] Once purged of its bad officers, the regiment performed well within the XIX Army Corps in operations in western Louisiana during April 1863, and returned to New York to be mustered out on June 25, 1863. During its entire service, twelve of the regiment's men were killed in action, three died of wounds, and thirty-four died from disease and other causes.

Despite being unable to acquire Zouave uniforms, the 6th New York continued to be known as Wilson's Zouaves. On April 23, 1861, each man was reported to have been given "a new thick grey shirt, and a tricolor cockade for his breast."[4] According to a regimental history, on departure from New York they paraded down Broadway attired in "gray jackets furnished by the State which were of the very worst sort of shoddy cloth."[5] Earlier, on May 18 *Harper's Weekly* described their uniform as "a gray shirt, gray pants, brown felt hat, belt, and brogans."

Initially commanding Company B, but not mustered in, Captain Walter Johnson was reported to be "a great expert in sword and bowie knife exercise," and he doubtless encouraged enlisted men in the regiment to carry knives like that brandished in this painting.[6] The figure also carries a Colt Model 1855 Side-hammer "Root" percussion pocket revolver. His waist belt is fastened with a small-sized Pattern 1839 oval "US" plate. The regiment was officially armed with Model 1840 muskets when it left for the front on June 15, 1861.

1. *National Republican* (Washington, DC), April 24, 1861, 3:5.
2. *Weekly Pioneer and Democrat* (Saint Paul, MN), May 8, 1863, 3:5.
3. *Buffalo Commercial Advertiser*, May 1, 1863, 2:2.
4. *New York Evening Express*, April 23, 1861, 4:1.
5. Gouverneur Morris, *The History of a Volunteer Regiment* (Veteran Volunteer Publishing Company, 1891), 31.
6. *New York Daily Herald*, April 27, 1861, 8:3.

Coppens's Battalion of Louisiana Zouaves

THE RECRUITMENT OF A BATTALION OF ZOUAVES commanded by George Auguste Gaston Coppens began several days before the secession of Louisiana from the Union on January 26, 1861. A report in the Richmond press after the unit reached the Confederate capital in June of that year noted that many members of the Battalion had served in the Crimean War and that "Twenty or thirty are New Orleans Irishmen, one hundred or thereabouts are Swiss, and quite a number are Germans, but the majority are American Frenchmen." Commenting on their appearance, the newspaper stated, "They are generally small, but wiry, muscular as cats, and brown as a side of sole leather."[1]

From January through March 1861, Coppens drilled his Zouaves regularly, with active service in mind, rather than put them in street parades or on military display. When he offered their services to Thomas O. Moore, then the governor of Louisiana, toward the end of February 1861, his offer was declined.[2] Journeying next to the new Confederate capital at Montgomery, Alabama, Coppens obtained a personal interview with President Jefferson Davis and Secretary of War Leroy P. Walker, who gladly accepted the "battalion of Louisiana Zouaves" into the ranks of "the Regular Army of the Southern Confederacy" and who immediately ordered it to Pensacola, Florida, where a Confederate force faced the Federal garrison in Fort Pickens.[3] The funds necessary for uniforming and equipping the Battalion were provided by Confederate purchasing agent J. W. Zacharie, father of Captain Howard H. Zacharie, commanding Company C of the unit, on the understanding that he would be reimbursed by the government.

Parrying with his musket, this Zouave wears the uniform received in New Orleans during April 1861. His red flannel fez has a deep-blue tassel. Similar in cut to that of the original French Zouaves, his loose dark-blue flannel jacket is edged and trimmed with yellow lace and braid, but is minus the characteristic trefoil or *tombeau* worn by most Zouave units.[4] Worn under it was a close-fitting collarless dark-blue flannel vest trimmed with yellow. Wrapped around his waist is a broad sky-blue merino-wool sash. His full red trousers are tucked into white canvas gaiters, over which are black "gutta percha" greaves.[5] Across his body, from left to right, is a blanket roll with a waterproof oilcloth cover that also served as a knapsack.

From Pensacola, Coppens's Zouaves proceeded to Virginia, where the unit was assigned to the Department of the Peninsula. Transferred next to the Army of Northern Virginia, it was expanded into the Regiment of Louisiana Zouaves and Chasseurs, and it fought in the Seven Days' campaign. Assigned to the 2nd Louisiana Brigade, it participated at Second Manassas and Sharpsburg, after which it was reorganized. It continued to serve in Virginia and North Carolina until December 1864.

1. *Daily Dispatch* (Richmond, VA), June 8, 1861, 2:6.
2. *New Orleans Daily Crescent,* March 29, 1861, 1:4.
3. Lee A. Wallace Jr., "Coppens' Louisiana Zouaves," *Civil War History* 8 (1962): 272.
4. Wallace, 272.
5. Ross Brooks, "Red Petticoats and Blue Jackets: 1st Confederate States Zouave Battalion, or Coppens' Louisiana Zouaves," *Military Collector & Historian* 45, no. 4 (Winter 1993): 149.

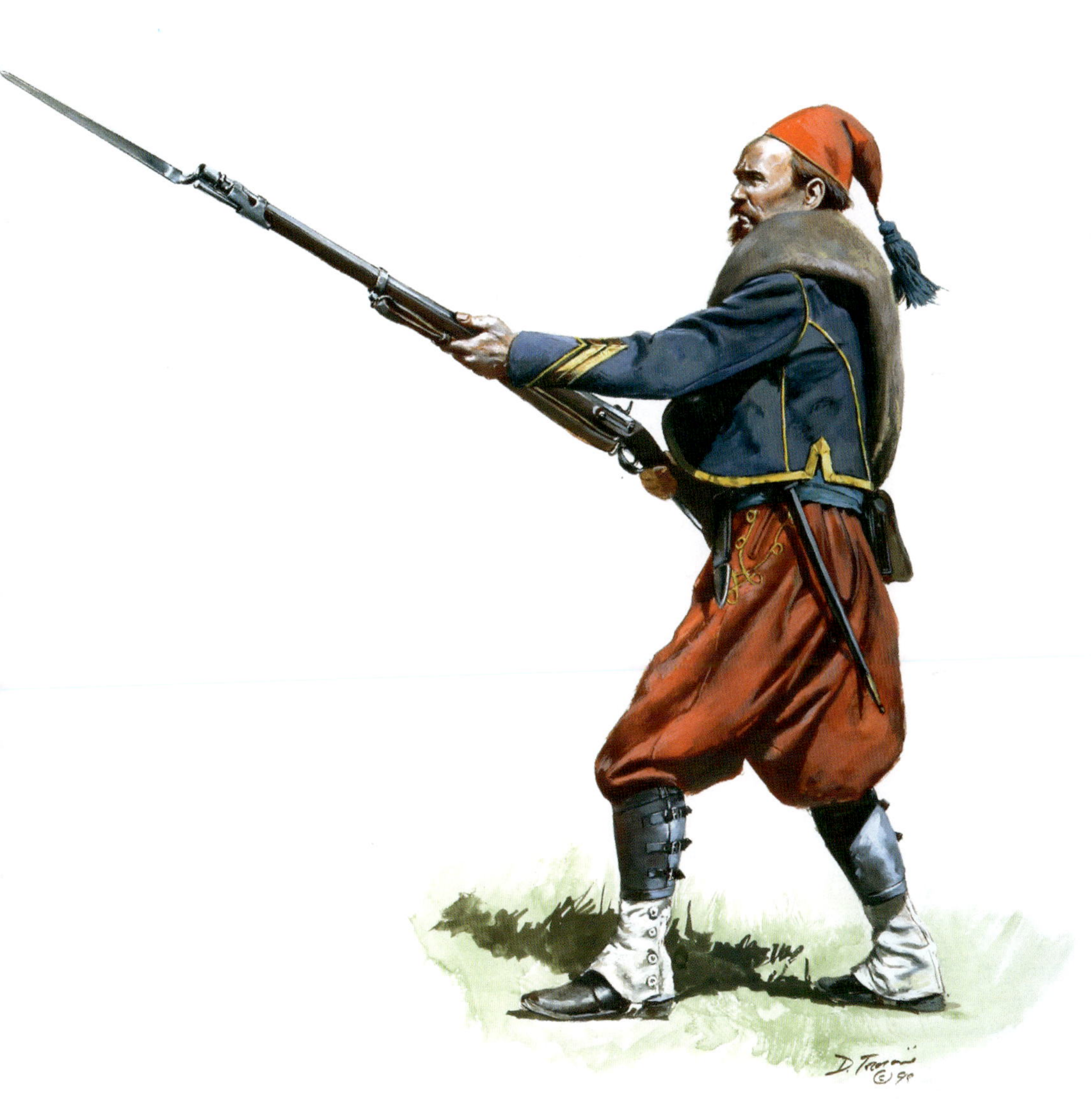

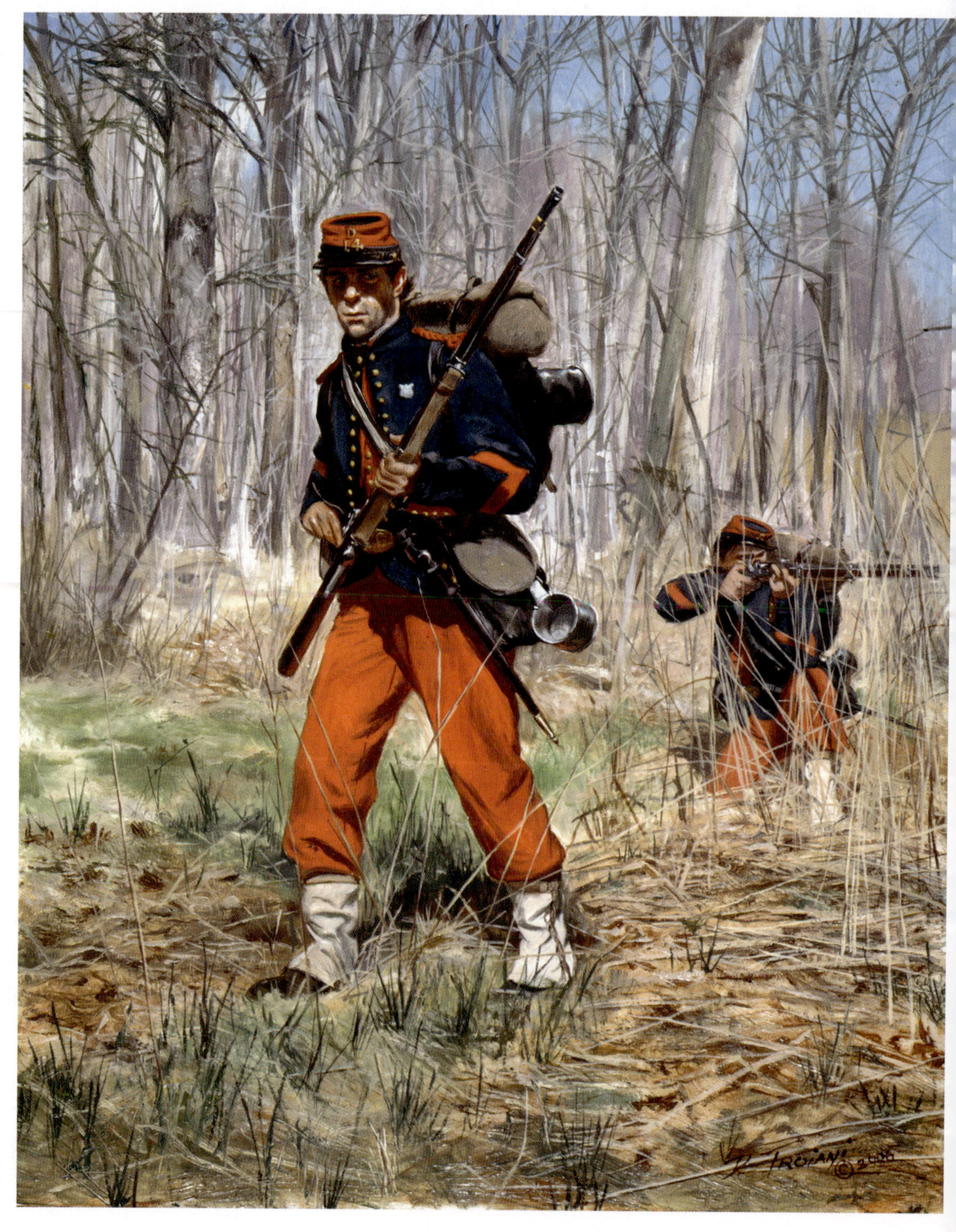

14th New York State Militia (14th Brooklyn)

THE 14TH NEW YORK STATE MILITIA (NYSM), ALSO KNOWN AS the 14th Brooklyn, first paraded in the uniform that would create its nickname, "the Red-Legged Devils," on April 18, 1861. Supplied by the City of Brooklyn, this uniform had been adopted by the Board of Officers in 1860 and was described in the regimental history as consisting of "red pants, white leggings, blue jacket and broad red chevrons and shoulder knots, and cap with blue band, red above and blue top."[1] Later, on May 12, 1861, this uniform was reported as consisting of "red pantaloons, blue jacket embroidered with red, and red and blue cap, similar to that of the Chasseur a Pied of France." The 14th NYSM paraded the next day in "large [dark] blue overcoats."[2]

The first uniform worn by the 14th NYSM did not fare well. On the occasion of its departure for Washington on May 18, 1861, a press reporter observed that it had "a very objectionable uniform, both on the score of color and durability. It was of a kind of red flannel, and though very striking on parade, will make its wearer a peculiarly conspicuous mark for sharp-shooters, while as an outside garment, it will shortly fray into rags."[3] On July 1, 1861, it was reported that "the whole regiment is to be newly uniformed, their old uniforms having become unserviceable."[4]

After heavy involvement at Bull Run, the uniforms of the 14th NYSM were in such a poor state that regulation blue uniforms were issued and worn for a short time. According to Colonel Alfred M. Wood, "the red pants were worn out . . . the army blue had to be substituted until others could be supplied by contract . . . the men were not pleased with them as 'they would not be found dead without red pants on.'" The central government soon supplied the distinctive uniform of the regiment via the New York Quartermaster Department and continued to furnish it during its term of service, which expired on June 14, 1864.[5]

The enlisted men of the 14th NYSM are depicted wearing chasseur-pattern coats with broad red sleeve chevrons and shoulder knots, with small brass buttons down the front edges and on red cuff patches. Brass buttons also adorned their red vests. Their chasseur-pattern caps have the company letter "D" on the red top and "14" on the dark-blue band. Baggy red trousers are tucked into white canvas leggings. A silver shield-shaped identification badge is pinned to the chest of the man at center. They are armed with Model 1855 rifle muskets and well equipped with cartridge box, cap pouch, canteen, haversack, and knapsack with mess tin and blanket roll attached.

Officially designated the 84th New York Volunteers on December 7, 1861, at its own request the regiment continued to be referred to as the 14th NYSM. It served with the Army of the Potomac through Pope's Campaign in Northern Virginia, the Maryland Campaign, the Chancellorsville and Gettysburg campaigns, and Grant's Overland Campaign. With ranks depleted, veterans and recruits of the regiment were transferred to the 5th New York Veteran Infantry on June 2, 1864. Twelve days later the 14th NYSM was mustered out of the service of the United States.

---

1. *The History of the Fighting Fourteenth*, published in commemoration of the fiftieth anniversary of the muster of the regiment into the United States service (1911), 213.

2. *New York Herald*, May 12, 1861, 5:2.

3. *New York World*, cited in *Charleston Daily Courier*, May 25, 1861, 1:2.

4. *New York Daily Tribune*, July 1, 1861, 7:6.

5. *History of the Fighting Fourteenth*, 237.

New York Independent Battalion (Les Enfants Perdus)

THE INDEPENDENT BATTALION, NEW YORK VOLUNTEER INFANTRY, was organized among immigrants in New York City beginning in August 1861, under the command of Lieutenant Colonel Felix Confort, who had served in the French army for about nineteen years and "had passed through the Crimean and Italian campaigns."[1] Nicknamed Les Enfants Perdus, meaning Lost Children, the unit was possibly named after units of French soldiers in the Crimean War engaged in what might be called a "forelorn hope" assignment, such as an assault on an impregnable position or a similar post of extreme danger in which they were likely to be cut off, killed, or captured.[2]

Initially hopeful of raising a regiment, Confort eventually had a seven-company, battalion-sized unit mustered in for three years on April 18, 1862.[3] A multinational unit, recruits were largely German, Swiss, Belgian, and Canadian. Of twenty-five officers, nine were French, six Belgian, five American, three German, one Irish, and one Scottish.[4]

This enlisted man wears an example of the first uniform issued to Les Enfants Perdus in 1862. This was reported in the New York press as being similar to that of the French *chasseurs a pied* and as resembling "in some respects the Zouave dress, [but] differs from it in a more comfortable arrangement of the loose pants and in the cap, which is a kepi, and not a fez. The jacket has short tunic lappels [sic], while the color of the uniform is a dark blue throughout, trimmed with yellow."[5] His shako has a round yellow worsted pompon and a brass American eagle at the front. His triple-breasted chasseur-pattern coat and pantaloons were made by Morrison, Haber & Co., of New York City, during February 1862. The coat is without the yellow plastron front and yellow worsted epaulettes originally included in the unit's full-dress uniform. His pants have yellow hussar-style knots and trim. White linen gaiters are worn under leather greaves. He is armed with a short Enfield rifle with a saber bayonet in a scabbard attached to his waist belt. Accoutrements include a cap pouch and a Pattern 1857 rifle musket cartridge box. His knapsack is of the French militia pattern with a blanket roll and a mess tin attached.[6]

From the outset, the Battalion appears to have been considered second rate, despite Confort's intention that they should serve as "tirailleurs and scouts." It left New York State on April 18, 1862, being assigned to the 4th Corps, Army of the Potomac, and served as garrison troops at Gloucester and Yorktown, Virginia, from May until December 1862. It was next transferred to the 18th Corps to conduct further garrison duty along the Carolina coast. By the end of 1862, it was down to about 250 men mainly due to desertion and disease. Three companies were detached, with a separate brigade for service along the Maryland and Delaware coast during 1863. By May 31 of that year, there were eight companies on duty on Port Royal Island. The unit's most active period of service occurred during the siege of Battery Wagner on Morris Island, South Carolina, from July through December 1863, in which four enlisted men were killed and six wounded.

1. *New-York Times*, June 3, 1862, 5:6.

2. *New York Ledger*, May 10, 1862, 8:5.

3. Frederick H. Dyer, *A Compendium of the War of the Rebellion* (Dyer Publishing Company, 1908), 1471.

4. Letter from a Belgian sailor in *Le Precurseur*, September 15, 1863.

5. *New York Herald*, December 7, 1861, 10:5.

6. NARA, record group 156, records of the Office of the Chief of Ordnance; Summary of Quarterly Returns of Ordnance of Volunteer Infantry Units.

7. John R. Elting, ed., "Collectors Field Book," *Military Collector & Historian* 22, no. 1 (Spring 1970): 26–27.

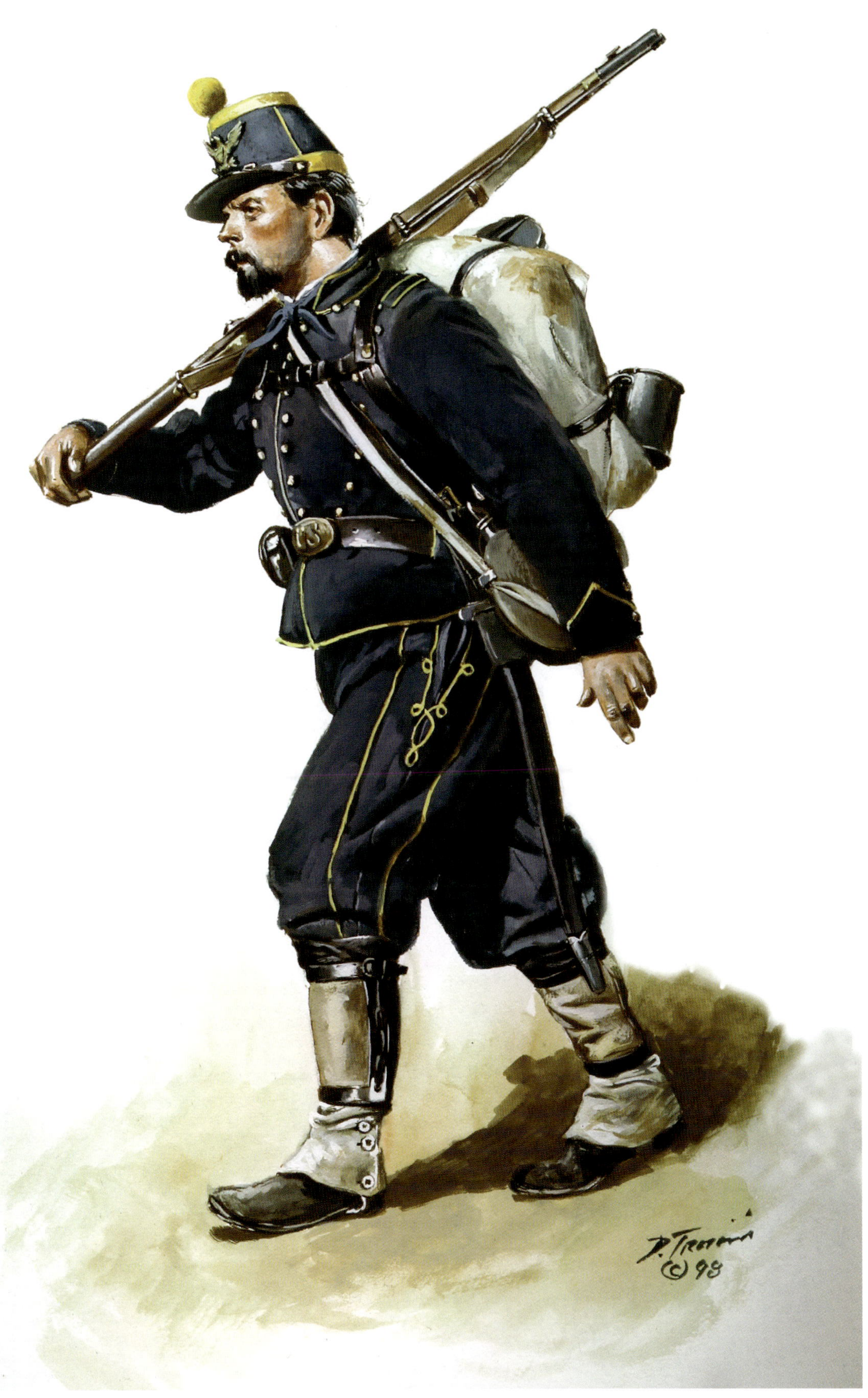

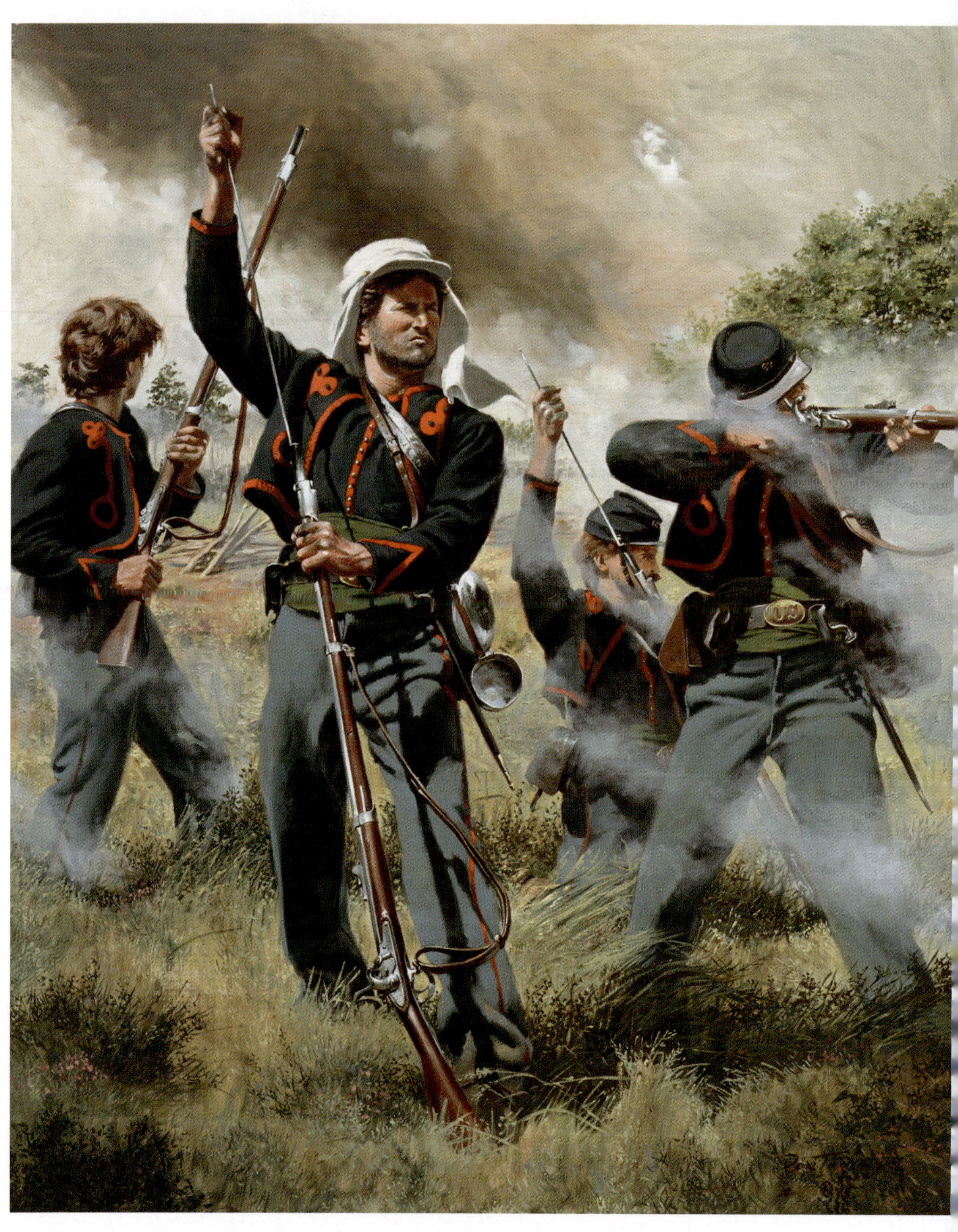

69th New York State Militia, Company K

Raised by political activist and Irish-American politician Thomas Francis Meagher, the Irish Zouaves were composed of recruits from the Phoenix Zouaves, which formed part of the military section of the Fenian Brotherhood of Irish exiles based in New York City and whose members wore a "full green uniform, bright with lace and gold fringe."[1] Recruitment of the Irish Zouaves, to be attached to the 69th New York State Militia (NYSM), commanded by Colonel Michael Corcoran, began with a gathering at Phelan's Billiard Saloon, off Broadway in New York City during the last few days of April 1861.[2] Being designated Company K, the Zouaves left to join the rest of the regiment encamped at Georgetown, DC, on May 23, 1861.

Assigned to the 3rd Brigade, 1st Division, Army of North-East Virginia, the 69th NYSM advanced from its camp at Centerville, Virginia, in the early hours of July 21, 1861, with Meagher serving as acting major and Lieutenant Edward K. Butler in command of the Irish Zouaves. During the Battle of Bull Run, among the Irish Zouaves, four men were killed, two were wounded, and nineteen went missing.[3] One of the wounded, Corporal John D. O'Keefe was involved in a desperate struggle to seize a Confederate flag, and, although captured, he managed to fight his way free and return to Centerville with a Rebel prisoner in tow.[4]

On departure for the front, the Zouaves were described as wearing "a loose navy blue jacket fringed with red, and pantaloons of a bluish gray, with caps *a la* Sixty-ninth regiment." On arrival in Washington, they were further reported to be uniformed in "a dark-blue Zouave jacket, gray Zouave pants, all trimmed with red, and blue Zouave cap."[5]

Shown in action at Bull Run and making good use of their converted Model 1816 muskets, which were fitted with the Maynard primer system, the Zouaves wear dark-blue jackets with red *tombeaux* and trim, plus matching vests. Their cadet-gray pantaloons have narrow red welts on the outer seams, and their dark-blue forage caps are of the same pattern as worn by the rest of the 69th NYSM, with the small brass numerals "69" at front. One man wears a white linen havelock cap cover of the type provided to the whole regiment by "the many patriotic ladies" of New York City, which included the wife of the Irish-born judge Charles P. Daly, who also presented the regiment with "a beautiful silken standard of the National colors."[6] Green waist sashes indicate their Irish heritage.

The battered 69th NYSM returned to New York City on July 27, 1861, where it was mustered out a week later, and a new volunteer 69th New York Infantry was formed. This became the nucleus of the famed Irish Brigade, commanded by Thomas Meagher as a brigadier general.

1. *New York Herald*, July 28, 1861, 1:5.
2. *Daily Missouri Democrat* (Saint Louis, MO), May 2, 1861, 2:4.
3. *New-York Tribune*, August 4, 1861, 1; and *The Sun* (New York, NY), July 29, 1861, 2:5.
4. *Irish American* (New York, NY), August 3, 1861, 2:4.
5. *New York Herald*, May 23, 1861, 8:1; and *National Republican* (Washington, DC), May 24, 1861, 3:2.
6. *Irish American Weekly* (New York, NY), June 15, 1861, 2:4.

Maryland Guard

ORGANIZED AS A FOUR-COMPANY BATTALION IN Baltimore during December 1859, the Maryland Guard was attached to the 53rd Regiment Infantry, Maryland Volunteer Militia. Two more companies were added during the next few months. Comprised of "the best class of young men," the unit had strict rules regarding temperance and behavior while in uniform. In February 1860, recruits were required to provide themselves with fatigue dress consisting of a "light-blue cloth cap, dark-blue jacket with standing collar and single row of buttons, and dark cloth pantaloons."[1]

The battalion paraded for the first time in full dress on October 19, 1860, for the Inauguration of Druid Hill Park in northwest Baltimore. According to Private McHenry Howard, of Company C, they wore "a dark blue jacket, short and close fitting and much embroidered with yellow; a blue flannel shirt with a close row of small round buttons (for ornament only) down the front, between yellow trimming; blue pantaloons very baggy and gathered below the knee and falling over the tops of long drab gaiters; small blue cap of the kepi style, also trimmed with yellow and, finally, a wide red sash, or band, kept wide by hooks and eyes on the ends."[2] The total cost of the full dress, which included an overcoat, full chasseur uniform, undress jacket, cap, knapsack, blanket, and body belt, was $42.48, which recruits had to pay within three months of joining the battalion.[3]

Held by this volunteer is a Model 1842 musket and rigid militia knapsack with a regimental number painted on the outer flap, plus a light-blue blanket with the letters "MG" in red strapped to it. His whitened buff leather waist belt has a plain rectangular plate. Throughout much of 1860 the battalion was without its own arms and borrowed muskets from other city militia companies.[4]

Members of the Maryland Guard were overwhelmingly secessionist in sympathy and fully expected to defend their city against Northern encroachment after April 1861. The battalion remained in uniform and under arms until May 1861, when Union forces occupied Baltimore. With their position untenable, the Maryland Guard dispersed. Many members of the unit made their way to Richmond, Virginia, where they enlisted in the Confederate army. Not destined to serve as a unit, two companies of Maryland men were ordered to go to Winchester to form the nucleus of the Confederate 1st Maryland Regiment, while a third became Company B, 21st Virginia Infantry. Both units served with distinction in the Army of Northern Virginia.

1. *The Daily Exchange* (Baltimore, MD), February 23, 1860, 1:3.

2. McHenry Howard in *Recollections of a Maryland Confederate Soldier and Staff Officer under Johnson, Jackson and Lee*, ed. James I. Robertson Jr. (Press of Morningside Bookshop, 1975), 1.

3. James Hennessey, "The Maryland Guard Battalion, 53rd Regiment, Maryland Volunteer Militia, 1860–1861," *Military Collector & Historian* 28, no. 4 (Winter 1976): 164.

4. *The Daily Exchange*, May 7, 1860, 1:2; and June 2, 1860, 2:1.

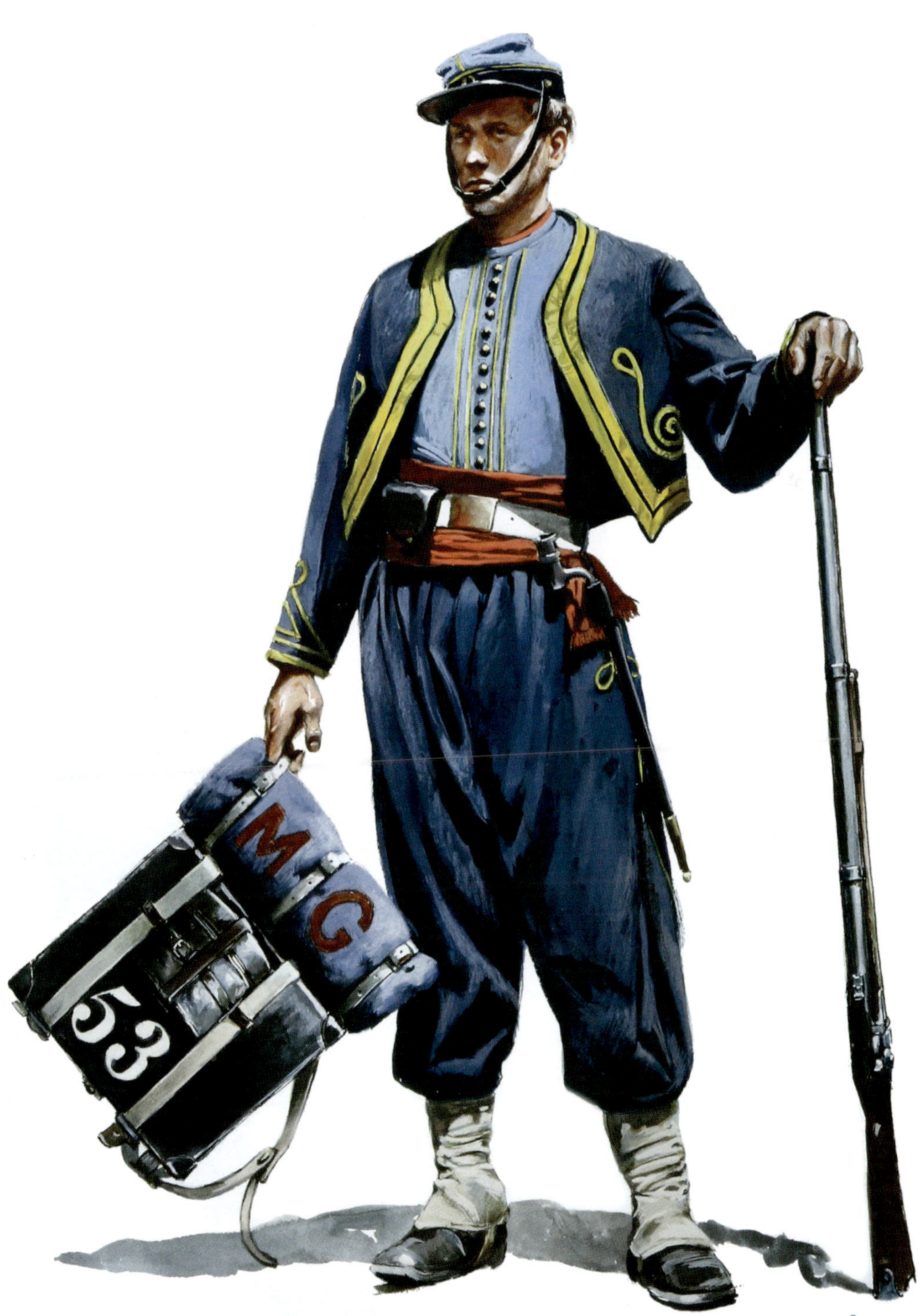

MC
53
D. Troiani
© 2000

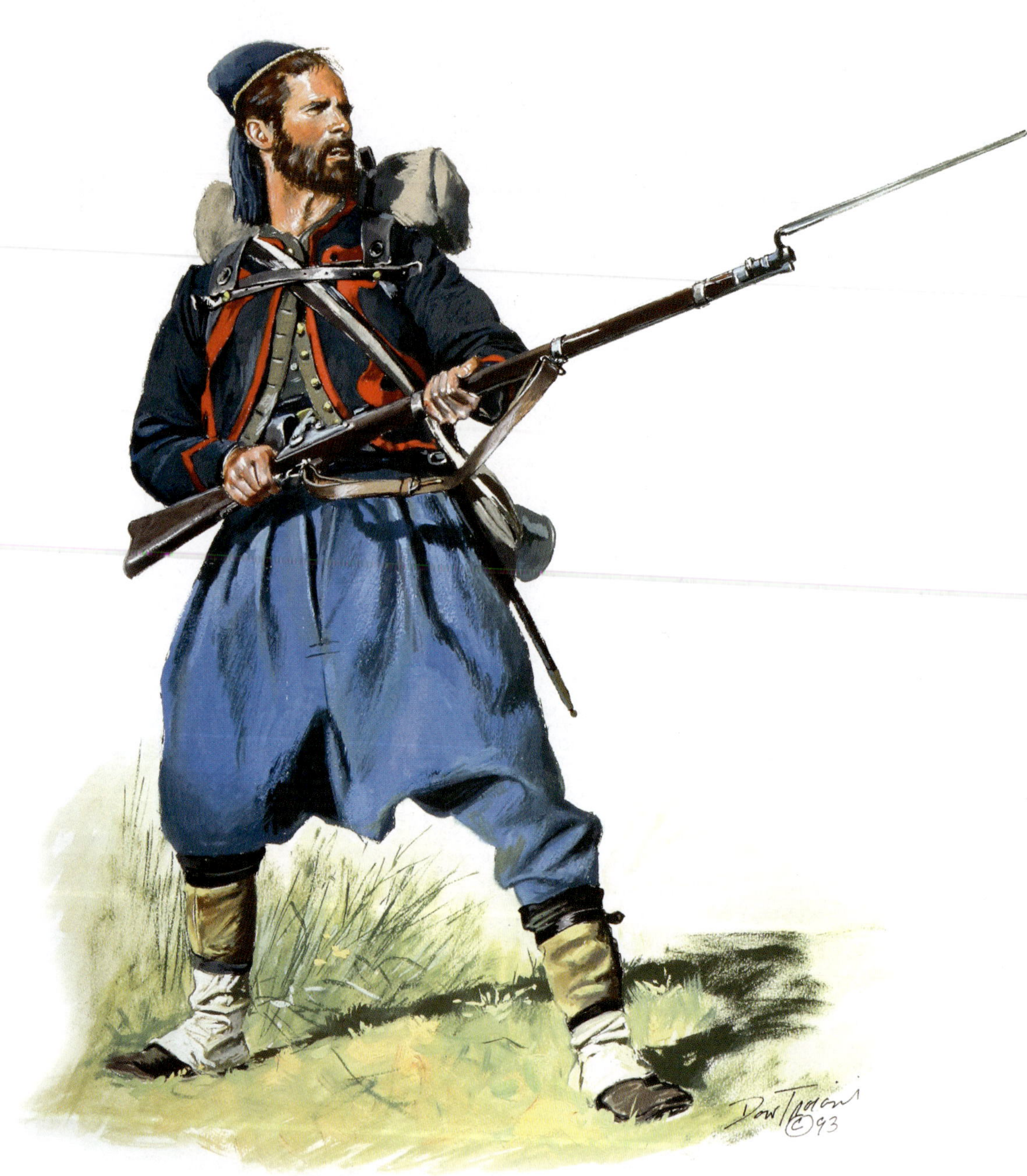

76th Pennsylvania (Keystone Zouaves)

THE 76TH PENNSYLVANIA, ALSO KNOWN AS THE "Keystone Zouaves," was recruited during August and September, 1861, and organized at Camp Cameron on October 18, 1861. Composed of previously independent companies, including the Lawrence Zouaves, the Sharon Zouaves, and the Curtin Zouaves, it was led by Colonel John M. Power, who originally commanded the Johnstown Zouave Cadets and was lieutenant colonel of the 3rd Pennsylvania Volunteer Militia (three months).

Although pre-enlistment uniforms were probably worn by some of the companies forming the Keystone Zouaves, the unit appears to have adopted a regimental uniform in September as, on the 4th of that month, a report in the *Philadelphia Inquirer* stated that it was made of "handsome army cloth" and consisted of a "dark blue cap and jacket, light blue pantaloons, and leather leggings, all in the Zouave style."[1] About three weeks later, a recruit using the pseudonym "Keystone" wrote from Camp Cameron, "All the men in the Zouave Regiment are now uniformed."[2] Based on photographic evidence, this uniform included a rather plain blue Zouave jacket with broad, light-colored facings around the edges and cuffs, underneath which was a plain pullover shirt with a placket front fastened by three or four small buttons. Headgear appears to have been a mixture of forage caps and tasseled fezzes, and sky-blue pants varied in style and cut. This uniform continued to be worn by the 76th Pennsylvania until replaced by uniforms in standard Federal blue before the end of 1861.

At the beginning of February 1862, a letter from a member of the regiment at Beaufort, South Carolina, mentioned that the Keystone Zouaves were "dressed in the French uniforms that the government has recently imported, and are decidedly neat."[3] This is the only evidence that the regiment received some of the ten thousand Pattern 1860 *chasseur a pied* uniforms acquired from France by the Federal Quartermaster Department.

It was not until November 1862 that the commander of the 76th Pennsylvania, by then Colonel DeWitt C. Strawbridge, requested a new set of Zouave uniforms, which were supplied by the Schuykill Arsenal in Philadelphia. Standing at "Charge—Bayonet" with a Model 1861 Springfield rifle musket, this Zouave wears an example of the uniform supplied. His dark-blue fez with yellow binding has a dark-blue tassel attached. His dark-blue wool jacket is edged with red binding with a red trefoil or *tombeau* at its front. Sewn inside this is a gray false vest with nine brass ball buttons attached. His pleated sky-blue pants are of full Zouave pattern and are tied below the knees via draw strings. Yellow leather greaves are worn over white canvas leggings.[4]

---

1. *Philadelphia Inquirer*, September 4, 1861, 1:6.
2. *Altoona Tribune*, September 26, 1861, 2:4.
3. *Wheeling Daily Intelligencer*, February 18, 1862, 1:4.
4. Uniforms courtesy of the Pennsylvania Historical and Museum Commission, Division of Historic Sites and Properties, and the Smithsonian Institution, Washington, DC.

11th Indiana Volunteers (Wallace's Zouaves)

A WEALTHY POLITICIAN, DIPLOMAT, AND AUTHOR, Lew Wallace was determined to raise a Zouave regiment to defend the Union. When the State of Indiana declined to supply more expensive Zouave-style uniforms, Wallace decided to pay for them himself. The uniform he acquired for the 11th Indiana Infantry, also known as Wallace's Zouaves, was purchased from Eli A. Hall, merchant tailor and clothier at 2 Odd Fellows Hall, Indianapolis, at $10 a suit, made from jeans cloth produced at the Ohio Premium Woolen Factory owned by George Merritt and William Coughlen.[1] Wallace also ordered six hundred "fatigue caps" at one dollar each from Meyberg & Hellman, Manufacturers and Wholesale Dealers in Hats, Caps, Furs and Straw Goods at 124 Walnut Street, Cincinnati, Ohio, on May 11, 1861.[2]

In his autobiography, Wallace stated, "There was nothing of the flashy, Algerian colors in the uniform of the Eleventh Indiana . . . Our outfit was of the tamest gray twilled goods, not unlike home-made jeans—a visor cap, French pattern, its top of red cloth not larger than the palm of one's hand; blue flannel shirt with open neck; a jacket Greekish in form, edged with narrow binding, the red scarcely noticeable; breeches baggy, but not petticoated; button gaiters connecting below the knees . . . The effect was to magnify the men, though in line two thousand yards off they looked like a smoky ribbon long-drawn out."[3]

Attaching a saber bayonet to his Model 1853 Enfield rifle, this Zouave wears the regimental uniform purchased by his commanding officer by the beginning of May 1861. His red-topped chasseur-pattern cap is quartered with red trim. Rather plain by Zouave standards, his gray jacket is edged with red braid, and his plain gray pantaloons are tucked in calf-length boots rather than gaiters. A collarless plain blue overshirt has two small buttons fastening its placket front. A knife with a deer-antler grip is attached to his belt.

Reporting the return of the 11th Indiana from three months' service in western Virginia on July 16, 1861, a newspaper correspondent wrote, "The clothes made three months ago for this regiment, after a severe service, show that the suits were made of good materials and well put together."[4] When the regiment was reorganized for three years on August 31, 1861, the state agreed to outfit it in the same style and color of uniform, with Eli Hall providing "606 jeans suits" made from cloth once again produced by Merritt and Coughlen, while a further 406 suits were supplied by Geisendorff & Co., who operated the Hoosier Woollen Factory near Indianapolis.[5] This uniform was eventually replaced by blue semi-Zouave uniforms of a different pattern in response to the War Department request of September 23, 1861, that no further gray uniforms should be issued to the Union Army. The 11th Indiana received its blue Zouave clothing during December 1861, and this was worn by the regiment throughout the remainder of the war.

1. *Indianapolis Directory and Business Mirror for 1861* (Bowen, Stuart & Co., 1861), 194.
2. "Report of John H. Vajen, Quarter-Master General of the State of Indiana," (Joseph J. Bingham, State Printer), 662.
3. Lewis Wallace, *Lew Wallace: An Autobiography*, vol. 1 (1906), 270.
4. *Indianapolis Daily Journal*, July 16, 1861, 3:1.
5. "Report of John H. Vajen," 666.

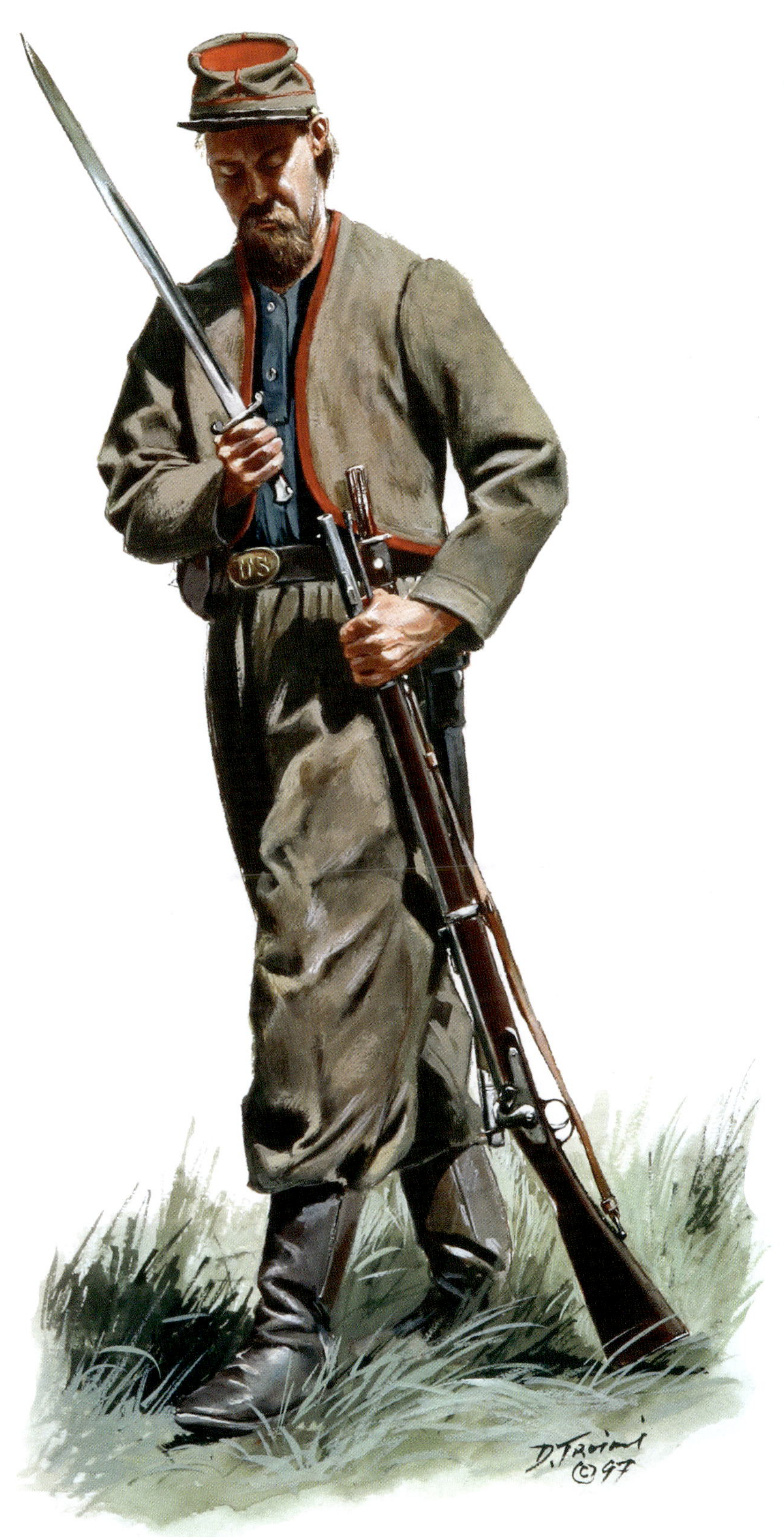

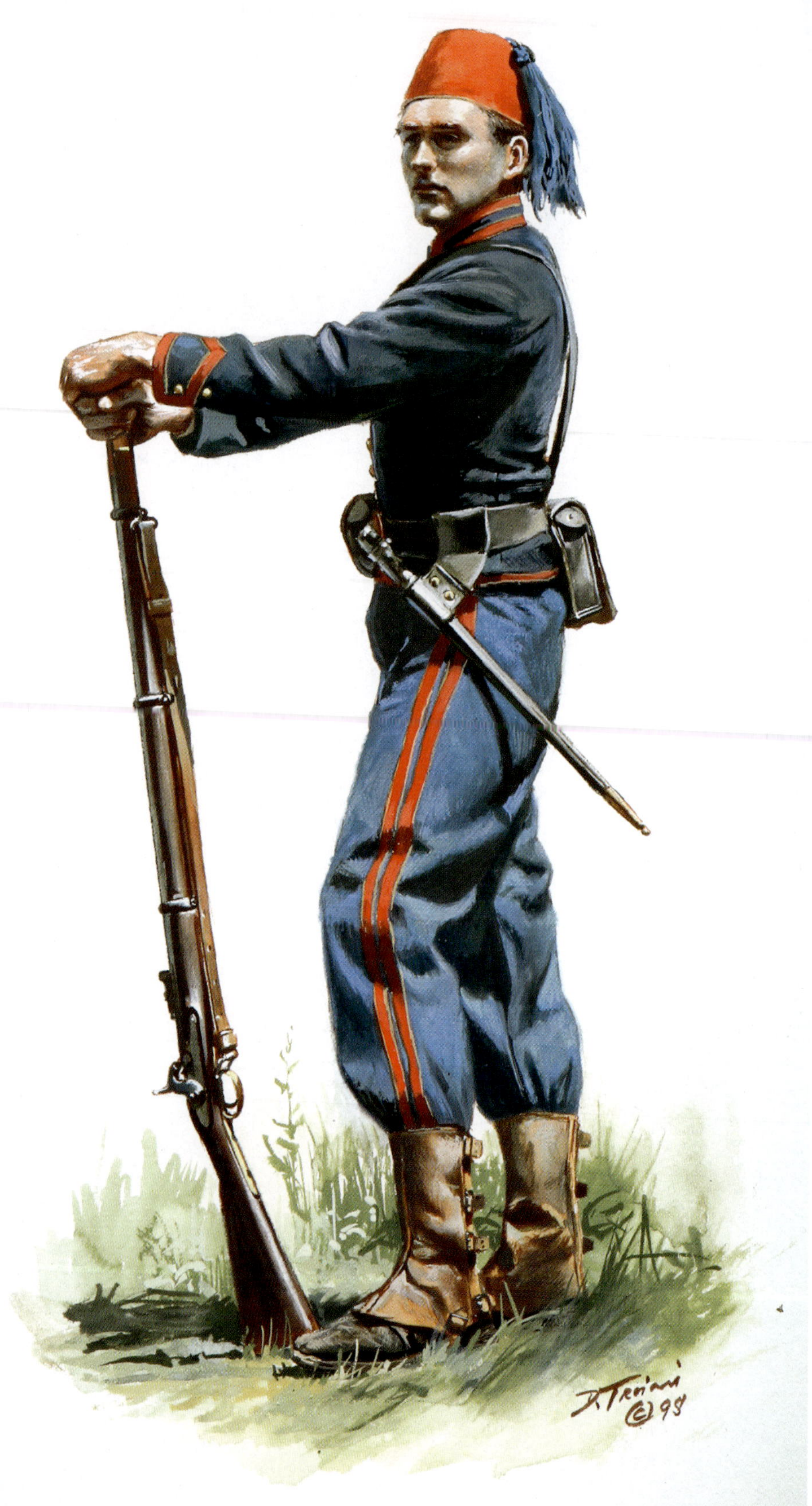

34th Ohio Volunteer Infantry (Piatt's Zouaves)

THE STATE OF OHIO ENLISTED TWO REGIMENTS OF Zouaves for three years' service. Known originally as Piatt Zouaves, or the 1st Zouaves, the 34th Ohio Infantry was organized in late July 1861 by newspaper editor and politician Abraham Sanders Piatt, who had expansive plans to recruit a brigade of Zouaves. The organization of the first regiment was complete within a month with the addition of a vivandière. Organization of the 54th Ohio, or 2nd Zouaves, progressed more slowly.

Piatt attracted recruits for both regiments with promises of Zouave uniforms, Maynard rifles, and service in the Western Department under General John C. Fremont. Made by Heidelbach, Seasongood & Co., of New York City, the nine-button jackets they received reached to the hips and were trimmed with half-inch red tape around collar, cuffs, and edges. Cut in a pleated chasseur style, with slightly narrower double red seam stripes, the pants were produced by A. & J. Trounstine, of Cincinnati. Also issued to both regiments were white buttoned leggings, "reaching some three inches above the ankle," manufactured at the Boot and Shoe Store of F. P. Haldy of Cincinnati, and "bright indigo blue" overcoats, apparently with lined capes.[1]

Headgear consisted of a rather square-shaped red fez with a light-blue tassel. Also worn was a drab gray felt hat, bound with red tape, of the same pattern as the Edmands hat issued to Massachusetts three-months regiments during May 1861. These were likely acquired directly from Haughton, Sawyer & Co., of Boston, or via their agent in Columbus, Ohio.

Though Piatt had requested Enfield rifles with sword bayonets for both regiments, the battalion companies of the 34th were furnished by the state with .69-caliber muskets rifled by Miles Greenwood of Cincinnati, while the two flank companies received "long" Enfields—in line with other Ohio regiments of this period. Sets of infantry equipments were of US pattern, but, as the regiments were of Zouaves, the quartermaster was instructed to "send no shoulder belts" to either, the cartridge boxes being worn initially on the waist belt; however, shoulder belts were added later.[2]

On September 15, 1861, the 34th Ohio departed from Camp Dennison for the Kanawha region, leaving behind just two full companies of the 54th and a demoralized company of artillery called the Lyon Battery, which was without guns or uniforms.[3] Not until mid-February 1862 was the 54th ready to march, under Colonel Thomas Kilby Smith. Although both regiments served with honor, the 34th in West Virginia and the 54th in the Army of the Tennessee, they were never reunited within a brigade.

1. Walter G. Smith, *Life and Letters of Thomas Kilby Smith, 1820–1887* (Putnam's, 1898), 187; and *Cincinnati Daily Commercial*, August 20, 1861, 2:5 and August 23, 1861, 2:5.

2. "*Correspondence to the Governor and Adjutant General*," Series 147-5: 122; "Quartermaster Orders to State Arsenal & Warehouse," Series 132, 1: 385, 2: 116, 120, 375, OHS; *Annual Report of the Quartermaster General to the Governor of the State of Ohio for the Year 1861* (Columbus: Richard Nevins, 1862); *Annual Report 1862* (1863); *Contracts—War Department for the Year 1861* (Washington, DC: GPO, 1862), 99, 119; Smith, *Kilby Smith*, 187.

3. "*Governor*," Series 147-7: 72, Series 147-9: 137, Series 147-10: 148; *Cincinnati Daily Commercial*, September 16, 1861, 2:6.

10th New York (National Zouaves)

ORIGINALLY FORMED IN NEW YORK CITY DURING December 1860 as an independent company-sized unit with Waters W. McChesney, a former member of the United States Zouave Cadets, as drill master, the Union Volunteers rebaptized themselves as the National Zouaves before the end of the year and adopted a Zouave uniform. Following news of the firing on Fort Sumter, the National Zouaves were expanded into a regiment with McChesney as colonel and were mustered in for two years on November 23, 1861, as the 10th New York Infantry.

This regiment's first wartime uniform was a hastily improvised "dark blue flannel costume, of the Zouave pattern, with grey fatigue caps."[1] Active service quickly wore this out and, sometime in June 1861, a new Zouave outfit was acquired, consisting of "jackets and pants . . . of blue pilot cloth, trimmed with red, with vest of the same cloth, trimmed with stripes of blue, and ornamented in front with a row of gilt buttons; a havelock of linen . . . and a blue sash with crimson border."[2]

During September 1861, a third Zouave-pattern uniform was issued to the regiment; it consisted of "light blue trousers, dark brown jacket, red vest, white canvas leggings and fez. The trousers and jacket were trimmed with red."[3] These uniforms were likely lost during the Peninsula Campaign of spring 1862, when the regiment's baggage was burned during the evacuation of the army's encampment at White House Landing.

On September 5, 1862, an order was issued for the procurement of a fourth Zouave uniform for the 10th New York. This was manufactured by William Seligman & Co., of New York City, who had supplied one of the earlier uniforms. Depicted is a private wearing an example of this uniform. A heavily trimmed dark-blue jacket, with an appliqued trefoil or *tombeau*, is worn over a red vest trimmed with six buttons. Light-blue chasseur-pattern trousers with double red seam stripes are tucked into white leggings. A white flannel turban is wound around a red fez with a blue tassel, and a blue sash is wrapped around his waist. He is armed with a Model 1842 Springfield smoothbore musket with a fixed bayonet.[4]

The 10th New York received a further issuance of Zouave uniforms in 1863 of "the same material and pattern" as those previously worn, which was presumably based on that worn during the previous year.[5] The regiment continued its efforts to maintain its Zouave appearance throughout the war and was mustered out at Munson's Hill, Virginia, on June 30, 1865, with 130 officers and enlisted men having died in action or from wounds and 89 having died by accident, during imprisonment, or from disease.

1. Charles Cowtan, *Services of the 10th New York Volunteers (National Zouaves) in the War of the Rebellion* (Charles H. Ludwig, 1882), 24–25.

2. *New York Herald*, June 1, 1861, 8:1.

3. Cowtan, 58.

4. Michael J. McAfee, "10th New York Volunteer Infantry Regiment ('National Zouaves'), 1861–1865, Plate No. 458–459, 'Military Uniforms in America,'" *Military Collector & Historian*, Company of Military Historians, 1977;

5. NARA, record group 94, regimental books and papers, 10th New York Infantry, book 21, entry 999.

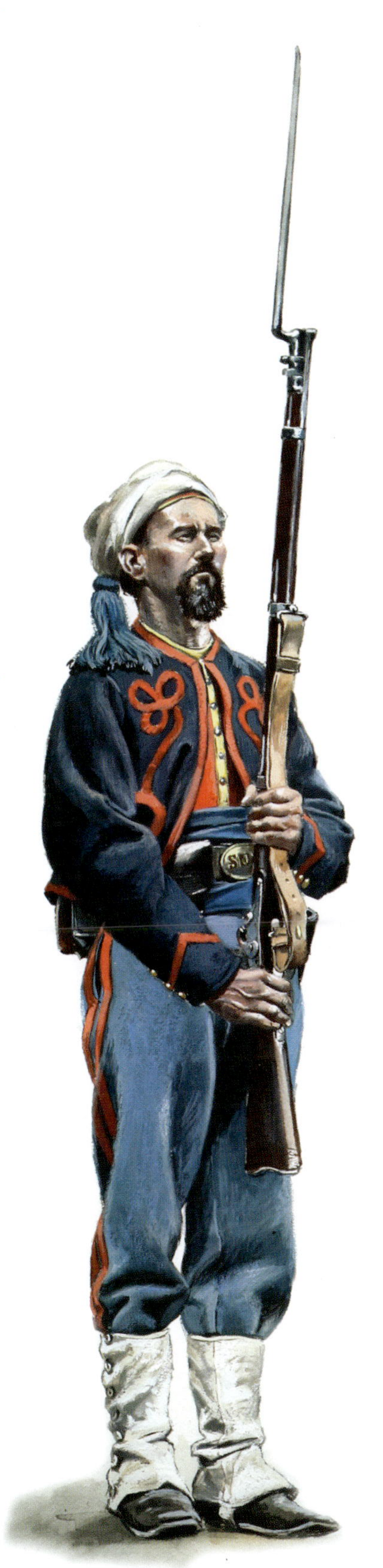

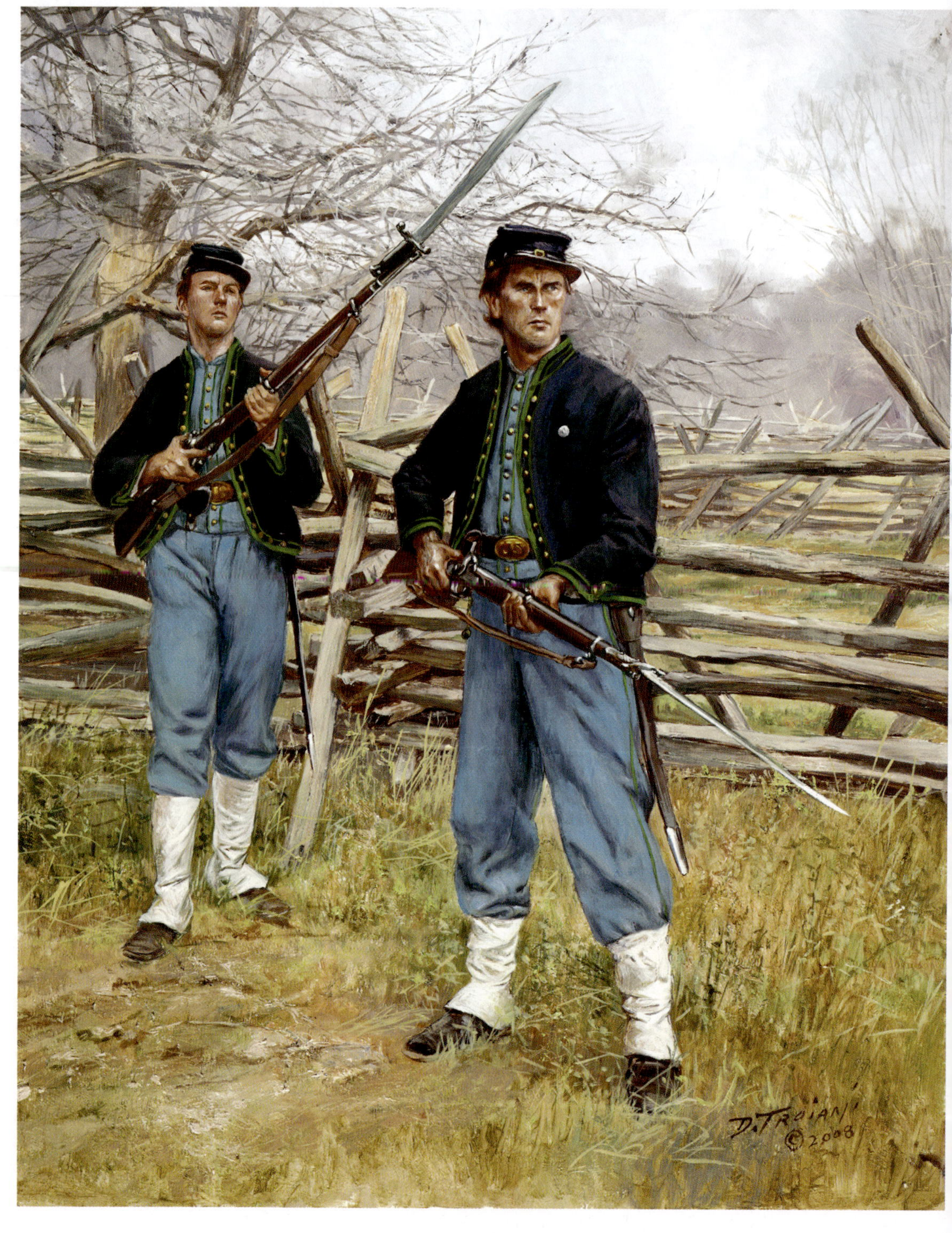

69th Pennsylvania Infantry, Companies I and K

THE BASIS FOR THE 69TH PENNSYLVANIA INFANTRY was the Irish-American 2nd Regiment, Second Brigade, First Division, Pennsylvania Militia, from which the 24th Pennsylvania, also known as "the Irish Brigade," was formed for three months' service in April 1861. Commanded by Welsh-born Colonel Joshua T. Owen, this unit served under Major General Robert Patterson on the Upper Potomac and in the Shenandoah Valley, but it saw little action. Reorganized for three years' service as the "Second California," Owen's Irish regiment was mustered in for three years by Colonel Edward D. Baker as the 69th Pennsylvania Infantry on August 19, 1861.[1]

On August 31, 1861, the 69th Pennsylvania received five hundred "uniforms, Minnie muskets, and accoutrements" for the five companies thus far recruited, the former including "a dark blue roundabout, trimmed in green."[2] On September 9, the Philadelphia *Press* reported, "The men . . . have their uniforms which are in marked contrast to that given them when away on three-months [sic] service. The pants are of light blue cloth; the jackets of dark-blue cloth, trimmed with green."[3]

Recruited as an "Independent Zouave Company" during September and October of 1861, the Reville Zouaves, also known as the Baker Guard Zouaves, became Company K of the 69th Pennsylvania. Commanded by Captain William Davis, who had previously served as a lieutenant in the largely Irish 69th New York State Militia, they also received "uniforms, of light and dark blue, trimmed with green."[4] By mid-October, a "Second Company of Independent Zouaves," which was probably the Tiger Zouaves, commanded by Captain James F. Anderson, had been attached to the regiment as Company I and was "in active service under Col. Baker, being within a few miles of Harper's Ferry" and being "employed on scouting parties."[5]

The Zouaves of the 69th Pennsylvania are shown wearing semi-Zouave–style uniforms. Although after the French Zouave pattern, the jacket has rounded edges and a low standing collar. Cuffs are slit, with ball buttons for decorative purposes only. A double row of wide and narrow green tape is sewn on the edges of the jacket front and around the collar and cuffs. Probably influenced by the original United States Zouave Cadets, the front edges of this garment were also ornamented with ball buttons. Their dark-blue chasseur-pattern forage caps are plain dark blue. Their sky-blue vest is trimmed with green braid and has a single row of nine buttons down its front. Sky-blue chasseur-pattern pants have green side seams and are tucked into white canvas leggings. They are armed with British Pattern 1855 Enfield rifles with saber bayonets.[6]

1. Samuel P. Bates, *History of the Pennsylvania Volunteers, 1861–5*, Vol. 2 (B. Singerly, State Printers, 1869), 697.
2. *Philadelphia Inquirer*, August 31, 1861, 8:4.
3. *The Press* (Philadelphia, PA), September 9, 1861, 2:8.
4. *Philadelphia Inquirer*, September 17, 1861, 8:1.
5. *The Press*, September 17, 1861, 1:5.
6. *Philadelphia Inquirer*, September 17, 1861, 8:1.

65th New York Infantry (1st US Chasseurs)

ORGANIZED AT CAMP TOMPKINS, NEAR THE FORT AT Willett's Point, New York, the 65th New York Infantry was mustered in for three years' service under lawyer and staunch states-rights Democrat Colonel John Cochrane on June 24, 1861. Also known as the First United States Chasseurs, this regiment adopted a uniform influenced by the French *Chasseurs de Vincennes* pattern, which included a *habit-veste*, or short coat, split on both sides of its skirt to provide more freedom of movement for the soldier. According to a New York City press report dated July 31, 1861, the uniform issued to the 65th New York consisted of "an army blue chasseur jacket, trimmed with light blue braid, cadet gray pantaloons and gray cap."[1] As this outfit was considered full dress, the regiment wore "the United States regulation dress" for field duty.[2]

Based on photographic evidence, Pattern 1858 uniform hats, otherwise known as Hardee hats, were also worn with full dress. Referring on July 29, 1861, to the 73rd and 74th New York infantry regiments of the Excelsior Brigade, a report in the *New York Tribune* commented, "So well adapted is the uniform of this regiment to military purpose, that already it has been imitated by several other regiments in process of formation."[3]

This corporal wears full dress, including a Hardee hat with a bugle-horn insignia; the numeral "1" in the loop, for "First U.S. Chasseurs"; and light-blue hat cord. His dark-blue chasseur-style coat is fastened by nine small buttons and is piped down its front, around its standing collar, and along the bottom edge of its skirts with light blue. Trefoil trim of the same color extends from its pointed cuff trim, and more trefoils extend diagonally on either side of splits in the skirt. Sleeve stripes are of a matching light blue. His trousers are plain rather than having half inch dark-blue side seam stripes, commensurate with the rank of corporal. This corporal is armed with an Enfield rifle with a sword bayonet attached, and his leather accoutrements include a Pattern 1861 cartridge box carried via a shoulder sling and an Allegheny Arsenal–pattern percussion cap pouch.

1. *New York Herald*, July 31, 1861, 8:3.
2. *New York Daily News*, June 26, 1861, 8:1.
3. *New York Tribune*, July 29, 1861, 7:2.

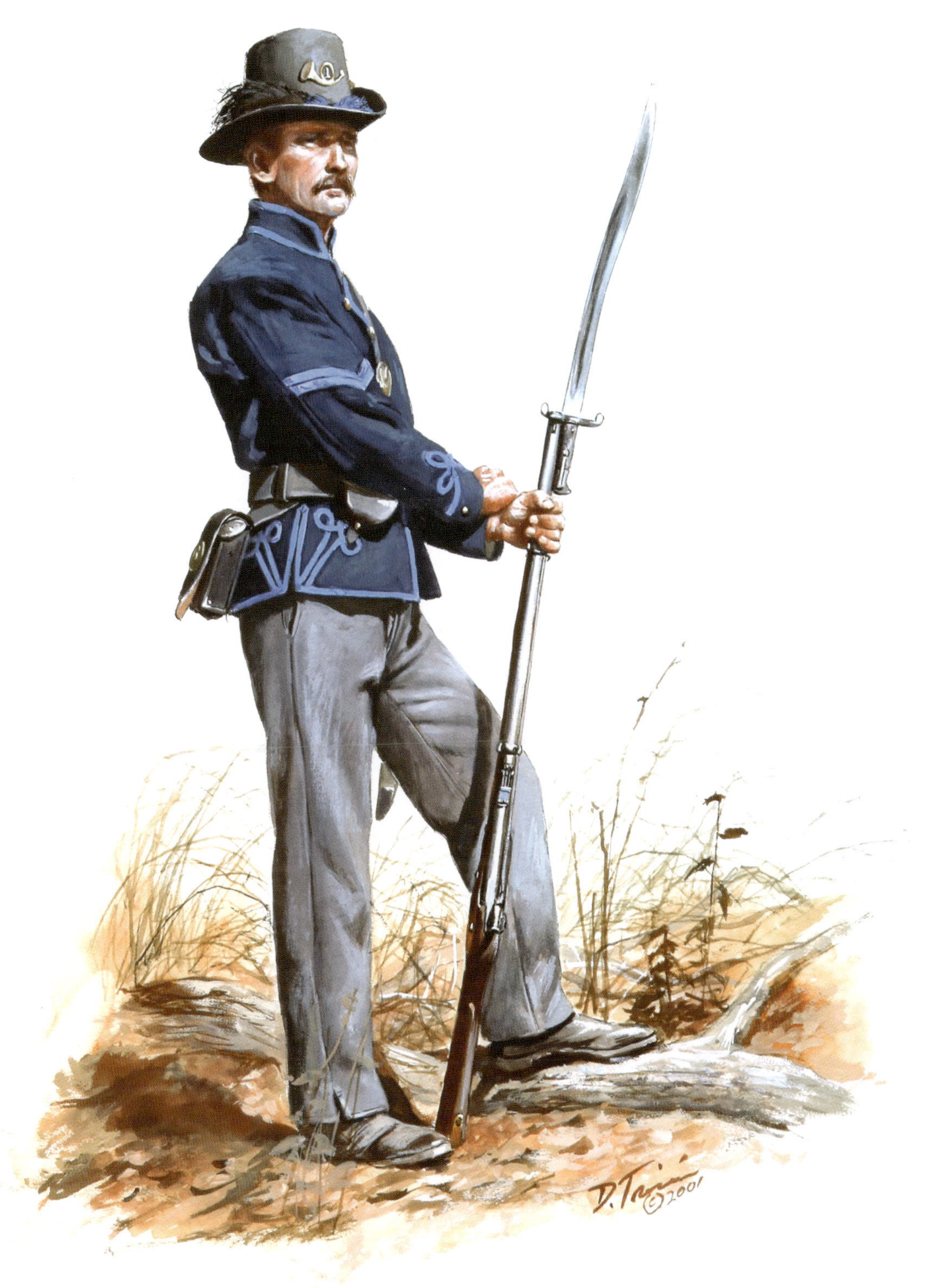

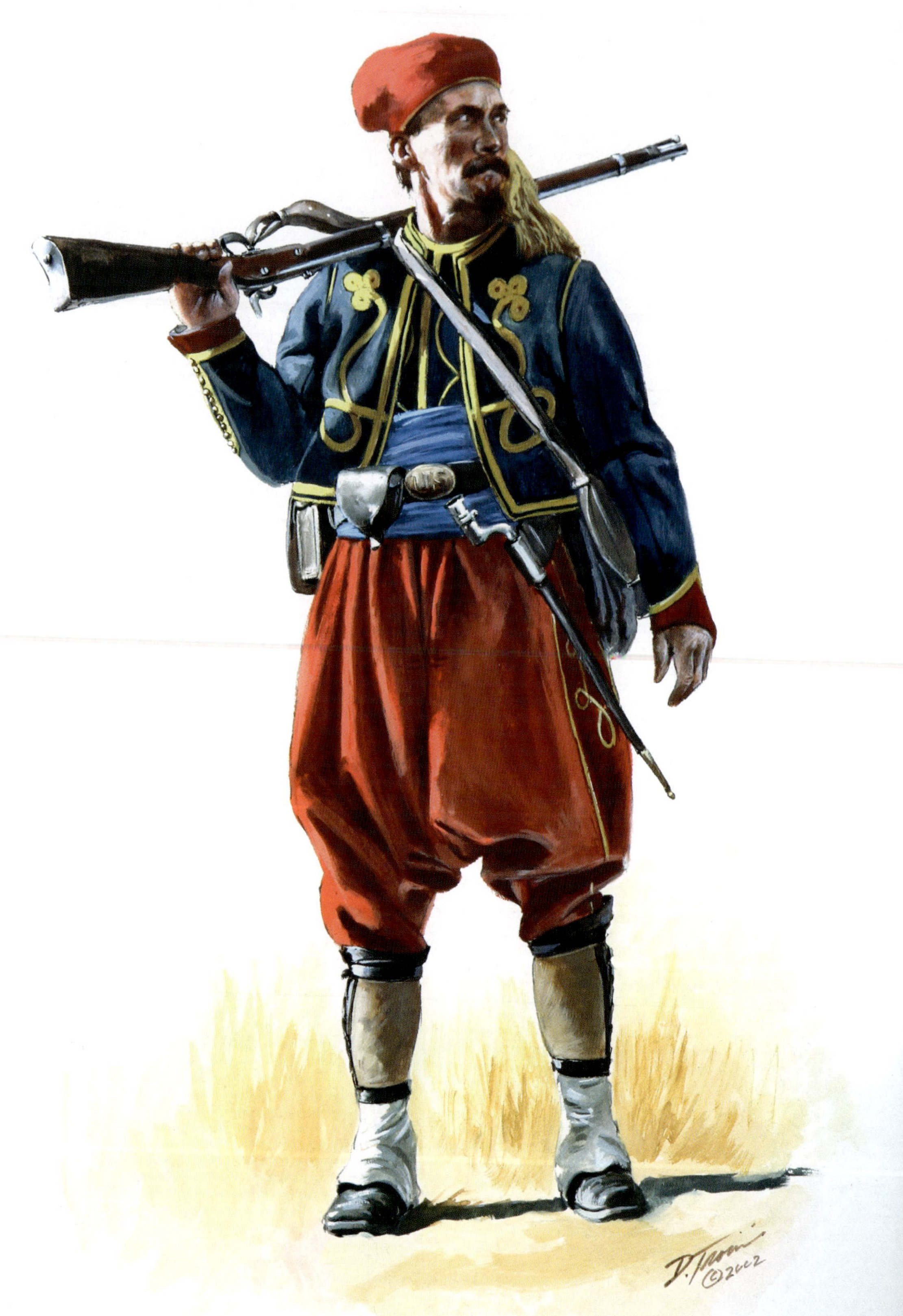

74th New York Volunteers (Zouave Company)

ORGANIZED AS THE FIFTH REGIMENT OF THE Excelsior Brigade by Brigadier General Daniel Edgar Sickles, the 74th New York Infantry was commanded by Colonel Charles K. Graham. While all other companies in this regiment wore chasseur-style uniforms, Company A, commanded by Captain John P. Glass, and Company B, under Captain Henry M. Alles, wore Zouave uniforms. Glass originally organized a company of Zouaves called the US Zouave Cadets after the original drill unit formed by Elmer Ellsworth. This company initially formed part of the First Regiment of Heavy Infantry, which was organized for home defense in Pittsburgh during May 1861.[1]

On June 7, 1861, the US Zouave Cadets left Pittsburgh to enlist in Sickles's Brigade and passed through Philadelphia en route for New York City, on which occasion the press reported, "A portion of them were uniformed, in red pantaloons and blue blouses. The majority, however, were dressed as citizens."[2] Designated Company A, 74th New York, this unit likely continued to wear Zouave uniforms after enlistment as, on August 9, 1861, the New York *Daily News* reported, "Company A (Zouaves) will wear uniforms similar to those worn by the Imperial Guard of Paris."[3]

Recruited by Captain Henry M. Alles, Company B of the 74th New York was mustered in at Camp Scott, Staten Island, on June 27, 1861, and was later described as "a company of French Zouaves, most of whom fought through the war in the Crimea." By August 1861, this company was reported to be "dressed in the exact costume of the Imperial Zouaves of the French army . . . Their uniform is of the most brilliant hues of red, blue, and yellow, slashed, braided, and trimmed in most tasteful, dashing, and expensive style."[4]

This Zouave private of Company B, 74th New York, wears a close representation of the uniform of the Imperial Guard Zouaves of the army of Napoleon III. His baggy red fez has a yellow tassel; his dark-blue jacket is richly edged and trimmed with yellow and has yellow trefoils or *tombeaux* at its front, plus red facings on cuffs; unusually, his dark-blue vest is also embellished with yellow trefoils or *tombeaux*; his full red wool pantaloons are trimmed with yellow cord around the pocket openings and have two parallel lines of yellow cord down each side. Dark-yellow leather greaves, or *jambières*, are worn over white canvas leggings. A wide light-blue sash is wrapped around his waist and worn under a waist belt fastened with a Pattern 1839 oval "US" plate, which supports a cartridge box and a cap pouch. Although the Zouaves of the 74th New York were intended to serve as skirmishers armed with "rifles and saber bayonets," they were issued Model 1861 Springfield rifle muskets.[5]

---

1. *Pittsburgh Post Gazette*, May 24, 1861, 3:2.
2. *The Press* (Philadelphia, PA), June 24, 1861, 3:1.
3. *Daily News* (New York, NY), August 9, 1861, 8:1.
4. *New York Tribune*, August 13, 1861, 8:1.
5. *New York Tribune*, August 13, 1861, 8:1.

41st New York Volunteers (De Kalb Zouaves)

FORMED IN NEW YORK CITY BY GERMAN-AMERICAN Emil Duysing on April 22, 1861, the De Kalb Zouaves were uniformed according to "the French bill of Zouave dress" and named in honor of the Prussian General Johann de Kalb, who lost his life in the War of Independence in 1780.[1] As they had not exceeded company strength after going into barracks amid the German community at Yorkville Park, New York City, during May 1861, the De Kalb Zouaves were designated Company A of an all-German regiment being recruited by Colonel Leopold von Gilsa and outfitted by the Union Defense Committee. As a result, the Zouaves became the nucleus of the DeKalb Regiment, which enlisted for three years as the 41st New York Volunteer Infantry.

After the 41st New York reached the Federal capital on July 10, 1861, the uniform of the De Kalb Zouaves was briefly reported in the press as consisting of a "dark blue jacket, (braided with red) and pantaloons with yellow and black leggings of the Turcos, the blue sash, red fez, and blue tassel."[2] Based on an example surviving in the collection at the Smithsonian Institution, the trim on the jacket worn by the De Kalb Zouaves was minus a trefoil and had a red insert in the *tombeau*. Also the sleeves were extensively embellished with elaborate yellow braid.[3]

Wearing the uniform adopted by the De Kalb Zouaves when the unit joined the ranks of the 41st New York, this Zouave wears a dark-blue jacket and pantaloons trimmed with red and has a matching dark-blue collarless vest. Tan leather greaves are fastened over white canvas leggings. His equipment includes a rigid militia-pattern knapsack with a mess tin attached. Strapped to its top is a rolled overcoat of "gray pilot cloth." He is armed with a Model 1842 Springfield musket with a fixed bayonet.

The De Kalb Zouaves continued to wear the Zouave outfit, at least for parade and full dress, into mid-1862, when the 41st New York adopted more regulation clothing. The company may have been issued replacement Zouave-style uniforms as Corporal Reinheld G. Winzer, who was killed at Gettysburg on July 2, 1863, was photographed in 1862 wearing a Hawkins's Zouave-style jacket and trousers of the pattern issued by the US Quartermaster Department to several other regiments during the war.[4]

---

1. *The World* (New York City, NY), April 27, 1861, 4:8; and *New York Herald*, June 9, 1861, 6:2.
2. *National Republican* (Washington, DC), July 11, 1861, 3:1.
3. National Museum of American History, Smithsonian Institution, AF.24944.01.
4. Drawing in the Anne S. K. Brown Military Collection, John Hay Library, Brown University, Rhode Island, based on a photograph in the New York State Collection, No. 1470.

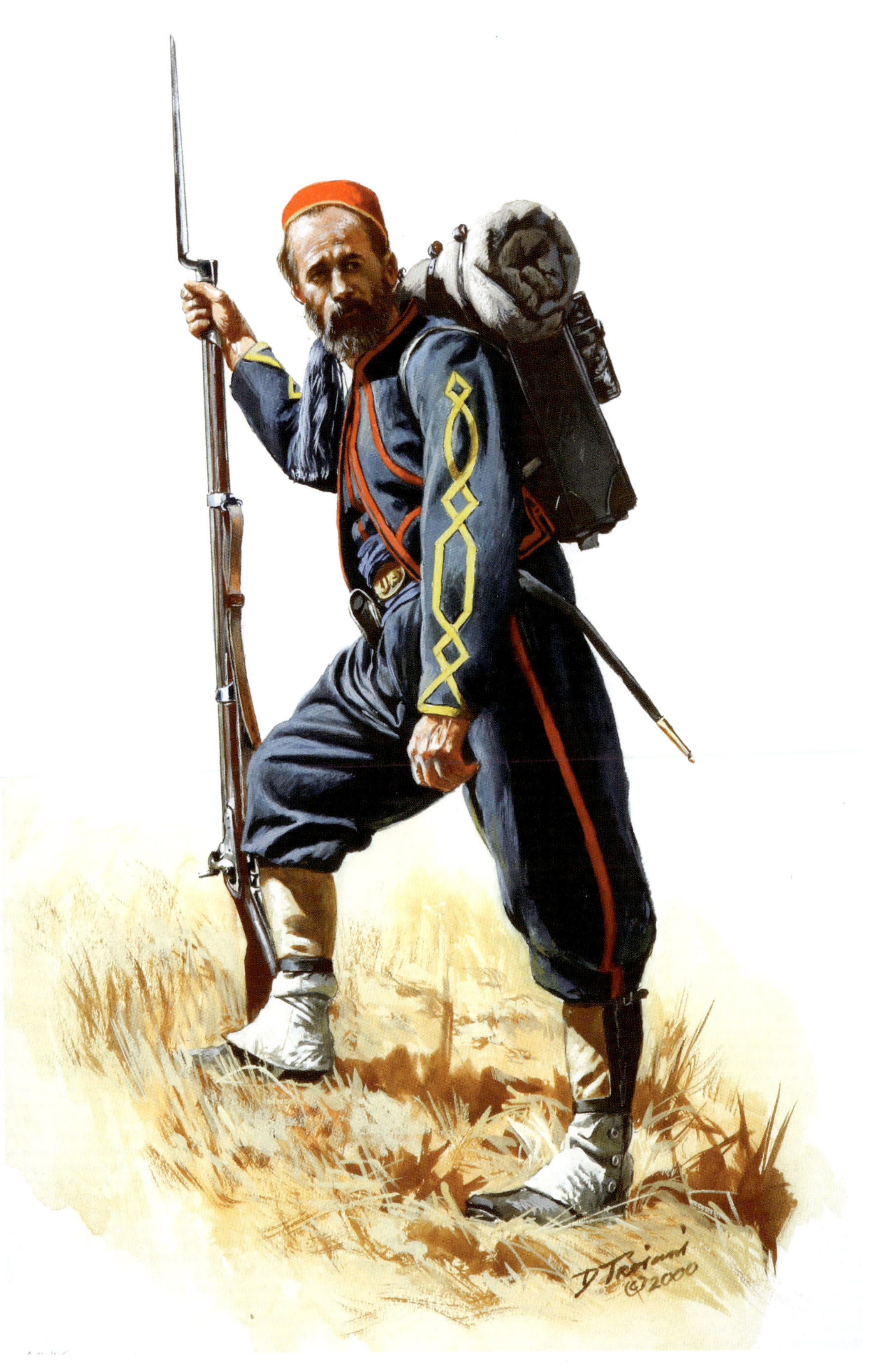

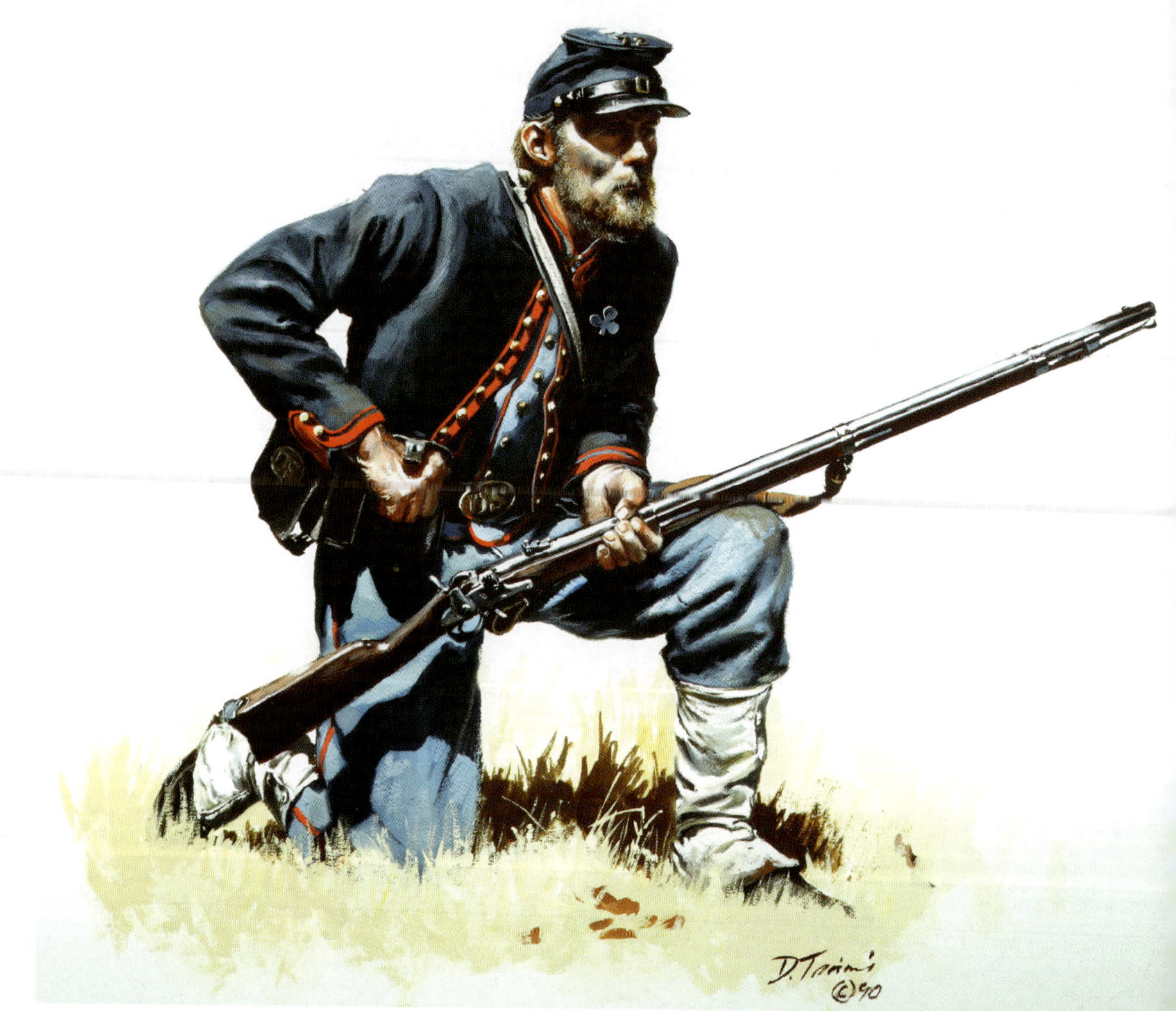

72nd Pennsylvania Infantry (Baxter's Zouaves)

RECRUITMENT OF A REGIMENT OF FIREMEN IN Philadelphia, Pennsylvania, by Colonel DeWitt Clinton Baxter began in early August 1861. Encamped at Haddington, near the old Bull's Head Tavern, the regiment was mustered in on August 10, 1861, and, on September 16, left for Washington, where it was assigned to Colonel Edward D. Baker's Brigade, Sedgewick's Division, Sumner's Corps. Having its origins in the "California Brigade" raised under direct authority of the President, this brigade was rated as a body of regular troops. After the death of Baker at Ball's Bluff on October 21, 1861, Baxter's Fire Zouaves, plus the other Pennsylvania regiments, were claimed by the Keystone State, renamed the "Philadelphia Brigade," and given numerical designations.[1]

Designated the 72nd Pennsylvania Infantry, the Fire Zouaves adopted at its inception a distinctive uniform that included a rounded Zouave jacket after the style introduced by Elmer Ellsworth for the United States Zouave Cadets in 1859. It lacked the customary *tombeaux* of the French Zouave jacket, but had sixteen brass ball buttons along each edge of the jacket front, placed between an outer strip of red tape and an inner one of twisted red cord. Its slit cuffs were similarly embellished with tape, cord, and two buttons. Light-blue vests were trimmed around the edges and pockets with red tape. Likewise, light-blue trousers had red tape trim on the outer seams and were tucked into white canvas leggings. Headgear originally consisted of dark-blue chasseur-pattern caps with red cord around the band and at the quarters and with a red circle of cord within the sunken crown of the cap top.[2] The 72nd Pennsylvania continued to wear its semi-Zouave uniforms throughout the war, being supplied via the Quartermaster Department at Philadelphia.

The Zouave pictured appears as he would have in the Battle of Gettysburg when posted in support behind the Angle during the artillery bombardment preceding Pickett's Charge on July 3, 1863, as part of the 2nd Brigade, Second Division, II Corps, commanded by Brigadier General John Gibbon. An appropriate white trefoil corps badge is attached to the breast of his jacket. His plain dark-blue forage cap also has a metal corps badge and the numerals "72" attached to its top. He is taking a percussion cap from a black leather pouch to prime his Model 1861 Springfield rifle musket. A black leather cartridge box is also attached to his waist belt, the latter being fastened by a Pattern 1839 "US" oval plate.

---

1. Frank H. Taylor, *Philadelphia in the Civil War, 1861–1865* (published by the City, 1913), 91.
2. Michael J. McAfee, "72nd Regiment, Pennsylvania Volunteer Infantry (Baxter's Fire Zouaves)," *Military Images* 11, no. 6, (May–June 1990): 27.

53rd New York Volunteers (D'Epineuil's Zouaves)

ORGANIZED IN AUGUST 1861 BY COLO-NEL LIONEL JOBERT D'Epineuil, an inefficient officer who managed to convince the War Department that he had served for seventeen years in the French Army, D'Epineuil's Zouaves was consolidated into the 53rd New York Volunteers on October 12 of that year. According to a press report, Colonel D'Epineuil believed his regiment should serve as "a pattern for the regular service, and prove to the officers of the Regular Army that such a corps would be advantageous as a permanent branch of the service." Their drill was that of "the Zouave Skirmishers, and their uniform that of the Blue Zouaves of France," or the 6th Regiment Imperial Zouaves.[1] Made by Brooks Brothers of New York City, via special contract with the War Department, the uniform received by D'Epineuil's Zouaves was described as a "red fez cap with a long yellow tassel, dark blue jacket trimmed with bright yellow braid, blue sash, and yellow and black leggings and duck gaiters." The officers' uniform was composed of a "dark blue coat with plain bell buttons, and heavily braided on the arm, dark blue vest, light blue pantaloons covered with rubber from knee down." Enlisted men also received a light-blue, short-hooded cloak, known as a capote.[2]

Recruits for the 53rd New York were gathered at Camp Leslie, named in honor of James Leslie Jr., chief clerk of the War Department, on Staten Island. D'Epineuil's Zouaves appeared on parade along Broadway for the first time on August 28, 1861.[3]

The regiment finally departed New York for the front on November 18, 1861, but problems appeared almost immediately. Its officers tended to ignore the conditions of the men under their command, causing numerous desertions from the ranks. Forming part of Burnside's Expeditionary Corps to the North Carolina coast, the Zouaves were placed aboard a steamer for what was intended to be a voyage of several days to Hatteras Inlet. They finally disembarked twenty-seven days later at Annapolis, after several botched attempts to pass through the shallow passage into Pamlico Sound. By that time, the discipline of the entire command had deteriorated beyond repair, with about four hundred men either being sick or having deserted. An inspection of the regiment found "rifle muskets in bad order . . . uniforms very dirty, and in many cases, filthy."[4]

Returning to Washington, DC, on January 26, 1862, Company A of the regiment was transferred to the 17th New York Volunteers, as Company G, and, on March 8, 1862, the rest of the unit was honorably discharged, being mustered out thirteen days later.

The enlisted man depicted wears the full Zouave uniform issued to the 53rd New York in August 1861, consisting of a red fez with a yellow tassel, a dark-blue jacket with yellow trim, light-blue pantaloons with yellow cord down the sides, a light-blue waist sash, and yellow leather greaves over white canvas gaiters. The letters "SNY" emblazon his Pattern 1839 oval waist belt plate. He is armed with a Pattern 1853 Enfield rifle musket of the type issued to his regiment in November 1861.

---

1. *New-York Times*, August 11, 1861, 8:5.
2. *New York Tribune*, September 12, 1861, 8:2; and *New-York Times*, September 12, 1861, 8:3.
3. *New York Tribune*, August 29, 1861, 8:3.
4. NARA, record group 94, regimental papers, 53rd New York Infantry.

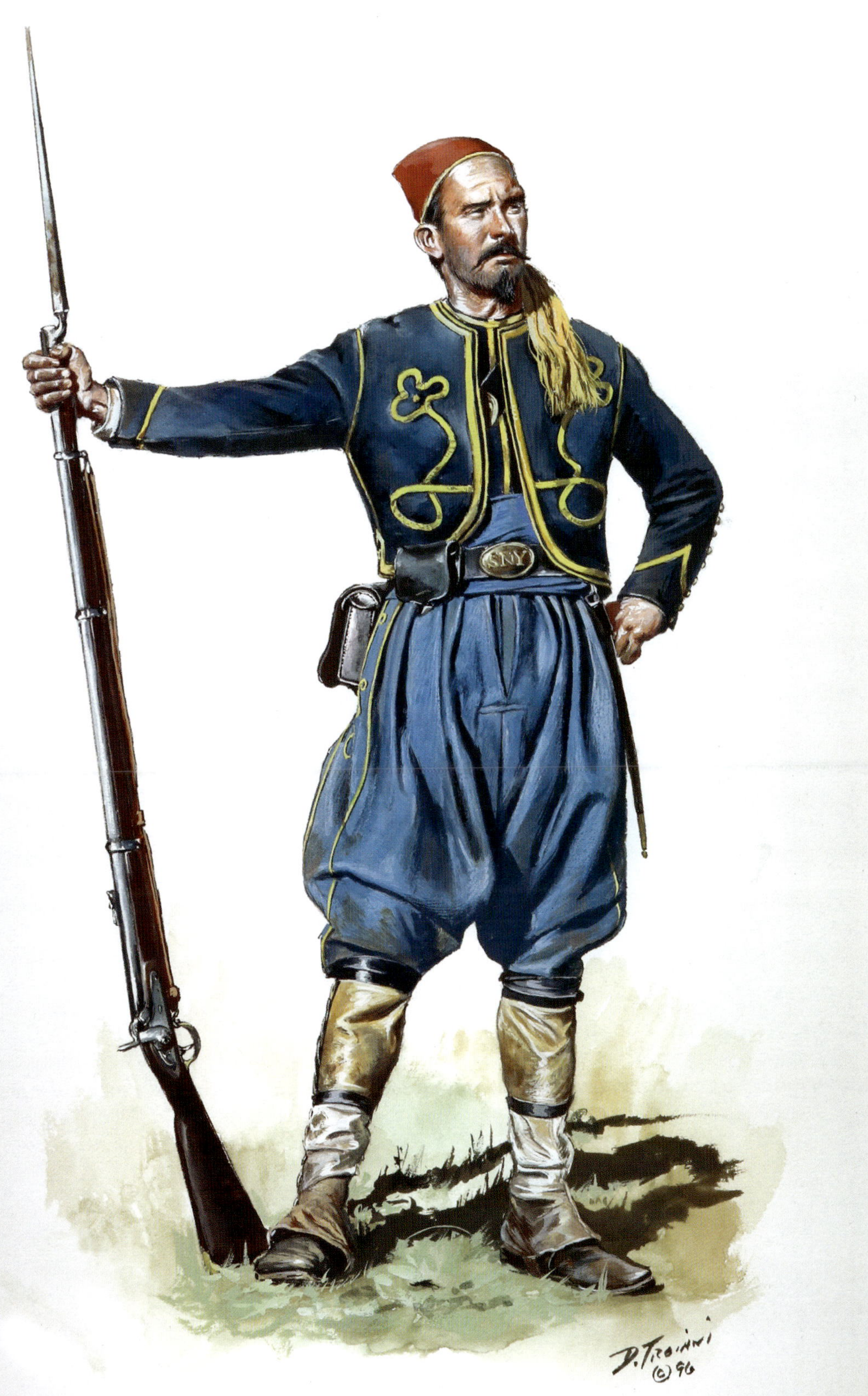

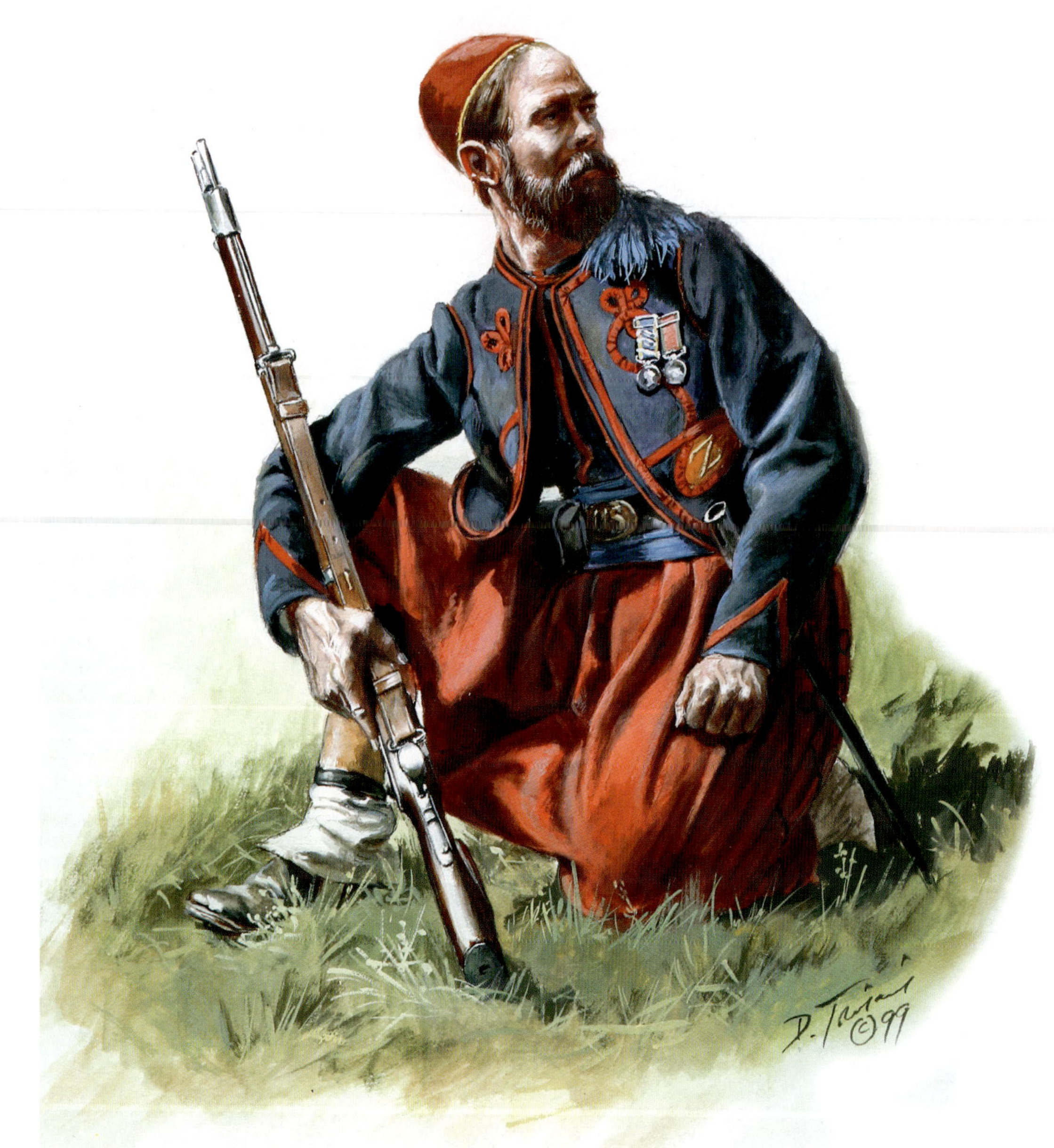

62nd New York Volunteers (Anderson Zouaves), Company I (Advanced Guard)

ONE OF THE REGIMENTS TO RECEIVE FINANCIAL AID from the Union Defense Committee of New York City, the Anderson Zouaves regiment was named in honor of Colonel Robert Anderson, hero of Fort Sumter. Its companies were mostly recruited in New York City, although volunteers also came from Albany, Troy, Brooklyn, and New Jersey.

Organized under special authority of the War Department, the regiment went into camp near Saltersville, New Jersey. It was mustered in for three years on June 30 and July 1, 1861, with Colonel J. Lafayette Riker in command, and was designated the 62nd New York Volunteers on October 19, 1861.

A news report published on June 2, 1861, described the uniform of the 62nd New York as "a blue Zouave jacket, with a red edge, on which is a row of brass-bell buttons. In the lower corners are the initials A.Z. The pants are blue and the leggins and gaiters similar to those of the French Zouaves."[1]

Called the Advance Guard of the regiment and commanded by Italian "soldier of distinction" Captain Charles G. La Fata, Company I was composed largely of "French adopted citizens" who originally formed the Zouave company of the 55th New York, or *Garde Lafayette*, but defected to the Anderson Zouaves in hopes of seeing action sooner. Some of these men had seen "the hard fought fields of the Crimean and Italian campaigns."[2]

Based on that of the French Imperial Guard Zouaves, their uniform consisted of a "red fez or skull cap with its long blue silk tassel, the immensely loose, red, baggy breeches, the leggins, gaiters, long blue scarf worn round the middle, the queer, tight cloth waistcoat with only one armhole— the left—in it, fastening on the right, and the short jacket." The men wore their hair "closely cropped and their necks bare." The officers had "dark blue uniforms, similar to those worn in the United States army."[3]

The remainder of the regiment wore the same Zouave-style jacket but with light-blue pants and either a red fez or a dark-blue forage cap. The whole regiment also received "dark grey seamless overcoats" produced by the Seamless Clothing Manufacturing Company of New York.[4]

A veteran of the French army, this enlisted man of the Advance Guard company of the 62nd New York wears an example of the full Zouave uniform that was originally worn by members of the 55th New York. His fez was made by the Seamless Clothing Manufacturing Company. The embroidered letter "A" in the *tombeau* on the right side of his jacket is not in view, but "Z" is seen in the tombeau on the left side. His full red pantaloons with dark-green piping were furnished by Brooks Brothers. Medals for service in the Crimean War are pinned to his chest.

1. *New York Tribune*, May 30, 1861, 8:3.
2. *New York Daily Herald*, June 19, 1861, 5:2.
3. *Evening Post* (New York, NY), July 11, 1861, 1:4.
4. Michael J. McAfee, "Uniforms & History: 62nd Regiment, New York Volunteer Infantry, 'Anderson's Zouaves,'" *Military Images* 12, no. 6 (May–June 1991): 31.

95th Pennsylvania Infantry (Gosline Zouaves)

ORIGINALLY COMMANDING COMPANY A, 18TH PENNSYLVANIA INFANTRY, in the three-months' service, John M. Gosline gained authority to recruit a regiment of infantry called the Gosline's Pennsylvania Zouaves, which was designated the 95th Pennsylvania Infantry by November 1861. All the companies, excepting a part of Company B, which contained a contingent from Burlington County, New Jersey, were recruited in Philadelphia.[1]

Of a modified Zouave pattern, and similar to that worn by the 23rd Pennsylvania and the 72nd Pennsylvania, the initial uniform worn by the regiment was made under contract to the Philadelphia clothing house of Rockhill and Wilson, the principal maker of uniforms in Philadelphia, by the Quartermaster Department. Upon departure for Washington, DC, on October 12, 1861, the Gosline Zouaves were reported as "clad in neat blue uniforms, trimmed in red."[2] A member of the regiment described the uniform as being of "the best material, heavy marine cloth. The jacket, which was of the sacque pattern, was open, and rounded at the waist, and trimmed with broad and narrow scarlet braid. Down each side was a row of brass buttons . . . The pants were of full length, not so wide as the regular 'Zouave Petticoat,' but just wide enough to harmonize with the pleated waist, in broad folds. The over shirt was of Navy flannel, with silver-plated buttons, corresponding with those on the jacket, but several sizes smaller. The cap was the McClellan style, braided with narrow scarlet braid. A pair of leather leggings nearly reaching the knees finished the uniform."[3]

The 95th Pennsylvania spent its entire term of service with the Army of the Potomac and, from September 1862 until muster out, as part of the VI Corps. While wintering by the Hazel River, Virginia, 245 original members of the regiment reenlisted, thus being the first unit in the Army of the Potomac to veteranize. In the fall of 1864, the veterans and recruits of the unit were organized into a battalion of four companies and were joined by a battalion of the 96th Pennsylvania, all of which were designated the 95th regiment. In December, the VI Corps joined the army in front of Petersburg and fought its final battle at Saylor's Creek three days before the Confederate surrender at Appomattox.

Manning the trenches outside Petersburg, this Zouave wears the red-trimmed jacket the Gosline Zouaves maintained throughout the war, although his trousers and forage cap are of regular Federal issue. His company letter "A" over the badge for the VI Corps is attached to his cap top, plus the metal letters "95PV." He is armed with a Model 1861 musket, and his equipment includes Mann's Patent 60-round cartridge box, which was trialed by only a few regiments during the final months of the war.

---

1. Taylor, *Philadelphia in the Civil War, 1861–1865*, 113.

2. *Philadelphia Inquirer*, October 14, 1861, 8:3.

3. G. Norton Galloway, *The Ninety-Fifth Pennsylvania Volunteers (Gosline's Pennsylvania Zouaves), in the Sixth Corps.* (Collins, printer, 1884), 8.

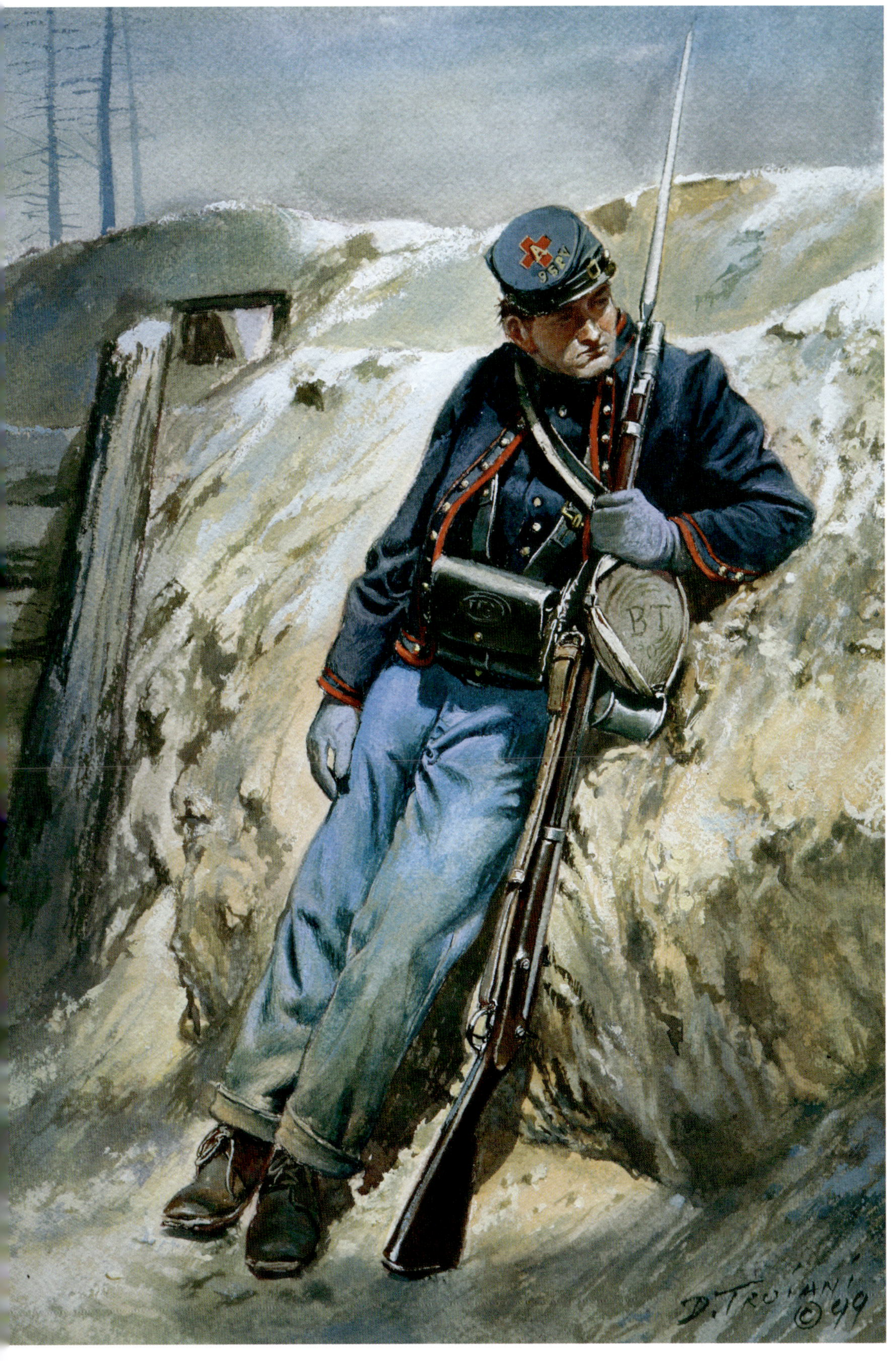
95 P.V

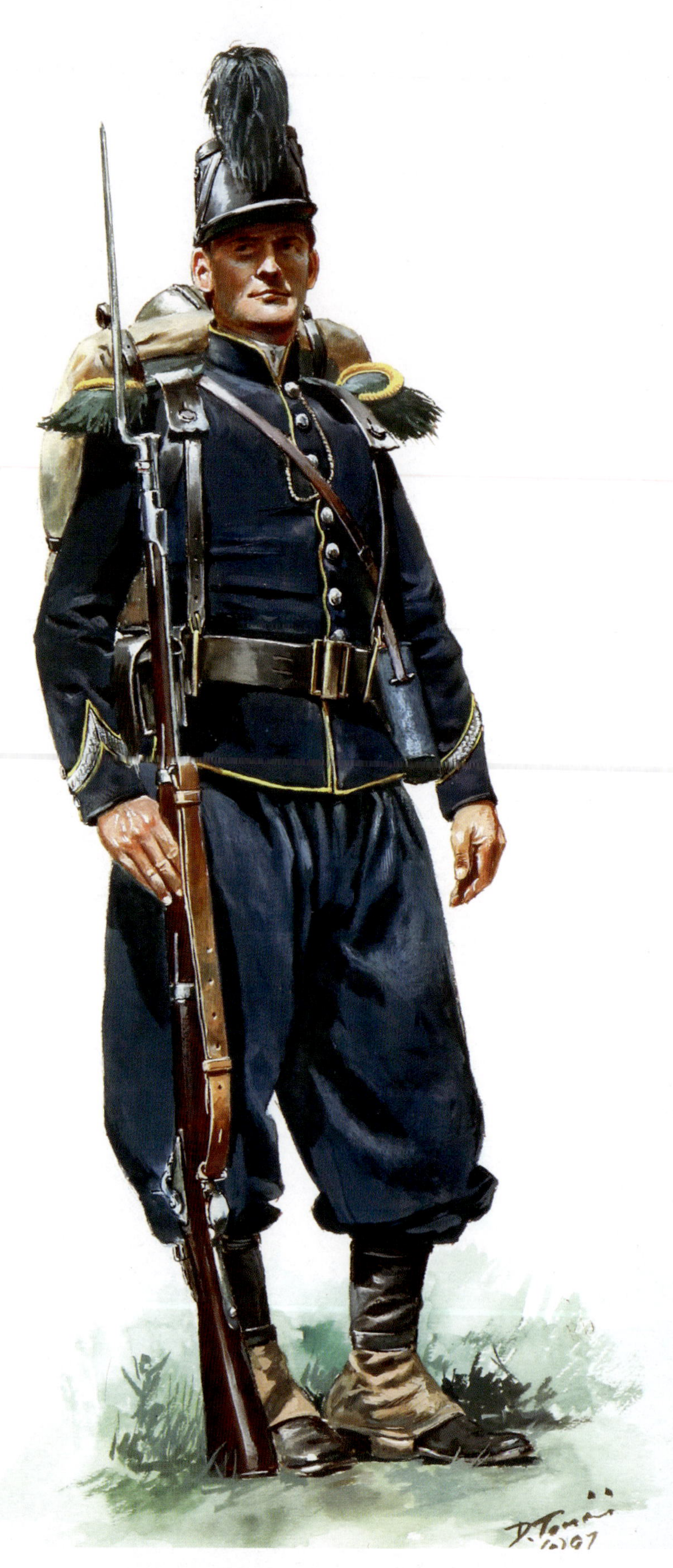

18th Massachusetts Volunteer Infantry, 1862

INTEREST IN ADOPTING THE UNIFORM OF THE FRENCH *chasseur a pied*, or light infantry, for the United States Army was expressed as early as 1855, when Quartermaster General Thomas Jesup sent for inspection a chasseur-pattern coat, worsted epaulets, trousers, an overcoat, and a knapsack to Major George H. Crossman, at the Schuylkill Arsenal.[1] Although not adopted, the idea and influence remained, and, with the outbreak of the Civil War, General Montgomery C. Meigs, the newly appointed quartermaster general, purchased on August 9, 1861, ten thousand complete *chasseur a pied* uniforms, plus numerous accessories, from the French firm of Alexis Godillot, the main supplier to the French army.

Upon receipt, these uniforms were awarded to various regiments, including the five best-drilled regiments in the Army of the Potomac following a review of the division of General Fitz-John Porter, at Bailey's Cross Roads, Virginia, on November 9, 1861. The units chosen on this occasion were the 18th Massachusetts, the 62nd Pennsylvania, the 83rd Pennsylvania, the 49th New York, and the 72nd New York.[2]

Members of the 18th Massachusetts received their French outfits on December 4, 1861, and three weeks later the Boston press reported, "At the grand review of McDowell's Division . . . Col. Barnes' Eighteenth Massachusetts attracted general attention in their new French Chasseur-a-pied uniforms. It is a gay and festive garb, and the men look finely in it, with their natty caps (like those of the 2d Battalion, M.V.M.) and small cock-tail fountain plumes; short-skirted coatees, with white buttons and yellow trimmings; baggy trowsers tucked into gaiters; hairy knapsacks &c. The other regiments look quite shabby by the side of these Napoleonic soldiers, and are anxious to have a little finery also."[3]

Worn by this enlisted man is the complete dress uniform received by the 18th Massachusetts. On campaign the fountain plume attached to the leather shako was replaced by a pompon. The cowhide knapsack with hair on the outside, cartridge box, belt, cloth-covered tin canteen, and all other accoutrements, except probably the bayonet scabbard, are French and were supplied as part of the complete outfit. The coatee was made of heavier wool than that found in US military garments, and the sleeves are narrow and close fitting. The French-made "eagle" coat buttons are of white metal. Full sky-blue trousers are tucked in leather gaiters. Fatigue jackets and caps, or *bonnets de police*, plus hooded capes, were also issued to all five regiments.

These European uniforms proved generally too small for the typical American soldier and are generally believed not to have been worn in combat. Nonetheless, the men of the 18th Massachusetts did not take kindly to leaving their distinctive dress in storage at Georgetown, DC, when McClellan finally began offensive operations on March 10, 1862, and they advanced toward Richmond in US regulation clothing. Following its seizure by Colonel Lafayette Baker, Provost Marshall of Washington, DC, such French finery was not worn again by the 18th Massachusetts.

---

1. NARA, record group 92, records of the Office of the Quartermaster General, LSB, Clo, vol. 14, 264–65.

2. *Boston Evening Transcript*, November 23, 1861, 4:1.

3. *Louisville Daily Journal*, December 5, 1861, 3:6; and *Boston Evening Journal*, December 26, 1861, 2:1.

114th Pennsylvania Infantry (Collis's Zouaves)

ORIGINALLY RAISED TO SERVE AS A BODYGUARD FOR Major General Nathaniel P. Banks, Collis's Zouaves were recruited by Charles H. T. Collis, ex-sergeant major of the 18th Pennsylvania Infantry (three months), who was requested by several veteran soldiers to form an independent company of infantry to be drilled as "Voltigeurs in the French army" and "uniformed similarly to the Zouaves D'Afrique."[1]

Recruitment began on July 25, 1861, and the unit was accepted by the War Department on August 13, at which time Quartermaster General Meigs issued orders that it should be uniformed in "the French Zouave costume."[2] After serving with Banks in the Shenandoah Valley, Collis's Zouaves were authorized to expand into a regiment on July 29, 1862, and were designated the 114th Pennsylvania Infantry.

As they had to wait until February 17, 1862, for their Quartermaster-issue Zouave clothing to be authorized, the first uniforms of Collis's Zouaves were likely made by local tailors in Philadelphia. The unit finally received government-issue outfits made from imported French cloth by the end of April 1862, and were described in the press as "quite picturesque in their new and jaunty blue, yellow and scarlet uniforms."[3]

Collis's Zouaves took part in every major campaign and battle of the Army of the Potomac, and Colonel Collis was awarded the Medal of Honor for bravery while leading the regiment at Fredericksburg in December 1862. With ranks much depleted by casualties, the 114th Pennsylvania often provided provost and guard duties at the Army of the Potomac Headquarters and mostly served in this capacity until the end of the war.

These Zouaves wear the regimental uniform issued to the 114th Pennsylvania in 1862. This consisted of dark-blue jackets with appliquéd red trefoils or *tombeaux*, plus red trim and edging. Sky-blue pointed cuffs were also piped with red trim and had narrow red trefoil trim on their sleeves above. Their dark-blue pullover vests had three or four buttons hidden by a flap edged in red. Their red fez caps were piped around the bottom edge with thin yellow lace and had a large yellow tassel. For full dress, this ensemble was surmounted by a white flannel turban. Waist sashes were in sky blue. Their madder-red heavyweight trousers of French woolen cloth were less baggy than the full Zouave style and were trimmed with yellow lace. These were tucked into tan leather greaves, or *jambières*, worn over white canvas leggings.[4]

Arms consist of Springfield rifle muskets, and accompanying accoutrements include a Pattern 1861 cartridge box, a percussion cap pouch, a Model 1858 canteen with a brown wool cover, and a black-painted canvas haversack.

1. *Philadelphia Inquirer,* July 25, 1861, 4:4.
2. *Philadelphia Inquirer,* August 15, 1861, 8:3.
3. *Philadelphia Inquirer,* April 29, 1862, 2:1.
4. NARA, record group 94, regimental books, 114th Pennsylvania Volunteers.

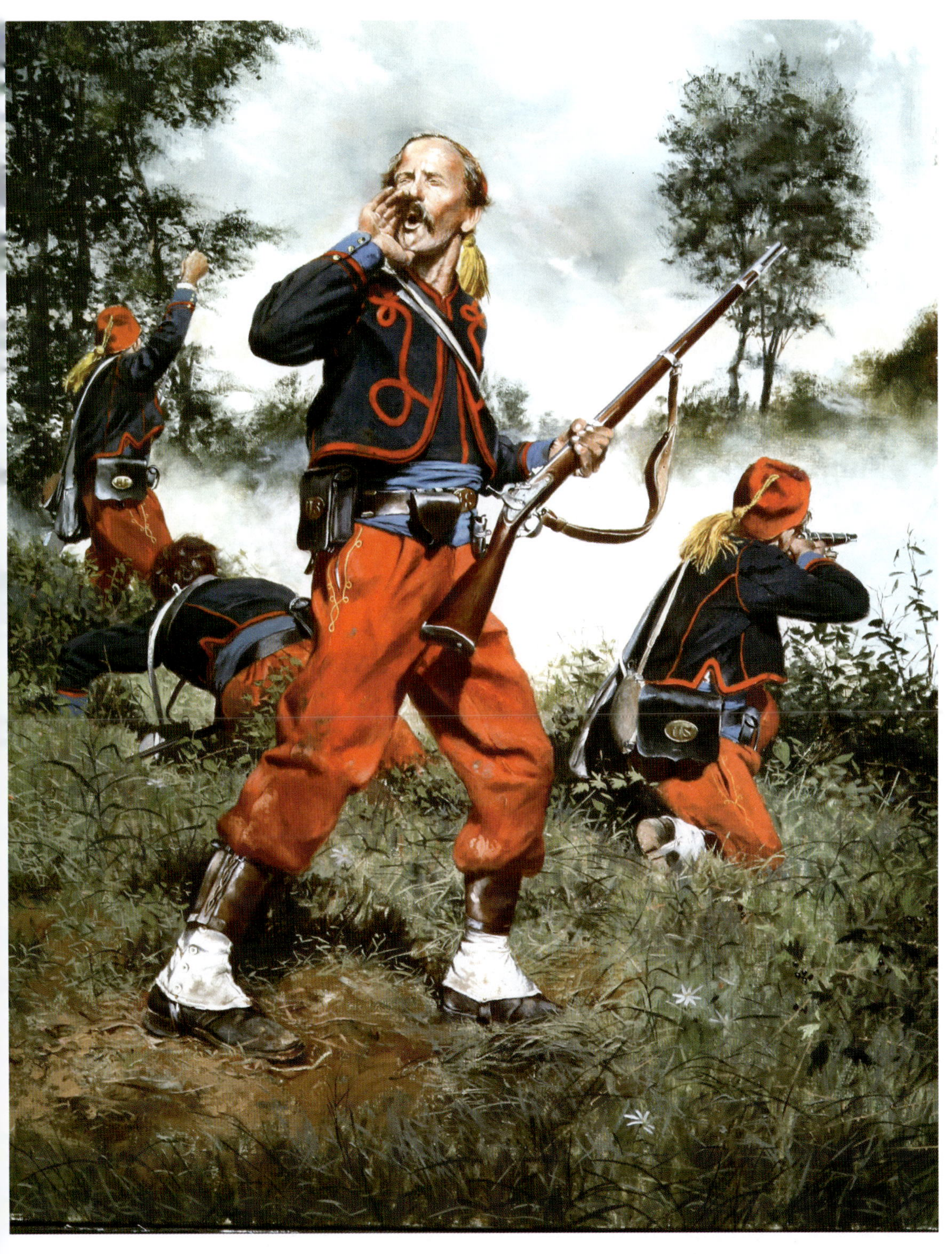

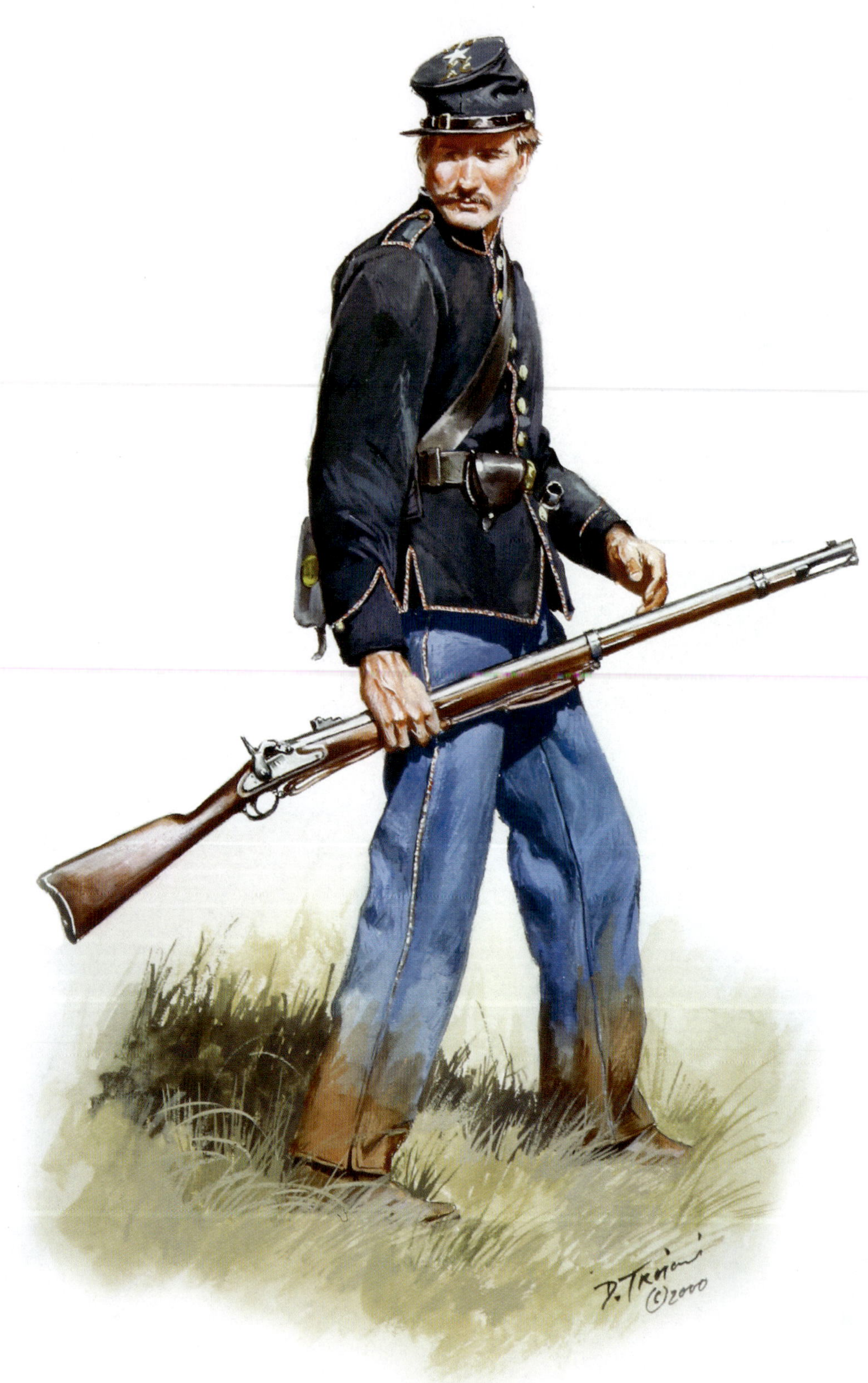

109th Pennsylvania Infantry (Curtin Light Guards)

NAMED FOR GOVERNOR ANDREW G. CURTIN, Curtin Light Guards were organized near Philadelphia during the winter of 1861–1862. Commanded by Colonel Henry J. Stainbrook, the regiment was designated the 109th Pennsylvania Infantry and mustered in for three years in May 1862. During the recruitment drive for this regiment, prospective volunteers were advised, "A special uniform [was] allowed by General McClellan."[1] This is a reference to a chasseur-pattern coat trimmed with a cord made of individual strands of red, white, and blue yarn twisted together in a candy-stripe fashion, and sewn around collar, shoulder straps, cuffs, and all edges. This trim was also added to the outer seam stripes of sky-blue trousers for all ranks.

The Curtin Light Guards remained in camp near Philadelphia, drilling and recruiting, until the unit left for Washington, DC, in May 1862. On June 2, it was sent to the Army of the Shenandoah, being assigned to Prince's Brigade, Auger's Division, Bank's Corps. With this force it fought at Cedar Mountain on August 9, 1862. There, fourteen men were killed; seventy-two were wounded; and forty went missing. During this action, Colonel Stainrook was struck in the groin by a fragment of shell that first hit a "body-plate" he was wearing. Also, the bugle insignia on his hat and one of his shoulder straps were shot away.[2]

Assigned to the Second Brigade, Second Division, XII Corps, 149 officers and men of the much-depleted 109th Pennsylvania were among those posted at the extreme right on the Rock Creek slope of Culp's Hill, at Gettysburg on July 2, 1863. They helped repulse the final Confederate charge on the third day of the battle.

This private of the 109th Pennsylvania appears as he would have done in 1863. The badge of the XII Corps, consisting of a five-pointed star, is attached to his cap top, above which are the numerals "109" and below which are the letters "PVAC," the last two letters relating to the Army of the Cumberland. His chasseur-style coat is piped and edged with red, white, and blue trim, as are his sky-blue kersey trousers. He carries a Model 1861 rifle musket.

---

1. *Philadelphia Inquirer*, December 26, 1861, 5:3.
2. *Philadelphia Inquirer*, August 16, 1862, 2:6.

146th New York Infantry (Zouaves)

IN EARLY 1863, IT BECAME APPARENT THAT ZOUAVE UNIFORMS would cease to be worn in the Volunteer Brigade of the Regular Division, V Corps, Army of the Potomac, with the expiration of the two-years' enlistment of the 5th New York Infantry, or Duryée's Zouaves, commanded by Colonel Cleveland Winslow. To avoid this, prompt action was taken and, during the first week of April 1863, Colonel Kenner Gerrard was ordered to go to Washington to supervise the manufacture of Zouave uniforms for his regiment, the 146th New York. Meanwhile, this regiment, which had been in service since October 10, 1862, began to adopt the Zouave drill.[1]

On May 1, 1863, the three-year enlistees of the 5th New York, whose terms of service did not expire at the same time as those of the majority of the regiment, were transferred to the 146th.[2] On June 3, 1863, members of the 146th New York received their Zouave uniforms, which consisted of "large baggy trousers, [light] blue in color, which were fastened at the knees; a fez cap, bright red in color . . . ; a long white turban which was wound round the hat, but worn only for dress parade; a red sash about ten feet long which was wound about the body and afforded great comfort and warmth; and white cloth leggins [sic] extending almost to the knees."[3]

In fact, the uniforms received by the 146th New York, also known as Garrard's Tigers, were a close copy of that worn by the Tirailleurs Algériens, or Turcos, of the French Army. With the turban around his fez, this Zouave wears parade dress. His light-blue jacket is edged with yellow trim and has traditional trefoil or *tombeau* lace on both sides of the breast and on the pointed cuffs. A matching vest has narrow yellow trim down the front on both sides of small buttons. Tucked into leather greaves over white canvas leggings, his voluminous trousers are in plain light blue and minus the yellow seam stripe that embellished that of the French Turcos. His fez has a yellow tassel. His sash is edged in yellow rather than being plain red. He is priming his Model 1842 rifle musket and is well equipped with a black rubberized canvas semirigid knapsack with a blanket roll attached.

Once outfitted as Turcos, members of the 146th New York wore no other type of uniform. By January 7, 1864, all the other regiments of the brigade, consisting of the 140th New York, plus the 91st Pennsylvania and the 155th Pennsylvania, had received Zouave uniforms, although only the 146th New York wore that of the Turco.[4] According to the regimental history, from that time forth, the brigade made "a dashing appearance on parade or in line of battle."[5] Members of the 146th New York wore their Turco dress from Gettysburg to Appomattox and proudly paraded for the final review in Washington, DC, wearing it during May 1865.

---

1. Mary G. Brainard, *Campaigns of the One Hundred and Forty-Sixth Regiment New York Volunteers* (G. P. Putnam's Sons, 1915), 309–10.

2. *Military Uniforms in America—Long Endure: The Civil War Period 1852–1867* (Presidio Press), 68.

3. Brainard, *Campaigns of the One Hundred and Forty-Sixth Regiment New York Volunteers*, 92.

4. Daniel J. Miller, *American Zouaves, 1859–1959: An Illustrated History* (McFarland & Company, Inc.), 308–9.

5. Brainard, *Campaigns of the One Hundred and Forty-Sixth Regiment New York Volunteers*, 158.

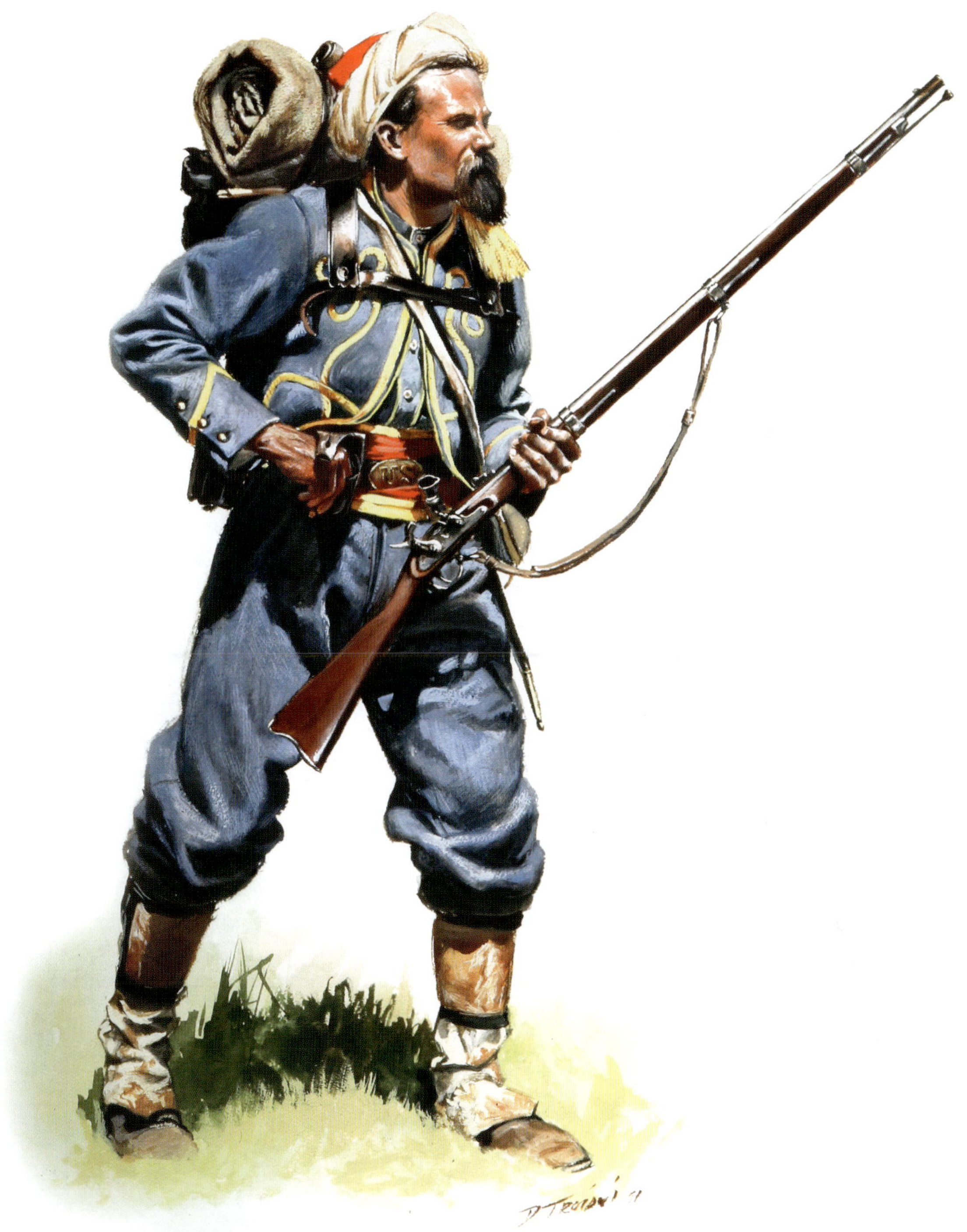

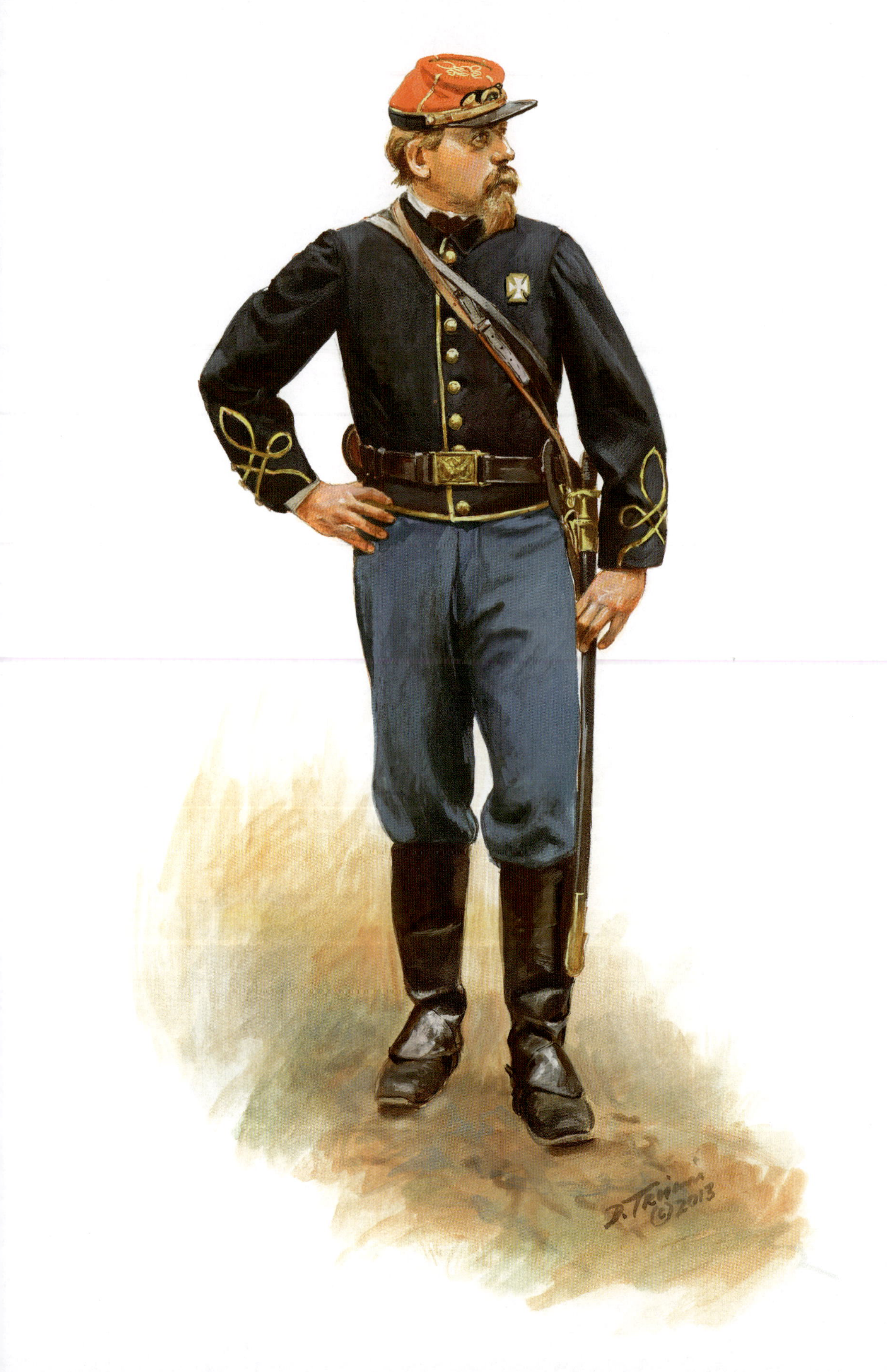

146th New York Volunteers, Officer, 1864–1865

AS WITH OTHER ZOUAVE REGIMENTS, OFFICERS OF THE 146th New York Volunteers, or Garrard's Tigers, often struck an elaborate and exotic appearance. This officer wears a nine-button jacket based on that worn by Captain William Fowler, Company C, 146th New York, who was mustered into this regiment as a first lieutenant after serving as a second lieutenant in the 173rd New York Infantry.[1] He was promoted to captain on December 22, 1864. Rank is indicated by three strands of gilt braid, forming a trefoil sleeve ornamentation. The jacket is also edged with wider gilt braid. He has a 2nd Division, V Corps, badge pinned to his chest.[2] His chasseur-pattern forage cap is based on that worn by Captain Joseph B. Cushman, who was mustered in as first lieutenant of Company K on October 10, 1862, and who was promoted to captain of Company C on October 29, 1863. He was discharged for disability on June 1, 1864. Of red wool with a dark-blue band, it is trimmed and quartered with three strands of gilt lace, also indicating rank, and has elaborately looped ornamentation on its top. At its front is a Pattern 1858 embroidered infantry officers horn, on a dark-blue patch, with "G3T" in its loop, which possible represents Garrard's Tigers of the Third Brigade. His sky-blue trousers are tucked into knee-high boots. His plain black leather belt is fastened with a Pattern 1851 "eagle" plate and supports a Model 1850 foot officer's sword and a holstered revolver.

1. New York State Military Museum and Veterans Research Center, Unit History 146th New York Infantry.
2. Don Troiani/Historical Image Bank.

164th New York Infantry (Corcoran Legion)

ORIGINALLY RECRUITED AS THE FOURTH REGIMENT of the Empire Brigade raised in New York City by General Francis B. Spinola in 1862, this all-Irish unit was also named the Phoenix Regiment, or the Corcoran Zouaves, after the Fenian activist Michael Corcoran, who was imprisoned in Richmond, Virginia, having been wounded and captured while commanding the 69th New York State Militia at the First Battle of Bull Run.[1] Following his exchange on August 15, 1862, Corcoran returned to New York and took command of the Empire Brigade, which was reorganized as the 155th, 164th, and 170th New York Infantry, and the 69th New York National Guard, also known as the Corcoran Legion.[2]

Commanded by Colonel John E. McMahon, the 164th New York left the State with the Legion on November 6, 1862, and served under Corcoran at Suffolk, Virginia, within Major General John J. Peck's Division, VII Corps, Department of Virginia, from December 1862, and was subsequently assigned to Corcoran's Division, VII Corps, from January 1863.

On February 20, 1863, First Lieutenant Joseph H. Abraham, 164th New York, writing under the pseudonym "Fenian," submitted a letter to the *Irish American*, advising readers, "Last Friday we received a new Zouave uniform . . . The suit is very handsome and durable. Pants, vest, and jacket are made of blue cloth, with red trimmings; fez also blue, with green tassel. The regular U.S. uniform is used for fatigue purposes, and the 'zou zou' uniform for 'dress parades' and gala occasions."[3]

Originally requested by Colonel Corcoran on October 13, 1862, and produced by the Quartermaster Department in Philadelphia, the Zouave suits received by the 164th New York were patterned after those worn by the 9th New York Infantry, or Hawkins's Zouaves, in 1861, the exception being dark-blue fezzes with green tassels.[4] Also received by the 164th were red waist sashes and white canvas gaiters. Based on photographic evidence, the Zouaves depicted have the brass numerals "164" pinned to the front of their fezzes.

1. *New York Herald*, October 5, 1862, 8:1.
2. *Buffalo Morning Express*, March 23, 1863, 3:1.
3. *Irish American* (New York, NY), March 7, 1863, 2:7.
4. NARA, record group 94, regimental books, 164th New York Infantry, vol. 20, 333.

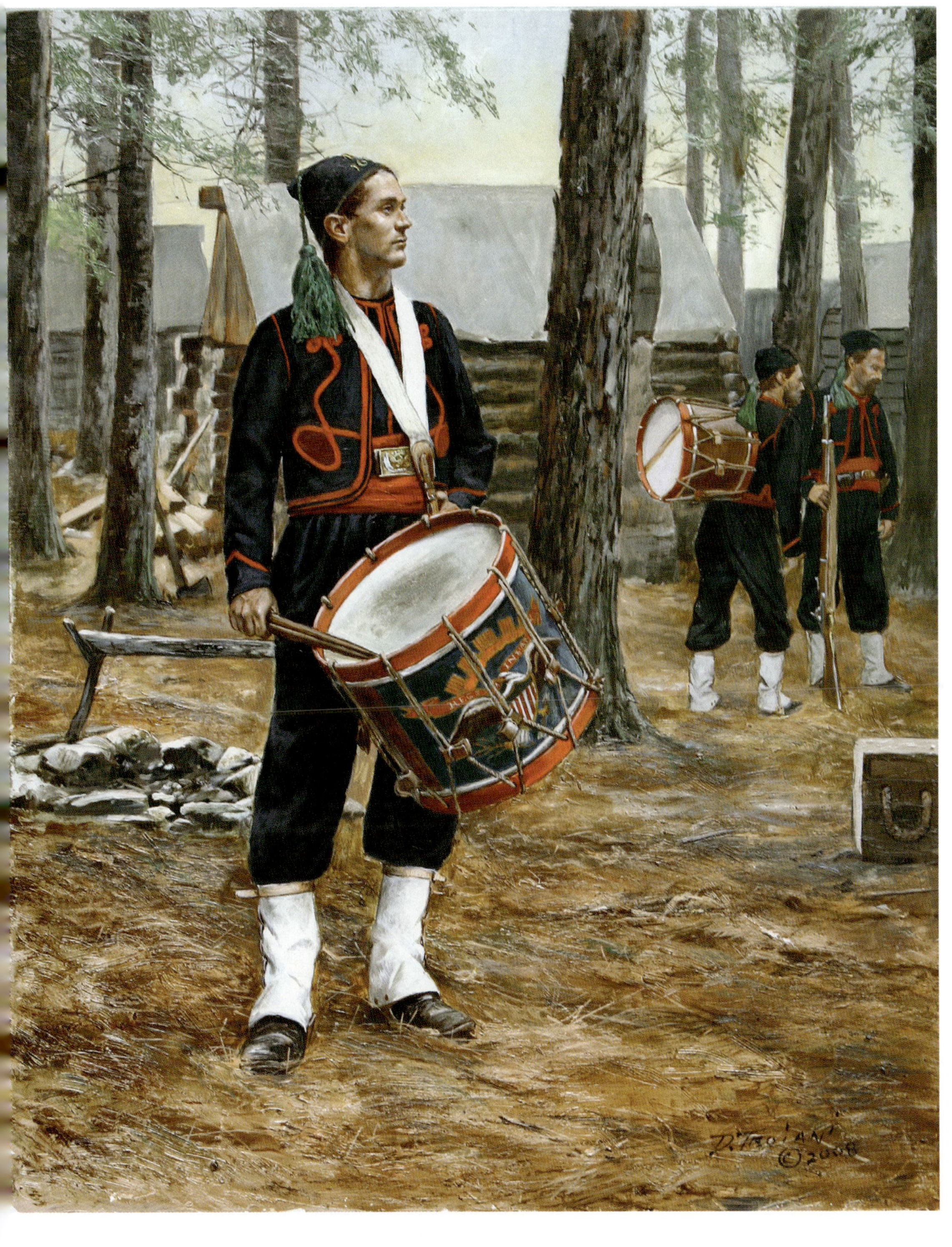

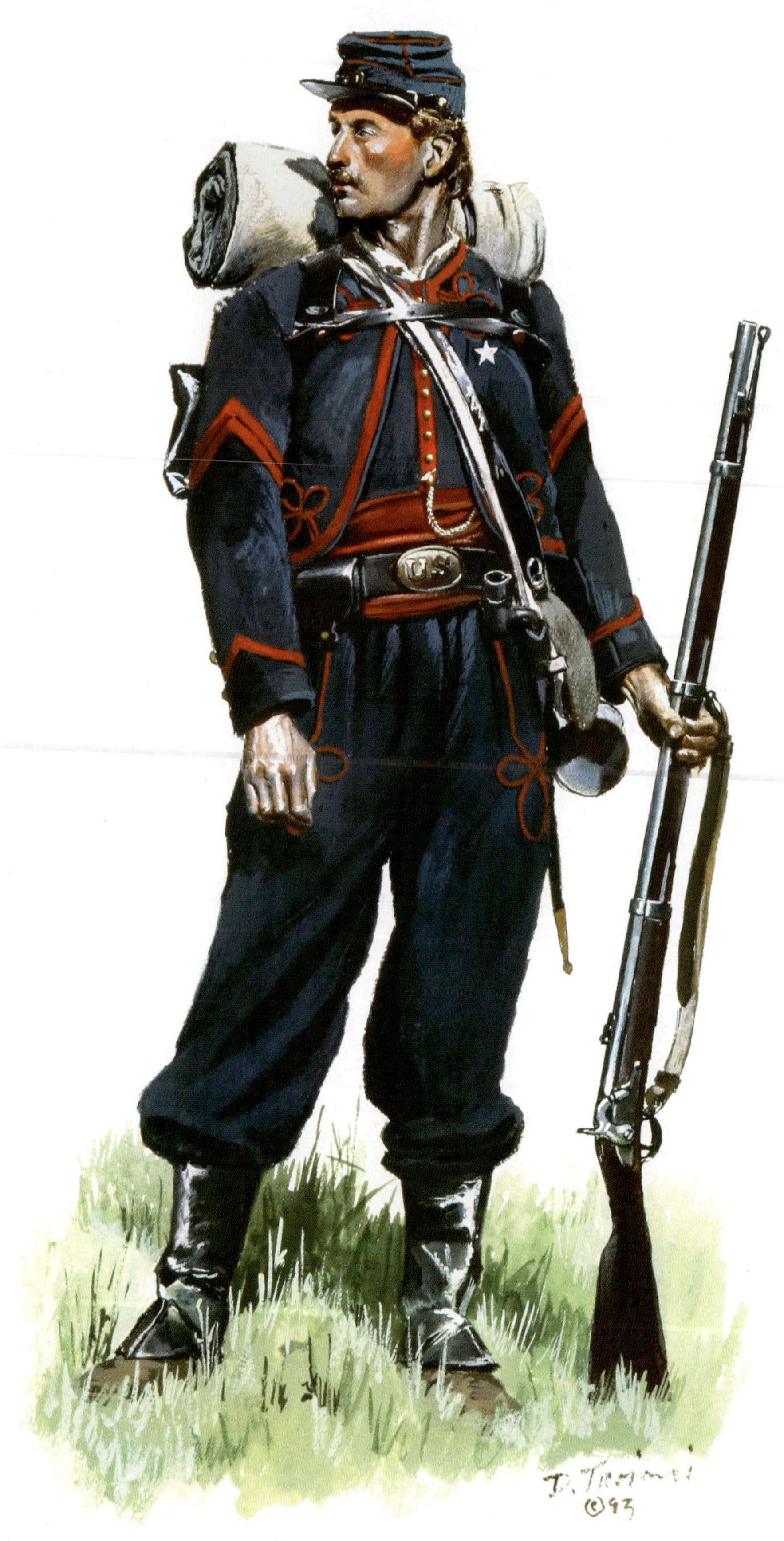

33rd New Jersey (Second Zouaves)

CLOTHING SUPPLIED TO TWO LATER WAR NEW JERSEY infantry regiments varied from the regulation uniform. Despite not favoring nonstandard clothing, the US Quartermaster Department relented when colorful uniforms might help induce recruits to enlist. Thus, in 1863 New Jersey State Quartermaster General Lewis Perrine procured through the US clothing department in New York what was known as the "Hawkins's Zouave uniform" for the 33rd and 35th New Jersey regiments, which were being recruited as Veteran Volunteers.[1]

The 33rd New Jersey, or Second Zouaves, enlisted for three years in Newark, New Jersey, during August and September 1863, under Colonel George W. Mindil. Recruits were encouraged to enlist or reenlist in "A Crack Corps of Volunteers" to be uniformed in "A Splendid Zouave Uniform."[2] A bounty encouraged many draft dodgers, who then disappeared from Camp Freylinghuysen as soon as they had received "$240 Cash." A total of 244 of 902 men managed to desert, initially earning the regiment the nickname "the mutinous 33rd." When the regiment left for the front on September 8, 1863, it was marched under armed guard to transport ships and dispatched to the South and the Midwest, where it was assigned to the 2nd Brigade, Second Division, XX Corps, Army of the Cumberland. Despite its poor start, the regiment performed well in the field, likely because a large portion of its men were seasoned veterans from other regiments.[3]

The corporal depicted wears the Hawkins's Zouave-pattern uniform, consisting of a dark-blue jacket, vest, and full-cut trousers with maroon trim. His jacket has small lace trefoils extending from the top corners near the neck and bottom front corners at the waist. His pleated trousers have a trefoil pattern of lace extending to about midway between the waist and the knee. The vest has a strip of small ball buttons attached to its front. His waist sash is deep red and his gaiters are black leather. Headgear consists of a chasseur cap that is piped and quartered with maroon trim; thus, the fez of the type worn by Hawkins's Zouaves was not worn. A five-pointed silver star-shaped XX Corps badge is pinned to his jacket. He is armed with a Model 1861 Springfield rifle musket.

The 33rd New Jersey spent its first months in service guarding bridges and performing fatigue duties, which took a toll on its uniforms. Replacements were requested in January 1864, but as the uniforms were of a distinctive pattern, they could not be readily supplied, and the regiment took to the field in mixed dress. As the Atlanta Campaign progressed, it was mostly issued regulation clothing, and by late summer it no longer wore Zouave uniforms. As a result, Colonel Mindil informed the Quartermaster Department that any surplus Zouave clothing in store could be issued to other regiments, including the 35th New Jersey, rather than to his own.

1. Lewis Perrine, *Annual Report of the Quartermaster General of the State of New Jersey for the Year 1863* (printed at the "True American" Office, 1864), 4.

2. *Newark Daily Advertiser*, August 1, 1863, 3:3.

3. Frederick Ray Jr., Roger C. Sturke, and Michael J. McAfee, "33rd Regiment, New Jersey Volunteer Infantry, '2nd Zouaves,' 1863–1865," *Military Collector and Historian* 31, no. 3 (Fall 1979): 128–29.

17th New York Veteran Volunteers

RECRUITED IN AND AROUND NEW YORK CITY DURING the fall of 1863, the 17th New York Veteran Volunteers, commanded by Colonel William T. C. Grower, consisted of men who had served in the original 17th New York Infantry, also known as the Westchester Chasseurs. Its ranks were also formed by a consolidation of veteran recruits who had originally enlisted for the reorganized 9th, 11th, and 38th New York, plus a new regiment called the Union Sharpshooters.[1] According to Quartermaster records, the Union Sharpshooters were to have received Zouave uniforms of the type issued to Duryée's Zouaves.[2] As recruiting for the 17th New York progressed, two of its fullest companies were made up of men from the original 9th New York, or Hawkins's Zouaves, and it was decided by the officers that theirs would become the uniform of the consolidated veteran regiment.[3]

As a result, the 17th New York was issued 339 each of "Jackets, Zouave infantry," "Trowsers, Zouave infantry," "Vests, Zouave infantry," "Sashes, Zouave infantry," "Fez caps, Zouave infantry," and "Leggings, pairs, infantry." Also received were 247 "Great coats, infantry," 280 "Blouses," 550 "shirts," and 340 "Shoes, pairs." The issuance of blouses, or sack coats, likely indicates that there was a need for fatigue uniforms for some duties.[4]

The 17th New York left New York City on October 18, 1863, and served with the XVI Corps in Mississippi and Alabama until August 1864, when it was transferred to the Army of the Cumberland and XIV Corps laying siege to Atlanta. As the unit left Atlanta and began the march to the sea, its members were mounted on mules. According to Private William B. Westervelt, Company K, "Worn out mules we left and took good ones in their place, while our cavalry were never so well mounted. All this was our gain and at the same time impoverished the South, as it left them no animals to work their land."[5]

The mounted Zouave wears a uniform patterned after that of Hawkins's Zouaves, which includes a red fez with a blue tassel, a dark-blue Zouave jacket, dark-blue chasseur-pattern trousers, and white canvas leggings. Private Westervelt recalled wearing a red shirt toward the end of the war.[6] He carries his musket slung over his shoulder, while much of his equipment is hung from the saddle on his mule.

According to the regimental history, the appearance of the 17th New York during the Grand Review at the close of the war on May 23–24, 1865, "in style, uniform and marching, bore such a similarity to the Hawkins' Zouaves that it was commented upon by many of the spectators who had been familiar with the appearance of the latter regiment."[7]

1. *Brooklyn Union*, October 16, 1863, 1:1.

2. NARA, record group 94, 17th New York Veteran Volunteer Infantry, vol. 22, 273.

3. Lt. Matthew J. Graham, *The Ninth Regiment New York Volunteers (Hawkins' Zouaves)* (E. P. Coby & Co., printers, 1900), 451–52.

4. Annual Report of the New York Quartermaster General, 1863. Statement B: Consolidated statement of all issues . . . from the 1st Day of January, 1863, to the 31st day of December, 1861. 17th New York Volunteer Infantry.

5. William B. Westervelt, *Lights and Shadows of Army Life* (C. H. Cochrane, 1886), 86.

6. Westervelt, *Lights and Shadows of Army Life*, 96.

7. Graham, *The Ninth Regiment New York Volunteers (Hawkins' Zouaves)*, 452.

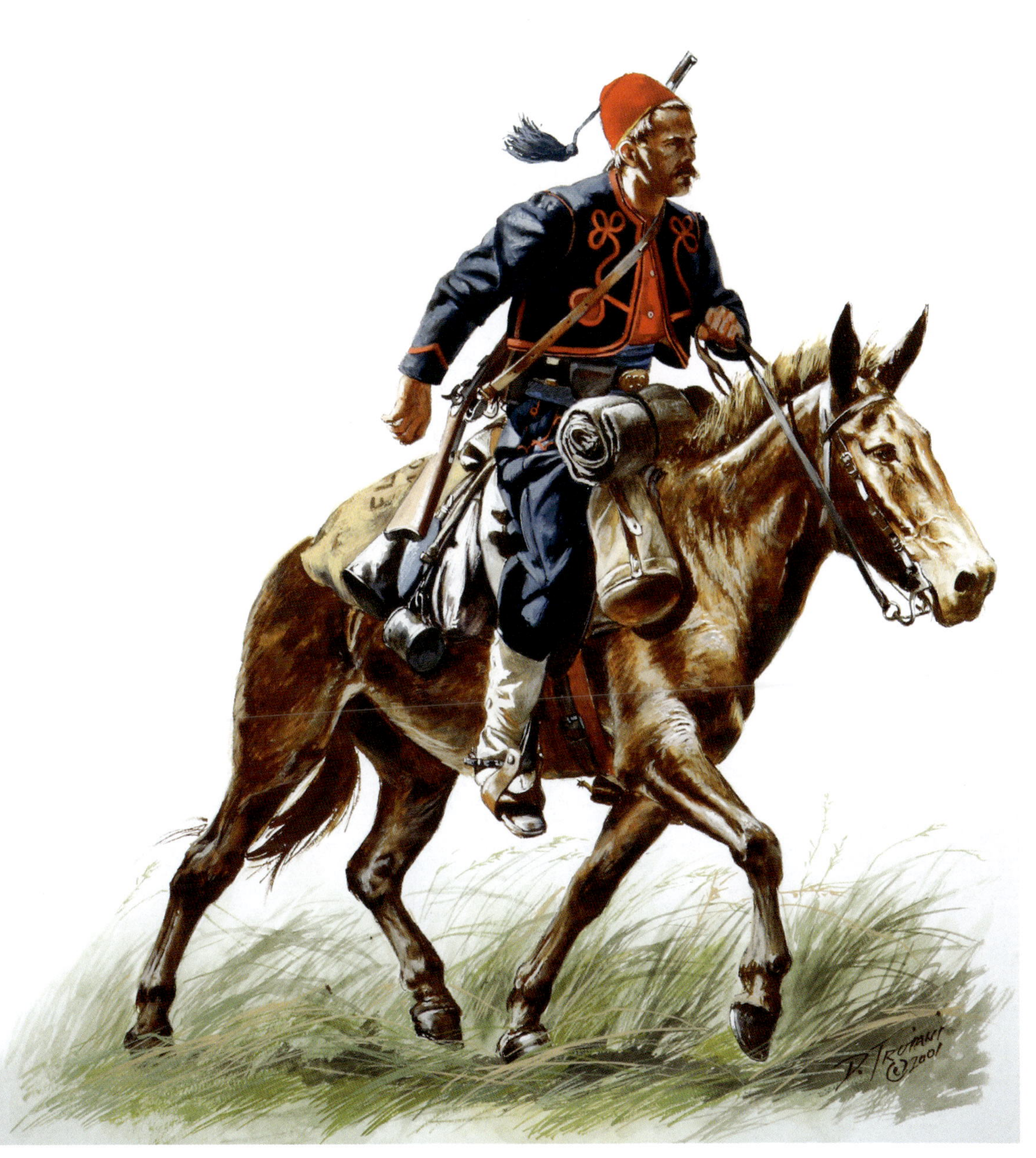

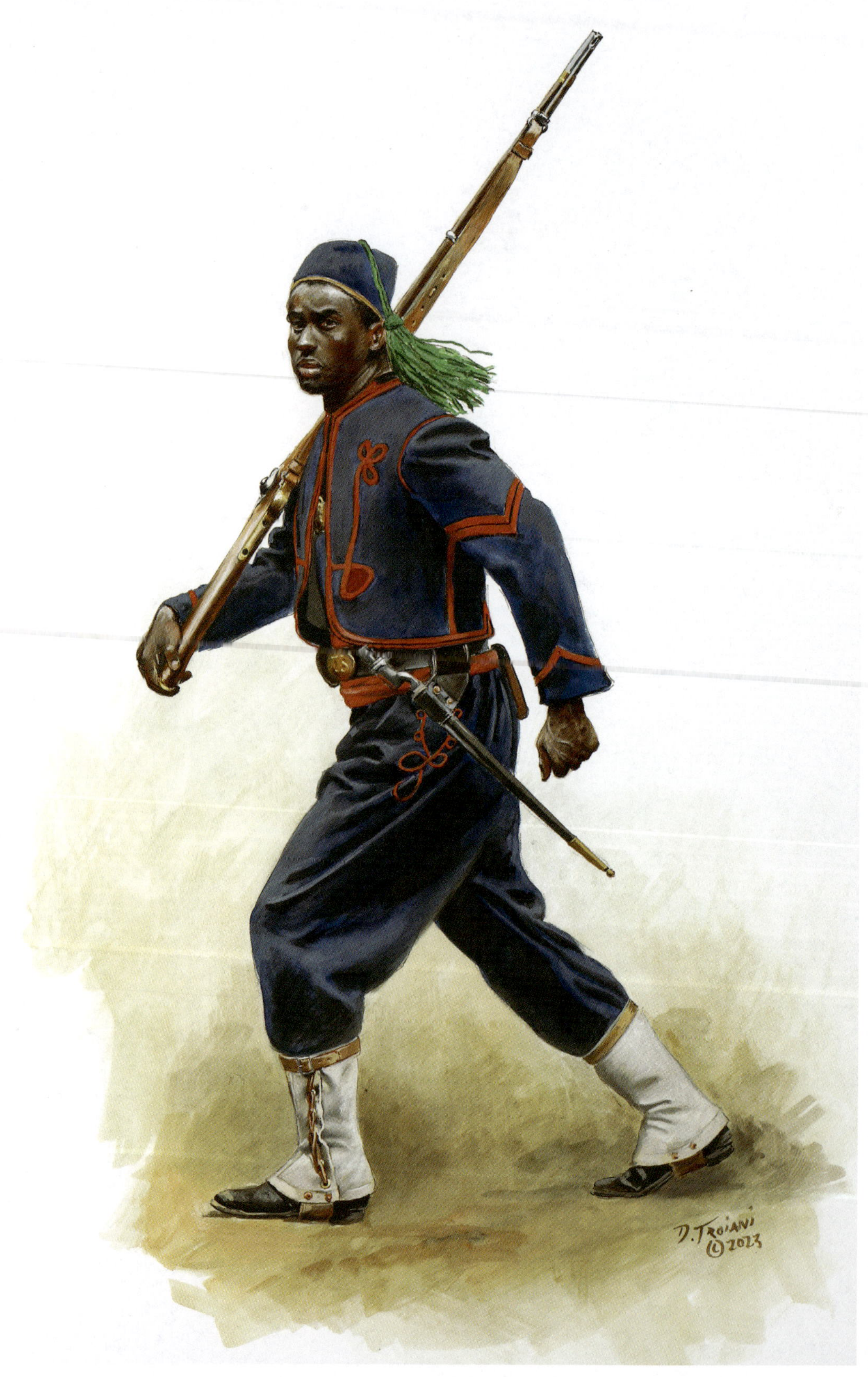

10th United States Colored Troops

COMMANDED BY COLONEL SPENCER H. STAFFORD, THE 10th United States Colored Troops was formed between November and December of 1863 on Craney Island, near Norfolk, Virginia, for three years' service. A lawyer before the war, Stafford was a captain in the 20th New York State Militia, the deputy provost marshal of New Orleans, and the colonel of the 1st Louisiana Native Guards before taking command of the 10th USCT. Stationed at Camp Hamilton, Fortress Monroe, from January until May of 1864, the 10th USCT was moved up the James River to Fort Powhatan aboard the ex-Confederate steamer *Planter*, where it joined the "African Brigade" commanded by Brigadier General Edward A. Wild.

On May 24, 1864, four companies of the 10th USCT helped defend fortifications at Wilson's Wharf from attack by Major General Fitzhugh Lee's cavalry. Prior to the action, Lee sent a flag of truce, informing Wild that, if the Black defenders surrendered, they would be "handed over to the authorities at Richmond as prisoners of war," rather than being returned or committed to slavery. Wild replied that he would "try to hold his position," which he did handsomely. During the six-hour battle, wave after wave of dismounted Confederate troopers attempted without success to dislodge the African Americans who "unflinchingly kept their position and fired murderous volleys into them, driving the enemy back with shattered and shrunken ranks, completely demoralized."[1] Confederate losses were approximately two killed and wounded, as opposed to six killed and forty wounded in the Union ranks.

The 10th USCT saw out the rest of the war in the trenches before Petersburg and performed guard duty at City Point, Virginia. On April 3, 1865, it was among the Black regiments that marched into Richmond, Virginia. Beginning in July 1865, it was stationed in Corpus Christi, Texas, where it remained until mustered out on May 17, 1866.[2]

The attire of this corporal of the 10th USCT is based on a newspaper report published in *The Anglo-African* of Norfolk, Virginia, on December 12, 1863, which described the Zouave dress of the 10th USCT while stationed at Craney Island as "blue, trimmed with red, and white leggins, cap blue with green tassel." Abolitionist editor Robert Hamilton went on to state, "The colored people of this city follow them in large numbers about the streets. Their uniform is exceedingly becoming, and make them the finest-looking soldiers we ever saw."[3]

Uniforms received by the 10th USCT were of the Hawkins's Zouave pattern selected as a standard Zouave dress being produced in quantity by the US Quartermaster Department during 1863–1864. The blue fez with a green tassel worn by the 10th USCT indicates they were surplus to requirements for the 164th New York, or Corcoran's Irish Zouaves.

---

1. *Nashville Daily Union*, June 3, 1864, 1:5.
2. NARA, record group 94, M1821, CMSR—Union—Colored Troops 8th–13th Infantry, 1861–1865, Introduction, 5.
3. *The Anglo-African* (Norfolk, VA), December 12, 1863.

5th New York Veteran Volunteer Zouaves

THE ORIGINAL 5TH NEW YORK INFANTRY, OR Duryée Zouaves, served with distinction for two years in the Army of the Potomac. When their term of service expired, there was a desire by many to continue their lineage. Recruiting notices, such as that titled "We still live—All quiet in the Army of the Potomac," resulted in the 5th New York Veteran Volunteer Infantry being reorganized for three years on May 25, 1863, with Colonel Cleveland Winslow in command.[1] The reconstituted unit initially entered Federal service as a four-company battalion, but, on October 14, 1863, it absorbed recruits intended for the 31st, 37th, and 38th New York infantry regiments, which failed to complete organization. Personnel from other regiments also swelled its ranks to form a complete regiment.

On August 24, 1863, Lieutenant Colonel D. H. Vinton, at the Office of Army Clothing and Equipage in New York City, requested sealed proposals for "One thousand uniforms of Duryée Zouave pattern" for the unit.[2] The initial uniform received was similar to that of the original Duryée's Zouaves, with the exceptions of the jacket, which was in sky blue as opposed to dark blue; the trousers, which were less baggy; and the gaiters, which were of leather rather than white canvas. During May 1864 the regiment received a second issue of clothing, including dark-blue jackets, baggier trousers, and white leggings with leather *jambières*, which more closely resembled that of the original regiment.

This Zouave wears an example of the uniform issued to the 5th New York Veteran Volunteers during the fall of 1863. He correctly wears his fez with a yellow tassel on the back of his head, and his ten-foot-long turban is wound about his head in the "canoe style" authorized by Colonel Winslow. His uniform suit consists of a sky-blue jacket trimmed with red braid and narrow chasseur-pattern red trousers trimmed with yellow cord, over which are worn leather gaiters. He is armed with a Springfield rifle musket, which replaced the inferior Enfield rifles his regiment carried prior to February 13, 1864.[3]

1. *New York Daily Herald*, June 4, 1863, 8:5.
2. *New-York Times*, August 27, 1863, 6:5.
3. NARA, record group 94, regimental books, 5th New York Veteran Infantry, February 13, 1864.

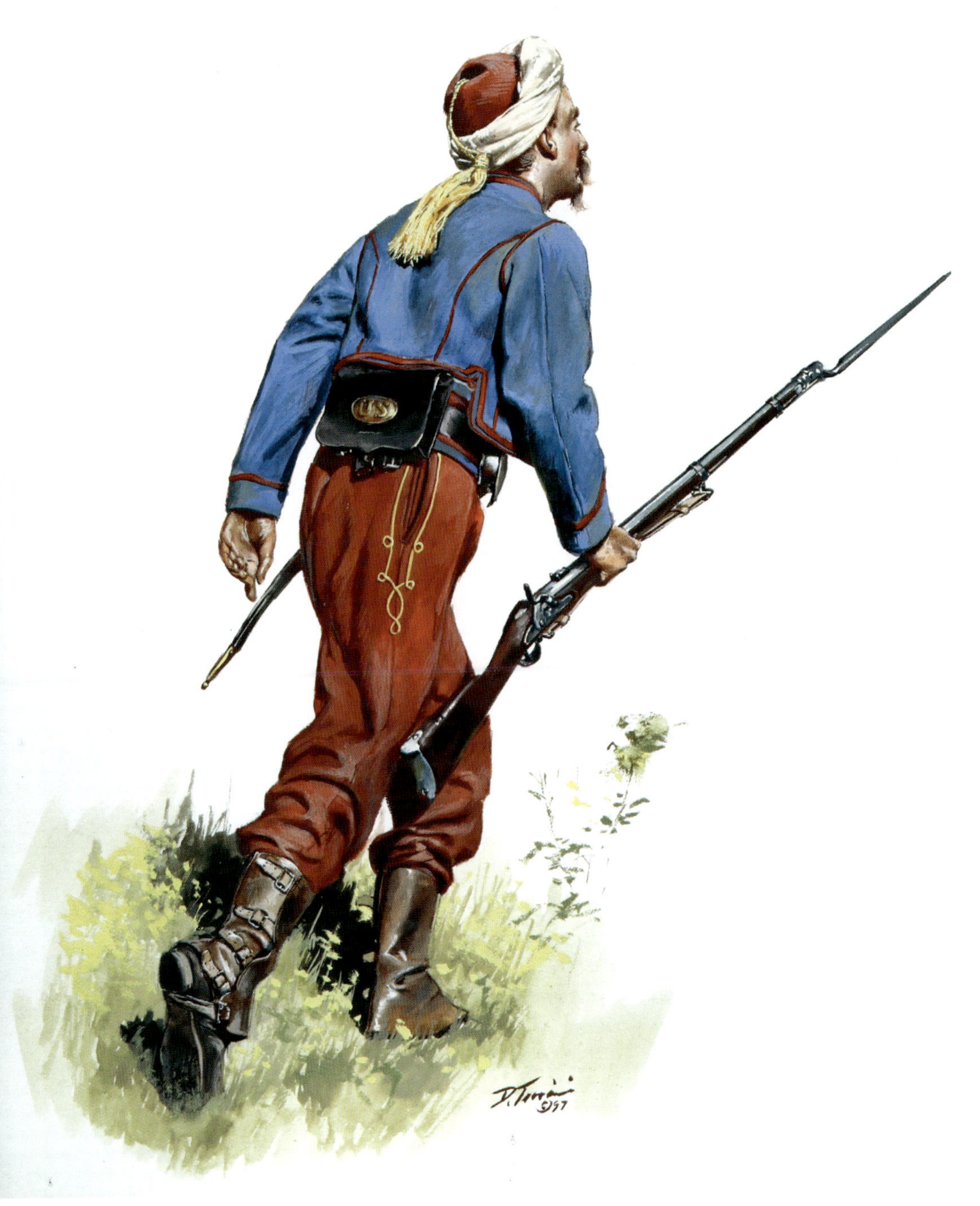

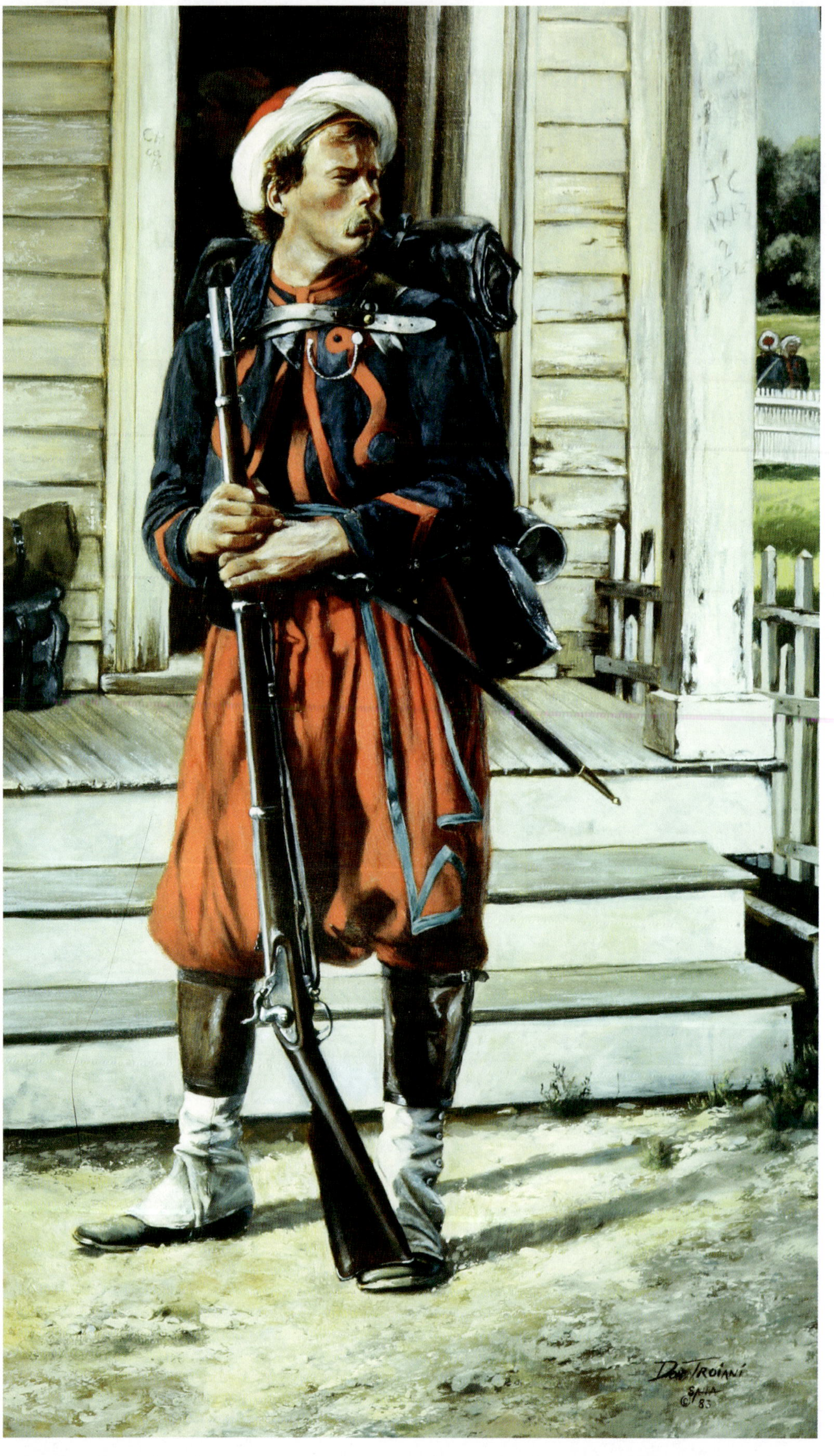

165th New York Infantry (Duryée's Zouaves)

THE REPUTATION OF THE 5TH NEW YORK INFANTRY, or Duryée's Zouaves, organized in 1861, inspired the formation of a new battalion of six companies. Designated the Second Battalion, Duryée's Zouaves, the unit was mustered into service as the 165th New York Infantry on November 28, 1862.[1]

Originally intended to form part of a four-regiment "Zouave Brigade" commanded by General Gouverneur K. Warren, it was assigned in January 1863 to the XIX Corps, Department of the Gulf, where it served under General Nathaniel Banks and saw its first action in the unsuccessful attack on Port Hudson on May 27, 1863. On this occasion the regiment's first commander, Lieutenant Colonel Abel Smith Jr., fell mortally wounded and the regiment suffered 107 other casualties, including the loss of four color bearers and five men of the color guard. During July 1864, the unit was transferred to Washington, DC, and, toward the end of the war, it served in the Shenandoah Valley. Following the Confederate surrender, it was placed on provost duty in Georgia and the Carolinas, and it was mustered out at Hart's Island, New York Harbor, on September 15, 1865.[2]

The uniform adopted by the 165th New York, and renewed after hard service on December 24, 1864, was in most respects that of the original Duryée's Zouaves, although the tassels on their fezzes were dark blue, as opposed to yellow, and the waist sashes worn were sometimes of plain red worsted rather than the blue-bound red of the 5th New York. Soldiers wearing Zouave dress, whether on parade or for fatigue, had to meet high standards under Lieutenant Colonel Smith. Prior to embarkation for Louisiana, an order was issued to the effect that "turbans will be folded neatly, the sash wound tight round the body at the full width showing the blue edge both at top and bottom, the ends tucked neatly in—the belt buckled tightly over it; the leggins whitened and the shoes blackened—the plates, belts & etc. neatly cleaned. Care must be taken in packing the knapsack—let it be as small and compact as possible, the overcoat rolled on top—the woolen blanket folded (inside of the rubber one, black side out); square with the knapsack; nothing will be allowed to dangle on the outside." A few days later, the Zouaves received the order, "Immediately after evening parade all turbans and white leggins will be taken off and not put on again until next morning; they will be placed in the knapsack."[3]

On guard duty in 1863, this fully equipped Zouave wears full dress, complete with white turban and leggings under leather greaves. His blue-bordered waist sash is neatly arranged, as per orders. He is armed with a Model 1863 Springfield rifle musket.

1. John A. Vanderbilt, John A. Murray, and Peter Biegel, *History of the Second Battalion, Duryée Zouaves* (Peter De Baun & Co., 1904), 9.

2. Vanderbilt, *History of the Second Battalion, Duryée Zouaves*, 42.

3. NARA, record group 94, regimental orders, 165th New York Infantry, January 4, and January 12, 1863.

155th Pennsylvania Infantry

ORGANIZED AT CAMP HOWE, NEAR PITTSBURGH, AND uniformed as a standard infantry regiment, the 155th Pennsylvania was mustered in for three years during September 1862. Serving with the Army of the Potomac, the regiment became one of several to the receive Zouave uniforms on January 19, 1864.[1]

With the expiration of the term of service of the 5th New York Infantry, or Duryée's Zouaves, on May 14, 1863, steps had been taken to ensure that Zouave uniforms would still be worn within the 2nd Division, V Corps, Army of the Potomac. In January 1864, three infantry regiments of Brigadier General Kenner Garrard's 3rd Brigade, 2nd Division, consisting of the 140th and 146th New York, plus the 155th Pennsylvania, were awarded the honor of exchanging their Federal-issue for Zouave uniforms due to their proficiency in Zouave drill and bayonet exercise.[2]

When published in 1910, the regimental history of the 155th Pennsylvania stated, "The exchange to the zouave uniform from the plain blue infantry uniform was enjoyed immensely by the men . . . not only on account of their having earned the recognition, but also because of the great beauty of the uniform and the greater comfort and other advantages it possessed over the regulation uniform."[3]

The Zouaves illustrated wear examples of the uniforms received, which were composed of a dark-blue–gray jacket with light buff-yellow *tombeaux* and trim, with a false vest front of the same color attached; wide dark-blue–gray pantaloons; a red fez and a white turban for full dress; a red flannel sash trimmed with yellow; and white canvas leggings. As an economy measure, the Quartermaster Department made up the Zouave uniform issued to this regiment by using surplus trousers supplied with the French chasseur uniforms purchased on August 9, 1861. Their Zouave jackets were fabricated from the talmas, or capes, also acquired with the chasseur outfits. These Zouaves have the red Maltese Cross badge of the V Corps on the trefoils on their jackets, and they carry Model 1861 rifle muskets.

For the remainder of the war, the men of the 155th Pennsylvania served with distinction in their colorful Zouave uniforms and Private William Montgomery, of Company I, was the last man killed in the Army of the Potomac, one hour before the Confederate surrender at Appomattox on April 9, 1865.[4]

1. H. Charles McBarron Jr. and Frederick P. Todd, "155th Pennsylvania Volunteer Infantry Regiment, 1864–1865," *Military Collector & Historian* 1, no. 3 (August 1949), 3–4.

2. Michael J. McAfee, *Zouaves: The First and The Bravest* (Thomas Publications, 1991), 42.

3. Charles F. McKenna, ed. and comp., *Under the Maltese Cross: Antietam to Appomattox* (The 155th Regimental Association, 1910), 224.

4. McKenna, 615.

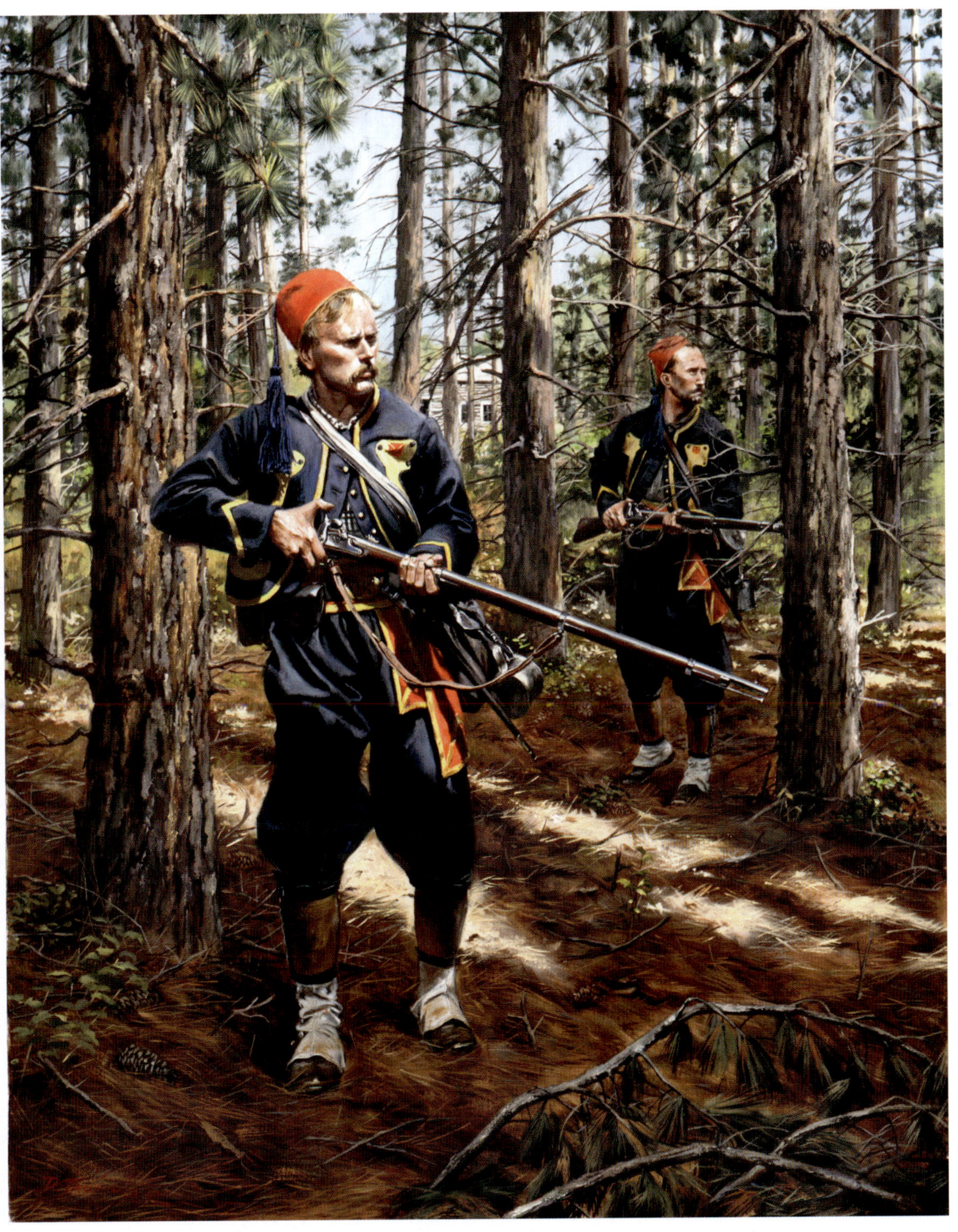

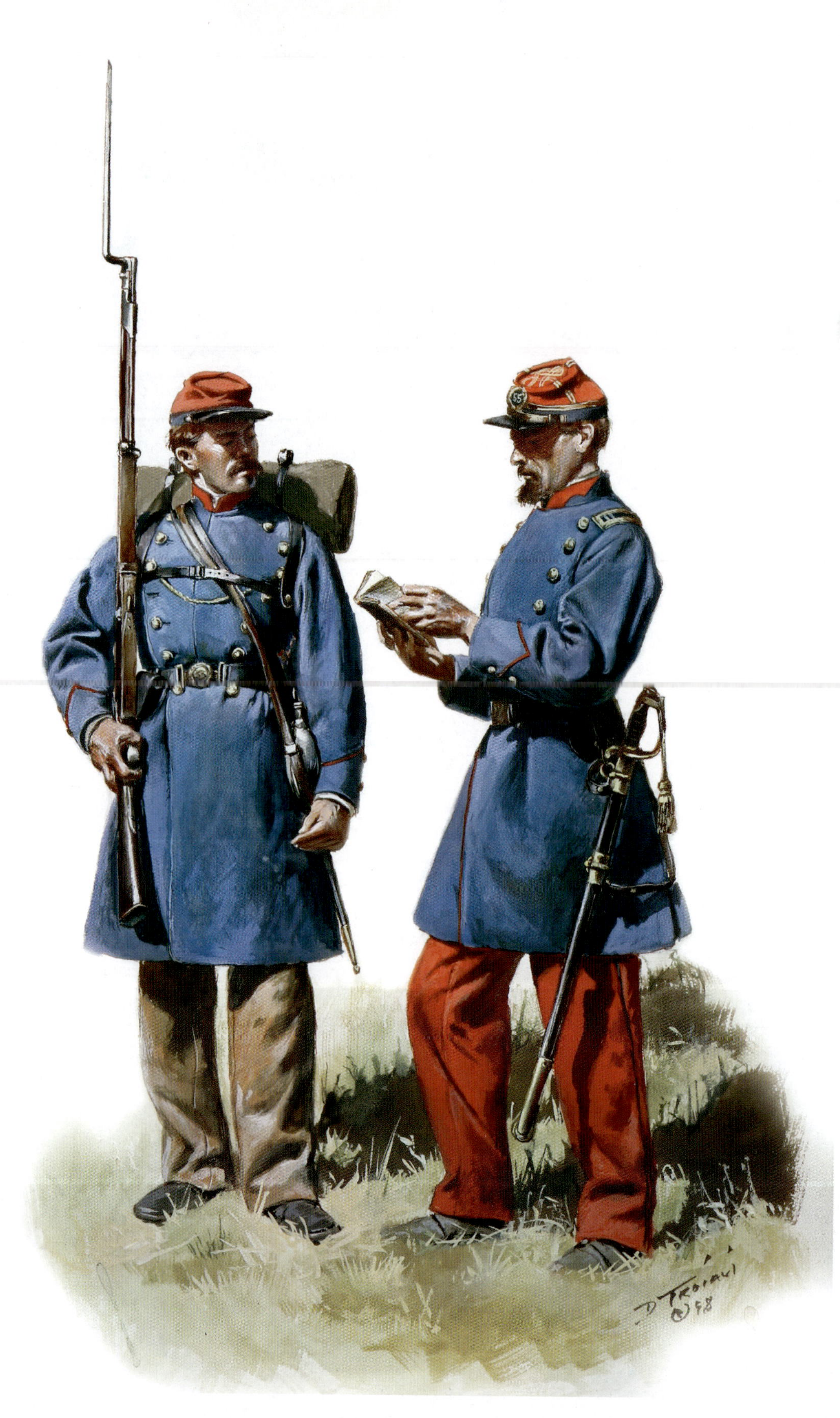

THE INFANTRY

55th New York (Lafayette Guard), 1861

NAMED FOR MARQUIS DE LA FAYETTE, THE FRENCH NOBLEMAN who fought for American Independence, the 55th New York Volunteer Infantry, or Lafayette Guard, mustered in for three years on August 28, 1861, with Colonel Baron Philipe Regis DeTrobriand in command. The nucleus of this regiment was several companies of the 55th New York State Militia, which had been accepted for three months' service but had failed to organize during the spring of 1861 under Colonel Eugene Le Gal.[1]

Proud of its Gallic heritage, under DeTrobriand, the 55th New York retained French-style uniforms of the type worn by its militia predecessors. Ordered from Brooks Brothers, of New York City, on August 23, 1861, the uniforms provided to enlisted men were "light blue overcoats trimmed with red cloth and lined with red twilled flannel" made of the "light blue Army Kersey" made at the Utica Woolen Mills in Oneida County, New York. Trousers were intended to be red, but, due to a lack of availability of red cloth, they were supplied in "Brown drilling." The regiment also received "dark blue jackets trimmed with red cloth," which were probably for fatigue wear.[2] Red chasseur-pattern caps had a dark-blue band. The Zou-ave company of this regiment was also fitted out by Brooks Brothers with dark-blue Zou-ave jackets and vests, scarlet Zouave trousers, and light-blue kersey hooded cloaks; for additional information, see Company I, or Advance Guard, 62nd New York Volunteers, in the previous chapter. On September 1, 1856, the press reported that the 55th New York "went away in heavy duck pantaloons and blue overcoats, except one company wearing French zouave uniforms."[3]

The enlisted man is shown as he would have appeared when the 55th New York departed for the front on September 1, 1861. He has a black leather waist belt with a two-piece clasp displaying the regimental number "55." His militia box knapsack is topped with a gray blanket roll, and a Pattern 1858 canteen is carried on his left hip. He holds a Model 1842 musket at "shoulder arms."

The officer's uniform was likely a private purchase and consists of a double-breasted coat trimmed in the same style as that of the enlisted man, with shoulder boards indicating the rank of first lieutenant, and plain red trousers. His cap is embellished with gold lace and has the regimental number within a gold wreath at front. A Model 1850 foot officer's sword is attached to his waist belt.

---

1. *New-York Times*, May 26, 1861, 8:2.
2. "Articles of Agreement," courtesy of Civil War Preservations.
3. *New York Tribune*, September 1, 1861, 5:3.

12th Tennessee Infantry

RECRUITED MAINLY IN GIBSON COUNTY BY Colonel Robert M. Russell, the 12th Tennessee Infantry was organized into state service at Jackson, Tennessee, on June 3, 1861. In September the regiment was ordered to go to Columbus, Kentucky, which was occupied by forces commanded by General Leonidas Polk. At the Battle of Belmont, Missouri, on November 7, 1861, the 12th Tennessee was part of a brigade also consisting of the 13th and 21st Tennessee, commanded by Colonel Russell. After the fall of Fort Donelson in February 1862, Columbus was evacuated and the 12th Tennessee moved to Corinth, Mississippi. Following this, the unit fought at Shiloh on April 6–7, 1862. It was consolidated with the 22nd Tennessee Infantry in June 1862 and with the 47th Tennessee Infantry in October of that year. It continued to serve in the Western Theater of the war, finally forming part of the 2nd Consolidated Tennessee Infantry, which consisted of remnants of nine regiments. When paroled at Greensboro, North Carolina, on May 2, 1865, there remained only fifty officers and men of the 12th, 22nd, and 47th Tennessee.[1]

Advancing into battle, this Tennessean wears an example of the uniform and headgear issued to the 12th Tennessee Infantry while stationed at Columbus, Kentucky. According to requisitions for clothing received during October 1861, the regiment was issued with various amounts of caps, coats, pants, flannel and cotton shirts, socks, boots, and blankets.[2] The coat worn is based on that produced by the Tennessee State Quartermaster Department established during May 1861 and was single-breasted with a solid facing color on the collar and pointed cuffs, the latter having two small buttons at the center.[3] Trouser seam stripes match the coat facing color, and his chasseur-pattern "army cap" has a dark band. Footwear consists of ankle or half-boots, as indicated in clothing requisitions. He carries a Model 1842 musket. A Pattern 1839 cartridge box is carried on his shoulder belt, and a frame buckle fastens his waist belt. Accoutrements include a tin drum canteen and a canvas haversack.

The uniform illustrated did not last long. Observing Tennessee volunteers, a Cairo correspondent of the *Missouri Republican*, who smuggled himself into Columbus as a clerk to a country merchant in October 1861, commented, "None of the uniforms of the soldiers were new, and a pinch will evidently come when they are worn out."[4]

1. *Tennesseans in the Civil War*, part 1 (Civil War Centennial Commission, 1964), 200.
2. NARA, M268, CMSR, 12th Tennessee Infantry, J. M. Wyatt, p. 17 for example.
3. Library of Congress LC-B8184-10038; and *Confederate Calendar 1988*, April, Robert M. Vawter collection.
4. *The Sun* (New York City, NY), October 21, 1861, 2:6.

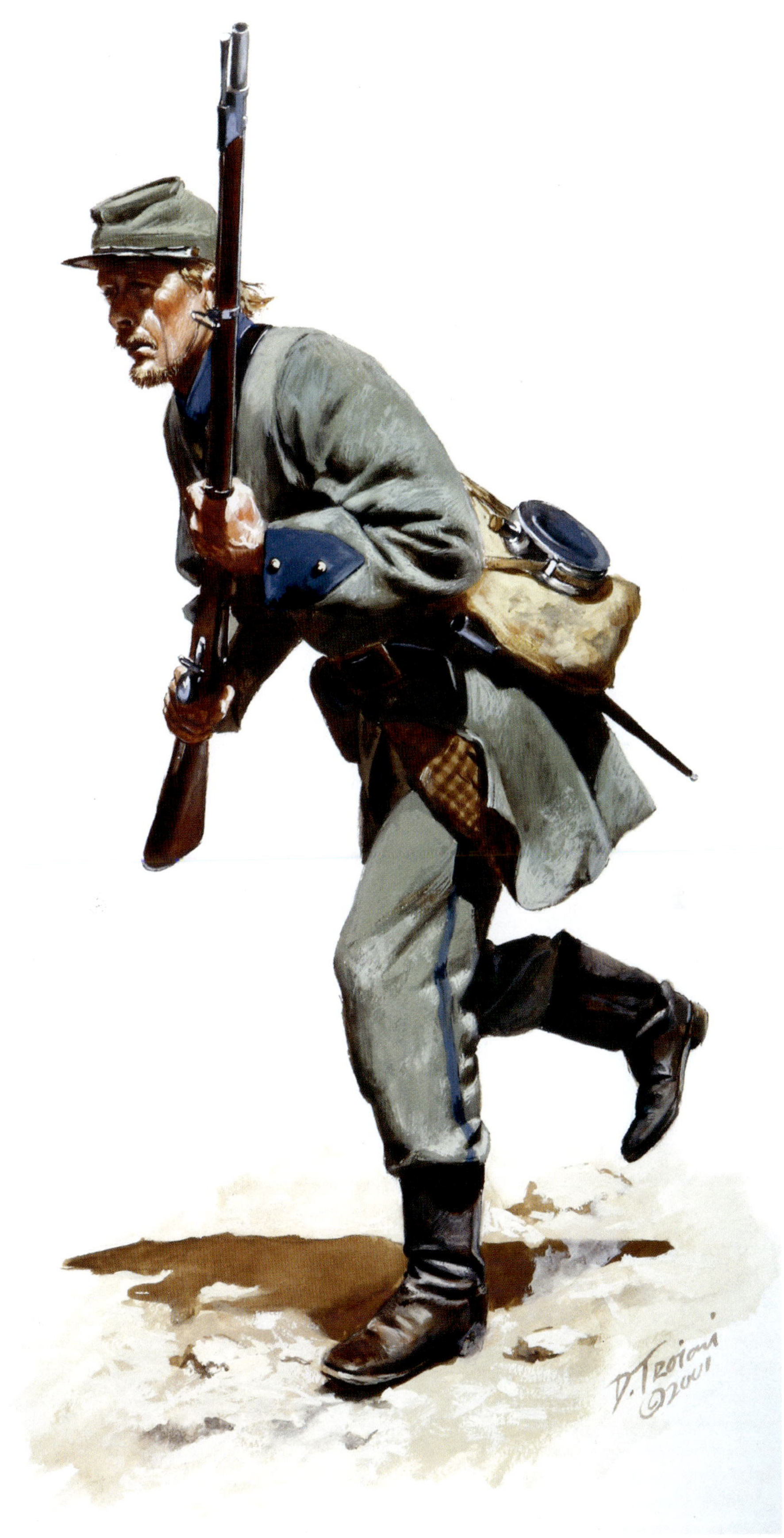

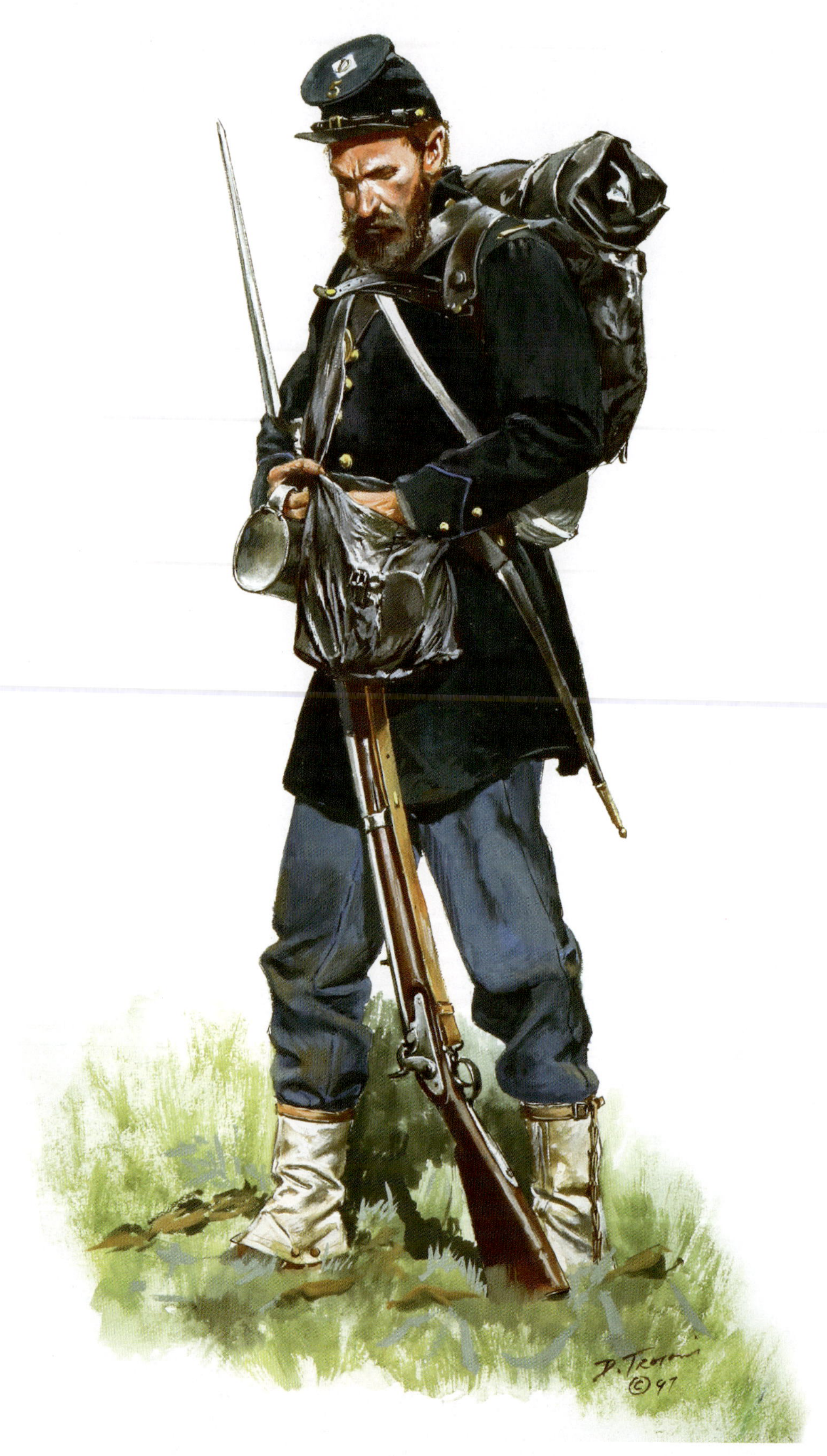

5th New Jersey Volunteers, 1863

ONE OF FORTY-FIVE MILITIA AND VOLUNTEER INFANTRY REGIMENTS provided to preserve the Union by New Jersey between 1861 and 1865, the 5th New Jersey Infantry was one of eight new regiments formed by Governor Charles Olden upon requisition of President Abraham Lincoln on July 24, 1861. It was mustered in under the command of Colonel Samuel H. Starr on August 22, 1861, and a week later left New Jersey for Washington, DC, where it performed duty in the defenses, being attached to Brigadier General Silas Casey's Provisional Division, Army of the Potomac.[1]

By April 1862 the 5th New Jersey was attached to the 3rd Brigade, 2nd Division, III Corps, Army of the Potomac, under the command of Colonel Starr, as senior colonel, and took part in the Peninsula Campaign, including the siege of Yorktown and the Battle of Williamsburg, during which Starr was wounded. It later took part in Pope's Campaign in Northern Virginia during August–September of 1862 and in the Battle of Fredericksburg toward the end of the year. Following the "Mud March" and the Battle of Chancellorsville from January through May of 1863, the 5th New Jersey arrived at Gettysburg as part of the Third Brigade, 2nd Division, of Major General Daniel E. Sickles's III Army Corps.

Commanded by Colonel William J. Sewell, the regiment formed part of Sickles's early afternoon attempt to advance his Corps into a salient on slightly higher ground in the Peach Orchard on July 2. As a result, it took huge casualties when Longstreet attacked as part of Lee's coordinated assault. Colonel Sewell was wounded. Captain Henry H. Woolsey took command for the rest of the action even though he was slightly wounded. Of the 221 men in the regiment who were brought to the field, 13 were killed, 65 were wounded, and 16 went missing.

The enlisted man of Company D, 5th New Jersey, appears as he would have on July 2, 1863. Unusually, his regiment was not resupplied with flannel sack coats that year, and he wears a uniform coat complete with a button and brass keeper on the shoulders to accommodate shoulder scales for dress occasions.[2] His high-crowned forage cap has the white diamond badge for the Second Division, III Corps, with the company letter inset. Below this is the brass regimental number "5." His sky-blue trousers are tucked into white canvas leggings. He is armed with a Model 1861 Springfield rifle musket with a russet leather sling and a fixed bayonet. Equipment includes a black rubberized canvas knapsack with a vulcanized rubber blanket roll strapped to its top. He clutches his tin cup and reaches into his India rubber haversack, which contains foodstuffs, including hardtack and beef jerky, plus personal hygiene utensils and keepsakes that remind him of home.

---

1. John Y. Foster, *New Jersey and the Rebellion* (Martin R. Dennis & Company, 1868), 17.

2. NARA, record group 393, Entry 202 Brigade Report, July 18, 1863; and Lewis Perrine, *Annual Report of the Quartermaster General of the State of New Jersey for the Year 1863* (printed at the "True American" Office, 1864), 63.

10th Tennessee Irish Legion

ORGANIZED AT FORT HENRY ON MAY 29, 1861, UNDER Colonel Adolphus Heimann, the 10th Tennessee Infantry, also known as "The Irish Legion," was accepted into Confederate service for one year on September 1, 1861.[1] Much of the early organization of Irish volunteers in the ranks of the 10th Tennessee was completed by Randolph M. McGavock, ex-mayor of Nashville, who was elected lieutenant colonel of the regiment. In particular, he recruited the Sons of Erin, which provided recruits for Companies F, D, and H of the 10th Tennessee during May 1861.[2] Uniforms worn by those Companies that joined the 10th Tennessee, such as the Pickett Rifles, commanded by Captain Boyd M. Cheatham, and the Irish Invincibles, commanded by Captain John G. O'Neill, were provided by the womenfolk of the communities in which they were recruited.[3]

As a result of hard service constructing batteries at Fort Henry, the first uniforms worn by the 10th Tennessee were in poor condition by the fall of 1861, and Lieutenant Colonel McGavock paid to replace them during September of that year. According to the diary of Private James Doyle, of Company D, "The jackets and pants were Confederate gray, with a scarlet line running down the pants legs. The hats [caps] were gray with scarlet trim, and . . . the insides of the jackets, as well as the shirts, were bright scarlet. The commissioned officers also got crimson and gold trimming on their jacket sleeves. The enlisted men took good care of the jackets for a while, but Fort Henry was still hot in the fall. Soon the area was swarming with ditch diggers in bright red shirts which stood out for miles around."[4]

The color bearer in this painting wears an example of the uniform provided by Lieutenant Colonel McGavock. He has a large "D"-guard knife attached to his belt via a leather frog, and other equipment includes a haversack and a tin drum canteen.

Originally presented on May 23, 1861, to McGavock's Sons of Erin, the flag he carries was made by Ladies Soldiers' Friends Society and painted by William J. Fry, of Nashville.[5] It was described in the *Nashville Union and American* the day after presentation as being of "the finest silk and satin, with a rich gold fringe. On one side was represented, in gilt, the Harp of Erin with a wreath of Shamrock most beautifully executed by Mr. Fry, our obliging artist; the other side was of the pattern of the flag of the Confederate states, differing from it only having fifteen instead of eight stars . . . [and was] inscribed with those glorious words—Go where glory awaits you."[6] The green field on the obverse side of the surviving flag measures 66 inches on the staff by 101 inches on the fly, exclusive of a 3-inch long fringe. This flag is held today in the collection of the Tennessee State Library and Archives.[7]

---

1. *Tennesseans in the Civil War*, part 1, 193.
2. *Nashville Union & American*, May 24, 1861, 3:2.
3. *Daily Nashville Patriot*, May 8, 1861, 3:1; and May 24, 1861, 3:1.
4. Diary of Private James Doyle, Company D, 10th Tennessee Infantry, 1861–1863, Private collection of Margaret Bailey, 15–16.
5. Stephen D. Cox, *Civil War Flags of Tennessee* (The University of Tennessee Press, 2020), 195.
6. *Nashville Union and American*, May 24, 1861, 3:3.
7. Howard Madaus Collection, US Army Heritage and Education Center, Carlisle, PA.

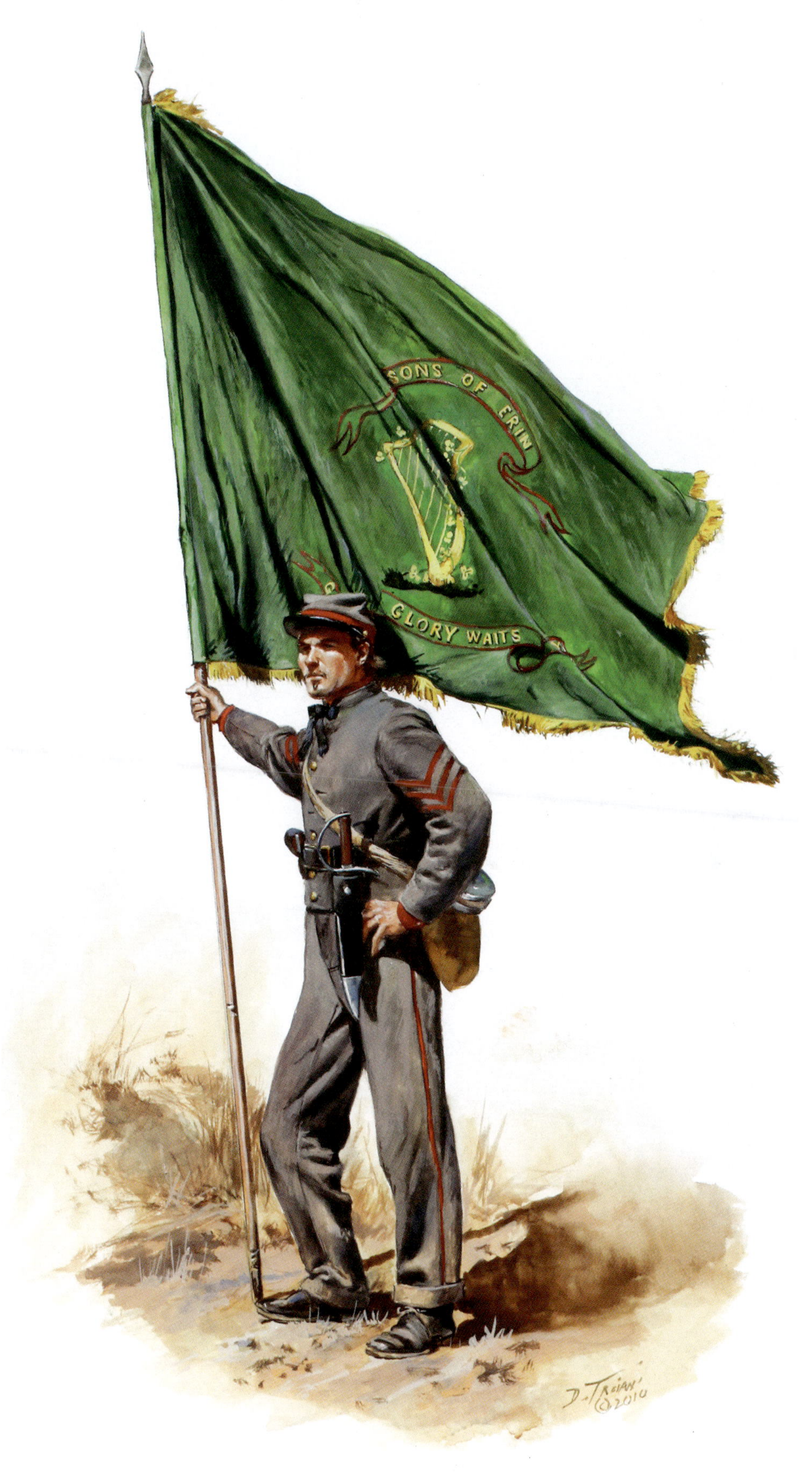
SONS OF ERIN
GLORY WAITS

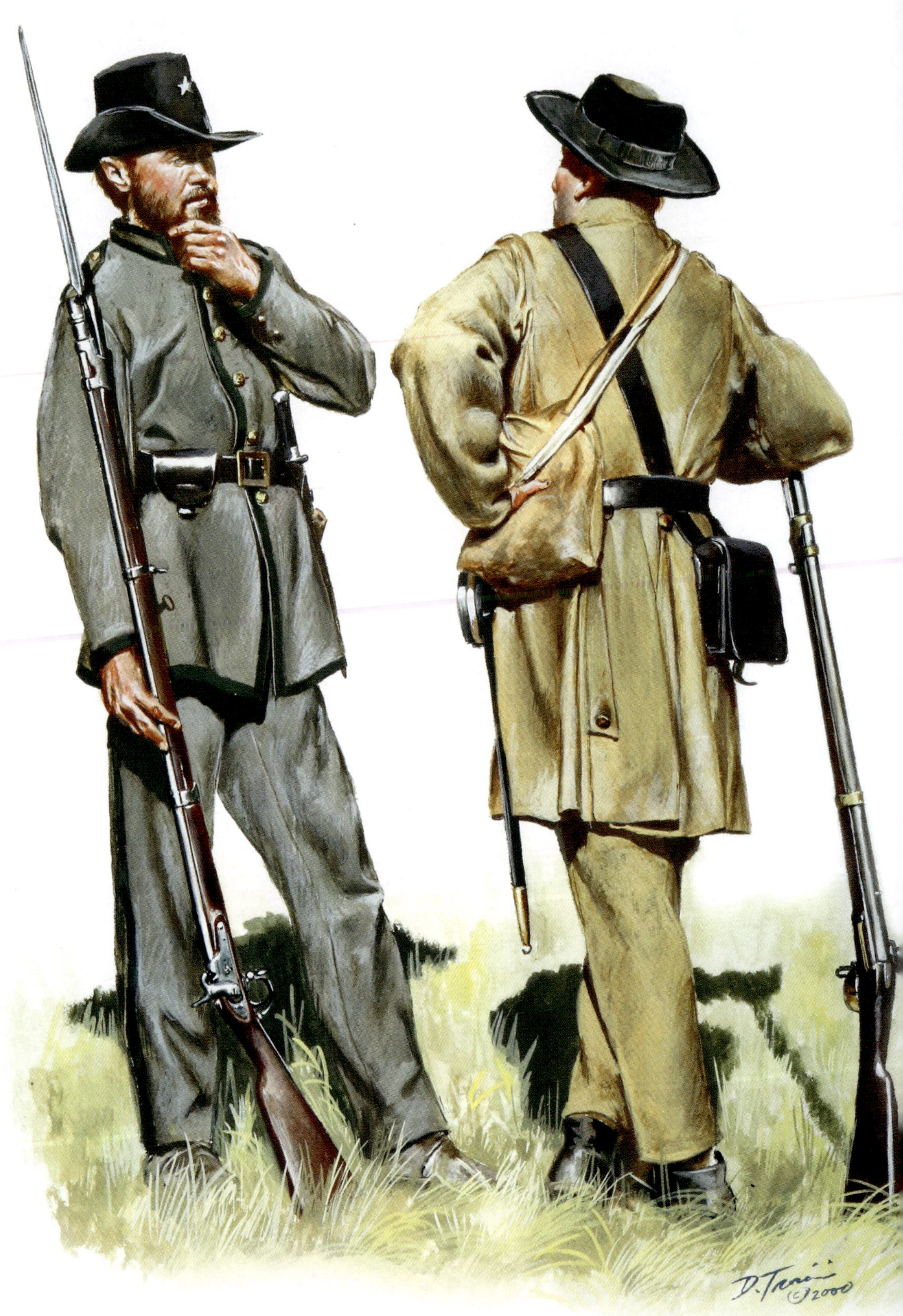

6th Texas Infantry, Company G, Travis Rifles

RECRUITED IN AUSTIN DURING AUGUST 1861, with Captain Rhoades Fisher elected to command, the Travis Rifles were mustered into Confederate service "for the war" as Company G, 6th Texas Infantry at Camp Henry E. McCulloch, four miles north of Victoria, on November 14, 1861. Provided by "the patriotic ladies" of Austin, their first uniform was of "a dark pepper and salt grey color . . . trimmed with green."[1] Based on photographic evidence, the six-button coats with short skirts and matching pants were made of a lightweight cassimere-type cloth. Although green trim often indicated the branch service color for a rifle unit, the original arms of the Travis Rifles were flintlock muskets, plus "belts, cartridge boxes etc.," probably obtained from the old US Armory in Austin. These weapons were converted to percussion muskets by an Austin gunsmith before the company left for Victoria.

The 6th Texas remained at Camp McCulloch until May 1862, during which time it was furnished with new uniforms of a "light brown color" from cloth manufactured at the State Penitentiary in Huntsville. On February 14, 1862, an unknown member of the regiment wrote "our measures all taken," which indicates that the cloth had likely arrived.[2] As a result, a total of 717 coats and 811 pairs of pants were issued shortly after.[3] With a nine-button front and pockets in rear skirts, the uniform coats with this uniform were likely based on the pattern of 1851 as worn by the US Army. Haversacks and canteens with straps were also issued at this time.

The conversion muskets carried by Company G were replaced on May 18, 1862, when the whole 6th Texas received new weapons. On this occasion, the Travis Rifles received eighty Mississippi Rifles, plus accoutrements consisting of eighty cap boxes, seventy cartridge boxes, forty bayonet scabbards, eighty waist belts with plates, "all in good Order."[4]

---

1. "Jim Turner Co. G, 6th Texas Infantry, C.S.A. from 1861 to 1865," *Texana* XII, no. 2: 149.
2. *Tri-Weekly Telegraph* (Houston, TX), February 14, 1862, 2:4.
3. NARA, record group 109, CMSR, Texas, Robert R. Garland, 149.
4. NARA, record group 109, CMSR, Texas, Darius Marsh, 58

16th New York Infantry, Corporal

ORGANIZED BY COMPANY IN SMALL TOWNS, THE 16th New York Infantry was assembled in Albany, New York, originally under the name 1st Northern New York Infantry. The regiment was mustered in for two years service as the 16th New York Infantry on May 15, 1861, with West Point graduate and Mexican War veteran Colonel Thomas A. Davies in command. Those who entered the ranks of the regiment later in the war would serve three years. According to a news report in May 1861, recruits for "the Northern regiment" were "composed of lumbermen, river drivers, farmers and mechanics," and all were "famous as unequalled marksmen."[1]

On June 15, 1861, the 16th New York received its uniforms, which consisted of New York State–pattern dark-blue jackets trimmed with sky blue, of the type produced via the May 1861 State contract; sky-blue wool kersey trousers; and dark-blue forage caps. The regiment also received 150 Model 1840 Springfield muskets converted to percussion. Ten days later a further six hundred muskets of the same pattern were issued, and the regiment was later that day ordered to go to New York, finally arriving in Washington, DC, on June 29, 1861, where it was attached to the 2nd Brigade, 5th Division, Army of Northeastern Virginia.

The 16th New York saw only limited action at Bull Run on July 21, 1861, following which it went into winter camp. With the commencement of McClellan's Peninsula campaign, it was ordered to go to York-town, Virginia, and, about five weeks after its arrival on May 3, 1862, every man in the regiment was presented with a straw hat. In a letter to his sister written on June 13, First Lieutenant Albert M. Barney, Company D, 16th New York, stated that Major Joel J. Seaver had "just presented to each member of the regiment a nice straw hat, with a ribbon round it, on which is printed the number of the regiment in gilt letters and figures. The officers' hats are bound with black, the others have no binding."[2]

These straw hats were provided by the wife of regimental commander Colonel Joseph Howland, via a ladies' aid society.[3] Given to the regiment at the same time were "rubber and woollen blankets, leggings . . . flags, and new instruments for the regimental band." The white straw hats proved a disadvantage for the 16th New York in battle as many men blamed their distinctive headgear for the number of head and upper-body wounds the unit suffered at Gaines Mill on June 27, 1862. This likely caused many men to revert to their state-issue forage caps, although some may have continued to wear their straw hat into 1863.

This corporal appears as he would have at Gaines Mill. The ribbon around his straw hat bears the designation "16 N.V.," and he wears leather leggings of the type received by his regiment prior to the battle. He is armed with a Pattern 1853 Enfield rifle musket, which replaced the Springfields in early July, 1861.[4]

1. *New York Daily Herald*, May 14, 1861, 1:3.
2. Newton Martin Curtis, *From Bull Run to Chancellorsville* (The Knickerbocker Press, 1906), 28.
3. *Buffalo Express*, February 3, 1862, 2:3.
4. Curtis, *From Bull Run to Chancellorsville*, 33.

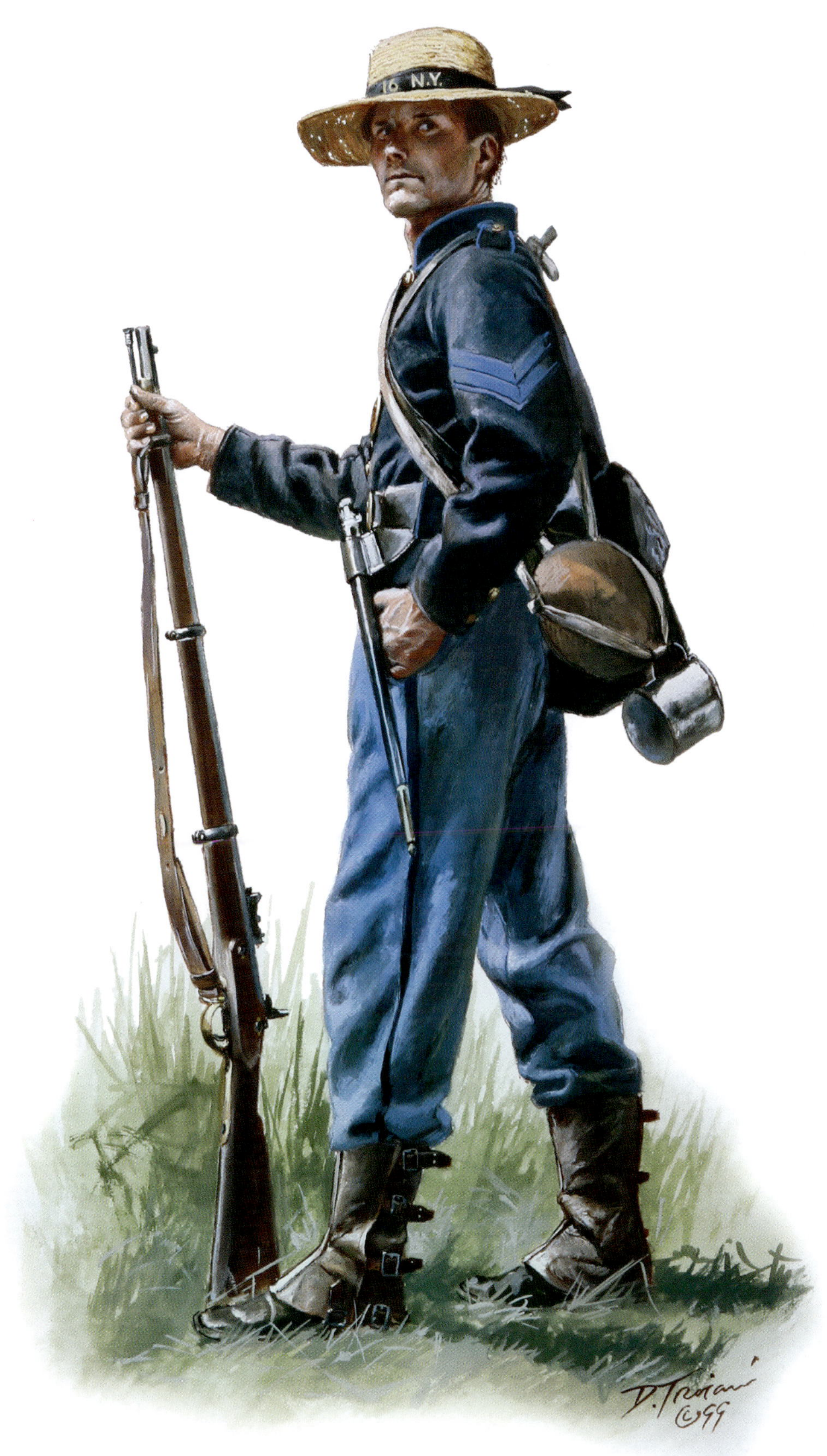
16 N.Y.

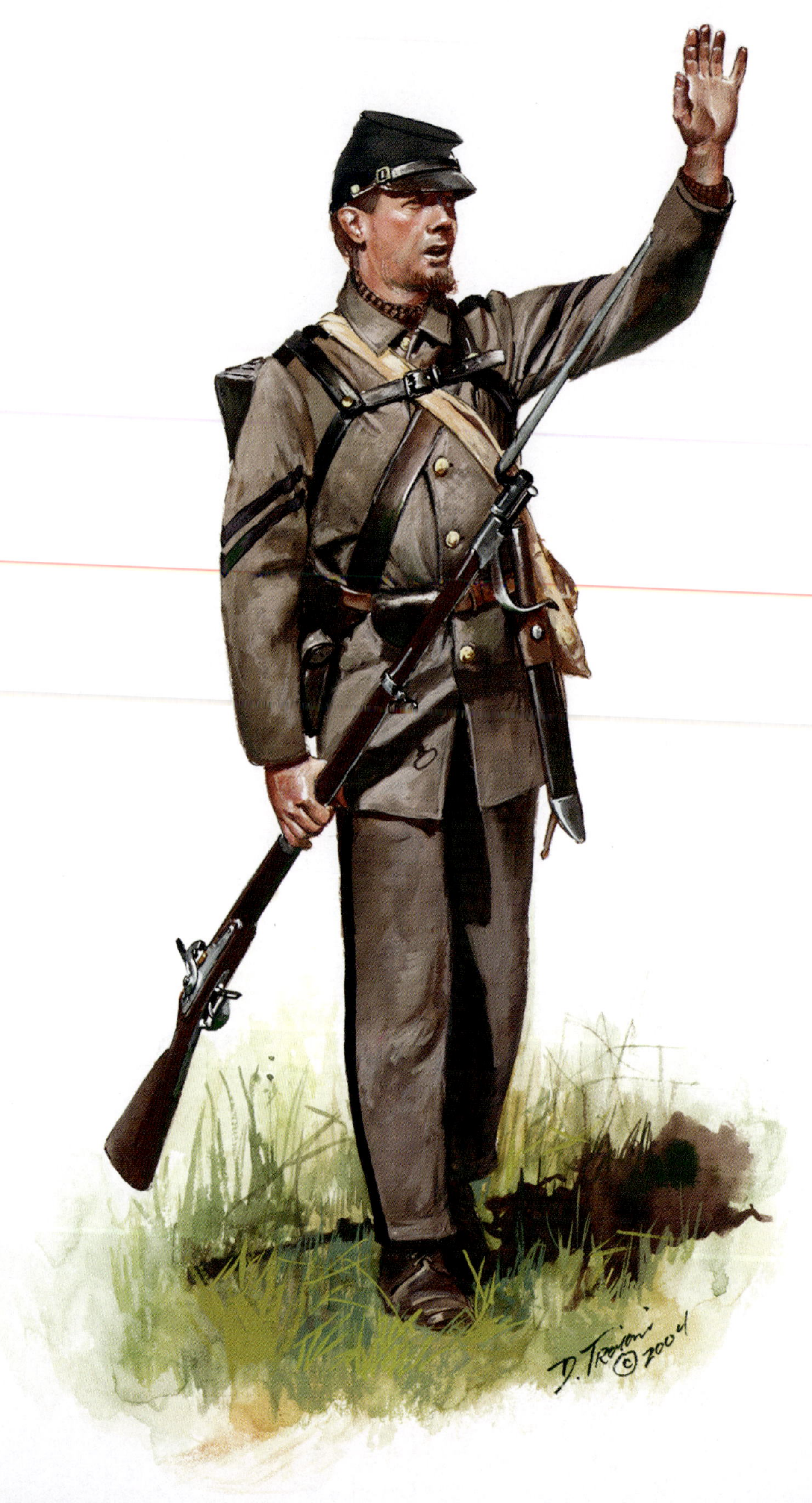

North Carolina Infantry Corporal, 1861

FROM THE OUTBREAK OF THE CIVIL WAR, NORTH CAROLINA was determined to maintain its states rights by clothing and equipping its troops sent to the front. On May 23, 1861, Governor John W. Ellis appointed a board of officers to determine a uniform for the regiments of state troops and volunteers being formed in the Old North State.[1]

On May 27, their findings were formalized in General Orders No. 1, which created a uniform thereafter referred to as the "state 1861 pattern." In its several variations, this uniform was worn by most North Carolina troops throughout the remainder of the conflict. Details were prescribed in "Uniform Dress and Equipment of the Volunteer and State Troops of North Carolina," which called for gray caps and sack coats and trousers of "North Carolina Manufacture" for all enlisted men. General officers and staff wore dark-blue frock coats and trousers, while regimental officers wore gray.

The six-button sack coats for enlisted men extended half way down the thigh and were made loose, with a falling collar and an inside pocket on each breast. The coats had a strip of cloth sewed on each shoulder, extending from the base of the collar to the shoulder seam. Of branch service color, this was black for infantry, red for artillery, and yellow for cavalry; the colors also applied to the chevrons and trouser seam stripes of noncommissioned officers. Regarding headgear, a gray dress hat was prescribed but rarely worn. Instead gray forage caps were issued under the state's first contract, although dark-blue caps were supplied via North Carolina's purchasing agent in Norfolk, Virginia.

From February 1862 the sack coat was modified by the removal of the skirt, producing a six-button jacket. Also eliminated were the shoulder facings, thus producing a garment similar to the Confederate Quartermaster-issue jacket. North Carolina continued to furnish her troops with uniforms throughout the war, even after the Confederate government discontinued the commutation system in October 1862 and began the issuance of uniforms from various clothing depots in several other Southern states.

Apart from relying on home production, North Carolina is believed to have imported, at an approximate total, gray wool cloth sufficient for 250,000 suits of uniforms and 12,000 overcoats; 50,000 blankets; and leather for 250,000 pairs of shoes. The imported cloth was generally a dark bluish-gray, which was quite distinct from the drab grays of the Confederate-made jeans cloth of the period. Sometimes referred to as "blue," or "English blue," it was manufactured by Peter Tait, of Limerick, Ireland.[2]

This North Carolina corporal wears the state uniform issued from mid-1861 until about February 1862. He is carrying a Model 1822 musket altered from flintlock to percussion. His plain brown leather accoutrements, knapsack, and canvas haversack have been supplied by the State. While the large "D"-guard bowie knife provides an air of invincibility, it likely proved more of a hindrance than a weapon as close-quarters combat proved to be a rarity on Civil War battlefields.

---

1. Ron Field, *The Confederate Army 1861–65 (5): Tennessee & North Carolina* (Osprey Publishing, 2007), 22–23.

2. Richard Warren, "Uniforms of the Confederacy: North Carolina State Issue Uniforms, 1861–1865," *Journal of the Confederate Historical Society* XVIII, no. 2 (Summer 1990): 45–52.

Confederate Infantry Officer, 1862

THIS CONFEDERATE INFANTRY FIRST LIEUTENANT WEARS A uniform based on that prescribed by and illustrated in the "Uniform and Dress of the Army of the Confederate States," as published in Richmond, Virginia, by Southern political organizer and soldier Blanton Duncan on June 6, 1861.[1] Unlike Federal officers of the same rank, his tailor-made cadet-gray uniform coat is double breasted, which was a feature reserved for field-grade and general officers in the Union army. Longer than the short-skirted version illustrated in the regulations, its two rows of seven fire-gilt General Staff buttons bear a raised "eagle" encircled by five-pointed stars.[2] His collar and cuffs have dark-blue branch-of-service facings for infantry, and rank is indicated by two horizontal gold bars on his collar and a European-style single strand "orna-ment of gold braid" on his sleeves. His gray chasseur-pattern uniform cap has an infantry branch-of-service dark-blue band and has a single strand of gold lace quartering its sides, forming a quatrefoil on its top. His sky-blue trousers have narrow nonregulation dark-blue welts on the outside seams.

Detached from its carrying straps, his Model 1850 company-grade infantry officers' sword is sheathed in a black leather scabbard with brass furniture. Swords for officers were often presented to them by their local community, or the men they commanded, in recognition of their patriotism and service. He is also armed with a holstered revolver attached to his plain black leather waist belt. The latter is not of the rectangular pattern prescribed in the regulations, but is fastened by circular two-piece plate with the letters "CS" at its center.

1. Frederick P. Todd, *American Military Equipage 1851–1872*, vol. II (The Company of Military Historians, 1977), 424.
2. Warren K. Tice, *Uniform Buttons of the United States 1776–1865* (Thomas Publications, 1997), 198–201.

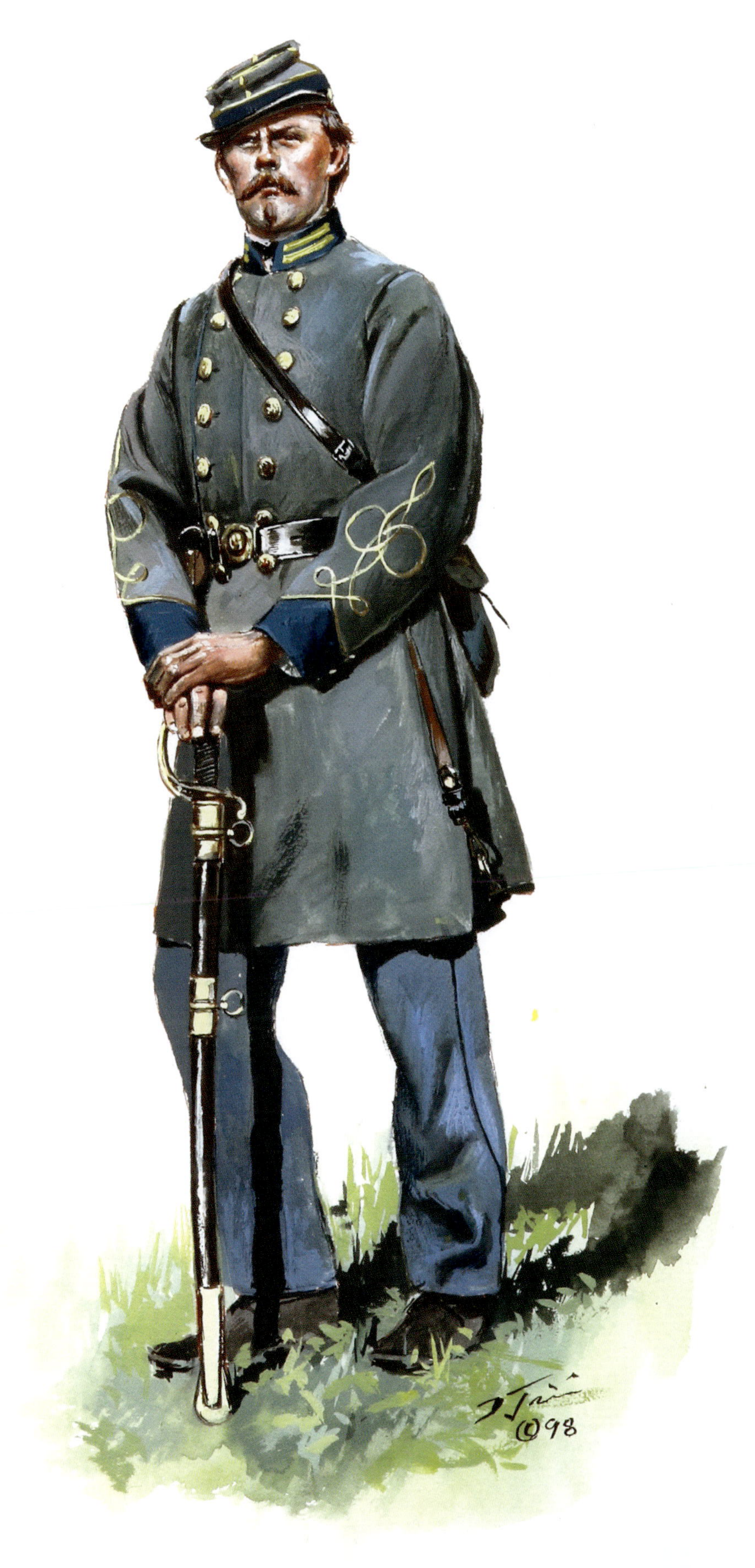

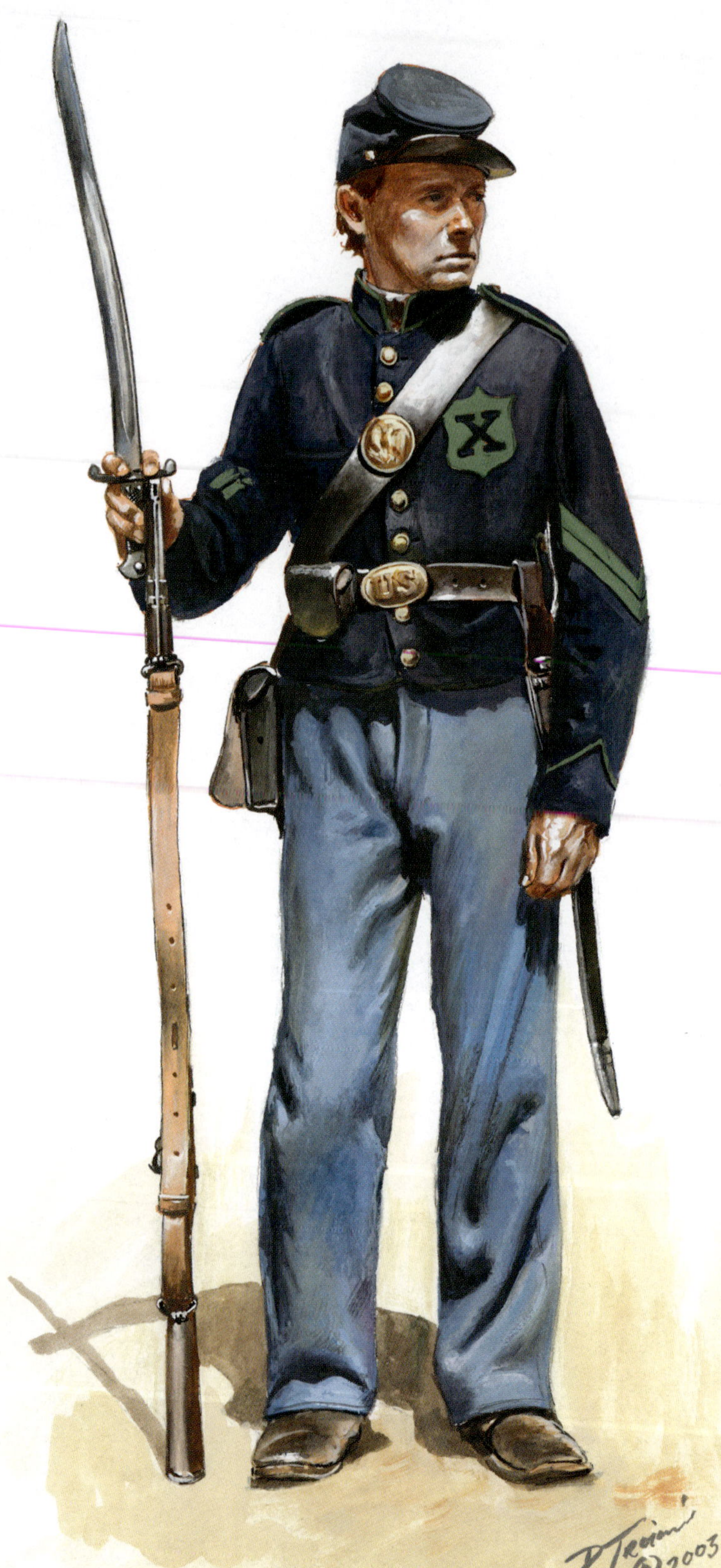

56th New York Volunteers (Tenth Legion), Sharpshooter Company

RECRUITED AT NEWBURGH, NEW YORK, DURING August 1861, the Tenth Legion was raised under the auspices and command of Colonel Charles H. Van Wyck, Representative of the Tenth Congressional District of New York State, and was named in honor of his district.[1] As with other Civil War legion-based units, it was initially a mixed command consisting of infantry, artillery, cavalry, and sharpshooters. The Tenth Legion was organized and received its numerical designation as 56th New York Volunteers on October 15, 1861, and was mustered in the service of the United States for three years thirteen days later. In January 1862 the 56th New York received a flag of "choice white silk" with an eagle in a wreath above which was a red scroll bearing the inscription "Our name is Legion."[2]

On November 2, 1861, the *New York Tribune* reported that the uniforms of this regiment, of blue New York State–contract pattern, had been "prepared with much care. Each soldier has a shield on his left breast, in which is cut an X. The infantry shield is blue, riflemen green, cavalry orange and artillery red." (*New York Herald*, November 2, 1861, 5:2.) Veterans who authored the regimental history wrote, "Uniforms were furnished to all of the members with the letter 'X' on the left breast . . . of which we were very proud, and nearly every one had his picture taken and sent home to his parents or family."[3]

Upon arrival in New York City on November 7, 1861, the 56th New York was reported as consisting of 1,452 men, which included two companies of cavalry, two of artillery, and one of sharpshooters, all of which wore "dark blue caps and jackets, and light blue pantaloons." Carried by the infantry and sharpshooter companies, arms consisted of short, two-band sergeant's Pattern 1856 Enfield rifles with "large sword bayonets" attached.[4] By the end of 1861, the artillery had been reorganized as the 7th and 8th New York Independent Batteries, and the two troops of cavalry were assigned to the 1st New York Mounted Rifles. The sharpshooter company remained with the unit as Company L, making it an eleven-company regiment rather the standard ten-company organization. When the sharpshooters were detached from the regiment in October 1862, they served as the Fifth Company of the 1st New York Sharpshooter Battalion, which served in Washington, DC, and Suffolk, Virginia, and, after April of 1864, with the Fifth Corps, Army of the Potomac.

The corporal depicted wears a jacket at variance with the state-pattern worn by the infantry companies of the 56th New York. His collar and shoulder straps have rifleman's green cord trim. Also, whereas most New York State jackets had plain cuffs, his have "V" shaped green trim. His sky-blue wool kersey trousers are without half-inch–wide green stripes on the outer side seams, which normally denoted the rank of corporal. The rifle company also had a distinctive marker or small flag featuring crossed rifles on a green field with ribbons above and below, which displayed the "Tenth Legion" name as well as its regimental designation "56th N.Y.S.V."

---

1. *New York Tribune*, October 8, 1861, 8:2.

2. *Evening Star* (Washington, DC), January 17, 1862, 3:2.

3. Joel C. Fisk and William H. D. Blake, *A Condensed History of the 56th Regiment New York Veteran Volunteer Infantry . . .* (Newburgh Journal Printing House, 1906), 13.

4. *New York Herald*, November 8, 1861, 5:1.

Cherokee Rangers, Company I, 19th Alabama Infantry

THE HUNTSVILLE PRESS GAVE MUCH ATTENTION TO the 19th Alabama Infantry encamped within the city limits until September 26, 1861. With measles and mumps rife within the camp, Colonel Joseph Wheeler, who later commanded the cavalry of the Army of Tennessee, ordered his regiment to be moved about five miles north to the Blue Springs Camp Ground. On October 2, 1861, the regular poetry column in *The Democrat*, of Huntsville, honored the 19th Alabama thus:

> "The 'Cherokees' is our name,
> We ask for neither wealth nor fame,
> But Freedom shall our motto be,
> And we'll shout 'DEATH or LIBERTY!'"[1]

At some point before it struck camp and left for Mobile, Alabama, on November 11, 1861, at least four companies of the 19th Alabama were clothed in homespun uniform suits, including an antiquated eight-button "swallow-tailed" coat.

Although while at Huntsville each company of the 19th Alabama was "instructed in the school of the soldier, company, battalion and manual of arms," it did so with borrowed arms.[2] Indeed the Cherokee Mountaineers, Company G, left Canton for Huntsville carrying "private arms—Rifles and Double barrel Shot Guns." The local paper the *Cherokee Mountaineer* commented, "persons having such arms are invited to join this company; or, if they cannot accompany their guns, to loan them to the Government, to be returned or paid for at the close of the war."[3]

One of three unarmed units assigned to reinforce the Gulf Coast defenses within the brigade of Brigadier General L. P. Walker in early November 1861, the 19th Alabama was likely armed while encamped at Mobile. Several members of the Cherokee Rangers, Company I, were photographed holding Model 1841 "Mississippi" rifles with sword bayonets that attached to the barrel by means of a socket at the end of the brass handle made by Horstmann Bros. & Company, of Philadelphia.[4] These men also wore locally made waist belts fastened with harness buckles.[5]

1. *The Democrat* (Huntsville, AL), October 2, 1861, 2:1.

2. *Supplement*, part 2, vol. 1, 520.

3. *Daily Chronicle & Sentinel* (Augusta, GA), August 13, 1861, 3:2, citing the *Cherokee Mountaineer*, August 10, 1861.

4. John M. Murphy and Howard Michael Madaus, *Confederate Rifles & Muskets* (Graphic Publishers, 1996), 503.

5. Private John Craig, 19th Alabama Infantry, Alabama Department of Archives & History, Q4223; Private Parris P. Casey, 19th Alabama Infantry, Library of Congress, Liljenquist Family Collection, LC-DIG-ppmsca-32626; Private Marcus Westbrook, 19th Alabama Infantry, Jack Westbrook collection.

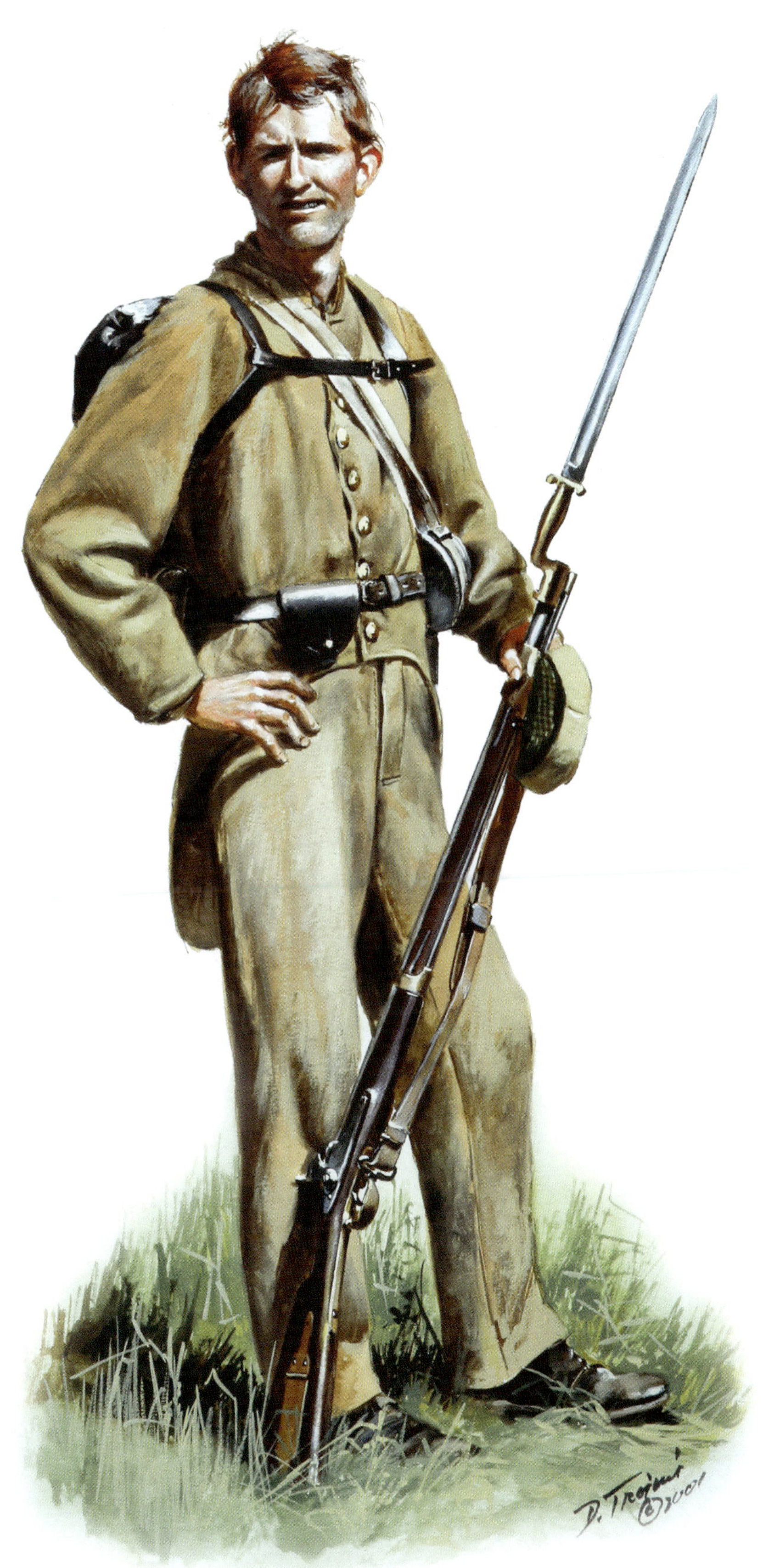

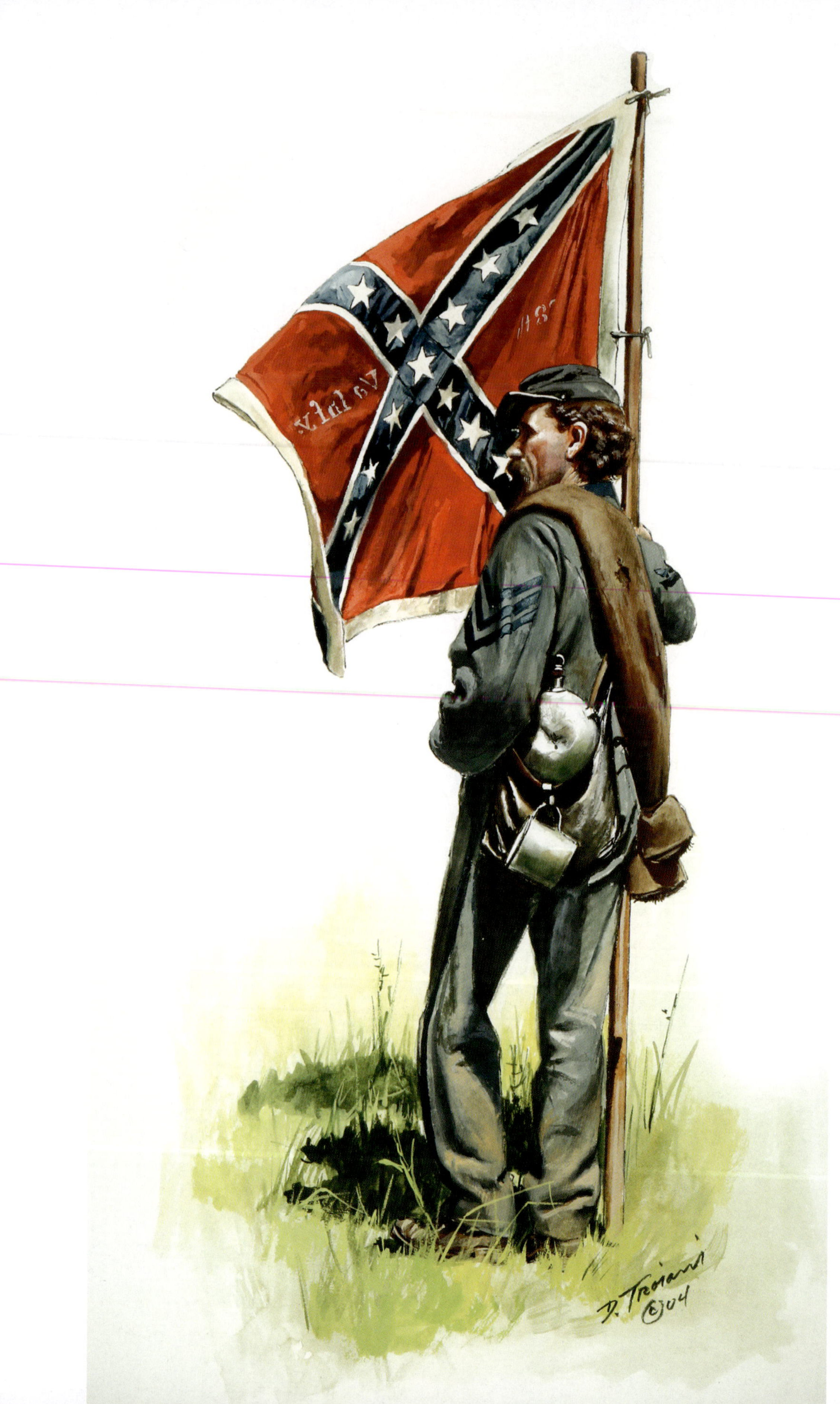

28th Virginia Infantry Color Bearer

THE 28TH VIRGINIA INFANTRY COMPLETED ITS organization at Lynchburg under Colonel Robert T. Preston on November 5, 1861, being recruited in Botetourt, Craig, Bedford, Campbell, and Roanoke counties.[1] Assigned to the 5th Brigade, Army of the Potomac, commanded by Colonel Philip St. George Cocke, it saw its first action at First Manassas, following which it was assigned to General Pickett's, Garnett's, and Hunton's Brigade, Army of Northern Virginia. As a part of Longstreet's corps, Pickett's Division, it fought at Second Manassas, Seven Days Battles, Sharpsburg, Gettysburg, siege of Richmond and Petersburg, and the retreat to Appomattox.

The color sergeant of the 28th Virginia wears a cadet-gray Richmond Depot Type III–style jacket. His trousers have a one-inch dark-blue seam stripe that is commensurate with his rank. A plain forage cap is also in cadet gray. His equipment includes of a plain tinned, heavy-gauge copper canteen of Confederate manufacture, an India rubber haversack, a tin cup, and a brown blanket roll, which likely contained extra clothing and personal items.

The Richmond Clothing Department issued third type battle flags to the units of Pickett's Division, Army of Northern Virginia, a few weeks prior to the Battle of Gettysburg. Made of bunting, those issued to infantry regiments were approximately forty-right inches square. As shown on the flag of the 28th Virginia, they had thirteen white cotton cambric stars in a blue saltire with a two-inch white bunting border. They were marked with a white-painted unit designation on the obverse side only of their red quadrants.[2]

The flag of the 28th Virginia was captured during the charge toward Cemetery Ridge at Gettysburg on July 3, 1863. Color Sergeant John J. Eakin relinquished it after being severely wounded three times in the upper arm and hand. The flag was grasped by an unknown private who was immediately shot, following which commanding officer Colonel Robert Allen grabbed it and was fatally wounded. The flag was next grabbed by Second Lieutenant John A. J. Lee, Company C, who stepped on top of the Union wall on Cemetery Ridge and began waving it. The flag staff was then shot in two, but Lee retrieved the flag and continued to wave it even after also being wounded. He was taken prisoner by Private Marshall Sherman, Company C, 1st Minnesota Infantry.[3]

Based on his own account, Private Sherman ran directly toward Lieutenant Lee and, holding his bayonet inches from the Confederate officer's chest, shouted, "Throw down that flag or I'll run you through," following which Lee surrendered and handed over the flag. Sherman was awarded the Medal of Honor for this action. According to another account by Private Daniel Bond, Company F, 1st Minnesota, the flag was discovered resting unguarded against a tree, and Sherman grasped it more quickly than Bond could.[4] Whatever the truth of the matter, the capture of the flag of the 28th Virginia was part of what became known as "the High Tide" of the Confederacy.

---

1. Lee A. Wallace Jr., *A Guide to Virginia Military Organizations* (H. E. Howard, Inc., 1986), 111.
2. Howard Madaus Collection, US Army Heritage and Education Center, Carlisle, PA.
3. *ORs*, series I, vol. 27, part 1, 425.
4. *Roanoke Times*, July 4, 2000, 1:34.

4th Texas Infantry, Hood's Division, 1863

RECRUITED IN TEXAS DURING JULY AND AUGUST of 1861, the 4th Texas Infantry completed its organization at Richmond, Virginia, on September 30, 1861. In a departure from tradition, the Confederate War Department appointed the field officers rather than allowing the men to elect them. As a result, Robert T. P. Allen, ex-superintendent of the Bastrop Military Academy, was selected to command the regiment. His harsh discipline soon made him very unpopular, and he resigned in October 1861, being replaced as colonel by West Point graduate and professional soldier John Bell Hood.[1]

As part of the Texas Brigade, the regiment fought in Hood's Division, Army of Northern Virginia, through the Seven Days Battles and at Second Bull Run, South Mountain, Sharpsburg, and Fredericksburg in 1862. At Sharpsburg, 57 of the regiment's men were killed, 130 wounded, and 23 captured, its worst losses of the war. Following the wounding of Hood at Gettysburg on July 2, 1863, the Texas Brigade became split, with the 4th and 5th Texas involved in the unsuccessful attack on Little Round Top. Transferred to the Western Theater with Longstreet's corps, the Texas Brigade fought at Chickamauga and Wauhatchie, before being transferred back east to play its part against Grant's Overland Campaign of 1864. Much reduced in numbers, the 4th Texas surrendered 15 officers and 145 men at Appomattox, having lost throughout the war 256 men, who were killed or mortally wounded; 486 men were wounded in battle, and 161 deaths were from disease.

This first sergeant of the 4th Texas wears a butternut-colored wool jean jacket with a medium-blue wool kersey collar and cuffs of the type produced by the Columbus Depot and received by the regiment while in Tennessee in 1863.[2] Unusually the cuffs were slightly pointed rather than straight. His tattered plain trousers are of the same color. His hat has a metal five-pointed "Lone Star" attached. His blanket roll has a waterproof cover, and accoutrements include a Confederate-made cartridge box, a cap pouch, a canvas haversack, and a wooden drum canteen. He is armed with an Enfield rifle musket.

1. Crute, *Units of the Confederate States Army*, 325.
2. NARA, M323, CMSR, 4th Texas Infantry, Richard M. Bomar, 62; Thomas C. Buffington, 65; Mat Beasley, 59.

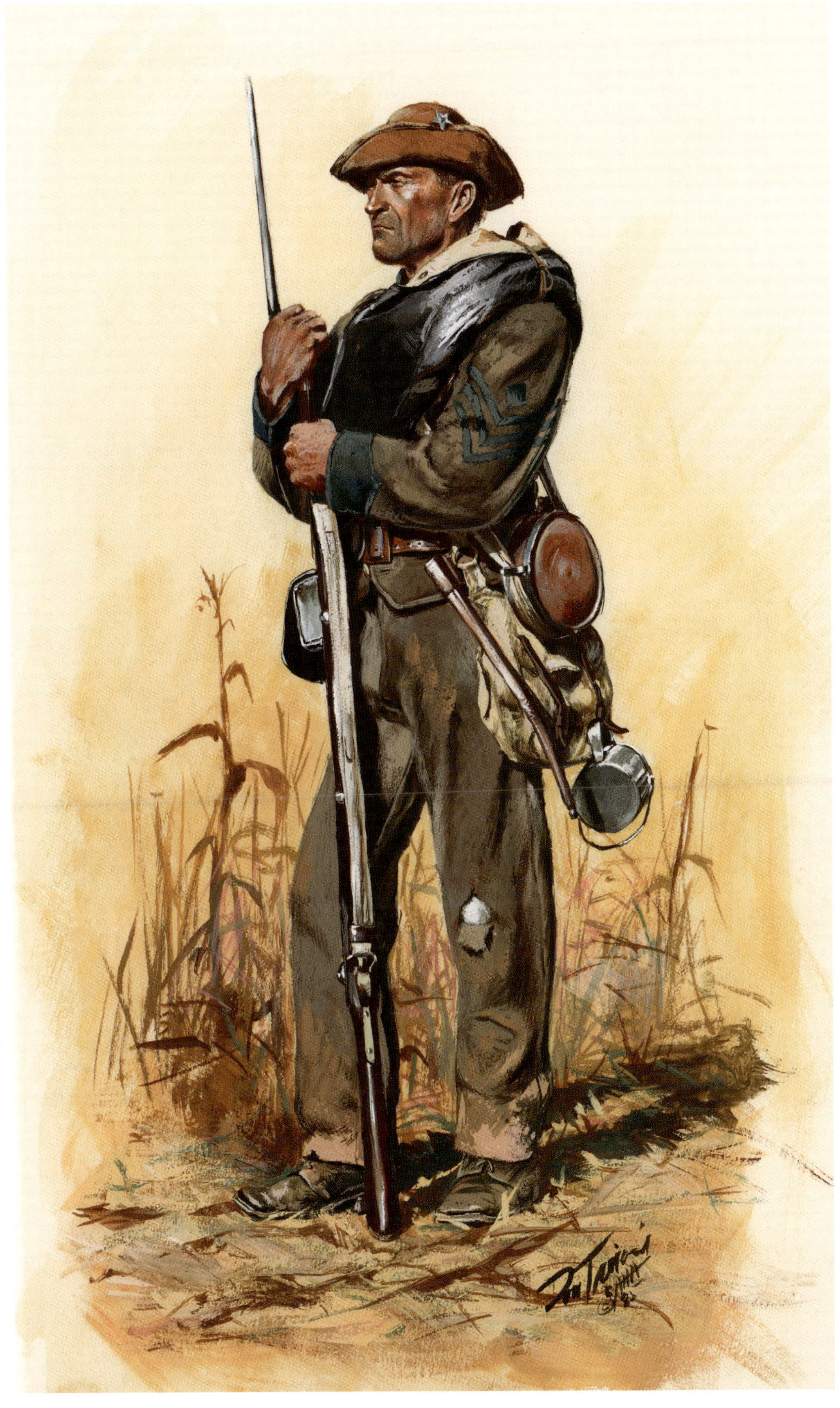

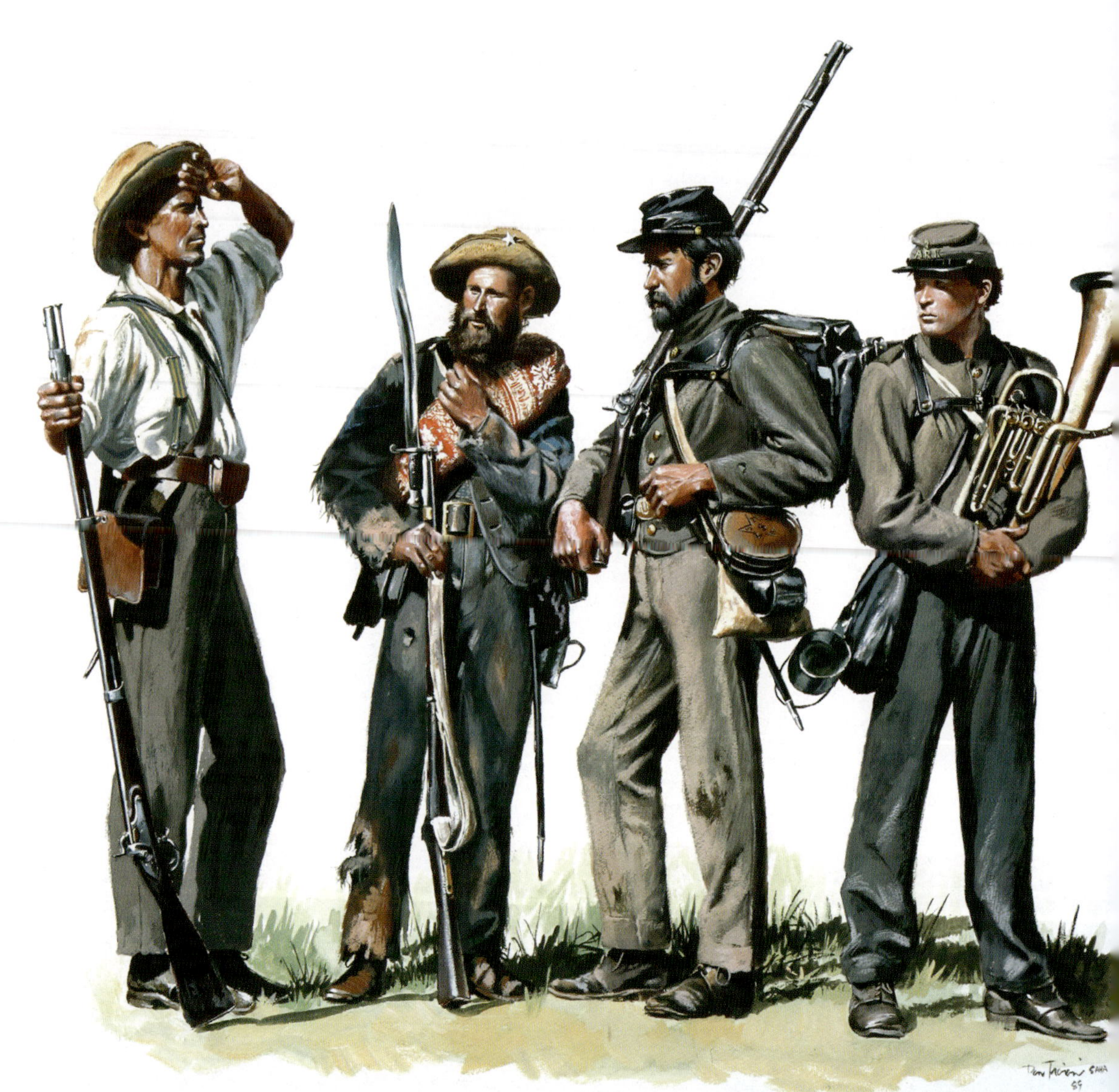

The Texas Brigade

COMPOSED OF THE ONLY TEXAS UNITS TO FIGHT IN THE Eastern Theater of the war, the Texas Brigade was organized on October 22, 1861, primarily through the efforts of politician and congressman John Allen Wilcox, who remained as the brigade's patron until his death in 1864. Command of the brigade was given to John Bell Hood on March 2, 1862; hence, it was often afterward called "Hood's Texas Brigade." Consisting of the 1st, 4th, and 5th Texas Infantry, it was joined by the 18th Georgia Infantry from November 1861, and the Hampton's Legion Infantry from June 1862, both of which were replaced by the 3rd Arkansas after the Battle of Sharpsburg in September 1862.

The uniforms worn by the Texas brigade in 1863 were much the same as those in general use in the Eastern Confederate army. In order to ensure as regular a supply as possible, each of the four regiments maintained its own separate depot in Richmond, where clothing was stored until needed. Prior to the summer of 1863, each unit was well provided for. The campaign that led to Gettysburg took its toll on the clothing and equipment of the Texas Brigade. Most items were resupplied when the brigade returned to Virginia and before it left with Longstreet's First Corps to temporarily reinforce the Army of the Tennessee.[1]

The four enlisted men depicted represent from left to right, the 1st, 5th, and 4th Texas as well as a musician of the 3rd Arkansas. They appear as they would have just prior to the attack on the Federal left flank on July 2, 1863. The private of the 1st Texas has removed the uniform coat he was issued earlier in the year, and wears his equipment, which includes a russet leather cartridge box, over a white cotton shirt. Distinguished by blue chevrons on the upper arms of his tattered cadet-gray jacket, the sergeant of the 5th Texas carries a homemade blanket roll and has a large frame buckle fastening his waist belt. He holds a short Enfield rifle with a saber bayonet that his unit received in 1861. During the first few months of 1863, the 4th Texas had received an extensive issue of clothing, which included forage caps with rain covers.[2] His wooden drum canteen bears a star with letters spelling Texas in its five points and surrounding the regimental number "4." The 3rd Arkansas musician wears a Richmond Depot Type 2-style–jacket, but with black facings on the collar, and cadet-gray trousers. His gray cap has the brass letters "ARK" and the numeral "3" at the front. He cradles an upright baritone or bass saxhorn with three string rotary valves.[3]

The arms carried by much of the brigade varied, consisting of .57- or .58-caliber rifle muskets. The 1st Texas received and carried a mixture of .69-caliber smoothbore muskets and rifle muskets, with the former continuing in service well into 1864.

While the brigade served in the Department of Tennessee during early 1864, and away from its clothing supply depots in Richmond, it was necessary to detail several shoemakers from the 4th Texas to make shoes and boots from leather obtained by the regimental quartermaster. During this period, for the 4th Texas alone, the detailed men manufactured 259 pairs of shoes and 22 pairs of boots.[4] The Texas Brigade returned east with Longstreet to participate in the fateful campaigns leading to Appomattox Court House on April 9, 1865.

---

1. Harold B. Simpson, *Hood's Texas Brigade: Lee's Grenadier Guard* (Texian Press, 1970).

2. NARA, record group 109, M323, CMSR, 4th Texas Infantry, Benjamin Reynolds, 25.

3. Robert Garofalo & Mark Elrod, *A Pictorial History of the Civil War Era* (Pictorial Histories Publishing Company, 1985), 21.

4. NARA, M323, CMSR, 4th Texas Infantry, Joseph D. Wade, 25.

Color Bearer of the 1st Texas Infantry

RECRUITED ACROSS TEN COUNTIES IN TEXAS, THE 1st Texas Battalion was formed in Richmond, Virginia, with Lieutenant Colonel Louis T. Wigfall in command. Expanded to twelve companies in August 1861, with Wigfall promoted to colonel, the unit was designated the 1st Texas Infantry and assigned to the Texas Brigade on October 22, 1861.

The 1st Texas played a critical role in defending Richmond during the Seven Days Battles in 1862. At Gaines Mill, when the regimental color bearer reached Federal lines he waved his flag from the breastworks to urge his comrades on. On September 17, 1862, the 1st Texas fought at Sharpsburg, the bloodiest day in American history. With Lee's army retreating, the 1st Texas was ordered to counterattack in a place known simply as "the Cornfield."[1] In the course of two hours, the regiment lost 186 of its 226 brought to the field. This amounted to an 82.3 percent casualty rate, which was the highest endured during the war by any unit, of the North or South. Eight Texans were killed carrying their flag before it was captured, with its staff shot in two, by a Federal soldier, who was awarded the Congressional Medal of Honor for his deed.[2]

Presented to the 1st Texas when it was organized in the summer of 1861, the Lone Star state flag depicted is reputed to have been made by the wife and daughter of Louis T. Wigfall. Measuring 55½ inches on the fly by 56 inches on the staff, its fringed field was made from three pieces of silk, with the blue vertical bar next to the staff having a five-pointed white silk star appliqued to its center, and the white-painted battle honors "SEVEN PINES" above and "GAINES FARM" below. In the remaining field, the battle honor "ELTHAM'S LANDING" was painted in gold-and-red lettering in the upper white bar, and "MALVERN HILL" in gold-and-green lettering in the lower red bar.

The flag was returned to the State of Texas on March 25, 1905, and until 1920 hung in the chamber of the Texas House of Representatives. Today it is preserved in the collection of the Texas State Library and Archives.[3]

1. Crute, *Units of the Confederate States Army*, 321–22.

2. *Memphis Daily Appeal*, October 31, 1862, 2:5.

3. Texas State Library and Archives Commission, Austin, TX, catalog no. M-13-80.

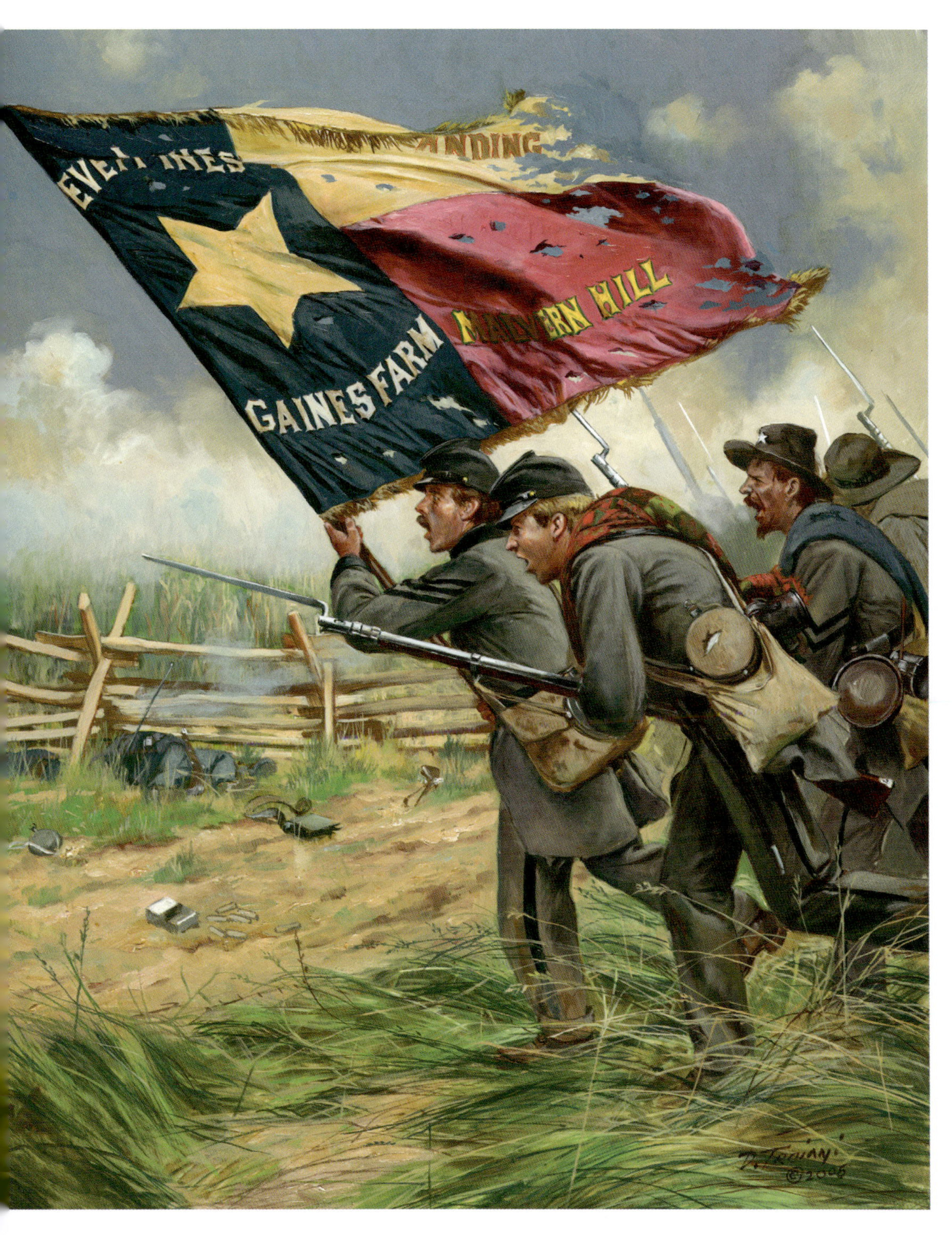
SEVEN PINES
GAINES FARM
MALVERN HILL
LANDING

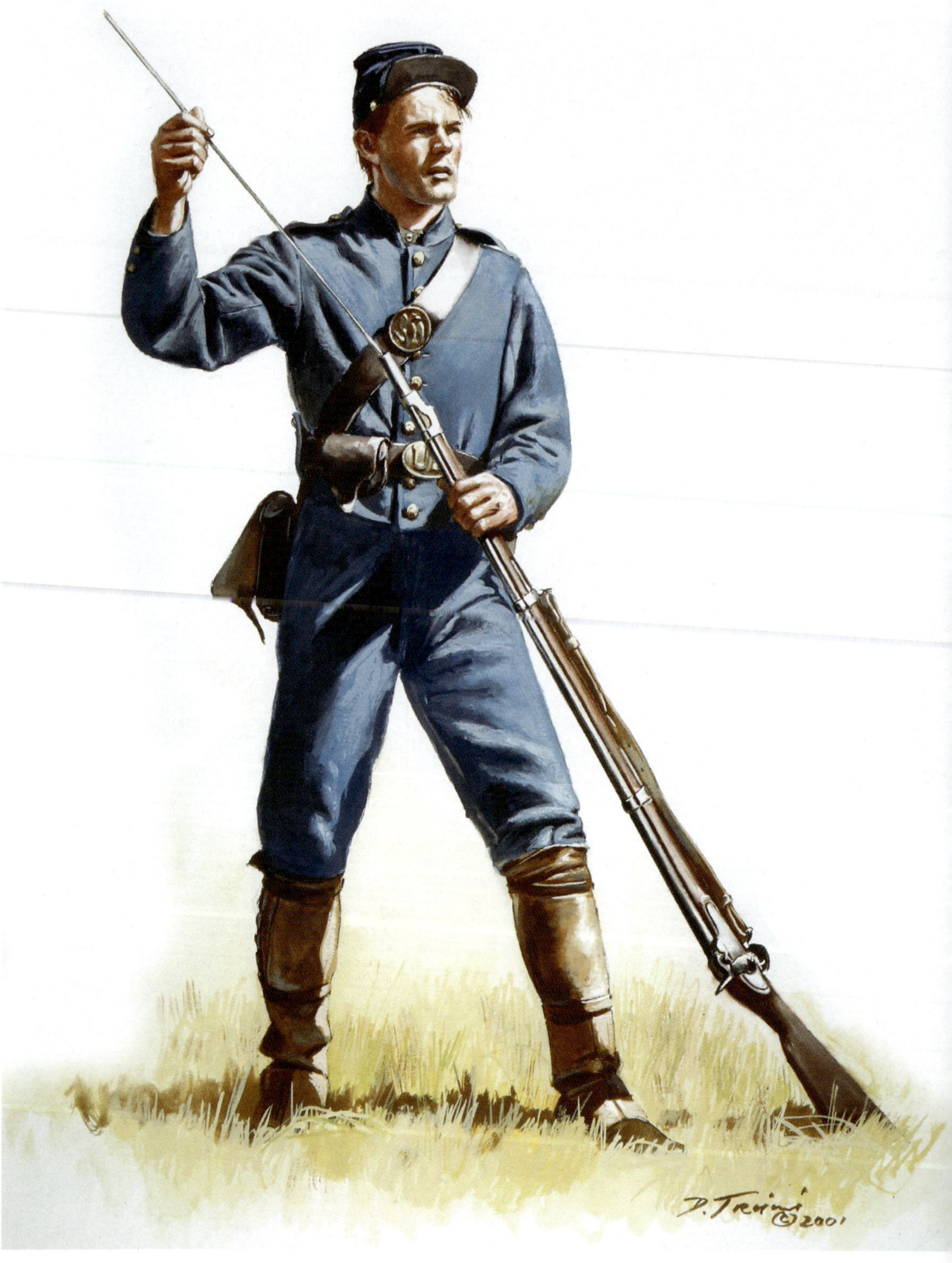

62nd Pennsylvania Infantry

ORIGINALLY KNOWN AS THE SECOND REGIMENT, Scott Legion, and designated the 33rd Pennsylvania Infantry, the regiment commanded by Mexican War veteran Samuel W. Black was organized at Pittsburgh beginning on July 4, 1861, and was mustered in on August 31, 1861. The unit was redesignated the 62nd Pennsylvania on November 18, 1861, after the 4th Reserves took precedence as the 33rd regiment. Attached to General George W. Morrell's Brigade, Fitz John Porter's Division, Army of the Potomac, the original 33rd Pennsylvania was garrisoned around Washington, DC, near Fort Corcoran until October 1861 and, then, as the 62nd Pennsylvania, at Falls Church, Virginia, until March 1862.[1]

In early August 1861, Colonel Black requested the same style of uniform as supplied to the first Scott Legion. The army contracted with the firm of George W. Colladay in Philadelphia, and, by August 31, 1861, an initial delivery of 247 pairs of sky-blue trousers and 449 sky-blue jackets was received. According to Major Jacob B. Sweitzer, the 33rd Pennsylvania received its uniforms on September 3, 1861; the uniforms consisted of "a pair of sky-blue pantaloons and a neat roundabout or jacket of the same color and material, and a dark blue cap besides a good serviceable overcoat, shoes, underclothing etc. Companies L [Chambers Zouaves] and M wore a dark blue blouse which distinguished them from the others as the flanking companies or skirmishers for the regiment."[2] A further description of the uniform was given by Private James Graham, who wrote, "The dress we are to ware [sic] on our intended march [is] to be our old sky-blue uniform repaired (they look rather bad but are as good as new), our shoes are low with leather gaiters and leather leggins [sic] over them reaching up to the knees."[3]

The private depicted wears a plain light-blue jacket, or "roundabout," based on the Pattern 1854 mounted service jacket, with shoulder straps and a single belt loop. Matching wool kersey trousers are tucked into knee-high leather leggings over gaiters. The leather visor on his dark-blue, 1861-type forage cap is worn pointing up. He is ramming a charge home in his Model 1842, .69-caliber Springfield musket. Black leather accoutrements include a Pattern 1839 cartridge box suspended from a shoulder belt with a round "eagle" breast plate; a Pattern 1850 Watervliet cap pouch; and Pattern 1839 "US" oval plate fastening his waist belt.

1. Samuel P. Bates, *History of the Pennsylvania Volunteers, 1861–5*, vol. 1 (Broadfoot, 1993), 636–64; and vol. 3, 451–88.

2. National Archives, record group 92, entry 2194, book 3; and record group 94, regimental books, 62nd Pennsylvania Infantry.

3. Colonel William H. Bartlett, *Aunt and the Soldier Boys* (Moore's Graphic Arts, 1970), 12.

42nd Pennsylvania Volunteers (Bucktails)

THE 42ND PENNSYLVANIA INFANTRY ORIGINATED AS THE Kane Rifles and was recruited in northwestern Pennsylvania in April 1861 by active abolitionist Thomas L. Kane. The regiment was accepted for three-year service by Governor Andrew G. Curtin as the 13th Pennsylvania Reserves. The original Kane Rifles, consisting of 350 "rugged backwoodsmen" armed with their own personal rifles, arrived in Harrisburg on May 2, 1861, clad in "red shirts trimmed with white and blue." Actually composed of the McKean County Rifles, Elk County Rifles, and Cameron County Rifles, these volunteers were also distinguished by a deer tail attached to their hats and caps.

According to their regimental history, Private James Landrigan, of the McKean County Rifles, noticed a deer's hide hanging outside a butcher's shop opposite the Bennett House at Smethport where Kane had his headquarters. Crossing the street, he pulled out a knife, cut off the tail, and stuck it in his cap. Upon the man's return to headquarters, Kane noticed the appendage on his headgear and announced that the force he was recruiting should be known as "Bucktails."[1]

On June 18, 1861, the Kane Rifles formed the nucleus of the Kane Rifle Regiment, or 1st Pennsylvania Rifles, and were accepted for three-year service by Governor Andrew G. Curtin as the 13th Pennsylvania Reserves, or the 42nd Pennsylvania Volunteer Infantry. A second and third regiment of Bucktails, the 149th and 150th Pennsylvania, were raised in 1862.

The 42nd Pennsylvania wore standard uniforms consisting of dark-blue sack coats and forage caps and dark-blue trousers, the latter being replaced by sky-blue kersey. Disappointed in having their personal rifles replaced by smoothbore muskets converted to percussion, by August 1861, the regiment received Enfield and Springfield rifle muskets. In the summer of 1862, these were replaced by double-set trigger Sharps Model 1859 breech-loading rifles, in acknowledgement of their rifleman status. These were replaced in 1864 by Spencer repeating rifles.[2]

This well-equipped first sergeant wears a deer's tail attached to the chin strap of his cap. Rank is indicated by three sky-blue chevrons, above which is a lozenge on upper sleeves and a one-inch–wide dark-blue stripe on his trousers, the latter being tucked into thick woolen socks to protect his ankles and chins. His equipment includes a tin-plated, oblate spheroid canteen with a gray wool cover and a leather strap, a waterproof haversack with a tin cup hanging from its buckle, and a nonrigid knapsack with a blanket roll. A leather sling is attached to his Sharps rifle.

---

1. Howard Thomson, *History of the Bucktails: Kane Rifle Regiment of the Pennsylvania Reserve Corps* (Electric Printing Company, 1906), 11.

2. "Long Endure: The Civil War Period, 1852–1867," in *Military Uniforms in America*, vol. III, eds. John R. Elting and Michael J. McAfee (Presidio Press, 1982), 70–71.

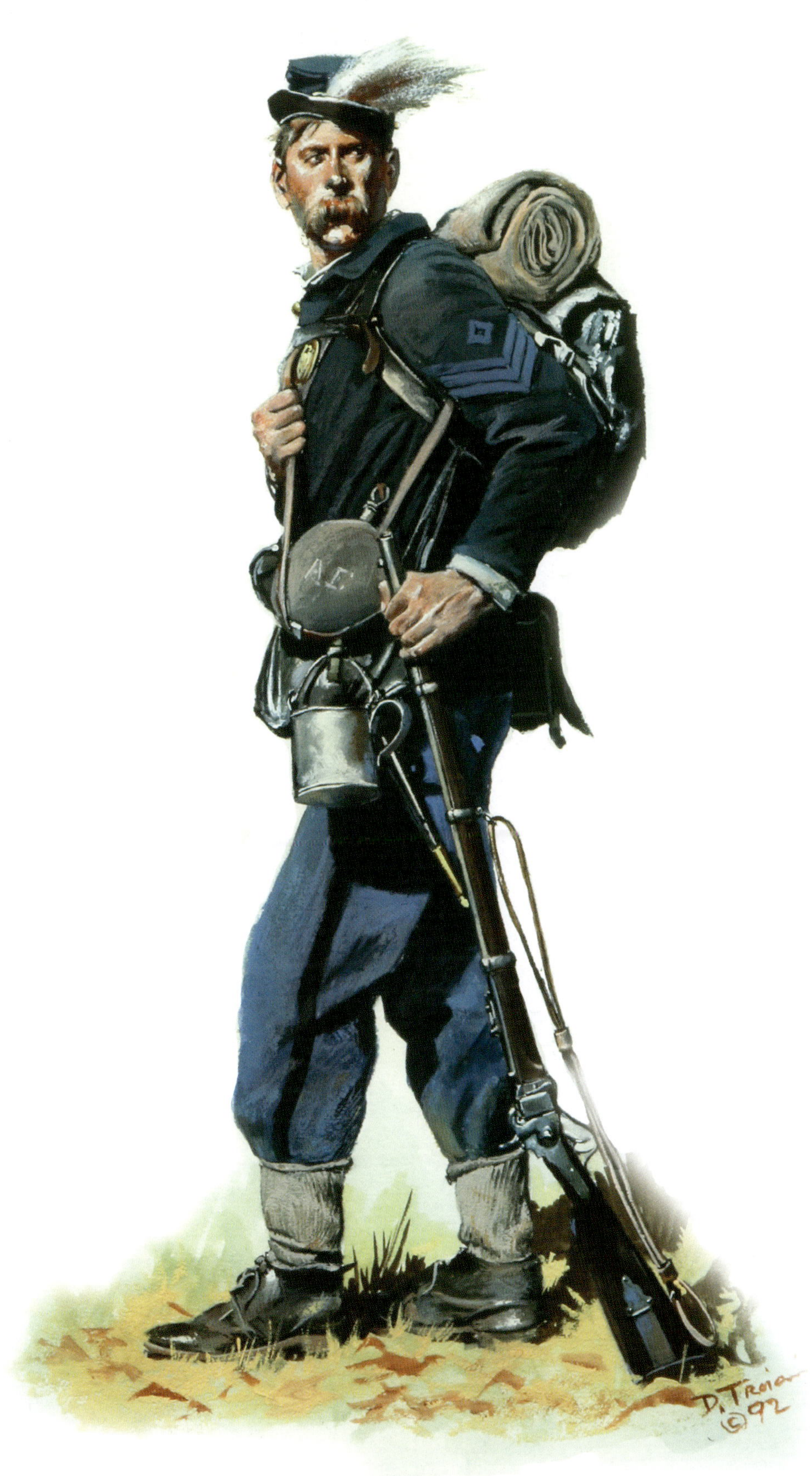

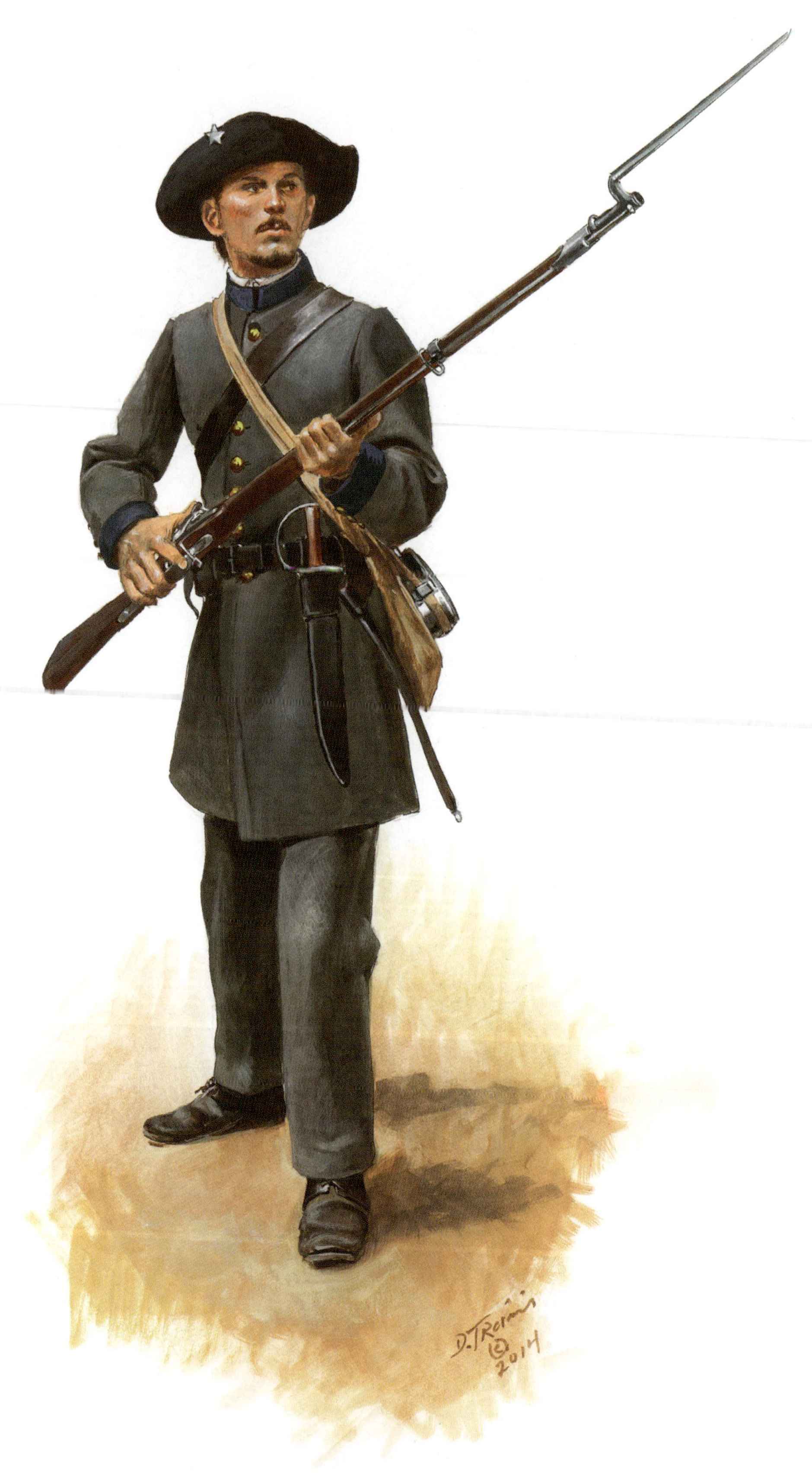

23rd Arkansas Infantry, 1862

THE 23RD ARKANSAS INFANTRY WAS ORGANIZED AT Memphis, Tennessee, on April 25, 1862, when Lieutenant Colonel Charles W. Adams's infantry battalion of five companies was combined with two companies of Major Simon P. Hughes's infantry battalion, and Captain Mitchell A. Adair's independent company. Appointed to command the regiment, Colonel Adams had served as a major and quartermaster of Arkansas state troops under Brigadier General Thomas Bradley. When the Provisional Army of Arkansas was dissolved and incorporated into the Confederate States Army later in 1861, Adams was appointed colonel of the 23rd Arkansas. The regiment was initially assigned to Brigadier General Darney H. Maury's Brigade of Major General Samuel Jones's Division, Army of the West, with Major General Earl Van Dorn commanding.[1] Following the Conscription Act of April 16, 1862, the 23rd Arkansas reenlisted "for 3 years or the war" at Camp Priceville, near Tupelo, Mississippi, with Colonel Oliver P. Lyles in command. The unit participated in the Iuka-Corinth campaign, after which it was assigned to Brigadier General William Beall's brigade, of Major General Franklin Gardner's Department of Mississippi and East Louisiana, and assigned to the garrison at Port Hudson, Louisiana.

At the end of the siege of Port Hudson on July 9, 1863, the officers of the 23rd Arkansas were sent to Johnson's Island Military Prison, while the enlisted men were paroled and returned to Arkansas. After being officially exchanged in the spring of 1864, the unit was converted to mounted infantry and took part in Price's Missouri Expedition. The 23rd Arkansas surrendered near Memphis, Tennessee, on May 16, 1865. The remains of the regiment were paroled at Wittsburg, Arkansas, nine days later.

This private of the 23rd Arkansas wears a uniform of the type paid for via the Confederate commutation system and made by local ladies aid societies in Little Rock from cloth fabricated at the manufactory set up at the State Penitentiary by the Military Board of Arkansas, which was established on May 15, 1861. Patterned after the prewar uniform of the US Army, the nine-button gray woolen jeans uniform coat has medium-blue facings on its standing collar and cuffs. The latter have three small buttons attached, with two of the same size on the rear waist. His gray trousers are made from jeans cloth. His black brimmed hat has a white metal, five-pointed star attached, as commonly worn by Mississippians and volunteers from other Southern States.

He is armed with a Model 1816/1822 musket altered to percussion. His equipment includes a cartridge box, a shoulder strap, a waist belt with a roller buckle, and a bayonet scabbard—all of the type issued to the regiment on May 15, 1862.[2] A large D-guard knife is attached to his waist belt, and an off-white canvas haversack and a tin drum canteen are slung over his shoulder.

---

1. "Louisiana and Arkansas," in *Confederate Military History*, vol. 10, ed. Clement A. Evans (Blue and Grey Press, 1975), 321.
2. NARA, M317, CMSR, Confederate, Arkansas, Charles W. Adams, 33.

2nd Wisconsin Volunteers

ACCEPTED INTO FEDERAL SERVICE FOR THREE YEARS on June 11, 1861, the 2nd Wisconsin Infantry sustained the greatest percentage of battle fatalities of all Northern regiments that fought in the Civil War. Of 1,203 men who served in its ranks, 238 were killed or mortally wounded in battle, amounting to 19.7 percent of its total number.[1] Originally clad in gray uniforms, some of these men were killed by friendly fire at First Bull Run on July 21, 1861.

Conforming to the order issued by Major General George Brinton McClellan in late August 1861, forbidding the purchase of any more gray uniforms for the Union Army, which he called "the rebels' color," the 2nd Wisconsin received blue uniforms while at Camp Kalorama, Washington, DC.[2] In celebration of the occasion, Private John Metcalf of Company G, the Belle City Rifles, wrote to the folks at home, "We are receiving our new clothes this morning. They are made of the regular U.S. cloth, such as the regulars wear, and I think we will make a better appearance than we did with our old ragged clothes."[3]

The uniforms issued consisted of Pattern 1858 frock coats with sky-blue trim on collar and cuffs; plain dark-blue trousers as per 1861 regulations; and black felt dress hats with brim looped up on the left with a Pattern 1858 brass "eagle" plate. Hat trimmings consisted of a Pattern 1858 "looped infantry horn" attached to the front of the crown with a regimental number inset; a single black ostrich feather; and a sky-blue worsted cord.

During the spring of 1862, the 2nd Wisconsin was organized into a brigade with the 6th and 7th Wisconsin and the 19th Indiana under the command of Brigadier General John Gibbon. In order to improve the morale and appearance of his brigade, Gibbon decided to extend the full dress already worn by the 2nd Wisconsin Infantry to the other three regiments with the addition of white canvas leggings.

Tearing the cartridge to load his .54-caliber Lorenz rifle musket, this private of the 2nd Wisconsin is shown as he would have appeared during the action at Turner's Gap, during the Battle of South Mountain, where Gibbon's command earned the nickname "The Iron Brigade." His equipment includes a black waterproof canvas haversack and nonrigid knapsack with blanket roll, plus Pattern 1858 canteen with blue wool cover and white cotton strap. Although in time their frock coats and leggings disappeared, these men clung to their dress hats throughout their service, also becoming known among the Rebels after Second Bull Run as the "Black Hat Brigade."[4]

1. William F. Fox, *Regimental Losses in the American Civil War, 1861–1865* (Albany Publishing Company, 1898), 14.
2. *Boston Herald*, August 22, 1861, 4:1.
3. *Janesville Daily Gazette*, September 28, 1861, 3:2.
4. *Wisconsin State Register* (Portage, WI), October 4, 1862, 2:2.

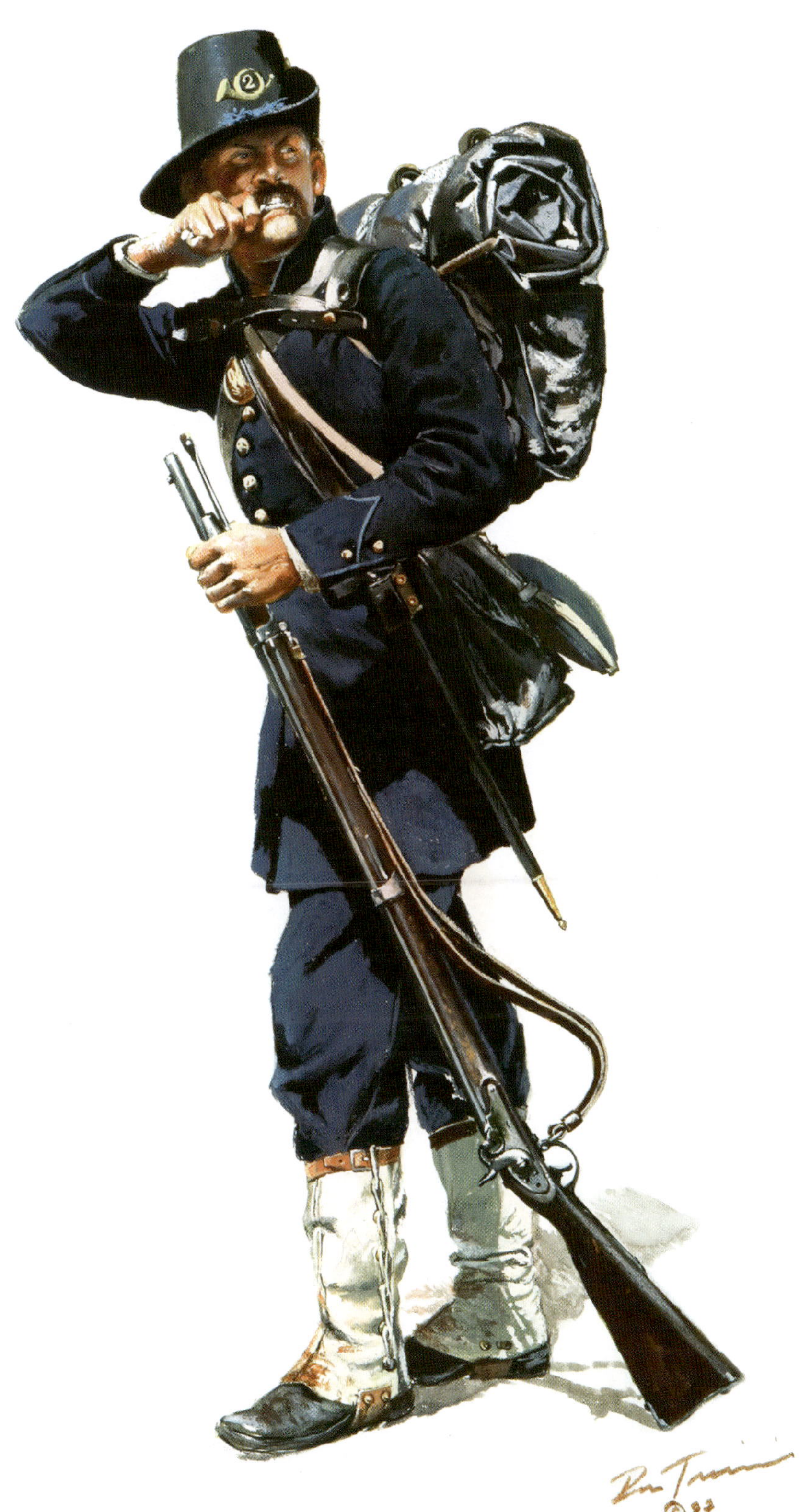

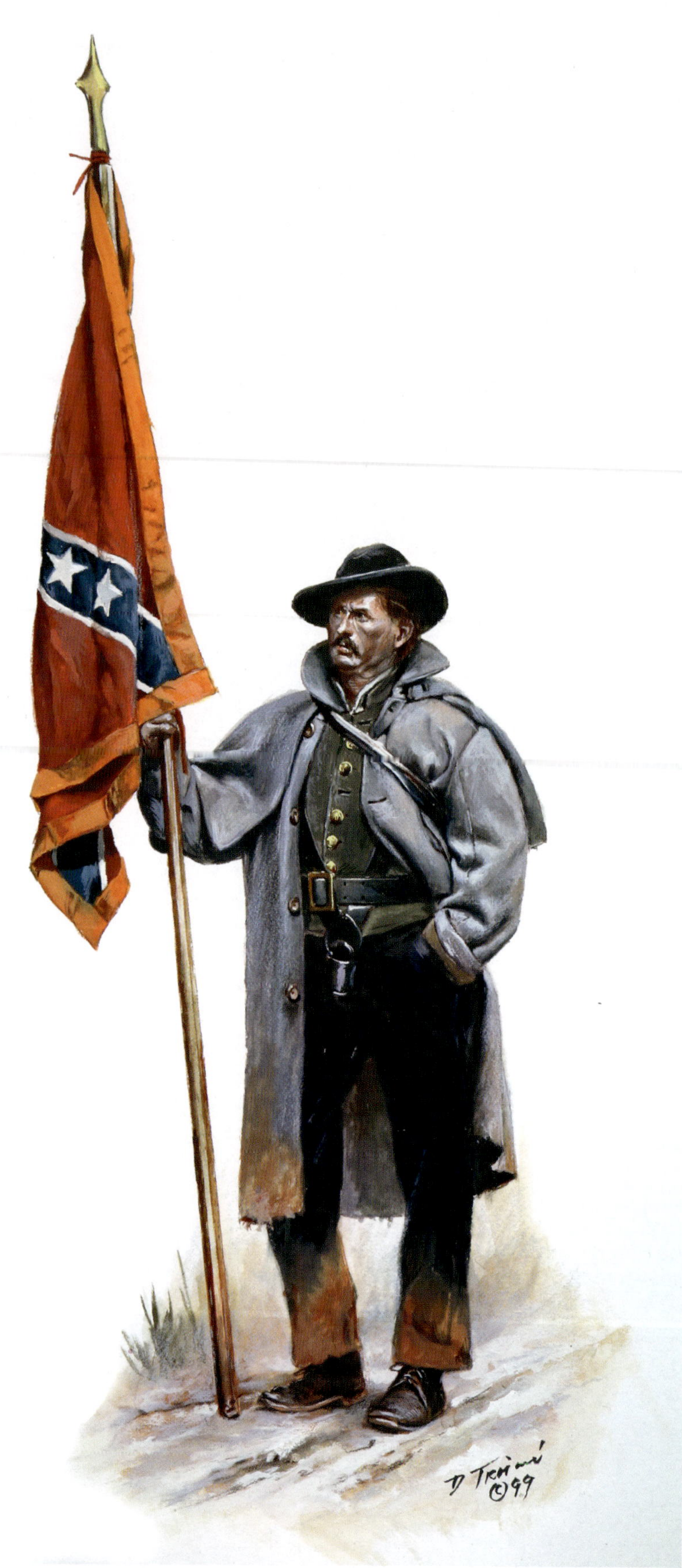

27th Virginia Infantry Color Sergeant, December 1862

ONE OF THE FIVE REGIMENTS THAT CONSTITUTED THE famed "Stonewall Brigade," the 27th Virginia Infantry was organized at Harpers Ferry on May 30, 1861, and was accepted into Confederate service under Colonel William W. Gordon on June 8, 1861. Made up of men from Alleghany, Rockbridge, Monroe, Greenbrier, and Ohio counties in Virginia, the regiment lay on Henry House Hill with the rest of the brigade, which was commanded by Thomas J. Jackson, and leapt up and charged under his command with bayonets fixed, thus turning the tide at the First Battle of Manassas on July 21, 1861, and earning its commander the sobriquet "Stonewall" Jackson. Although Jackson soon went on to higher command, the regiments he originally commanded remained together and gained further glory as the hard-fighting "Stonewall Brigade."[1]

The color sergeant of the 27th Virginia wears a uniform of the type supplied by the Richmond Clothing Bureau beginning in September 1861. His overcoat is of English manufacture and would be needed for the approaching Virginia winter of 1862–1863. His darker-gray woolen jacket is a product of the Richmond Bureau and likely of the second pattern minus the trim on the collar and cuffs. It would, however, have sergeant's black chevrons sewn on the sleeves. Made of wool-cotton cloth known as cassimere, his black trousers are of the type listed in several "Special Requisition" documents found in the records of the regiment.[2] Both hats and caps were issued to Virginia units during the mid- and later stages of the war. His shoes are of English manufacture and among those run through the blockade. His waist belt is fastened with a large brass frame buckle, and a belt with a leather socket for carrying the flag aloft is slung around his neck and secured under his belt.

The flag he holds is of the Second Bunting issue of the battle flag of the Army of Northern Virginia, issued from the Richmond Clothing Bureau beginning in June 1862. Measuring forty-eight inches square and distinguished by an orange wool border, it had a red wool bunting field, a blue bunting cross, and white cotton stars. Attached to a Confederate-issue octagonal staff, it was issued to the 27th Virginia on August 4, 1862, while the regiment was resting and training in camp at Gordonsville, Virginia.

---

1. Lowell Reidenbaugh, *27th Virginia Infantry* (H. E. Howard, Inc., 1993), 9.
2. NARA, M324, CMSR, Lieutenant Jacob Miley, 25; Captain Alfred M. Edgar, 69; and Lieutenant Andrew C. Shawver, 57.

19th Tennessee Regiment, 1862

THE 19TH TENNESSEE INFANTRY WAS FORMED FROM companies of men in the counties of East Tennessee during May and June 1861. Assembled at Knoxville, they were organized into a regiment in the Provisional Army of Tennessee on June 11, 1861, with Colonel David H. Cummings in command. Ordered to go to Cumberland Gap, Virginia, they were mustered into Confederate service on August 15, 1861.[1]

Although the regiment received ample supplies of clothing and equipment from home communities and ladies' aid societies during September and October of 1861, the obsolete flintlock muskets it was issued left much to be desired. Unfortunately the regiment's first major action at Fishing Creek, Kentucky, on January 19, 1862, was unsuited to the arms they carried. Regimental chaplain David Sullins recalled that, "the rain poured down so they could not fire at all. Several of them, after trying repeatedly to fire, just broke their guns over a fence or around a tree, and went off in disgust."[2] With 125 men killed and 404 wounded or missing, the Confederates conducted a nighttime retreat toward Nashville, abandoning large amounts of equipment and supplies.

During the next few months, the tattered clothing of the 19th Tennessee was replaced by that issued via the Nashville Quartermaster Department. Suits supplied were predominantly made up of eight-button frock coats of heavy gray jeans and plain jeans pants of various colors. Also many of the flintlock muskets carried by the 19th Tennessee were exchanged for percussion muskets. Within several weeks those who still carried flintlocks had an opportunity to exchange them for more efficient arms on the battlefield of Shiloh, where the regiment lost about 25 percent of the four hundred men present for duty. After the battle an unidentified member of Company H, commanded by Captain Willie Lowry, wrote, "Our Regiment was perfectly intoxicated with excitement—I thought it was glory enough for one day. I exchanged my gun there and got an Enfield rifle."[3]

Appearing as he would have prior to the action at Shiloh, the enlisted man of the 19th Tennessee in this painting wears a plain eight-button frock coat of gray jeans and brown jeans pants. His military cap is in cadet gray with a black band. He shoulders a Model 1816 flintlock musket and has a large D-guard knife attached via a leather frog to his waist belt. Accoutrements include a Pattern 1857 .69-caliber cartridge box for round ball cartridges and a semirigid black-painted canvas knapsack.

1. *Tennesseans in the Civil War*, part 1, 214–15.
2. David Sullins, *Recollections of an Old Man: Seventy Years in Dixie, 1827–1897* (The King Printing Company, 1910), 212.
3. *The Athens Post*, April 25, 1862, 2:3.

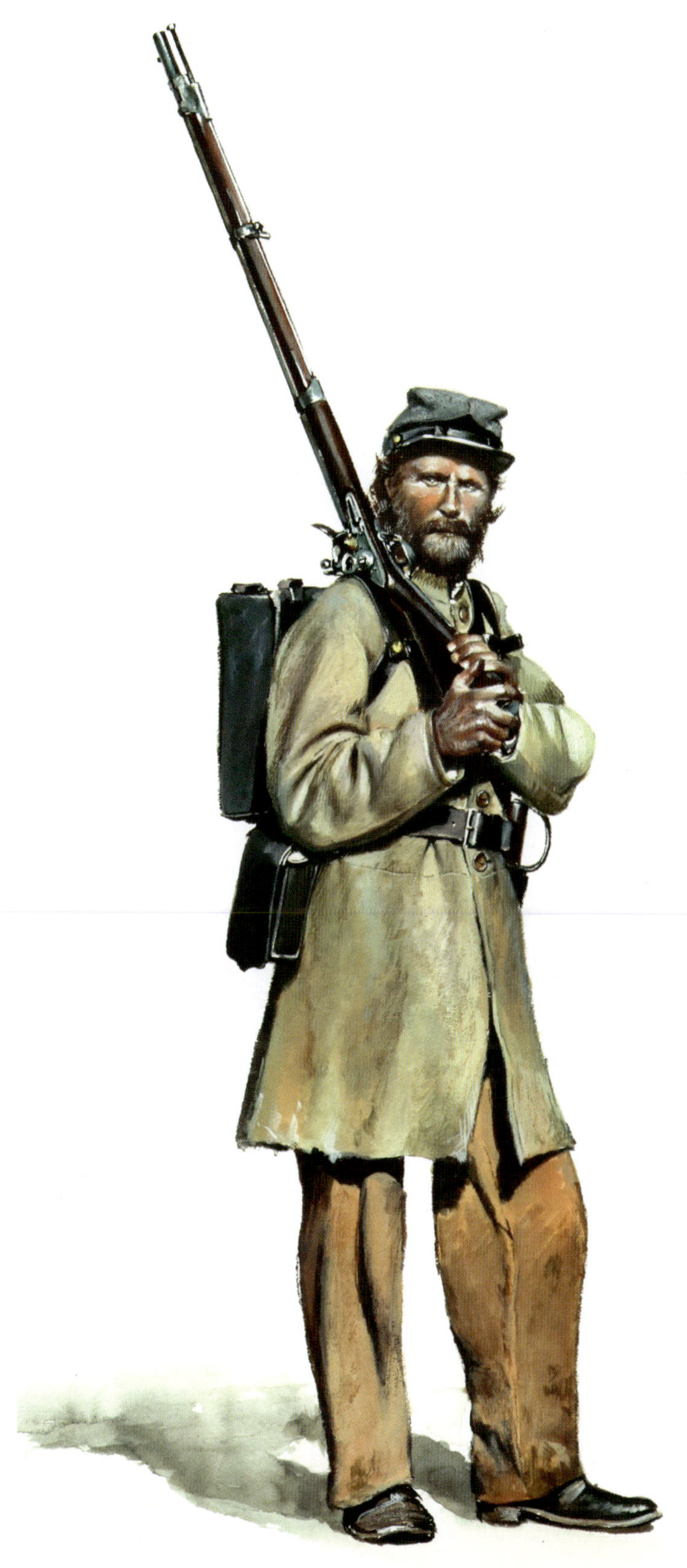

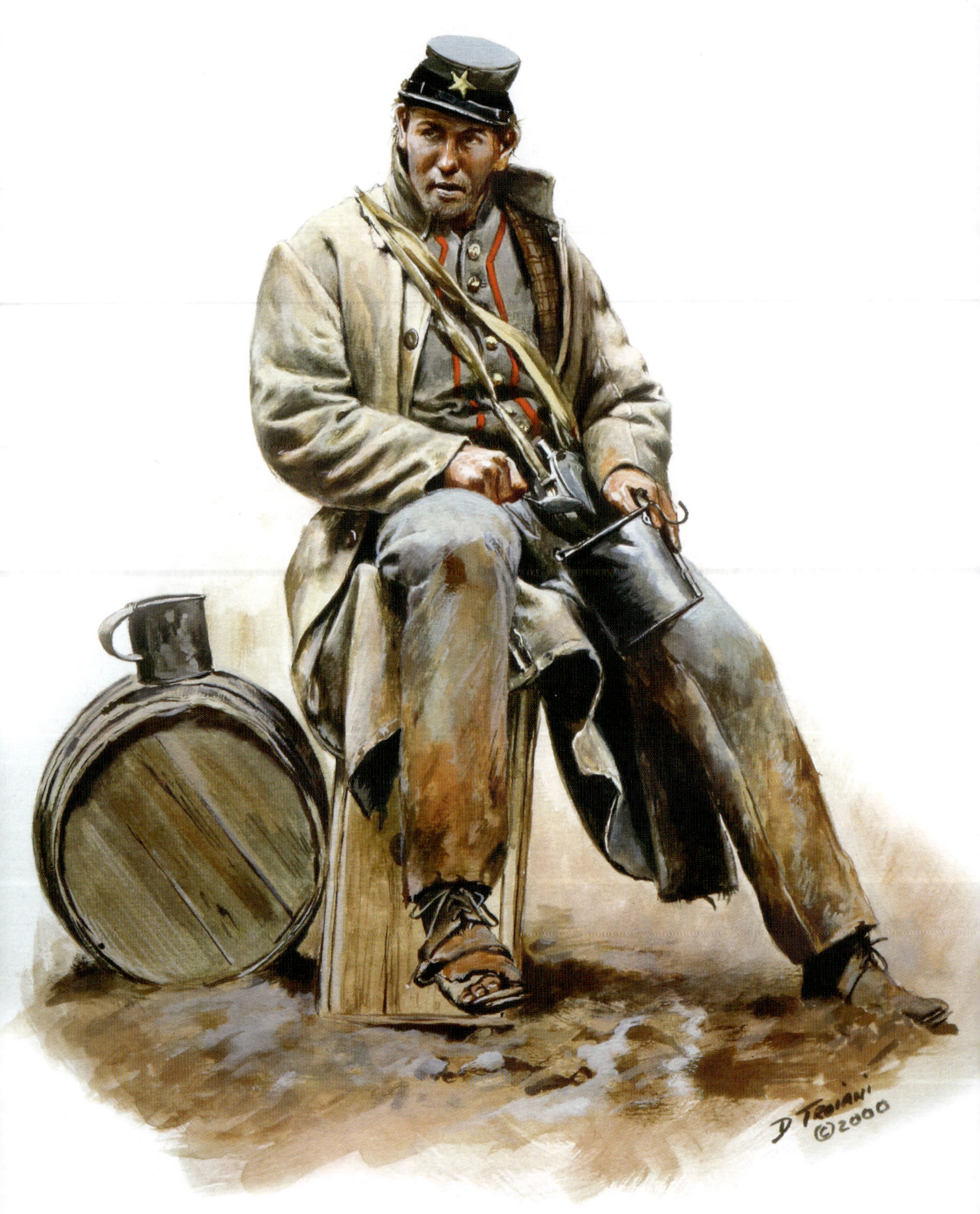

14th Mississippi Infantry, 1862

BASED ON SOME OF THE 650 CONFED-ERATES OF THE 14th Mississippi Infantry captured at Fort Donelson in the Cumberland River on February 16, 1862, this enlisted man bears the crestfallen demeanor of a prisoner of war. On February 15, his regiment was part of the Confederate breakout attempt, twice being ordered to make a bayonet charge to punch through the enemy lines. It succeeded, only to be ordered back to its trenches and required to surrender.

During the four-day siege and battles of Fort Donelson, seventeen members of the 14th Mississippi were killed, eighty-five were wounded, and ten went missing.[1] On Confederate soldiers' arrival at Chicago, Illinois, en route for the Camp Douglas prison camp on February 21, 1862, their clothing was described in the press as "lacking all the characteristics of infantry, cavalry, or artillery costume, in being wholly ununiform in color, cut, fashion and manufacture."[2]

Still showing some semblance of the varied dress supplied to the Fort Donelson garrison during the winter of 1861–1862, this man wears a cap with a five-pointed star at its front, as sported by many Mississippians during the early stages of the war. His jacket has unusual red trim as seen in an image of the three Adams brothers who enlisted in Company I, Monroe Volunteers, 14th Mississippi, on May 30, 1861. He wears a thin "white cotton [osnaburg] overcoat" with check lining and large wooden buttons.[3] His frayed and mud-stained trousers were once of sky blue, and his brogan-style shoes have parted from their soles, revealing bare feet where socks have worn through. His remaining accoutrements consist of a tin drum canteen and a cotton haversack.

Of the journey to Chicago, Private Militon A. Ryan, Company B, 14th Mississippi, recalled, "We had all our cooking utensils with us, camp kettles, skillets, ovens, frying pans, coffee pots, tin pans, tin cups and plates. We had them on our heads, on our backs, swinging from our sides, and in our hands."[4] This Mississippian is spooning some form of sustenance from a tin camp pot while, devoid of coffee, his tin cup rests on a nearby barrel.

After spending about eight months at Camp Douglas, the 14th Mississippi was exchanged on October 16, 1862. Eventually receiving Confederate Quartermaster-issue clothing, it participated in some of the bloodiest battles of the Western Theater, including the siege of Vicksburg, the Atlanta Campaign, and Hood's Nashville Campaign, finally ending its war service near Durham Station, North Carolina, on April 26, 1865.

1. Dunbar Rowland, *Military History of Mississippi, 1803–1898* (The Reprint Company, Publishers, 1978), 222.

2. *Chicago Tribune*, February 22, 1862, 4:2.

3. Thomas M. Arliskas, *Cadet Gray and Butternut Brown: Notes on Confederate Uniforms* (Thomas Publications, 2006), 31.

4. "Reminiscences of Milton Asbury Ryan, Company B, 14th Mississippi Infantry," Carter House Collection, Franklin, Tennessee.

11th Mississippi Color Bearer

IRISH-BORN COLOR SERGEANT WIL-LIAM O'BRIEN, Company C, 11th Mississippi Infantry, fell nobly while bearing the battle flag of his regiment at Gettysburg on July 3, 1863. The 11th Mississippi was established in Corinth, Mississippi, with Colonel William H. Moore in command, and was mustered into service at Lynchburg, Virginia, on May 4, 1861.[1] The regiment saw action at First Manassas in 1861, and in 1862 fought at Seven Pines, Gaines's Mill, Malvern Hill, Second Manassas, South Mountain, and Sharpsburg, in which Colonel Phillip F. Liddell was mortally wounded.

The 11th Mississippi was assigned to guard the Division wagon train near Cashtown, Pennsylvania, on the first day at Gettysburg. They rejoined General Joseph R. Davis's brigade of Heth's division, Third Army Corps, on July 2, which brigade was held in reserve due to its heavy casualties the day before. On the third day, Davis's brigade took part in the charge up the slope to Cemetery Ridge with the 11th regiment on its extreme left flank. When Brockenbrough's brigade, which was to its right, took heavy fire and collapsed well short of the Union lines, the 11th Mississippi became exposed as the left-flank regiment for the remainder of the charge. Color Sergeant O'Brien and a handful of men managed to reach the stone wall and were captured or killed there. Regimental casualties were reported as 32 killed and 170 wounded.[2]

The color sergeant depicted wears a tattered felt hat and a gray Richmond Depot Type II–style jacket, or "roundabout," with shoulder straps and dark-blue chevrons on upper sleeves, underneath which is a gray vest and a white cotton shirt. Plain gray trousers are tucked into thick woolen socks. A brown woolen blanket roll, a waterproof haversack, and a tin cup complete his equipment.

The battle flag carried was captured by First Sergeant Ferdinando Maggi, Company C, 39th New York Infantry, also known as the Garibaldi Guard, who received special recognition for his action. Depicted held by the color sergeant is the flag of the 11th Mississippi, which is of the Third Bunting–pattern issued by the Richmond Clothing Depot prior to the Gettysburg Campaign. Bearing thirteen white cotton cambric five-pointed stars on its dark blue saltire or St. Andrew's cross, it measured approximately 48 inches square with a 1¾-inch white bunting border on three sides. The battle honors "MANASSAS," "SEVEN PINES," "GAINES FARM," and "MALVERN HILL" are painted in yellow-gold stylized Gothic lettering on its red quadrants. It is secured to a plain staff via ties through three whipped eyelets that pierce the two-inch–wide white bunting border on the hoist edge.[3]

The captured flag was sent with thirty others by Major General George G. Meade to Brigadier General Lorenzo Thomas, Adjutant-General, Washington, DC, on July 10, 1863. It was transferred to the Confederate Memorial Literary Society (Museum of the Confederacy) in 1906 as War Department capture no. 039.[4] It is held today in the collection of the American Civil War Museum at Tredegar, Virginia.

---

1. Rowland, *Military History of Mississippi*, 53–55.
2. Rowland, *Military History of Mississippi*, 56.
3. Howard Madaus Collection, US Army Heritage and Education Center, Carlisle, PA.
4. *ORs*, series I, vol. 27, part 1, 85.

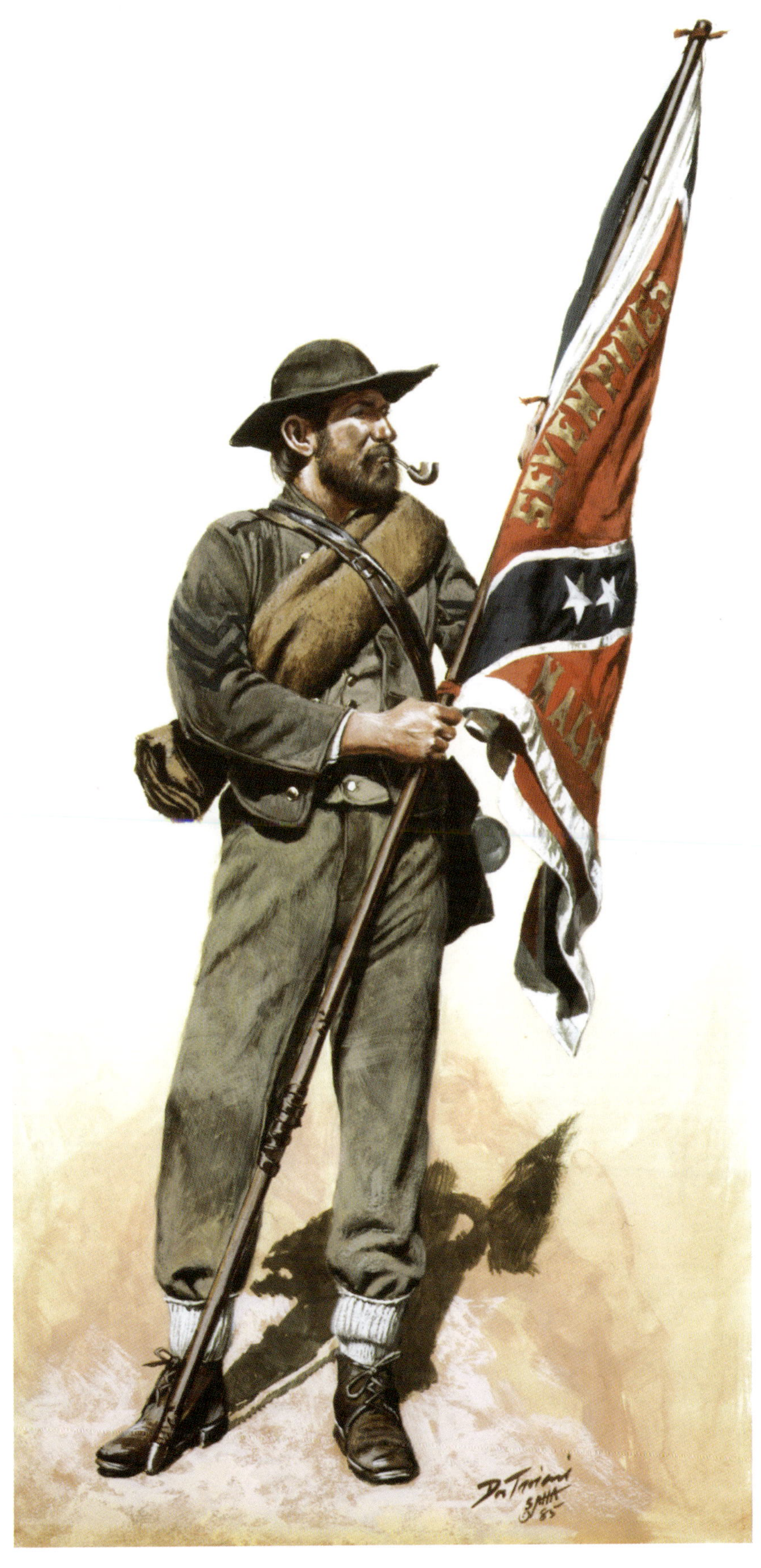

SEVEN PINES
MALV

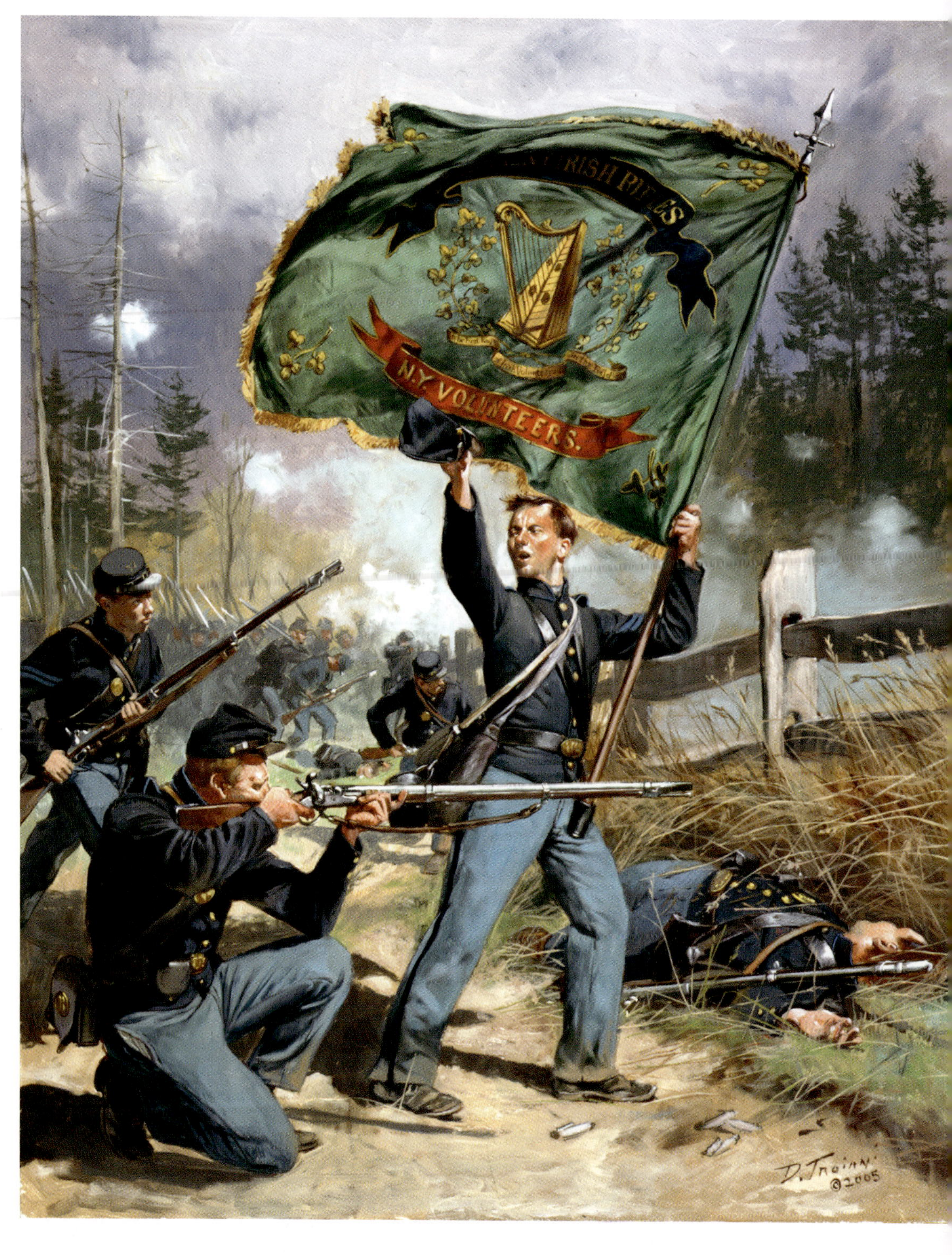
IRISH RIFLES
N.Y. VOLUNTEERS.

37th New York (Irish Rifles)

DECLARED "THE CRACK IRISH REGIMENT IN the field," following the return of the 69th New York State Militia from three months' service on August 3, 1861, the 37th New York Infantry, or Irish Rifles, had been mustered in for two years in New York City on June 6 and 7, 1861, with the 75th New York State Militia forming its nucleus.[1] Departing New York on June 23 for Washington, DC, it participated in the first movement to Manassas, Virginia, in the Reserve Brigade of McDowell's Army, following which it went into winter quarters near Bailey's Crossroads. Assigned to the 3rd Brigade, 1st Division, III Corps, in March 1862, it embarked for Fortress Monroe following which it was involved in siege operations before Yorktown and Williamsburg, sustaining 95 killed, wounded, or missing in the latter engagement. Following this, the regiment saw action at Second Bull Run and Fredericksburg. Its heaviest losses were at Chancellorsville in May 1863, when a further 222 officers and men were killed or wounded or went missing. The regiment was mustered out at New York City on June 22, 1863.

Showing elements of the 37th New York rallying around their flag at Chancellorsville after a surprise Confederate attack on May 3, 1863, the color sergeant holds the green silk regimental flag aloft. Measuring 71½ inches on the fly by 58 inches on the staff, this was presented to the regiment on June 23, 1861, accompanied by two green silk guide flags, which also bore a representation of the Irish Harp.[2] The Irishmen are uniformed in New York State–issue jackets with sky-blue trim around the collars and shoulder straps, sky-blue trousers, and dark-blue forage caps, and are armed with Model 1842 muskets.

1. *New York Daily Herald*, August 10, 1861, 8:5.
2. *New York Daily Herald*, June 23, 1861, 5:1.

The Irish Brigade Band

AT THE OUTBREAK OF THE CIVIL WAR, CITY AND town brass bands throughout the North were in great demand to serve as regimental bands in the Union army. An inspection of some of the camps by the US Sanitary Commission during the fall of 1861 revealed that 143 out of 200 regiments examined, or nearly 75 percent, had bands.[1] However, by the closing months of 1861, the Federal government began to experience financial difficulties and soon realized that it could no longer afford for volunteer regiments to have bands. The first adverse order affecting regimental bands was issued by the War Department in October 1861, which order forbade the mustering in of new regimental bands and prohibited the enlistment of bandsmen to fill vacancies. In July 1862, the War Department issued General Order No. 91, which directed that all regimental bandsmen be mustered out of service within thirty days. Bandsmen who had been mustered in as musicians were to be discharged from the service or, with their own consent, to be transferred to brigade bands.[2]

Established in August 1862, the Band of the Irish Brigade was led by Edward Manahan, whose Brass Band had been attached to the 69th New York State Militia since 1854.[3] When they accompanied General Thomas Meagher when he left for Harrison's Landing, Virginia, aboard the steamer *Key West* to rejoin his command on August 10, 1862, the *Irish American* reported, "The members wear a tasteful gray uniform faced with green, and make quite a handsome appearance. They will be a great addition to the Brigade, and will cheer the tedium of camp life with some of the fine old music of Fatherland, to which every true Celt is so passionately attached."[4]

Based on this description plus photographic evidence, this bandsman wears a uniform coat with dark-green facings on the collar, a chasseur-pattern cap with a dark-green band and with brass numerals of his old regiment attached to its front, and a narrow welt of green cord on the outer seams of his trousers. He is playing an upright bass saxhorn.

1. *A Report to the Secretary of War of the Operation of the Sanitary Commission* (McGill & Witherow, Printers, 1861), 41.

2. Robert Garofalo & Mark Elrod, *A Pictorial History of Civil War Era Musical Instruments & Military Bands* (Pictorial Histories Publishing Company, 1985), 53–54.

3. *Irish American Weekly* (New York, NY), July 8, 1854, 2:8.

4. *The Irish American* (New York, NY), August 16, 1862, 2:6.

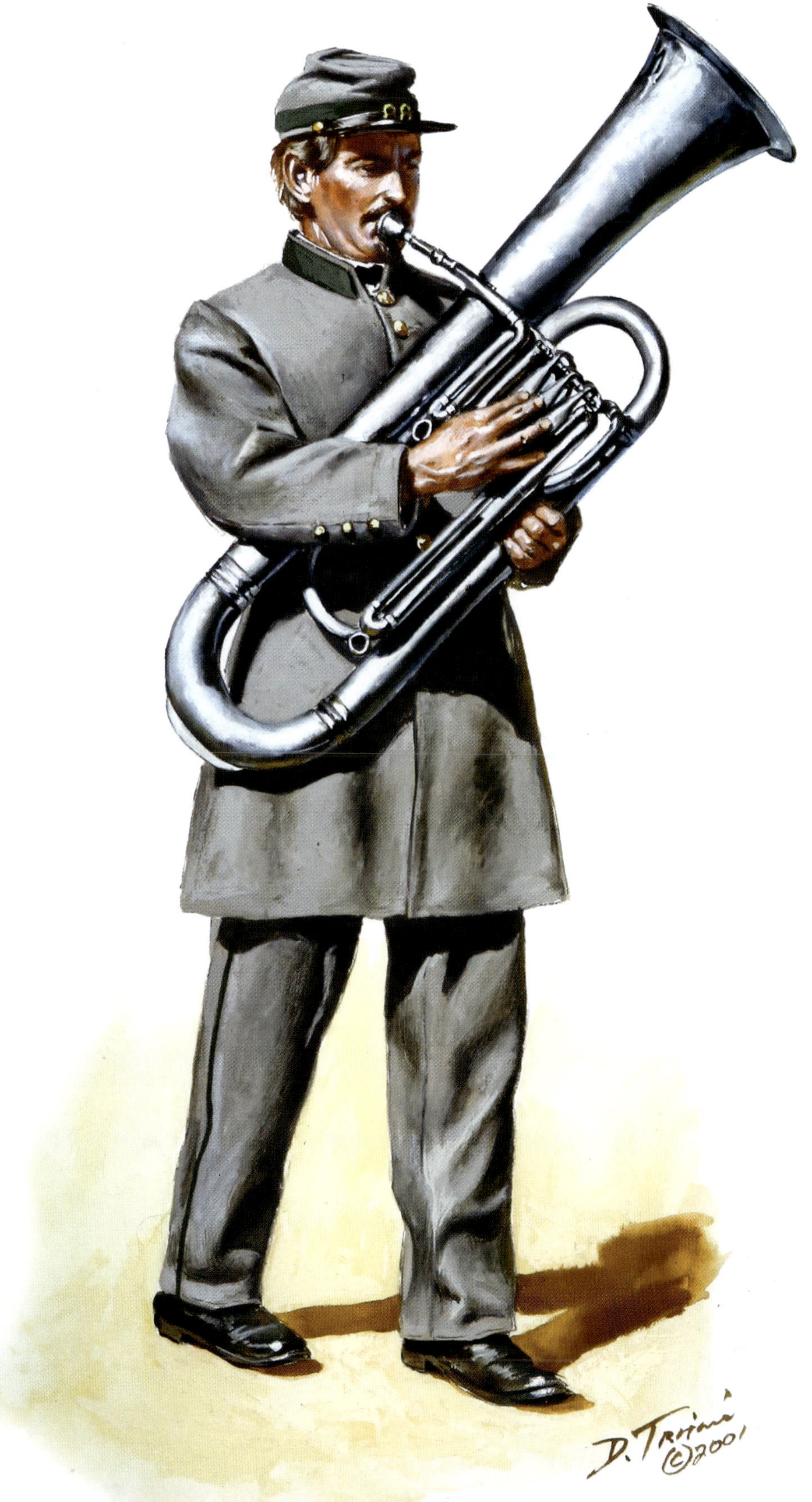

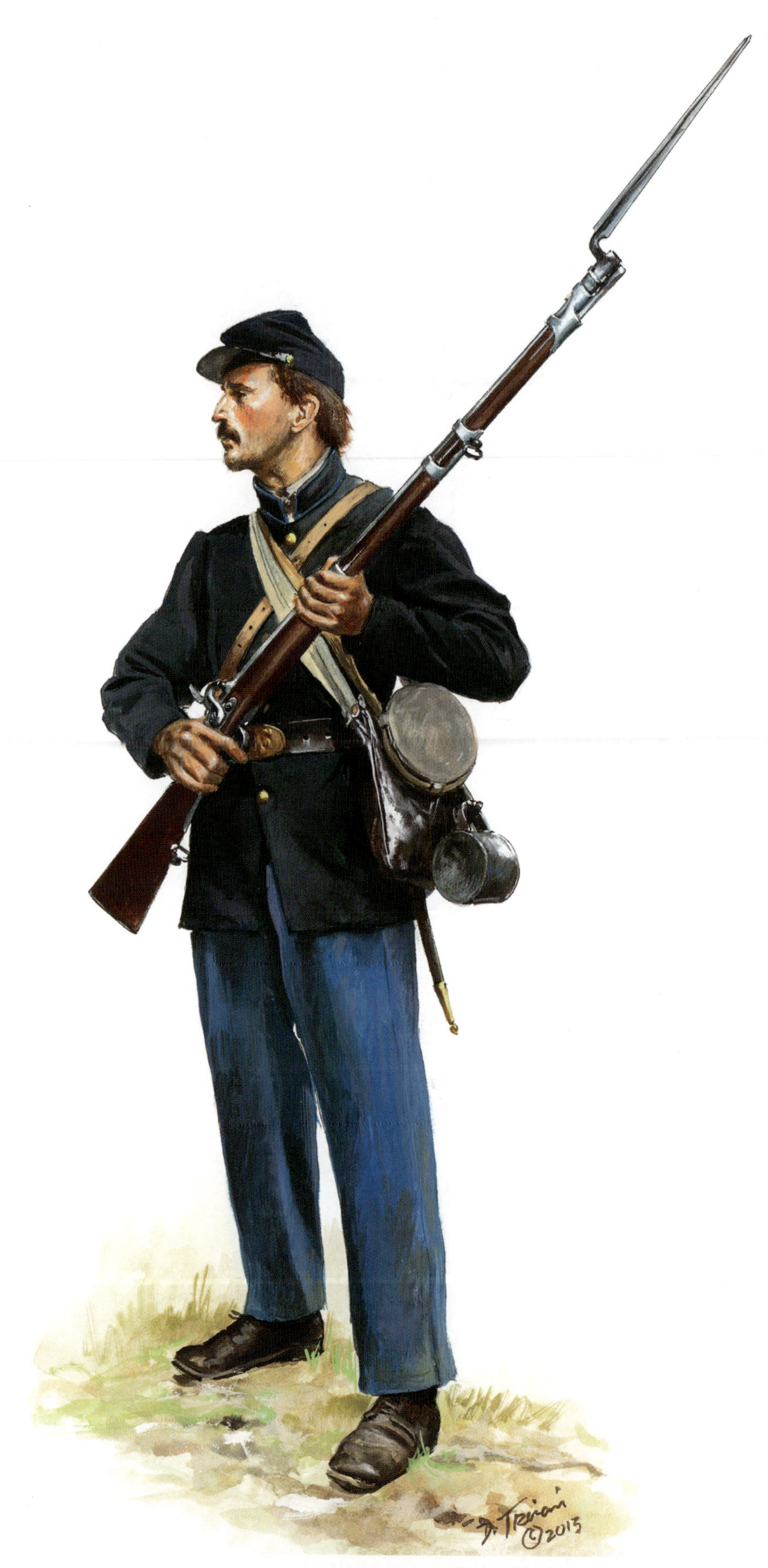

15th Wisconsin Infantry

LIKE MOST STATES FACED WITH THE IMMENSE TASK of uniforming and equipping its volunteer soldiers in 1861, Wisconsin was forced to scramble and make do with whatever materials were on hand. Its first eight regiments, largely drawn from the state militia, were dressed in a variety of gray clothing, including some uniforms hastily procured from the New York firm E. D. Eaton by state agents W. D. Bacon and Lysander Cutler, who were dispatched there when the state's supply of cloth for uniforms was exhausted.[1] These uniforms proved to be of poor quality, with the 2nd Wisconsin, for example, becoming known as the "Ragged Second."

Thereafter, as supplies became available, the state's soldiers were issued a distinctive five-button sack coat of dark-blue cloth with a standing collar piped in lighter-blue cord supplied by the New York City firms Kohner & Brothers and Mackin & Brother.[2] Their new trousers were of sky-blue cloth, and the newer regiments were issued blue forage caps. Some regiments evidently had round, black hats.

This private of the 15th Wisconsin Infantry wears an example of the blue state-issue uniform issued during the fall of 1861. Made of dark-blue kersey, his mid-thigh length coat is fastened with five evenly spaced state buttons. Its standing collar is trimmed with a sky-blue kersey piping and has a hook and eye closure at its base.[3] His forage cap is of the type supplied to Wisconsin on September 2, 1861, by hatters Duryee, Jaques & Co., of 2 Beaver Street, Newark, New Jersey.[4] Trousers are plain sky-blue kersey.

His equipment includes a tin drum canteen and a painted haversack with an unpainted cloth sling. Like many Western soldiers he has received a foreign import shoulder arm consisting of a "Saxon" Model 1851 and 1857 rifle musket. Purchasing agent George Schuyler bought twenty-seven thousand of this weapon in Dresden in 1861. Unlike many of the imported weapons, these were considered to be totally serviceable and were classified as a first-class weapon.

The 15th Wisconsin needed dependable arms. Organized at Camp Randall, near Madison, Wisconsin, in December 1861 and January 1862, with recruits from a largely Scandinavian immigrant population, the "Scandinavian Regiment" would see full service in the war. After leaving the state on March 15, 1862, it first served in the siege of Island No. 10 where two of its companies remained in garrison after its capture. The remainder of the regiment was later engaged in the Battle of Perryville and fought at the battles of both Stones River and Chickamauga. At Missionary Ridge it was the first to take Orchard Knob, and it later served gallantly in the battles of Resaca, Kennesaw Mountain, Peachtree Creek, and Jonesboro. By the time the 15th Wisconsin was mustered out of service at the end of 1864 or in early 1865, it had lost 194 officers and men in action.

---

1. Ron Field, *The Union Army 1861–65*, vol. 3, Midwestern and Western States (Osprey Publishing, 2024), 13.

2. *Wisconsin Daily Patriot* (Madison, WI), September 11, 1861, 3:3.

3. Robert A. Braun, "Wisconsin's 5-Button Fatigue Blouse," *Military Images* XXIII, no. 1 (July–August 2001): 21–22.

4. *Wisconsin Daily Patriot*, September 3, 1861, 3:3.

Confederate Drummer

AT THE START OF THE CIVIL WAR, OFFI-CIAL AGE LIMITS were ignored regarding drummers, who were often young boys; they also were sometimes treated as mascots. As the conflict wore on, drummers were more likely to be adult men and were recruited like the common soldiers. As an essential part of military routine in camp, the drum and fife would signal important activities, such as reveille, surgeon's call, fatigue call, meals, roll call, retreat, and lights out. The drum and fife were as useful outside of camp; on the march and in the field, there were twenty-four different drum calls, according to Casey's *Infantry Tactics*. When amid the roar of battle, the officers' shouted commands were often drowned out in the din and chaos, and the beat of the drum could convey the order to aim and fire.

According to the *Drummer's and Fifer's Guide* published in May 1862, "the field music should always appear neat and clean, and should pay particular attention to . . . those placed in command over them, and should never engage in conversation, or leave their position in line without permission."[1]

A shortage of medical orderlies often necessitated another important aspect of field service for the musician. When battle appeared imminent, musicians and sometimes drummers might expect to be detailed to assist the regimental surgeon as stretcher bearers. Stacking their instruments, they would await orders to carry the seriously wounded off the battlefield to a field dressing station.

Surveying the scene prior to battle, this Confederate drummer has his instrument slung over his shoulder and his drum sticks at the ready. Unless acquired from a prewar militia unit, most Confederate drums tended to have shells that were plainer than those on Union instruments. The example in this painting has a plain shell and red wooden rims. The wooden rim of a similar Confederate drum, which was captured on the Wilderness battlefield, was "worn by beating it, instead of the head during night marches."[2]

He wears a patched Columbus Depot–pattern jacket with dark-blue collar and cuffs; a chasseur-pattern forage cap with dark-blue piping; and ragged gray trousers. Like other seasoned soldiers, he carries spare clothing and other essentials in a simple blanket roll over his shoulder. A wooden drum canteen has his initials carved on its side, and a tin cup is suspended from his blanket roll tie.

---

1. George B. Bruce, *Drummer's and Fifer's Guide; or Self-Instructor* (New York, May 1862).

2. J. Craig Caba, *United States Military Drums, 1845–1865: A Pictorial Survey* (Civil War Antiquities & Americana, 1977), 102.

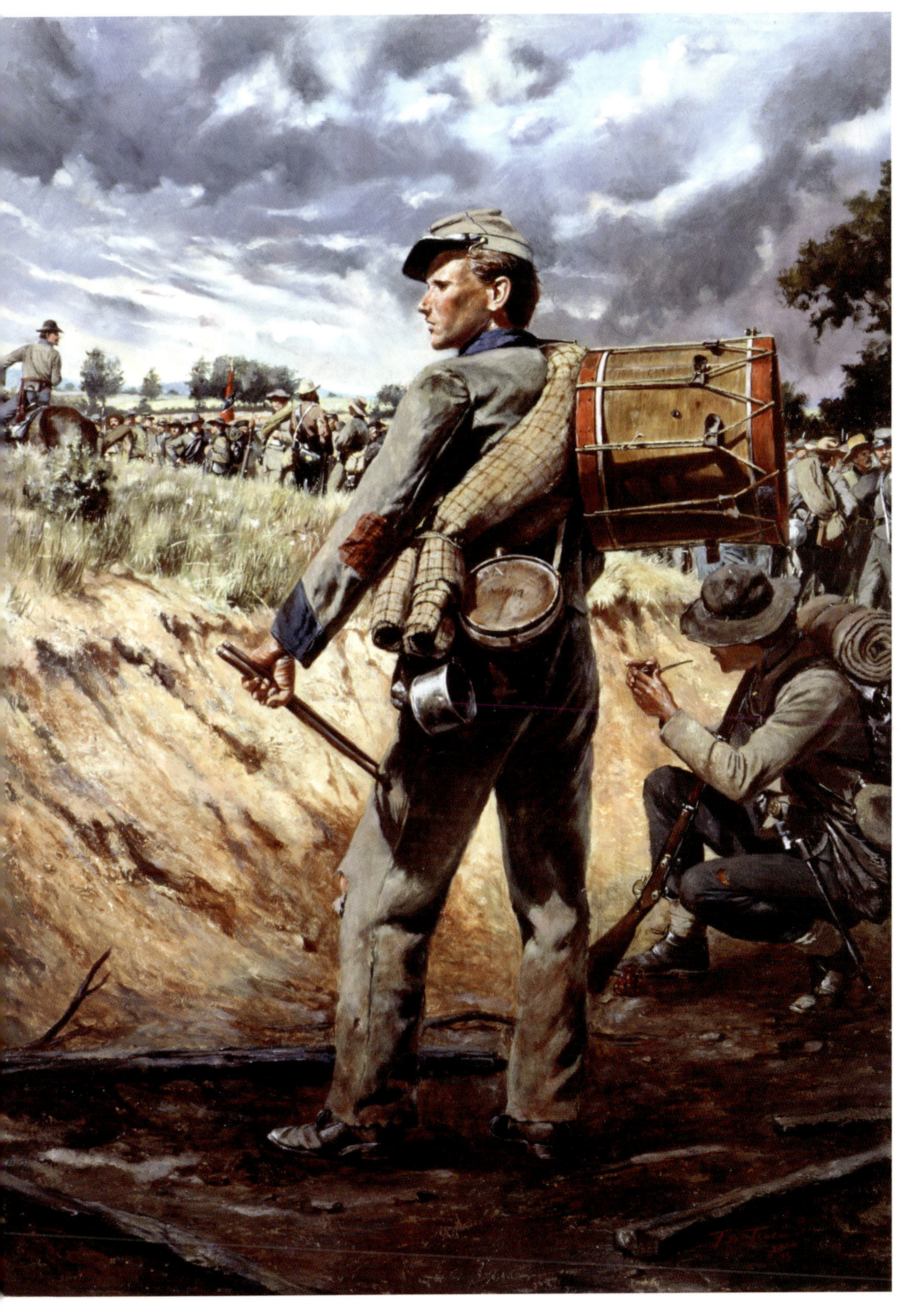

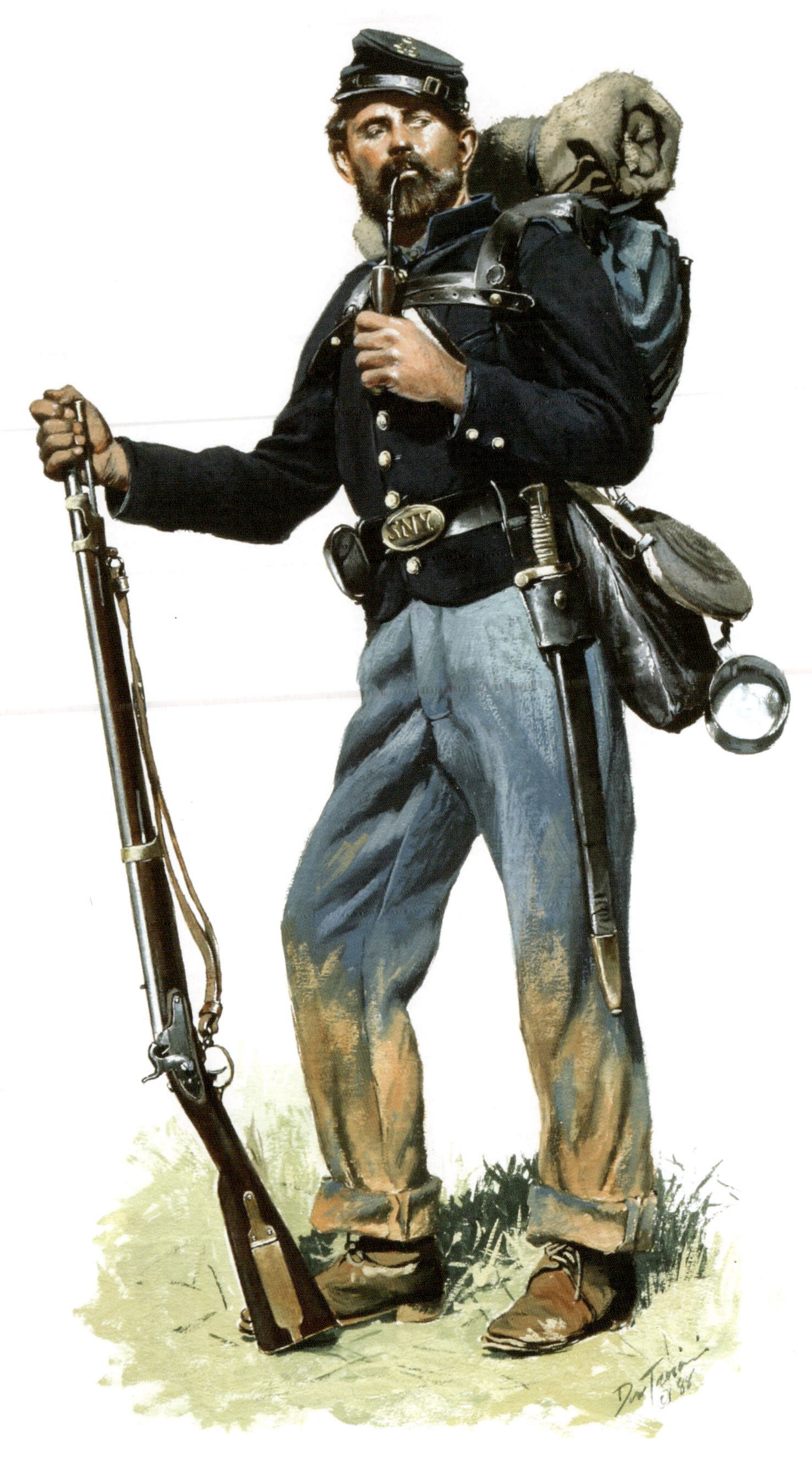

45th New York Infantry, 1863

THE 45TH NEW YORK INFANTRY, OR FIFTH GERMAN RIFLES, was organized in New York City with Colonel George Von Amsberg, a veteran of the Hungarian Revolution, in command. Recruited wholly among the German population of the city, and with orders given in German, it was mustered in for three years on September 9, 1861.[1] Considered a rifle regiment, the unit was initially clothed in a dark-green uniform coat, trousers, and a forage cap and was armed with the Model 1841 rifle.

The regiment left the State on October 9, 1861, and was assigned to Julius H. Stahel's Brigade, Blenker's Division, Army of the Potomac. Transferred to the Mountain Department under General John C. Frémont in April 1862, it served there until May 1, 1862. Following the Battle of Cross Keys, many of the regiment were sick due to constant marches with insufficient food. In August it fought at Second Bull Run and, later in the year, at Fredericksburg. At Chancellorsville, seventy-six of its men were killed or wounded or went missing. Assigned to the 1st Brigade, 3rd Division, XI Corps, it was heavily involved in all three days' fighting at Gettysburg. Taking into action 447 officers and men, the regiment lost 324, who were killed, wounded, or missing.

Appearing as he would have at Gettysburg, this battle-hardened private of the 45th New York wears a dark-blue New York state-issue jacket with sky-blue trim around the collar and shoulder straps; sky-blue pants; and a dark-blue cap with the regiment numbers and the company letter affixed to its top. Missing is the division's blue crescent-moon badge, which the regiment appears not to have received prior to the battle. A gray blanket roll is strapped to his nonrigid knapsack, which, according to a directive from divisional commander Major General Carl Schurz, carried an extra pair of shoes, a set of underwear, an overcoat, and a shelter half.

With its ranks supplemented and reorganized after Gettysburg, the 45th New York was transferred west in October 1863 and fought at Wauhatchie, Tennessee. It was next involved in fighting in Chattanooga and in the Rossville Campaign. During the Atlanta Campaign in the spring of 1864, it was assigned to the 3rd Brigade, 1st Division, XX Corps, with which it served until July, being in action in the battles of Resaca, Dallas, and Kennesaw Mountain. Attached to the Department of the Cumberland in Nashville in July 1864, it remained there until the close of the war.[2]

The original three-year volunteers who did not reenlist were mustered out on October 8, 1864, while the rest of the unit was retained as a veteran regiment until June 30, 1865, when it was consolidated with the 58th New York and with it mustered out in Nashville on October 1, 1865.

---

1. *New York Daily Herald*, August 24, 1861, 5:1.
2. *The Union Army*, vol. II (Federal Publishing Company, 1908), 82.

53rd Georgia Infantry, 1863

DEPICTED ON THE SECOND DAY OF THE BATTLE OF Gettysburg, this private of the 53rd Georgia Infantry is tearing open a paper cartridge in preparation for loading his .69-caliber smoothbore Model 1842 musket. Forming part of General Paul J. Semmes's brigade, of Lafayette McLaw's division, the Georgians lost eighty-seven men in the struggle for Rose Hill during Longstreet's assault on the Federal left and center. The brother of Commander Raphael Semmes, the famed Confederate commerce raider, General Semmes was mortally wounded during this action.

Organized in May 1862, with Colonel Leonard T. Doyal in command, the 53rd Georgia fought in the battles of South Mountain and Sharpsburg, with twelve men killed and sixty-three wounded in the latter action. Their commanding officer, Lieutenant Colonel Thomas Sloan, was captured and died of his wounds in a Federal hospital.

Arriving in Gettysburg with 422 officers and men, the regiment was reasonably well clothed, armed, and equipped.[1] This soldier wears a wool jean, Richmond Depot Type 2 jacket with wooden buttons, which reflects a shortage of brass ones in the Confederacy at that time. A shortage of leather is also illustrated by the painted canvas shoulder belts that support his Richmond-made cartridge box and haversack. According to archival records, only 80 percent of Semmes's brigade had been issued with canteens.

After the Battle of Gettysburg, the 53rd Georgia went west with Longstreet's Corps and fought in the battles of Chattanooga and Fort Sanders, before returning east in March 1864 to take part in the battles leading to the fall of Petersburg and the evacuation of Richmond. Most of the regiment was captured at Saylor's Creek on April 6, 1865, and only sixty-four of its officers and men surrendered in Appomattox six days later.[2]

---

1. NARA, M266, CMSR, Andrew J. Phillips, 34; Daniel McLucas, 40.
2. Crute, *Units of the Confederate States Army*, 113.

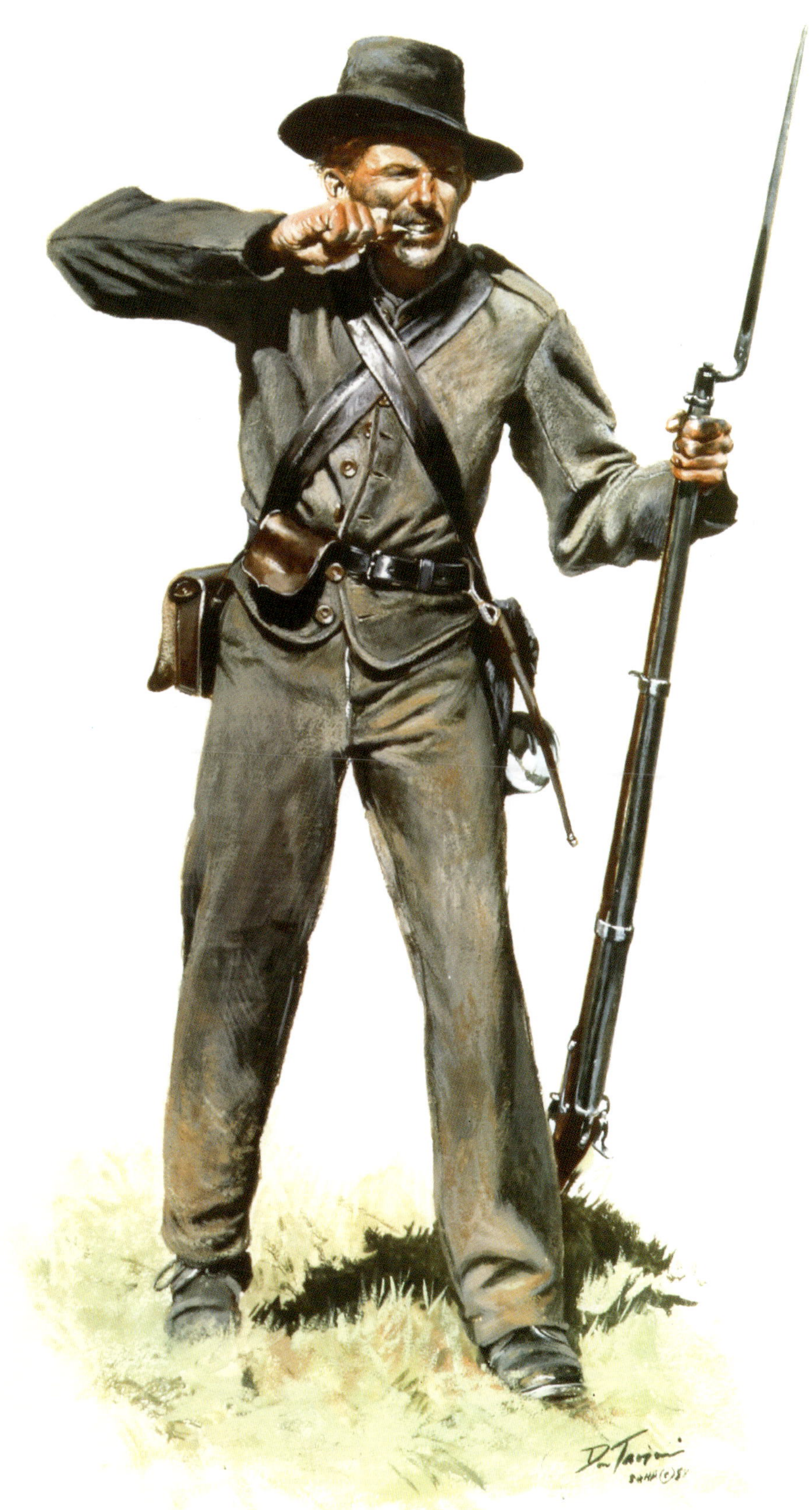

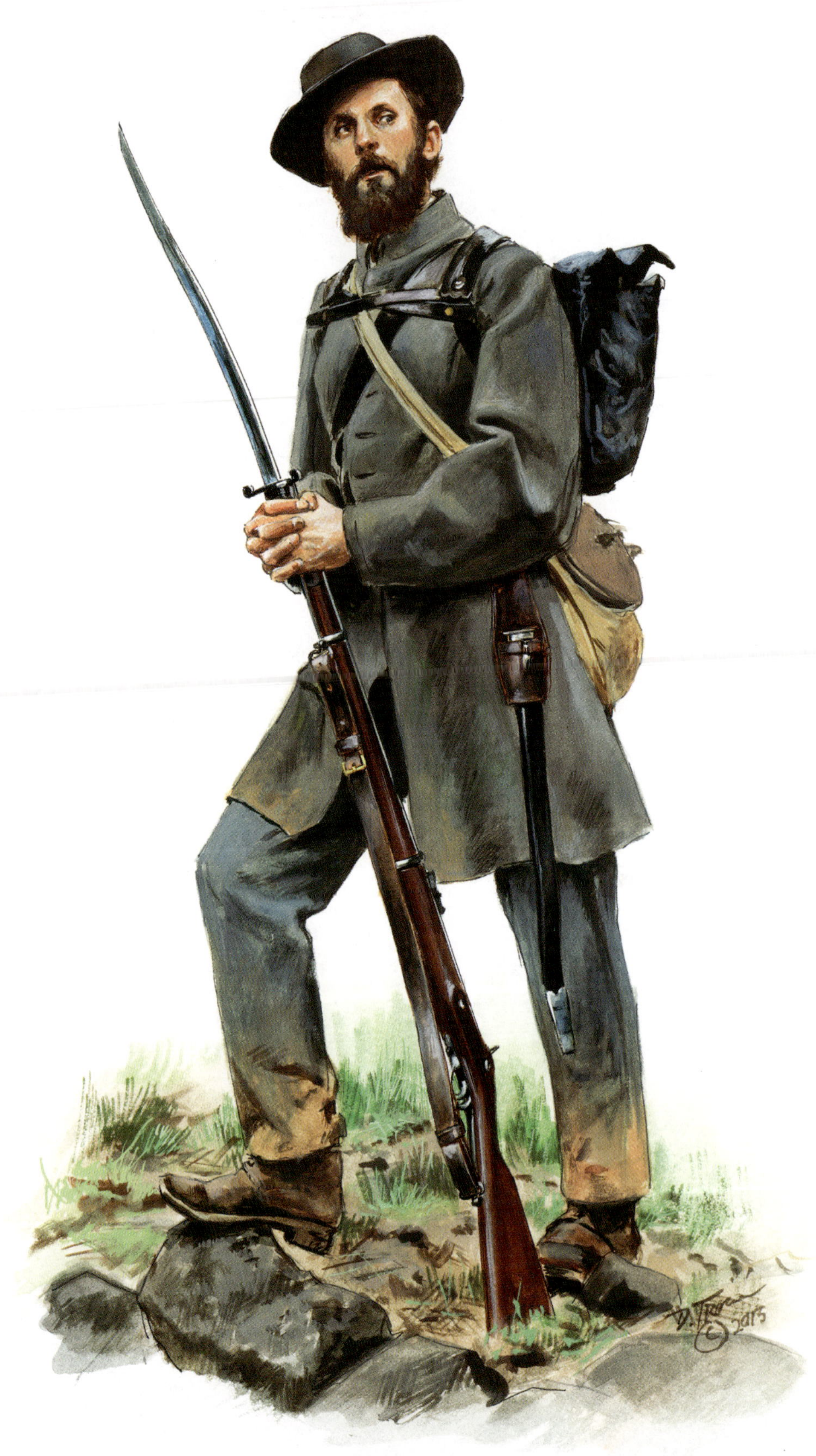

16th Georgia Infantry, Private, Company A, 1863

ORIGINALLY COMMANDED BY COLONEL HOWELL COBB, one of the founders of the Confederacy, the 16th Georgia Infantry was recruited in the northeast part of the State in July and August 1861. Comprised of men from Madison County, Company A was named the Madison County Greys. During the next four years the 16th Georgia would earn more than its share of glory as part of Wofford's Brigade in Longstreet's Corps of the Army of Northern Virginia. At Gettysburg on July 3rd, 1863, the regiment played an important part in driving Union forces from the Peach Orchard and into the hotly contested Wheatfield.

This private of Company A has fixed a saber bayonet to his Enfield rifle, with which his regiment was issued shortly after arriving in Richmond, Virginia, in October 1861, and is waiting for orders to move forward.[1] He carries a captured Federal knapsack and a cloth-covered canteen along with a Confederate-issue off-white canvas haversack. His Enfield-type cartridge box is slung on his right hip, and a leather frog on the left side of his waist belt supports his bayonet scabbard.

While most Confederate regiments went into the 1863 Gettysburg Campaign wearing the Quartermaster-issue jacket, many men still retained a uniform coat. Georgia troops were among those well supplied with clothing by their home state. In early 1863 the State Quartermaster's Department at the Columbus Depot reported it had over seven thousand coats on hand for issue.[2] "Special Requisitions" of clothing to the 16th Georgia listed in the personal service records confirm a predominance of coats until after Gettysburg when, as required, the more practical and less expensive jacket would take their place. For example, Captain Henry C. Nash, commanding Company A, received seventy-three coats on May 30, 1862.[3] The records of Private William L. Glenn, Company A, who died of a gunshot wound on June 11, 1863, list his effects as "1 Hat, 2 blankets, 1 coat, 1 [pair] pants, 1 [pair] drawers, 1 pair shoes."[4] That a number of the men of the 16th Georgia were of high proficiency with their Enfield rifles is verified by the fact that some were selected in June 1863 to form the 3rd Battalion of Georgia Sharpshooters.

---

1. NARA, M266, CMSR, James S. Gholston, 49. This record is a receipt for ninety-five Enfield rifles, each with a sword bayonet, ninety-five cartridge boxes, ninety-five waist belts, ninety-five gun slings, and ninety-five bayonet frogs on October 18, 1861.

2. Ron Field, *American Civil War: Confederate Army* (Brassey's, 1996), 48.

3. NARA, M266, CMSR, Henry C. Nash, 22.

4. NARA, M266, CMSR, William L. Glenn, 10. It is likely that Glenn was wounded at Chancellorsville and died in Richmond.

21st Ohio Volunteer Infantry

FOLLOWING THREE MONTHS' SERVICE, THE 21ST OHIO Volunteer Infantry reenlisted for three years under Colonel Jesse S. Norton at Camp Vance in Findlay, Ohio, on September 19, 1861. Notable volunteers in this regiment were Captain Americus V. Rice, who would become a brigadier general by the end of the war. Among its enlisted men was Private Thomas W. Custer, who would win the Medal of Honor and later fight and die with the 7th Cavalry in the Battle of Little Bighorn.

The 21st Ohio served throughout the war in the West. While campaigning in Tennessee in early 1862 as part of the Army of the Ohio, nine of its number, plus two civilians and thirteen men from two other Ohio regiments, volunteered to take part in a secret mission known as the Andrews's Raid, named for civilian James J. Andrews, who led the expedition. Slipping behind enemy lines in civilian clothing, they hijacked the Confederate locomotive, "The General," but were captured attempting to escape after the engine eventually lost steam pressure and came to a halt. Eight of the raiders, including Private John M. Scott, Company F, 21st Ohio, were hanged, while eight, including five men from the regiment, managed to escape. The remaining raiders, among them three more members of the unit, were released in a prisoner exchange the next year. In recognition of their bravery, Congress awarded most of those involved, including all nine of the 21st Ohio, with the newly created Medal of Honor.[1]

On May 28, 1863, the 21st Ohio exchanged 350 Enfield rifle muskets for the same number of Model 1855 Colt revolving rifles, which had been turned in by Berdan's Sharpshooters. The latter weapons were a major factor in the stubborn defense of Chickamauga performed by Major General George Thomas's XIV Army Corps on September 20, 1863.[2] Although effective in battle, the Colt revolving rifle was generally considered to be unreliable and dangerous as it tended to shoot splinters of lead into the left wrist and hand of the person firing it. On February 9, 1864, Brigadier General Richard W. Johnson desired to standardize the small arms in his division and directed that all regiments armed with other than Enfield and Springfield rifle muskets should turn them in. As a result, by the summer, the 21st Ohio was armed mostly with Enfields combined with a small number of Springfields.

Loading his Colt revolving rifle, this corporal of the 21st Ohio wears a four-button sack coat and sky-blue trousers. His high-crowned black felt hat is unadorned with regimental or corps insignia. His accoutrements include a waist belt with a Pattern 1839 oval "US" plate and a shoulder belt with a Pattern 1826 round "eagle" plate, plus a black waterproofed nonrigid knapsack.

---

1. William Pittenger, *Daring and Suffering: A History of the Andrews Railroad Raid into Georgia in 1862 . . .* (The War Publishing Co., 1887).

2. John D. McAulay, *Rifles in the U.S. Army* (Andrew Mowbray Publishers, 2003), 16.

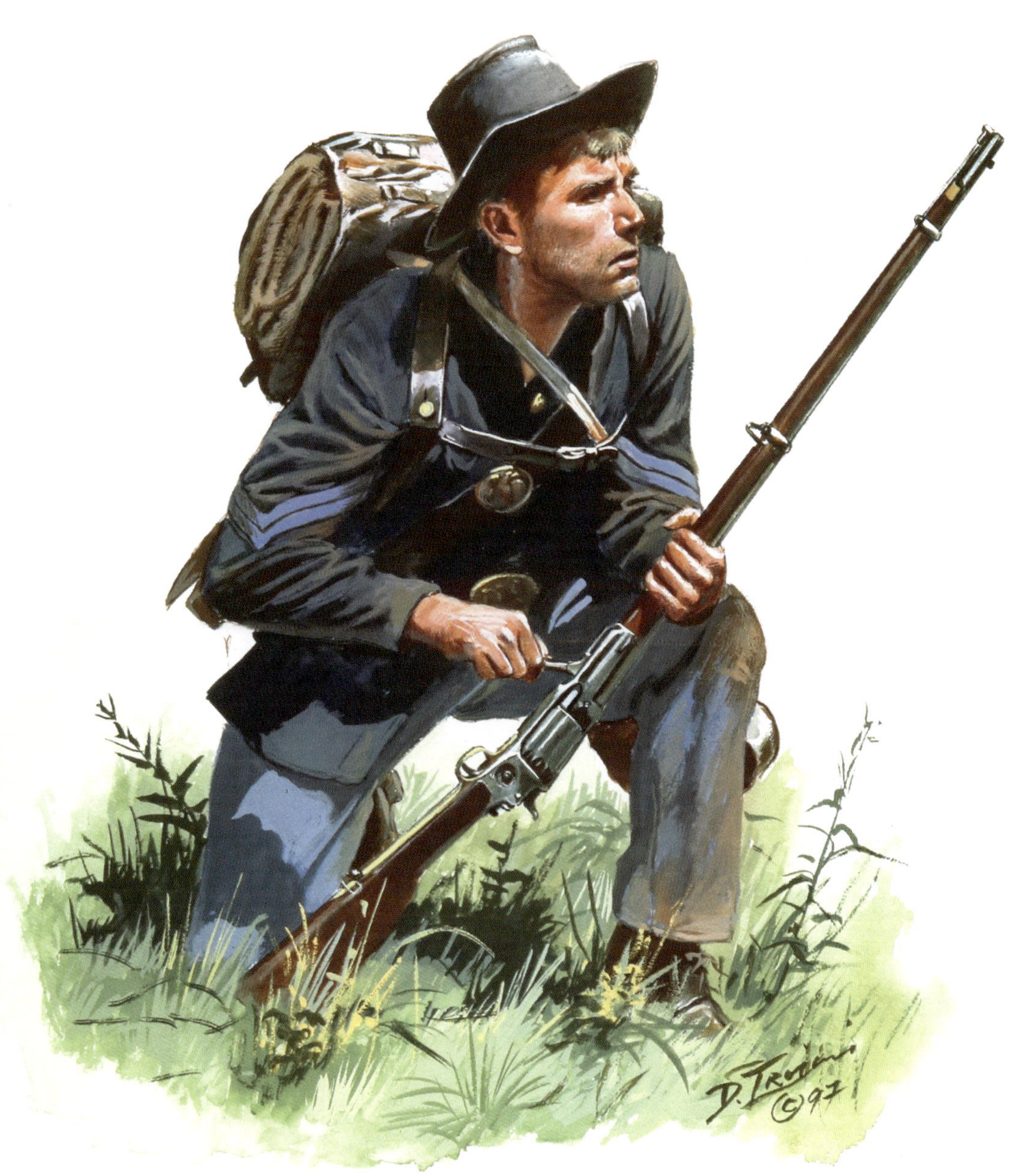

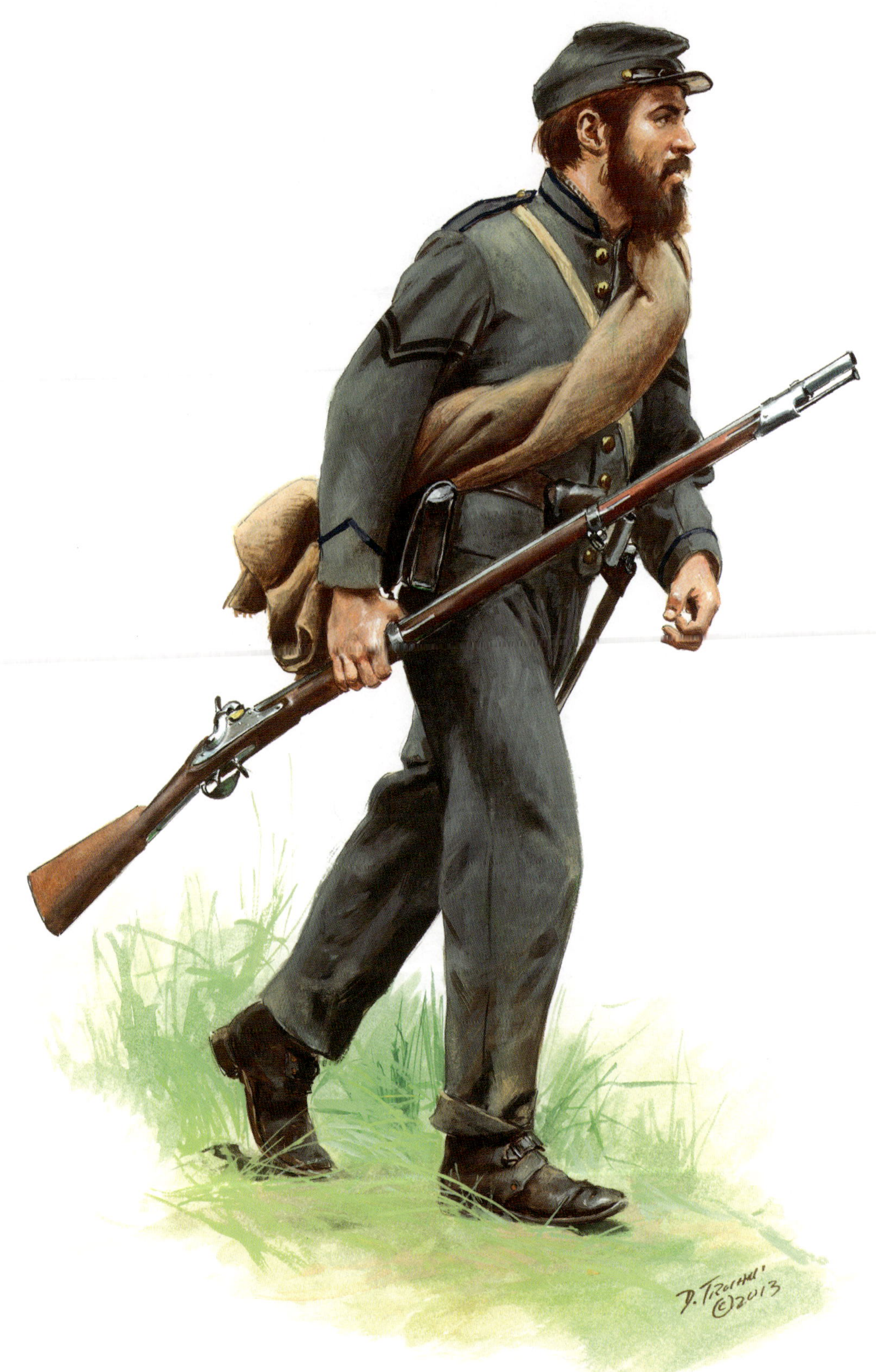

47th North Carolina Infantry, Corporal, Company A, Chicora Guards, Spring 1863

THE CHICORA GUARDS WERE RE-CRUITED IN Nash County, North Carolina, with Captain John W. Bryant in command, and mustered into state service at Camp Mangun on April 11, 1862, as Company A, 47th North Carolina Infantry.[1] The regiment was assigned to General James G. Martin's Brigade, Department of North Carolina, in July 1862. During September it was assigned to James J. Pettigrew's Brigade, French's Command, Department of North Carolina and Southern Virginia, and built fortifications at Drewry's Bluff on the James River. They also guarded the railroad south of Petersburg. Prior to the Gettysburg Campaign, this brigade joined Major General Henry Heth's Division, III Corps of the Army of Northern Virginia. The 47th North Carolina marched 250 miles between May 26 and June 30, 1863, prior to fighting at Gettysburg. It was in the initial battle at Seminary Ridge on the first day and on the left of Pickett's Charge on July 3. Bringing 567 men into the field, it suffered 35 percent casualties.

This corporal of the Chicora Guards wears a comparatively new uniform having been issued a complete outfit on May 12, 1863, prior to the Gettysburg Campaign.[2] His jacket is of the first pattern manufactured at the Richmond Quartermaster Depot.[3] Although the blue trim indicates infantry, his black chevrons may indicate that the jacket was a close copy manufactured in his home state. Made from the same cloth as his jacket, his plain cap and trousers suggest they came from the same source. Of particular significance are his shoes, which are English Army issue run though the Union naval blockade. Four hundred pairs had been received at Goldsborough, North Carolina, and issued to Pettigrew's Brigade on January 18, 1863.[4]

The soldier is armed with a Model 1822 .69-caliber musket, which has been altered to percussion. His accoutrements are of Confederate manufacture. Although the 47th North Carolina was issued knapsacks, he is outfitted in light marching order with a blanket roll, which contains all he required for a short time.

The 47th North Carolina went on to participate in the Bristoe and Mine Run campaigns in 1863 following which it went into winter quarters at Orange Court House. It fought at the Wilderness, Spotsylvania Court House, Cold Harbor, and Siege of Petersburg in 1864, surrendering with Lee's Army of Northern Virginia at Appomattox Court House on April 9, 1865, with only 5 officers and 72 men.

1. *Supplement*, part II, vol. 49, 285.
2. NARA, M270, CMSR, Lieutenant John H. Thorp, 95.
3. Jensen, "A Survey of Confederate Central Government Quartermaster Issue Jackets," part 1, 113.
4. NARA, M331, Confederate officers, 1861–1865, Captain John F. Divine AQM, 125.

20th Tennessee Infantry, Summer 1863

ORGANIZED AT CAMP TROUSDALE UNDER COLONEL Joel A. Battle on June 12, 1861, the 20th Tennessee Infantry was ordered to East Tennessee and Kentucky as part of the brigade commanded by Brigadier General Felix K. Zollicoffer. It saw its first action at Fishing Creek on January 19, 1862, where it sustained 110 casualties. After service at Vicksburg and Baton Rouge, the regiment was assigned to the Army of Tennessee and fought at Murfreesboro from December 31, 1862, to January 2, 1863, during which it was on the receiving end of the first significant use of repeating rifles in battle as part of the force that attacked the Union Lightening Brigade commanded by Colonel John T. Wilder. Later in the year it suffered 88 casualties out of 183 men engaged at Chickamauga on September 18–20, 1863.[1]

This private of the 20th Tennessee appears as he would have looked prior to the battle at Chickamauga. Regimental records indicate that a regular supply of quartermaster-issue uniform items were received, including jackets, pants and shirts, plus hats rather than the caps received by most Confederate regiments. Also, unlike most Southern units, this regiment wore a small brass badge on the hat or jacket bearing the regimental designation "20th TENN."

As a general rule, units of the Army of Tennessee received clothing and ordnance from depots in the Deep South such as Columbus and Macon, Georgia. Hence, the soldier shown here wears a wool jean jacket with dark blue wool kersey facings on collar and cuffs of the type manufactured at the Columbus facility.

He is armed with a Pattern 1853 Enfield rifle musket with russet leather sling, which his regiment received in place of flintlock muskets in 1862.[2] Equipment includes a waist belt with a rectangular solid cast "CSA" plate supporting a percussion cap pouch and cartridge box. Also carried is a wooden drum canteen, haversack with tin cup attached, plus knapsack and blanket roll.

---

1. *Tennesseans in the Civil War*, part 1, 218.
2. John M. Murphy and Howard Michael Madaus, *Confederate Rifles & Muskets* (Graphic Publishers, 1996), 64.

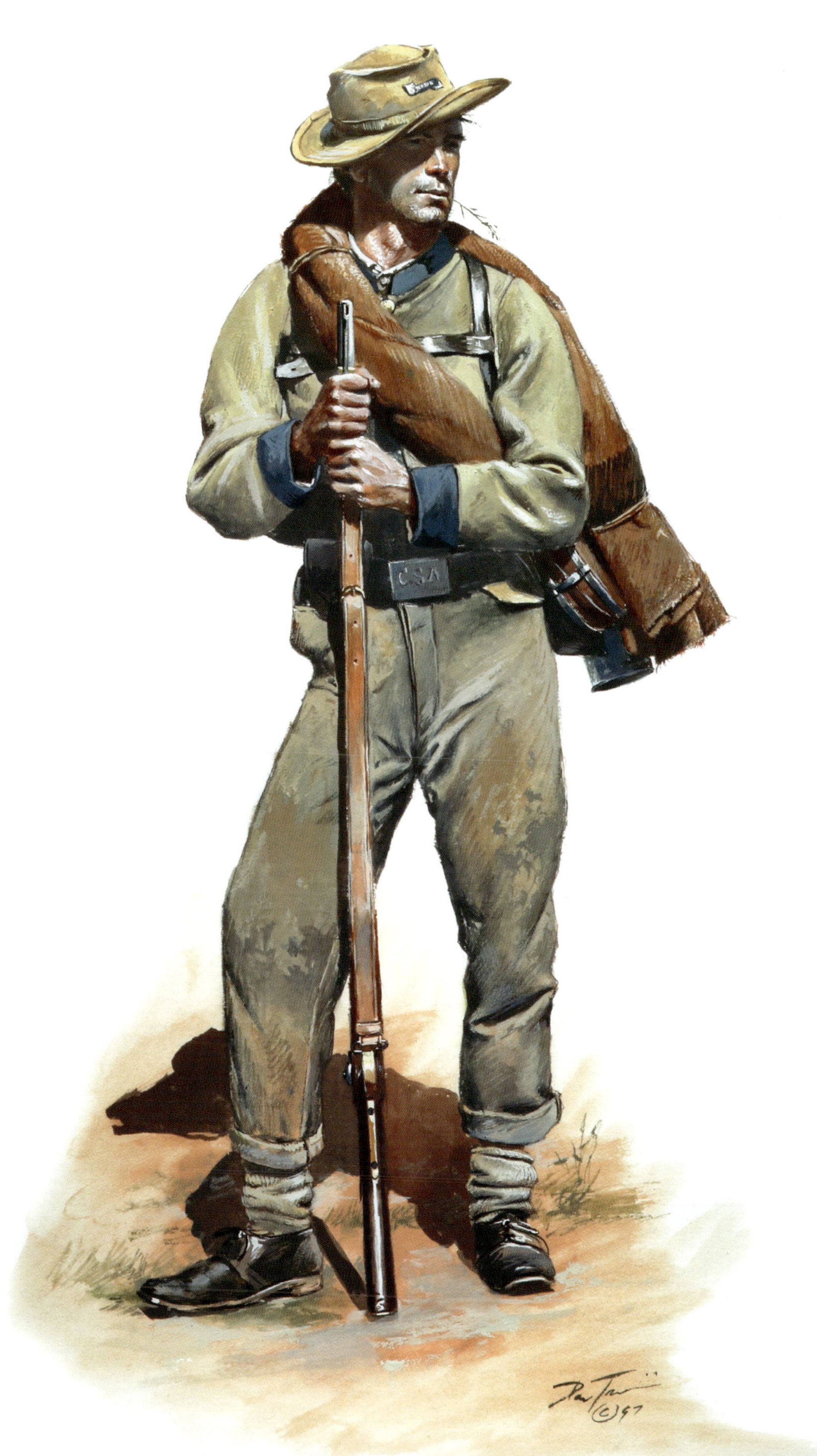

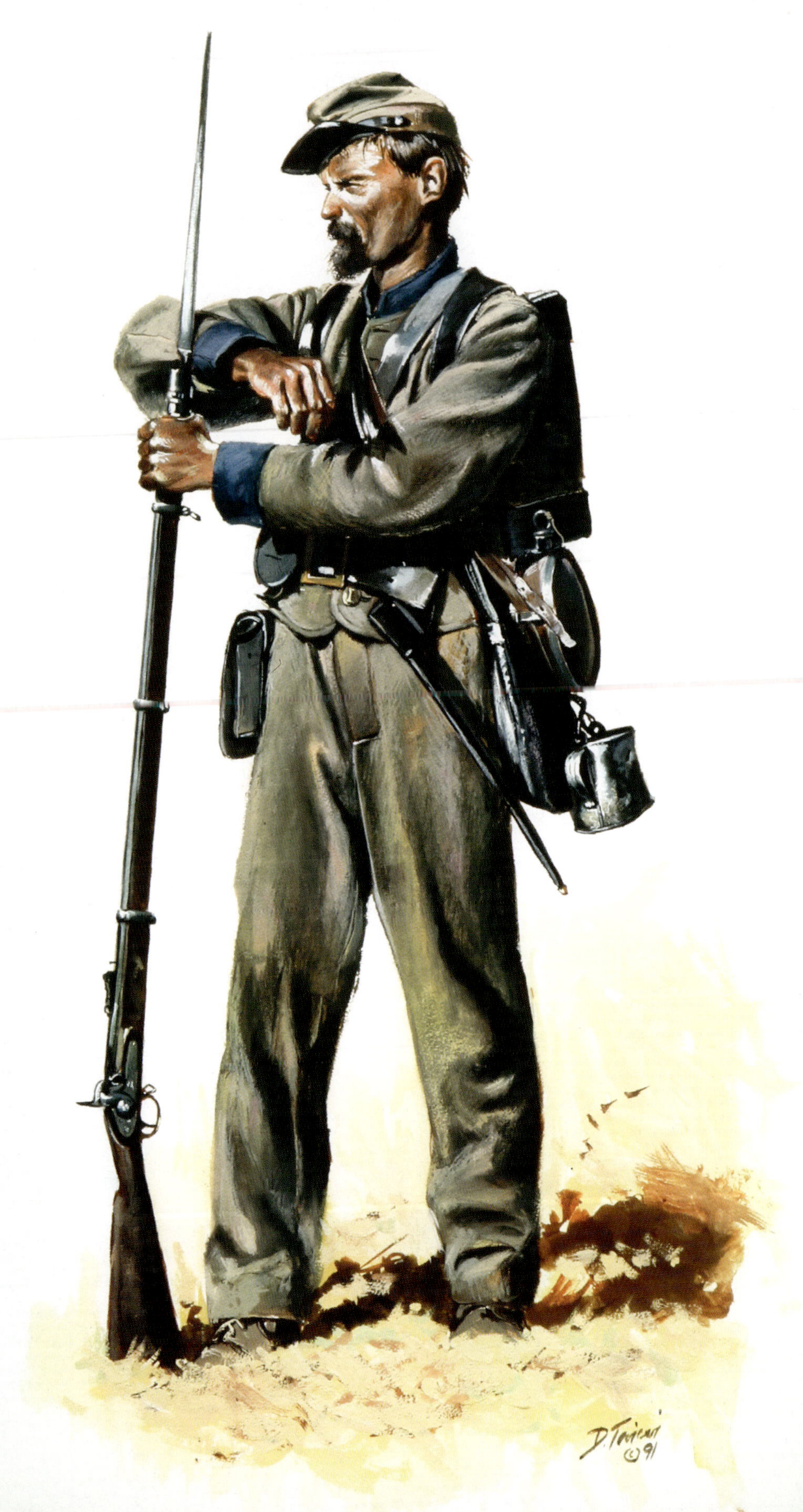

29th Alabama Infantry

COMMANDED BY COLONEL JOHN F. CONOLEY, THE 29th Alabama Infantry was one of the finest veteran regiments in the Confederate army of the West, with 1,100 men in its ranks by the beginning of 1864. The unit had been organized at Pensacola, Florida, in February 1862, and was likely created by the addition of two companies to the 4th Battalion Alabama Infantry, which had been recruited with seven companies at Camp Breckinridge, Montgomery, Alabama, on November 16, 1861. Serving as artillery, the 29th Alabama remained at Pensacola for over a year until it moved into Camp Lee near Pollard, Alabama.

In the summer of 1863 the regiment was ordered to Mobile where it remained until the spring of 1864. Joining the Army of the Tennessee, it was assigned to Cantey's and Shelley's Brigade and participated in numerous actions from Reseca to Nashville. At Resaca it lost about 100 killed or wounded, and sustained further heavy losses at New Hope Church and Peach Tree Creek. Nearly half the regiment was killed or wounded in the fierce and protracted assault on the Federal lines near Atlanta on July 28, 1864. Ordered into Tennessee with General Hood, it again lost very heavily at Franklin and Nashville. What remained of the 29th Alabama was moved into the Carolinas; and was engaged at Kinston and Bentonville with further losses. Less than 90 men surrendered on April 26, 1865, at Greensboro, North Carolina.[1]

This battle-hardened and well-accoutred infantryman of the 29th Alabama wears a Columbus Depot Type 2 jacket of gray wool jean with medium blue collar and straight cuffs of the same material, which would have had a five or six button-front. His plain trousers are of jean cloth.[2] The band on his military cap is likely faded from medium blue also. Suits of clothing of this type were issued to his regiment while at Mobile during the last few months of 1863. For example, Company C received "46 Jackets, 54 Pairs Pants, 133 Shirts, 118 pairs bootees, 14 hats."[3]

He is armed with a Pattern 1853 Enfield rifle musket, with socket bayonet attached. Equipment includes a waist belt with brass frame buckle; Confederate-made Pattern 1861 cartridge box and percussion cap pouch with shield-shaped outer flap; wooden drum canteen with metal rim; water proofed haversack with battered tin cup attached to its buckle; and semi-rigid militia-style knapsack.

1. Crute, *Units of the Confederate States Army*, 22.

2. Leslie D. Jensen, "A Survey of Confederate Central Government Quartermaster Issue Jackets," part 2, *Military Collector & Historian* XLI, no. 4 (Winter 1989): 166–67.

3. NARA, M311, CMSR, 29th Alabama Infantry, Company C, Captain John M. Hanna, 38.

76th Ohio Infantry

ORGANIZED AND MUSTERED IN AT CAMP SHERMAN, Newark, Ohio, from October 1861 to February 1862, the 76th Ohio Infantry was uniformed in standard Federal uniforms for much of its service. The uniform was remembered as "a dark blue blouse, light blue pants, forage caps, low, broad soled shoes ('bootees' the government styled them) and blue overcoat with cape. Each soldier carried a gray woolen blanket and a rubber blanket."[1]

After two years of hard service in the West, primarily as part of the XV Corps in the Army of the Tennessee, the 76th Ohio became a veteran regiment in January 1864. To celebrate this status, the veterans bought themselves a new uniform. According to Private Charles A. Willison, "On the 27th [of January] the officers held a meeting to discuss the adoption of a new uniform for the Regiment. It was deemed desirable that the veterans be all clothed alike with some kind of a zouave jacket that they might make a fine appearance on their return to Ohio. A Regimental fund of about seven hundred dollars had been created which it was considered best to expend for this purpose. The officers decided on the style most appropriate to be a short dark blue jacket with rounded corner, no collar and trimmed in sky-blue binding."[2]

The 76th Ohio was originally armed with "old second-hand Belgian rifles, a short, heavy, clumsy arm, with a vicious recoil." During December 1862, however, the unit received Springfield rifle muskets, which they retained through the rest of their service.[3]

1. Charles A. Willison, *Reminiscences of a Boy's Service with the 76th Ohio* (The George Santa Publishing Company, 1908), 13.
2. Willison, *Reminiscences of a Boy's Service with the 76th Ohio*, 144.
3. Willison, *Reminiscences of a Boy's Service with the 76th Ohio*, 14.

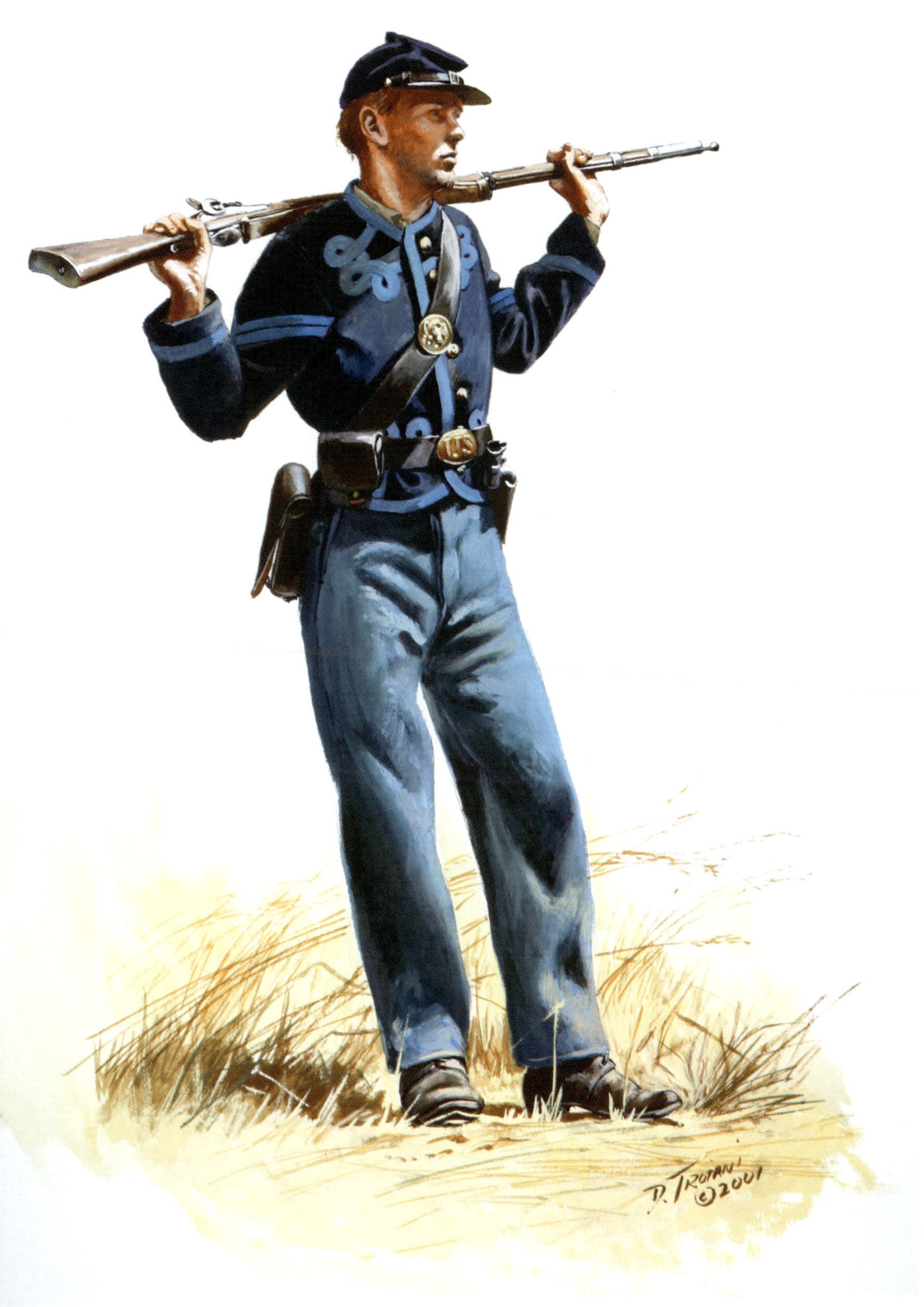

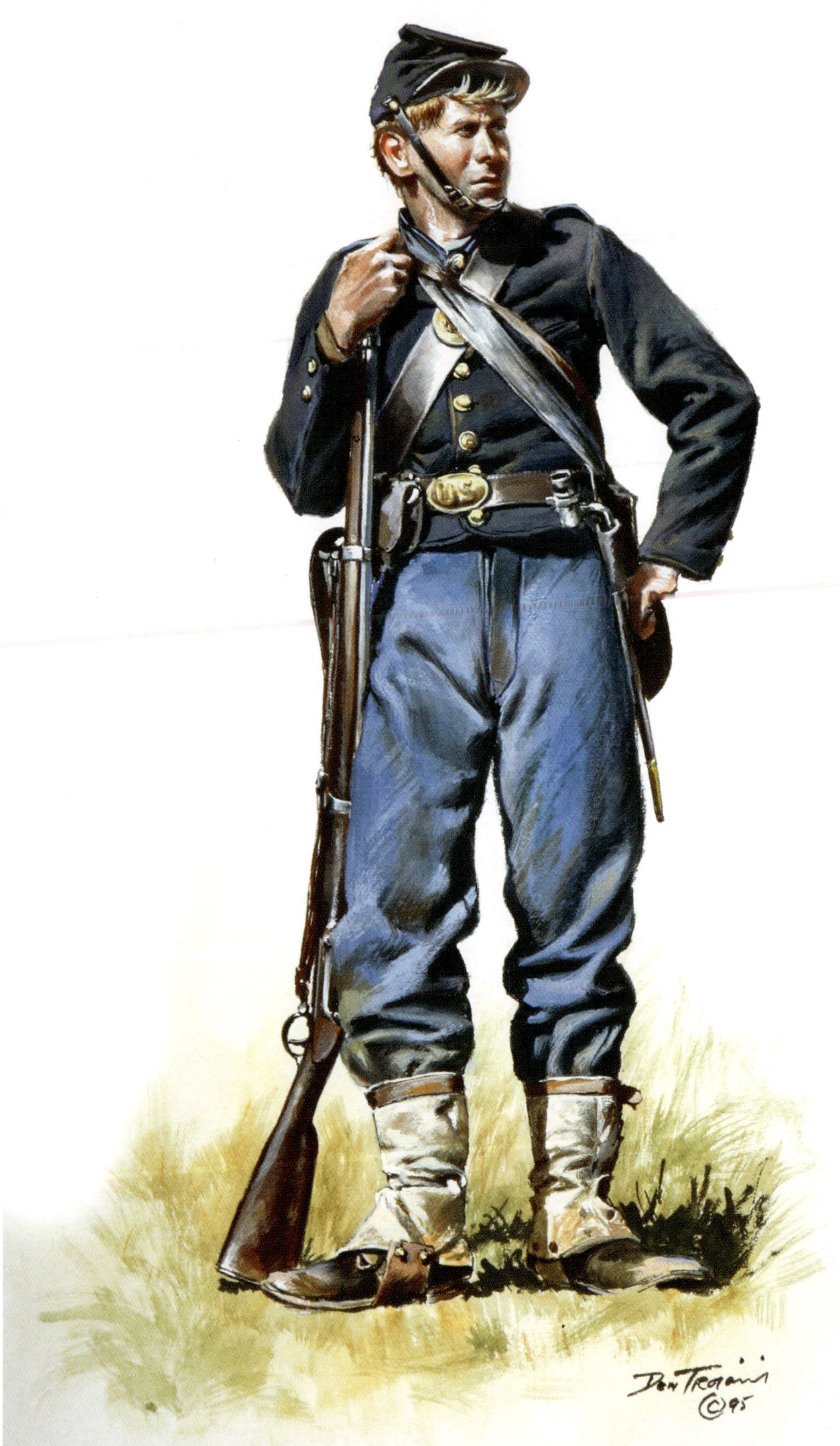

MUSTERED INTO SERVICE AT FORT SCHUYLER, NEW YORK, when the government approved the commissioning of an Irish Brigade in September 1861, the 88th New York Infantry was initially composed of the 2nd and 4th New York under the command of Colonel Baker and Colonel Thomas F. Meagher, respectively. However, the two commanders agreed to combine the two units that were designated the 88th New York Infantry, after the 88th Regiment of Foot, a British Army unit composed largely of Irishmen. The regiment was also known as the "Faugh a Ballaghs," and the "Fourth Irish." Along with the other regiments in the Irish Brigade, the 88th New York was presented with a green regimental flag known as the "Irish Colors" bearing a gold-painted harp, shortly after Fredericksburg and while still attending to their wounded.[1]

The regiment left the state on December 16, 1861, and served with Meagher's Brigade, Sumner's Division, Army of the Potomac, from December 1861, which became Richardson's brigade, 1st Division, II Corps, Army of the Potomac, from March 1862. During the second day at Gettysburg the Irish Brigade, as part of John C. Caldwell's division, II Corps, took up position at the Wheatfield and stood against several attacks from Longstreet's corps. Although they eventually broke, they were commended for holding on for so long.

This private wears a New York State pattern jacket with sky-blue trim on collar and shoulder straps. His sky-blue wool kersey trousers are tucked into white lace-up canvas gaiters. His forage cap is plain dark blue. He is armed with a Model 1863 rifle musket, and has a Pattern 1839 oval "US" plate on his waist belt, and round Pattern 1826 "eagle" plate on his shoulder belt.

---

1. New York State Military Museum and Veterans Research Center, Unit History 88th New York Infantry.

1st South Carolina Volunteer Infantry, US Colored Troops

THE FIRST ATTEMPT TO RECRUIT A SOUTH CAROLINIAN Black regiment to fight for the Union occurred in March 1862 when Major General David Hunter took command of troops in the Department of the South. On April 3 he wrote to Secretary of War Edwin M. Stanton requesting "50,000 muskets, with all the necessary accoutrements, and 200 rounds for each piece." Concerning clothing, he required "50,000 pairs of scarlet pantaloons," adding unsympathetically "this is all the clothing I shall require for these people."[1] Although he managed to conscript about 500 black men, he lacked the necessary political support and was forced to disband them in August 1862, retaining only one company in service.

However, Hunter's plan was revived under Brigadier General Rufus Saxton, who supervised contraband affairs in the Department of the South. His request for permission to recruit and arm five thousand black quartermaster employees euphemistically termed "laborers" was granted. As a result, with the aid of Massachusetts Governor John A. Andrews, Saxton recruited and organized the 1st South Carolina Volunteer Infantry and appointed as its commander Thomas W. Higginson, a radical abolitionist and former ally of John Brown.[2]

Commanded by white officers, early recruits were largely Gullah men from the South Carolinian and Georgian Sea Islands including one hundred men from Hunter's original regiment, and were deployed almost two months before the Emancipation Proclamation was issued by President Lincoln on January 1, 1863. The regiment was redesignated the 33rd United States Colored Troops on March 26, 1864, and served as such until the end of the war. Although the unit was not involved in major battles, it saw extensive action along the South Carolina, Georgia and Florida coast in 1862–1863, and was involved in the Battle of Honey Hill, South Carolina, on November 30, 1864.

This private of the 1st South Carolina Volunteer Infantry wears a pair of the red trousers of the type originally supplied to Hunter's regiment during May 1862.[3] These would be replaced by regulation sky-blue in February 1863 at the request of the unit, who felt they were being set apart from white regiments. The rest of his uniform is regulation US Army pattern. He is armed with a Model 1842 Springfield musket. Accoutrements include a cartridge box carried on a shoulder belt bearing a Pattern 1826 "eagle" plate. A Pattern 1839 oval "US" plate fastens his waist belt on which is slid a percussion cap pouch plus socket bayonet and scabbard.

---

1. *ORs*, series 1, vol. 6, 264.

2. "The Black Military Experience," in *Freedom: A Documentary History of Emancipation, 1861–1867*, series II, ed. Ira Berlin (Cambridge, UK: Cambridge University Press, 1982), 39–40.

3. *New-York Times*, May 1, 1862, 2:1.

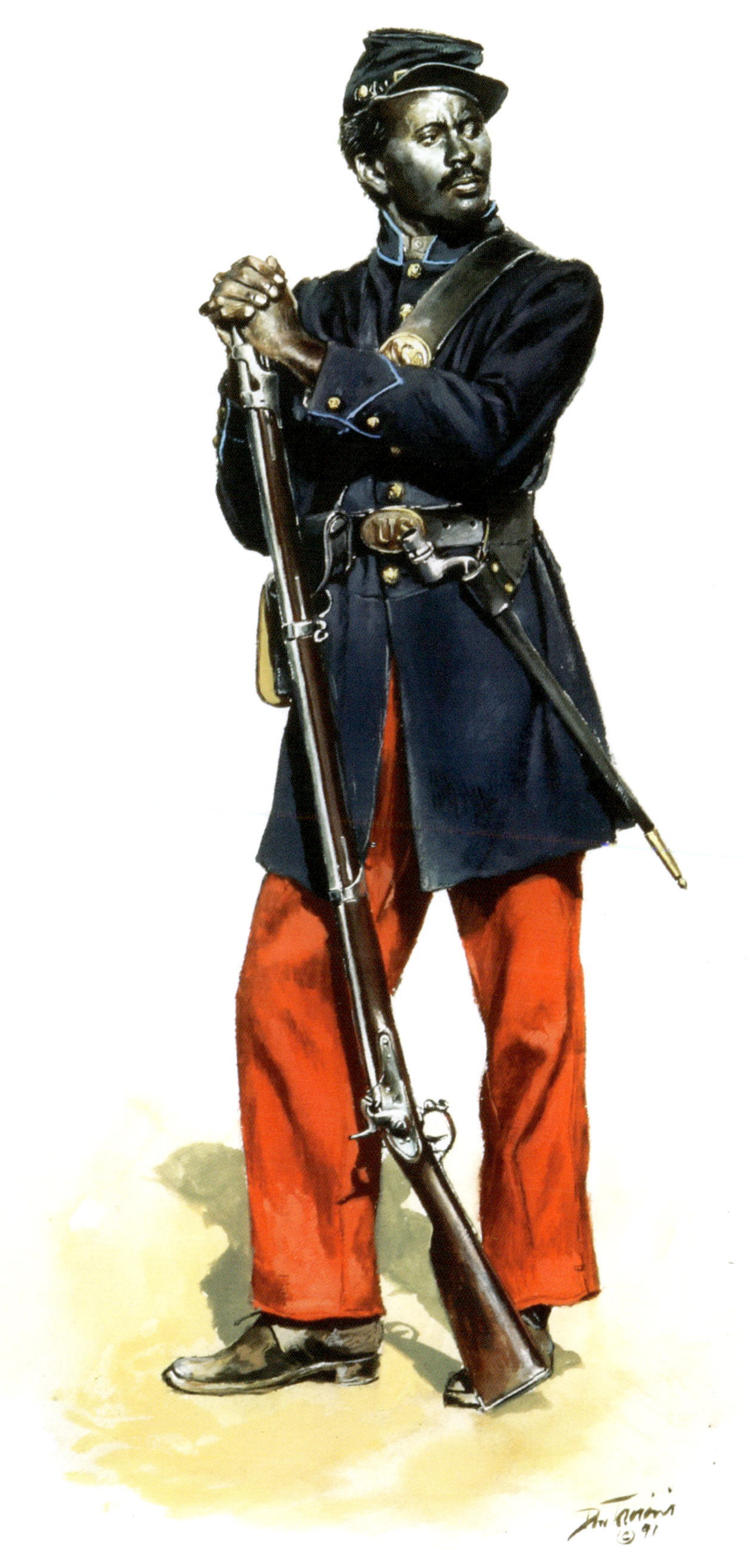

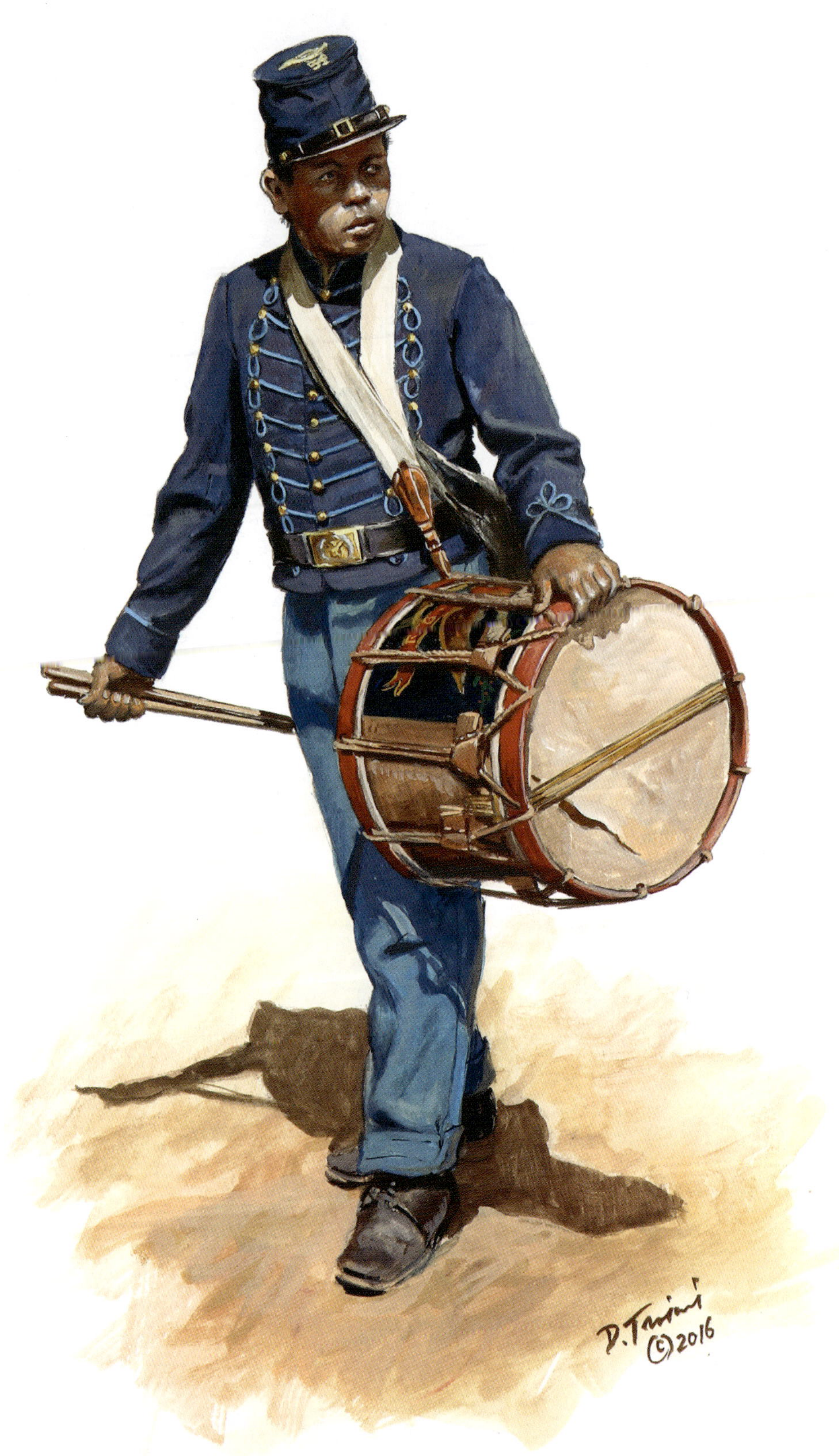

54th Massachusetts Infantry Drummer

ALTHOUGH NOT THE FIRST REGIMENT OF BLACK SOLDIERS to be raised in defence of the Union, the 54th Massachusetts Infantry is probably the most recognizable. Not strictly composed of volunteers from the Bay State, its ranks consisted of freemen of color from several Northern states, plus a small number of ex-slaves, who gathered at Camp Meigs in Readville, Massachusetts, beginning on February 21, 1863. As more men volunteered than were needed for one regiment, the surplus became the nucleus for another African American infantry regiment, the 55th Massachusetts.[1]

With mostly all white officers, the 54th Massachusetts was commanded by Colonel Robert Gould Shaw, who had served as a private in the 7th New York State Militia during the spring of 1861, and then as a captain of Company K, 2nd Massachusetts Infantry. Many of his fellow officers of the 54th had seen prior service in other regiments. Thus, led by veteran officers it left camp on May 28, 1863, departing for South Carolina after a grand review for Massachusetts Governor John A. Andrew. In the regiment's first battle near Seccessionville on July 16, it lost fourteen killed, eighteen wounded, and three missing. But compared to its next action this was a mere skirmish. Two days later, on July 18, 1863, the regiment reported to Morris Island where it joined the assault on Battery Wagner ordered by Brigadier General George C. Strong that evening, with Colonel Shaw agreeing to "lead the column" attack despite the exhausted state of his men.[2]

Advancing across a narrow sand bar into intense artillery and musket fire, the regiment met with devastating opposition suffering 42 percent casualties. Colonel Shaw and two other officers were among thirty men killed. One hundred and forty-nine were wounded, including eleven officers. Fifteen men were captured and fifty-two were missing in action. Sergeant William H. Carney, Company C, 54th Massachusetts, became the first black American soldier to be awarded the Congressional Medal of Honor for grasping the regimental flag when the color bearer was shot down, planting it on the parapet of the fort, and bringing it back to the Union lines, despite being "twice severely wounded."[3] The regiment continued to serve in South Carolina and Georgia until war's end, returning to Boston in August of 1865.

The light blue trim on the jacket of this drummer is based on a photograph of John Gooseberry, Company E, 54th Massachusetts, which was published in the regimental history. While unusual, this style of trim was not unique and field musicians of other regiments wore similar jackets. The rest of the regiment was uniformed and equipped according to federal regulations and were armed with Enfield rifle muskets received on April 30, 1863. On the evening of the assault on Battery Wagner, Colonel Shaw was described as wearing a "close-fitting staff-officer's jacket, with a silver eagle denoting his rank on each shoulder. His trousers were light blue; a fine narrow silk sash was wound around his waist. . . . Upon his head was a high felt army hat with cord."

---

1. The Adjutant General, ed. and comp., *Massachusetts Soldiers, Sailors, and Marines in the Civil War*, vol. IV (printed at the Norwood Press, 1932), 657.

2. Luis F. Emilio, *History of the Fifty-Fourth Regiment of Massachusetts Volunteer Infantry, 1863–65* (The Boston Book Company, 1894), 72.

3. Emilio, *History of the Fifty-Fourth Regiment of Massachusetts Volunteer Infantry, 1863–65*, 77.

4th United States Colored Troops, Private, 1864

ORGANIZED AT BALTIMORE, MARY-LAND, FROM July 15 to September 1, 1863, the 4th United States Colored Troops served in Virginia and fought at the Battle of the Crater at Petersburg on July 30, 184. Later involved in the move toward Richmond, it took part in the fight at Dutch Gap on September 7, Chaffin's Farm from September 28 to September 30, and the Fair Oaks on October 27 and October 28. Three men of the regiment received the Medal of Honor for their actions at Chaffin's Farm. At the war's end, the men of the 4th USCT witnessed the surrender of the army of General Joseph E. Johnston at Bennett, or Bennitt, Place, North Carolina, on April 26, 1865. The unit served out the rest of its term in the Department of North Carolina, and was mustered out on May 4, 1866.[1]

This well equipped private is dressed for winter campaigning. He wears a sky-blue infantry enlisted man's overcoat, underneath which would be his uniform coat and sky-blue trousers. His forage cap bears an XVIII Corps badge and Pattern 1858 infantry horn insignia with regimental number "4" attached to its top. He is armed with a Pattern 1853 Enfield rifle musket.

---

1. *Supplement*, part II, vol. 77, 319.

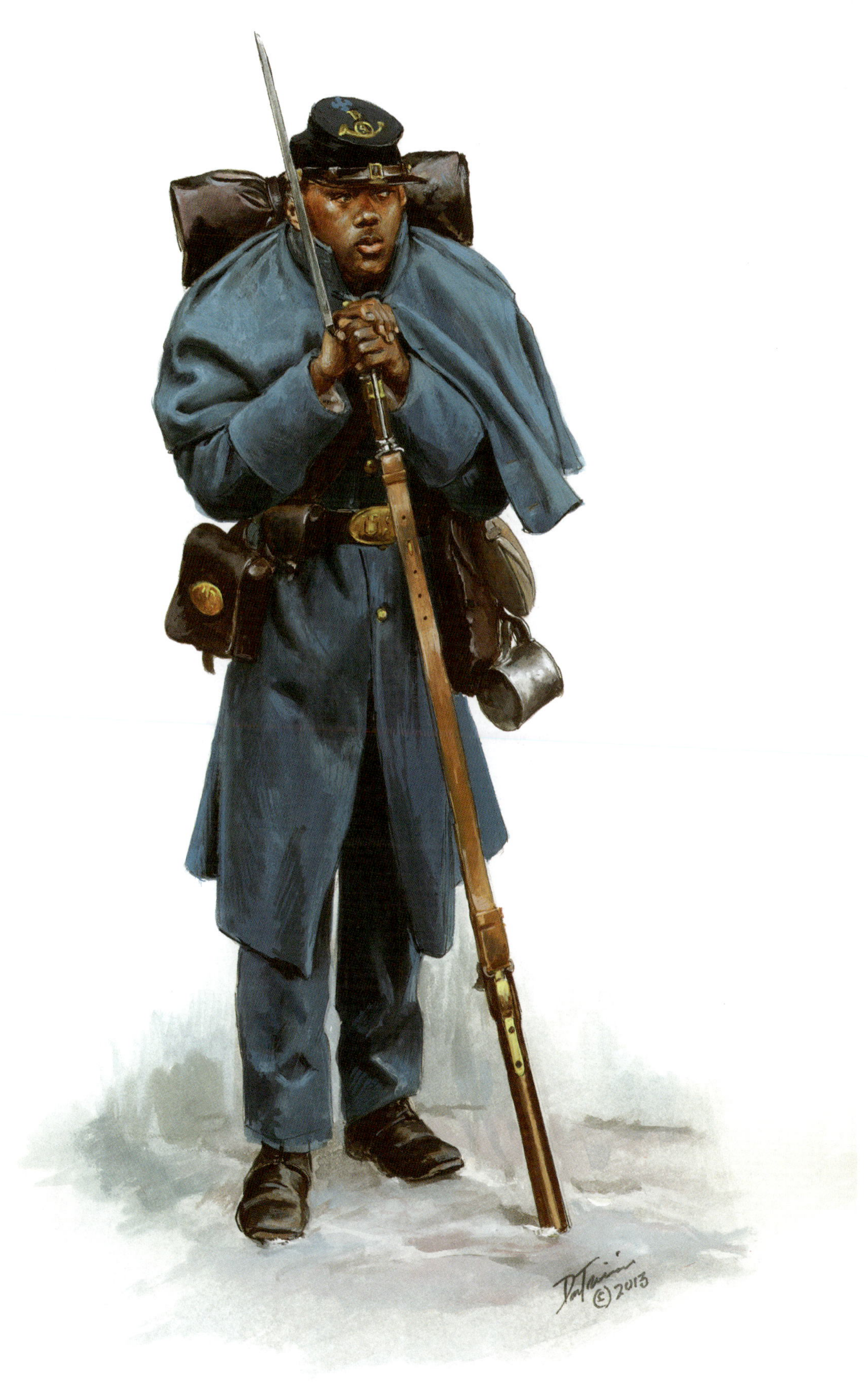

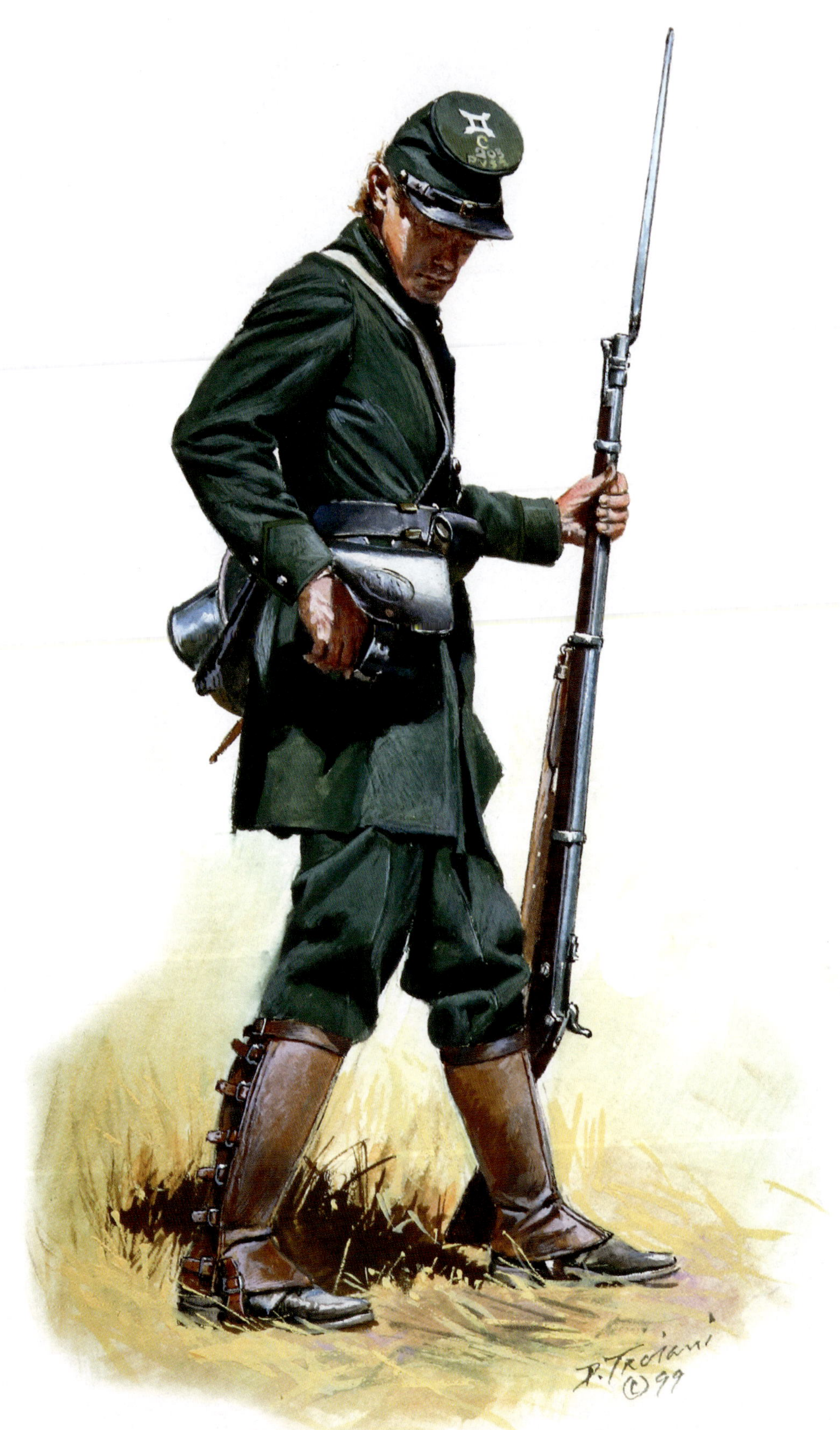
P. Troiani
©99

203rd Pennsylvania Infantry (Birney's Sharpshooters)

RECRUITED AT THE SUGGESTION OF GENERAL DAVID Bell Birney to serve in his division of the Army of the James, the 203rd Pennsylvania Infantry was organized for one year's service at Camp Cadwalader, near Philadelphia, on September 10, 1864, with Colonel John W. Moore in command. The regiment left for the front twelve days later and arrived in front of Petersburg on September 27 where it was assigned to 2nd Brigade, 2nd Division, X Corps.[1]

Enlisting at a time when the service of the renowned Berdan's Sharpshooters was coming to an end, the Union army Quartermaster Department had a surplus of dark green uniforms which, with the backing of General Birney, were issued to the 203rd Pennsylvania.[2] Unlike Berdan's Sharphooters, who had received Sharps breech-loading rifles, the Pennsylvanians were issued with Springfield rifle muskets, which were most likely the improved model of 1864. Their accoutrements included Pattern 1864 cartridge boxes with embossed "US" on the outer flap rather than the brass plate, and were carried on a black leather shoulder belt minus Pattern 1826 round "eagle" plate.

Birney originally intended that the 203rd Pennsylvania should only serve as sharpshooters, but after his death from disease on October 18, 1864, the unit was regarded as infantry and served as a line regiment. Involved in the grand assault on Fort Fisher on January 15, 1865, the regiment lost both its colonel and lieutenant colonel, plus 44 killed and 145 wounded, nearly half its number.[3]

Loading his Springfield rifle musket, this private wears the full Berdan's Sharpshooters surplus uniform complete with leather leggings, but has brass letters and numerals, plus X Corps badge, attached to his cap top.

1. Samuel P. Bates, *History of Pennsylvania Volunteers, 1861–5* (B. Singerly, State Printer, 1871), 578.

2. NARA, record group 92, records of the Office of the Quartermaster General, entry 2182, Washington Depot to Schuylkill Arsenal, September 23, 1864.

3. Bates, *History of Pennsylvania Volunteers, 1861–5*, 579.

2nd Maryland Infantry, C.S.A., 1864

THE 2ND MARYLAND INFANTRY, FOR-MERLY KNOWN AS the 1st Maryland Battalion, was composed of volunteers from the border state of Maryland who, despite their home state remaining loyal to the Union, chose instead to fight for the Confederacy. This regiment was largely made up of volunteers from the earlier 1st Maryland Infantry, which was disbanded at Gordonsville, Virginia, in August 1862, its initial term of service having expired.[1] Unable to return home to Maryland having effectively committed to the Confederacy for the duration of the war, many Marylander secessionists joined Virginia units, while others determined to form a new Maryland infantry regiment. Five companies had been recruited by the end of September 1862, and a further two were added by early 1863 enabling their organization to be mustered in to the Confederate army as the 1st Maryland Battalion, Lieutenant Colonel James R. Herbert commanding. Containing eight companies by March 1864, the unit was officially redesignated the 2nd Maryland Infantry.

Following arduous service in the Shenandoah Valley, the 2nd Maryland Battalion found itself at Gettysburg on July 1, 1863, as part of Ewell's II Corps, and suffered one third casualties during the unsuccessful assaults on Culp's Hill. Following the retreat from Gettysburg, it was brigaded with all other Maryland units in the Army of Northern Virginia to form "The Maryland Line" under Brigadier General Bradley T. Johnson. Although broken up and assigned to different commands for the spring ,offensive of 1864, they were still referred to as Maryland Line units. The 2nd Maryland Infantry fought through the Virginia campaign and by the fall of 1864 were in the trenches outside Petersburg.

During the early days of formation, the 2nd Maryland was considered to be well supplied with uniforms, and continued to draw large quantities of clothing from the Confederate quartermaster department during 1864, which included forage caps, jackets, trousers, overcoats and shoes. Nonetheless, the general appearance of the unit was decidedly ragged by February 1864 when secessionist and ex-Marshall of Police of Baltimore, Colonel George P. Kane, visited them in the trenches, and purchased replacement uniform clothing and headgear for them.

This Maryland private is depicted having been uniformed in 1864. His chasseur-pattern forage cap is trimmed with a branch-service band of infantry dark blue. His jacket is of the type run though the Union naval blockade having been supplied by the thousand to the Confederacy that year by Peter Tait & Company, of Limerick, Ireland.[2] Of dark blue-gray cloth and with dark blue collar, some of its issued Confederate infantry "I" buttons have been replaced by those of the private's home state. He is armed with a Pattern 1853 Enfield rifle musket, and accoutrements include a Pattern 1860 Enfield cartridge box on black leather shoulder belt. A nonrigid, black water-proofed knapsack and rolled light-blue overcoat rest at the foot of the tree.

---

1. Frederick P. Todd, "State Forces," in *American Military Equipage 1851–1872*, vol. II (Chatham Square Press, Inc., 1983), 889.

2. NARA, M346, Confederate Citizens File, Peter Tait & Co., 3.

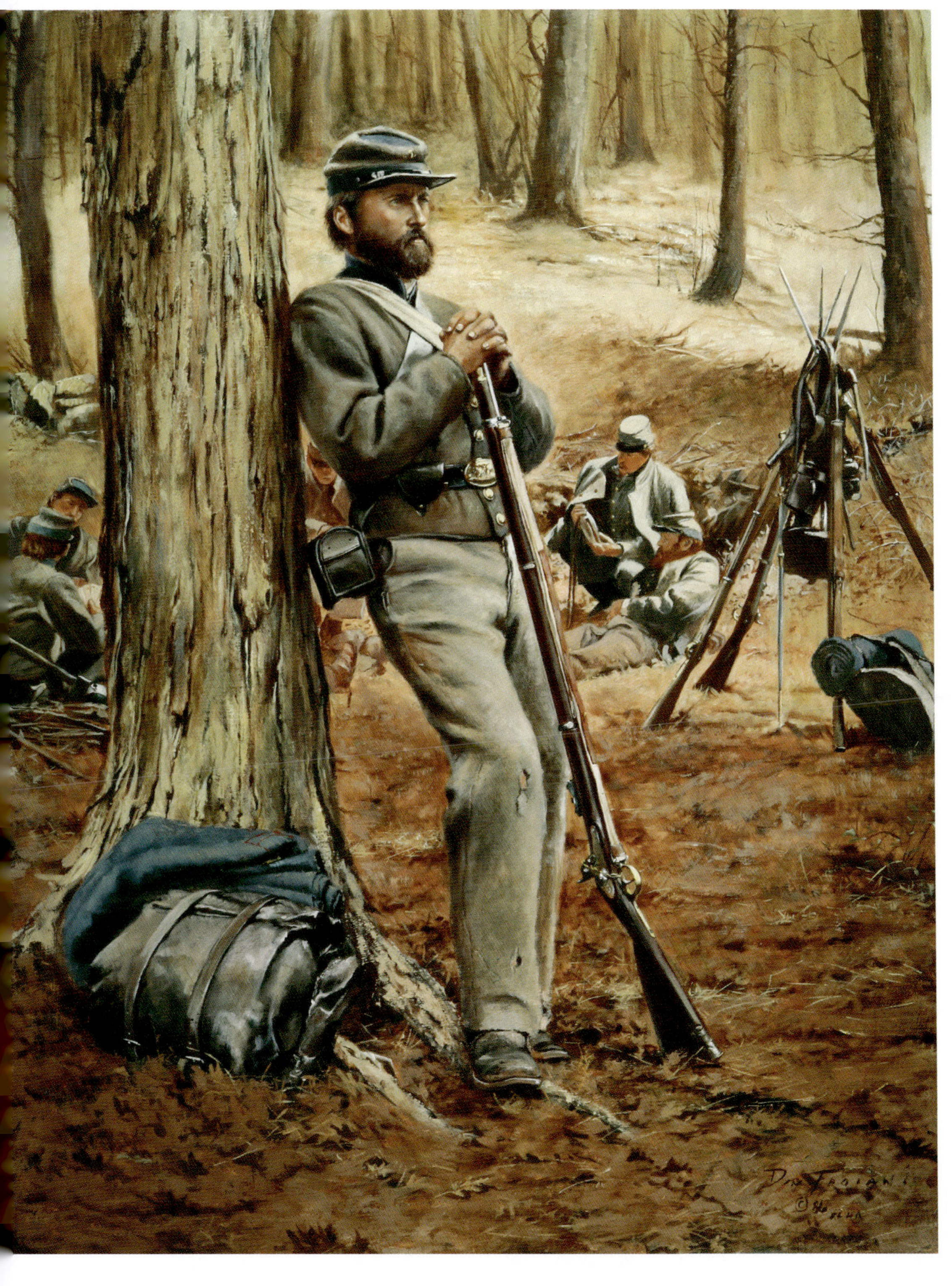

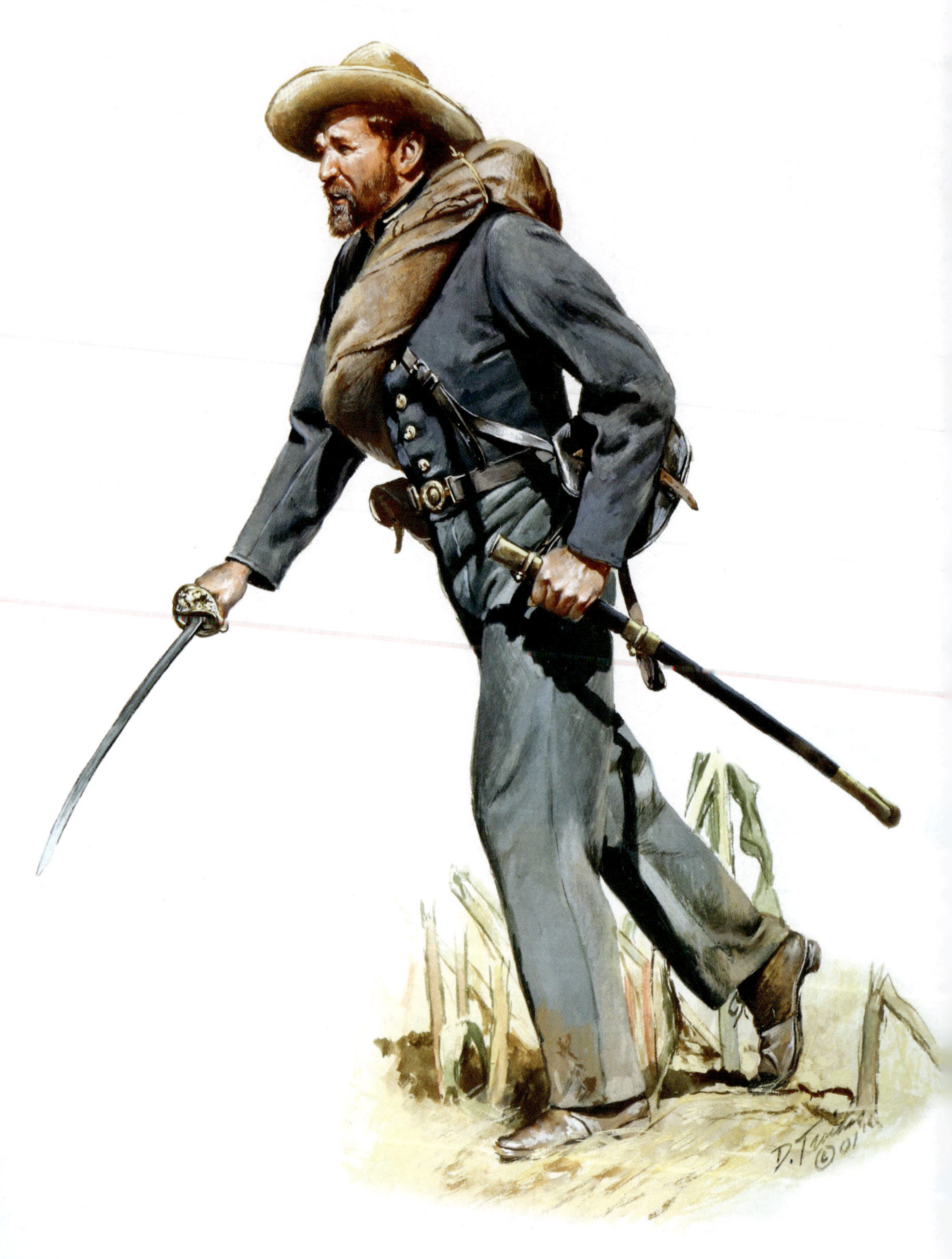

Confederate States Infantry Officer, 1865

BY 1865, IT WAS DIFFICULT TO DISTIN-GUISH LINE OFFICERS from enlisted men in the Confederate armies. This was as much by design as it was a lack of access to military tailors to produce regulation dress. The only ways of distinguishing this officer from his men was the bars on his collar, and the sword he carried. This lack of rank insignia offered some protection from Federal troops and sharpshooters who might find difficulty discerning his officer status in the smoke of battle. This captain wears a specially tai-lored cadet gray jacket with gold bars on the collar, and plain sky-blue enlisted man's wool kersey trousers. As with enlisted men, he wears a blanket roll, which also contains his few personal belongings. His accoutrements include a privately purchased leather haversack containing a few morsels of food. Armed with a Model 1850 Foot Officer's sword, he carries a holstered revolver attached to his waist belt, which has a two-piece wreath and tongue plate.

31st United States Colored Troops

THE 31ST UNITED STATES COLORED TROOPS WAS FORMED by consolidation with the 30th Connecticut Volunteers via Special Orders No. 180 issued by the Adjutant General's Office, War Department, on May 18, 1864. Following difficulties appointing an executive officer, with Major Theodore H. Rockwood being relieved of command, and Major James H. Lane arrested, command of the 31st USCT devolved upon Captain Thomas Wright. Eventually on June 22, 1864, Lieutenant Colonel William E.W. Ross was appointed to command the regiment.[1]

Stationed near Petersburg during July–August 1864, the regiment took part in the Battle of the Crater on July 30 as part of the Second Brigade, Fourth Division, IX Corps, Army of the Potomac. According to Major Thomas Wright, the regiment was so affected by the "great loss of officers" including Lieutenant Colonel Ross shot through the left leg, and himself struck by a piece of shell in the side, that it fell back in disorder.[2] Two other officers and 17 enlisted men were killed, plus 47 wounded during the action.

The regiment mainly performed picket duty near Chaffin's Farm until the end of the year when it was transferred to the Third Brigade, Second Division, XXV Army Corps on December 30, 1864. Moved across the James and Appomattox rivers to the extreme left of the Army of the Potomac, it took part in the operations near and across Hatcher's Run. On April 2, 1865, it occupied the Confederate works and took part in the advance on Petersburg the next day. Joining in the pursuit of the enemy, it participated in the operations resulting in the surrender of the Army of Northern Virginia at Appomattox Court House on April 9, 1865.[3]

Attached to the First Brigade, Third Division, X Army Corps, the 31st USCT served in troop transports off the coast of Texas operating at Brazos Santiago and Corpus Christi until August 1865, when it was transferred to the District of New Berne, North Carolina, until honorably discharged and mustered out on November 7, 1865. During its service the regiment sustained two officers and thirty-five enlisted men killed, while one officer and nineteen enlisted men were wounded in action. A further one hundred men died of disease.

This enlisted man of Company D, 31st USCT wears a four-button sack coat, sky-blue infantry-pattern trousers, and Pattern 1858 cap with brass "looped infantry horn" insignia with regimental numerals "31" inset, above which is the company letter "D" and IX Corps green shield-shaped badge. He is armed with a Model 1864 Springfield rifle musket with fixed bayonet, as issued to at least three companies of the regiment at its organization in May 1864, and accoutrements include a Pattern 1858 canteen with cloth cover painted with "D 31."

1. *Supplement*, part II, vol. 77, 700.
2. *New York Evening Post*, August 16, 1864.
3. *Supplement*, part II, vol. 77, 701.

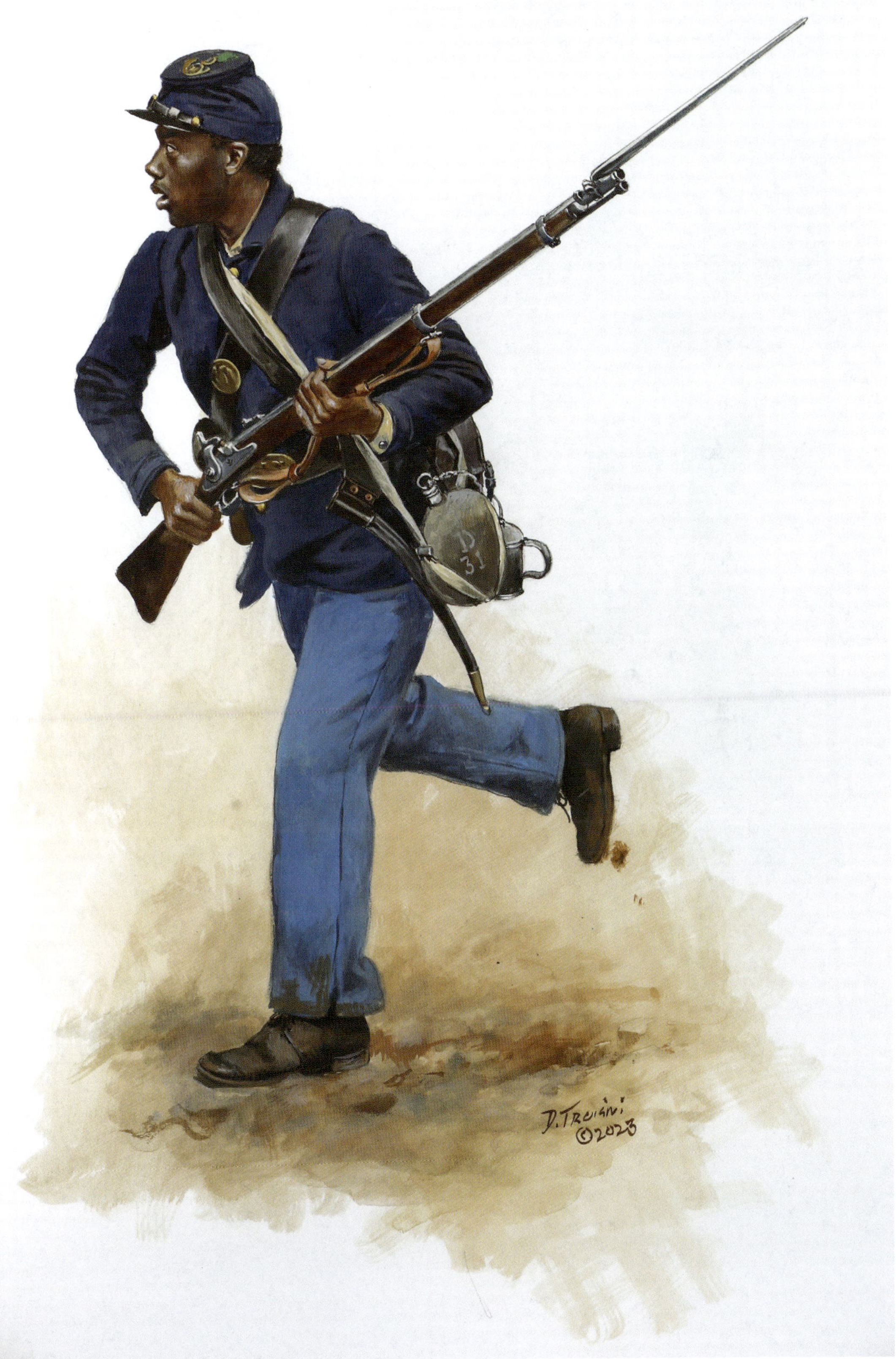

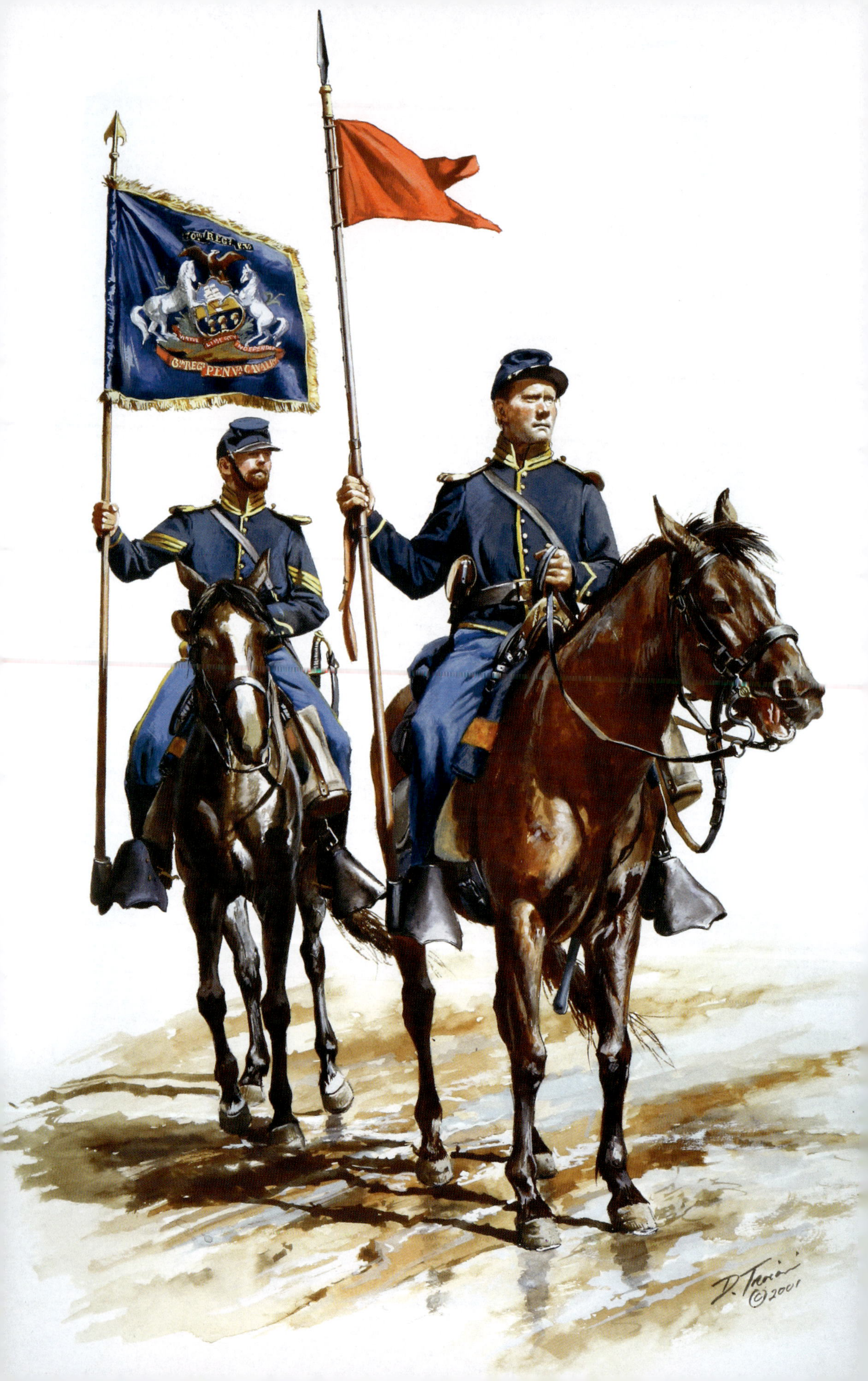
70th REGt INFy
6th REGt PENNa CAVALRY
VIRTUE LIBERTY INDEPENDENCE

THE CAVALRY

6th Pennsylvania Cavalry, 1861–1865

THE 6TH PENNSYLVANIA CAVALRY, OR 70TH REGIMENT of Pennsylvania Volunteers, was raised by Colonel Richard H. Rush during the summer and fall of 1861. Originally known as the Philadelphia Light Cavalry, the unit was initially armed with .44-caliber Colt Army Model 1860 revolvers and a mixture of Model 1840 and 1860 sabers. Under orders from Major General George B. McClellan, it was transformed into a lancer regiment on November 30, 1861. Based on advice from the Duc de Chartes, Comte de Paris, and Major Von Hammerstein, then all on McClellan's staff, the type of lance adopted was the Austrian pattern. This weapon consisted of a 9-foot-long staff made of Norwegian fir, and an 11-inch, three-edged blade, topped with a scarlet swallow-tailed pennon. Made in Philadelphia by Isaac Broome, 1001 "Lances, with pennon & strap," at $6 each, were supplied to the War Department by December 1861.[1] Subsequently known as Rush's Lancers, each company in the regiment was issued with lances plus twelve Sharp's carbines for picket and scout duty. It was not until May 1863 that the regiment gave up its lances in favor of carbines. Participating in the Peninsula Campaign, Antietam, and Fredericksburg, it went on to fight in every subsequent battle of the Army of the Potomac to Appomattox.

The uniform worn by Rush's Lancers was the US regulation cavalry model with minor variation. Brass shoulder scales were worn by enlisted men as late as May 1862. Trousers were sky-blue as opposed to dark blue prescribed for the army since 1858. Full dress headgear, also worn by several other Pennsylvania units, initially consisted of a stiff, high-crowned Havelock hat patented by master hatter Charles Lacroix Pascal on December 10, 1861, and produced by Sullender & Pascal, of Philadelphia.[2] Forage caps subsequently worn by this unit had more horizontal than vertical leather visors. Some enlisted men sported either the brass letters "RL" and regimental number "6," or brass crossed sabers, on the crown. All leather was black, and half boots were worn under their trousers.

Horse equipment includes a Pattern 1859 McClellan saddle; black leather stirrup straps; wooden stirrups and black leather stirrup hoods; canvas nose bag; black saddle bags; halter-bridle; and dark blue dragoon horse blanket with broad orange band around the edge folded under the saddle. A leather socket attached to the off-side stirrup hood designed to accommodate the staff of the color bearer was also used to support and carry the weight of the lance.

Bearing the coat of arms of Pennsylvania, the standard of Rush's Lancers came close to being captured during the cavalry fight at Brandy Station on June 9, 1863, when the bearer was shot from his horse. Caught before it fell to the ground, it was scooped up and carried from the field to be borne proudly until the end of the war.[3]

---

1. Bruce S. Bazelon and William F. McGuinn, *A Directory of American Military Goods Dealers & Makers 1785–1885* (REF Typesetting & Publishing, 1987), 10.

2. Ron Field, "A Field Guide to Havelock Hats in the Civil War: Ugly as the Devil," *Military Images* 23, no. 1 (Winter 2015): 55.

3. Richard A. Sauers, *Advance the Colors: Pennsylvania Civil War Battle Flags*, vol. 1 (Capitol Preservation Committee, 1987), 191.

Sussex Light Dragoons

THE SUSSEX LIGHT DRAGOONS WERE ORGANIZED UNDER Captain Benjamin W. Belches at Waverly in Sussex County, Virginia, during January 1861, and mustered into State service for a period of 12 months at Suffolk, Virginia, on April 22, 1861. Temporarily attached to the 5th Virginia Cavalry, they were assigned with seven other companies to the 16th Battalion Virginia Cavalry under Major Belches on June 26, 1862. With the addition of another company on July 29, the designation of this unit was changed to the 13th Virginia Cavalry, under Colonel John R. Chambliss Jr., and the Sussex Light Dragoons served with that command as Company H until the end of the war.[1]

Much of the information used to produce this interpretation of a mounted second lieutenant and private of the Sussex Light Dragoons was drawn from period photographs. The full dress is based on images of Private Rufus K. Harrison, which shows a nine-button dark blue uniform coat with a narrow piping at the collar and cuff, and Corporal Robert T. Bendall, whose coat is without trim. A group image of Privates Richard L. Dobie and James R. Parham, plus an unidentified soldier, show examples of headgear consisting of a high-crowned dark blue forage cap, quartered with yellow piping, with gilt letters "SLD" over crossed sabers at front. The men in the latter image also wore for fatigue purposes plain gray woolen shirts with small, rectangular plastrons fastened by four buttons on each side.[2]

The officer wears knee-high boots and holds a .36-caliber Colt Navy revolver. He also has a single-shot pistol in a pommel holster attached to his saddle, and likely carries a cavalry officer's saber. The private is armed with a Model 1840 US Heavy Dragoon saber and holds a privately owned shotgun. Accoutrements consist of cavalry belts with shoulder straps and two-piece wreath and tongue for the officer and rectangular Virginia State belt plate for the enlisted man.

The names of 178 men appear on the rolls of the Sussex Light Dragoons. Fifty-one were killed or wounded. Of these, 21 were killed on the battlefield, or died in hospital; 16 were discharged, being disabled by wounds, and 14 returned to duty. Fifty-seven men of the unit laid down their arms at Appomattox Courthouse on April 9, 1865.[3]

---

1. Wallace, *A Guide to Virginia Military Organizations 1861–1865*, 44.
2. For images of Bendall, Dobie, and Parham, see the collection of the American Civil War Museum, catalog no. 0985.13.02189 and 1954.001.
3. "Sussex Light Dragoons," *Southern Historical Society Papers* 25 (1876): 275.

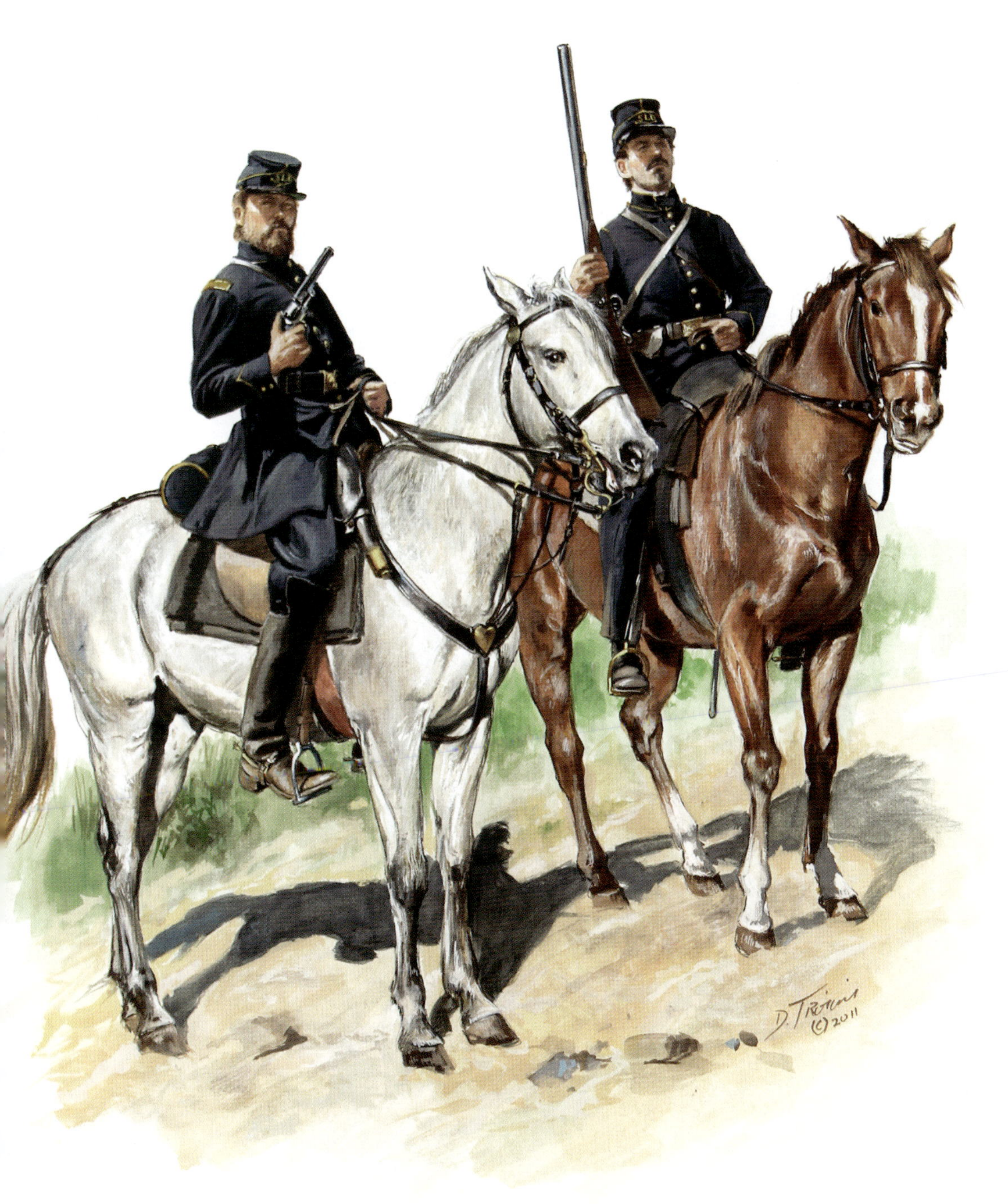

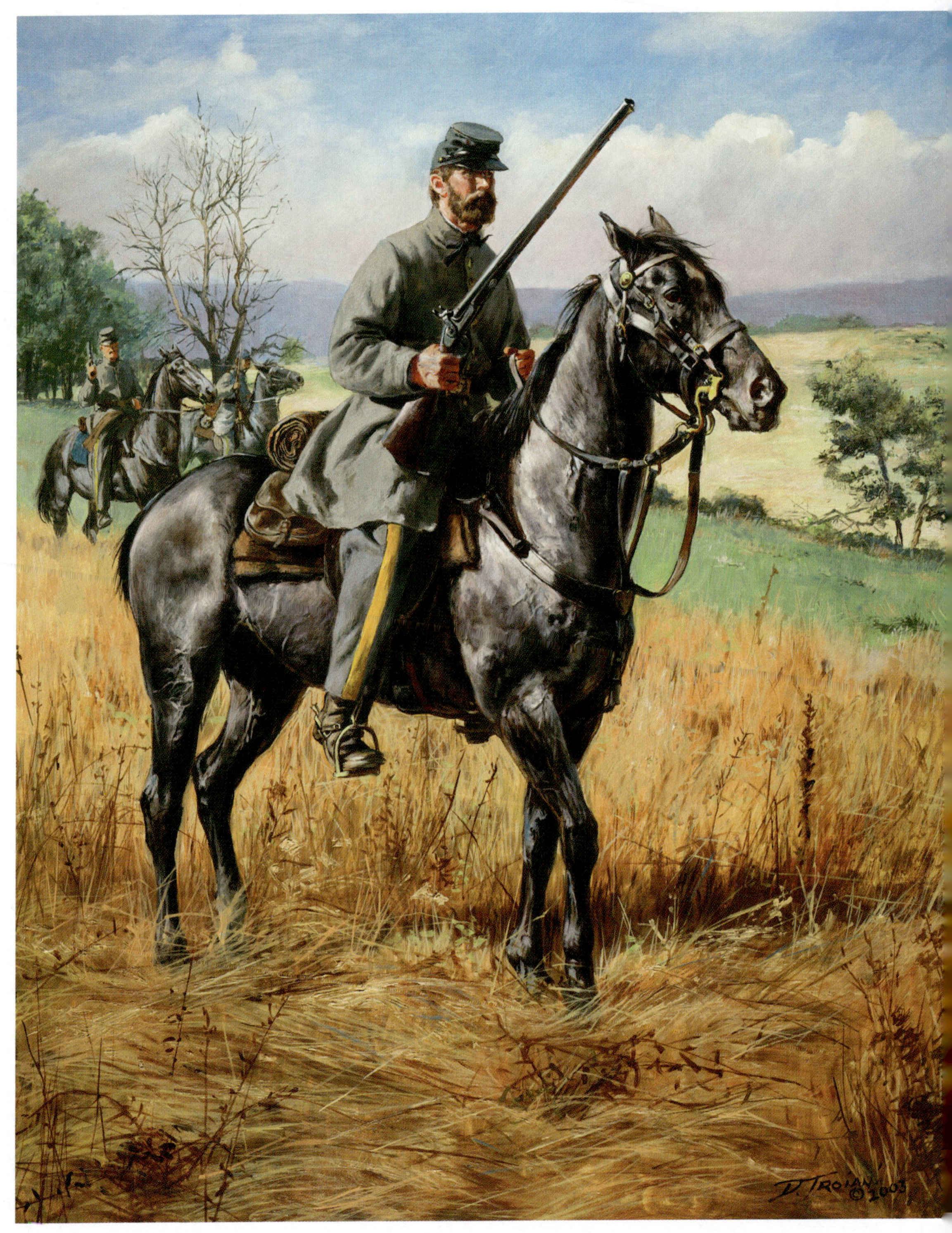

4th Virginia Cavalry, Black Horse Troop

COMPOSED LARGELY OF THE SONS OF WEALTHY PLANTERS, the Black Horse Troop was recruited in Fauquier County, Virginia, during June 1859. Commanded by Captain William H. F. Payne, they were ordered with other troops to occupy Harpers Ferry and seize the US Government Arsenal on April 1, 1861. Entering state service for one year later that month, they became Company H of the 4th Virginia Cavalry on September 4, 1861.

Describing the Union defeat at First Manassas on July 21, 1861, a Northern newspaper correspondent wrote that retreating troops expected any moment that "the 'black horse' cavalry would be upon them."[1] Fear of the Black Horse Troop among Union troops stemmed from a skirmish at Fairfax Court House on June 1, 1861, when a detachment of the 2nd US Cavalry under Lieutenant Charles H. Tompkins clashed with Confederate cavalry and infantry. Both Northern and Southern press falsely reported that Tompkins's unit was "cut to pieces" by the Black Horse Troop.[2] In fact casualties were light on both sides, and the Troop arrived too late to take part in the action. Nonetheless, rumors continued to spread and Union troops who subsequently spied any body of Confederate horsemen on July 21, 1861, assumed they must be the dreaded Black Horse Troop. In fact, the unit was held in reserve with Lieutenant Colonel Thomas T. Munford's Squadron, and only descended on panic-stricken Union troops endeavoring to cross Cub Run toward the end of the battle, turning retreat into a complete rout with men screaming "the Black Horse Cavalry are coming!"

Prior to the Civil War, the Black Horse Troop wore dark blue uniforms based on 1858 State Regulations, but adopted field service clothing in 1861 which consisted of gray nine-button uniform coats and gray or sky-blue trousers with broad yellow stripes on the outer seams.[3] Regarding headgear, the company was issued 87 caps on October 2, 1861, being "without caps" and wearing hats before that date. Ninety pairs of pants were received on the same occasion.[4]

On patrol in October 1861, these Black Horse Troopers are armed with a mixture of double-barrelled shot-gun, Sharps carbines and pistols. Horse equipment includes a halter-bridle with running martingale; breast strap and crupper; and Jenifer saddle. A post-war reminiscence of the Black Horse Troop stated, "All members did not have black horses, but there were many black horses in the company."[5]

The Black Horse Troop served with the Army of Northern Virginia throughout the war. Refusing to surrender at Appomattox Court House on April 9, 1865, the few survivors of the company simply dispersed and rode home.

1. *Rutland Weekly Herald and Globe*, July 26, 1861, 2:6.
2. *Daily Evening Express* (Lancaster, PA), June 25, 1861, 3:5; and *Alabama Beacon* (Greensboro, AL), June 14, 1861, 2:8.
3. *Fauquier Historical Society Bulletin* 1, no. 1 (June 1923).
4. NARA, M224, CMSR, Fourth Virginia Cavalry, Alexander D. Payne, 60 and 62.
5. *Alexandria Gazette*, July 19, 1899, 1:3.

Trooper, 12th Virginia Cavalry, 1863

A CONFEDERATE CAVALRY REGIMENT HAD A SIMILAR company, squadron and battalion organization to that of the Union army, but was smaller since the company was officially made up of only about 88 officers and men instead of approximately 100, and there were only 10 companies in the regiment as opposed to 12. Thus, Confederate regiments initially had an official strength of about 880 men. At its inception on June 21, 1862, the 12th Virginia Cavalry consisted of a total of 646 troopers. Company A was the largest with 104 men while Company H the smallest with only 42 men.[1]

As with many Confederate regiments, the 12th Virginia Cavalry was issued a variety of clothing toward the end of the war. Although this mainly included jackets, the type and color of cloth used for these, and trousers, occasionally varied greatly. For example, while at Atlee Station, on the Virginia Central Railroad, on June 6, 1864, Company G received 30 pairs of trousers of which 17 were gray, 8 light blue, and 5 dark blue. Also received were 35 jackets, consisting of 18 gray and 17 black.[2] Other companies were issued similar assortments at that time. Also prevalent was a mixture of headgear, which included issue "military caps" and brimmed hats. Footwear consisted predominantly of shoes rather than boots.

Previous to reorganization in June 1862, the ten companies of the 12th Virginia had served as the 7th Virginia Cavalry. By mid-September 1862, the regiment formed part of the Laurel Brigade, originally commanded by Turner Ashby, and subsequently by Thomas L. Rosser, which also consisted of the 7th and 11th Virginia Cavalry, 35th Battalion Virginia Cavalry, also known as "the Comanches," and Chew's Battery, Virginia Horse Artillery.[3]

The 12th Virginia carried a great variety of arms. A regimental ordnance return dated March 31, 1863, while the regiment was stationed at Front Royal lists ammunition received for Enfield rifles, Colt Army and Colt Navy revolvers, Colt revolving rifles, Sharps, Robinson, Merrill, Hall and Smith carbines.[4] A number of English Kerr revolvers were acquired at a later date.

Depicted in 1864, these troopers of the 12th Virginia wear a mixture of quartermaster-issue jackets and pants. The man in the foreground holds an English Kerr revolver, and has a Sharps carbine slung by his side. A heart-shaped Laurel Brigade insignia is attached to the crown of his hat. The trooper at the rear is armed with a Colt Navy revolver and carbine. The horses of the Laurel Brigade were described in an inspection report produced by Rosser as "tolerably good," although on a divisional level they were assessed as being "in bad condition owing to the scarcity of forage."

---

1. Dennis E. Frye, *12th Virginia Cavalry* (H. E. Howard, Inc., 1988), 2.
2. NARA, M324, CMSR, 12th Virginia Cavalry, First Lieutenant William F. Anderson, 47.
3. Wallace, *A Guide to Virginia Military Organizations 1861–1865*, 53–54.
4. NARA, M324, CMSR, 12th Virginia Cavalry, Colonel Asher Waterman Harman, 33.

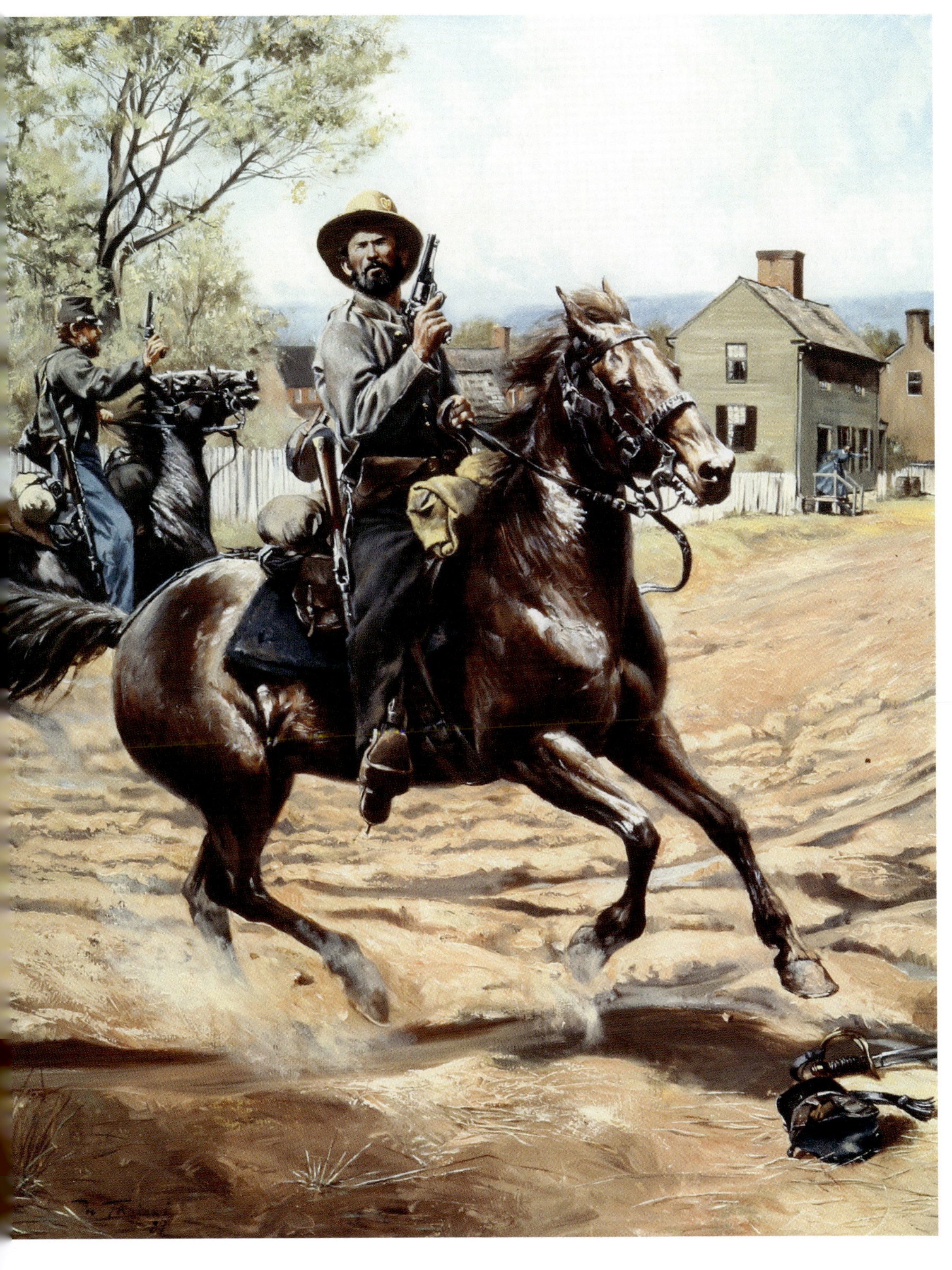

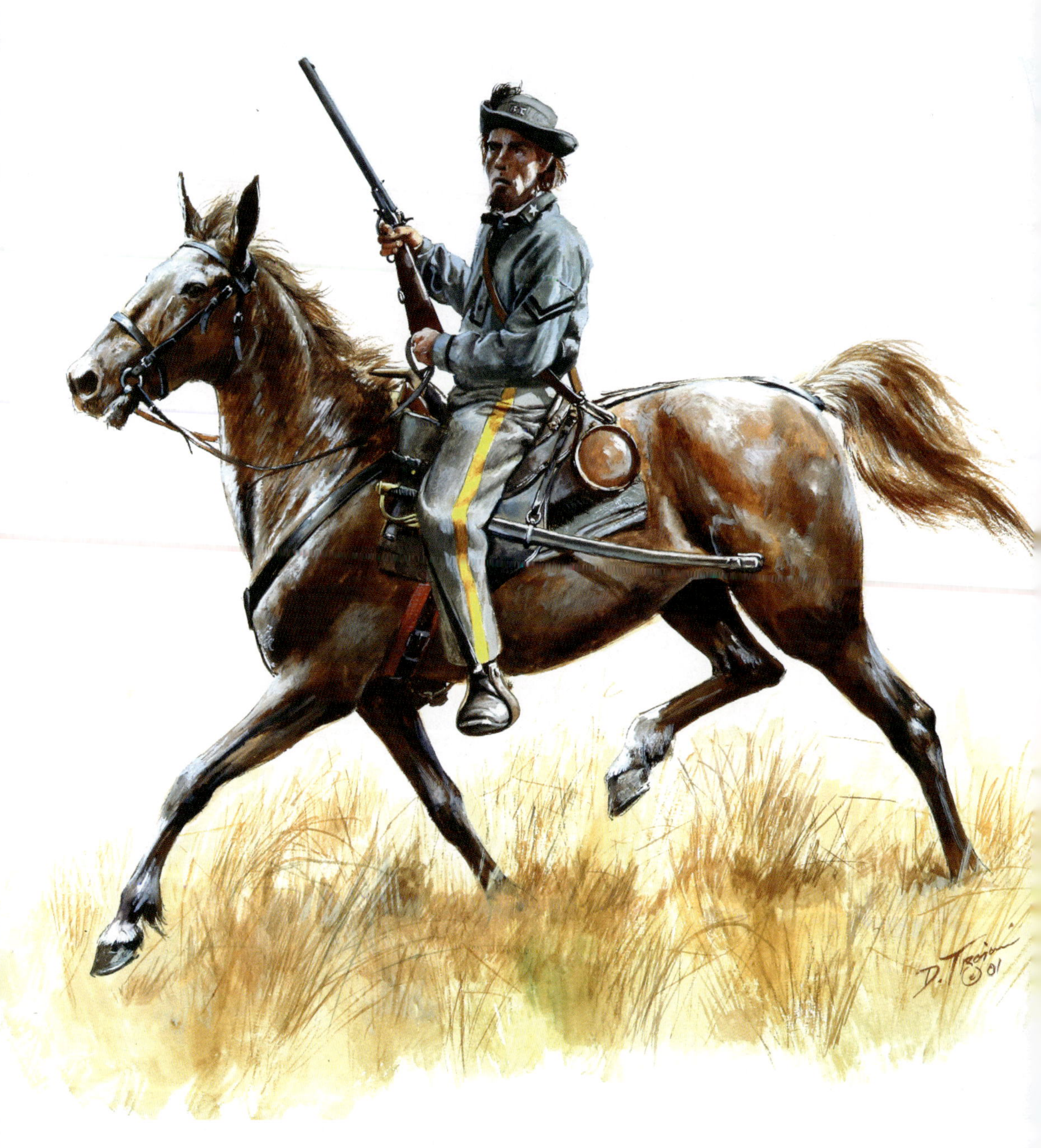

Bolivar Troop, Mississippi Cavalry

ORGANIZED IN BOLIVAR COUNTY, MISSISSIPPI, ON October 29, 1860, in response to the prospect of Abraham Lincoln being elected president of the United States, the Bolivar Troop was commanded by Captain Frank Armstrong Montgomery, and joined the ranks of the Army of Mississippi established in January 1861. Mustered in at Prentiss, Mississippi, on March 20, 1861, the Troop became Company A, 1st Battalion of Mississippi Cavalry about three months later. When that unit was expanded into a regiment on April 2, 1862, it was redesignated as Company H, and served in that capacity for the remainder of the war fighting in at least one hundred engagements, skirmishes, and battles.

When originally formed in 1860, the Bolivar Troop proposed to adopt a uniform consisting of "foraging cap, red flannel shirts, and deep blue pants," although there is no evidence to confirm that this was received by the end of the year.[1] Based on photographic evidence and a description of Fifth Sergeant Frank A. Gayden when he was captured near Charleston, Missouri, on August 13, 1861, this corporal wears a uniform loosely based on that prescribed for cavalrymen of the Army of Mississippi which, for fatigue dress, consisted of a blue flannel shirt with a star of white on each side of the collar.[2]

His headwear consists of a gray felt hat with low crown and narrow brim pinned up on the right and decorated with a black ostrich feather plume and wide silk band to which is fastened the yellow metal old-script letters "BT." His blue-gray pull-over shirt has black trim around its placket front, collar and cuffs, and black chevrons on his sleeves. A five-pointed white star decorates either side of his falling collar. Although variation in the color of trousers appears to have existed within the ranks of the Troop, those worn by this corporal are light gray with broad yellow stripes down the outer seams.

The Bolivar Troop were originally armed with "pistols and sabres" issued by the state of Mississippi when the unit was organized.[3] The corporal also carries a Maynard breech-loading carbine supplied by the state in January 1861, and has a narrow nonregulation brown leather sling over his shoulder to accommodate this weapon. A metal scabbard holding his saber is attached to his saddle by leather straps. Each man in the Bolivar Troop provided his own horse. The corporal is seated on a privately purchased Texas-style saddle. The rest of his equipment consists of a single-rein leather bridle, breast collar and crupper strap; leather and red cloth girth or surcingle; leather stirrup straps; and wooden stirrups. A wooden drum canteen is attached to his saddle plus a leather boot for his carbine.

1. *Daily Vicksburg Whig*, October 30, 1860, 1:1; and *Weekly Vicksburg Whig*, November 14, 1860, 3:3.
2. *Southern Military Manual*, J. L. Power, Jackson, MS, and H. P. Lathrop, New Orleans, 1861, 106.
3. *Weekly Vicksburg Whig*, November 14, 1860, 3:3.

Union Cavalry Bugler

THE COMPANY BUGLER WAS ESSENTIAL TO THE Union cavalry regiment. In the field, he listened for bugle calls from the chief, or sergeant, bugler who accompanied the regimental commander. After confirming with his company commander, he relayed the bugle call to his company. When maneuvering in the battlefield, he needed to know and relay any one of fourteen different calls, consisting of nine "Gait and Directional Calls," and five "Fight and Rally Calls." Often the target for enemy fire in battle, he was required to stay near the company commander who remained behind his company, while the platoon commanders led the troopers from the front.[1] Hence, the bugler would be armed with only a revolver and saber for self-defense.

Bugle calls were not always understood by some cavalry troopers, especially in the confusion of battle. Private George W. Peck, 4th Wisconsin Cavalry, recalled, "In camp we got so we could tell 'assembly,' and 'surgeon's call,' and 'tattoo,' and quite a number of others, but the calls of battle were Greek to us."[2]

This bugler wears a Pattern 1854 dark blue wool uniform jacket bound with yellow branch of service trim on collar, cuffs and back seams, and is fastened by twelve small "General Service" buttons at the front and two on each cuff. His standing collar has two yellow false buttonholes terminating in small buttons of the same pattern on each side. It also has yellow worsted lace forming a "herringbone"-pattern of trim down its front. His plain sky-blue kersey wool mounted-pattern trousers, with reinforced seat and inner legs, are tucked into black leather half boots. The strap on his forage cap is worn under his chin to prevent the loss of his headgear at a gallop or canter. The yellow worsted cord attached to his bugle is looped around his neck to prevent its loss. His black leather waist belt is fastened with a Pattern 1851 "eagle-wreath" plate, and carries a holstered revolver, saber, and cavalry cartridge box. Horse equipment includes a Model 1859 McClellan saddle over an orange-trimmed dragoon saddle blanket.

---

1. George B. McClellan, *Regulations and Instructions for the Field Service of the U.S. Cavalry in Time of War* (J. B. Lippincott & Co., 1861), 123, 130.

2. George W. Peck, *How Private Geo. W. Peck Put Down the Rebellion, or the Funny Experiences of a Raw Recruit* (Belford, Clarke & Co., 1887), 302.

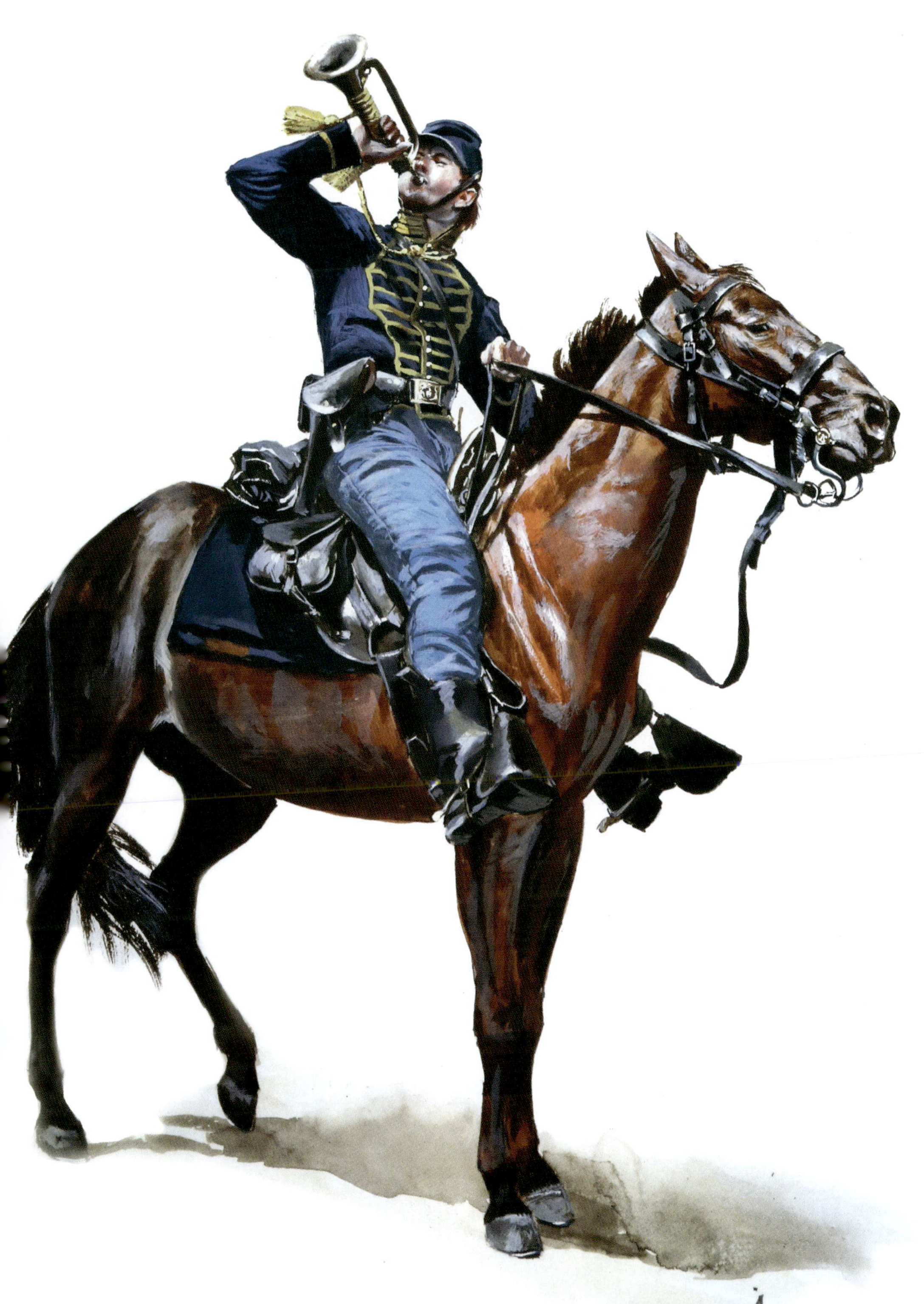

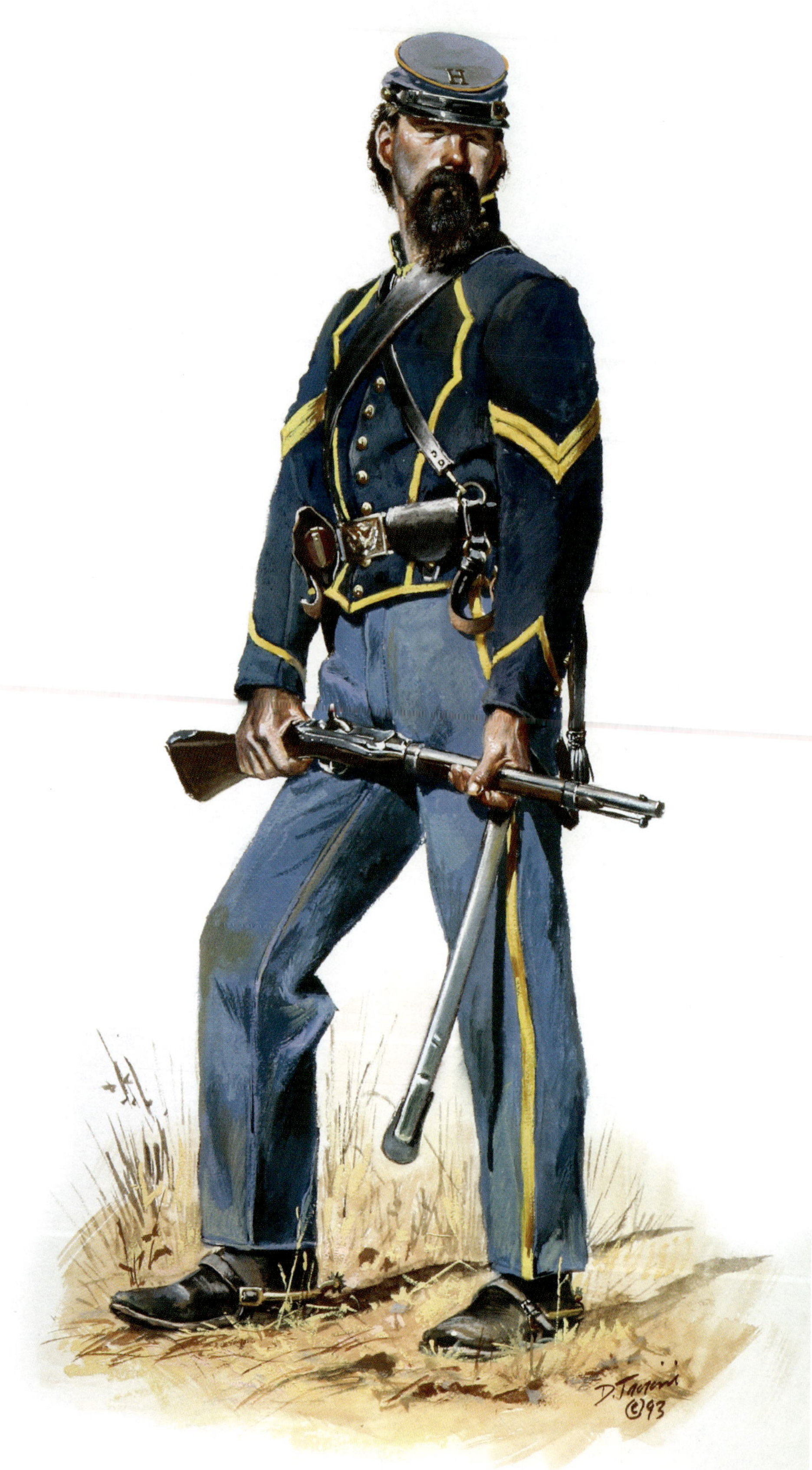

2nd Missouri Cavalry (Merrill's Horse)

THE 2ND MISSOURI CAVALRY, ALSO KNOWN AS Merrill's Horse, was raised under the authority of Major General John C. Fremont, commander of the Department of the West, and was organized at Benton Barracks from August 25 to December 11, 1861, by ex-regular army officer Lewis Merrill. Graduating from West Point twentieth in the class of 1855, Merrill was assigned to duty as second lieutenant with the 2nd US Dragoons, and served in Missouri, Kansas Territory, and with the Utah Expedition. In 1861 he was appointed a first lieutenant and, following his regiment's reorganization as the 2nd Cavalry, was appointed a captain on October 1, 1861.

Meanwhile, appointed Chief of Cavalry Staff under General Fremont, Merrill was promoted to Colonel of Volunteers and, on August 23, 1861, tasked with raising and organizing the 2nd Missouri Cavalry, more popularly known as Merrill's Horse. The first company to enter the ranks of this regiment called themselves the Knights of Saint Louis and swore to be "the protectors of the women and children" of the city.[1] Recruited on August 18, 1861, under Captain E. James Bennett, they became Company A of Merrill's regiment. Another eight companies were quickly raised between September 3 and December 11, 1861, with companies B through G also being recruited in Saint Louis, and in Cincinnati, Ohio, while companies H and I, with companies L and M added later, were raised in Battle Creek, Michigan. As a result, the regiment was unofficially organized into a Missouri squadron, Ohio squadron, and Michigan squadron.[2]

Merrill ensured that his regiment wore a distinctive uniform throughout its period of service, and ordered that any additions or alterations to it were prohibited. Their dress consisted of a Pattern 1854 mounted service jacket with nonregulation yellow trim across the chest and a mid-blue forage cap with orange trim around its top in recognition of Merrill's prewar service in the 2nd Dragoons. Besides sleeve chevrons indicating rank, this corporal has half-inch wide yellow welts on the outer seams of his sky-blue mounted service trousers. Boots with spurs are worn under his trousers in regulation fashion.

He is armed with a Model 1843 Hall carbine, Model 1860 cavalry saber, and holstered Colt Army revolver. Equipment consists of an Allegheny Arsenal-pattern cap pouch and pistol cartridge box on a belt with Pattern 1851 "eagle" plate.

1. *Sunday Morning Republican* (Saint Louis, MO), August 18, 1861, 2:6.
2. *Chicago Tribune*, March 25, 1863, 2:4.

1st North Carolina Cavalry, October 1861

THE 1ST NORTH CAROLINA CAVALRY, ALSO KNOWN as the 9th Regiment N.C. Troops, as it was the ninth regiment formed in the state, attracted much admiration when it arrived in Richmond, Virginia, on October 18, 1861. Raised entirely at the expense of the state, it was organized at Camp Beauregard, Ridgeway, Warren County, North Carolina, on August 12, 1861, under Colonel Robert Ransom. This regiment wore uniforms prescribed for cavalry in "Regulations for the Uniform Dress and Equipments of the Volunteer and State Troops of North Carolina" published in Raleigh on May, 24, 1861.[1] Made by the Rock Island Mills, near Charlotte, North Carolina, the uniform for enlisted men consisted of a sack coat of Cadet gray cloth of North Carolina manufacture extending half way down the thigh, and made loose, with falling collar, and an inside pocket on each breast. A strip of yellow cloth was sewn on each shoulder representing the cavalry branch service color.

Pantaloons of the same cloth were made loose and reinforced in the seat and inner leg for mounted troops, with yellow stripes on the outer seams, one-inch wide for sergeants and noncommissioned staff of regiments; three-fourths of an inch wide for corporals, and half an inch wide for privates.

Although gray hats were prescribed for full dress, Brigadier General Lawrence O'Bryan Branch, State Quartermaster General, informed Governor John Ellis on May 28, 1861, that Cadet gray forage caps were easier to supply and ordered eight thousand from W.H.C. Lovitt, of Norfolk, Virginia, some of which the 1st North Carolina Cavalry received.[2]

Depicted are members of Company A, 1st North Carolina Cavalry commanded by Captain Thomas A. Crumpler, armed with the artillery version of Colt's revolving carbine. Most of the rest of the regiment received breech-loading carbines adapted from Model 1819 Hall flintlock rifles that had been shortened, converted to percussion, and otherwise adapted for cavalry service. Arms also included US Model 1840 Heavy Cavalry Sabers, and single-shot pistols carried in saddle holsters. Accoutrements were composed of white buff leather belts supporting a black leather cap pouch and cartridge box. On September 10, 1861, the regiment received from the Quartermaster General and Paymaster's Office at Raleigh, North Carolina, one thousand saddles and one thousand bridles and martingales as part of their horse equipment.

---

1. Richard Warren, "North Carolina State Issue Uniforms, 1861–1865," *Confederate Historical Society Journal* 18, no. 2 (Summer 1990): 45.

2. Quartermaster and Paymaster's Department, Letter Book, May 19, 1861–April 10, 1862, Branch to Marshall Parks, May 28, 1861, & Branch to Lovett [sic], August 5, 1861, North Carolina Department of Archives & History.

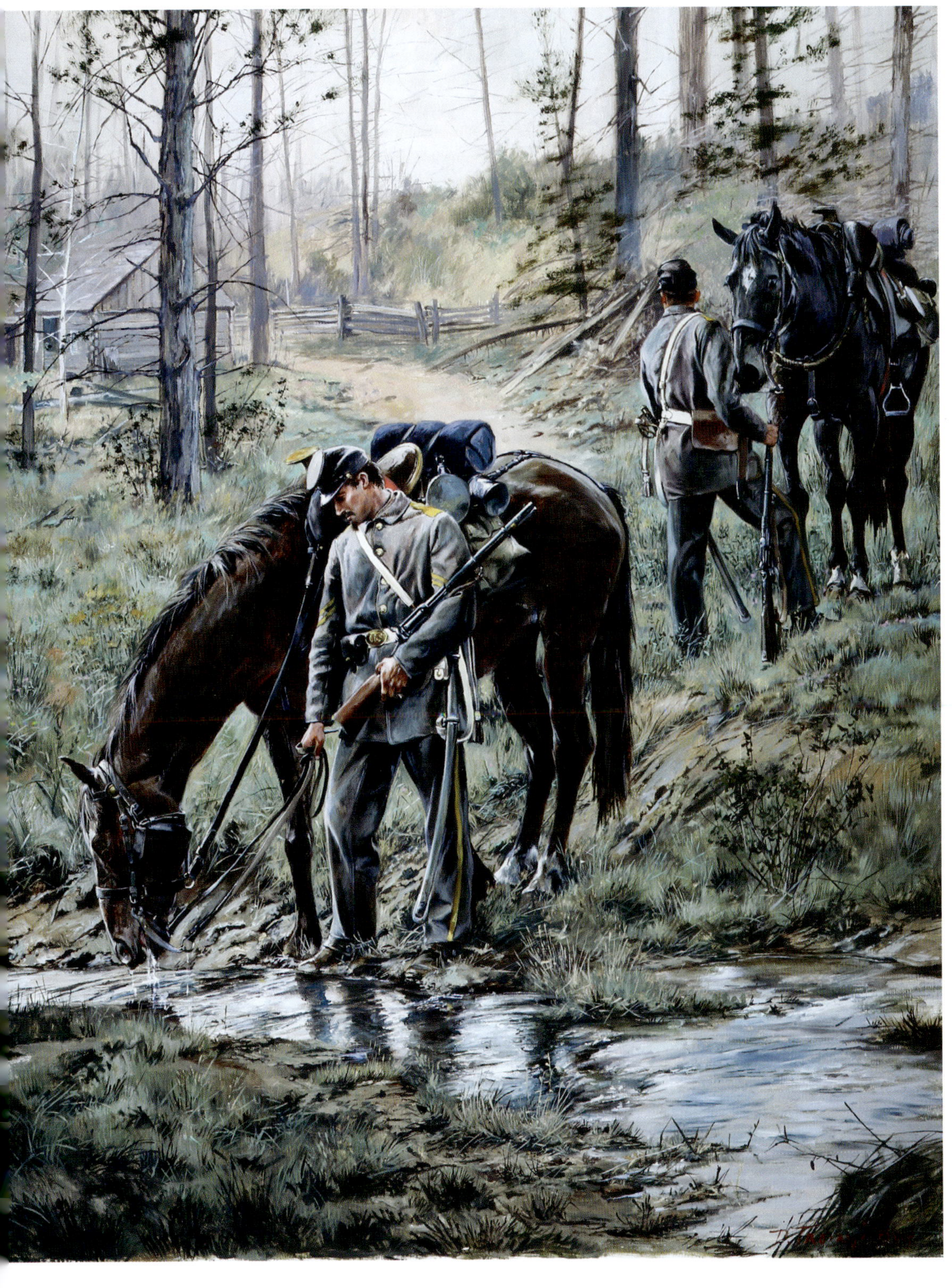

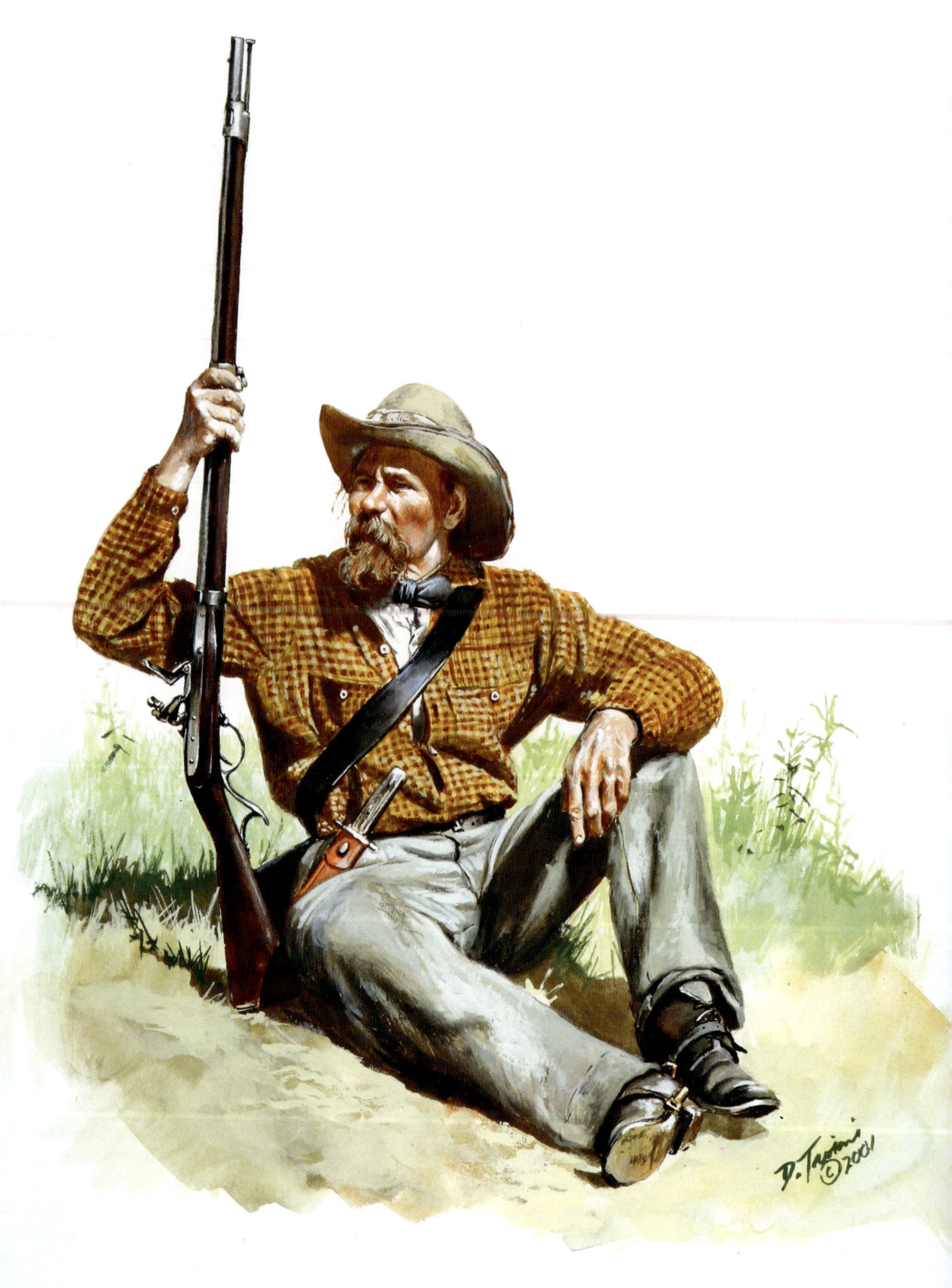

1st Arkansas Mounted Rifles, Company D, 1861

COMPANIES FORMING THE 1ST ARKANSAS MOUNTED RIFLES were gathered on the grounds of St. John's College, Little Rock in May 1861 and the regiment was organized at Fort Smith on June 16 with Colonel Thomas J. Churchill in command. Forming Company D, the Augusta Guards were originally raised as a volunteer militia company in the 34th Regiment, Arkansas State Militia, in Jackson County on December 28, 1860.[1] Led by Captain Charles H. Matlock, who was appointed lieutenant colonel of the regiment, the Augusta Guards arrived at Little Rock on May 24, 1861.[2]

The regiment fought at Wilson's Creek on August 10, 1861, and Elkhorn Tavern on March 7–8, 1862, following which it turned its horses in and served throughout the rest of the war dismounted. It participated in the Heartland Offensive of August through October 1862, which failed to draw neutral Kentucky into the Confederacy, and was later engaged at Stones River from December 31, 1862, to January 2, 1863. Assigned to the Army of Tennessee, it fought at Chickamauga, and participated in the Atlanta Campaign through Georgia as part of the force attempting to stop Sherman's "march to the sea." The 1st Arkansas Consolidated Mounted Rifles surrendered with the Army of the Tennessee at Greensboro, North Carolina, on April 26, 1865.

Clothing at first received by the Augusta Guards and the rest of the 1st Arkansas was likely produced by "the local ladies of Little Rock" who had been making uniforms for volunteers since at least May 4, 1861, which was two days before the state seceded from the Union.[3] Based on the clothing account book for Company D all they received until early 1862 was overshirts, trousers, and shoes. The lack of headgear indicates the men were expected to acquire their own, which largely consisted of brimmed hats. Some items supplied to the Augusta Guards may have been received via the Central Committee of Jackson County, which furnished clothing for its local volunteers. In addition, on November 12, 1861, the Military Board of Arkansas paid merchants Pool, Pulliam & Co., of Jackson, for $380 for clothing, some of which likely went to the company.[4]

Over a white shirt and necktie, this private of Company D wears a checked or plaid wool overshirt with small buttons fastening its pockets, cuffs, and placket front. His trousers are plain gray jeans. His drab-colored felt hat is privately purchased. He holds an unaltered flintlock Hall's rifle likely acquired from the Little Rock Arsenal.[5] Accoutrements consist of an early war .69-caliber cartridge box with "US" plate removed suspended from a plain black bridle leather shoulder belt, and a waist belt with small frame buckle. Attached to his belt is a hunting knife with a one-piece stag antler handle and German silver cross-guard in red leather sheath. Spurs are strapped to his brogans.

---

1. Arkansas Military Department records, List of Commissioned Officers of the Militia 1827–1862, Arkansas History Commission, microfilm roll 38-8, 149.

2. *Des Arc Semi-Weekly Citizen*, May 24, 1861, 4:1.

3. *Arkansas True Democrat* (Little Rock, AR), May 9, 1861, 2:3.

4. "Minutes Book of the Military Board of Arkansas, 1861–1862," Military Board of Arkansas Records, Arkansas State Archives, Little Rock, AR, 146, 208.

5. NARA, record group 109, record of Ordnance and Ordnance Stores Issued, Ordnance Depot, Corinth, MS, February–May 1862, War Department Collection of Captured Confederate Records.

Fremont Body Guard

FORMED IN SAINT LOUIS, MISSOURI, ON AUGUST 12, 1861 by authority of Major General John C. Frémont, commanding the Western Department, the original Fremont Body Guard was led by Captain Charles Zagonyi, a Hungarian émigré, and was intended to be "the crack company of the West."[1] Initially recruited and quartered at the Saint Louis Riding School, the unit was expanded into a battalion of four companies within a month with Zagonyi promoted to major. Companies A and B were raised in Saint Louis with First Lieutenants Walter S. Newhall and Napoleon C. G. E. Westerborg in command respectively. Company C was largely recruited in Cincinnati, Ohio, by Captain James L. Foley. Company D contained recruits from Missouri and Illinois with Second Lieutenant James M. Goff in command.

This private wears the uniform furnished to the Fremont Body Guard via US assistant quartermaster Major Justus McKinstry by the beginning of September 1861. Reported as being a "black jacket and pants, with yellow stripes, of the finest woolen cloth," it was noted by *Frank Leslie's Illustrated Newspaper* artist Henri Lovie as consisting of "black tight jackets & pants."[2] This man's plain high-crowned forage cap and *Stulpstiefel* or "top boots" with spurs are based on Lovie's published illustrations.[3]

Armed as his unit was during their only engagement with Confederate troops, at Springfield, Missouri, in October 1861, he holds a Colt Navy revolver with detachable stock, and Model 1840 cavalry saber. A Remington Beal revolver is carried in a saddler holster. Fastened with a Pattern 1851 rectangular "eagle" plate, his belt supports a Watervliet Arsenal cap pouch and pistol cartridge box. His Grimsley saddle with quilted seat depicted, plus other horse equipment, is based on that supplied by Condict, Woolley and Co., of 52 Lake Street, Chicago.[4]

During their fight on October 25, 1861, 150 of the Fremont Body Guard charged a mixed Confederate command of 2,100 infantry and cavalry sounding the battle cry of "Frémont and the Union" and successfully drove the enemy off with a loss to themselves of 6 killed, 27 wounded, and 10 missing.[5] Despite their bravery in action, the unit were disbanded on November 26, 1861, following their refusal to be broken up and transferred to other cavalry units.

1. *Daily Missouri Democrat* (Saint Louis, MO), August 13, 1861, 2:5; and *Hartford Courant* (Hartford, CT), August 15, 1861, 2:4.

2. *Chicago Tribune*, September 6, 1861, 2:7; and Henri Lovie, "March from Tipton—Second Day," *The Becker Collection*, CW-HL-MO-10/15/61.

3. *Frank Leslie's Illustrated Newspaper* (New York, NY), November 23, 1861, 11, 13.

4. *Chicago Times*, August 16, 1861, 4:1.

5. *ORs*, series 1, vol. 3, 251.

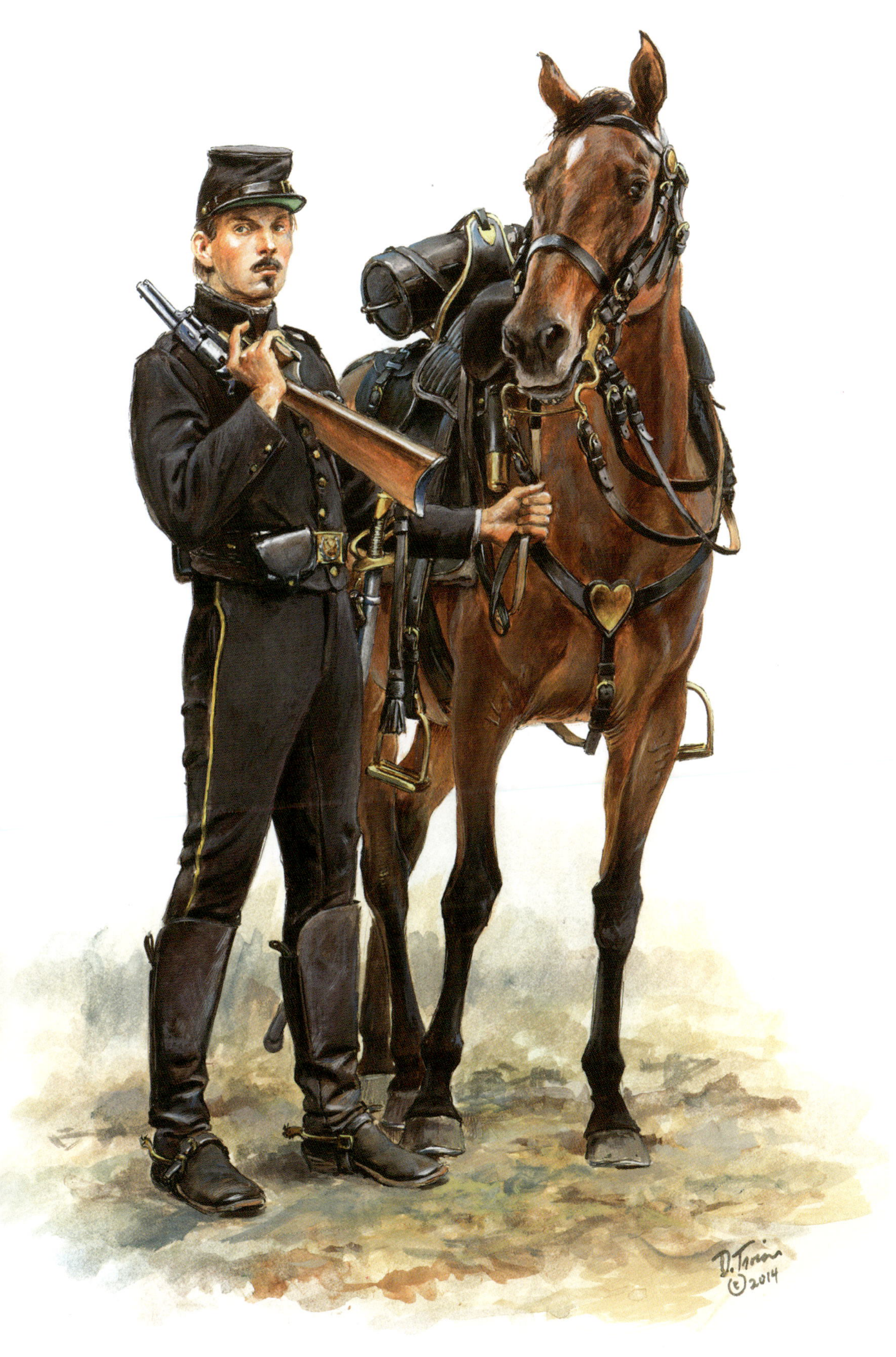

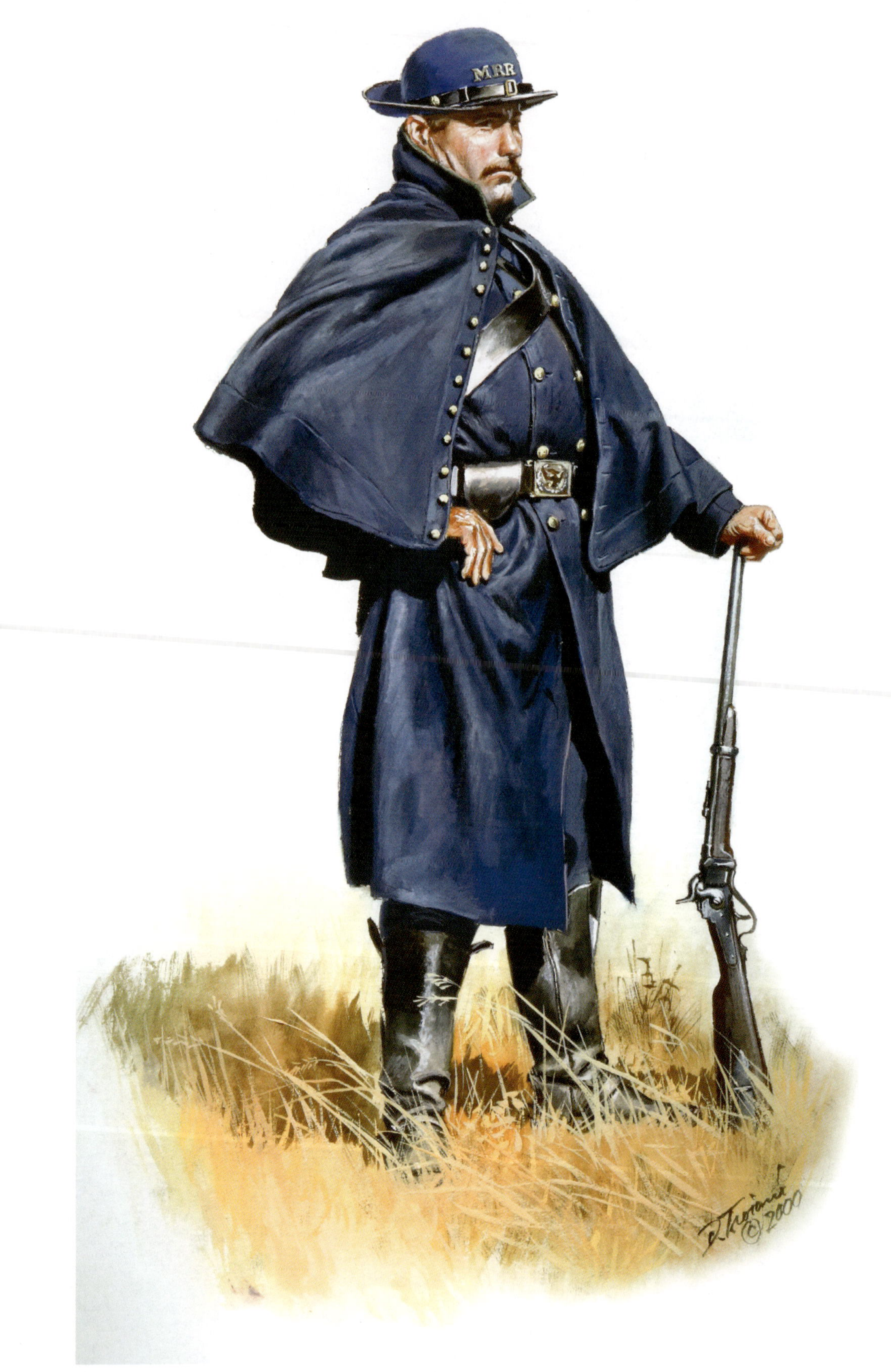

Mounted Rifle Rangers, January 1862

RECRUITED BY CAPTAIN S. TYLER READ FOR Major General Benjamin F. Butler's expedition to the Gulf of Mexico, the Squadron of Mounted Rifle Rangers was assembled at Camp Chase, near Lowell, Massachusetts, from September through December 1861. According to Read, recruits were to be "Equestrians and Marksmen" and furnished "a Horse, Rifle, Long Sabre, Pistols, Uniform and Full Equipments." The Squadron was to be composed of "PICKED MEN, none under five feet, nine inches in height, or weighing more than 165 pounds."[1] The first company was mustered into service under Read on November 17, 1861. A second company organized under Captain James McGee mustered in at Camp Chase on December 27, 1861.[2]

The Mounted Rifle Rangers served as unattached cavalry until June 1862 when they were designated companies A and B, 2nd Battalion Massachusetts Cavalry. Although attached to the 3rd Massachusetts Cavalry, on June 17, 1863, the first being known as Read's Company and the second as Company L, both continued to serve independently in advance of the main army on raiding and reconnaissance missions in Louisiana.

This member of the unit wears the uniform hat and nonregulation overcoat received by the Mounted Rifle Rangers on December 5, 1861.[3] Made by the Seamless Clothing Manufacturing Company of New York City, and based on that patented by Jonathan F. Whipple, his Havelock hat consists of seamless piece of felt, with a brim running around the back and sides for the protection of the head and neck, plus leather visor and brass letters "MRR" at the front. Made by Pierce Bros. & Co., of Boston, the overcoat was described as being of "dark blue cloth" with collar "trimmed with green cord."[4] The jacket worn underneath was also trimmed green and had brass shoulder scales attached for full dress. Footwear consists of tall Wellington-style boots.

He holds a Sharps carbine and is also armed with a saber. Pistols were issued to the Mounted Rifle Rangers from the Ordnance Depot in New Orleans in June 1862 Horse equipment received by both companies included McClellan saddles and regulation bridles.[5] Black horses were originally supplied, but most of these were lost in shipwrecks caused by gales experienced during the voyage to Ship Island, Mississippi, in February 1862. These were replaced by general mounts mostly transferred from artillery batteries several weeks later.[6]

1. *Boston Herald*, September 26, 1861, 2:6.
2. The Adjutant General, comp., *Massachusetts Soldiers, Sailors, and Marines in the Civil War*, vol. 6 (Norwood Press, 1933), 329.
3. *National Aegis* (Worcester, MA), December 7, 1861, 4:5.
4. *Boston Evening Journal*, December 31, 1861, 4:6.
5. NARA, record group 94, regimental papers, 3rd Massachusetts Cavalry, report dated June 3, 1863.
6. *Boston Morning Journal*, December 17, 1861, 4:5; and February 11, 1862, 4:5.

1st Cherokee Mounted Rifles, 1862

THE CHEROKEE NATION COMMITTED TO THE Confederate cause on August 21, 1861, when principal chief John Ross addressed about four thousand Cherokee braves in the public square at Tahlequah, a small village just west of the Illinois River in Oklahoma Territory, and announced that an alliance with the Confederacy was both "expedient and desirable."[1] Four days later, the Executive Committee of the Cherokee Nation wrote to Brigadier General Benjamin McCullough, commanding the District of the Indian Territory, informing him of the creation of a Cherokee mounted regiment led by John Drew, a mixed blood military and political leader and member of the Executive Committee. Designated the 1st Cherokee Mounted Rifles, this unit was composed of full-blood Cherokees, who mostly did not own slaves and had little sympathy for Southern white people, although Drew was a slave-owner.

Meanwhile, an independent command designated 1st Cherokee Mounted Rifles composed of mixed-race Southern Rights supporters was recruited by Colonel Stand Watie during July 1861 to defend the northern border of the Territory against Kansas "Jayhawkers."

Both Drew's and Watie's units appear in official correspondence as either the 1st or 2nd Cherokee Mounted Rifles depending on the politics of the author and/or recipient. To halt further confusion, each Cherokee regiment was eventually referenced by the name of its commander.[2] Both units fought at Pea Ridge, or Elkhorn Tavern, Arkansas, in Brigadier General Albert Pike's Indian Brigade on March 7–8, 1862, where they captured a Federal battery. Most of Drew's regiment deserted and joined the Union army following the Confederate defeat at Old Fort Wayne, or Beattie's Prairie, Indian Territory, on October 22, 1862. The remaining members of the unit combined with Waite's and were reorganized as the 1st Regiment Cherokee Mounted Rifles at Webbers Falls during December 1862. At that time, various companies of Watie's combined command were issued "suits of clothing," plus caps, overshirts, and shoes.

This enlisted man of Watie's regiment wears a butternut jeans jacket and matching pants. His forage cap is topped with feathers, and he has a red overshirt. His boots were likely captured from a Union cavalryman. He brandishes a shotgun, and accoutrements consist of a powder flask and buckshot bag. A wooden handled scalping knife is carried in his waist belt. The war paint on his face indicates his Cherokee heritage, and the simple rope halter on his mount suggests his prowess as a horseman.

---

1. *Daily Dispatch* (Richmond, VA), September 13, 1861, 1:4.

2. W. Craig Gaines, *The Confederate Cherokees: John Drew's Regiment of Mounted Rifles* (Louisiana State University Press, 1992), 15.

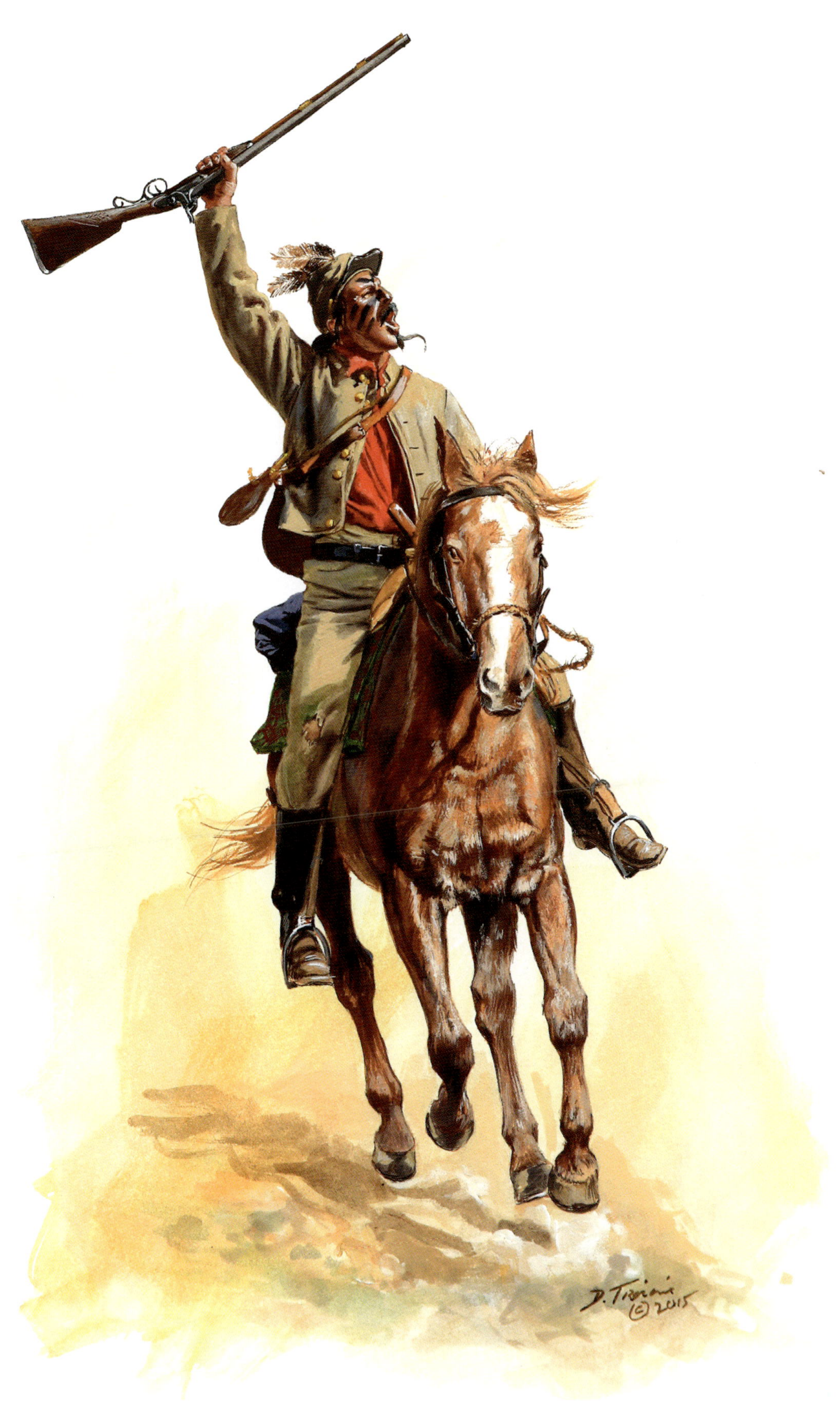

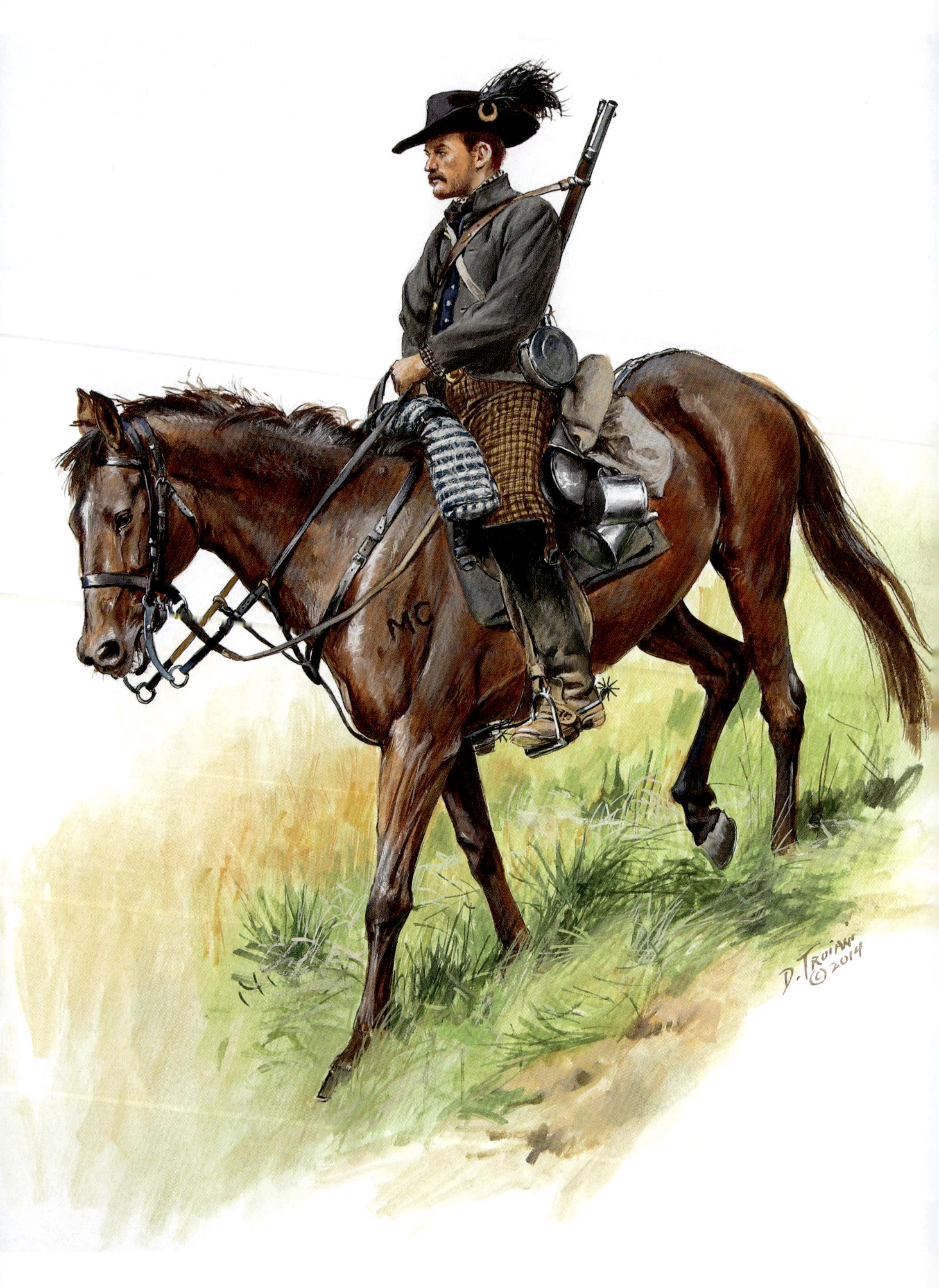

2nd Kentucky Cavalry (Morgan's Raiders)

KNOWN AS "THE THUNDERBOLT OF THE CONFEDERACY" because of the lighting raids he led behind Federal lines, John Hunt Morgan was born in Huntsville, Alabama, in 1825, but espoused his mother's home state of Kentucky. Known only as John Morgan or John H. Morgan prior to and during the Civil War, he enlisted in the 1st Kentucky Cavalry at the outbreak of the Mexican War and, serving under Zachary Taylor, distinguished himself at the Battle of Buena Vista in 1847. He later became a successful hemp manufacturer, and raised and commanded the Lexington Rifles, which were regarded as "the best drilled company in the State."[1]

During the secession crisis, Morgan supported the Confederacy and in September 1861 led about 400 Kentucky State Guard carrying 150 arms passed Federal lines to join forces with Brigadier General Simon B. Buckner at Bowling Green.[2] Appointed colonel of the 2nd Kentucky Cavalry on April 4, 1862, his unit was part of the Reserve Corps at Shiloh, following which it was attached to Brigadier General Joseph Wheeler's division of General Braxton Bragg's Army of Tennessee.

During the summer of 1862 Morgan began the first of several daring raids into Federal territory, which eventually forced some 20,000 Union troops to be detached from the front to guard communication and supply lines. On July 4, he led a thousand-mile ride through Kentucky destroying railroad and telegraph lines, seizing supplies, taking prisoners and generally wreaking havoc. Appointed a brigadier general on December 11, 1862, he conducted his most ambitious raid against General Bragg's explicit orders in July 1863 leading 2,400 men crossed the Ohio and riding over 1,000 miles along the north bank of the river. Terrorizing local defenses in southern Indiana and Ohio for three weeks, he was captured on July 26, 1863, at New Lisbon, Ohio, by Union cavalry under Brigadier General Edward H. Hobson.

Sent to the Ohio State Penitentiary in Columbus rather than to nearby Camp Chase, he escaped on November 27, 1863, by tunneling underground and made his way back into Confederate lines.[3] Appointed head of the Department of Southwestern Virginia and East Tennessee on June 30, 1864, he was killed in a surprise Federal attack at Greenville, Tennessee, on September 4, 1864.[4]

With an Enfield rifle slung across his back, this member of Morgan's raiders has provided himself with a mixture of clothing and equipment. Although his gray jacket shows no indication of rank, his boots are of officer quality. His black felt hat is embellished with a black ostrich feather plume and has a crescent-shaped insignia pinning up its brim in emulation of his commanding officer. His tin drum canteen is typical of those issued to the Western Confederate army, while his saddle and personal items were possibly obtained from a captured Union soldier. The comforter attached to the front of his saddle was likely found hanging on a clothes line on an Ohio farmstead, while his trousers may well have been confiscated from the stock of an Indiana general store. His mount is branded "MC" denoting Morgan's Cavalry.

1. *Louisville Daily Courier*, August 27, 1860, 1:4.
2. *Nashville Union and American*, October 8, 1861, 2:2.
3. *Daily Ohio Statesman* (Columbus, OH), December 10, 1863, 1:4.
4. NARA, M331, CMSR, Confederate Officers, 1861–1865, John Hunt Morgan, 47.

Trooper, 7th Virginia Cavalry, 1863

ORIGINALLY FORMED IN JUNE 1861 BY COLONEL ANGUS W. McDonald Sr., the 7th Virginia Cavalry was attached to the command of Thomas "Stonewall" Jackson in the Shenandoah Valley, and was initially tasked with guarding the fords across the upper Potomac River.[1] In the spring of 1862 the regiment took part in Jackson's Valley Campaign, where the exploits of its new commander, Turner Ashby, became famous for his exploits in both Union and Confederate armies. Near the conclusion of that campaign, Ashby was mortally wounded near Harrisburg, Pennsylvania, and Colonel Richard Henry Dulany took command of what continued to be called Ashby's Cavalry, which had swelled to twenty-nine companies. In June 1862, the 7th Virginia was reorganized and reduced to the normal regimental size of ten companies, while ten formed the 12th Virginia Cavalry; and seven others became the 17th Battalion Virginia Cavalry. Also one company was transferred to the 14th Virginia Cavalry, and another became J. W. Carter's Battery, Virginia Artillery.

The 12th Virginia next joined the 11th and 12th Cavalry, plus the 35th Battalion Virginia Cavalry, also know as "the Comanches," to form what Brigadier General Thomas L. Rosser named "The Laurel Brigade," after the mountain laurel which blooms throughout most of Virginia during May/June every year. As a result, some members of the brigade wore a heart-shaped insignia with a laurel leaf inset.

Under Rosser's command, the Laurel Brigade took part in the Confederate victory near the small township of Buckland Mills on October 19, 1863, where Stuart's Cavalry Division attacked the Federal cavalry under General Judson Kilpatrick. The Federals were driven back in total confusion several miles, and the fight became known as the "Buckland Races."[2]

Tending his mount after the victory near Buckland Mills, this Trooper holds a Richmond Arsenal Second Model "New Jenifer" saddle with nonregulation red wool surcingle draped over it.[3] He wears an infantry-pattern overcoat with elbow length cape, underneath which would be a round jacket and trousers of the pattern issued from the Richmond Clothing Depot.[4] Manufactured in Richmond and issued to the 7th Cavalry during the spring and summer of 1863, a Robinson carbine, copied from the Sharps carbine, hangs from a shoulder sling under his overcoat cape.[5] A saber is suspended from his waist belt, and spurs are strapped over his high cavalry boots.

---

1. Richard L. Armstrong, *7th Virginia Cavalry Lynchburg,* Virginia Regimental History Series (H. E. Howard, Inc., 1992), 3.

2. Ron Field, *Confederate Cavalryman versus Union Cavalryman: Eastern Theater 1861–65* (Osprey Publishing, 2015), 40–55.

3. Ken R. Knopp, *Confederate Saddles & Horse Equipment* (Publisher's Press, Inc., 2001), 67.

4. National Archives, record group 109, M324, regimental personnel files of the 7th Cavalry, file of First Lieutenant Derich D. Pennybacker.

5. John M. Murphy and Howard M. Madaus, *Confederate Rifles and Muskets* (Graphic Publishers, 1996), 636–37.

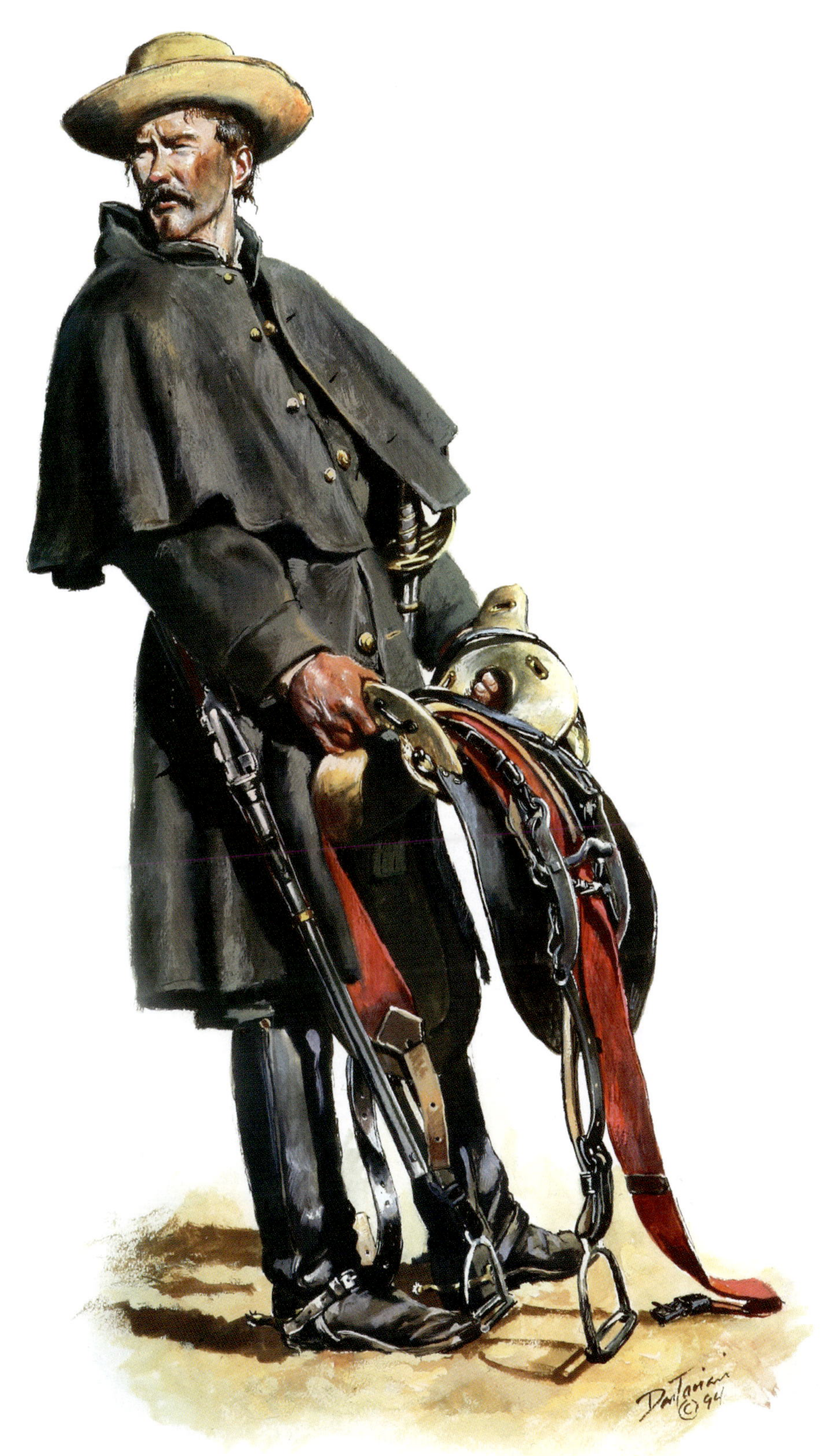

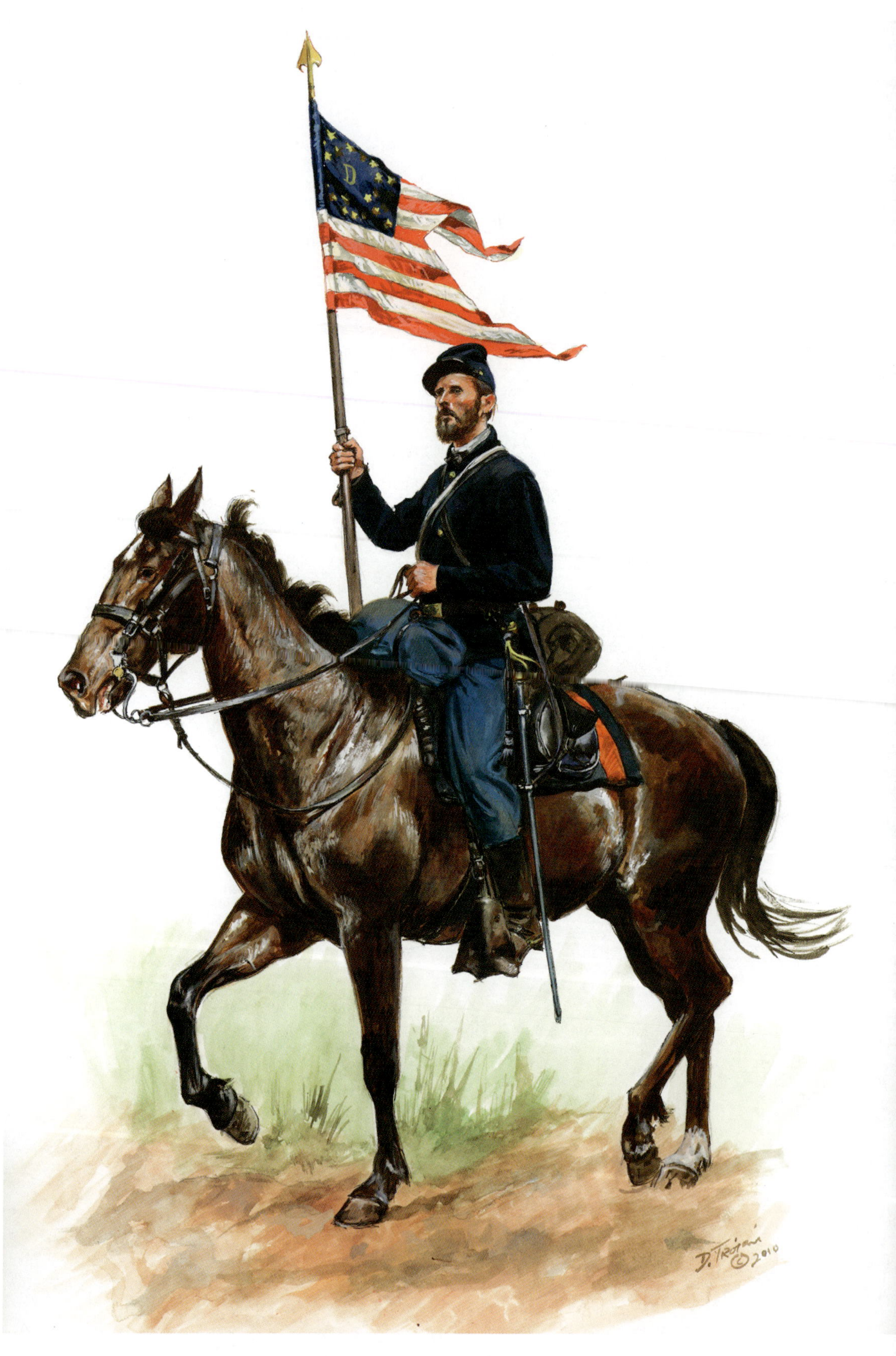

Guidon Bearer, Company D, 4th United States Cavalry, 1863

THE 4TH UNITED STATES CAVALRY WAS ORIGINALLY FORMED in 1855 as the 1st US Cavalry. At that time there were in the service five mounted regiments consisting of the 1st and 2nd Dragoons, the 1st Mounted Rifles, and the 1st and 2nd Cavalry. With the outbreak of the Civil War, it was determined via an Act of Congress, dated August 3, 1861, to renumber these regiments making them all cavalry. As senior regiments, the Dragoons and Rifles redesignated the 1st through 3rd Cavalry, and the old cavalry regiments were redesignated the 4th and 5th Cavalry.[1] At that point the new 4th Cavalry was initially broken up with Companies A and E serving with the Army of the Potomac until November 1862, when the regiment was reunited.

In January 1863, the 4th Cavalry was attached to 1st Brigade, 2nd Division, Cavalry Corps, Army of the Cumberland, which also consisted of the 4th Michigan Cavalry, 7th Pennsylvania Cavalry, plus 1st Middle Tennessee Cavalry, with Irish-born Colonel Robert H. G. Minty as their brigade commander. Following a saber charge it made at Shelbyville, Tennessee, during the Tullahoma Campaign, on June 27, 1863, which shattered Wheeler's entire cavalry corps, this organization became known as "The Saber Brigade."[2]

This trooper is holding the guidon of Company D, 4th US Cavalry, and is ready for the order to advance. He wears a dark blue four-button sack coat, sky-blue wool kersey trousers, dark blue forage cap, and calf-length leather boots. His equipment is standard cavalry issue with waist belt fastened by a Pattern 1851 "eagle" plate. His folded sky-blue overcoat is strapped to the front of his Model 1858 McClellan saddle and his rolled blanket is attached to its back. The dragoon saddle blanket with an orange stripe is covered by his saddle bags. Nicknamed the "Old Wristbreaker" because of its two and a half pound weight, his weapon is a Model 1840 Cavalry saber.

As Federal cavalry regiments carried only a silken regimental standard, the absence of the US colors was made up for by the swallow-tail silken guidon with stars and stripes issued to each company, which was adopted in 1862. The guidon measures three feet five inches on the fly and two feet three inches on the staff.[3]

1. Ron Field, *The Union Army 1861–65 (1): The Regular Army and the Territories* (Osprey Publishing, 2024), 17.
2. *New York Herald*, July 8, 1863, 6:4.
3. George H. Crosman, Earl J. Coates, Frederick C. Gaede, *The 1865 Quartermaster Manual* (Arbor House, 2013), 211.

5th Texas Mounted Rifle Lancers

THE ROMANTIC NOVELS OF SIR WALTER SCOTT stirred the Southern imagination with their tales of brave knights and sturdy yeomen. Jousting at hoops with blunt lances became a popular form of sport and competition among many mounted militia companies. The first Confederate lancers, and those who saw the most extensive Civil War service, came from Texas. During the early part of the war no fewer than five Texas mounted regiments were armed wholly or in part with the weapon. One of these was the 5th Texas Mounted Rifles commanded by Colonel Tom Green, which boasted two lancer companies. Captain Willis L. Lang joined the regiment with Company B containing seventy-three men. Company G was organized by Captain Jerome B. McCown, a forty-one-year-old Alabamian who earlier served under Colonel Jack Hay's Texas Rangers during the Mexican War. The impression created by the dash and glitter of the Mexican lancers of that conflict clearly remained with him and, on September 12, 1861, he enrolled the Jackson Cavalry as lancers in Green's regiment.

Organizing at San Antonio, the 5th Texas was assigned to the Army of New Mexico under the command of Brigadier General Henry H. Sibley, an alcoholic ex-major of the US 2nd Dragoons, to invade unionist New Mexico. In preparation for their expedition, on September 9, 1861, the Quartermaster's Department at San Antonio issued the whole of Sibley's Brigade with 6,000 caps, 3,000 cap covers, 6,000 coats, 9,000 trousers, 6,000 pairs bootees, and 3,000 pairs of boots.[1]

With his original uniform clothing worn out, the lancer depicted wears a plain gray jacket and trousers of loose-woven wool-jean or jean cloth of the type provided by local citizens and ladies aid societies by early 1862, His brimmed hat is of civilian origin. The lance he carries is of the type manufactured especially for his regiment at Yorktown, DeWitt County, Texas, and issued to Lang's company on or about October 23, 1861.[2] With a 12-inch blade mounted on a slender 9 foot long shaft, it is topped with a red pennon measuring 8 by 17 inches. Additional armament consists of a holstered Colt Navy revolver attached to his waist belt, which has a frame buckle.

Although the lancer companies within his command quickly became Sibley's pride and joy, they suffered greatly when ordered to make a charge against what was thought to be an inexperienced New Mexico infantry company on the Union extreme right at Valverde Ford on February 21, 1862. As McCown's company apparently failed to receive the order, Lang's was the only unit to conduct the charge. Of approximately fifty lancers involved, nine were killed and eleven wounded, while Lang was shot six times and died soon after. Almost all of the horses were killed or disabled. When the survivors returned to the Confederate line, the lancer company was rearmed with shotguns and musketoons and continued to participate in the fight.

The New Mexico campaign shattered Sibley's command. After reorganization, the 5th Texas took part in the capture of Galveston on January 1, 1863, and in the numerous actions in Louisiana during the next two years, including the battles of Mansfield and Pleasant Hill. It finally moved to Huntsville, Texas, and was disbanded before the surrender in June 1865.

---

1. NARA, M331, CMSR, Confederate officers, Henry Beaumont, A.Q.M, Sibley's Brigade, 21.

2. NARA, M323, CMSR, Fifth Cavalry, 5th Mounted Volunteers, Second Regiment, Sibley's Brigade, Willis L. Lang, 15.

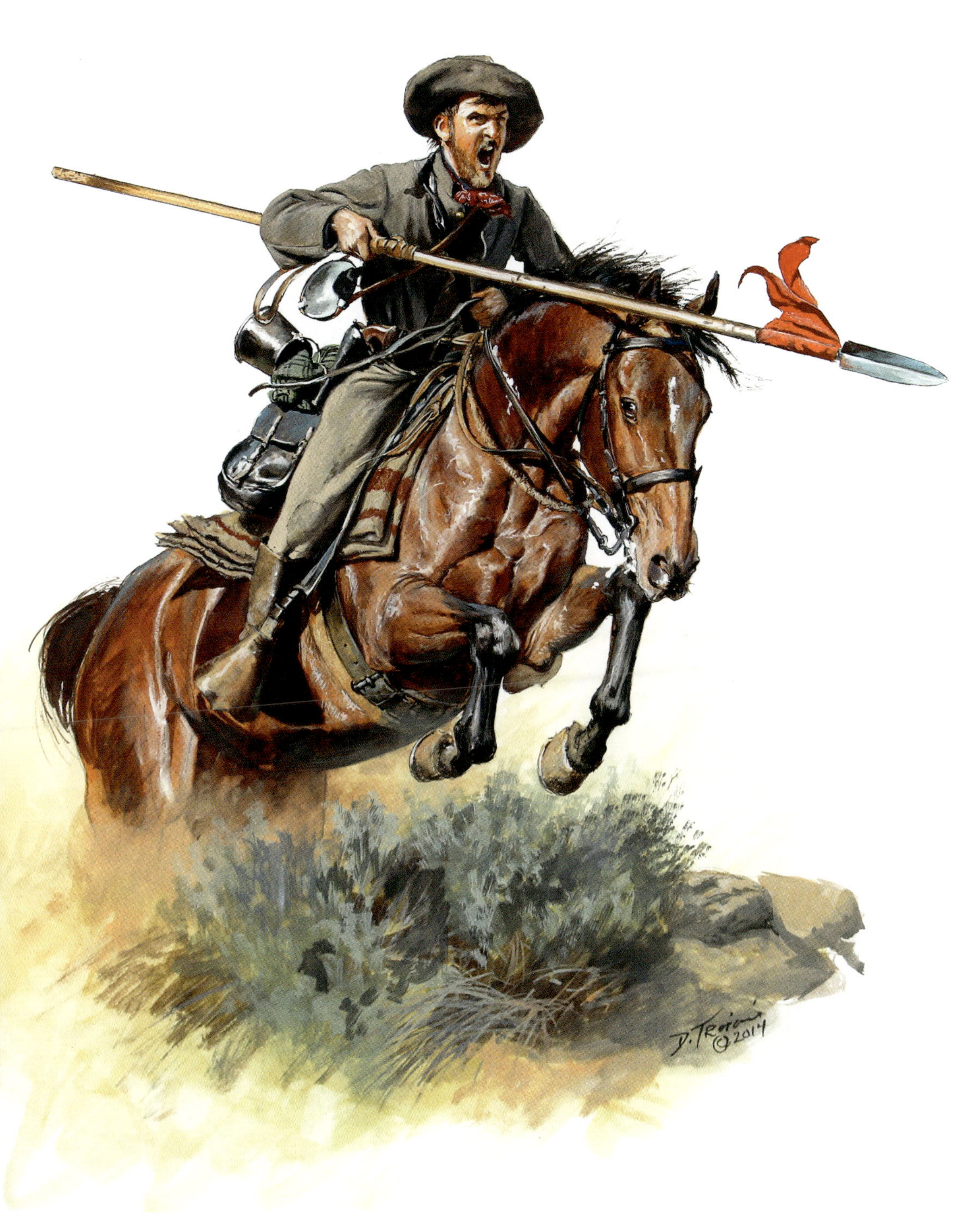

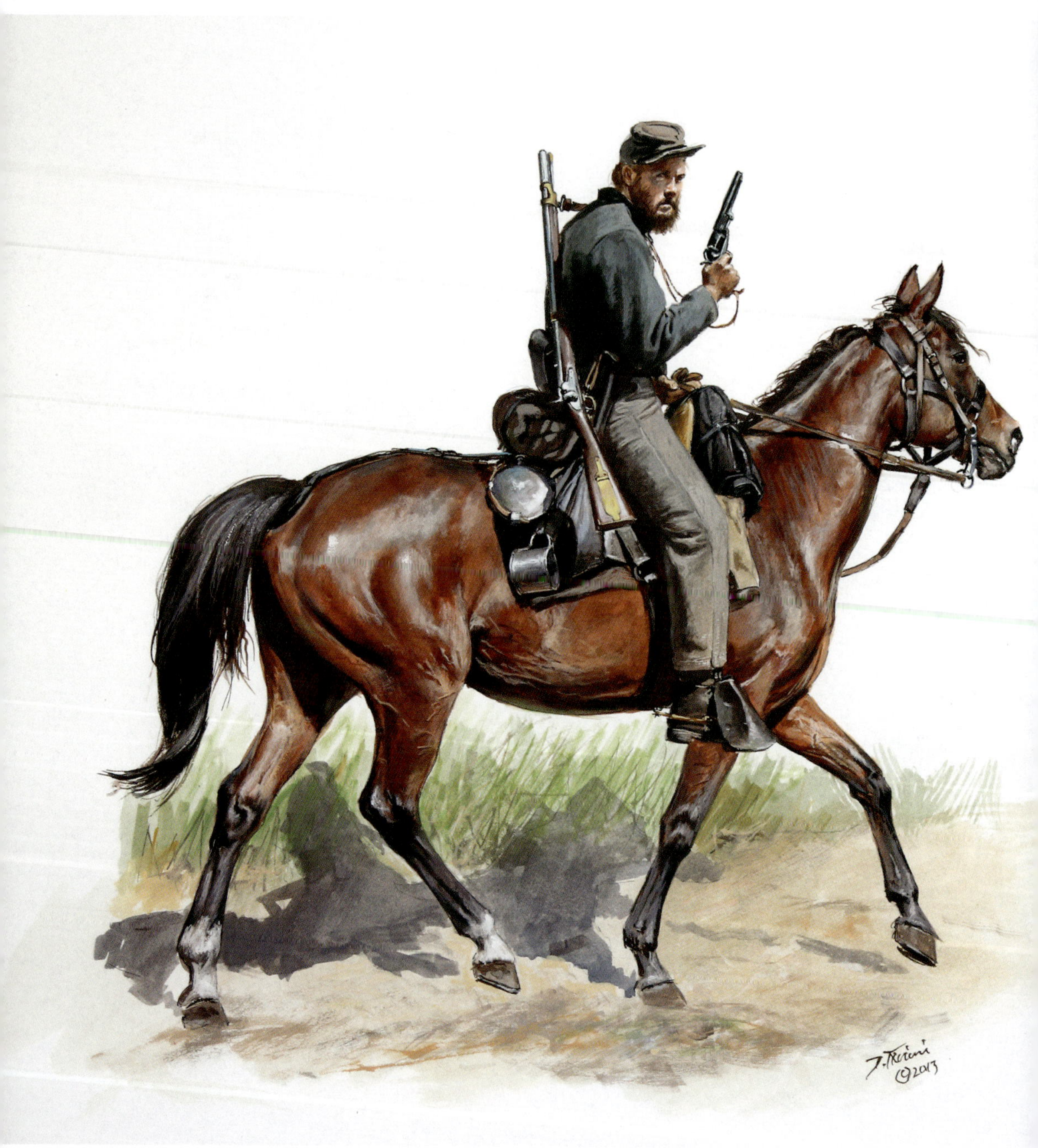

34th Virginia Cavalry Battalion Private, Gettysburg, July 1863

RAISED IN THE APPALACHIAN MOUN-TAIN REGION of southwestern Virginia, as well as adjoining areas of what became West Virginia, plus Tennessee, Kentucky and North Carolina, the 34th Virginia Cavalry Battalion was originally organized during June 1862 as the 1st Battalion, Virginia Mounted Rifles. It was absorbed into the 34th Virginia Cavalry Battalion in December 1862 with Major, later Lieutenant Colonel, Vincent A. Witcher in command.[1]

During 1863 the 34th Battalion gained a notorious reputation for its fierce skirmishes and raids on the Northern sympathizing communities in western Virginia, resulting in Colonel Witcher becoming known in the South as "a daring and successful partizan ranger," while the men under his command were described as "a hard, rough-looking bat-tallion [sic] of mountaineers."[2] During May 1863 the battalion was assigned to General Albert G. Jenkins's Brigade, Cavalry Division, Department of East Tennessee, which was selected by General Robert E. Lee to serve as an advanced guard for the Army of Northern Virginia during its invasion of Pennsylvania beginning on June 15, 1863.

On what became known as the East Cav-alry Battlefield at Gettysburg on July 3, 1863, the 34th Virginia fought dismounted with 332 officers and men. Short of ammunition, the unit retired across the Rummel Farm occupying a barn in their rear. Reinforced at about 3 p.m., Witcher was ordered for-ward and drove back the Federal line seiz-ing a battery. Although attacked by the 5th Michigan Cavalry armed with seven-shot Spencer repeating rifles, Witcher recalled, "the 34th Battalion, which had alone rallied with me, opened fire . . . sweeping down its ranks with a most deadly fire."[3] Toward the end of the day, Witcher's battalion provided flanking and enfilading fire at the charging columns of Federal cavalry.

During 1862, the 34th Virginia Cavalry Battalion was without a quartermaster but grasped every opportunity to cloth itself in the face of a shortage of Confederate sup-ply. In October they raided stores in Guy-andotte, Western Virginia, and seized "boots, jeans, hats, clothing &c."[4] During a raid into Kentucky, Witcher's men took possession of a store at Carter Court House and, accord-ing to a press report, "the Virginia boys were well shod from its contents."[5] By early 1863, Confederate womenfolk were supplying the battalion with clothing, including shirts, coats and hats.[6] By mid-1863, the unit was in receipt of jackets and pants possibly via the Wytheville Depot.

The mounted private depicted wears a Cadet gray jacket and plain gray cap and pants. He holds a Model 1851 Colt Navy revolver with lanyard attached and has a Model 1841 Mississippi rifle slung over his shoulder. Footwear consists of brogans over which are strapped spurs. A blanket roll and valise, plus most of his equipment, are attached to his saddle.

---

1. Wallace, *A Guide to Virginia Military Organizations*, 66.
2. *Abingdon Virginian*, April 24, 1863, 2:1; and *Rockingham Register*, November 6, 1863, 2:1.
3. Harlan H. Hinkle, *Grayback Mountaineers: The Confederate Face of Western Virginia* (iUniverse, 2003), 117.
4. *Nashville Daily Union*, October 16, 1862, 1:6.
5. *Daily Journal* (Wilmington, NC), November 24, 1862, 3:1.
6. *Staunton Spectator*, February 17, 1863, 1:7.

8th Texas Cavalry, Terry's Texas Rangers

THE 8TH TEXAS CAVALRY, ALSO KNOWN AS TERRY'S Texas Rangers, was formed as a result of the successful service of B. Frank Terry and Thomas Lubbock who led a company of Rangers as scouts and partisans under General P. G. T. Beauregard at First Manassas on July 21, 1861. As a reward, President Jefferson Davis commissioned Terry as a colonel and Lubbock a lieutenant colonel, with authority to recruit a ten-company regiment to serve as Texas "Rangers" for "the war." Originally intended for service in Virginia, the regiment was instead placed under the command of General Albert Sydney Johnston for service west of the Mississippi, and later served in the Army of Tennessee. After Terry was killed near Woodsonville, Kentucky, on December 17, 1861, and Lubbock died of typhoid fever on January 9, 1862, the regiment was consecutively commanded by Colonels John Wharton, Thomas Harrison, and Gustave Cook throughout the remainder of its service. It fought in approximately 275 engagements including Shiloh, Murfreesboro, Chattanooga, and Chickamauga, and earned a reputation as one of the most effective mounted regiments in the Western Theater of the war.

Originally consisting of picked men recruited throughout Texas into companies such as "Waul's Confederates" and "the Lubbock Scouts," the men of the 8th Texas Cavalry were armed with "two Colt's revolvers, a double-barrel gun or rifle, with a saber bayonet [Bowie knife] each."[1] This corporal wears an example of the nine-button cadet gray jackets at times issued to his unit and likely made in his home state. The red trim was noted by emigrant artist Carl G. von Iwonski who produced a painting of Terry's Texas Rangers circa 1864. Tucked into leather top boots are plain brown cotton jeans trousers. His slouch hat has a metal "Lone Star" insignia attached to its turned-up brim. He holds a double-barrel shot gun, and carries one revolver in a belt holster and another in a saddle holster also with "Lone Star" decoration.

Horse equipment includes a "Texas" saddle patterned after that developed in the 1830s by Richard Hope; a three-buckle bridle headstall with single-rein bit; a surcingle and crupper strap; and "teardrop" pattern bent wood stirrups. A captured Federal indigo blue wool dragoon-pattern horse blanket with broad orange band is folded under the saddle.[2]

1. *New Orleans Daily Crescent*, October 12, 1861, 1:4.
2. Knopp, *Confederate Saddles & Horse Equipment*, 95, 113, 131.

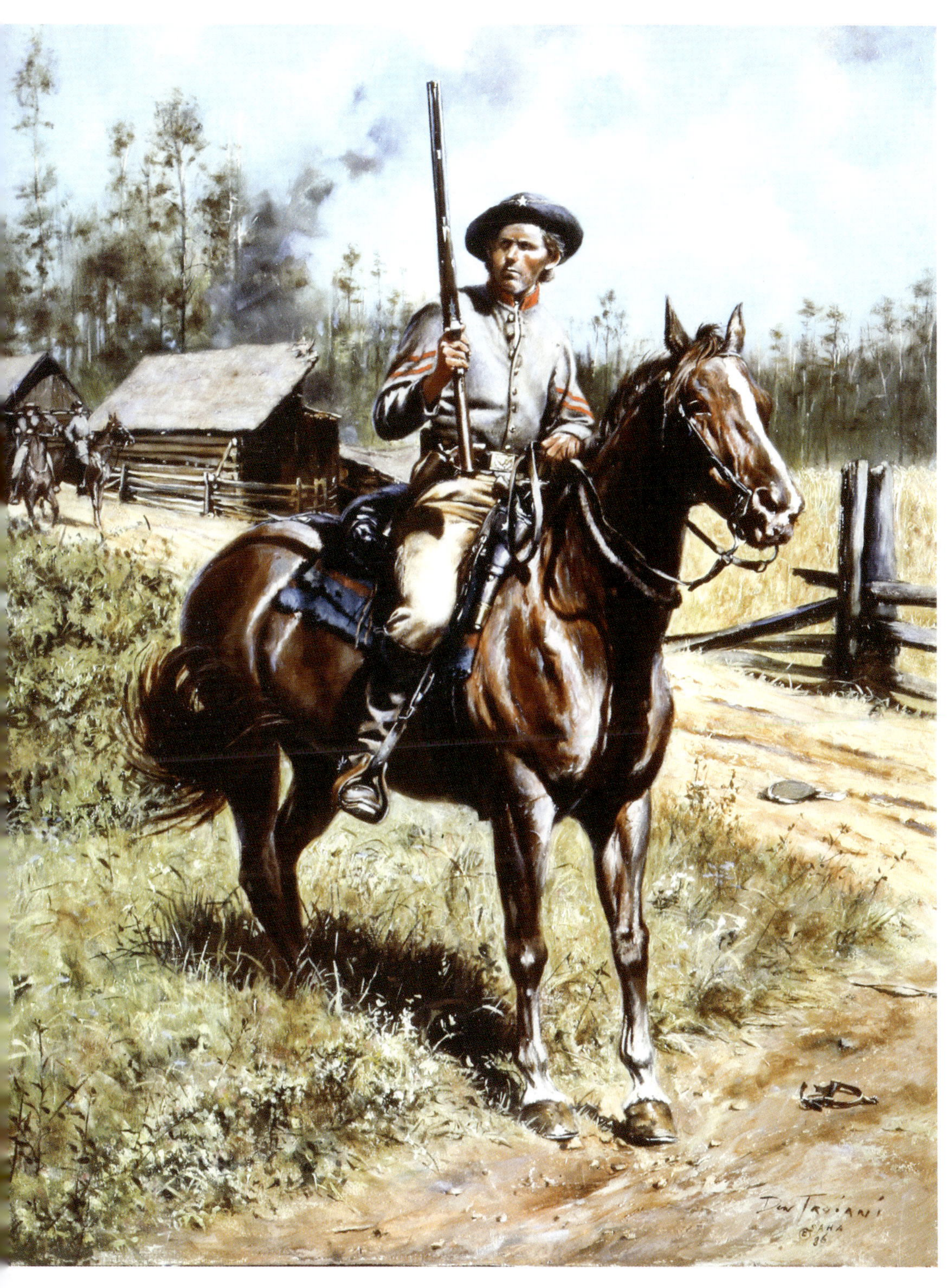

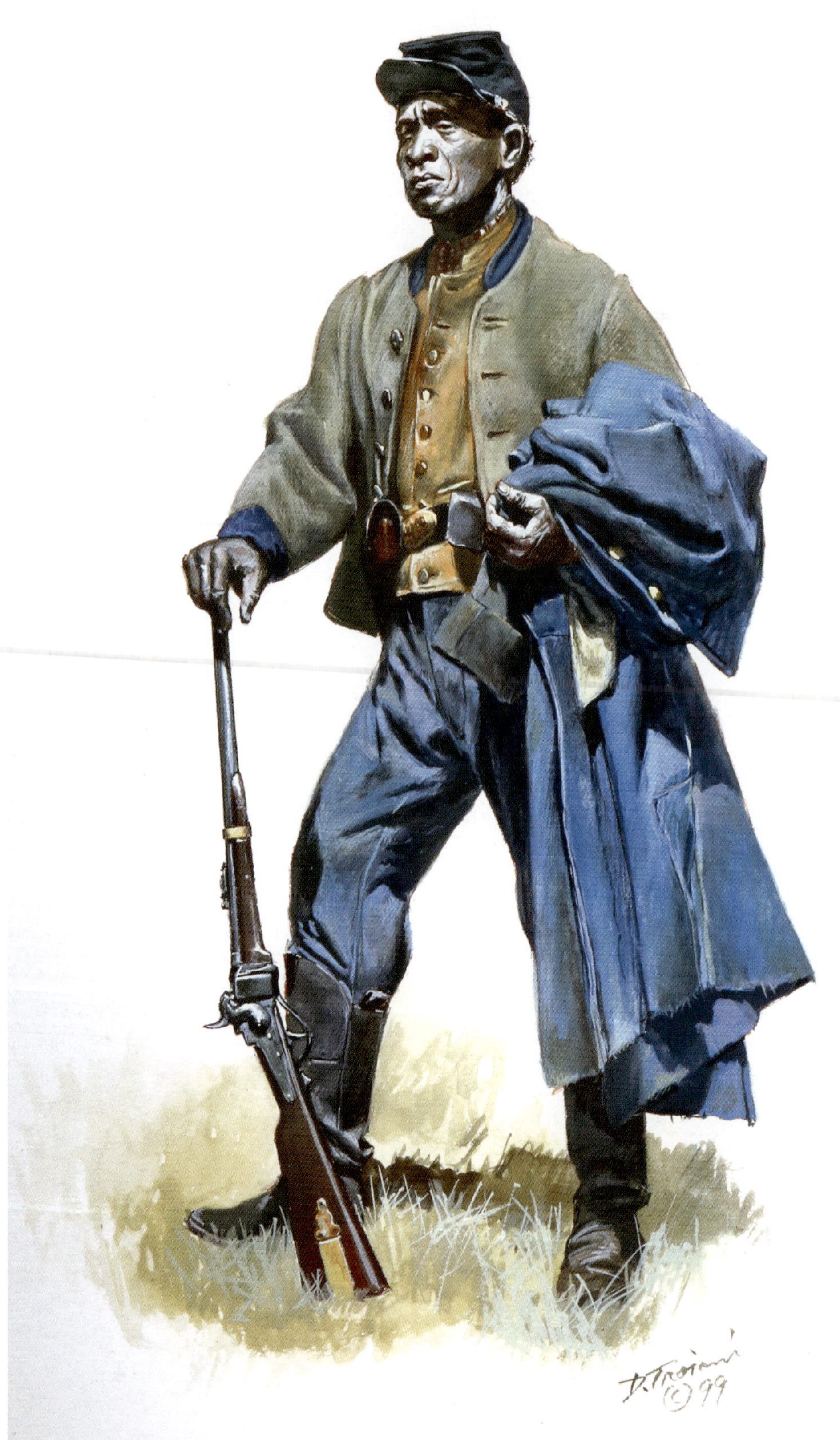

4th Tennessee Cavalry, Black Trooper, Chickamauga, September 1863

ALTHOUGH NEVER OFFICIALLY MUS-TERED INTO THE Confederate army, numerous blacks served in and supported Southern units. At the outset of war, many faithful black servants accompanied their masters to the front. Remaining behind the battle lines, these men had ample opportunity to arm and equip themselves from casualties and prisoners. In September 1863, during the battle of Chickamauga, fought on September 18–20, 1863, the 4th Tennessee Cavalry, commanded by Colonel William S. McLemore, was dismounted to fight as infantry, and every fourth man was detailed to serve as horse-handlers. During the early part of the battle it became evident to Colonel McLemore that he would need every man in the firing line, and so he ordered Captain and Quartermaster Joseph B. Briggs to return to the horse-handlers at the rear and bring them up to the front after placing the horses and wagon teams in charge of the numerous black servants owned by the men of his regiment.

On reaching the horses, Briggs was surprised to find the blacks, who numbered about 40 men, organized, armed, and equipped, under the command of Daniel McLemore, the colonel's servant, and demanding the right to go into action. Failing to dissuade them, Briggs led them up to the line of battle, which was just preparing to assault the troops of the Union XIV Corps, commanded by Major General George H. Thomas. Believing they would be of service in caring for the wounded, he held the blacks back behind the line.[1]

According to a story in the *Savannah Morning News*, published on January 28, 1885, when "the advance was ordered the negro company became enthused as well as their masters, and filled a portion of the line of advance as well as any company of the regiment. While they had no guidon or muster roll, the burial after the battle of four of their number and the care of seven wounded at the hospital, told the tale of how well they fought."[2]

The black Confederate trooper shown here is largely outfitted with items of Union uniform that he likely acquired during the months of campaigning with his master's regiment. His Union forage cap and mounted-service trousers, plus tall boots, were taken from some unfortunate Federal trooper. His gray infantry jacket with dark blue facings on collar and cuffs is of the style worn by the famed Orphan Brigade of Kentucky. His brown vest may have been given him by the officer he served. His checkered shirt is of the type issued in large quantity to the Army of Tennessee. A Federal-issue overcoat is folded over his arm, and he wears Federal accoutrements found in abundance on the battlefield. He is armed with a Sharps carbine and Colt navy revolver.

---

1. Charles Kelly Burrow, ed. and comp., et al., *Black Confederates* (Pelican Publishing Company, 2001), 128.
2. *Savannah Morning News*, January 28, 1885, 2:8.

3rd New Jersey Volunteer Cavalry (Hussars) (Butterflies)

THE 3RD NEW JERSEY VOLUNTEER CAVALRY WAS the only full-strength hussar regiment to experience extensive Civil War service. Originally designated the 1st Regiment US Hussars, it was raised by Colonel Andrew J. Morrison during the first three months of 1864 in response to President Lincoln's call for 300,000 new volunteers. A soldier of fortune who claimed to have served with Garibaldi, Morrison designed the hussar uniform worn by his regiment. Made by the firms Halsey, Hunter & Company and N. Perry Company, of Newark, New Jersey, it was based on that of a troop of Austrian Army Hussars. Morrison insisted that his regiment should be armed only with Model 1860 cavalry sabers, although it eventually also carried carbines and revolvers.

Assigned to Major General Ambrose Burnside's IX Corps, the 3rd New Jersey Cavalry initially had little chance to build a reputation as a fighting unit as its showy uniform made it ideal for orderly, courier and escort duty. With their dark blue jackets overloaded with yellow braid, the regiment was held in low regard by its comrades. According Private John McElroy, Company L, 16th Illinois Cavalry, they were referred to as "daffodil cavaliers" because of their flamboyant uniform.[1] The regiment also became known as the "Butterflies" after being presented with a dark blue flag fringed in gold with a stylized butterfly at its center.

Part of the Cavalry Corps, Army of the Potomac in the Shenandoah Valley by late August 1864, the Hussars proved themselves in battle at Winchester, Cedar Creek, Five Forks, Saylor's Creek and Appomattox under the more efficient command of Lieutenant Colonel William P. Robeson Jr. After a final spell in the Washington defenses, they were mustered out between May and August 1865, having lost 3 officers and 47 enlisted men killed or mortally wounded, and 2 officers and 105 men from disease.[2]

The headgear of the regiment consisted of an unusual form of "pill box" cap with chinstrap, which differed from the cylindrical European version by having a soft top. Worn at a tilt, the top and bottom edges of the cap band were trimmed with yellow cord within which was the numeral "3" in a wreath. Mounted pattern trousers of all enlisted ranks had broad yellow welts on the outer seams. This Hussar also wears the showy yellow-lined sky blue hooded cloak or talma issued to his regiment for full dress and cold weather, instead of an overcoat. This could be fastened by three tabs edged with yellow cord and buttoned at either end. It could also be worn thrown back over one shoulder in the form of a pelisse. Footwear consists of nonregulation Napoleonic-style boots to which Model 1860 cavalry sabers are attached.

---

1. John McElroy, *Andersonville: A Story of Rebel Military Prisons* (Blade Printing & Paper Co., 1870), 434.

2. Frederick H. Dyer, *A Compendium of the War of the Rebellion*, vol. 2 (reprint, Thomas Yoseloff, 1959), 1354.

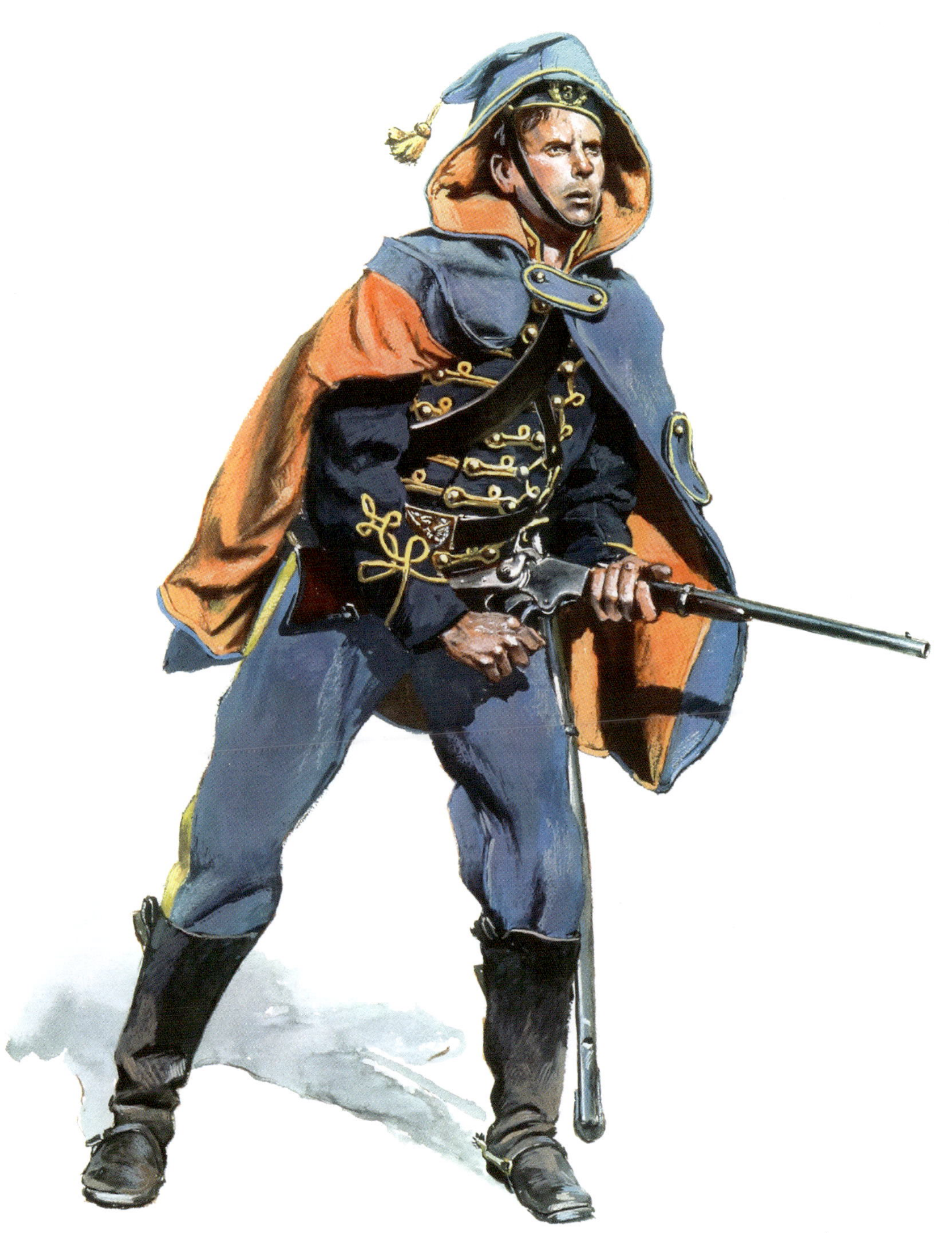

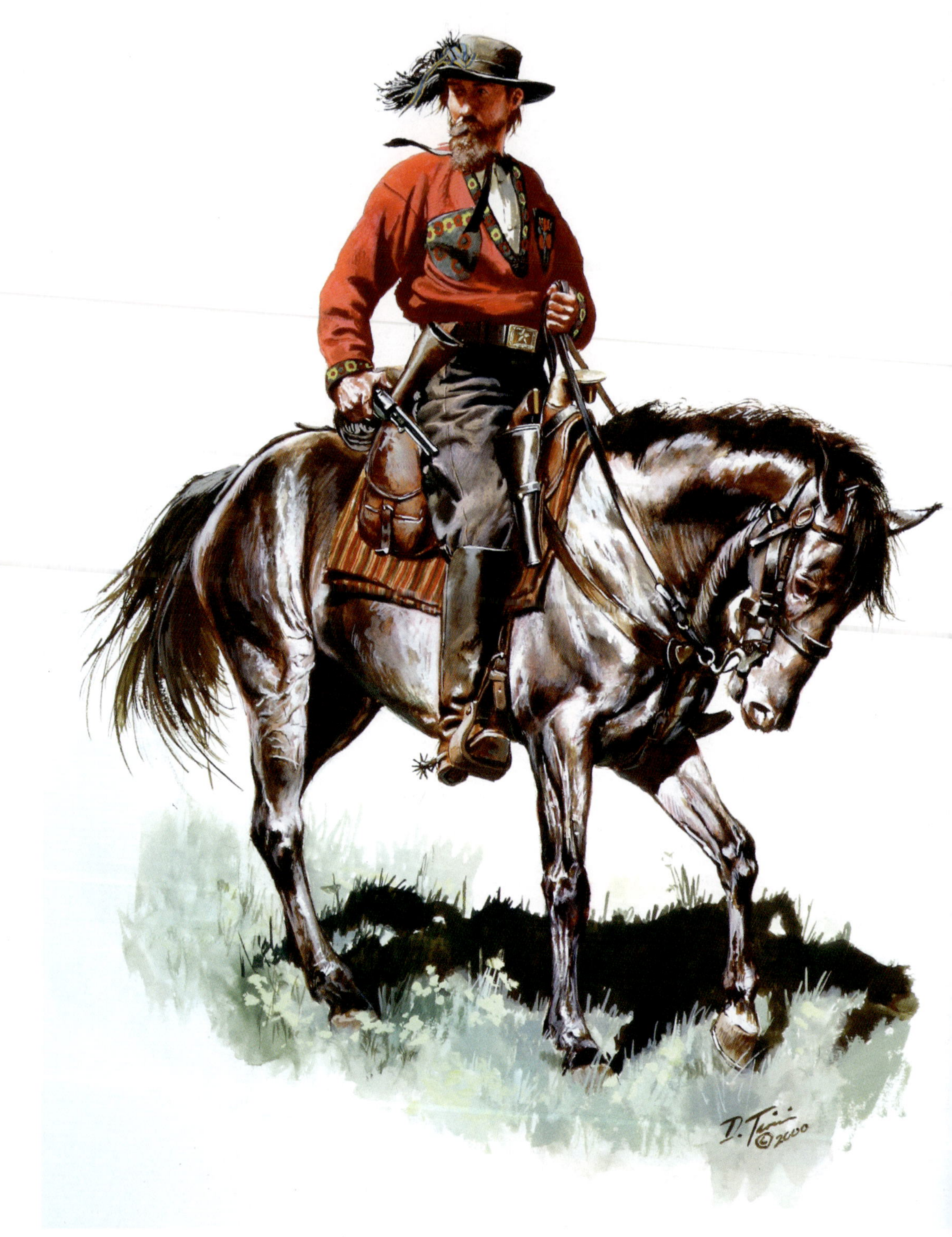

Quantrill's Guerillas

A SCHOOLTEACHER AND GAMBLER BEFORE THE Civil War, William Clarke Quantrill espoused the Confederate cause and joined a small band of Cherokee that fought under General Sterling Price at Wilson's Creek on August 10, 1861. Following this, he turned to guerrilla warfare forming a small pro-Confederate band of "Bushwackers," which became known as "Quantrill's Guerrillas." Their first main action occurred on February 22, 1862, when they attacked a detachment of the 2nd Battalion Ohio Cavalry near Independence, Kansas, under Major George W. Purington, killing one soldier and wounding three.[1]

In March 1862, Quantrill joined forces with Colonel John T. Hughes, 1st Regiment, 4th Division, Missouri State Guard, and took part in an attack on Independence, Missouri, known as the First Battle of Independence. As a result, the guerrilla leader was commissioned a captain of Partisan Rangers, while he and his men were declared outlaws by the Union forces. Skirmishes and raids continued as Quantrill's band increased in numbers to include Cole Younger, William T. "Bloody Bill" Anderson, and Frank and Jesse James.

The most significant event in Quantrill's guerrilla campaign occurred on August 21, 1863, when he attacked Lawrence which for several years had been the stronghold of antislavery forces in Kansas and a base of operations for incursions into Missouri by "Jayhawkers" and pro-Union forces. It was also the home of antislavery senator James Henry Lane. Quantrill attacked with approximately 450 guerrilla fighters as Lane escaped through a cornfield in his nightshirt. The guerrillas killed about 150 men and boys, and left most of Lawrence in flames. A survivor of the Lawrence Massacre, Joseph Savage described the appearance of Quantrill's men as wearing "Low-crowned, broad brimmed hats—all alike nearly—unshaven—stoop-shouldered—all without coats—nearly all wore red flannel shirts much begrimed with camp-grease and dirt."[2]

Typical of Quantrill's band when they attacked Lawrence, the guerrilla in this plate has feathers and ribbons in his hat. Worn over a regular shirt and neck-tie, his scarlet overshirt is lavishly decorated by a wife or sweetheart with floral-patterned embroidery around its low-cut V-shaped neck, large patch pockets and cuffs.[3] His baggy gray trousers are tucked into high-topped boots. A rectangular "five star" plate fastens his waist belt. He holds a .44-caliber Colt Navy revolver drawn from a belt holster, while another revolver is carried in a pommel holster.

After committing further depravations through 1864, Quantrill was eventually ambushed and captured in western Kentucky by guerrilla hunter Edwin W. Terrell, and died of wounds in a military prison at Louisville on June 6, 1865.

1. *Leavenworth Times*, February 23, 1862, 2:1.
2. William Elsey, *Quantrill and the Border Wars* (Connelly Pageant Book Co., 1909), 347.
3. Elsey, *Quantrill and the Border Wars*, 317–18.

First Sergeant, 6th Regiment United States Colored Cavalry

ONE OF SIX MOUNTED AFRICAN AMER-ICAN REGIMENTS, the 6th Regiment US Colored Cavalry was organized at Camp Nelson, Kentucky, on October 24, 1864, with Colonel James F. Wade in command. Like other Black regiments, its ranks were filled with ex-slaves and freedmen. Attached to the 1st Division, District of Kentucky, Department of Ohio, it took part in Stoneman's Raid into Southwestern Virginia, from December 10–29, 1864. The regiment continued in service within the Military District and Department of Kentucky until December 1865, and Department of Arkansas until mustered out on April 15, 1866.[1]

African American cavalrymen took much pride in their uniforms and appearance, as did their infantry and artillery counterparts. This First Sergeant wears a forage cap; Pattern 1858 four-button sack coat; and mounted service trousers with reinforced seat and inner leg. Rather than being sewn directly on, rank insignia consisting of yellow lozenge within three chevrons was applied to a dark blue flannel patch, which was then sewn on the sleeves of his coat. His rank is also indicated by 1½ wide stripes on the outer seams of his trousers. A sky-blue over-coat is rolled and attached to the front of the pommel of his saddle. Footwear consists of Napoleon-style boots with regulation brass spurs. The leather saber knot attached to his 1860 light cavalry saber is wrapped around his wrist so he would not lose the weapon if knocked out of his hand. A revolver is holstered on his waist belt and a Model 1863 Sharps carbine is carried in a leather thimble attached to his saddle.

Horse equipment consists of a Pattern 1859 McClellan saddle and combined bridle and halter with cavalry curb bit. A leather valise is attached to the back of the saddle cantle. A woolen-webbing saddle girth fastens his saddle around the girth of his mount. Buckled on the rings on the rear of his saddle, a crupper strap is secured around the tail of his mount to prevent the saddle slipping forward. Pattern 1859 saddlebags are attached by leather stays to the saddle skirts. Wooden stirrups are covered with black leather stirrup hoods. An off-white nose-bag for feeding his mount hangs from the front of his saddle skirts. A dark blue dragoon-pattern horse blanket has a broad orange woven border.[2]

---

1. *Tabular Analysis of the Records of the U.S. Colored Troops and Their Predecessor Units in the National Archives of the United States,* Special List No. 33, National Archives and Records Service General Services Administration, compiled by Joseph B. Ross, FS Library Book 973 M2rt Film:1036062 Item 21, Washington, DC, 1973.

2. *The Ordnance Manual for the Use of the Officers of the United States Army* (J. B. Lippencott & Co., 1861), 155–63.

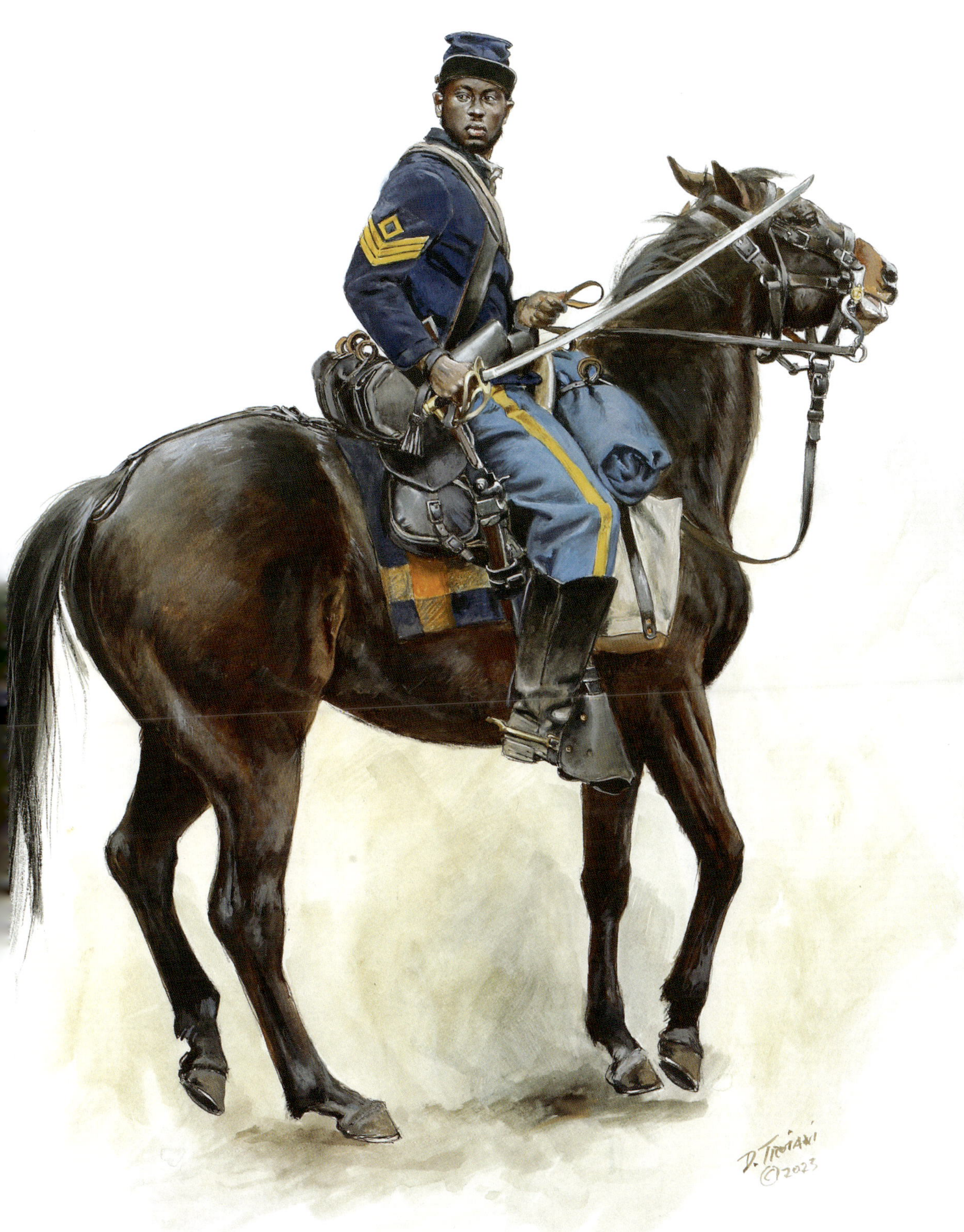

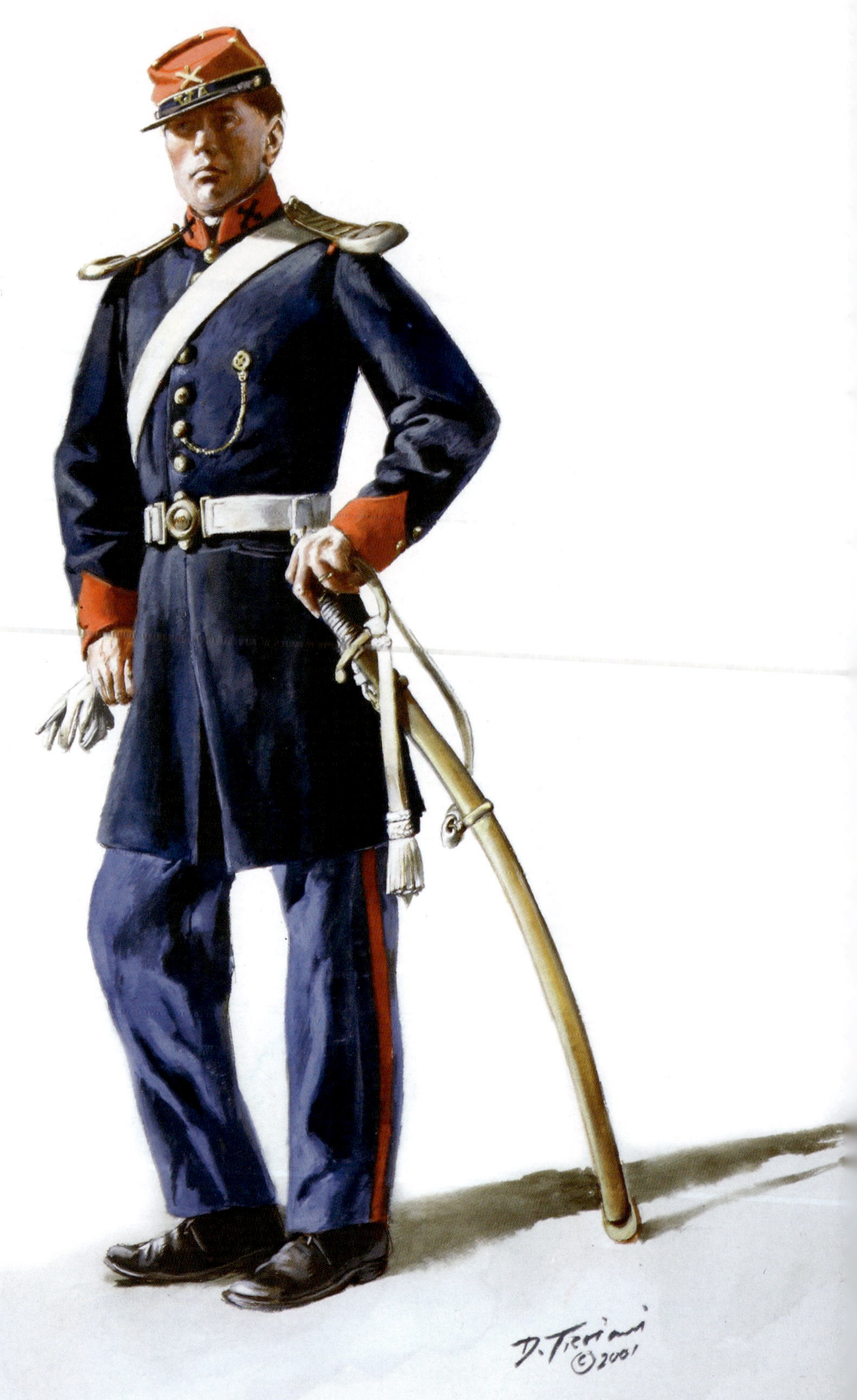

THE ARTILLERY

Washington Artillery of New Orleans, 1860–1861

ORGANIZED AS A VOLUNTEER MILITIA COMPANY IN 1838 and later nick-named "The Game Cocks" by President Jefferson Davis, the Washington Artillery became a two-company unit on January 17, 1861, and by March had expanded into a four-company battalion. A fifth company was formed as a reserve on May 27, 1861. A sixth company did not leave the state.[1] The Washington Artillery prided itself on being proficient in both infantry and artillery tactics, and possessed both cannon and muskets in its arsenal. For efficiency, drill, and discipline it was one of the most proficient organizations of citizen soldiery in the Southern States.[2]

Based on the French artillery of the 1850s, much of the dress uniform worn by the Washington Artillery at the beginning of the Civil War was likely adopted in 1854 when the press reported on the Quarterly Parade of the volunteer militia of the Crescent City. The *Daily Delta* described the corps as wearing "new uniforms . . . with a very complete and fine brass band."[3] At members' expense, their full dress uniform consisted of Pattern 1851 dress caps with red band and pompon; and nine-button dark blue uniform coats with brass shoulder scales and scarlet facings on collar and cuffs. Crossed cannon of blue cloth were stitched on each side of the standing collar. Pants were sky blue with one-inch wide scarlet seam stripe. Officers generally wore a plain coat and the same style of pants as the enlisted men, except for a gold cord at the centre of their red seam stripes.

During November 1860, the Washington Artillery paraded for the first time wearing "neat, new red caps, or *kepis*," which had dark blue bands and gold braid for all ranks.[4] These were "ornamented with a pair of cross-cannon, with the letters W.A, in front."[5] Waist and shoulder belts were of white webbing, the former fastened with a two-piece plate bearing the letters "WA." Small crossed cannon ornamented the outer flap of their cartridge boxes, and rolled red blankets were strapped to militia-pattern knapsacks painted with the script letters "WA."

The pin worn on the chest of this private's coat, which is seen in a number of contemporary images of members of the unit, is composed of a circular cannoneer's belt bearing the motto "Try Us," inset with crossed cannon, from which hangs a miniature brass "Tiger's Head," the whole being attached via a fine chain to one of the Pelican buttons on his coat.

The Battalion of Washington Artillery was mustered into Confederate service on May 26, 1861, and left for Virginia the next day under the command of Major James B. Walton. The First and Second Companies were armed with Model 1840 Light Artillery sabers and revolvers for "close quarters," and had two 6-pounder and two 12-pounder howitzers each. The Third and Fourth Companies were armed with Springfield muskets, which were turned in on arrival in Richmond, following which the Third Company received two 12-pounders and two 24-pounder howitzers, and the First Company received a rifle battery, handing their original guns over to the Fourth Company.

---

1. Arthur W. Bergeron Jr., *Guide to Louisiana Confederate Military Units 1861–1865* (Louisiana State University Press, 1989), 14.

2. William Miller Owen, *In Camp and Battle with the Washington Artillery of New Orleans* (Ticknor and Company, 1885), 3.

3. *The Daily Delta* (New Orleans, LA), November 3, 1854, 2:3.

4. *The Daily Picayune* (New Orleans, LA), November 23, 1860, 2:1.

5. "Constitution and By-Laws of the Battalion of Washington Artillery" (Bulletin Book and Job Office, 35 and 37 Gravier Street, 1861), 6.

Washington Artillery of New Orleans, 1861–1862

THE PRIDE OF THE CRESCENT CITY, THE BATTALION of the Washington Artillery of New Orleans arrived in Richmond, Virginia on June 4, 1861, and elements of the unit played an important part in the Confederate victory at Manassas on July 21, 1861. With red flannel bands tied around the left upper sleeves of their dark blue uniform coats to distinguish themselves from the predominantly blue-clad Union army, all four companies served with distinction in General Beauregard's Army of the Potomac.

While encamped near Centreville during the fall of 1861, the battalion received a new fatigue uniform, which unit historian Lieutenant William M. Owen recorded as consisting of "jackets and pants, 'made to order' by [William] Ira Smith & Co." A clothing manufacturer in Richmond since 1849, Smith's store was at 114 Main Street, and he would go on to supply the Confederate Quartermaster Department with overcoats and gray cloth into 1862.[1] According to Owen, each man in the Washington Artillery was "measured for his suit, and they came, properly labeled, to their owners." Made of cloth from the Crenshaw Woolen Mill, their outfit was "a bluish-gray in color, and gave the command a neat and distinctive appearance."[2] As a result, the "blue cloth dress uniforms" of the battalion were sent to Richmond where they were retained for "swell occasions" when the artillerists were on furlough.[3] The red caps they wore when they departed from New Orleans continued in use while their white gaiters soon fell out of favor being replaced by cavalry boots.

The red-trimmed round jackets worn by these artillerists are of the pattern soon after produced by the Richmond Clothing Depot. That of the sergeant has a battalion pin with crossed cannon and "Tiger's Head" attached. His sky-blue trousers have non-regulation narrow red stripes on the outer seams. Leaning against one of the battalion's 12-pound Napoleons, he holds a Model 1840 Light Artillery saber. A leather gunner's haversack and tin drum canteen hang over its brass gun tube.

---

1. National Archives, record group 109, M346, Confederate Citizens File, 1861–1865, William Ira Smith, documents 6 and 18.

2. Owen, *In Camp and Battle with the Washington Artillery of New Orleans*, 54.

3. Owen, *In Camp and Battle with the Washington Artillery of New Orleans*, 50.

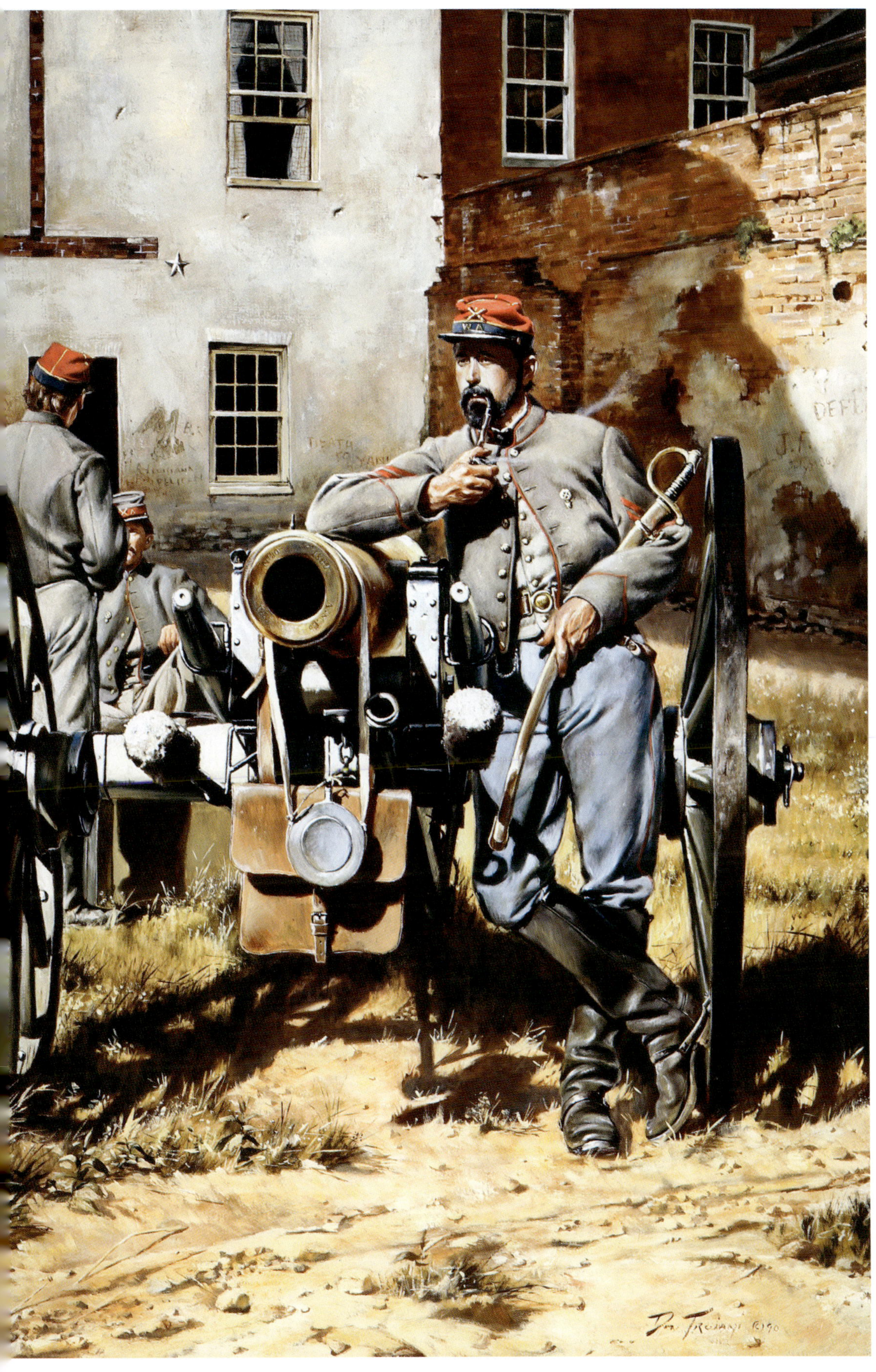

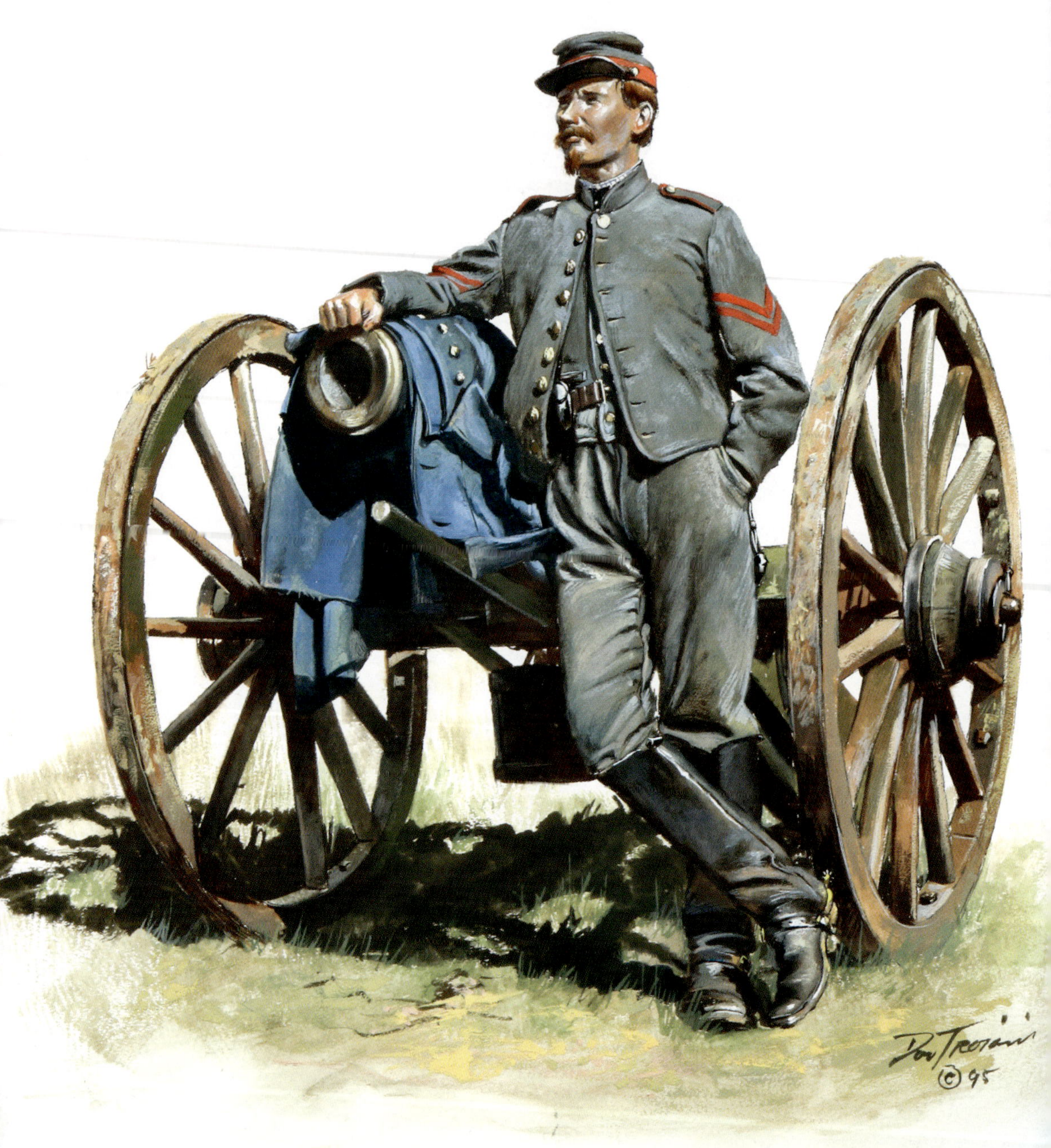

First Company, Richmond Howitzers, 1863

ORIGINALLY FORMED ON NOVEMBER 9, 1859, AS THE "Howitzer Battery," commanded by Captain George Wythe Randolph, the original company of the Richmond Howitzers were first called into action ten days later as a result of the John Brown Raid on Harper's Ferry. Quickly armed with muskets by the state and as yet without uniforms, they were sent along with other Richmond volunteer militia companies to Charlestown in response to rumors of a plot to rescue Brown during his trial and execution. By July 4, 1860, the unit had been designated Company H, 1st Regiment of Virginia Volunteers and had been provided with six Dahlgren 12-pounder Boat Howitzers, one of which was rifled. Two other companies of Richmond Howitzers were formed in May 1861, but the three units never served together as a battalion.[1]

By the summer of 1863, the First Company was armed with two 10-pounder Parrot rifled guns and two Napoleon 6-pounders as part of Colonel Henry C. Cabell's Artillery Battalion, Army of Northern Virginia, and was in action at Chancellorsville and Gettysburg. During the former action it lost two men killed and two wounded. With Longstreet's Corps at Gettysburg, it took part in the general artillery fire proceeding Pickett's assault. During July 2 and 3 the rifle section fired about 600 rounds, and the two Napoleons expended 264 rounds. On the latter day the company again lost two men killed and two wounded, plus ten horses killed.

Leaning on the muzzle of one of the unit's guns, this corporal wears headgear and clothing that was typical of an artillerist of the Army of Northern Virginia in 1863. His cap is based on that worn by Private Robert William Royall who served in the battery from April 21, 1861, until his surrender in Burkville, Virginia, April 24, 1865. Of a chasseur pattern as produced by the Richmond Clothing Bureau, it has a branch service red band, and also a red crown. The chin strap on Royall's cap had lined Roman "I" (infantry) buttons and a visor made of pasteboard, covered with enameled cloth, with a machine-stitched welt around the outer edge.

His partially trimmed jacket is based on the second-pattern produced at Richmond, and has a nine-button front, no buttons on the cuffs, belt loops, and red piping around the shoulder straps.[2] Under this is a privately purchased cadet gray vest. His matching trousers are devoid of the seam stripes officially prescribed for a corporal. His fine quality boots are likely of English origin, as is the belt worn under his jacket. Draped over the gun barrel is a sky-blue overcoat likely captured from the Yankees.

---

1. Louis H. Manarin and Lee A. Wallace Jr., *Richmond Volunteers 1861–1865* (Westover Press, 1969), 3–11.
2. Jensen, "A Survey of Confederate Central Government Quartermaster Issue Jackets," part 1, 114.

Confederate Artillery Officer, Spring 1863

THE ARTILLERY OF THE ARMY OF NORTHERN VIRGINIA was dubbed "the Long Arm of Lee" by historian Jennings C. Wise, and this light artillery captain proudly represents that branch of service.[1] According to the 1861 regulations, artillery officers and men were to wear double-breasted uniform coats, or "tunics," but by 1863 most wore a jacket, which was more practical in the field. However, red facing color on his collar and cuffs adhere to regulations and show that artillery was his branch of service.[2] This is embellished by red cord on his jacket edges. His rank of captain is indicated by three horizontal gold bars on his collar front, and a European-style double stranded "ornament of gold braid" on his sleeves. According to regulations, the buttons on his jacket would bear the letter "A," although those of General Staff pattern with raised "eagle" encircled by stars were often preferred. A gray vest is fastened by a single row of smaller buttons. His sky-blue trousers have nonregulation one inch-wide red welts on the outer seams.

As overcoats were not provided for officers in the 1861 Confederate regulations, this officer wears the double-breasted version prescribed for enlisted man. Its cape extends only to the elbows, indicating it is of infantry pattern. Cadet gray in color, for reasons of economy it has only two buttons on its cape. His jaunty red chasseur-pattern uniform cap has two strands of gold lace around the band, which also quarters its sides and forms a quatrefoil on its top.

Footwear consists of top boots of fine leather reaching to the knees. His plain black leather waist belt is fastened by a circular two-piece plate with raised "eagle" motif, and has attached a revolver in black leather holster and light artillery saber. Binoculars are carried in a leather case.

---

1. Jennings Cropper Wise, *The Long Arm of Lee or History of the Artillery of the Army of Northern Virginia* (J. P. Bell Company, Inc., 1915).

2. *Uniform and Dress of the Army of the Confederate States.*

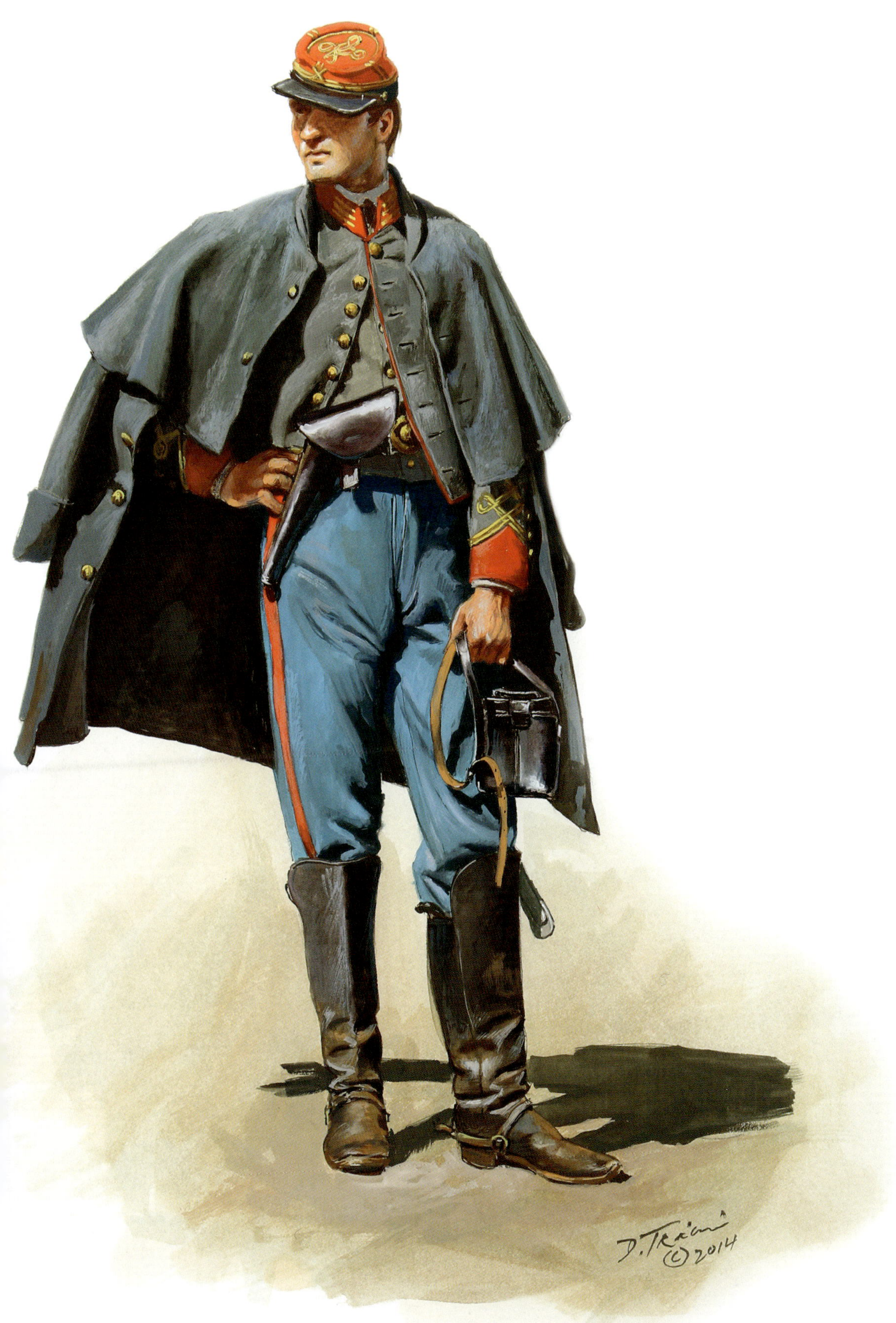

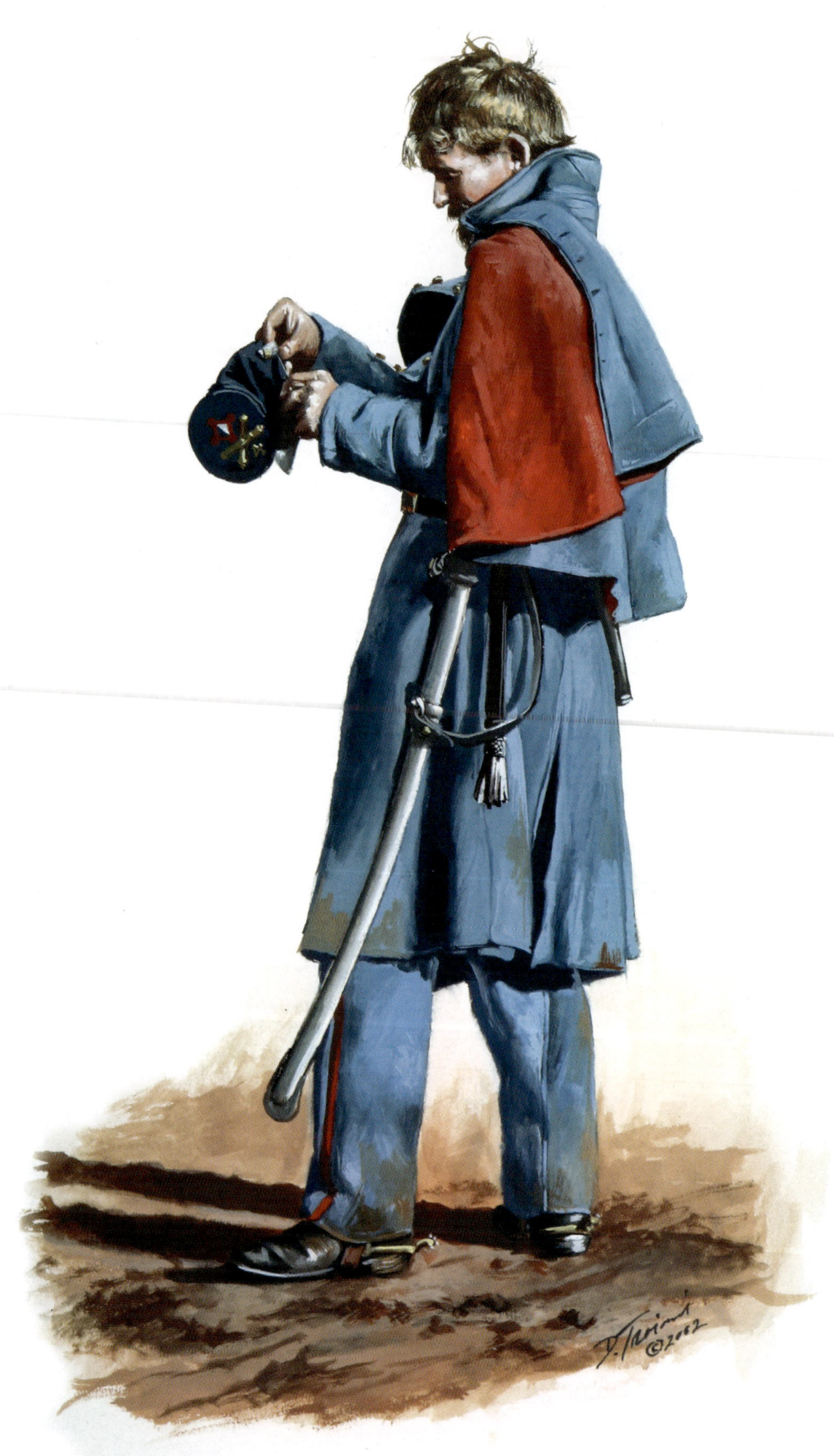

Corporal, Battery D, 4th New Jersey Light Artillery, December 1864

ONE OF THE FINEST DRESSED UNION ARTILLERY UNITS outside the Regular Army, the 4th New Jersey Light Artillery was commanded by Captain George T. Woodbury who was a stickler for detail and discipline. Enrolled and mustered in on September 16, 1863, the battery of six 12-pounder bronze Napoleon guns was organized at Trenton, New Jersey. Stationed at Camp Barry, the artillery camp of instruction in the District of Columbia until February 29, 1864, it was moved to Camp Kearney at Gloucester Point, Virginia, until May 1864. It saw its first action at Bermuda Hundred and fought outside Petersburg and Richmond until the war's end. When Richmond fell, the battery was the first organization to represent New Jersey when elements of the Union Army entered the city on April 2, 1865.[1]

While at Gloucester Point Captain Woodbury procured for the enlisted men in his command "red flannel linings for overcoat capes, at the price of $1.30 a piece." A circular issued to the battery stated, "They will be put in by the Company tailor and the cost deducted from the pay of the men next pay day. The material is the same as that in the original coat furnished the Battery before leaving the state, having been procured from the firm who made the Company uniforms."[2]

Also while at Gloucester Point, and in preparation for the battery's assignment to the Second Division, X Corps, at Bermuda Hundred, Virginia, Woodbury issued General Orders No. 1 on April 26, 1864, stating, "The enlisted men of this command will immediately reduce their clothing to the following allowance; viz. 2 forage caps, 2 Artillery jackets, 2 pairs trousers, 2 pairs shoes or boots, 2 shirts, 2 pairs of drawers, 3 pairs of stockings, 1 blanket, 1 overcoat and 1 rubber blanket or gum overcoat. All clothing in excess of this allowance will be immediately packed, plainly marked and turned over to the QM Sgt."[3]

Resigning in August 1864 due to disability, Woodbury was succeeded by First Lieutenant Charles R. Doane who was promoted to captain in command of the battery. When corps badges were issued to the X Corps while the Battery was in the trenches outside Richmond, Doane maintained the exacting discipline established by his predecessor. On October 31, 1864, he issued General Orders No. 17. Allowing no room for deviation, it stated, "Corps badges will be furnished on application to the QM Sgt. And every enlisted man is required to provide himself at once. The figure 4 will be placed below the cross cannon [on the cap top] and the badge above with one of its points upward and the opposite end directed toward the centre of the cross cannon. Care will be taken that the points are well stitched down."

Likely in order to ensure that the corps badge and brasses were displayed at all times, Doane added to his order, "The wearing of glazed covers for caps is strictly prohibited and chiefs of Detachments will be held responsible that their men conform to this order and likewise that their clothing is at all times kept neat and uniform."[4]

---

1. *Supplement to the Official Records of the Union and Confederate Armies*, part II, vol. 39, 672–74.
2. National Archives, record group 94, regimental books, New Jersey Light Artillery Batteries.
3. Regimental books, New Jersey Light Artillery Batteries.
4. Regimental books, New Jersey Light Artillery Batteries.

Watson's Battery, 1861

ORGANIZED AT NEW ORLEANS, LOUI-siANA, IN EARLY August 1861, the Watson Battery also known as Watson Flying Artillery, was uniformed and equipped by wealthy planter Augustus C. Watson, of Tensas Parish, at a cost of about $50,000. Originally commanded by Captain Allen A. Bursley, Watson enlisted in the unit as a high private, or wealthy man who preferred to serve in the ranks. Formed among members of "the first families of the French districts of New Orleans," the Watson Battery was composed of 120 officers and men, and the battery consisted of four rifled 6-pounders, plus two rifled 12-pound howitzers, "all fine bronze pieces, with carriages and appointments complete, and the finest horse to be found in the state."[1]

After Augustus Watson persuaded Daniel Beltzhoover, chief of staff to General Twigg's Department of Alabama, Mississippi, and East Louisiana, to take command of the Battery in April 1862, the unit became dissatisfied with his harsh leadership and began to break-up with some men resigning to join the Louisiana Point Coupe Battery.

The Watson Battery fought at Belmont, Missouri, on November 7, 1861, where it lost two guns and sustained heavy casualties. It next served at Shiloh and then Corinth, and helped cover the Confederate retreat at Tuscumbia River Bridge on October 5, 1862. Forming part of the garrison at Port Hudson in early 1863, it served as heavy artillery until captured on July 9, 1863. After parole, some of its men were merged into the 1st Louisiana Heavy Artillery and the original unit was disbanded.[2]

The first uniform worn by the Watson Battery consisted of a chasseur-pattern cap with yellow trim. Affixed to its crimson red band was a small militia crossed cannon insignia with metal letters "W" and "B" either side in honor of their founder. The harsh command of Captain Beltzhoover in 1862 caused some men to remove the "W" from the caps. The roundabout jacket worn by this artilleryman is steel gray faced and edged in crimson red. Its sleeves are adorned with a French cuff with yellow piping outlining eight small ball buttons and topped with trefoil trim. Matching trousers have a wide crimson red welt down the outer seams. He is armed with a Model 1840 light artillery saber. The two-piece plate fastening his belt likely bore the Pelican state seal. His horse is feeding from a duck canvas nose bag with leather bottom well attached to its bridle.

---

1. *Daily Picayune* (New Orleans, LA), August 12, 1861, 1:7; and *Daily True Delta* (New Orleans, LA), August 13, 1861, 1:7.
2. Bergeron Jr., *Guide to Louisiana Confederate Military Units 1861–1865*, 36–37.

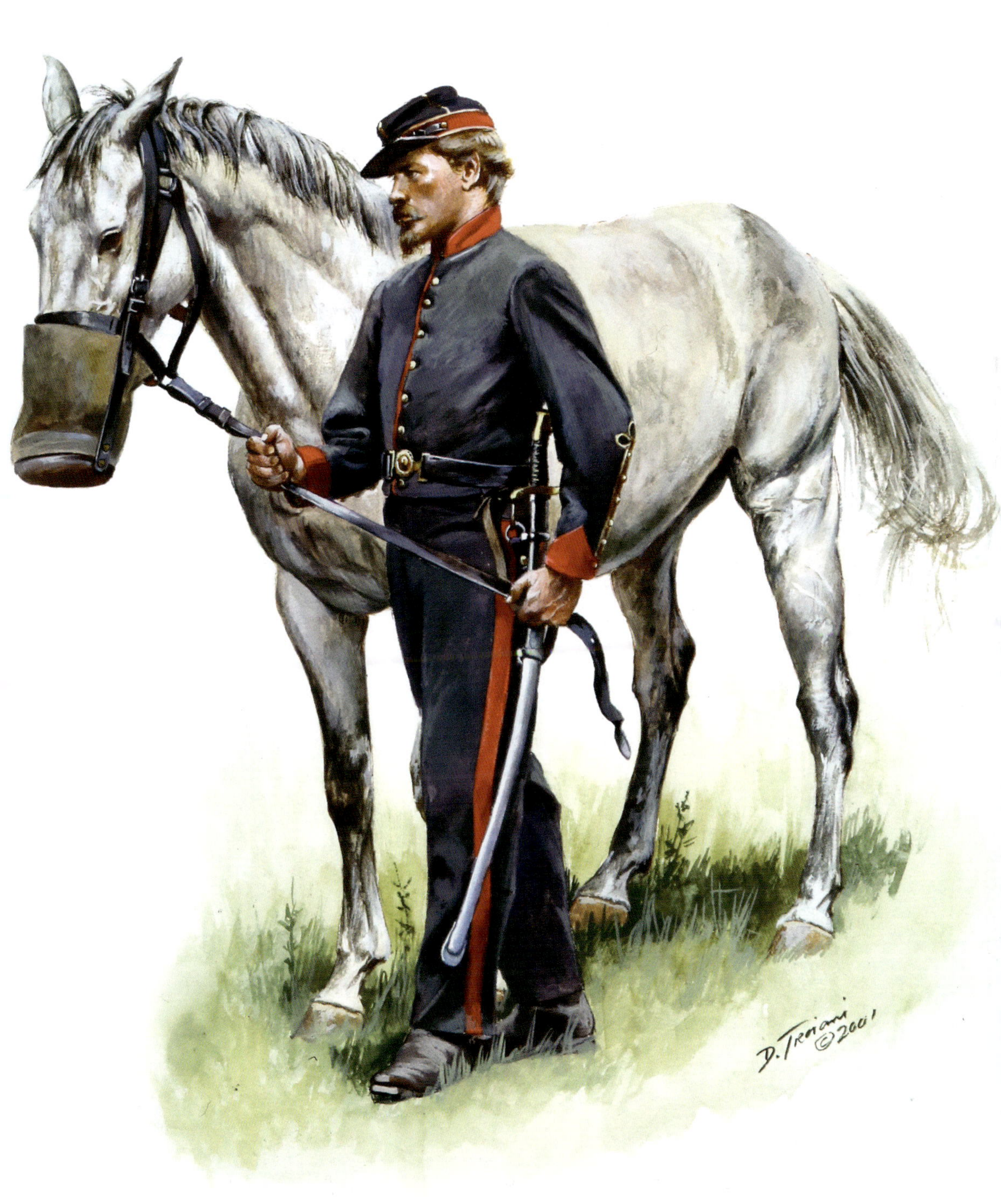

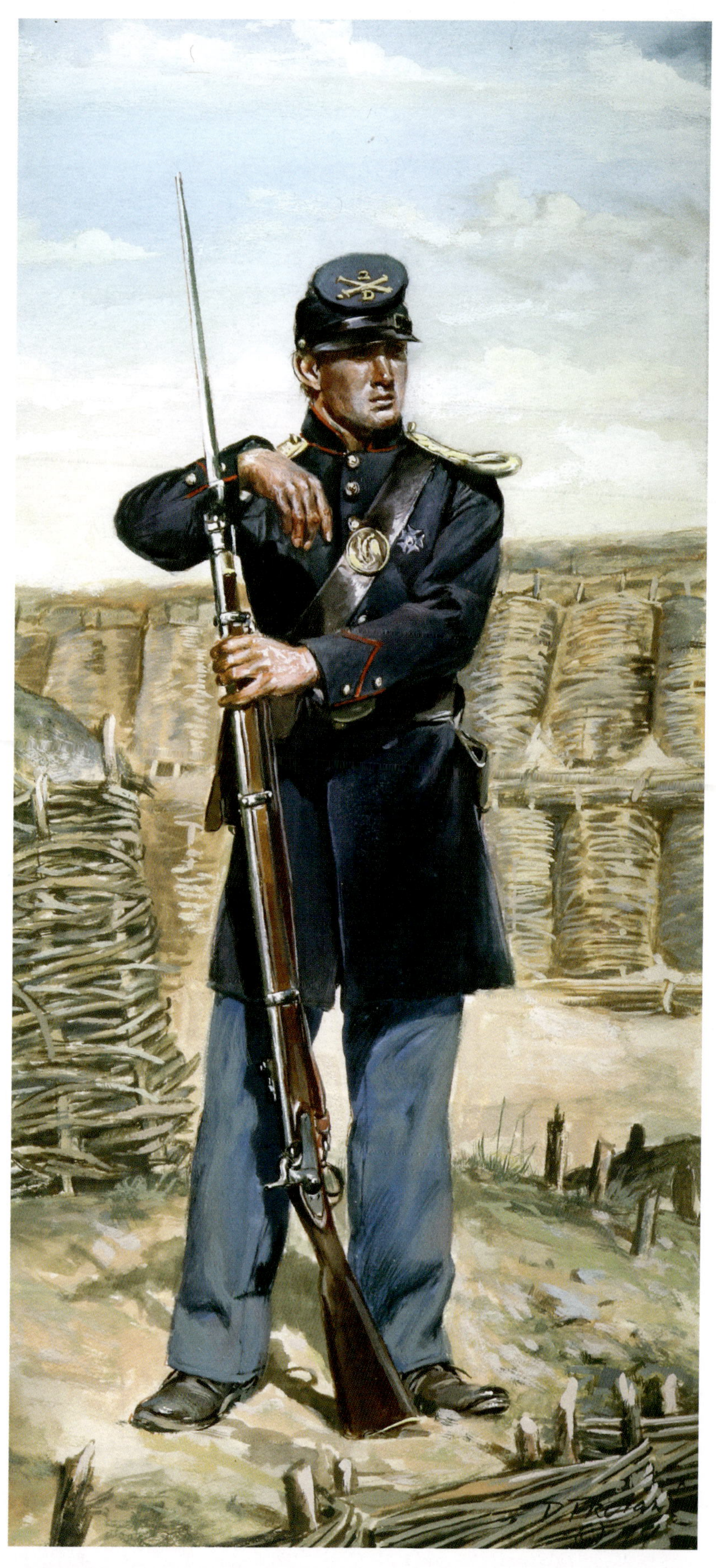

2nd Connecticut Heavy Artillery, 1864

ORIGINALLY ORGANIZED AS THE LITCHFIELD COUNTY Regiment, the 19th Connecticut Infantry was changed to the 2nd Connecticut Heavy Artillery by order of the War Department on November 23, 1863. It performed garrison duty in the defenses near Alexandria, Virginia, until May 1864 when it was sent to fight as infantry in the Army of the Potomac. Assigned to the Second Brigade, First Division, VI Corps, the regiment was in action at Cold Harbor on June 1 leaving 323 men on the field, 129 of them dead or mortally wounded, including Colonel Elisha S. Kellogg. After participating in the opening stages of the Siege of Petersburg in June 1864, it was transferred to the Shenandoah Valley where it suffered further heavy losses at Cedar Creek on October 19, 1864. Moved back to Petersburg, it took part in the final breakthrough on April 2, 1865, and the subsequent Appomattox Campaign, following which it was sent to North Carolina to assist Major General William T. Sherman in forcing the surrender of the Army of Tennessee on April 26, 1865.[1]

Following conversion to artillery, the regiment was ordered on January 1, 1864, to turn all early issue "hats and light artillery jackets" over to the regimental quartermaster who provided in their stead caps and artillery pattern frock coats. This order stated further that "no men . . . will be allowed to wear a hat of any kind."[2]

This private of Company D, 2nd Connecticut Heavy Artillery, has a Pattern 1858 crossed cannon insignia, plus regimental and company designation, attached to his cap top. His Pattern 1851 frock coat has artillery branch service red trim around collar and cuffs, and has nine gilt Connecticut state seal buttons at front, two at waist level in back, and two smaller buttons of the same pattern on each cuff. His enlisted man's brass shoulder scales have seven scalloped surfaces on an edged strap with rounded end and a half-round crescent. He wears sky-blue dismounted pattern kersey wool trousers. Footwear consists of brogans or bootees with smooth exterior of blackened leather that reaches high upon the ankle.

He is armed with a Pattern 1853 Enfield rifle musket with russet leather sling, and has fixed his socket bayonet. His waist belt is fastened by a Pattern 1839 "US" oval plate and carries a cap pouch and bayonet frog with scabbard. His cartridge box is suspended on a shoulder belt with Pattern 1826 "eagle" plate attached.

---

1. Stephen R. Smith et al., *Record of Service of Connecticut Men in the Army and Navy of the United States during the War of the Rebellion* (Press of the Case, Lockwood & Brainard Company, 1889).

2. Regimental Order and Letter Book, Connecticut 2nd Heavy Artillery, Order No. 1, January 1, 1864, regimental papers, record group 94, National Archives.

11th United States Colored Heavy Artillery, Private, 1864

ORGANIZED AT DUTCH ISLAND, IN NARRAGANSETT BAY, Providence, Rhode Island, with Lieutenant Colonel Nelson Viall in command, the 14th Rhode Island Heavy Artillery was mustered in for three years' service on August 28, 1863, following General Orders 143 issued by the War Department on May 22, 1863, authorizing the establishment of regiments of colored troops. The regiment was changed to the 8th United States Colored Heavy Artillery on April 4, 1864, but because a unit with the same designation had already been established in Kentucky, it was redesignated the 11th US Colored Heavy Artillery on May 21, 1864. Consisting of fifteen companies, it was organized into three battalions, which were assigned to the XIII Corps, Department of the Gulf, and served as garrison troops in separate locations with regimental headquarters at Greenville, moved to Plaquemine, Louisiana, on March 4, 1865, and to Donaldsonville on June 25, 1865.[1]

Unlike other colored regiments, the many of those in the ranks of the 11th US Colored Heavy Artillery had never known the yoke of slavery as most were free men in their native state. An inspection report dated August 10, 1864, commented on the superior nature of the regiment and made special note of the fact that "the men are almost all free, and not freed men."[2] It also noted that the majority of the regiment were literate, and that they were all well uniformed. For such men to go and fight in the South took special courage, as capture left open the possibility of being made a slave.

Although it was a heavy artillery unit, this regiment was issued with light artillery pattern jackets.[3] Holding a handspike, this private wears a jacket with red trim on collar, cuffs and jacket edges, and keepers for brass scales on his shoulders. His forage cap has a Pattern 1858 Artillery insignia on its top, plus unit designation. As was regulation for all regiments of heavy artillery, his accoutrements are for infantry service. The 11th US Colored Heavy Artillery was mustered out at New Orleans on October 2, 1865.

---

1. *Supplement to the Official Records of the Union and Confederate Armies*, part II, vol. 77, 230–31.
2. NARA, record group 94, regimental books, 8th US Colored Heavy Artillery.
3. Howard University, staff, MSRC, "US Colored Troops Clothing Account Books Collection," Book 141–39.

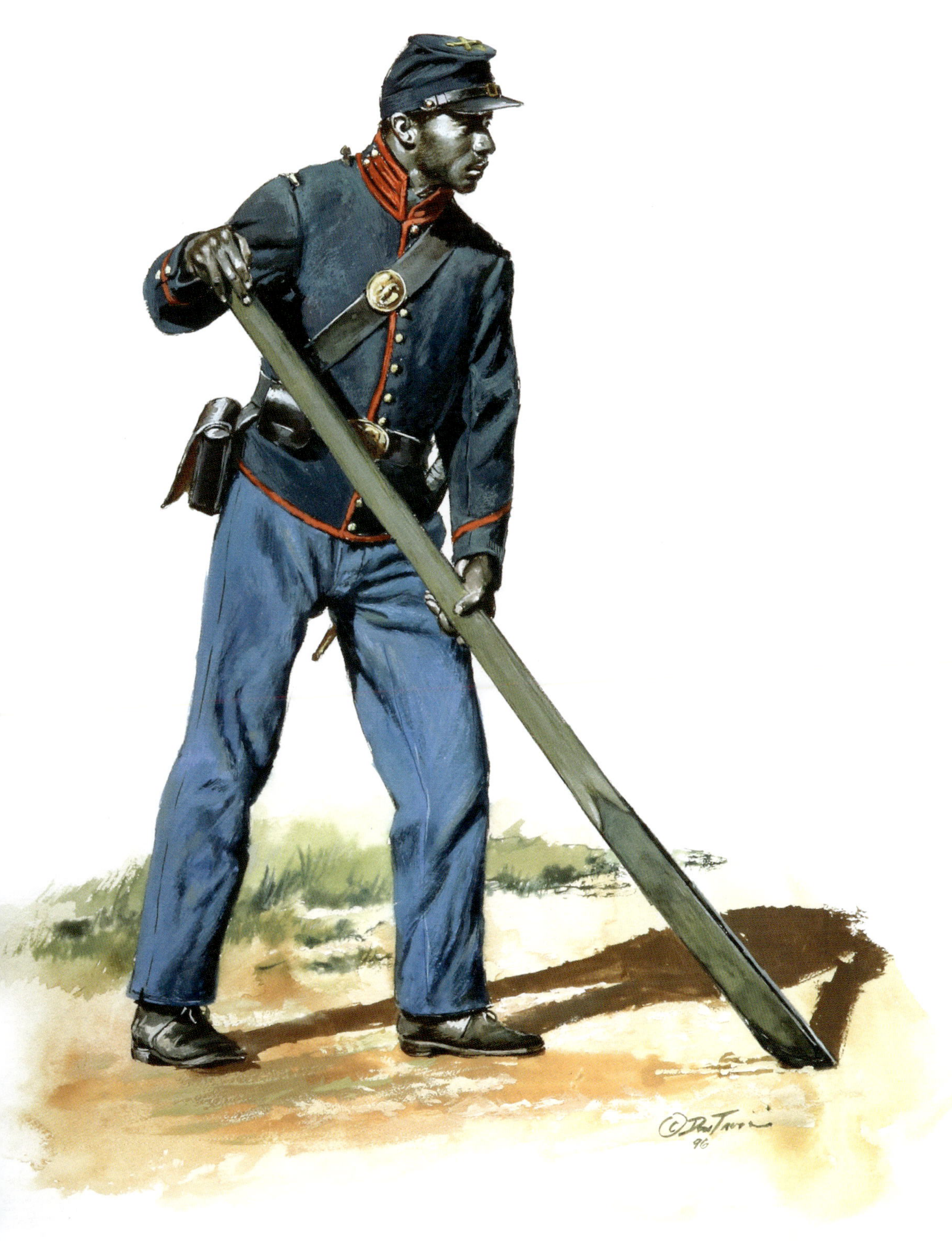

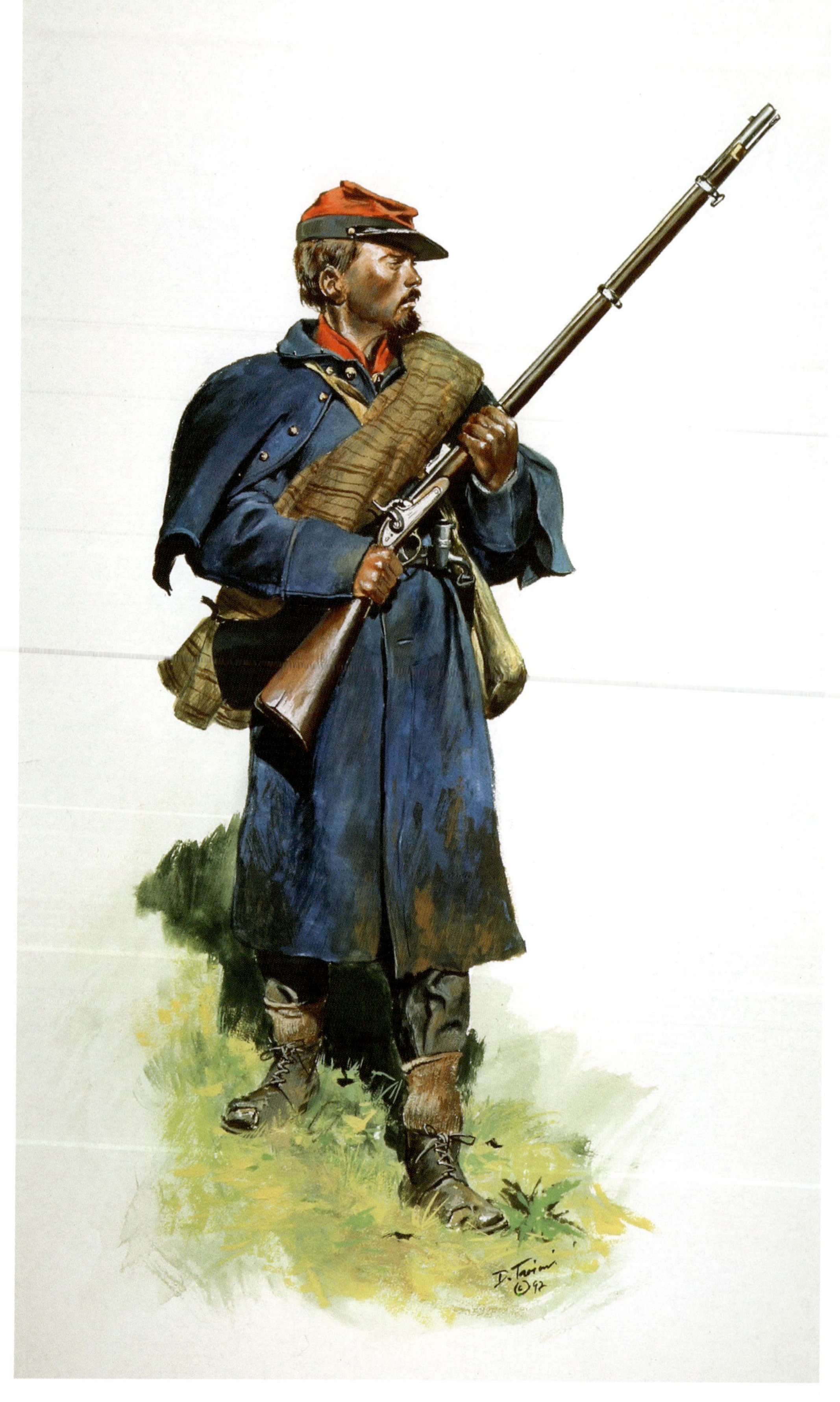

Crutchfield's Virginia Heavy Artillery

A STUDENT AND LATER PROFESSOR AT THE VIRGINIA MILITARY Institute before the Civil War, Stapleton Crutchfield served as Lieutenant General Thomas J. "Stonewall" Jackson's chief of artillery with the rank of colonel during 1862–1863. Wounded and losing a leg at Chancellorsville on May 2, 1863, he was transported in the same field ambulance that carried Jackson after his fatal wounding by friendly fire the same day. On January 18, 1865, Crutchfield was again assigned to the Army of Northern Virginia commanding the artillery units in the defenses of Richmond, Virginia, including the Chaffin's Bluff line. With the collapse of Petersburg and imminent evacuation of Richmond on March 25, 1865, Crutchfield ordered his heavy artillerymen to spike and abandon their guns. The units under his command, including the 10th, 18th, 19th, and 20th Virginia Artillery battalions, plus the Chaffin's Bluff garrison, were hastily organized into an infantry brigade to serve in the division of Major General George Washington Custis Lee, and joined the retreating Confederate army.[1]

Low on supplies and light in marching order, many of the men under Crutchfield's command had been wearing sky-blue Federal overcoats, which had served them well in the Richmond trenches. But when they took to the field they were in danger of being mistaken for the enemy and exposed to friendly fire.

Of the action at Saylor's Creek on April 6, 1865, where Crutchfield's brigade took up a position on the left of the Confederate line, Major Robert Stiles, who had commanded the artillery at Chaffin's Bluff, recalled, "I had cautioned my men against wearing 'Yankee overcoats,' especially in battle, but had not been able to enforce the order perfectly—and almost at my side I saw a young fellow of one of my companies jam the muzzle of his musket against the back of the head of his most intimate friend, clad in a Yankee overcoat, and blow his brains out."[2]

Shortly after this, in the heavy fighting that ensued, Crutchfield was killed and several men died as a result of "friendly fire" from others in their brigade who, seeing blue Yankee overcoats, mistook them for the enemy.

The Confederate heavy artilleryman depicted wears a Federal infantry-pattern overcoat over a round jacket with red facings on the collar. A product of the Richmond Clothing Bureau, his forage cap has a red top and cadet gray band. An indication of hard campaigning during the last days of the war, his brogans are worn out although thick woolen socks help protect his feet. Whatever personal effects he may have are wrapped in his thin blanket roll. He is armed with a British Pattern 1853 Enfield rifle musket. At Saylor's Creek, 7,700 Confederate troops, amounting to about one fifth of the remaining retreating Confederate army, was taken prisoner or became casualties. The number of killed or wounded in its ranks is unknown.

---

1. "Crutchfield's Artillery Brigade," in *Southern Historical Society Papers*, vol. 25, ed. Reverend J. William Jones, 38.
2. Robert Stiles, *Four Years under Marse Robert* (The Neale Publishing Company, 1903), 333.

COMMANDERS AND SPECIAL BRANCHES OF SERVICE

Lieutenant General Ulysses S. Grant

FOLLOWING THE REORGANIZATION OF THE ARMY of the Potomac at Brandy Station, Virginia, Lieutenant General Ulysses S. Grant reviewed the VI Corps, commanded by Major General John Sedgewick, on April 18, 1864. On this occasion he was described by Lieutenant Colonel Theodore Lyman, aide-de-camp to Major General George G. Meade, as being "neatly dressed in the regulation uniform, with handsome sash and sword, and the three stars of a lieutenant-general on his shoulder. He is a man of a natural, severe simplicity, in all things—the very way he wears his high crowned felt hat shows this: he neither puts it on behind his ears, nor draws it over his eyes; much less does he cock it on one side, but sets it straight and very hard on his head. His riding is the same . . . he sits firmly in the saddle and looks straight ahead, as if only intent on getting to some particular point."[1]

Generally keen on formal dress, Grant was photographed wearing the correct uniform following his appointment as brigadier general on July 31, 1862. As the war and his military career progressed, he became less concerned about regulations. He wore a short blue jacket on Lookout Mountain in late 1863. In mid-June 1864, according to General Horace Porter, the weather was too hot to wear the uniform coat, so he, and most of his staff, ordered "thin, dark blue flannel blouses to be sent to them to take the place of the heavy uniform coats which they had been wearing." After trying them on, Porter noted: "The general's blouse, like the others, was of plain material, single-breasted, and had four regulation brass buttons in front. It was substantially the coat of a private soldier, with nothing to indicate the rank of an officer except the three gold stars of a lieutenant-general on the shoulder-straps. He wore at this time a turndown white linen collar and a small, black 'butterfly' cravat, which was hooked on to his front collar-button."[2]

Grant also received a pair of light, neatly fitting calfskin boots, to which he seemed to take a fancy, and thereafter wore them most of the time in place of his heavy top-boots, putting on the latter only when he rode out in wet weather.

Reviewing the troops of the Army of the Potomac, Grant is shown with his regulation dress coat open, with two rows of buttons placed in threes on its front, while three stars grace his shoulder straps. With the exception of a gold cord with acorn ends, his hat is plain and devoid of "US" insignia within a wreath at front or "eagle" plate looping-up the brim on the right side. His plain dark blue trousers are regulation for a General Officer. His blue wool officer's shabraque, or saddle cloth, with heavy gold trim is embroidered with two stars and an eagle at its swallow tail ends.

---

1. George R. Agassiz, ed., *Meade's Headquarters 1863–1865, Letters of Colonel Theodore Lyman from the Wilderness to Appomattox* (The Atlantic Monthly Press, 1922), 83.

2. General Horace Porter, *Campaigning with Grant* (The Century Company, 1897), 203–4.

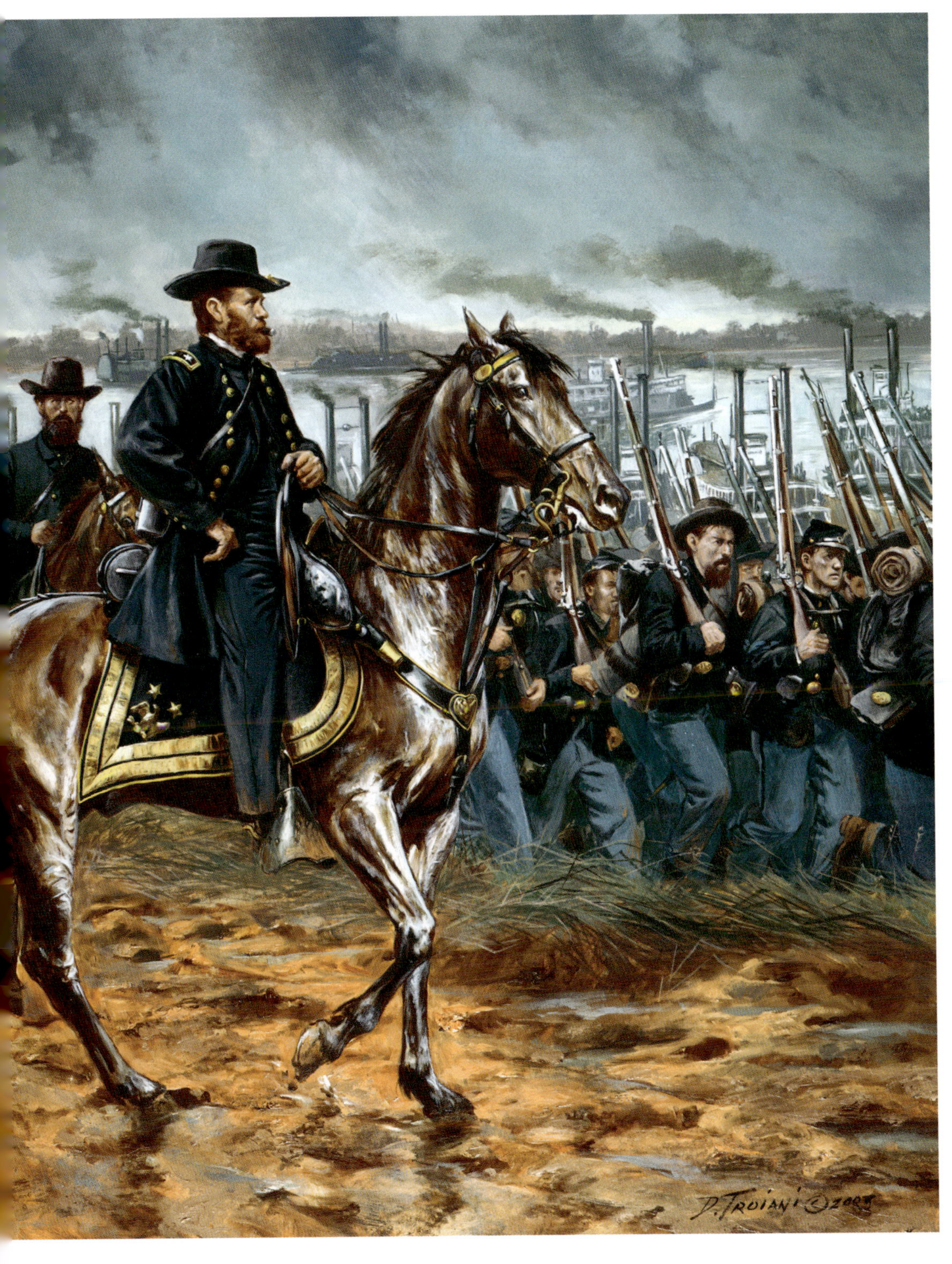

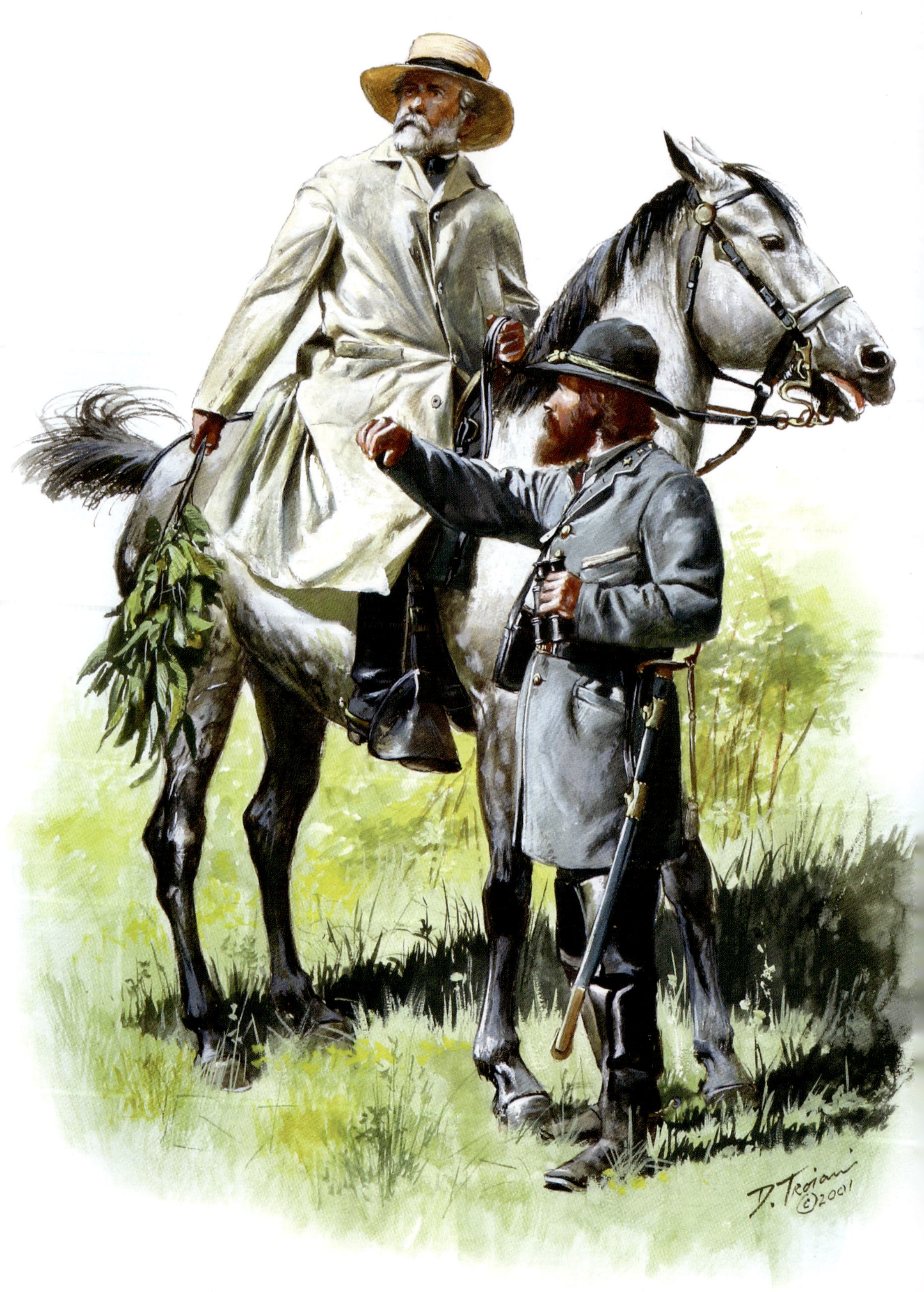

Generals Robert E. Lee and A. P. Hill, Gettysburg Campaign, 1863

DESPITE THE PUBLICATION OF THE "UNIFORM AND Dress of the Army of the Confederate States" on June 6, 1861, many Confederate generals either designed their own unique uniforms or put together a combination of clothing based on what could be acquired at the time. A case in point is General Robert E. Lee who seldom wore a fully prescribed general officers' uniform. On several occasions he was described wearing simpler garb. Soon after taking command of the Army of Northern Virginia on May 31, 1862, he was observed by staff officer Major G. Moxley Sorrel, who wrote, "The General was always well dressed in gray sack-coat of Confederate cloth, matching trousers tucked into well-fitting riding-boots—the simplest emblems of his rank appearing, and a good, large black felt army hat completed the attire of our commander. He rarely wore his sword, but his binoculars were always at hand."[1]

At Gettysburg on July 1, 1863, First Lieutenant James P. Smith, aide-de-camp to General Richard S. Ewell, recalled that Lee was "plain and neat in his uniform of gray. Hat of gray felt with medium brim and boots fitted neatly coming to the knee with a border of fine leather."[2]

A guest of the Confederate army in 1863, British army officer, Lieutenant Colonel Arthur J. L. Fremantle commented of Lee at Gettysburg, "he generally wears a long grey jacket, a high black felt hat, and blue trousers tucked into his Wellington boots. I never saw him carry arms; and the only mark of his military rank . . . three stars on his collar."[3]

Based on these descriptions and photographic evidence, Lee wore the minimum of rank insignia, which consisted of three stars on his collar, indicating the rank of colonel, and no sleeve braid. But he was at pains to protect his clothing from the rigors of campaigning. At Chancellorsville, First Sergeant Charles C. Cummings, Company B, 17th Mississippi Infantry, recalled that he wore "a long linen duster, which so enveloped his uniform as to make it invisible; added to this . . . he wore a broad-brimmed straw hat."[4]

Nevertheless, for the surrender at Appomattox Court House on April 9, 1865, Lee wore regulation dress of a Confederate general, which he kept for important occasions. However, eleven days later he posed for Matthew Brady's camera in his plain frock coat with three stars on the collar once again.[5]

One of Lee's most trusted commanders, Lieutenant General Ambrose P. Hill also preferred less regulation dress. Soon after his appointment as Major General on May 26, 1862, a fellow officer noted, "It was his habit when on the march to wear what was called a hunting-shirt," without a coat or any insignia of rank visible.[6] At Mechanicsville during the next month, Hill was described by First Lieutenant John W. Jones as, "Dressed in a fatigue jacket of gray flannel, his felt hat slouched over his noble brow . . ."[7] In consultation with able lieutenant A. P. Hill, Lee is depicted in his duster and carrying "a bush in his hand with which he brushed flies from his horse," the latter as recalled by Lieutenant J. Winder Laird.[8]

1. G. Moxley Sorrel, *Recollections of a Confederate Staff Officer* (The Neale Publishing Company, 1905), 74.

2. James Power Smith, "General Lee at Gettysburg," in *Gettysburg Sources*, comp. James L. McLean Jr. and Judy W. McLean (Butternut and Blue, 1986), 36.

3. Arthur J. L. Fremantle, *Three Months in the Southern States* (W. Blackwood, 1863), 253–54.

4. Judge C. C. Cummings, "Chancellorsville, May 2, 1863," *Confederate Veteran* 23, no. 9 (September 1915): 405.

5. Ron Field, *Silent Witness: The Civil War through Photography and its Photographers* (Osprey Publishing, 2017), 284–87.

6. "Lt. Gen. A. P. Hill," *Southern Historical Society Papers*, vol. 19 (Southern Historical Society, 1891), 178–79.

7. J. William Jones, "Gen. A. P. Hill," *Confederate Veteran* 1, no. 8 (August 1893): 234.

8. Unpublished diary of Lieutenant J. Winder Laird, 2nd Maryland Infantry.

Lieutenant Colonel Joshua L. Chamberlain

ON NOVEMBER 3, 1862, LIEUTENANT COLONEL JOSHUA L. Chamberlain wrote a letter to his wife Fanny describing the condition of the 20th Maine Infantry, and his own rude health despite the harsh life on campaign with the Army of the Potomac. Having been held in reserve during the battle of Antietam on September 16–17, 1862, the 20th Maine with the V Corps was ordered to march toward Falmouth en route for Fredericksburg, Virginia. Crossing the Rappahannock River, Major General Ambrose Burnside failed in his attempt to march on Richmond and instead fought the bloody battle of Fredericksburg.

The 20th Maine was bivouacked at Snicker's Gap, in the Blue Ridge Mountains, in bitterly cold weather when Chamberlain settled down under his talma to write a letter in which he described his appearance to his wife as "a stout looking fellow—face covered with beard—with a pair of cavalry pants on—sky blue—big enough for Goliath, and coarse as a sheep's back—said fellow having worn storm and ridden his original suit quite out of the question—enveloped in a huge cavalry overcoat (when it is cold) of the same color and texture as the pants; and . . . the identical flannel blouse worn at Portland—cap with an immense rent in it . . . a shawl and rubber talma strapped on behind the saddle and overcoat (perhaps), or the dressing case, before—two pistols in holsters, sword about three feet long at side—a piece of blue beef and some hard bread in the saddlebags."[1]

The 20th Maine would lose four men killed and 32 wounded charging the deadly Confederate defences on Marye's Heights at Fredericksburg on December 13, 1862, and spent the next day and two nights lying in the open in front of enemy positions. It was one of the last regiments to retreat back across the Rappahannock serving as a rear guard for the army.

Chamberlain's greatest military achievement would occur during the second day at Gettysburg when he repulsed the Confederate attack on the Union left flank on Little Round Top. Awarded the Medal of Honor for this action, he was promoted to brigadier general and served with further distinction through the rest of the war.

Based on the description provided in his letter, he is depicted here as a lieutenant colonel. His forage cap has at its front an officer's Pattern 1851 infantry looped "horn" with regimental numerals "20" inset. He wears a mounted enlisted man's sky-blue overcoat and knee-high boots. He is armed with a Model 1850 Foot Officer's sword, and has two pistols, only one of which can be seen, in saddle holsters. Horse equipment includes a McClellan saddle, bridle and halter with running martingale, and breast strap with decorative shield-shaped plate.

---

1. Thomas Desjardin, *Joshua L. Chamberlain: A Life in Letters* (Osprey Publishing, 2012).

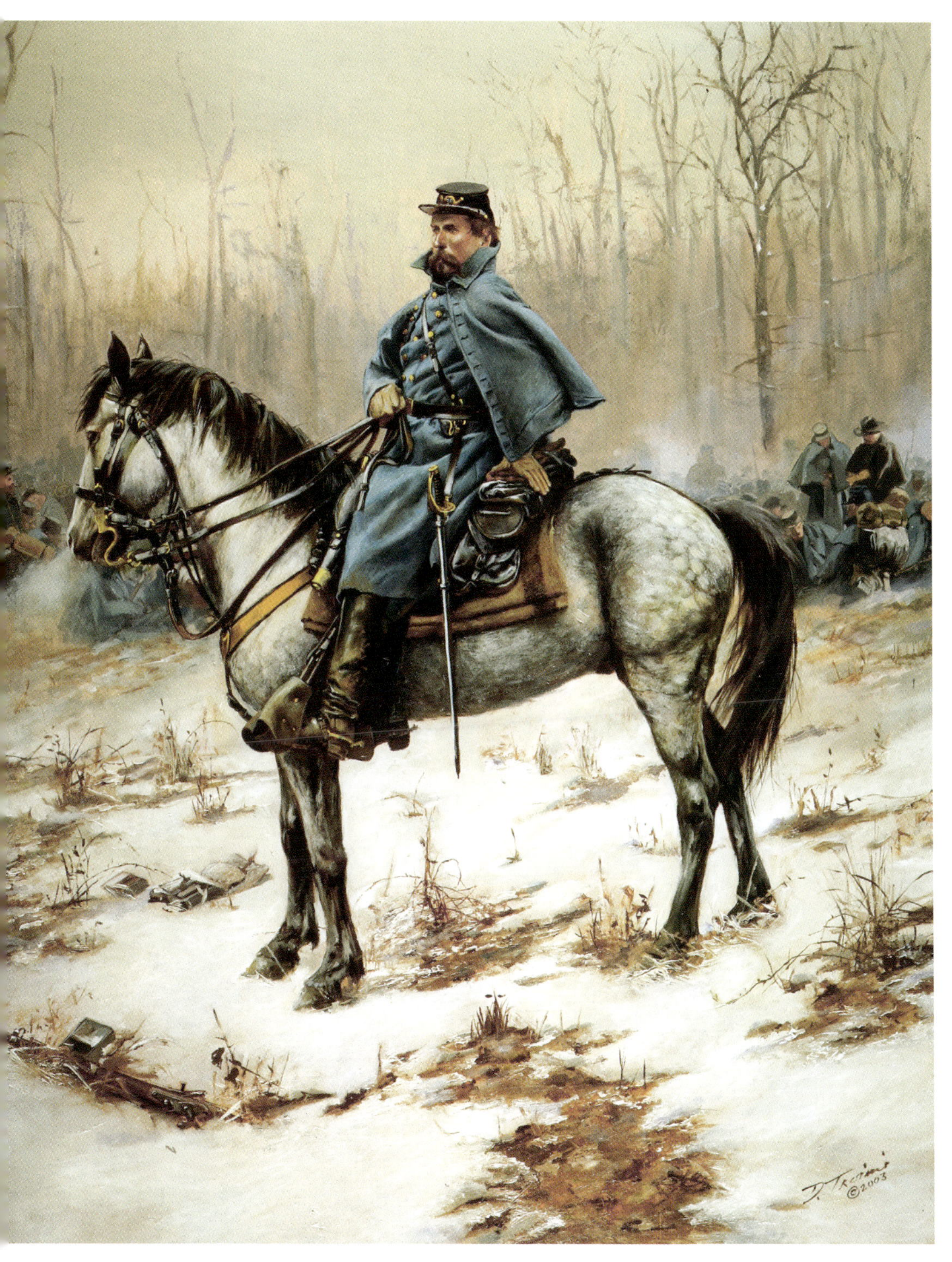

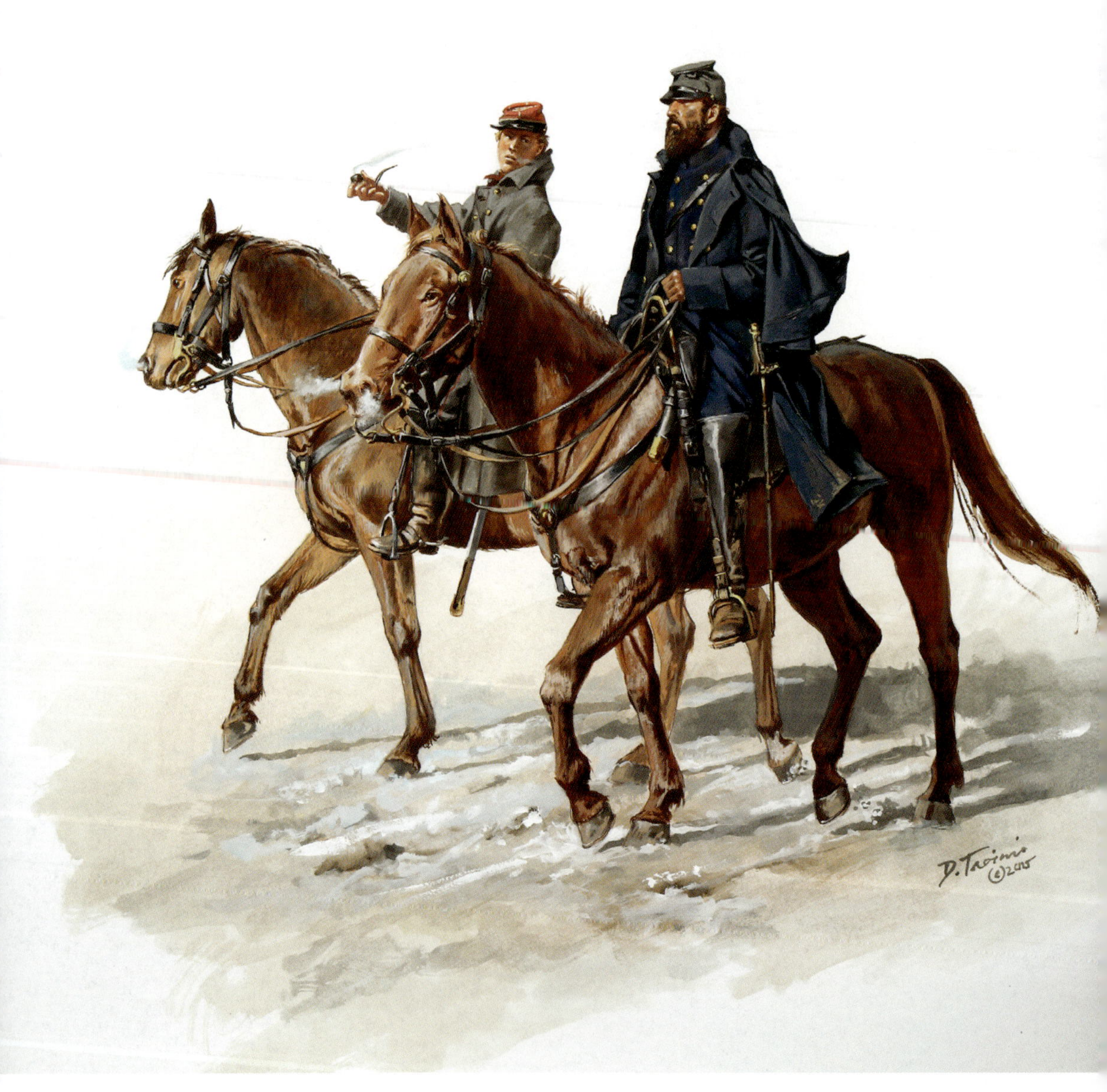

Jackson and Pendleton

BASED ON A PHOTOGRAPH TAKEN IN APRIL 1863 by Minnis & Cowell, in Richmond, Virginia, Major General Thomas J. Jackson, generally known as "Stonewall Jackson," is portrayed in countless artistic impressions from the 19th century to present times as wearing a full dress gray general's uniform. In fact, Jackson was notoriously indifferent to the niceties of military fashion. After a chance encounter with him, Corporal Joseph B. Polley, Company F, 4th Texas Infantry, described him as "a particularly seedy, sleepy-looking old man whose uniform and cap were very dirty."[1]

In the aftermath of the First Battle of Manassas, First Lieutenant William M. Owen of the Washington Artillery recalled seeing Jackson riding around on the battlefield, and wrote, "He was very quiet, plain-looking man, dressed in a blue military coat, and wore the shoulder-straps of a colonel in the United States army. His cap was of the old army pattern [the 1839 pattern forage cap], in vogue during the Mexican war,–blue cloth, flat on top."[2]

In December 1861, Private, John H. Worsham, Company F, 21st Virginia Infantry recalled seeing Jackson in Winchester and noted that he had "full dark whiskers and hair, dressed in a uniform, wearing a long dark blue overcoat with a large cape, his coat reaching to his boots, which were worn outside of his pants in regular military style, and on them were bright spurs. His head was covered by a faded gray cap, pulled down so far over his face that between the cap and whiskers one could see very little of it."[3]

Jackson continued to wear a federal-style uniform until the spring of 1862, although his Mexican War–style cap seems to have been replaced with a gray forage cap. An aide-de-camp to General George H. Steuart, First Lieutenant McHenry Howard stated that "he wore at the time, if not during the valley campaign, a dark blue uniform, his dress as a professor at V.M.I. [Virginia Military Institute]. His cap of the high kepi kind, high but the upper part not stiff and showing as you faced him the small round top falling to the front and almost resting on the visor which was well down over his eyes . . ."[4]

During August 1862, Jackson was noted by a Mississippi volunteer wearing a uniform of "common gray, sort of faded cassimere coat, pants and hat, the coat slightly braided on the sleeve . . . just enough to be perceptible, the collar displaying the mark of Major General."[5]

He appears to have wore this until the Fredericksburg Campaign, when General J. E. B. Stuart presented him with a regulation full dress general's uniform. However, he may have worn his dark blue overcoat until the time of his death, as in her memoir, his wife wrote, "The remains were carefully prepared by the loving hands of the staff-officers, the body being embalmed and clothed in ordinary dress, then wrapped in a dark-blue military overcoat . . ."[6]

Depicted with his faithful aide, First Lieutenant Andrew Swift "Sandie" Pendleton, Jackson appears as he would have done during the winter of 1861–1862.

---

1. *Confederate Veteran* 4 (February 1896): 158.

2. Owen, *In Camp and Battle with the Washington Artillery Battalion of New Orleans*, 41.

3. John H. Worsham, *One of Jacksons Foot Cavalry* (The Neale Publishing Company, 1912), 54.

4. McHenry Howard, *Jackson during the Valley Campaign, Recollections of a Maryland Confederate Soldier and Staff Officer* (Williams & Wilkins, 1914), 79.

5. An English combatant, *Battlefields of the South*, vol. 2 (John Bradburn, 1864), 459.

6. Mary Anna Jackson, *Memoirs of Stonewall Jackson* (The Prentice Press, 1895), 458.

Colonel John B. Gordon

TYPICAL OF MANY SUCCESSFUL CON-FEDERATE COMMANDERS, John B. Gordon was promoted through the ranks and elected colonel of the 6th Alabama Infantry during the reorganization of the Confederate army in May 1862. Experiencing his first combat in command of his regiment at Seven Pines a few weeks later, he took over brigade command when Brigadier General Rober Rhodes was wounded. Colonel Gordon was himself wounded in the eyes at Malvern Hill on July 1, 1862, recovering sufficiently to be wounded five times more at Sharpsburg while holding the vital sunken road, or "Bloody Lane." Miraculously nursed back to reasonable health by his wife, he was promoted to brigadier general at the request of Robert E. Lee, ranking from May 7, 1863. He went on to further prove his bravery and command credentials at Gettysburg on July 1, when his brigade and other units drove the Union XI Corps from Barlow's Knoll. On May 8, 1864, Gordon was given command of Early's division in Lieutenant General Richard S. Ewell's corps, being promoted to major general on May 14. His success in turning back the massive Union assault at Spotsylvania Court House prevented a Confederate rout, following which he served in the Valley Campaigns of 1864. Returning to Lee's army around Richmond and Petersburg, he led the attack on Fort Stedman on March 25, 1865, where he was again wounded. At Appomattox Court House, he led the last charge of the Army of Northern Virginia, capturing the entrenchments and several pieces of artillery at his front just before the surrender.[1]

Depicted as a colonel of the Confederacy, Gordon wears a regulation gray frock coat with two rows of seven General Staff buttons, plus dark blue infantry facings and trim. Rank is indicated by three small gold stars on his collar, and three rows of gold braid on his sleeve ornamentation. Tucked in knee high boots, his sky-blue trousers have narrow light-colored nonregulation welts on the outer seams. Armed with sword and revolver, he wears leather gauntlets and holds a brimmed hat with gold cord and Pattern 1858 infantry officer gold bullion "horn" in oval black patch.

---

1. John H. Eicher and David J. Eicher, *Civil War High Commands* (Stanford University Press, 2001), 260.

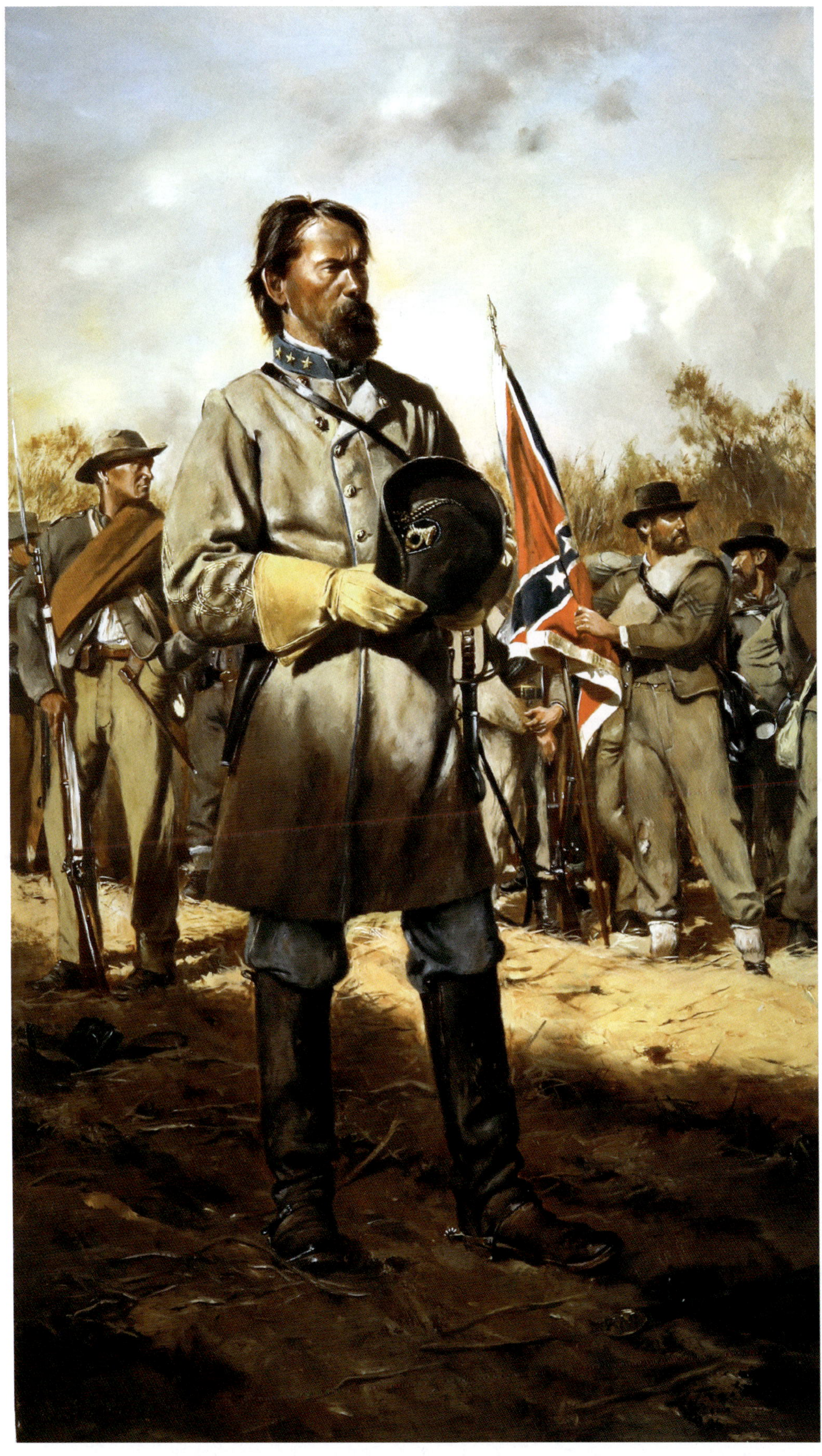

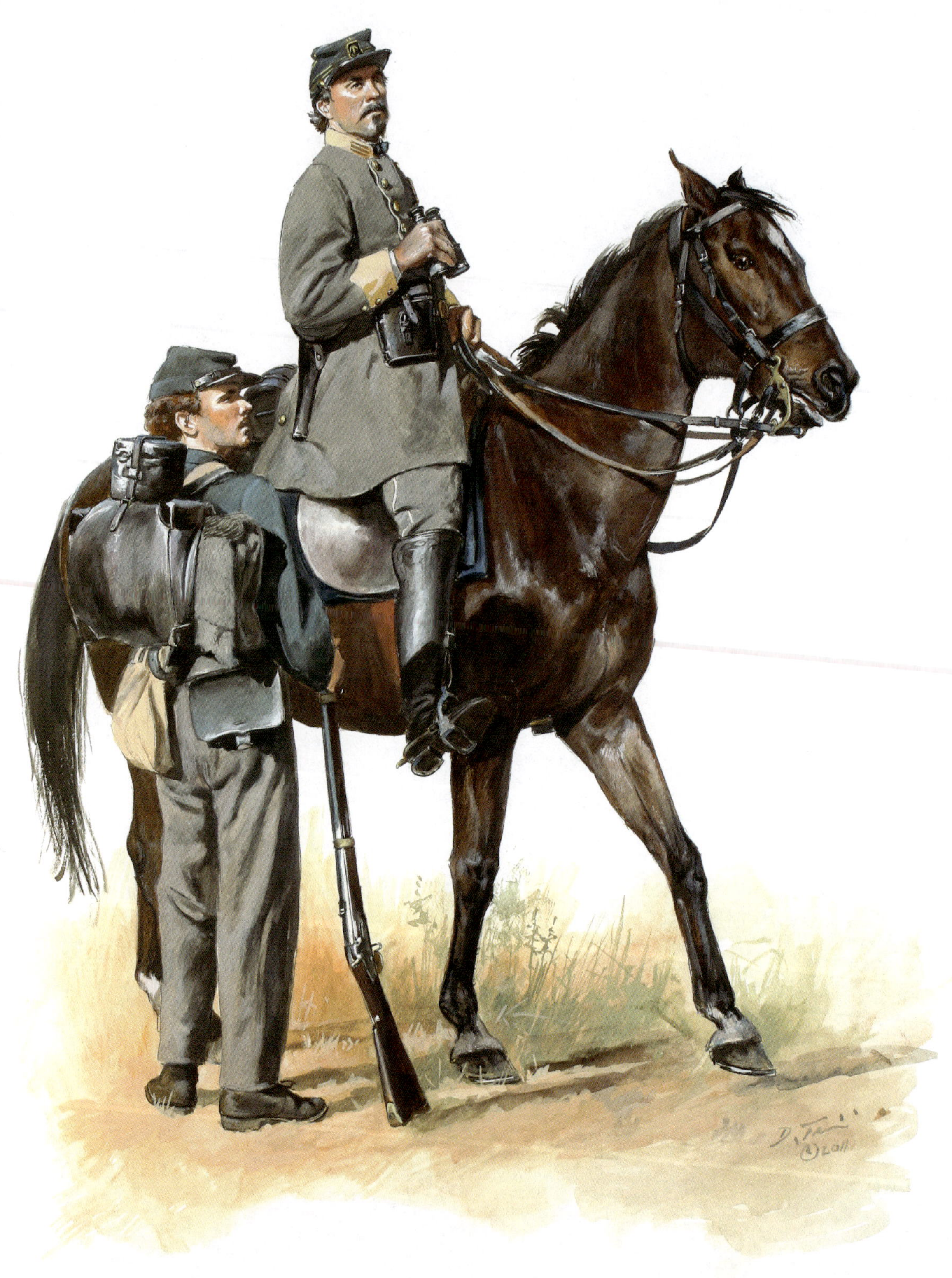

1st Regiment Engineer Troops Army of Northern Virginia

THE FORMATION OF THE 1ST REGI-MENT ENGINEER Troops, Army of Northern Virginia, began on September 5, 1863, when recruits, or those that provided them, were offered a $50 bounty.[1] Both Colonel T. M. Randolph Talcott and Lieutenant Colonel William W. Blackford were handpicked by General Robert E. Lee to organize and form the regiment. Talcott had been a railroad engineer before the war and served with the A.N.V. as an artillery officer and as an aide on Lee's staff. Blackford had been the acting chief engineer for the Virginia and Tennessee Railroad prior to the war.

From a mixture of veterans and conscripts, these officers were able to assemble a very effective engineer unit. In his war memoir, William Blackford wrote, "We had miners, sailors, carpenters, blacksmiths, masons, mechanics of all sorts, and farmers. With these the ten companies in the regiment were filled to about their quotes of 100 men each, making a splendid body nearly 1,000 strong."[2]

The Regiment was armed and drilled as infantry and while on campaign served as such except when required for specialist duties. Its two companies of pontoniers, or builders of pontoon bridges, performed a particularly valuable role during the Overland Campaign of 1864. Its sappers and miners strengthened defenses around Richmond and Petersburg during the closing months of the war. When the end came in April 1865 the 1st Engineers marched with Lee's retreating army and fired one of the final volleys of the conflict.

The mounted captain of engineers in this painting has buff facings on his double-breasted coat which were prescribed for Engineer officers in 1861.[3] The enlisted soldier wears a jacket and cap of blue gray kersey of the type made by Peter Tait & Co. of Limerick, Ireland, and imported through the Union naval blockade to the Confederacy. His gray trousers are of more locally made goods. His knapsack is the British Pattern 1856 as supplied by S. Isaac, Campbell & Company of 71 Jermyn Street, London, England. Strapped to its top is a Pattern 1854 mess tin in its black painted canvas cover. A Confederate-made cartridge box and haversack are also carried. He is armed with a .58-caliber rifle produced at the Cook & Brother Armory in Athens, Georgia, and issued during March 1864.[4] Although this weapon was generally fitted with a saber bayonet, these were not supplied to the 1st Regiment Engineer Troops as they would likely have been an encumbrance rather than an asset when considering the duties the unit was expected to perform.[5]

1. *Richmond Whig*, September 8, 1863, 2:6.
2. W. W. Blackford, *War Years with J. E. B. Stuart* (Charles Scribner's Sons, 1946), 251.
3. *Uniform and Dress of the Army of the Confederate States*, 3.
4. NARA, Confederate Government, CMSR, First Confederate Engineer Troops, T. M. Randolph Talcott, 56, 58, 60.
5. Murphy and Madaus, *Confederate Rifles & Muskets*, 133–60.

Army of the Potomac Pioneers, Summer 1863

AS THE CIVIL WAR ENTERED ITS THIRD YEAR BOTH Union and Confederate armies realized the value of organized units of skilled, reliable soldiers who would act as a supplementary force to the established Engineer regiments. These men, termed "Pioneers" were drawn from each regiment and wore the distinctive crossed hatchet insignia in branch of service color on each upper sleeve adopted in 1863.[1] Initially, one man per company was assigned to a battalion of pioneers, but in 1862 this was increased to two men per company. By 1864, one man in every fifty was drawn from the ranks of a brigade for pioneer duty.[2]

Exempt from ordinary fatigue duty and drill, the role of the Pioneer often required them to move ahead of the Army assuring the route of march was open for wagons and artillery to follow and if necessary working to establish temporary breastworks. While most tools were carried in wagons, the individual Pioneer would carry one of the selected tools of his trade in a specially designed sling. In his history of the Fifth Massachusetts Infantry, Alfred S. Roe recalls members of the 10th Connecticut at the battle of Whitehall, North Carolina, on December 16, 1862 "with characteristic Yankee industry, anxious for something to do, four of their pioneers swam the river, its waters being ice cold, having their axes strapped upon their backs, and commenced felling trees into the stream."[3]

Although not intended to serve in a combat role, the Pioneers could often find themselves in close contact with the enemy. For this reason they were lightly armed. Orders issued by the 1st Division, III Corps, Army of the Potomac, on April 6, 1863 provided that the Pioneer Corps of that Division would be armed with "Sharps carbines, Cartridge boxes for Sharps Carbines, Cartridge box belts for Sharps carbines, gun slings, ball cartridges (60 r[oun]ds.) each."[4] To ease carrying, a sling was devised that would fit through the sling swivel at the butt of the carbine with a small socket that would pass over the barrel. The 6th New York Cavalry regimental books contain Special Order No. 25, issued on March 18, 1863, which states, in reference to the Pioneers, "They will carry no arms except a revolver and that on their belt."[5]

The cavalry sergeant of the 6th New York Cavalry in this plate carries an axe with leather cover attached to a strap over his right shoulder. The infantryman of the 5th Michigan has a spade attached behind his knapsack and blanket roll.

1. *Revised United States Army Regulations of 1861* (Government Printing, 1863), 473.
2. James Lancel McElhinney, *Manual for the Instruction of Civil War Pioneer Troops* (Bent, St. Vrain & Co., 2004), 14.
3. Alfred S. Roe, *The Fifth Regiment Massachusetts Volunteer Infantry* (Boston, MA: Fifth Regiment Veteran Association, 1911), 173.
4. NARA, record group 393, entry 3873: Circulars 1st Division, III Corps, April 6, 1863.
5. NARA, record group 94, regimental books, 6th New York Cavalry.

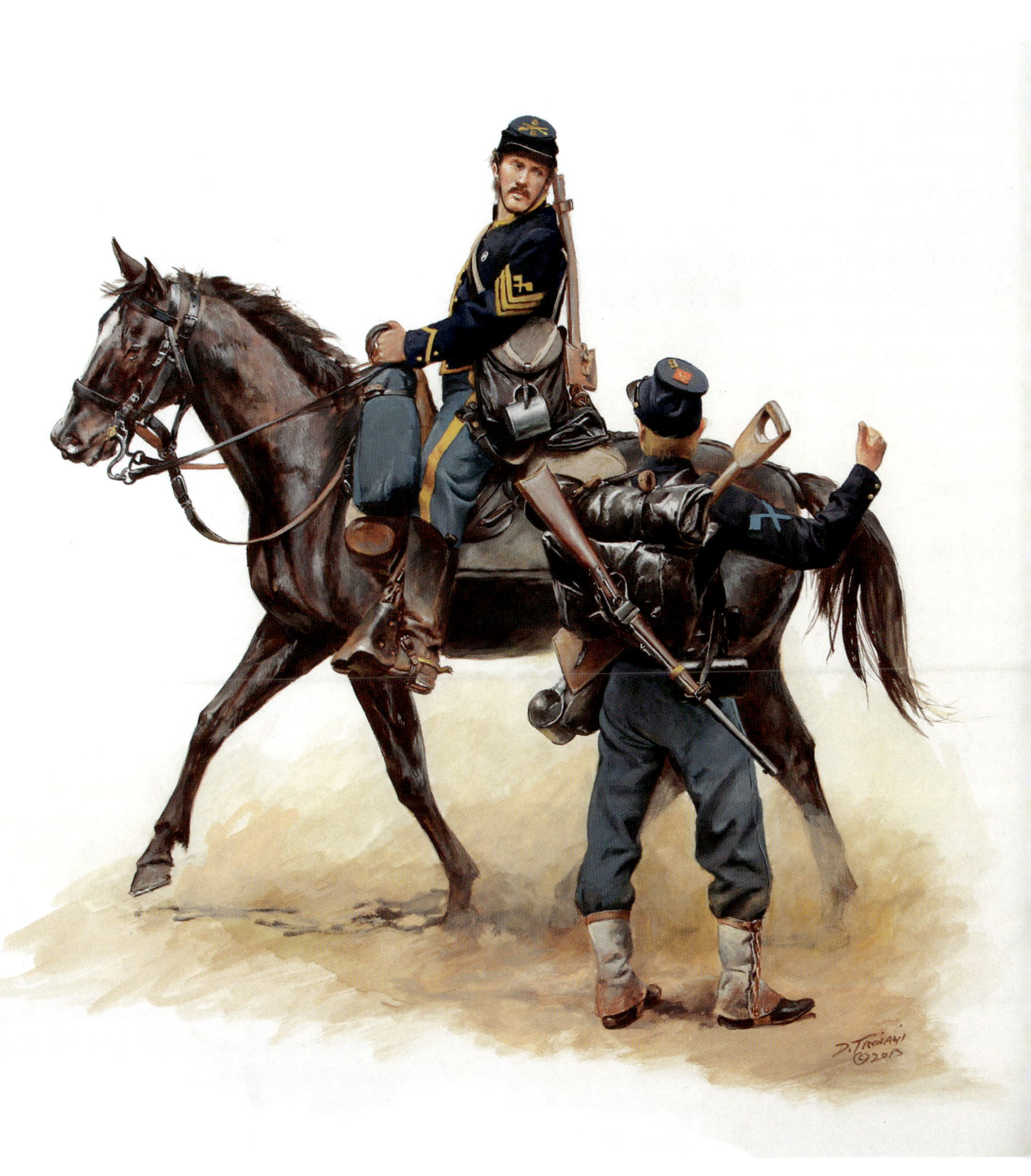

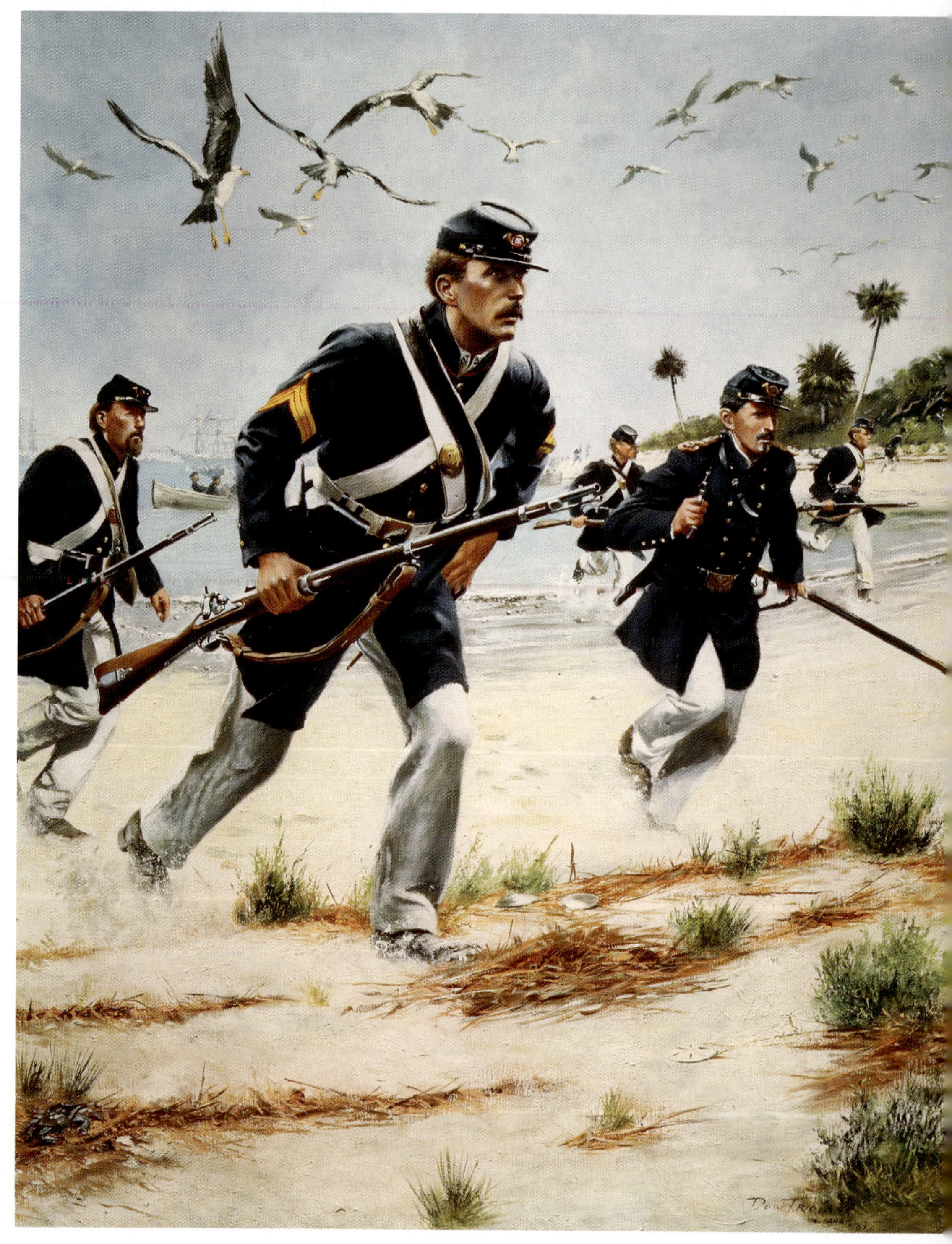

United States Marine Corps, 1861–1865

THE UNITED STATES MARINE CORPS CONDUCTED A number of amphibious assaults during the Civil War. For example, on August 28, 1861, 100 Marines waded ashore through the raging surf to spearhead General Benjamin F. Butler's attack on Forts Hatteras and Clark on the North Carolina coast. The Navy Fleet Brigade formed by Rear Admiral John Dahlgren consisting of 400 Marines and sailors took part in the abortive attack on Fort Sumter on September 8, 1863. During November and December 1864, the Fleet Brigade made two landings on the South Carolina coast to assist the troops of Major General John G. Foster in destroying the Charleston and Savannah Railroad to prevent Confederate reinforcements from reaching Savannah in anticipation of Sherman's "March to the Sea." Finally on January 15, 1865, 400 Marines and 1,600 sailors took part in the Second Battle of Fort Fisher, which led to the capture of Wilmington, North Carolina, and closure of the last main Confederate port of entry for blockade runners.[1]

These Marines running ashore from surfboats wear undress uniforms, which would have been prescribed for field service. The officer's headgear consists of a French-style kepi with black band and black ribbed silk trim with a quatrefoil knot in the crown, plus cap ornament with gold embroidered bugle horn on scarlet ground with silver, Old English "M" at the center of the bugle loop. The kepis worn by enlisted men were plain with false embroidery-type, brass stamped cap ornament.

Shoulders of the double-breasted officer's frock coat are adorned with gold Russian knots with scarlet underlining. The single-breasted uniform coats of enlisted men have scarlet trim on the bottom collar seam. The sergeant's rank is denoted by points up sleeve stripes of yellow lace on red background above the elbow. Trousers worn by all ranks are of white linen for warm weather service.[2]

The officer is armed with a Colt Navy revolver and M1850 army foot officer's sword. His sword belt is fastened with a Pattern 1851 eagle-wreath plate. Enlisted men are armed with M1855 rifle muskets with Maynard tape primer system, and socket bayonets. Accoutrements consist of whitened buff leather shoulder belts supporting the black leather cartridge box and bayonet scabbard. Oval-shaped breast plates are worn on the bayonet belt, and waist belts with black percussion caps attached are fastened with an unadorned rectangular plates. They also have Pattern 1858 tin canteens with a brown cloth cover carried on white cotton slings, and water-proofed black canvas haversacks.

---

1. Ron Field, *American Civil War Marines 1861–65* (Osprey Publishing, 2004).

2. Charles H. Cureton and David M. Sullivan, *The Civil War Uniforms of the United States Marine Corps: The Regulations of 1859* (R. James Bender Publishing, 2009).

Confederate States Marine Corps, 1861–1865

ON FEBRUARY 21, 1861, THE PROVISIONAL GOVERNMENT of the Confederate States passed an act creating a Navy Department with Stephen R. Mallory as the Secretary of the Navy. On March 16, 1861, another Act of the Congress established the Confederate States Marine Corps, and authorized the creation of a headquarters organization consisting of a major, quartermaster, paymaster, adjutant, sergeant major, and quartermaster sergeant, and a battalion of six companies, each of which was to consist of a captain, first lieutenant, second lieutenant, four sergeants, four corporals, two musicians, and one hundred men. On May 20, 1861, and after an enlargement of the Confederacy with the secession of Virginia, Arkansas, Tennessee, and North Carolina, an Amendatory Act increased the Marine Corps from battalion to regimental strength of 46 officers and 944 enlisted men. Three days later, Lloyd J. Beall was appointed colonel and commandant of the Corps, and served in this capacity until the end of the war.[1]

During the summer of 1862, a Marine battalion consisting of Companies A, B, and C established a permanent camp at Drewry's Bluff, Virginia. Other companies were organized at Naval Stations such as Mobile, Savannah, and Pensacola. Marine detachments were assigned to various vessels of the C.S. Navy from these locations during the course of the war.

No uniform regulations for the C.S. Marine Corps have been located and, given the numerous changes that occurred during the war, it is unlikely that any were ever prescribed. The Marine First Lieutenant peering through binoculars wears a chasseur-pattern forage cap and double-breasted cadet gray frock coat with Russian-style shoulder knots identical to those worn by officers of the US Marine Corps, plus dark blue facings on collar and cuffs. A Model 1852 Naval Officer's sword is slung from his waist belt.

Uniforms for enlisted Confederate marines initially consisted of US Marine Corps clothing from Federal stores seized at Pensacola, Florida. The first issue of Southern-made goods in September and October of 1861, was composed of navy blue satinette uniform coats and jean trousers. Gray became the predominant uniform color toward the end of 1862. On December 13 of that year stores were turned over to the Corps Quartermaster including "60 grey cloth uniform coats."[2] A notice in the Mobile press reported that when Private George W. Jackson of Company F deserted from that Station in January 1863 he was wearing "*a grey coat and black pants*."[3] In contemporary photographs, Privates Allen P. Ham and William G. B. Hosch, of Company E, wear single-breasted gray coats.

The enlisted men of the Marine detachment depicted at sea in this painting wear gray coats with dark blue trim on collar and cuffs, with white cotton trousers. British-made coat buttons have a Roman letter "M" in a plain field. Gray forage caps have dark blue bands. Copying the Uniform Regulations of the United States Marine Corps, the corporal's chevrons are points-up above the elbow. These men are armed with imported British Pattern 1853 Enfield rifles with saber bayonets, and are equipped with matching accoutrements including Pattern 1861 ball bags carrying ten loose paper cartridges plus orthodox cartridge boxes carrying further wrapped rounds. Waist belts are fastened with British-made "snake" buckles.

---

1. Ralph W. Donnely, *The Confederate States Marine Corps: The Rebel Leathernecks* (White Mane Publishing Company, 1989), 3.

2. Donnely, *The Confederate States Marine Corps: The Rebel Leathernecks*, 296.

3. *Mobile Advertiser and Register*, January 24, 1863, 2:6.

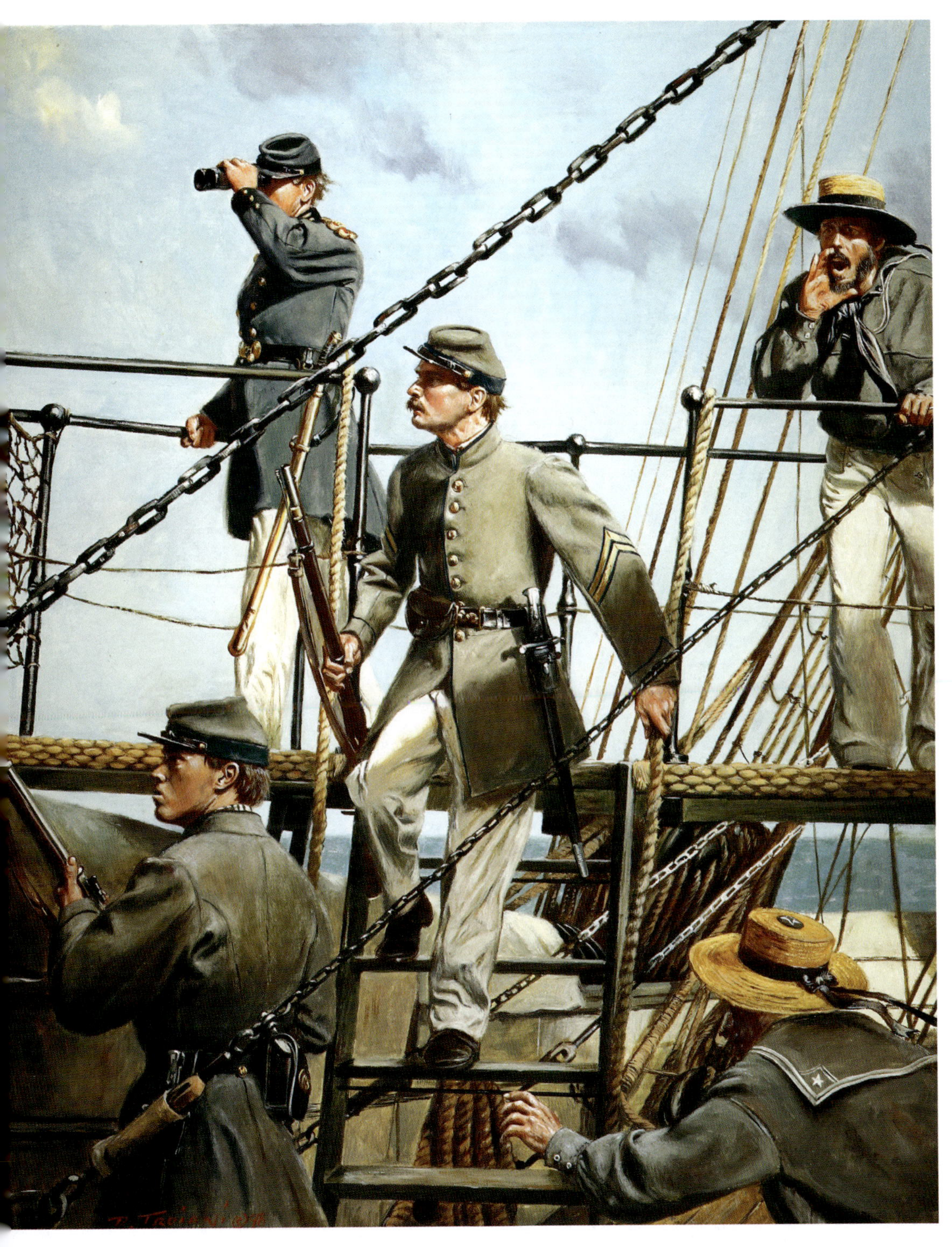

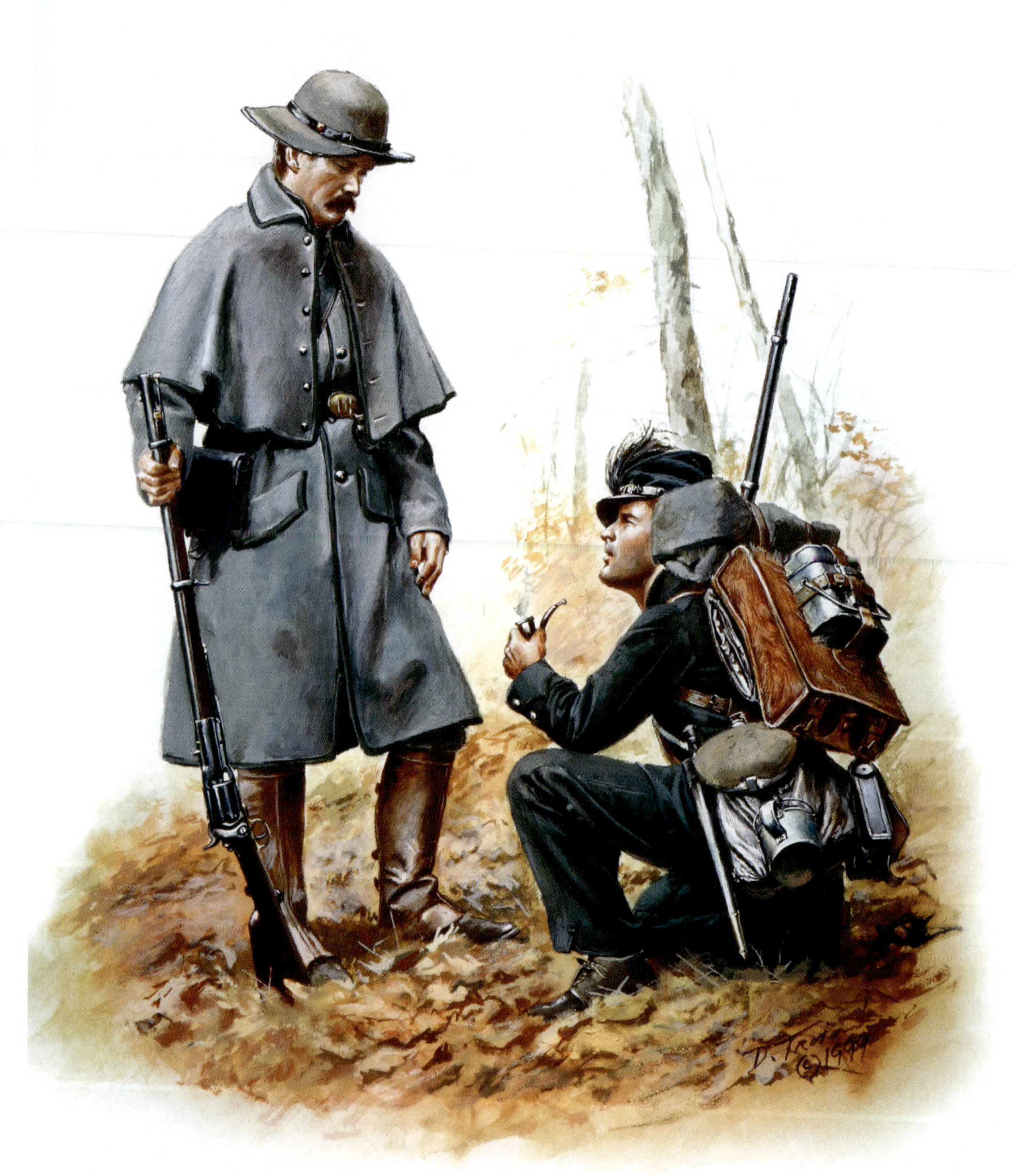

Berdan's Sharpshooters, 1862

THE UNITED STATES SHARPSHOOTERS WERE ORGANIZED FROM August 1861 to March 1862 by Colonel Hiram Berdan, with "crack rifle shots" from all Northern states being recruited. As the response was greater than expected, two regiments were formed. The 1st Regiment had the regulation ten companies, comprising four from New York; three from Michigan; one each from Vermont, New Hampshire, and Wisconsin. Company A was composed of Swiss and German recruits. The 2nd Regiment never had more than eight companies composed of two each from New Hampshire and Vermont; one each from Minnesota, Michigan, Pennsylvania, and Maine.[1]

Of the first uniform received by the Sharpshooters, First Lieutenant Charles A. Stevens of Company G, 1st Regiment, wrote, "Our uniform was of fine material, consisting of dark green coat and cap with black plume, light blue trowsers (afterward exchanged for green ones) and leather leggins, presenting a striking contrast to the regular blue of the infantry. . . ."[2] Made from dark green kersey at the Schuylkill Arsenal, the uniform coat had a single row of nonreflective hard rubber buttons down its front, produced by the Novelty Rubber Company of New York, and emerald or medium green trim on the collar and cuffs. The forage cap was plain dark green, while trousers were sky-blue.

The standing Sharpshooter wears additional winter clothing issued in 1862 for "outpost duty or in bad weather," which consists of a patent waterproof "Havelock" hat and an "Austrian-gray overcoat" edged with green, both of which were made by the Seamless Clothing Manufacturing Company.[3] The hat had a visor at the front and flaps that protected the back and sides of the wearer's neck. Made of Austrian-gray felt, his overcoat is edged with green around the collar, cape, lower pocket flaps, and coat edges, and has five hard rubber buttons down its front and six smaller ones on its cape. Russet leather leggings, fastened with eight buckles and straps, are worn over his sky-blue trousers.

The original Sharpshooter recruits were instructed to bring their own target rifles, but the first skirmishes with the enemy demonstrated that these weapons were unsuitable although several companies continued to use them. This man is armed with a Colt Model 1855 revolving rifle in lieu of the Sharps rifles his regiment was waiting for. Equipment consists of a Pattern 1839 shoulder belt and Pattern 1855 cartridge box with plates removed. A cap pouch and bayonet in a scabbard are carried on his waist belt, which has a Pattern 1839 oval "US" plate.

The man kneeling wears a full dark green uniform consisting of forage cap with black ostrich feather plume attached to the chin strap, uniform coat and trousers. Equipment includes a knapsack of the type purchased from Tiffany & Co., of 550 Broadway, New York City, described at the time as of "the style then used by the Prussian army, being of leather tanned with the hair on and, although heavier than the regulation knapsack, were roomy and fitted the wearer's back well. Each had strapped to its outside a small cooking kit which was found compact and useful."[4] His rolled overcoat is strapped to its top, and a woolen blanket wrapped inside a rubber one is folded neatly and inserted behind his knapsack straps. Also carried is a cloth-covered Pattern 1858 canteen and a waterproof haversack with a tin cup attached.

1. John R. Elting, "The United States Sharpshooters," *Military Collector and Historian* VI, no. 3 (1954), 57.

2. C. A. Stevens. *Berdan's United States Sharpshooters in the Army of the Potomac, 1861–1865* (The Price-McGill Company, 1892), 5.

3. Stevens, *Berdan's United States Sharpshooters in the Army of the Potomac, 1861–1865,* 5.

4. Wm. Y. W. Ripley, *The Vermont Riflemen in the War for the Union, 1861–1865: A History of Company F, First United States Sharp Shooters* (Tuttle & Co., 1883), 20.

Berdan's Sharpshooters, 1863–1864

BOTH REGIMENTS OF UNITED STATES SHARPSHOOTERS FOUGHT well in the Army of the Potomac throughout most of the Civil War. Although regarded as infantry, they served tactically as skirmishers rather than fighting in regular battle lines. Describing their tactics, the contemporary press stated they "advance before the body of the army and scour the ground as skirmishes, covering themselves behind trees, rocks, or any shelter that may be formed and picking off the enemy at each fire."[1]

At Antietam, the 2nd Regiment operated as an independent unit reporting to the headquarters of the 1st Brigade, also known as the "Iron Brigade of the East," 1st Division, I Corps. Later it was assigned in turn to the II and III Corps, serving alongside the 1st Regiment. Also in the Battle of Antietam, the 1st Regiment was listed as an independent unit reporting directly to 1st Division Headquarters, V Corps. In 1863, it was transferred to the III Corps, fighting in the battles of Chancellorsville and Gettysburg, following which it was transferred to the II Corps in 1864.[2]

By September 1863 the gray overcoats issued in 1862 had been replaced. According to Charles Stevens, while the Sharpshooters were encamped near Culpeper, Virginia, "a large amount of green clothing, with overcoats (which were the regulation blue) . . . were received and distributed."[3] Cap plumes were likely discarded earlier, with none surviving in any great quantity beyond 1862.

However, while the Sharpshooter regiments continued to proudly wear their dark-green uniforms throughout most of their service, large quantities of dark-blue, four-button sack coats were issued for field service.[4]

In action in 1863, these Sharpshooters wear their sack coats with otherwise dark-green headgear and trousers. Red diamond badges on their cap tops indicate their attachment to the 1st Division, III Corps, during the Gettysburg Campaign. They are armed with New Model 1859, breech-loading Sharps rifles, the issuance of which did not begin until April 1862 and was not complete for both regiments until toward the end of the following month.[5]

The 1st Regiment was mustered out of service beginning in August 1864, mostly due to their term of enlistment having expired. In September the greatly reduced 1st Regiment was formed into a battalion that lasted until December 31, 1864, when the men whose enlistment had not expired were transferred to the Second Regiment, the exception being the Michiganders who were sent to the 5th Michigan Infantry. The Second Regiment was mustered out on February 20, 1865, and the men whose term of enlistment had not expired were transferred to infantry regiments of their respective home states. A total of 532 officers and men of the combined USSS regiments died in battle or from mortal wounds, while a further 254 were lost to disease.

1. *Detroit Free Press*, August 9, 1861, 1:1.
2. Philip Katcher, *The American Civil War Source Book* (Arms and Armour Press, 1992), 161.
3. Stevens (1892), 354.
4. NARA, record group 92, Quartermaster letters sent and received, 472, 629.
5. Earl J. Coates and John D. McAulay, *Civil War Sharps Carbines & Rifles* (Thomas Publications, 1996), 19.

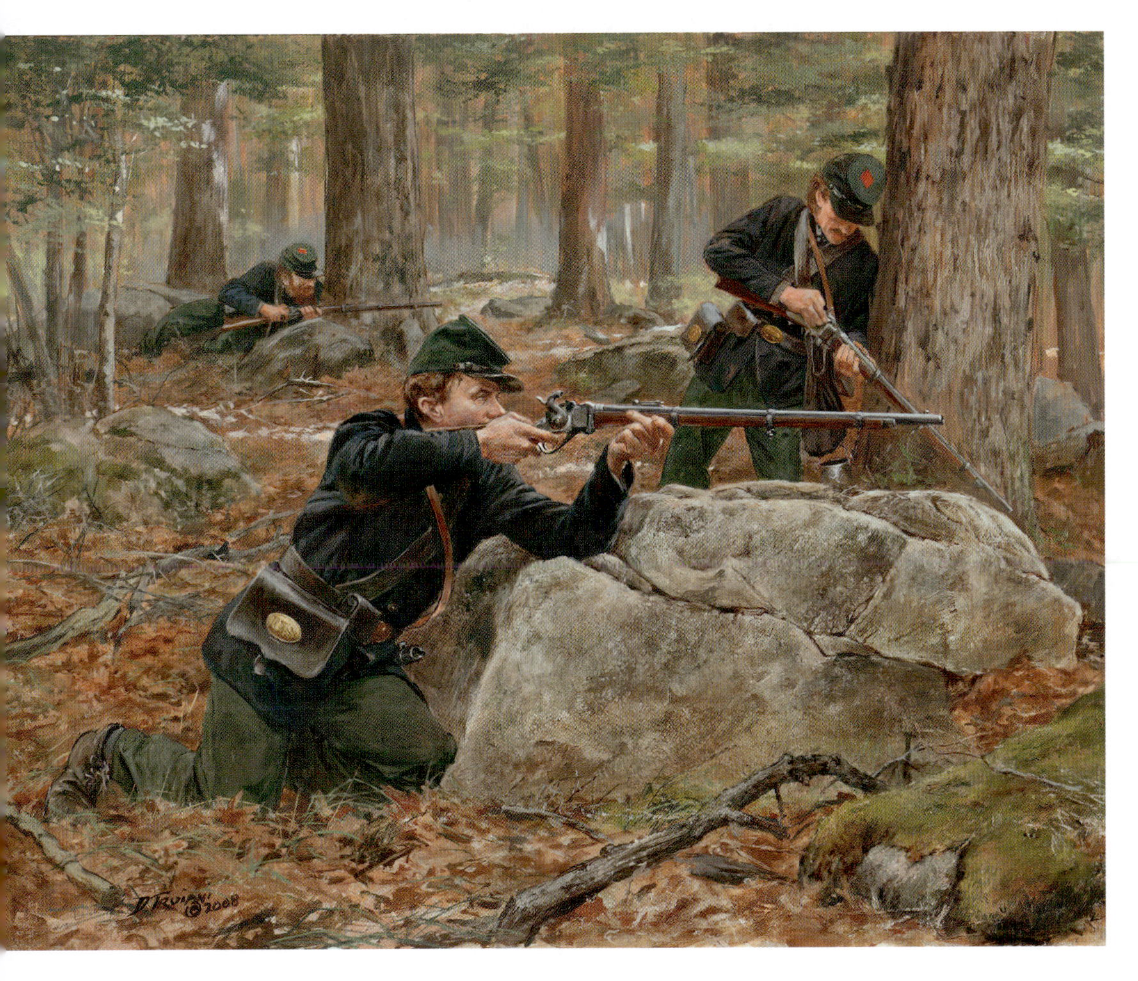

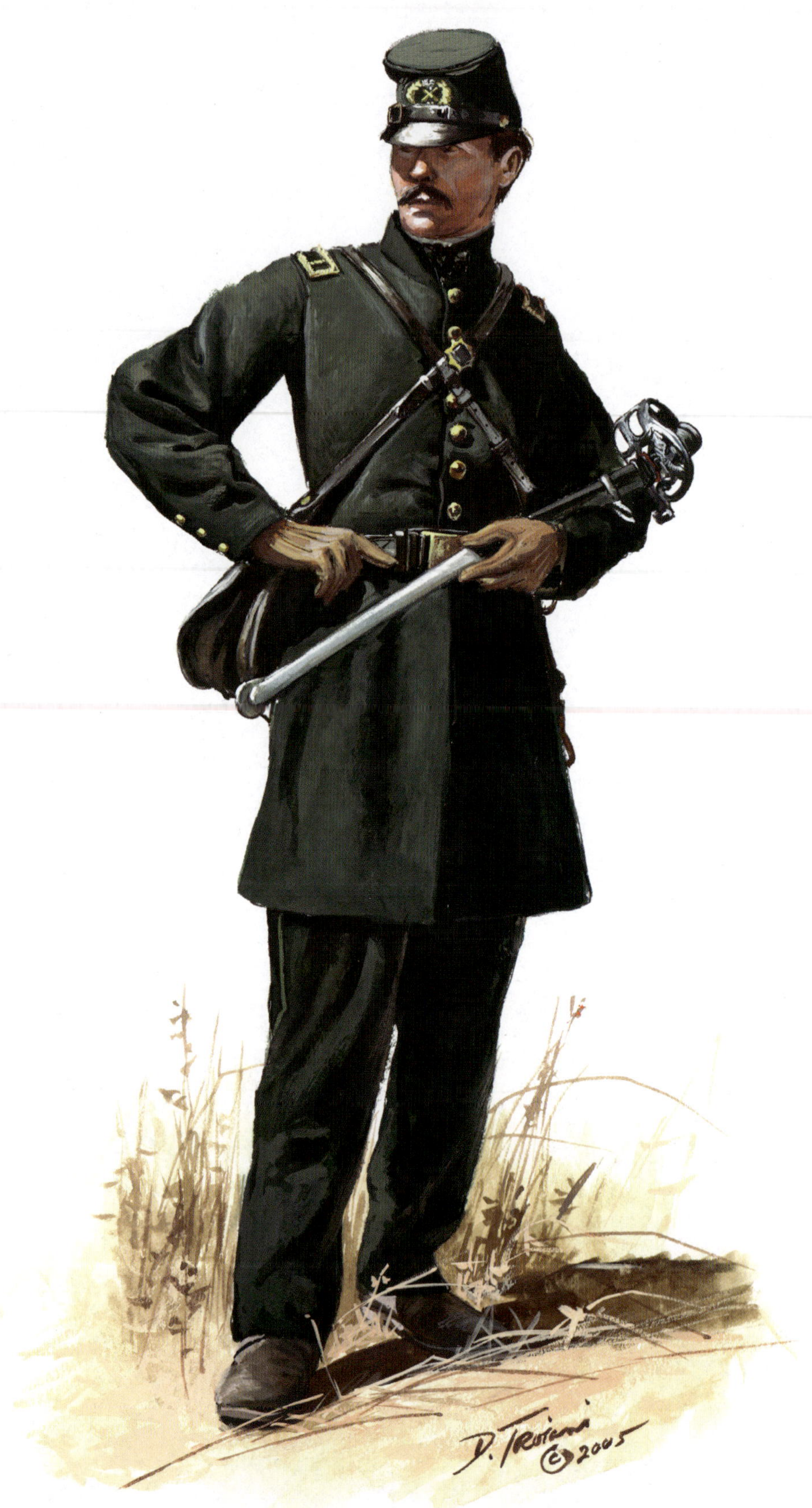

Officer of Berdan's Sharpshooters, 1862

THIS COMPANY-GRADE OFFICER OF BERDAN'S SHARPSHOOTERS wears a dark-green full-dress uniform that is made of slightly better-quality cloth than are those of enlisted men under his command and consists of a single-breasted coat with nine dulled metal buttons and shoulder boards indicating the rank of first lieutenant. His matching trousers have a narrow dark-green welt down the side seams. His tall-crowned McDowell-style forage cap has at its front the insignia of his unit, which consists of crossed carbines with old English silver lettering, with "US" above and "SS" below, set in a wreath of laurels.[1]

For fatigue purposes some officers wore blue flannel sack coats in the field. One officer took pride in their simple garb, stating "The officers' uniforms, though made with more care and of finer cloth, were not much different from those of the soldiers and just as simple by comparison. The insignia were no glittering epaulets, only a narrow band edged with gold braid and fastened on the shoulders, showing the different badges of rank."[2]

Wearing kid-leather gloves, this officer cradles a foreign imported sword, and his leather accoutrements include a privately purchased haversack and map case. His plain black leather belt is fastened with a Pattern 1851 "eagle" plate.

1. Elting, "The United States Sharpshooters," 57–61.
2. Henry K. Meier, ed., *Memoirs of a Swiss Officer [Rudolf Aschmann] in the American Civil War* (Berne and Frankfurt, 1972).

Veteran Reserve Corps, Corporal, 8th Regiment, March 1864

AUTHORIZED BY THE WAR DEPART-MENT VIA General Order No. 105 on April 28, 1863, the Invalid Corps was recruited mainly from partially disabled soldiers in general hospitals and convalescent camps in the various states in an attempt to retain reasonably effective men in the service as staff or guards in army hospitals.[1]

Commanded by Provost Marshall General James B. Fry, the Corps was initially organized into 240 separate numbered companies. Between October 10, 1863, and February 24, 1864, these were reorganized into the 1st through 24th regiments, Invalid Corps, although about 188 companies remained unassigned to regiments. A regiment normally comprised ten infantry companies, six in its 1st Battalion and four in the 2nd Battalion. The ranks of 1st Battalion companies were filled with those who could handle a musket and make light marches, These men were used for guard duty on railroads, bridges, and government property and for guarding prisoners of war or drafted men. Those who were less physically able served in the 2nd Battalion companies as clerks, cooks, or ancillary hospital nurses.

Unfortunately, the name Invalid Corps proved unpopular as "I.C." was jokingly referred to as "Inspected and Condemned," with reference to the term used by inspectors who condemned meat as not fit for human consumption, and, on March 18, 1864, via General Order No. 111, the Invalid Corps was redesignated the Veteran Reserve Corps.[2]

On May 15, 1863, General Order No. 124 prescribed a uniform for enlisted men of the Invalid Corps and, subsequently, of the Vet-eran Reserve Corps, an example of which is worn by this corporal. The mounted service–pattern sky-blue jacket has dark-blue trim around the collar, the cuffs, and the skirts, which reached about four inches below the waist belt. His sky-blue trousers and dark-blue forage caps were of regulation pattern.[3]

The corporal is armed with a Model 1842 .69-caliber Springfield rifle musket. Others were issued with long arms, including Austrian, Prussian, and French smoothbore muskets. His accoutrements are of regulation infantry pattern and include a cartridge box and a percussion cap pouch. Haversacks, canteens, and knapsacks were issued as required. Regarding insignia, enlisted men of the Corps wore the brass infantry bugle on their cap tops.

Several Veteran Reserve Corps regiments saw action. On June 20, 1864, the 18th Regiment took part in the defense of White House, Virginia, against Confederate cavalry that served under Major General Wade Hampton. Twice during the engagement an aide rode up to Colonel Charles F. Johnson with the question, 'Will your invalids stand?' 'Tell the general,' was the answer, 'that my men are cripples, and they can't run.'"[4] When the Confederate Second Corps, Army of Northern Virginia, commanded by Lieutenant General Jubal Early, attacked the Federal capital during July 11–12, 1864, the 9th Regiment was brought into action at Fort Stevens. Ordered to charge, the regiment drove the enemy some distance and maintained a sharp skirmish until night, with five men killed and seven severely wounded.[5]

1. Thomas O'Brien and Oliver Diefendorf, *General Orders of the War Department Embracing the Years 1861, 1862 & 1863*, vol. 2 (Derby & Miller, No. 5 Spruce Street, 1864), 120.

2. *ORs*, series 3, vol. 4, 188.

3. O'Brien and Oliver Diefendorf, *General Orders of the War Department Embracing the Years 1861, 1862 & 1863*, 135.

4. *ORs*, series 3, vol. 5, 555.

5. *ORs*, series 3, vol. 5, 553.

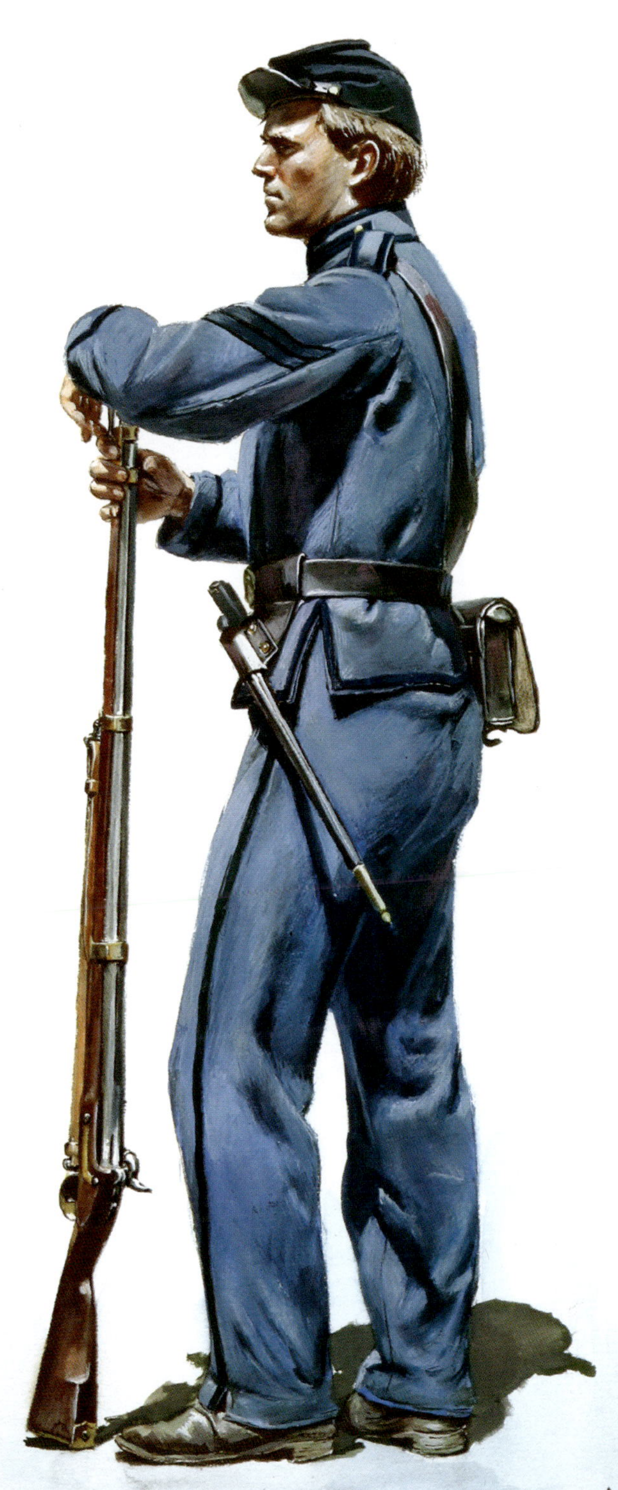

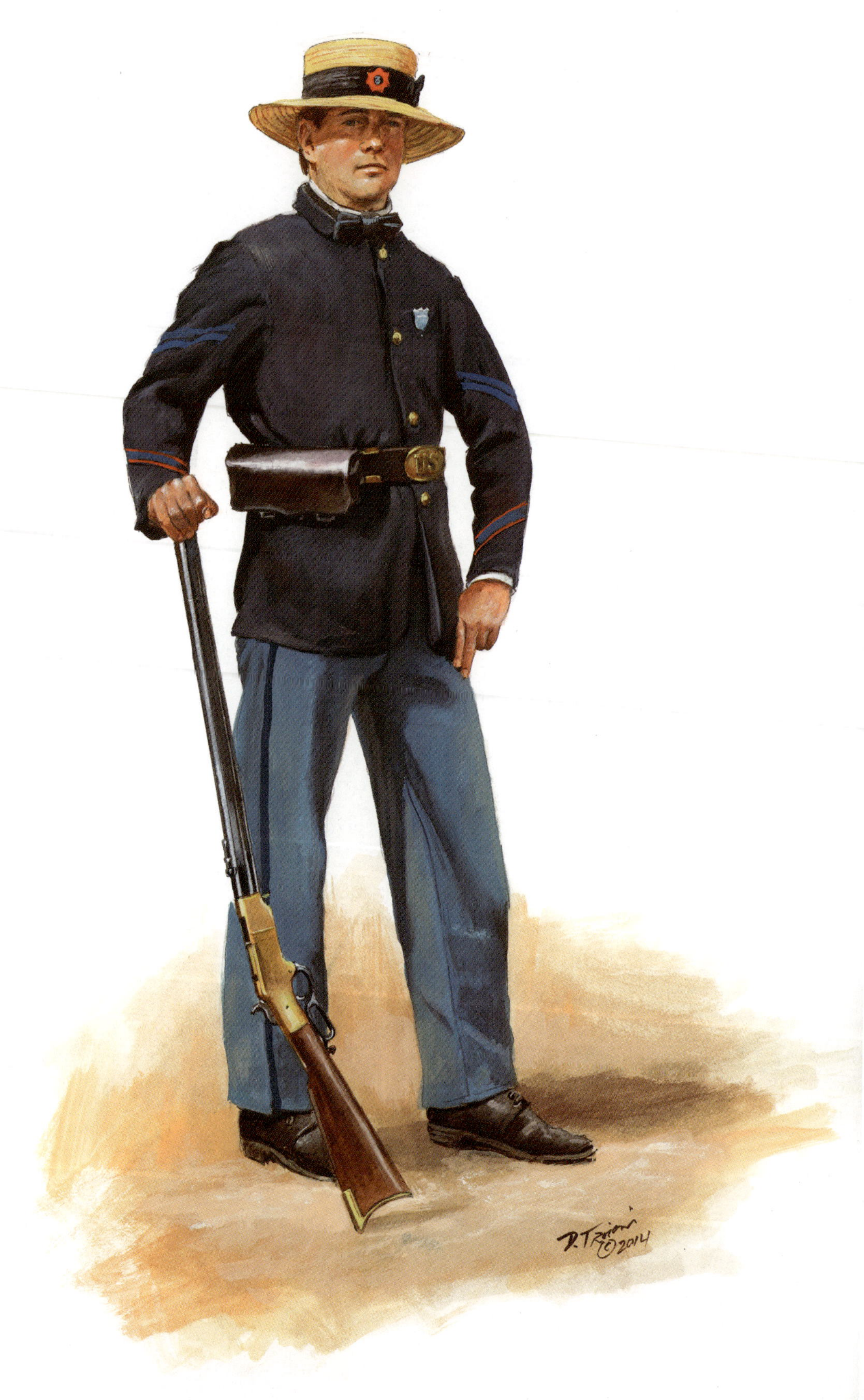

Corporal, 3rd US Veteran Volunteers, Summer 1865

ON NOVEMBER 29, 1864, THE *NEW-YORK TIMES* PUBLISHED a notice titled "A New Army Corps—Hancock's Veterans," and stating, "It will be seen that, by authority of the War Department, Gen. [Winfield S.] HANCOCK is empowered to raise an Army Corps, which is to consist of twenty thousand infantry, to be enlisted for not less than twelve months, from among that class of discharged soldiers who have served two years in the army. The organization of the corps is to commence on the first day of December, and to continue until the first day of the incoming year. There is thus but one full month within which the proposed organization is to be completed."[1]

The article continued with the promise that enlistees would receive a $300 bounty and the latest breech-loading arms. This induced formation of a total of nine Veteran US Volunteer Infantry regiments and one engineer regiment, to be organized at Camp Stoneman, DC, between December 1864 and June 1865.

On June 15, 1865, I Veteran Corps Headquarters issued the following order: "Straw hats of uniform pattern are allowed to be worn by the officers and enlisted men of this Command under the following restrictions. The uniform cap must be worn at Guard Mount, Review, inspections and dress parade . . . After the Guards have marched on Regimental Commanders may allow the men to change their caps to straw hats and their Uniform Coats to Blouses, during the heat of the day. The straw hats must have the Corps Badges in front and on the black ribbon with the number of the Regiment in white metal in the centre of the Corps Badge. The tie of the ribbon on the left side."[2]

Regarding the promised firearms, the 2nd, 4th, 5th, and 6th US Veteran Volunteers receive Model 1863 Sharps rifles.[3] However, the 3rd regiment was initially issued muzzle-loading rifle muskets, but these were replaced on May 19, 1865, by .44-caliber, 16-shot, lever-action Henry repeating rifles, which had already earned a wartime reputation as a fearsome weapon in the hands of a select few Union regiments. All old cartridge boxes, cap pouches, and appendages were exchanged for cavalry cartridge boxes, which were worn on the waist belt.

The 3rd US Veteran Volunteers completed organization in March 1865 and saw service in the Washington, DC, defenses and the Shenandoah Valley, and were mustered out by detachments from March 6 to July 20, 1866.[4]

This corporal has the badge of the Veteran Corps, adopted on May 10, 1865, consisting of a seven-pointed star with the numeral "3" inset, attached to the black silk ribbon around his straw hat. The IX Corps badge pinned to his sack coat indicates previous service, as do the service stripes on his lower sleeves. He is armed with a Henry repeating rifle.

1. *New-York Times*, November 29, 1864, 4:4.
2. NARA, record group 94, Regimental Order Book, 6th US Veteran Volunteers.
3. Coates and McAulay, *Civil War Sharps Carbines & Rifles*, 94.
4. Dyer, *Compendium of the War of the Rebellion*, 245.

Federal Surgeon, 1861–1863

PRIOR TO APRIL 1861, THE PERSONNEL OF THE MEDICAL Department of the US Army comprised the surgeons, assistant surgeons, civilian physicians hired on contract, and hospital stewards. At any level of service, from regiment to army corps, surgeons and assistant surgeons were considered members of the headquarters staff. Hence it was difficult to distinguish them from staff officers of equivalent rank in other departments.[1] At the beginning of the conflict there were about one hundred commissioned medical officers within the small Regular Army. By 1865 this had increased to five hundred commissioned medical officers and approximately two thousand contract physicians.[2]

The uniform of army surgeons and assistant surgeons in 1861 consisted of a dark-blue Pattern 1858 frock coat with gilt epaulets for full dress bearing in the crescent on the strap the silver letters "MS" within a gold embroidered laurel wreath. Surgeon's shoulder straps sometimes had the silver embroidered letters "MS" at the center, although this was not prescribed in regulations during the war. Officers' pattern forage caps and hats often bore a small nonregulation insignia at the front consisting of a gold bullion wreath and the silver letters "MS" embroidered on a black velvet ground. Dark-blue trousers had a 1/8th-inch–wide buff welt in the outside seam. An emerald-green silk waist sash, if worn, was the most distinctive aspect of their dress.

Usually worn only for dress occasions, the Medical Staff sword prescribed for surgeons and assistant surgeons had a straight blade; a pineapple-shaped pommel; no knuckle guard; a specially moulded grip, bearing oak-leaf and acorn devices and a national eagle; and a scrolled quillon, bearing two shields, the obverse having the letters "MS" in Old English letters and the reverse plain. Sword belt plates were of the pattern worn by general and staff officers.[3] The surgeon depicted holds a pair of leather gauntlets behind his back and wears high-topped boots that are strapped around the back of his legs to keep them up. Spurs indicate his mounted role.

1. Katcher, *The American Civil War Source Book*, 173–76.

2. *New-York Times*, July 2, 1865, 2:2.

3. *Regulations for the Uniform and Dress of the Army of the United States, 1861* (George W. Bowman, Public Printers, 1861), 9–11.

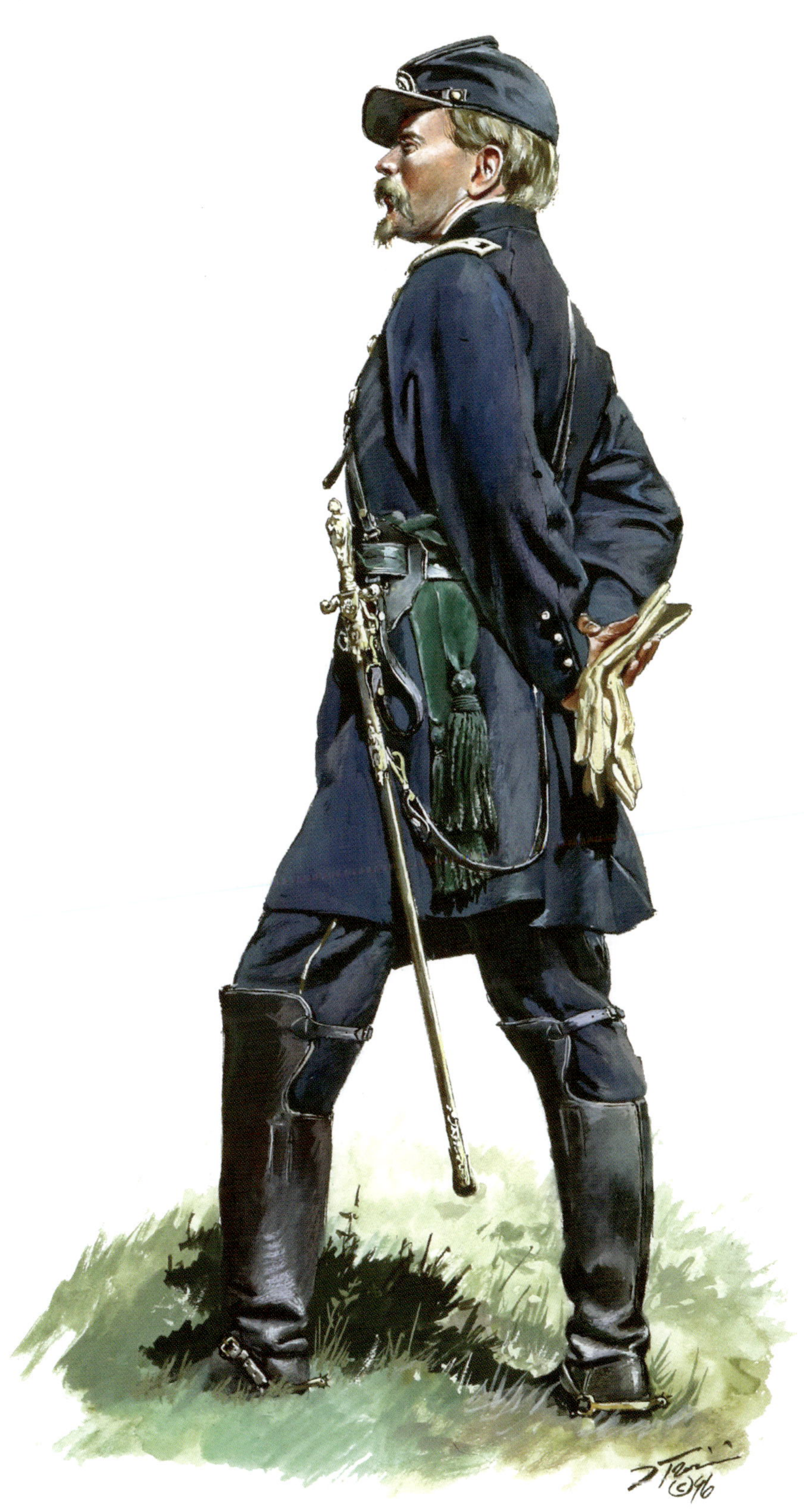

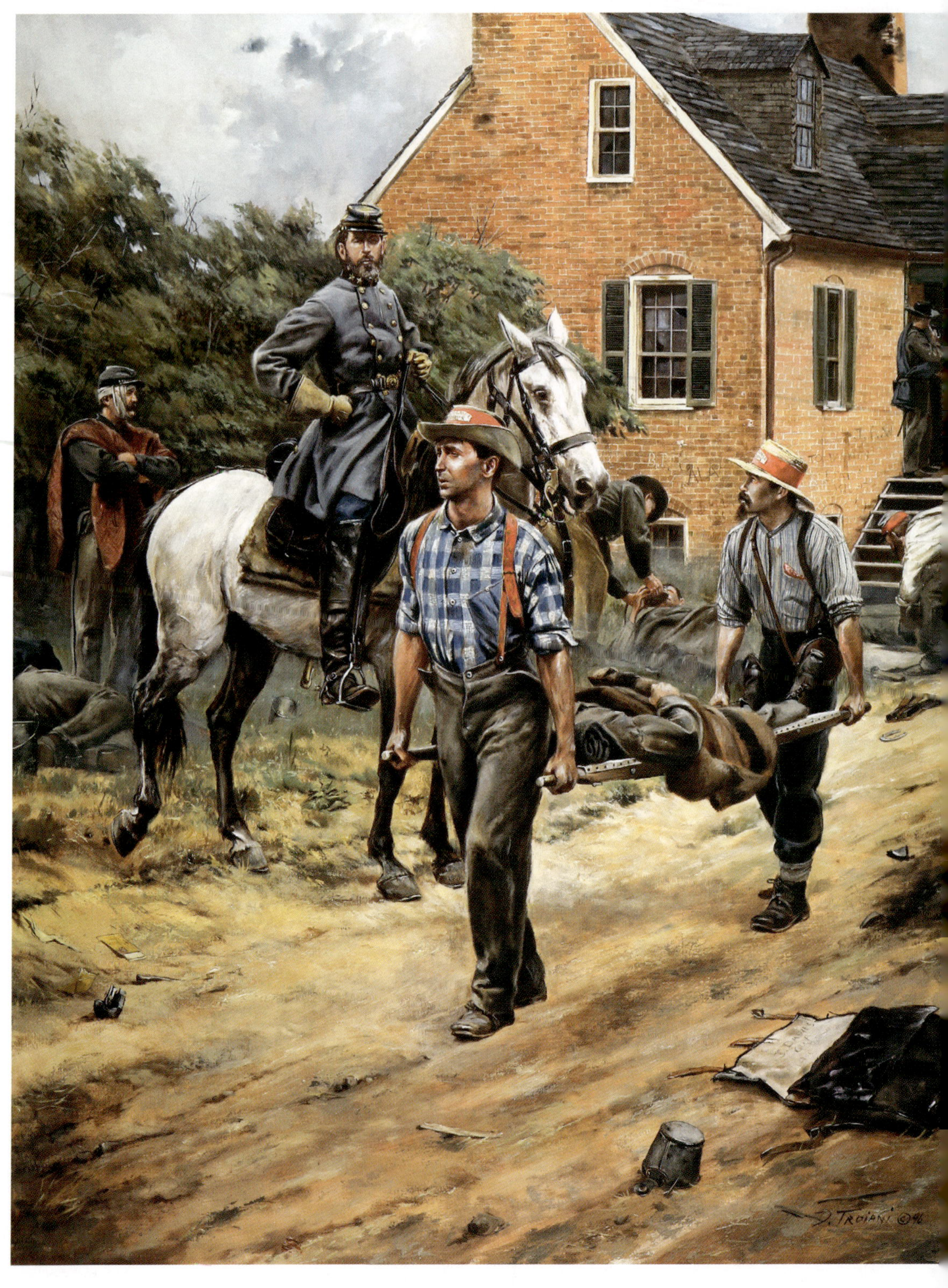

Confederate States Medical Service

MODELED ON THAT OF THE FEDERAL ARMY, THE MEDICAL Service of the Confederate States assigned a surgeon and an assistant surgeon to each regiment of infantry and cavalry. Senior-ranking surgeons would serve at brigade or division level. All were nominally under the overall supervision of the surgeon general, Samuel P. Moore. The uniform of the Confederate surgeon was similar to that of line officers, except that the facings on the coat collar, cuffs, and trousers seam stripe were black. A green silk net waist sash was worn with full dress.[1] The letters "MS" were sometimes embroidered in gold on the cap front. The mounted senior surgeon with the rank of lieutenant colonel depicted in this scene at a Confederate field dressing station wears an officer's pattern chasseur cap and a double-breasted frock coat with the medical branch of service indicated by his black collar. Leather gauntlets cover his black cuff facings.

Although there were no regulations concerning a uniform for the men detailed as hospital orderlies or nurses, there is evidence that some wore in their hats "a red badge," representing the Confederate ambulance corps. In July 1863, Lieutenant Colonel Arthur J. L. Freemantle, a British observer with the Army of Northern Virginia, described Semmes's and Barksdale's brigades on the march during the Gettysburg Campaign as follows: "In the rear of each regiment were . . . a certain number of unarmed men carrying stretchers and wearing in their hats the red badge of the ambulance corps—this an excellent institution, for it prevents unwounded men from falling out on pretense of taking wounded to the rear."[2] The hospital orderlies shown bearing the stretcher are distinguished by broad red ribbons around their hats upon which is attached a patch with the lettering "Ambulance Corps."

Furthermore, copying the Regulations of the Army of the United States, 1861, the Confederate army adopted the following order: "The ambulance depot, to which the wounded are carried or directed for immediate treatment, is generally established at the most convenient building nearest the field of battle. A *red flag* marks the place, or the way to it, to the conductors of the ambulance and to the wounded who can walk."[3] Hence, a red bunting flag measuring about three feet on the hoist by four and a half feet on the fly would likely be fluttering above the building in the rear.

---

1. *Uniform and Dress of the Army of the Confederate States*, 3, 4.
2. Freemantle, *Three Months in the Southern States*, 234.
3. *Regulations for the Army of the Confederate States, 1862* (MacFarland & Ferguson, 1862), 72–73.

Sergeant of Ordnance, 1863

ESTABLISHED IN 1812, THE ORDNANCE DEPARTMENT OF THE United States Regular Army of 1861–1865 was commanded by the chief of ordnance, General James W. Ripley, and consisted of forty officers, seventy sergeants of ordnance, fifteen military storekeepers, and about four hundred enlisted men, most being employed as technicians at the armories and arsenals. Hundreds of civilians also worked within the Department as clerks and laborers, their numbers increasing from approximately one thousand to nine thousand by 1865.[1]

The most senior noncommissioned officer grade in the Ordnance Department, and one which could be earned only after many years of service, the sergeant of ordnance served as a caretaker of ordnance and other stores at military installations throughout the United States. From about May 1854, ordnance sergeants were authorized to wear for dress a uniform coat with nine "Ordnance Corps" buttons, trimmed with crimson lace on collar and cuffs, and noncommissioned-staff brass shoulder scales. Trousers were dark blue, later sky blue, with 1½-inch–wide crimson lace on the outer seam. Their Hardee hat had a Pattern 1851 brass "flaming bomb" in front, a single black ostrich feather plume, and crimson cord. Rank was displayed by three silk crimson chevrons. A red worsted sash was worn under a plain black leather sword belt fastened by a Pattern 1851 rectangular "eagle" plate. This ordnance sergeant has four service stripes, or half-chevrons, on his lower sleeves indicating four periods of five-year service in the army.[2] He wears white dress gloves and holds a Model 1840 noncommisioned officers' sword.

Most Ordnance Department privates wore the same full dress minus rank insignia and enlisted-pattern shoulder scales and trousers without seam stripes. Fatigue clothing for all noncommisioned officers and enlisted men included a dark-blue jacket trimmed with crimson, which, when not available, was supplemented by cutting the skirts of a frock coat. Sack coats, and forage caps with "flaming bomb" insignia on the top, were also worn for undress. Ordnance enlisted men were armed and equipped as infantry.

---

1. Field, *The Union Army 1861–65 (1): The Regular Army and the Territories*, 40.
2. *Regulations for the Uniform and Dress of the Army of the United States, 1861*, 14.

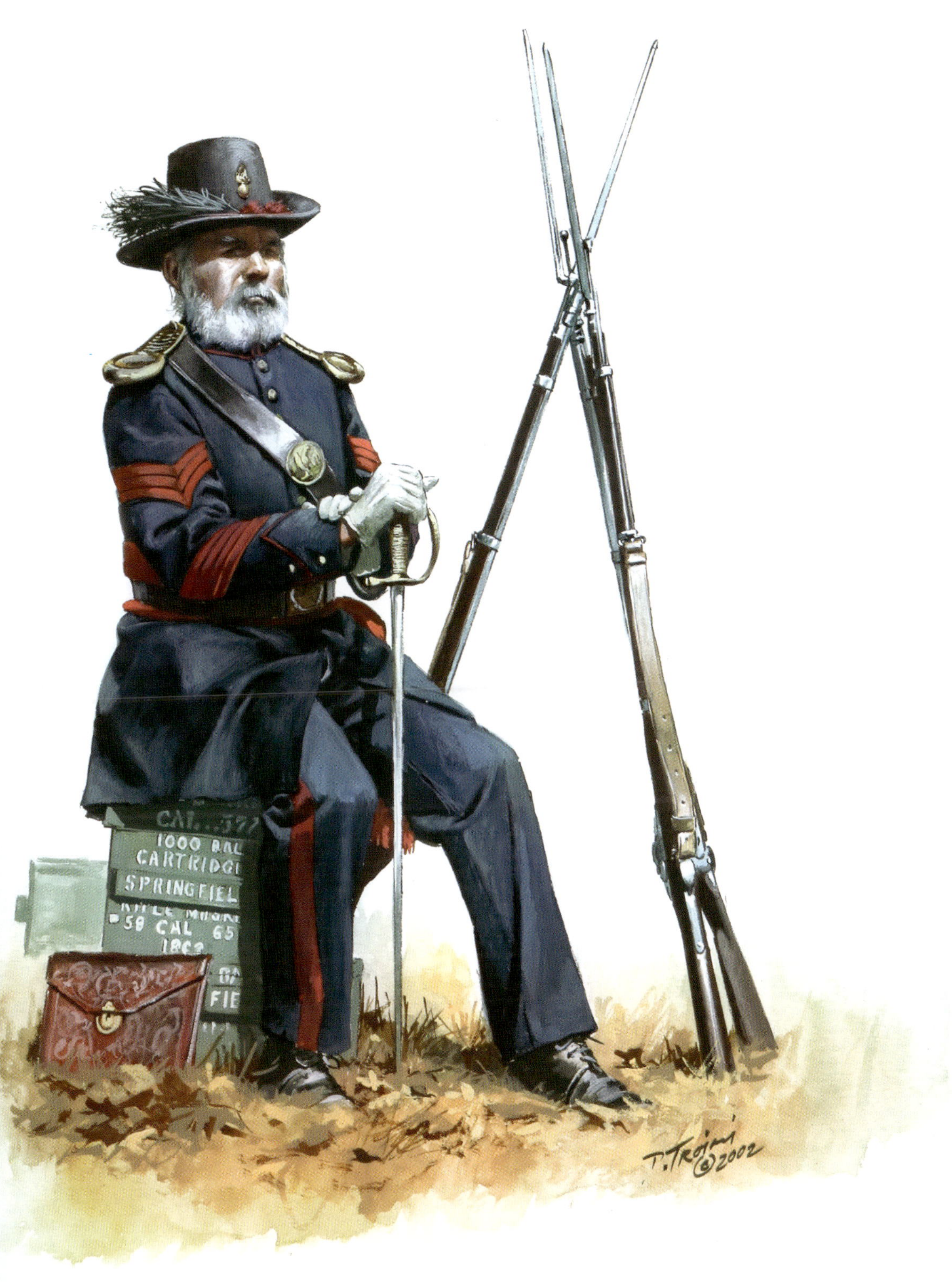

CAL. .57
1000 BAL
CARTRIDGE
SPRINGFIEL
RIFLE MUSKE
58 CAL 65
FIE

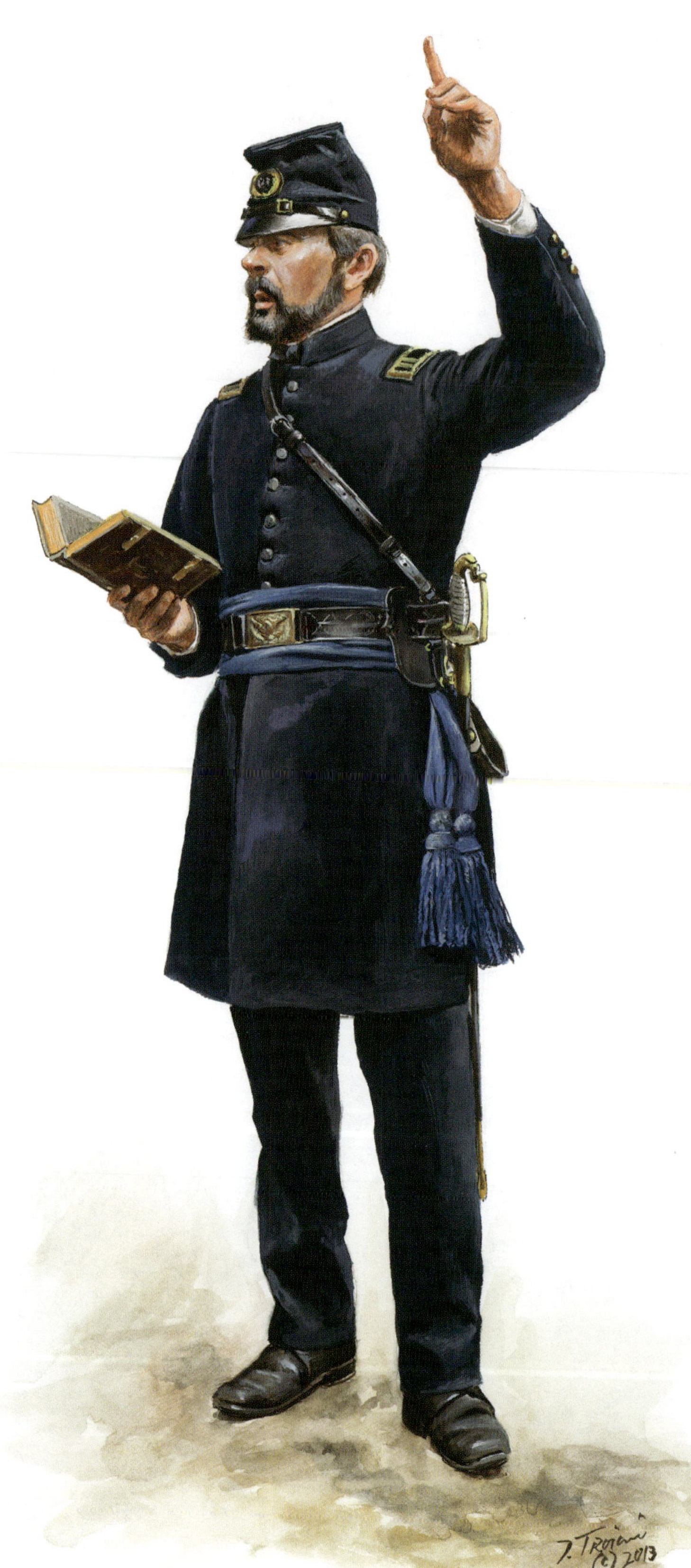

Union Army Chaplain

REGIMENTAL CHAPLAINS WERE NOT A PART OF THE United States Army's regular establishment at the outbreak of the Civil War, although numerous militia units recruited chaplains for the moral and social benefit of the soldiers. With the creation of a vast number of volunteer regiments in 1861, chaplains were added to their regimental staff. Some of these were poorly qualified and, despite regulations and orders concerning their merits, were a mixed bag of individuals. They ranged from thieves who stole regimental funds and cowards who shirked their duties to men who sincerely tended to the spiritual and physical welfare of their flocks. Some were even known to fight alongside the men of their regiment, and four chaplains were awarded the Medal of Honor during the war.[1]

It was not until the issuing of US Army General Order No. 102, on November 25, 1861, that an acknowledged uniform was established for Union army chaplains. This consisted of a plain black nine-button frock coat and trousers with a black hat or cap. Usually chaplains chose the staff insignia, consisting of the letters "US" in a wreath, to trim their headgear. In 1864 their uniform was modified via General Order 247, which added "herringbone black braid around the buttonholes." Chaplains often wore the shoulder straps of a staff captain as this was their equivalent rank.[2]

Nonetheless, there continued to be considerable latitude taken in chaplains' dress, even to the wearing of a sword—a practice that resulted in the death of Chaplain Horatio Howell of the 90th Pennsylvania Infantry at Gettysburg. The chaplain depicted wears a regular officer's dark-blue line frock coat with nine cloth-covered buttons, matching plain dark-blue trousers, and a Pattern 1859 forage cap with staff insignia at its front. His rank of captain is indicated by two bars on his shoulder straps. His waist belt is fastened with a Pattern 1851 eagle-wreath plate under which is a mid-blue silk sash, and he carries a circa 1800–1830 "eaglehead" infantry officer's sword.

---

1. Michael J. McAfee, "Army Chaplains," *Military Images* (March–April 2009): 25–30.

2. "Regulations and Notes for the Uniform of the Army of the United States, 1861," comp. Jacques Noel Jacobsen Jr., (Manor Publishing, 1978).

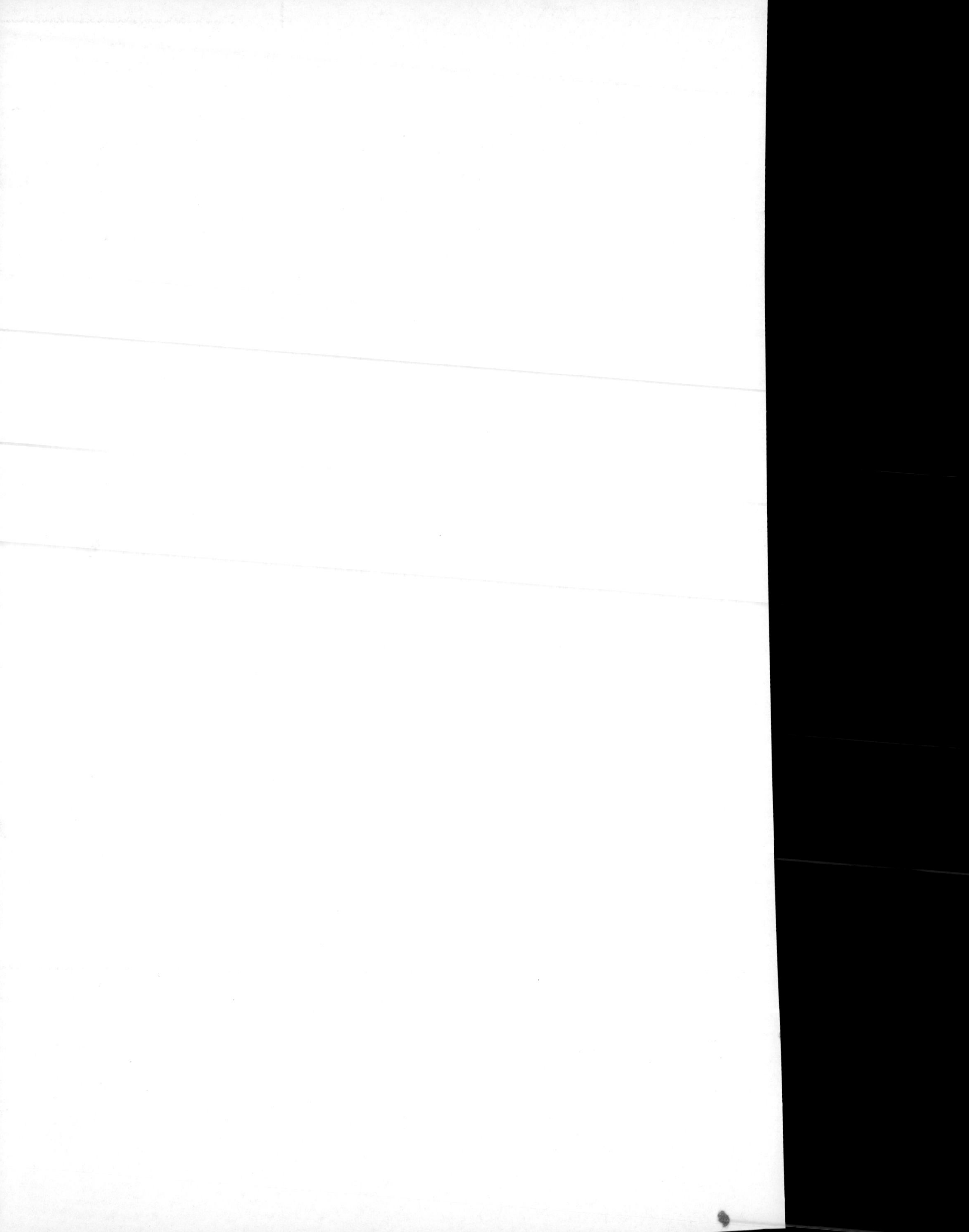